MOTOR LEARNING
Concepts *and* Applications

MOTOR LEARNING
Concepts *and* Applications

third edition

Richard A. Magill
Louisiana State University

ᴡᴄᴃ
Wm. C. Brown Publishers
Dubuque, Iowa

Book Team

Editor *Chris Rogers*
Developmental Editor *Sue Pulvermacher-Alt*
Designer *K. Wayne Harms*
Production Editor *Barbara Rowe Day*
Photo Editor *Mary Roussel*
Visuals Processor *Vickie Werner*

wcb group

Chairman of the Board *Wm. C. Brown*
President and Chief Executive Officer *Mark C. Falb*

wcb

Wm. C. Brown Publishers, College Division

President *G. Franklin Lewis*
Vice President, Editor-in-Chief *George Wm. Bergquist*
Vice President, Director of Production *Beverly Kolz*
Vice President, National Sales Manager *Bob McLaughlin*
Director of Marketing *Thomas E. Doran*
Marketing Communications Manager *Edward Bartell*
Marketing Manager *Kathy Law Laube*
Manager of Visuals and Design *Faye M. Schilling*
Production Editorial Manager *Colleen A. Yonda*
Production Editorial Manager *Julie A. Kennedy*
Publishing Services Manager *Karen J. Slaght*

Dedicated to my wife
Susan Faust Straley
and to our daughter
Straley Elizabeth Magill

Contents

Preface

*T*he first edition of this textbook was developed to provide a basic introduction to the complex field of motor learning. This goal, which was continued in the second edition, characterizes this third edition as well. The focus of the book continues to be on skill acquisition with primary consideration given to the learning process, the cognitive and motor processes underlying the learning of skills, and factors that influence skill learning. To provide the most complete view possible of skill acquisition, issues related to the control of skilled motor performance are also considered, although to a lesser extent than those related to skill learning. The book continues to be directed toward the student preparing for a career in which motor skill instruction is an important part of the job, as is the case with physical education teachers, coaches, dance instructors, physical and occupational therapists, and instructors in military and industrial training settings. The goal of this text is to provide these persons with a foundation for understanding the characteristics and capabilities of the persons with whom they will work, the learning process and how different factors influence the course of learning, and the effectiveness of various instructional strategies.

One of the exciting aspects of developing the third edition is that it demonstrates the vitality of the field of motor learning, both as an area of research and as an important part of the preparation of teachers of motor skills. The explosion in research output since the publication of the first edition in 1980 is apparent when one observes the increase in research articles related to motor learning issues in a variety of research journals, as well as the increase in the number of journals devoted to the study of human learning and of motor skill learning. Although on the one hand this increase in research activity is encouraging and exciting to see, on the other hand it poses a unique problem for the author of an introductory textbook: there is a wealth of information related to the learning and control of motor skills. This information covers a wide range of issues from a variety of perspectives. As a result, decisions had to be made to delimit the scope of this textbook. The effect of those decisions is that many issues related to the control of skills, especially from neurophysiological and biomechanical perspectives, either have been given cursory consideration or have not been discussed at all. However, this edition includes what are considered to be essential elements for establishing an appropriate foundation for understanding motor learning for the students for whom this text is intended.

A number of changes will be noted in this edition compared with the second edition. One important change is a reorganization and expansion of what was Chapter 1 in the second edition. That chapter is now two chapters (Chapters 1 and 2) that are organized as an introduction to motor skills and

research (Chapter 1) and an introduction to learning (Chapter 2). The benefit of this reorganization is that it highlights the significance of these components of the study of motor learning and allows for a more complete discussion of concepts related to them. For example, in Chapter 1, the discussion of how motor skills are measured has been expanded and is more representative of measurement techniques and variables currently found in the motor learning research literature. In Chapter 2, more emphasis has been placed on developing the important issue of defining and measuring learning by extending the discussion of how the learning inference is made. Also, the discussion of learning stages has been expanded and strengthened by incorporating Gentile's model into the discussion.

There has been a major overhaul on the chapter on attention (Chapter 4). An important improvement is the addition of the notion of alertness to the concept of response preparation and the development of a broader discussion of variables influencing alertness and preparation. The discussion of attention as limited capacity has been expanded to consider a wider variety of views of attention limitations. Also, a discussion of automaticity has been added. In the concept related to selective attention, consideration has been given to the role of conscious awareness and learning motor skills.

The memory chapter (Chapter 5) has been significantly reworked to incorporate several new findings and theoretical viewpoints that have developed since the publication of the second edition. For example, there is now a discussion of different types of information stored in memory that is particularly relevant for motor learning, such as the distinction between information needed to know "what to do" and information needed to know "how to do" a skill. The concept about influences on remembering and forgetting has been reorganized and expanded to reflect much new research information.

The chapter on knowledge of results (KR) (Chapter 7) includes a more complete discussion of defining KR and distinguishing it from other sources of feedback. Also, there is an expanded discussion concerning the content of KR and what is involved in deciding what information to give as KR. The issue of the frequency of providing KR has resurfaced in the research literature and is discussed more fully in this edition. Questions have been forwarded in much of the research literature concerning the interaction between KR and feedback information that can be obtained visually by the learner. This issue is given attention in this chapter and provides an interesting interface with the discussion in Chapter 3 on the role of vision in the control of movement. Also, the use of various types of KR, which includes what some refer to as knowledge of performance (KP) and augmented feedback, is discussed more extensively in this edition. The discussion of the KR intervals has been greatly revised to reflect recent research findings as well as recent theorizing concerning the processing activities engaged in during these intervals. An attempt has been made as well to make this discussion of the KR intervals more relevant to instructional applications.

Finally, the chapter concerning practice (Chapter 9) has undergone several changes. A new concept on modeling as a form of instruction has been added. Modeling has seen an impressive increase in research activity in recent years and is present as an issue that has relevance for providing effective skill instruction as well as for providing insight into the role of vision in skill learning. The concept on practice variability has been greatly revised to incorporate many new ideas and research findings related to this issue, such as the relationship of contextual interference to skill learning and the role of making errors early in practice in learning. The concept on practice distribution has been drastically revised to reflect current thinking that has emerged about this issue and skill acquisition.

Every attempt has been made to maintain the essential characteristics that have been so popular in previous editions. The concepts approach has been maintained as has the presentation of how the concept under consideration applies to specific skill learning or performance situations. There has been a concerted effort to expand the type of application examples to relate to the widest range of motor skills and motor skill performance context situations possible. As in previous editions, controversial issues are underplayed so that the introductory student of motor learning will not get side-tracked by controversy and can focus on concepts of motor learning that are generally acknowledged. Alternative views on various issues are considered with the view to encourage the student to consider reasonable alternative explanations for research findings.

Before concluding, I would like to thank and credit a number of people who have provided invaluable assistance and support in the development of this third edition. First, I want to thank the many persons who critiqued the second edition and the first draft of this third edition. Some volunteered this input while others were solicited by the editors at Wm. C. Brown Publishers: Ian Franks, University of British Columbia; Stephen Langendorfer, Kent State University; Tim Lee, McMaster University; Priscilla MacRae, Pepperdine University; Virginia Peters, Central State University; Malvin Rau, Springfield College; and Richard K. Stratton, Virginia Tech. Many useful suggestions were provided and incorporated into this edition. I would like to especially single out Tim Lee and Beth Kerr for their significant input into this edition. Much appreciation is extended to several student workers at LSU, particularly Kathleen McKinell and Melissa Morrison, who helped so much in various aspects of the development of the final product. Also, thanks goes to two of my graduate students, Kellie Green and Britta Schoenfelder, for their help in organizing the indexes. As I did in the past two editions, I want to again thank the students who have been in my motor learning classes over the years. They not only are a constant source of encouragement to continue to teach and do motor learning research, but they also have provided invaluable information for this text so that it can be relevant to their needs. Finally, I again am very grateful to my wife Susan Straley for her support and tolerance of

me while I worked on this third edition. The arrival of our daughter, Straley Elizabeth, since the last edition has provided even greater challenges than before to complete this work. Without their support and encouragement, this third edition could not have been done.

Richard A. Magill
Baton Rouge, Louisiana

MOTOR LEARNING
Concepts *and* Applications

Unit 1

Motor Skills and Learning

Introduction to Motor Skills and Motor Learning Research 1

Concept 1.1
Motor skills can be classified into general categories.

Concept 1.2
The measurement of motor performance is a critical part of understanding motor learning.

Concept 1.3
The scientific method, or research, is an important tool in understanding the learning and performance of motor skills.

Concept 1.1   Motor skills can be classified into general categories

Application

Playing a piano, dancing, learning to walk with an artificial limb, throwing a baseball, hitting a squash ball, operating a wood lathe, and piloting an airplane are all rather diverse and unique skills. However, each of these is a motor skill. In this text you will be confronted with information that will help you understand how we produce and control motor skills such as these, as well as how we can teach motor skills.

As you venture through this study, you will find that it will be helpful to be able to draw general conclusions and make applications that can be related to a broad range of motor skills. You will inevitably find that this is preferable to being limited to making specific statements about each skill. In the discussion section of this concept, you will be presented with a starting point for making these kinds of general statements. That starting point involves knowing what motor skills are and how they can be classified into broad categories that emphasize the similarities rather than the distinctions among skills.

For example, piloting an airplane and playing the piano seem quite distinct from each other. However, based on at least one of their underlying components, some similarity or common elements can be seen between these skills; and this is important for designing instruction. Both tasks involve serial responses. That is, in order for the tasks to be carried out, a certain number of distinct movements must be performed in a very specific order. If any part of the movements is forgotten, or if the order is improperly arranged, the probability for successful performance of these skills is diminished. In this way, then, generalizations can be made concerning the learning of skills involving serial responses. Two seemingly diverse skills such as piano playing and piloting an airplane thus become related when those generalizations are applied to specific motor skills.

Discussion

As you begin your study of motor learning, it is important to discover some essential information about the skills that are the focus of this book. In this discussion, we will address two aspects of this information. First, we will consider what motor skills are and what distinguishes them from other skills. Second, we will discuss how motor skills can be classified into categories that identify common characteristics of various skills. We will discuss three different methods that have been developed to classify motor skills. As you have just read, this classification process is beneficial in enabling us to better understand what motor skills are as well as to apply theoretical knowledge about how we control and learn motor skills to the instruction of motor skills.

Before specifically defining what is meant by the term *motor skill,* it will be helpful to first consider the "skill" part of that term, a term that is often misunderstood. The word *skill* can be used in different ways in different contexts. For instance, its meaning when used as "That running back is a tremendously skilled performer" is rather distinct from its meaning when the term is used as "foul shooting is a basketball skill essential to the game." Each of these uses of the term skill is appropriate.

Skill as an act or task. When *skill* is used in connection with the example of foul shooting in basketball as a skill, the term denotes an act or task that has a specific goal to achieve. Piano playing, welding, swimming, shooting a rifle, and serving a tennis ball are all examples of skills in the motor domain. The use of the term *skill* in this manner is quite straightforward and causes little confusion with regard to its meaning. In this text, when the term skill is used to refer to a *motor skill,* it denotes *an act or a task that has a goal to achieve and that requires voluntary body or limb movement to be properly performed.*

This definition indicates several characteristics about a skill as we will use the term. First, there is a goal to achieve, which means that skills have a purpose. Second, skills are performed voluntarily, which indicates that we do not consider reflexes to be skills. Although an eye blink may have a purpose and can be classified as a motor act, it is not a skill in the sense that we are using the term. Finally, a motor skill requires body or limb movement to accomplish the goal of the act or task. This characteristic specifies that when we use the term skill, we are referring to a specific type of skill. Although reading and calculating math problems are skills, they are not motor skills and are not the focus of this text. Our interest is in motor skills that all have in common the property that each needs to be learned in order to be properly executed. Walking, while a fundamental and relatively simple motor skill, requires learning by the child who is attempting to move in his or her environment by this new and exciting means of locomotion. Walking is also a skill that must be acquired by the therapy patient who is learning to walk with the aid of an artificial leg.

With regard to a more theoretical concern related to the use of the term skill, when a skill is referred to in this text, it is used in the same sense that motor learning and control theorists use the term *action.* That is, an action is viewed as a goal-directed response that consists of body and limb movements. What's important here is that a variety of movements or movement patterns can produce the same action. For example, if we think of hitting a baseball with a bat as an action, then it is easy to see that no one pattern of movement must be produced to achieve the goal of this action, which is to hit the ball with the bat. The person can achieve this goal by using a variety of movement patterns, even though some may be better than others. It should be noted, however, that there are some exceptions, where an action goal can only be

achieved by a very limited set of specific movement patterns. These exceptions involve skills where performance criteria are established and must be met in order for the goal to be achieved, as in a gymnastics trick or a dive.

Skill as an indicator of quality performance. Probably a more confusing and ambiguous use of the term *skill* occurs when it is used to refer to a skilled performer. In this use of the term, *skill* is a *qualitative expression of performance.* Here the word connotes a degree of proficiency that is often subjectively determined. However, that proficiency can be expressed by some statement relating to *productivity or characteristics* of the performer. For example, we consider basketball players skilled free-throw shooters if they are successful in 80% of the free throws they attempt. We likewise consider tennis players skilled servers if 60% to 70% of their first serves are good. These examples indicate that skill is judged by productivity of performance. What should be most apparent in these examples is that the use of the term *skill* in relation to productivity is very relative to the context of the performance. The "skilled" professional tennis player is judged by a much more stringent set of criteria to be acclaimed "skilled" than is the high school player. This seems especially apparent when the person's peers are the ones doing the judging.

A second means of expressing that an individual is a skilled performer is on the basis of certain characteristics of the person's performance. These characteristics can include such things as the consistency of performance, the use of meaningful cues rather than being distracted by nonmeaningful cues, and the anticipating in advance what response should be made.

These characteristics can be adequately illustrated with some examples in sports activities. If a golfer sinks several difficult putts during a round of golf, we would hesitate to say that he or she is a skilled putter until we have observed him or her for many rounds of golf. If this golfer continued to make many difficult putts, we would be more justified in labeling that person a skilled putter. Thus, the consistency of a high level of performance is critical to consideration of the golfer as "skilled."

If we compare a skilled and an unskilled baseball or softball batter, one of the important differences we would observe would be the use of meaningful cues. The skilled batter has learned to ignore cues that are not important or are meaningless. While a pitcher who includes many irrelevant movements may confuse the unskilled batter, these same moves will have little disrupting effect on the skilled batter.

If a football quarterback must wait until the opposing linemen are on top of him before knowing what to do with the ball in an option situation, we would not be justified in calling that person a skilled quarterback. On the other hand, the quarterback who can anticipate what to do on the basis of something he has observed in the linemen in advance of when he must respond by keeping the ball or pitching it out, then the label "skilled" can be more aptly applied to that individual.

These three characteristics have been used only as examples of the criteria that we often use in the process of determining whether or not a person is a skilled performer. Undoubtedly other characteristics are considered. The use of these three should be sufficient to establish the point that we use the term *skill* to express a quality of performance and that the quality of performance is often based on certain characteristics.

The word *skill*, then, when designating the quality of performance is typically based on how well the individual accomplishes the goal of the task. This can be established by measuring the outcome of performing the task or by observing certain characteristics of the performance that lead to the successful outcome.

Ability

The term *ability* will also be used often throughout this text. It is a term that we hear in many conversations in the educational or athletic setting. We will be considering this term more specifically in Chapter 6 when individual differences are discussed. However, it will be beneficial to define the term here to help develop the foundation on which you can base your study of motor learning. Edwin Fleishman (1972, 1978) has been responsible for developing much of the present understanding of the relationship between human abilities and the performance of motor skills. He has defined the term *ability* as a "general capacity of the individual" that is related to the performance of a variety of skills or tasks. For example, the ability that Fleishman has labeled "spatial visualization" has been found to be related to the performance of such diverse tasks as aerial navigation, blueprint reading, and dentistry. In a sport context, the ability (or capability) of "speed of movement" can be seen as an important component in performing a variety of skills in football, baseball, tennis, and track. A motor ability therefore, is *a general trait or capacity of an individual that is related to the performance of a variety of motor skills.*

As you will see in Chapter 6, there are many different motor abilities. The level of success a person can achieve for a motor skill is in large part dependent on how those abilities related to performing the skill are characterized in the individual. That is, a person with a high degree of all the abilities required to successfully play golf can be expected to have good potential to be an excellent player. You will learn more about the relationship between abilities and performance in Chapter 6.

Motor Skill Classification Systems

The general approach of this text is to present motor learning concepts that can be applied to a variety of motor skill contexts. However, as you have seen in the discussion thus far, there is an extremely large number of possible motor skills that can be performed. It would make the task of applying these concepts to motor skill learning and performance situations much simpler if motor skills themselves could be organized in such a way as to eliminate the need to apply concepts to specific skills. Fortunately, this organizational system has been established. However, there are several different organizational schemes that

have been developed to classify motor skills into distinct groups. In this section we will consider three different skill classification systems that have been developed and are used rather extensively, although each tends to be used in certain contexts.

Classifying motor skills into general categories is based on determining what components or elements of a skill are common or similar to components of another skill. Each of the methods of classification that will be discussed has led to the presentation of a dichotomy. That is, skills are classified as being one of two categories. Rather than considering these two categories as unique and unrelated so that all motor skills must fit into one or the other category, consider each of the two categories as an extreme end of a continuum. This approach suggests that skills can be classified as being more closely allied with one category than with the other without having to totally fit into that one category exclusively.

An analogy may be helpful. The concepts "hot" and "cold" are two categories of temperatures that we typically consider as distinct. However, it is more accurate to place these terms at the ends of a continuum since there are degrees of hot or cold that do not fit exclusively in one or the other category. By considering hot and cold as anchor points on a continuum you can maintain the distinction of these two concepts while at the same time allowing more accurately to relate various temperature levels that do not fit in only one or the other category.

As you can see from this analogy, the benefit of considering these classification system categories as anchor points at the opposite ends of a continuum allows the complex nature of motor skills to be accommodated while maintaining an emphasis on the common characteristics of the wide range of skills being classified. You will also find it helpful to keep in mind that the primary purpose for developing classifications is to provide a convenient vehicle to aid in the process of making generalizations. If this point is understood, then the problems that may appear in these classifications will be less important.

Many approaches have been developed to classify motor skills. Each classification system is based on the general nature of motor skills relating to some specific *aspect of the skills*. We will consider three systems, in which motor skill classification is based on (1) the precision of the movement; (2) defining the beginning and end points of the movement; and (3) the stability of the environment. As each of these is discussed, consider how the various examples fit along the continuum anchored by the two categories. Think of additional examples that would fit these categories. Remember that some motor skills will fit very easily into one or the other category. In other cases, you will find that a particular skill is more like one category than the other, even though it doesn't meet all the characteristics implied by that category.

In addition to discussing the two categories in each classification system, we will also consider the typical context in which the use of the system is popular. As you will see, the different classification systems seem to have appeal

or relevance for a particular use. For example, one classification system is more common in elementary physical education while another is common in physical therapy and adapted physical education. Within these settings, specific classification systems provide a more convenient means of classifying the motor skills involved in these instructional contexts.

Classifying motor skills on the basis of the precision of movement involved in the skills has led to the development of two categories: gross motor skills and fine motor skills. *Gross motor skills* are characterized as involving large musculature and a goal where the precision of movement is not as important to the successful execution of the skill as it is for fine motor skills. Fundamental motor skills, such as walking, jumping, throwing, leaping, etc., and most sports skills are considered to be gross motor skills. While precision of movement is not an important component, the smooth coordination of movement is essential to the skilled performance of these tasks.

Precision of
Movement

   Fine motor skills are skills that require control of the small muscles of the body to achieve the goal of the skill. Generally, these skills involve hand-eye coordination and require a high degree of precision of movement for the performance of the particular skill at a high level of accomplishment. Writing, drawing, piano playing, and watchmaking are examples of fine motor skills.

   Skills like the ones presented here are relatively easy to categorize. However, when skills such as pitching or hitting a baseball and riding a bicycle are considered, where do they belong? Here is where the continuum helps the categorization process. Obviously, skills such as these involve large musculature to a great extent, but a high degree of movement accuracy is also required. On the basis of the characteristics of skills classified as gross or fine, it would seem likely that pitching or hitting a baseball and riding a bicycle are more closely related to the gross end of the classification continuum.

Where this classification system is used. The use of the gross-fine distinction for motor skills is popular in a number of settings. One of these is special education or adapted physical education, where the training or rehabilitation of motor skills is typically related to working with gross or fine skills. In therapy settings, this classification system is also commonly used. Physical therapists typically work with patients who need to rehabilitate gross motor skills such as walking, whereas occupational therapists deal with patients who need to learn fine motor skills. Finally, individuals who are involved in early childhood motor skills development research also find the gross-fine categorization useful. Thus, the classification of motor skills according to the precision of the movement, which is in turn based on the type of musculature primarily involved in achieving the goal of the movement, appears to be a popular and useful means of classifying motor skills.

Another means of classifying motor skills is on the basis of how clearly defined the beginning and end of the skill are. If there are clearly defined beginning and end points, then the skill is categorized as a *discrete* motor skill. If the skill has rather arbitrary beginning and end points, the category label is *continuous*. *Discrete motor skills* include such movements as throwing a ball, flipping a light switch, depressing the clutch of an automobile, or hitting a typewriter key. Each of these movements has defined beginning and end points that the performer must adhere to if he or she is to perform the task successfully. Discrete skills can be put together in a series. When this occurs, we consider the skill to be a *serial motor skill*. Starting a standard shift automobile is a good example. In this situation, a series of discrete motor tasks must be performed. The clutch must be depressed, the key must be turned to start the engine, the gear shift must be put into first gear, the accelerator must be properly depressed as the clutch is let out as the car finally begins to move forward. Playing the piano can also be considered as a serial motor skill, since discrete movements of striking the piano keys must be accomplished in a definite, serial order. Many sports skills can also be considered serial skills. Performing a dance routine or a floor exercise routine in gymnastics, and shooting an arrow in archery each consists of a specific series of movements that must be performed in a specific order for the proper execution of the skill. In a serial skill, each part or phase of the skill is both a stimulus and a response; it is a response to the immediately prior movement and a stimulus for the movement that immediately follows it.

Continuous motor skills have arbitrary beginning and end points. The performer, or some external force, determines the beginning and end point of the skill rather than the skill itself. Steering an automobile is a good example of a continuous motor skill. Tracking tasks, like tracking a blip on a radar scope or following a revolving dot on a pursuit rotor, are also continuous tasks. Sport skills such as swimming or running can be considered continuous in that the beginning and end points of the task are determined by the performer and not specified by the task itself.

Where this classification system is used. The use of this classification system has been especially prevalent in the motor skills research literature. Researchers have found, for example, that certain phenomena about how we control movement is applicable to discrete skills but not to continuous skills, or vice versa. This distinction between discrete and continuous skills seems to be especially popular with researchers who view the performance of motor skills from a human engineering perspective. You will become more acquainted with this approach as you progress through this text.

In 1957, a British experimental psychologist, E. C. Poulton, presented a classification system for motor skills as they were related to the industrial setting. The basis for the classification was the stability of the environment in which

the skill was performed. If the environment was stable, that is predictable, then Poulton classified the skill as *closed*. If, on the other hand, the skill involved an ever-changing, unpredictable environment, the skill was classified as *open*. Gentile (1972) expanded this classification system to make it applicable to instruction of sport skills. Rather than considering open and closed skills as dichotomous, Gentile suggested these terms were anchor points of a continuum. One end of the continuum includes skills that take place under fixed, unchanging, environmental conditions, or *closed skills;* some examples would be bowling, golf, archery, and weightlifting. *The object in each of these situations waits to be acted upon by the performer.* In bowling, the pins are not going to move from their location, and the performer is not required to begin action until he or she is ready to do so. This is typical of closed skills. Conversely, *open skills,* at the other end of the continuum, involve such skills as tennis ground strokes and hitting a baseball or racquetball—actions that take place in a temporally and/or spatially changing environment. For these tasks to be performed, *the performer must act upon the object according to the action of the object.* During a rally the racquetball player cannot stand in one spot and decide when he or she will respond to the ball. To be successful, the player must move and act as the ball's spatial location and speed demand.

Another set of terms has been used interchangeably with the open-closed skills categories. The term *self-paced task* or skill is synonymous with the closed-skill category. Self-paced is an equally appropriate label if the performer's pace of when and how to initiate the required action is determined by the performer. The other extreme is the *externally* or *forced-paced task* or skill, which is synonymous with the open skill. Here the initiation of action is determined by an external source, the stimulus. The performer is forced into action.

A four-category classification system. An interesting extension of this open-closed classification system was presented by Gentile, Higgins, Miller, and Rosen (1975). This system is especially helpful in further identifying where a motor skill belongs on the open-closed continuum. Gentile et al. suggested that rather than considering a dichotomous classification system, four types of categories could be identified. These categories involve two types of variations from one response attempt to the next, change or no change, and two types of environmental conditions during execution of the movement, stationary and in motion. These are presented in a 2 × 2 diagram in Figure 1.1–1. Note that a skill is classified according to how it fits the intersections of any two of these types of movement conditions. An example of skills in each of the four categories is presented in Figure 1.1–2.

In keeping with our continuum approach, it is interesting to arrange Gentile's 2 × 2 diagram in a continuum configuration. This is presented in Figure 1.1–2. Note that the no-change/stationary conditions category becomes the anchor point on the closed end of the continuum. The change/in-motion condition category is the anchor for the open end of the continuum.

Response-to-Response Variability

	No Change	Change
Stationary	**Category 1** The object of the response remains stationary, and there is no change in response requirements from one response to the next.	**Category 3** The object of the response remains stationary, and the response requirements change from one response to the next.
In Motion	**Category 2** The object of the response is in motion, and there is no change in the response requirements from one response to the next.	**Category 4** The object of the response is in motion, and the response requirements change from one response to the next.

Environmental Conditions

Figure 1.1-1
A 2 × 2 diagram representing the four-category classification system presented by Gentile, Higgins, Miller, and Rosen.

The change/stationary conditions category becomes an in-between point on the continuum that is closer to the closed- than to the open-skill end. On the other hand, the no-change/in-motion conditions category falls on the open side of the continuum. It should be noted that the category numbers are in keeping with the Gentile designation. As a result, they do not follow a consecutive order on the continuum.

An advantage of presenting this four-point continuum can be seen when there is a need by a teacher or coach to determine how to modify an open skill, such as hitting a baseball thrown by a pitcher, for purposes of teaching this skill in progressively more difficult steps. An example of this approach is included in Figure 1.1–2. Notice that at the closed end of the continuum, the ball is batted from a batting tee. In this situation, the ball, or stimulus, is stationary and remains in the same place on each practice attempt. The next level for modification keeps the ball stationary but requires that it be batted from different heights on each practice attempt, thus presenting a varying situation from one attempt to the next. The third level of modification goes back

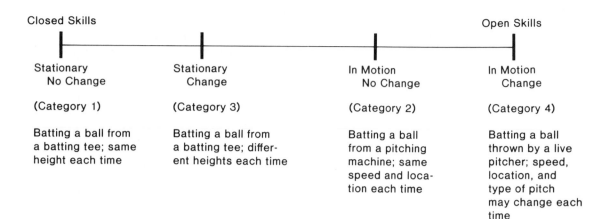

Closed Skills			Open Skills
Stationary No Change	Stationary Change	In Motion No Change	In Motion Change
(Category 1)	(Category 3)	(Category 2)	(Category 4)
Batting a ball from a batting tee; same height each time	Batting a ball from a batting tee; different heights each time	Batting a ball from a pitching machine; same speed and location each time	Batting a ball thrown by a live pitcher; speed, location, and type of pitch may change each time

to a no-change situation for each practice attempt but puts the ball in motion. This can be easily done by using a pitching machine, with which the speed and location of the pitch can be kept the same on each pitch. Finally, the open end of the continuum is reached by having a live pitcher pitching the ball with a different pitch on each practice attempt. A further discussion of the use of this approach to teaching open skills will be considered in Chapter 9 where specific practice-related issues are presented.

Where this classification system is used. The use of the open-closed classification system has found a large degree of popularity in instructional methodology contexts. It is not uncommon, for example, to find references to open and closed motor skills in textbooks related to teaching methods of physical education (e.g., Singer & Dick, 1980) or in research journal articles related to teaching motor skills (e.g., Del Rey, Wughalter, & Whitehurst, 1982). A likely reason for this popularity in using the open-closed skills classification system by those interested in teaching motor skills is that these skill categories are readily adaptable to the types of skills that are taught in instructional settings. Also, skills in these categories have in common characteristics that follow principles of instruction that are based on motor learning research. As such you will find this classification system frequently referred to in various parts of this book. This system has become commonly used in the motor learning research literature due to its simplicity and its ability to accommodate complex "real-world" skills as well as laboratory skills.

Motor skills have been defined as skills in which physical movement is required to accomplish the goal of the task. The word *skill* can be considered either a synonym for the word *task* or as an indicator of the quality of a performer's achievement in performing a particular motor skill. There is a wide variety of motor skills. Skills as diverse as throwing a football and playing the

Figure 1.1-2
The four categories from the Gentile et al. system placed on a continuum having closed- and open-skill categories as its extremes. Four different types of ball-batting tasks are presented to show how the categories are different.

Summary

piano are included under the general label of motor skills. One means of increasing the ease with which we can apply learning concepts and principles to instruction in motor skills is to develop general categories of such motor skills that are based on some common features of various motor aptitudes. Three categories or classification systems have been discussed, and each system is based on a general, common characteristic of motor skills. One system is based on the precision of the movement required by the skill; here, skills are classified as either gross or fine. Second, a system that is based on the distinctiveness of the beginning and end points of a skill considers it as either discrete or continuous. The third system is based on the stability of the environment in which the skill is performed; this environment may be stable, or closed; or it may be very changeable, or open.

Related Readings

Gagné, R. M. (1973). The domains of learning. *Interchange, 3,* 1–8.

Harrow, A. J. (1971). *A taxonomy of the psychomotor domain.* New York: David McKay.

Higgins, J. R. (1977). *Human movement: An integrated approach.* St. Louis: Mosby. (Read chapter 2.)

Holding, D. H. (1981). Skill research. In D. H. Holding (Ed.), *Human skills* (pp. 1–13). New York: John Wiley & Sons.

Newell, K. M. (1978). Some issues on action plans. In G. E. Stelmach (Ed.), *Information processing in motor control and learning* (pp. 41–54). New York: Academic Press. (Read pp. 41–43.)

The measurement of motor performance is a critical part of understanding motor learning

Application

As a person teaching motor skills, you must be able to determine whether or not the people you are teaching are learning the skills being taught. An important part of making that decision will be based on what motor performance characteristics are measured and what tests are given to allow you to make a decision about learning. For example, suppose you are a physical education teacher teaching a tennis unit. If you are teaching your students to serve, what will you look for to assess their progress of learning the serve? You could observe a number of possible performance characteristics. You could compare the number of serves that correctly land in the proper service court with the number of serves attempted. Or, you could mark the service court in some way so that the "better" serves, in terms of where they land, are scored higher than others. Or, you could establish a measure that is concerned with the student's serving form. These are just three different performance measurements that could be made. You can probably think of others. To assess student learning, you must first establish a performance measure, or measures, on which you will base your assessment.

In the discussion that follows, we will focus on this issue of measuring motor performance. It will help to consider this discussion as the first step in a two-step process of assessing learning. The first step is to establish the performance characteristics to be measured. The second step involves using these measures in an appropriate test that will allow an evaluation of the learning that took place as a result of the students' practice. This second step will be the focus of the first concept of the next chapter.

Because the goal of this book is to present motor learning concepts that have been derived from experimental research, the discussion of motor performance measures will be directed primarily to those measures that have been used in research, where understanding motor skill learning is the primary goal. The discussion of measures related to assessing motor performance in your particular area of application, such as physical education, physical therapy, dance, and so on, is the basis for a tests and measurements course, therefore, we will not discuss that topic here. The intent here is to provide you with a brief introduction to motor performance measurement as it relates to motor learning research, which should help you better understand the various concepts presented in this book. As you will see, however, although this discussion relates primarily to motor performance measurement concerns involved in motor learning research, much of this discussion will be directly applicable to your own instruction situations.

Discussion

There are a variety of ways to measure motor performance, some of which have already been mentioned. It is helpful to organize the various types of motor performance measures into two categories. These categories relate to different levels of performance observation. The first category is called *response outcome measures*. The performance measures included in this category are measures that indicate the product or result of a motor performance. For example, you may want to measure how far a person ran in a certain amount of time, or how many points a person scored. To answer these questions, response outcome measures are used. However, notice that these measures do not tell us anything about how the limbs or body behaved in producing these results, or how the nervous system functioned while the response was being made. If we want to know something about these characteristics, then measures in the category called *response production measures* should be used. These measures can tell us a number of different things about how the nervous system was functioning, how the muscular system was operating, or how the limbs or joints were acting before, during, or after the response was made. Although additional categories of measures could be developed, these two encompass the types of motor performance measures that will be found in this text. Examples of the two categories of motor performance measures are presented in Table 1.2–1.

Most of the measures in the response output category are well known to you and need no further explanation, although some may be new to you and will need to be explained. This is also likely the case for the response production measures category. In the remainder of this discussion, we will look more closely at some of these measures. In particular, we will discuss measures that are popular in motor learning research and frequently seen in the research literature. In the discussion of each measure, you will see how each measure is determined, how each is used in a motor learning research setting, and the problems that exist related to that measure.

Reaction Time

A popular response latency performance measure in motor learning research has been *reaction time* (RT). Figure 1.2–1 shows that RT is the interval of time between the onset of a signal (stimulus) and the initiation of a response. It is important to note that RT does not include the response itself. When RT is measured, there is usually, but not always, a warning signal followed by a signal that indicates a response should be made.

Also, there is always some means for making the appropriate response. For example, the signal to respond may be a light, buzzer, shock, or word on a screen. As such, the signal may be presented to any sensory source, i.e., vision, hearing, touch, etc. The response may be any particular movement. For example, the subject may be required to lift a finger off a telegraph key, depress a keyboard key, speak a word, or kick a board. The response, then, may be required from any body part or even the entire body.

Table 1.2-1

Two categories of motor skill performance measures

Category	Examples of Measures	Performance Examples
1. Response outcome measures	Time to complete a response e.g., sec., min., hr.	Amount of time to: Run a mile; Type a word
	Reaction time	Time between starter's gun and beginning of movement
	Amount of error in performing criterion response e.g., AE, CE, VE	Number of cm off target in reproducing a criterion limb position
	Number or percentage of errors	Number of free throws missed
	Number of successful attempts	Number of times the beanbag hit the target
	Time on/off target	Number of seconds stylus in contact with target on pursuit rotor
	Time on/off balance	Number of seconds stood in stork stance
	Distance	Height of vertical jump
	Trials to completion	Number of trials it took until all responses correct
2. Response production measures	Displacement	Distance limb traveled to produce response
	Velocity	Speed limb moved while performing response
	Acceleration	Acceleration/deceleration pattern while moving
	Joint angle	Angle of each joint of arm at impact in hitting ball
	Electromyography (EMG)	Time at which the biceps initially fired during a rapid flexion response
	Electroencephalogram (EEG)	Characteristic of the P300 for a choice RT response

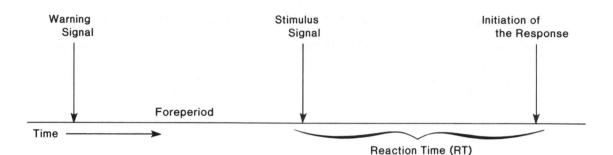

Figure 1.2-1
The time intervals and events related to the typical measurement of reaction time (RT). RT is always the time interval between the onset of the stimulus signal and the initiation of the response.

There are several ways to establish an RT situation. These are depicted in Figure 1.2–2. One is *simple* RT. Here only one signal and one response are required. For example, Figure 1.2–2 indicates that a light will come on and the subject is to lift a finger from a telegraph key. Another type of RT is *choice* RT. In this situation, there is more than one signal to which the subject must respond. Additionally, each signal has a specified response that must be made. The example in Figure 1.2–2 indicates that a subject must respond to the red light by lifting the index finger from a telegraph key, the blue light by lifting the middle finger, and the green light by lifting the ring finger. If the specified response is not made, the attempt is considered an error and typically redone. Another type of RT is *discrimination* RT. Here there is also more than one signal, but only one response is to be made. In Figure 1.2–2, this is illustrated by the subject's response of lifting a finger from the telegraph key only when the red light comes on. If the blue or green light illuminates, no response is to be made. While there are other types of RT situations presented in the research literature, these are sufficient for our needs.

An important point to keep in mind about RT as it is used in motor learning research is that RT is typically used as a dependent measure (performance measure) to represent the time a person takes to process information in order to produce a required response. That is, the experimenter will look at how RT changes as a function of the influence of some variable so that some conclusion can be made about the influence of that variable on the cognitive or motor processing that occurred between the onset of the "go" signal to move and the beginning of the actual observed movement. A longer RT signifies that more information processing was required than for a shorter RT (e.g., if you want to know if it takes longer to process information related to producing a movement that has three component parts compared with a movement that has only one part). That is, would preparing a movement where you must move your arm from point A to B to C to D as fast as possible take longer than preparing a movement from point A to B? Because RT measures only the time between the "go" signal until the movement actually begins, the length of time it takes to make these two movements (which is called movement time, or MT) would not be important. However, the RT would be important because

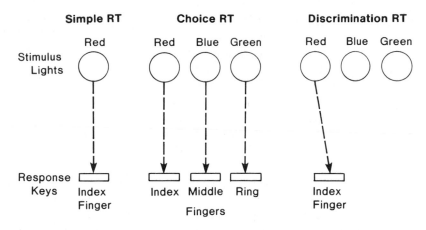

Figure 1.2-2
Three different types of reaction time (RT) test situations: simple RT, choice RT, and discrimination RT.

a longer RT for the three-part movement than for the one-part movement would indicate that something different occurred internally causing the person to take longer to begin moving after the "go" signal occurred. This information could then be used by the researcher as a base from which to develop more research to determine why there was a longer RT time.

Two response measures closely related to RT are movement time (MT) and response time. MT is defined as the interval of time between the initiation and completion of the movement required in a response. It is measured beginning where the RT measurement stops. Response time is the total time interval involving both RT and MT.

Movement Time and Response Time

An example of how RT, MT, and response time intervals are involved in a common everyday situation will help you understand how these are measured and what intervals of time they involve. Suppose you were interested in knowing how long it took an individual to move his or her foot from the accelerator to the brake pedal of a car in response to the sudden appearance of an obstacle in the road. The total amount of time from the appearance of the obstacle until the person contacted the brake is the response time. This response time consists of the RT, the time from the appearance of the obstacle until the person's foot begins to move from the accelerator, and the MT, the time it takes to begin moving from the accelerator until contact with the brake is made.

As you will see in many of the research examples used throughout this text, the use and distinction of these measures is important. Response time should not be considered as synonymous with reaction time, which, unfortunately is common in much of the popular literature. The need for distinction among these measures will become more apparent as you see how they provide useful dependent measures from which inferences can be made related to the learning and control of movement skills.

Error Measures   Measuring the amount of response error has been one of the more prominent measures used in motor learning research. One reason for this is that many tasks used in motor learning research require subjects to make an accurate movement to a target or to move a certain distance in a specified amount of time. In each of these situations, *accuracy* is the goal of the movement. In the first case, spatial accuracy is the goal whereas in the latter case, temporal accuracy is the goal. As a result, the amount of error the subject makes in relation to achieving the spatial or temporal goal becomes a meaningful performance measure.

Consider first the goal of spatial accuracy, which has been the goal of many experimental tasks used in motor learning research. For example, a popular task has been the linear positioning task.

This task requires the subject to move his or her arm or leg to a specified position in space. Typically, the subject moves a lever or sliding handle along a trackway until the desired limb position is reached. The subject may be required to repeat a positioning movement previously performed or demonstrated, or the subject may be required to learn to move the lever or handle to a particular location on the trackway. In these situations, error is recorded as the amount of distance between the subject's positioning response and the criterion or target position.

An example of the limb-positioning response measurement situation is illustrated in Figure 1.2–3. Suppose that the criterion in this example is the 60-cm mark on the trackway. As illustrated, the subject moved to the 40-cm mark. As a result, the subject's score becomes -20 cm ($40 - 60 = -20$). That is, the subject undershot the target, or criterion position, by 20 cm.

Now, let's look at the goal of temporal accuracy. Here the goal is to be as accurate as possible in making a movement in an exact amount of time. The amount of error in these situations is the difference between the subject's movement time and the criterion or target time that was established as the temporal goal for the movement. For example, if the criterion time is 300 msec for moving the right arm a distance of 20 cm, and the subject moves in 350 msec, the amount of error equals 350 (subject's time) $-$ 300 (criterion time) $= +50$ msec. In other words, the subject moved too slowly by 50 msec.

Many of the experiments you will study in this text use tasks like these where amount of error is the performance measure reported. To assist you in interpreting and understanding the results of these experiments, we will consider the measurement of amount of error in more detail.

Reporting the amount of error scores. The amount of error made in responses such as in the examples just presented can be reported in five different ways, each leading to a different interpretation of the data. To help you put this into perspective, consider the following example. Suppose that a subject is required

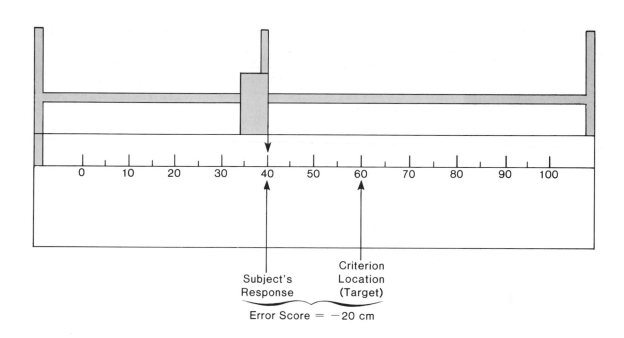

Subject's
Response

Criterion
Location
(Target)

Error Score = −20 cm

to learn to move the handle of the apparatus illustrated in Figure 1.2–3 a distance of 20 cm in 300 msec. It should be noted that in an experiment like this subjects are typically not told in advance what the criterion movement time is. Subjects are instructed to reduce their error to 0, which would indicate they have moved in the exact amount of time. To assist them in reaching this goal, the experimenter tells the subjects their error for an attempt after it is completed. In our previous example, the subject would have been told that the error for that trial was "50 msec too slow."

Table 1.2–2 presents an example of one subject's responses for six trials of practice for a timing task like the one just described, the five different error measures, and how each measure is calculated. Each measure is based on the six practice trials. In the first row under the trial numbers are the subject's movement times. The criterion time (300 msec) is in the second row. The third row presents the difference between these times for the six trials and is labeled *constant error* (*CE*). This measure indicates the signed deviation from the target or criterion. As such, CE represents both the amount and direction of the error. The next row indicates another measure that can be derived from the subject's response. This is *absolute error* (*AE*) and is the unsigned deviation from the target or criterion. Here, the amount of error and not the direction of that error is represented. The average AE for the six trials is calculated by averaging the six CE scores without their algebraic signs. The

Figure 1.2-3
Drawing of a linear positioning apparatus showing the sliding handle that moves freely along the trackway. Scaled along the side facing the experimenter are the measurement values (typically in cm) used to score the response. In this example, the subject has moved the handle to the 40-cm mark.

Table 1.2-2

An example of calculations for five error measures for one subject performing six trials of a timing task where each trial has a movement time goal of 300 msec.

		Trial						
Subject 1	1	2	3	4	5	6	Total	$\overline{X}$
Movement Time	75	596	104	243	411	216	—	—
Criterion Time	300	300	300	300	300	300	—	—
CE	−225	+296	−196	−57	+111	−84	−155	−25.8[a]
AE	225	296	196	57	111	84	969	161.5[b]
VE								180.4[c]
E								182.2[d]
|CE|								25.8

$$[a]\,\overline{CE} = \frac{\Sigma(X - \text{Criterion Value})}{k} \qquad [b]\,\overline{AE} = \frac{\Sigma|X - \text{Criterion Value}|}{k}$$

$$[c]\,VE = \sqrt{\frac{\Sigma CE^2 - \frac{(\Sigma CE)^2}{k}}{k}} \qquad [d]\,E = \sqrt{CE^2 + VE^2}$$

where: X = the subject's score for the trial (Movement Time in the above example)

k = number of trials

next row presents the *variable error* (*VE*) measure. This score represents the variability, or consistency, of the subject's responses. The calculation of this score is simply the standard deviation of the subject's six CE scores.

These three scores, AE, CE, and VE, represent the three primary pieces of error information that are essential in this situation. Note that CE and AE are actually mean scores, that is, they represent the average CE and AE for

the trials. However, when CE and AE are reported in the research literature, the bar above the CE and AE labels (as shown in the formulas in Table 1.2–2), which designates a mean value, are dropped and not included as a part of the CE and AE error measures.

AE represents a general measure of the amount of error. It is a composite score that is mathematically derived from both CE and VE. As such, it does not permit interpretation about whether the error is due to a tendency to inaccurately undershoot or overshoot or due to a lack of consistency in the response from trial to trial. To provide this type of interpretation, CE and VE must be considered. CE enables the researcher to discuss the *bias* of the subject's responses. That is, did the subject tend to move too slow (a positive average CE) or too fast (a negative average CE)? Finally, VE allows the researcher to discuss something about the *consistency* of the subject's responses across the practice trials. VE is actually the standard deviation about a person's own CE. Thus, a large VE indicates inconsistency in the responses whereas a low VE indicates consistent responding for the trials being considered.

While these three error measures provide the essential kinds of information researchers want from these response situations, there has been some controversy concerning the validity of two of the measures. Specifically, CE, while agreeably measuring bias, has problems when averaged across a group of subjects. The principal concern is that when a number of subjects are considered, it is possible that subjects' scores can cancel out each other. That is, if one subject had an average CE score of -13 and another subject had a $+13$, the result would be 0, which would not be an accurate reflection of bias-related error. To accommodate this problem, Henry (1974) and Schutz (1977) argued that after a subject's CE was calculated, to get a group CE value, the absolute value of each subject's CE score should be averaged. This new measure, termed absolute CE ($|CE|$), is considered to be the more valid representation for the amount of bias for a group of subjects. The direction of that bias for a group can be determined by comparing the number of $+$'s and $-$'s for the individual CE scores.

Another validity issue related to error measures is the appropriateness of the use of AE as a representative performance error measure. Traditionally, only AE was reported as the dependent measure in the research literature. However, a very influential article by Robert Schutz and Eric Roy (1973) presented information that indicated some problems with using AE as an only error score. The primary problem was that AE is a score that has CE and VE as components. Thus, the use of AE alone made the results of an experiment difficult to interpret. Schutz and Roy suggested that only CE and VE be used. In 1974, Franklin Henry, although agreeing with Schutz and Roy that AE was an inadequate dependent measure, disagreed that CE and VE should be

used. Rather, Henry suggested the use of a total error score that he labeled as E. E is a composite score that is calculated as follows:

$$E = \sqrt{CE^2 + VE^2}$$

Henry (1974) believed that the advantage of using E is that it reflects the contributions of both components VE and CE. AE does not adequately reflect that contribution.

There are several theoretical problems associated with the use of error scores.[1] These problems deal with such issues as which score is the proper one to use, how each score should be interpreted, and so on. Other scores have been suggested as alternatives to these three that we have just considered. However, when referring to group performance, we will consider AE, VE, and |CE| as basic performance measures for tasks that involve error scores considered in relation to a target or criterion. In this text these scores will always be used to refer to some specific aspect of a performance. Absolute error is a measure of magnitude or amount of error, constant error is a measure of response biasing, and variable error is a measure of response consistency. |CE| and VE help to interpret and explain AE; that is, was the large AE due to response biasing or to inconsistent responding over trials, or both? Or was the small AE due to almost no response biasing or to very consistent responding, or both?

Relating error measures to teaching. At this point it is quite reasonable for you to conclude that all of this discussion about error measures has little to do with the needs of people instructing others to learn motor skills. To eliminate that conclusion, consider the following example. Suppose you are teaching an archery or riflery class, where target accuracy is the critical measure of performance. Further, suppose you have two students with target accuracy for six shots that look like those in Figure 1.2–4. It is important to note here that in order to illustrate the point about the potential for the different error scores to be informative to a teacher, the target-accuracy example in Figure 1.2–4 is based on the actual value of the points for each ring, rather than a calculated error score. Thus, the terms AE, VE, and CE as used in this example are analogous to the scores discussed in the preceding section. The application to teaching is the same whether error scores or number of points scored are used.

Both of these students have identical total AE and E scores of 2.0 and 2.16 respectively. However, if we arbitrarily cut the targets in half so that we can evaluate response bias, the right half can be considered + and the left half −, the CE and VE scores are remarkably different. Student A has a CE score of 0, and Student B's CE score is +2.0. Obviously, response bias is a problem for Student B. On the other hand, VE for Student A is 2.16, and for Student B it is 0.81, half more than the variability problem of Student A's responses. For the teacher, then, the AE, or actual target values, would be

1. For those interested in investigating that debate, the articles by Schutz and Roy (1973), Henry (1974), Schutz (1977), and Spray (1986) cited in the Related Readings section will be helpful.

Motor Skills and Learning

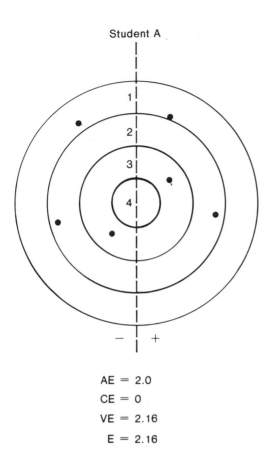

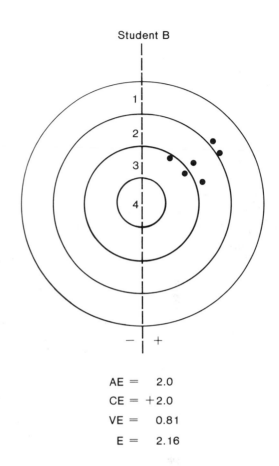

Student A	Student B
AE = 2.0	AE = 2.0
CE = 0	CE = +2.0
VE = 2.16	VE = 0.81
E = 2.16	E = 2.16

Figure 1.2-4
An example of two sets of scores from a target-accuracy task where the AE scores are the same but the CE, VE, and E scores are different.

misleading. The two students have different problems that require different types of correction. That is, Student A is having difficulty being consistent from one shot to the next. This could be caused by a variety of problems, such as not focusing on the target, lack of steadiness before shooting, etc. Student B, on the other hand, has a simpler problem. Here the problem seems to be one of aim where the student needs to adjust his or her aim to the left a bit.

Some laboratory tasks require a subject to make a joystick or movable lever to follow a specified pathway, as was seen in the displacement curve in Figure 1.2–5. While the displacement curve provides descriptive information about the pathway traversed by the subject, the researcher may also wish to determine how accurately the subject moved in relation to the criterion pathway. One source of this information is found by determining the amount of error between the subject's pathway and the criterion pathway. This calculated error measure is known as *root-mean-squared error* (*RMSE*). It might be helpful to think of RMSE as AE for a continuous task.

Tracking
Performance
Error

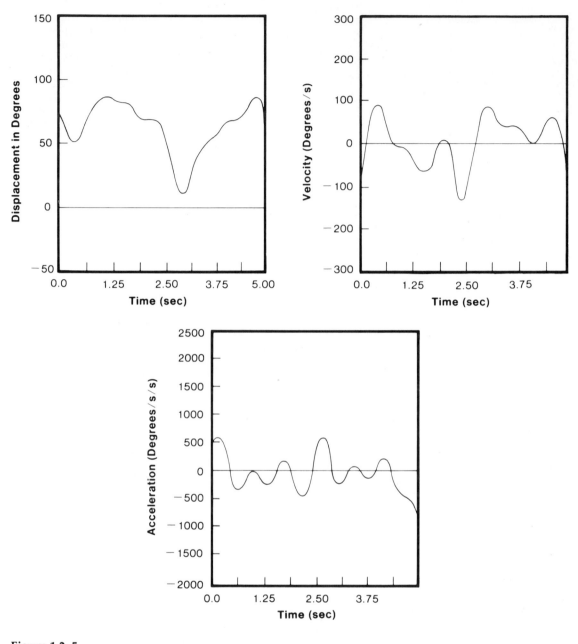

Figure 1.2-5
Recordings of
displacement,
velocity, and
acceleration for a
tracking task.

Motor Skills and Learning

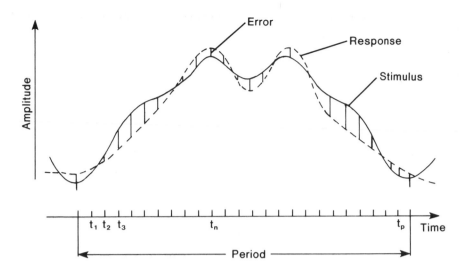

Figure 1.2-6
The difference between the subject's response and the stimulus at each specified time interval is used to calculate one root-mean squared error (RMSE) score.

An example of calculating RMSE is presented in Figure 1.2–6. The solid line indicates the criterion pathway the subjects were required to follow with a movable lever. The dashed lines represent an example of a subject's actual response on one trial. The computer is programmed to record the subject's position in relation to the criterion pathway at specified intervals of time, such as every 1/1000 sec (1 msec). These error values are then averaged for the total pathway to yield the RMSE.

Kinematic Measures

Increasingly popular measures of motor skill performance are kinematic measures. *Kinematics* refers to a description of movement without regard to force or mass. Commonly used kinematic measures typically describe movement location, velocity, and acceleration. Movement location can be kinematically described in a number of ways. For example, one can attach light-emitting diodes (LED) to a limb and then, by using a computerized camera system, record the pathway of the limb in performing a movement. Currently available systems for doing this type of analysis include Selspot, WATSMART, and Motion Analysis System. An example of a handwriting movement described by this method is presented in Figure 1.2–7.

Another kinematic method of describing movement location involves marking the performer's body at specific points of interest, filming that person while performing the movement, and then noting the location characteristics of each marked body point. This final part is usually quantified by using a digitizer, which indicates the X–Y coordinates of each marked part of the body. By observing the frame-to-frame changes of each point of interest, the researcher can obtain specific information about the movement.

Movement location information can also be represented graphically by means of displacement values of the movement, as seen in Figure 1.2–5. In

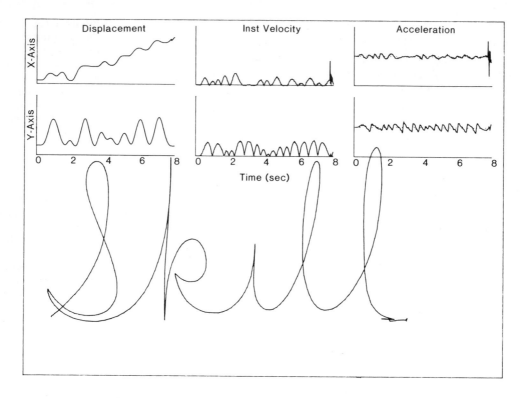

Figure 1.2-7
Handwriting described by attaching light-emitting diodes to the limb and using a computerized camera system to show the movement's pathway.

this example, displacement represents the movement of a joystick through a prescribed movement pathway that was shown to a subject on a computer monitor. The curve in this graph represents the pathway taken by a subject by moving the joystick in an attempt to follow the prescribed pathway.

Velocities are typically determined by calculating movement speed per unit of time, which can then be graphically represented in the form of a velocity–time curve, as depicted in Figure 1.2–6. Here, the number of degrees of movement made by the subject is plotted over the amount of time taken to perform the total movement. Finally, acceleration can also be graphically represented. An acceleration curve is also presented in Figure 1.2–6. Here, the speeding up and slowing down of the movements are recorded as the subject moves.

Kinematic measures are useful descriptors for researchers. They enable researchers to describe movements more completely, thus allowing them a better understanding of the influences of variables of interest on the performance of motor skills. Examples of the use of such measures will be seen in various parts of this book.

EMG Measures

Movement involves electrical activity in the muscles. This electrical activity can be measured by *electromyography* (*EMG*). This is accomplished by attaching electrodes on the skin over the muscles of interest and then recording

Motor Skills and Learning

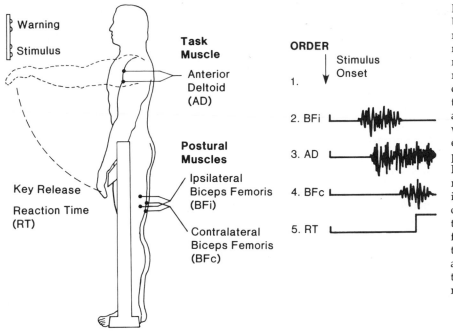

Figure 1.2-8
Using EMG recordings to measure a movement response. The figure on the left shows the reaction-time apparatus and where each electrode was placed to record the EMG for each muscle group of interest. The figures on the right show the EMG recordings for each of the three muscle groups and the reaction-time interval for the response.

the electrical activity by means of a polygraph recorder or a computer. Each muscle of interest can be recorded individually. Figure 1.2–8 shows some EMG recordings for electrical activity in the ipsilateral biceps femoris (BFi) and contralateral biceps femoris (BFc) of the legs and the anterior deltoid (AD) of the shoulder girdle for a task that required subjects to move their arm from the reaction-time key, on a signal, to a position directly in front of their shoulders. The EMG signals presented for these muscles show when electrical activity began in the muscles. This can be seen by the increase in the frequency and height of the traces for each muscle. The actual beginning of movement off the RT key is designated in this diagram by the vertical line at the end of the RT recording (line 5 of this figure).

An interesting use of the EMG and RT measures has been to *fractionate* RT. This can be done by observing the time at which the muscle shows increased activity after the stimulus has occurred. The period of time between the onset of the stimulus and the beginning of the increase in EMG activity is called the *premotor time*. The period of time beginning with this increase in EMG activity and the actual beginning of limb movement is called the *motor time*. In this way, the RT is "fractionated" into two parts. This measurement method has been popular because most researchers agree that the premotor time is a measure of the receipt and transmission of information from the environment, through the nervous system, and to the muscle itself (i.e., the "cognitive" component of RT). The motor time, on the other hand,

indicates the lag in the muscle to overcome the inertia of the limb following receipt of the command to contract. We will refer to this in more detail in later sections.

The Speed-Accuracy Measurement Problem

One additional performance measure that needs to be highlighted involves a relatively common measurement problem. This measure of performance problem occurs in any skill that requires both speed and accuracy, such as in fencing. The fencer must be accurate with the foil and quick as well. Suppose you were plotting the daily performance of the fencer to determine the progress he or she was making in learning to lunge. Would you measure the accuracy of each lunge, the speed of each lunge, or both?

A similar concern exists for any skill requiring both speed and accuracy, such as piano playing or tennis serving. Obviously, this is not only a measurement problem but one that should be considered in the area of how to practice. Does the performer emphasize speed, accuracy, or both in practice when learning the skill? At this point, however, only the measurement problem will be considered.

When only one measure of performance is desired, several options are available in the speed-accuracy situation. The simplest is to choose one over the other, depending on which is more important in the experimental problem. However, in this case valuable information is lost, and the measure when considered alone is generally not a valid one. A second option is to calculate a score that is based on a combination of the two measures. This second alternative is the preferrred one and the one you will most often find reported in the research literature.

Two common methods of combining these measures are related to the type of task used. When the task involves speed for its completion but considers errors that are made, the suggestion is to add the number of errors and the time to complete the task and divide by two. If the task involves speed for completion but considers points scored, as with a target, then multiply the time to complete the task by the total points in order to obtain the speed-accuracy score.

From this discussion it should be apparent that to determine the amount of learning that has taken place in any situation, an adequate performance measure is first required. The suggestions that have been made here should help you to understand why a particular measure is selected. Although most performance measures are simply selected because the task being learned can only be measured one way, there are certain instances where several measures can be used for one task. When this latter situation occurs, the guidelines discussed next should be applied.

How adequately a person can measure learning will be dependent on the nature of the skill or task that is being observed. In the practical setting of a physical education class, the skill to be observed is readily defined by what is being taught. What is important in this situation is the performance measure selected, on the basis of which the learning inference will be based. In an experimental setting, both the task and the performance measure must be selected by the experimenter. Since you will be reading about many experiments that deal with the learning and performance of motor skills, it will be helpful for you to understand the basis for the selection of the tasks and performance measures for these experiments.

There appear to be four major criteria for judging the appropriateness of a motor task and/or performance measure for any learning situation. These four criteria are (1) objectivity, (2) reliability, (3) validity, (4) novelty. The first three criteria are standard concerns that can be found in most tests and measurement textbooks. These three conditions are essential as criteria for performance measure selection in either the instructional setting or the experimental setting. The fourth criterion, however, is unique to the task selection process of the learning experiment.

Objectivity means simply that two different people should be able to arrive at a similar score for performance. In the examples presented in Table 1.2–1, objectivity is generally no problem. It can become a problem when you measure a performance according to such abstract and subjective terms as "good," "bad," "fair," "excellent," etc., when no objective measuring criteria are available.

Reliability refers to the repeatability of the test and results, the certainty of obtaining a similar performance score on the task if the subject is tested a second time. Control must be used to ensure that measures are as reliable as possible. *Validity* indicates whether the task or performance score actually measures what you want it to measure. Thus, for motor learning experiments, you must consider whether the task is motor; that is, does the task demand physical movement to be successfully accomplished? You must also consider whether the task you use accurately reflects the factor in question in the experiment, e.g., strength, coordination, or balance.

The fourth criterion is of particular importance in the learning experiment. The *novelty* of the task, that is, how familiar the task is to the subjects, is essential to the learning experiment to avoid the problem of using subjects who have had different amounts of experience with the task. A novel task, then, is one with which subjects have had no previous experience. The benefit of the novel task can be seen in an example of an experiment that is designed to assess or measure the effect of a fatigue on learning a motor skill. If a basketball free throw is used, misleading results could occur if all subjects had varying prior experiences in free-throw shooting. It would be difficult to attribute any observed performance differences to the effects of fatigue. The differences could also be attributed to different skill levels of subjects at the

beginning of the experiment. Using a novel task such as bouncing a basketball into the hoop with the nonpreferred hand would help avoid such ambiguous results.

Summary

An essential element in understanding motor learning is the measurement of motor performance. All concepts presented in this text are based on research in which motor performance was observed and measured. Measuring motor performance is also important for a teacher of motor skills because it is essential that the performance of students is evaluated as they practice and perform the skills being taught. An important part of this evaluation process is measuring motor performance. In this concept, the discussion has focused on considering different ways that motor performance can be measured, and some guidelines for selecting appropriate measures were presented. Because there are so many kinds of motor performance measures, they were organized into three categories. Response output measures can be subdivided into three categories in which time, error, and magnitude of a response are measured. Limb and joint measures include kinematic measures that describe the biomechanical characteristics of limbs and joints as they move. Finally, EMG measures provide a look at the muscle level of a movement by measuring the electrical activity related to the muscle's involvement in a movement. Motor performance measures are not without their problems. Several of these have been discussed, with particular attention given to error measures and speed-accuracy measures. Four criteria should be considered when judging the appropriateness of a task to be used in a motor learning experiment or for selecting a performance measure to evaluate motor skills: objectivity, reliability, validity, and novelty.

Related Readings

Atha, J. (1984). Current techniques for measuring motion. *Applied Ergonomics, 15*, 245–257.

Heatherington, R. (1973). Within-subject variation, measurement error, and selection of a criterion score. *Research Quarterly, 44*, 113–117.

Henry, F. M. (1967). "Best" versus "average" individual scores. *Research Quarterly, 38*, 317–320.

Henry, F. M. (1974). Variable and constant performance errors within a group of individuals. *Journal of Motor Behavior, 6*, 149–154.

Schutz, R. W. (1977). Absolute, constant, and variable error: Problems and solutions. In D. Mood (Ed.), *The measurement of change in physical education* (pp. 82–108). Boulder, Co.: University of Colorado.

Schutz, R. W. & Roy, E. A. (1973). Absolute error: The devil in disguise. *Journal of Motor Behavior, 5*, 141–153.

Spray, J. A. (1986). Absolute error revisited: An accuracy indicator in disguise. *Journal of Motor Behavior, 18*, 225–238.

Thomas, J. R. & Nelson, J. K. (1985). *Introduction to research in health, physical education, recreation, and dance.* Champaign, IL: Human Kinetics. (Read chapters 13 & 14.)

The scientific method, or research, is an important tool in understanding the learning and performance of motor skills

As you progress through this book, you will find that each chapter includes a series of *concepts* related to the topic of that chapter. These concepts should be considered as generalized statements about a particular issue, statements that have been developed by synthesizing research findings. As such, these concepts can be thought of as similar to principles or general conclusions. The role of research is important in the development of these concepts. It is from information gained from research activity that evidence is provided from which a concept can be generated. In the discussion that follows, you will be introduced to the scientific method, the foundation upon which research in motor learning is based. By becoming familiar with this method of scientific inquiry, you will be better able to understand the process involved in obtaining the information on which the concepts in this book are based.

A further benefit of studying the scientific method can be seen in the following example. An often perplexing question for many people involved in providing motor skill instruction to individuals or groups is "Why did you teach that skill the way you did?" Suddenly the instructor is required to consider the basis or rationale for decisions that were made when developing the instructional approach that was employed. Why was the instruction sequenced as it was? Why did the group practice like that? Why did you have them use that instructional aid? Why did you say what you did to them? We could go on and on with similar probing questions, but the point can be made with these few examples. How often do we really consider the reasons *why* we structure an instructional setting as we do? This very basic question is at the heart of this book. The primary intent of the study of motor learning is to acquaint you with both the learner, the learning environment, and the process of learning in such a way as to provide you with a basis for your instructional decisions. Furthermore, it is also the intent of this study to provide you with a foundation for understanding how movement decisions are made and controlled and how various environmental variables influence movement even when that movement is quite apart from the instructional setting.

In order to answer effectively the types of questions we have here, we must first understand how such questions can be investigated. Throughout this book you will encounter many reports of research. The purpose of such encounters is to provide you with an opportunity to see for yourself how the very perplexing questions related to the how's and why's of motor behavior are investigated, so that the answers which we so urgently seek when confronted with the need for instructional decisions can be found. It is through careful

use of research that we can begin to uncover the clues concerning the mysteries of motor behavior. It is hoped that through the following discussion you will see what research is about and that you will feel more confident as you read about various research reports in the ensuing chapters of this book.

Knowledge is based on the gathering of reliable information. But this type of information about motor behavior, like any other domain of science, can only be obtained through the application of carefully planned and conducted research. This discussion, then, should help you to better understand the processes involved in that research, so that you can better determine for yourself the appropriateness of the generalizations concerning the processes of learning and performing motor skills, which are made in later chapters.

Discussion

When we are confronted with the "why" questions formulated in the previous section, we are limited to certain methods of determining our answer, which we can assume is based on some knowledge. We generally limit our acquisition of knowledge to such means as intuition, common sense, tradition, or personal experience. The teacher who uses a particular teaching method because that is the way he or she was taught is basing knowledge on personal experience or tradition. These means can be very powerful and beneficial. They are certainly not to be disparaged. A problem, however, is that these methods of obtaining information are very subjective. The rationale for decisions or the understanding may be different for one teacher than for another. There is no objective basis for such decisions. Thus, when knowledge is so subjective, it is difficult to generalize to a variety of situations and individuals. It should be stated, however, that when the subjective means just mentioned are combined with the objective method we are about to discuss, a very useful approach to gaining and using information has been achieved.

Clearly the need is to base knowledge on some objective means of gathering information. This objective means is termed the *scientific method,* the basis for research in the motor domain. It will become apparent that the application of the scientific method to the understanding of motor behavior is often very difficult. However, the need to know and understand that behavior provides a strong incentive to overcome such difficulties and to approach the study of human motor behavior as scientifically as possible.

The Method of Science

At the core of science is the need for *observation.* Since our concern here is motor behavior, the initial point for understanding the method of science is to know that observation of motor behavior is the primary element in such study. Observation of behavior can be a rather elusive concept. What is meant by observation? How should it occur? How do we know what to look for? And so on. These questions are all important to the basic understanding of the scientific method; as you study this section, answers to these questions should become more apparent.

The primary goal of science is to understand our universe. To accomplish this primary goal, three subgoals of science are important: to *describe, explain,* and *predict.* These three goals are hierarchically listed and form the basis for the several possible forms of research in motor behavior. Describing motor behavior simply indicates that a statement of what behavior has occurred can be made. For example, a group of boys learned to walk through a maze in an average time of 10 minutes. The next level of understanding in science involves explaining why the observed behavior occurred. Here we are not only concerned with stating that the group of boys learned to walk through the maze in 10 minutes but we also want to know why. Perhaps they received a reward, while another group of boys who received no reward took an average of 20 minutes to learn the maze. Finally, we want to be able to predict motor behavior. From our example we would predict that when a reward is available, children will learn a complex task, like walking through a maze, more quickly than when no reward is available. Successful prediction can be seen as achieving the primary goal of science, because to successfully predict demonstrates an understanding of a phenomenon. Prediction is the ability to generalize results of careful observation from one setting and to apply them to another setting. If the prediction or generalization is correct, results in the new setting should resemble the results from the previous setting. Prediction is based on the attainment of the goals of description and explanation. These goals can only be achieved through the careful observation of behavior. This observation can occur in very natural settings, such as on the playground, in the gymnasium, or in the therapy room; or it can occur in a laboratory where the essential elements to be observed can be specifically controlled and manipulated.

The experiment. The primary means of observation employed in the motor behavior research you will find throughout this book is the *experiment.* As much as possible, the primary purpose in the experiment is to control as many elements as possible, except for the ones that are the focus of observation in that experiment. These elements that need to be controlled or released to act naturally are called *variables.* In any experiment the experimenter must determine what variable he or she is interested in so as to observe its effects on some type of behavior. This variable of interest is termed the *independent variable.*[2] The example of the boys' learning to walk a maze with or without a reward is a good example to consider here. The purpose of such an experiment is to determine the influence of rewards on the learning of a motor skill. The variable of interest to the experimenter is rewards. Thus the experimenter manipulates this variable by intentionally changing its use for different groups of subjects; that is, one group of subjects would get a reward following each trial while a second group, the control group, would not receive any reward at all. If the group receiving the reward learns to perform the task better than the other group, and if other possible influencing variables have been controlled

2. *Dependent variables,* which were considered in Concept 1.2, are the performance measures used in an experiment. In the example experiment, the number of minutes required by a subject to learn to walk through the maze is the dependent variable.

by keeping them equal between the groups, then the experimenter has answered his or her basic question concerning a particular variable that influences learning.

This quite simple example of an experiment illustrates how observation is used in a controlled experiment. The procedures to be followed, the task to be performed, the location of the experiment, and so on, are all decisions the experimenter must make. He or she will make those decisions on the basis of his or her own knowledge of the particular area of study the experiment is related to. The experimenter must be very careful in these decisions, for they will have a great influence on what the results will be and what he or she can say about those results.

Relationships and experiments. Every experiment includes a basic concern for relationships, primarily between either the independent and dependent variable or two dependent variables. If the relationship of interest is between the independent and dependent variables, the experiment is primarily concerned with a *causal relationship*. The goal here is to determine cause and effect. In our example of the rewards experiment, the goal of that experiment was to determine the effect of rewards (the independent variable) on the learning of walking through a maze (the dependent variable). It is essential in experiments of this type that all variables be similar between groups, except for the independent variable. Then, if differences between groups do occur, you can be quite certain that the cause of the performance differences between groups was due to the only variable that was different between the groups.

Sometimes it is not the experimenter's intention to determine a causal relationship between variables; rather, the interest is more in a *noncausal relationship,* that is, in how two dependent variables are related to each other. For example, the question might be raised, if a person reacts quickly to a sound will he or she also move very quickly? The problem being investigated is whether the reaction time and the speed of movement are related to each other. The cause-and-effect relationship between these two variables is not of interest here. The experimenter manipulates no variables. He or she simply tests subjects on two tasks, one measuring reaction time and the other measuring speed of movement. The two performance scores (the dependent variables) are then correlated; a high correlation indicates a strong relationship, while a low correlation shows little if any relationship.

Conclusions. It is important to understand the distinction between causal and noncausal relationships, each of which can be investigated through controlled experimentation. You will encounter both types of experiments throughout this book. As you consider these types of relationships, you should become aware that understanding the difference between causal and noncausal relationships is related to the type of *conclusion* that can be made on the basis of the results of an experiment. The conclusion that a fast reaction time *causes*

fast speed of movement could *not* be made from the experiment described, even if the relationship between the two was found to be strong, because the experiment was designed to consider noncausal relationships. Thus, the conclusion about the relationship between the two variables must be always stated in a noncausal manner. For example, if the results show a high relationship, the conclusion could be that reaction time and speed of movement are highly related to each other, although we could not say anything about the cause of these results. However, in terms of prediction, it would be possible to say that if a person had a fast reaction time, he or she also had fast speed of movement.

Conclusions that suggest cause can only be validly made when the experiment has been designed as a cause-and-effect type of experiment. If the experimenter has manipulated a particular variable to observe the effects of that manipulation on some behavior, then a cause-and-effect experiment has been designed.

An example of this type of experiment is the one described earlier where the children were required to learn to walk through a maze. The variable manipulated in that experiment was availability of a reward. Suppose that one group of subjects is given a reward after each trial that is better than the previous best trial while the other group receives no rewards as they practice the skill. In this experiment, all conditions are the same except the availability of a reward. That is, all subjects practice the same skill, receive the same instructions, and so on. Therefore, if the results show that the reward group learned the skill faster than the no reward group, then a causal conclusion can be made about the benefit of rewards. We can have confidence in this conclusion because the availability of rewards is the only thing that differed about the conditions related to practice and performing the skill. Any observed difference in performance between the two groups must therefore be attributed to the reward availability variable.

Generalization. Generalizations are important to science. A major goal of every experiment is that the conclusion can be taken beyond the specific experiment and applied to general situations involving similar variables. This book is filled with generalizations; in fact, each concept that is presented in every chapter is a generalization. These generalizations are made by synthesizing the research evidence that is available as a result of many experiments. The presentation of much consistent research evidence that has controlled and manipulated variables in a variety of ways and settings provides generalizations that become generally accepted. When the results are reliable or consistent, generalizations can be made with some degree of confidence. This is the ultimate goal of science, for generalizations permit prediction. However, further experiments based on the predictions may indicate that some modifications of the generalizations are necessary. Thus the process of science continues in the search for absolute prediction. When human behavior is of concern,

however, such absolute prediction is very improbable. Nevertheless, generalizations in which we can be quite confident can be made; but it is only through careful observation by means of controlled experimentation that these generalizations can be developed.

Types of research. An important aspect of the research process that is related to the issue of generalization concerns the type of research conducted. That is, does the research have generalization goals that are primarily theoretical or primarily applied? Put another way, does the researcher want the experiment to have impact on a theoretical issue or does the researcher want the experiment to have impact on solving a "real" problem? If the goal of the experiment is directed primarily to a theoretical generalization, then this research is categorized as *basic* research; if the research is directed primarily toward answering an immediate problem that a practitioner faces, then the research is classified as *applied* research. Both basic and applied research are valuable to furthering our knowledge of motor learning.

An example of a basic research experiment would be one that investigates how a learned motor skill is represented in human memory. As you will see in Chapters 3 and 5, this question has been the basis of much motor learning research. The answer to this question does not have direct application to the teaching of skills, but it does increase our understanding of processes responsible for motor performance. An example of an applied research experiment is one that attempts to solve the problem a teacher might confront during a class. For example, when teaching the tennis serve, should the serve be demonstrated to the class to help them learn it? The experiment designed to answer this question would provide an immediate answer about the efficacy of using demonstration as a teaching strategy for tennis serving.

There are two points to emphasize about the distinction between basic and applied research. First, these two types of research should be thought of as end points on a continuum, which allows for research to be classified as some combination of the two. Much of the research you will read about in this book falls somewhere along the continuum, rather than in either one category or the other. In this type of research it is possible to make a generalization to both theory and to real-world problems. The degree of generalization possible to either of these depends on where along the continuum between basic and applied the research falls. The second important point to remember about the basic-applied research distinction is that each type of research has strengths and weaknesses. One type should not be thought of as "better" than the other. Rather, one type may be preferable for a certain type of generalization goal than the other.

Summary

When you are confronted with the need to provide a rationale to support your approach to teaching, you would like to have a more objective basis than intuition or tradition can provide. The scientific method provides a cogent means

of obtaining information that can be used as a solid foundation for supporting instructional decisions. The scientific method is based on objective observation; through observation the goals of science, which are to describe, explain, and predict, may be attained. The primary means of observation in the scientific method is the experiment, which includes independent and dependent variables. Independent variables are those variables in which the experimenter is interested in determining the influence on the dependent variable. In a broad sense all experiments are concerned with relationships between variables. Causal relationships involve relationships between the independent and the dependent variables. Noncausal relationships are concerned with the relationship between dependent variables. These relationships determine the type of conclusion that can be made from any experiment. Generalizations are essential to the scientific method, for they are statements that go beyond the narrow limits of any one experiment. In this book, the concepts that are presented and discussed in each chapter are generalizations which have been made on the basis of information obtained through the scientific method.

Finally, both basic and applied research will be found in the research literature related to motor learning. Basic research is designed to provide generalizations that can be related to theoretical issues whereas applied research is designed to provide generalizations that can help answer specific problems that a practitioner might face. Both types of research are valuable for furthering our understanding of motor learning.

Related Readings

Anderson, B. F. (1971). *The psychology experiment: An introduction to the scientific method.* Belmont, California: Brooks/Cole. (Read chapter 2.)

Arnold, R. K. (1982). Research on sport skill: Is it applicable to coaching? *Motor Skills: Theory into Practice, 6,* 93–102.

Campbell, D. T., & Stanley, J. C. (1963). *Experimental and quasi-experimental designs for research.* Chicago: Rand McNally. (Read pp. 1–6.)

Christina, R. W. (1989). Whatever happened to applied research in motor learning? In J. Skinner (Ed.), *Future directions in exercise/sport research.* Champaign, IL: Human Kinetics. (Read pp. 413–424.)

Prytula, R. E. (1975). The concept of organ use revisited in the gluteus maximus. *Perceptual and Motor Skills, 40,* 289–290.

Thomas, J. R., & Nelson, J. K. (1985). *Introduction to research in health, physical education, recreation, and dance.* Champaign, IL: Human Kinetics. (Read pp. 3–17.)

Study Questions for Chapter 1

1. What is the meaning of the term *skill* when it is used to refer to a motor skill? What is another use of the term *skill?*
2. What is the difference between a dichotomous classification system and a classification system that involves a continuum of categories?
3. What distinguishes (a) a gross from a fine motor skill? (b) a discrete from a continuous motor skill? (c) a closed from an open motor skill? Give three examples of motor skills for each category.

4. How does the Gentile 2×2 classification system differ from the two-category open and closed skills classification? Is the Gentile approach an improvement over the two-category system? Why or why not?
5. Cite three examples of different measures of motor performance that can be classified as response outcome measures. Cite three examples of response production measures.
6. Describe how simple RT, choice RT, and discrimination RT situations differ. How does MT differ from RT?
7. What different information can be obtained about a person's performance by calculating AE, CE, and VE when performance accuracy is the movement goal?
8. What information can kinematic measures of performance provide that other forms of performance measures cannot?
9. What information about a movement can be provided by using EMG?
10. Name three important criteria that should be considered when a performance measure must be selected. Explain why each is important.
11. What is meant by the *scientific method* of obtaining information? How does this method differ from other methods of obtaining information?
12. What is the difference between the *independent* and the *dependent* variables in an experiment?
13. What is the difference between a *causal* and a *noncausal* relationship? Why is this distinction an important one when doing motor learning research?
14. What is the difference between *applied* and *basic* research?

Introduction to Motor Learning

2

Concept 2.1
Learning can be inferred from practice observations, retention tests, and transfer tests.

Concept 2.2
The learning of a motor skill occurs in stages.

Concept 2.3
A theoretical basis is necessary for the advancement of knowledge about how we learn and control motor skills.

Concept 2.1 Learning can be inferred from practice observations, retention tests, and transfer tests

Application

In any profession involving motor skills instruction, a typical requirement is that the instructor make some assessment of whether or not the students are learning what is being taught. For example, suppose you are a physical education teacher teaching a tennis unit. If you are teaching your students to serve, what will you look for in their serves that will help you assess their progress in learning. How can you be certain that what you are observing is the result of learning and not just luck?

These questions relate to an important aspect of learning that must be considered when skill learning is assessed. That is, we must make an inference about learning. We do not directly observe learning. We directly observe behavior, which in this case is motor performance. It is from this performance observation that we must determine if the observed behavior reflects learning of the skill being practiced. Thus, the determination of whether or not a skill has been learned involves a two-part process. First, there must be observation of performance of the skill under conditions where an appropriate evaluation of learning can take place. Second, there must be a translation of that observation into a meaningful conclusion about learning, based on what has been observed.

In the discussion that follows, the problem of how to assess learning will be approached from two general directions. First, a definition of learning will be established. This is a critical step as it is important to know what learning is before attempting to determine how to evaluate whether or not it has taken place. Then, the focus will shift to considering different ways that the learning inference can be made. The primary concern will be to establish the appropriate conditions under which performance should be observed. As you will see, when inappropriate conditions are established, inappropriate conclusions about learning usually result. Three learning assessment methods will be discussed so that you will be able to make confident conclusions about learning.

The importance of making appropriate conclusions about learning can be illustrated in several different ways. For example, if you are a teacher, you will undoubtedly want to base a student's grade, at least in part, on how well he or she has learned the skills you taught in class. As a teacher you will also want to know if a particular teaching strategy is more effective than an available alternative. The more desirable teaching strategy is the one that leads to more effective learning of the skill being taught. A similar problem occurs in a physical therapy setting where it is important to know that the techniques used to help patients learn certain skills will lead to better learning than other

available techniques. It is critical to keep in mind that unless you are able to confidently assess learning, it is difficult to derive valid conclusions that are applicable to any of these situations.

Two important terms are important for you to keep distinct in this discussion and throughout this book: *performance* and *learning. Performance* can be thought of most simply as *observable behavior.* In terms of motor skills, observable behaviors include such things as hitting a baseball, shooting a basketball, running a mile, tracing through a maze, dancing a waltz, or operating a lathe. Each attempt to hit a ball, shoot a basketball, and so on, is a performance. We can usually quantify performances such as these for evaluation purposes by using one or more of the motor performance measures described in Concept 1.2. Additionally, a performance may include behaviors of greater magnitude than these examples. For example, playing an entire game of basketball may be considered a performance. The behavior of interest to the observer, then, becomes the basis for specifically defining a performance.

Learning, on the other hand, is an internal phenomenon that cannot be observed directly; it can only be inferred from a person's behavior, i.e., performance. It is common for us to make inferences about a person's internal states based on observations of their behaviors. For example, when someone smiles (an observable behavior), we infer that he or she is happy. When someone cries, we infer that he or she is sad, or perhaps very happy. When a person's face gets red, we believe that person is embarrassed. Notice that in each of these situations, certain characteristics about the individual's behavior are specifically identified as the basis for making a particular inference about some internal state that we cannot directly observe. However, because we must make an inference based on observed behavior, it is possible to make an incorrect inference. If a student sitting beside you in class yawns during the lecture, you might infer that person is bored when in fact he or she is very interested but is also very tired because of lack of sleep the night before. In the same way, then, because we must infer on the basis of observed behavioral characteristics that learning is occurring or has occurred, we must select the most appropriate behavioral characteristics to observe and then observe these characteristics under appropriate circumstances.

An important question to consider, then, is What performance characteristics should be identified in order to confidently infer that learning has taken place? Probably the key indicator of learning is that performance changes should occur as learning occurs. This means that the performance measure being used should show distinct changes as the person practices the skill. Two performance characteristic changes are especially important to look for.

First, performance of the skill should show *improvement* over time. This means that the person can exhibit a greater degree of skill at some later time

Performance
Changes during
Learning

than at some previous time during which performance of the skill was observed. However, note that this improvement should be marked by persistence. That is, the improvement that has been observed should not last for just a short time or for one performance. Rather, the improvement should continue over a long period. A person who is judged to have learned something should not only be able to demonstrate the improved performance today, but also tomorrow, next week, and so on. It is important to note that learning should not be limited to performance improvement. There are instances when bad habits result from practice. In these situations, the observed performance does not improve and actually worsens. However, because this text is concerned with skill acquisition, we will focus on learning as involving the improvement in performance.

The second characteristic that should change when learning occurs is that performance should become *increasingly more consistent*. This means that trial-to-trial, or attempt-to-attempt performances should reveal decreasing fluctuations. Early in practicing a new skill, a person is likely to be very inconsistent in performing the skill. On one attempt, the measured response may be better than the previous one whereas on the next attempt it may be worse. However, eventually the performance becomes more consistent.

These two characteristics of performance changes during learning are both important in making inferences about learning and are also closely interrelated. The first characteristic is concerned with the improvement in performance and the persistence of that improvement whereas the second characteristic involves how consistent that change in performance becomes. Together, these characteristics emphasize that motor learning is a process in which many physical and psychological changes are taking place.

Learning Defined

On the basis of the characteristics of performance related to learning, it is possible to develop a general definition for the term *learning* that we can use as the basis for all that follows in this book. Accordingly, learning is defined as *a change in the capability of the individual to perform a skill that must be inferred from a relatively permanent improvement in performance as a result of practice or experience*. This does not mean that once a skill is learned it will be performed perfectly every time it is attempted. Remember the example about making an incorrect inference on the basis of observed performance. How a person performs a skill is dependent on a number of variables in addition to the degree to which it is learned. We will discuss a number of these performance variables throughout this text. What this definition does mean, however, is that the person has increased his or her capability, or potential, to perform that skill. Whether or not the skill is actually performed in a way that is consistent with how well it is learned will be due to a number of factors, such as the maturation level of the person, the anxiety created by the situation, and so on. As a result, it is critical that the methods used to assess learning allow an accurate inference about learning to be made.

Now that you are familiar with some important performance characteristics that should be associated with learning a motor skill, it is important to establish the conditions under which these characteristics should be observed. Of interest are methods that can be used to assess learning so that an accurate inference can be made about learning. Three such methods will be discussed: *practice observations, retention tests,* and *transfer tests.* Consider the following examples of situations you have undoubtedly experienced.

Once again, suppose you are a physical education teacher teaching a tennis serve to your class. In Concept 1.2 several possible performance measures were discussed that could indicate tennis serving performance and provide a quantitative means for evaluating students' progress. For example, you could simply record the number of legal serves made by the students during the class periods. Or you could establish an accuracy measure whereby you give different point values to balls landing in different locations in the service court. You might even develop a serving form measure that is only concerned with the form the students use as they serve. The selection of the performance measure is an important step in assessing learning. However, after that measure has been selected, you must determine the conditions in which the students will perform so that you can assess their progress.

One way to set up a learning assessment evaluation situation is to observe the students' performance each day for a specified period. The students could record the number of legal serves, if that is the performance measure you have selected, that they make each day out of 20 attempted serves. After several class periods, you can look at these records and determine if the expected performance improvement and consistency changes are occurring.

Another way to assess learning of the serve would be to give the students a serving test several days after serving practice has ceased. Then, a few days after that, test them again. Based on the record of serving performance your students have been keeping and on their scores on these tests, you can assess how well the performance scores they made during practice persisted after a period of limited or no practice. According to the definition of learning stated earlier, they should be able to serve better during these tests than they were able to before they began practicing the serve.

One additional means of determining how well the serve has been learned is by having the students use the serve in situations different from those in which they have been practicing. For example, during a game, can the student serve in a manner consistent with how he or she did during practice? For certain skills, it is important that they be learned in such a way that they can be performed in a variety of situations. A person who can only serve effectively in practice conditions that are unlike a game situation will not become a successful tennis player.

These three examples demonstrate that learning can be inferred from performance observations that take place in different circumstances. These three situations provide the basis for three different types of learning assessment methods. The first situation was an example of asesssing learning by

using practice observations. The second situation was an example of using a retention test, and the third situation described the use of a type of transfer test. Each of these methods is useful and is preferred for certain situations. The following sections will consider the important features of these three learning assessment methods and provide information that will enable you to select the appropriate method for the various situations you may encounter as you teach skills.

Practice Observations

A useful method to assess learning is to keep a performance record throughout the period during which the new skill is being practiced. The record should be of the performance measure you have chosen for the skill. There are several ways to graphically represent this record so that performance changes resulting from practice are readily apparent. Two methods will be discussed here. The first is the performance curve, which is especially useful to graphically represent performance when the performance measure is one of the response outcome measures discussed in Concept 1.2. The second graphic presentation method is useful for more complex performance measures, such as the kinematic measures discussed in Concept 1.2.

Performance curves. Sometimes incorrectly referred to as a learning curve, the performance curve plots the progress made by a person or a group of persons during a certain period. It provides a graphic picture or illustration of the performance changes that have taken place. Both improvement in performance and in performance consistency can be observed on a performance curve.

Before discussing how to interpret a performance curve, it will be helpful to first consider how a performance curve is constructed. Figure 2.1–1 is an example of a performance curve for one person practicing a motor skill requiring the person to knock down a small wooden target with a hand-held bat while a moving light traveling along a long trackway reaches the target. This is known as an anticipation timing task and is designed to simulate in the laboratory the skill of striking an object moving toward the subject, such as hitting a baseball or tennis ball.

Three features of this person's performance curve need to be considered to understand how a performance curve is constructed. First, the *vertical axis* of the graph, which is also referred to as the *y-axis* or the *ordinate,* is the performance, or dependent, measure used to assess performance of the skill. In Figure 2.1–1, this measure is CE, or constant error, which was discussed in Concept 1.2. Because the task requires the person to make an accurate timing response, a useful performance measure is the timing error the person makes, which is the difference between when the person struck the object and when the light reached the target. A negative error value indicates the object was struck too early, whereas a positive error value indicates the object was struck too late. It is important to note that the vertical axis is always marked in equal

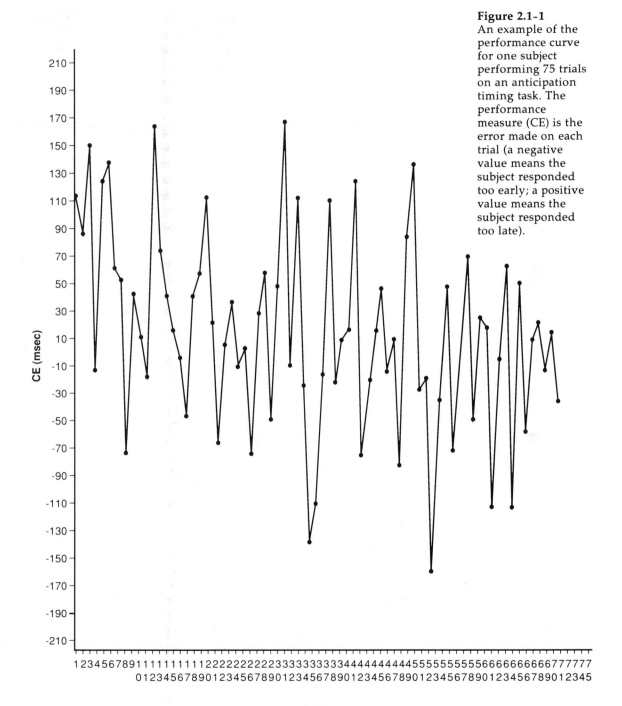

Figure 2.1-1
An example of the performance curve for one subject performing 75 trials on an anticipation timing task. The performance measure (CE) is the error made on each trial (a negative value means the subject responded too early; a positive value means the subject responded too late).

units, which are determined by the person making the graph. Also notice that the bottom of this axis, where it intersects the horizontal axis, is always assumed to have the value of 0. Thus, performance measures should be represented on the vertical axis progressing from smaller to larger values.

Second, the *horizontal axis* of the graph, also referred to as the *x-axis* or the *abcissa,* typically represents the time over which the performance was observed. In the graph in Figure 2.1–1, this measure is trials. Each trial represents a new attempt at performing the skill. The person represented by this performance curve performed 75 trials. Again, notice that the units along this axis are of equal size. It is also important to notice that the point of intersection between this axis and the y-axis is assumed to be 0. The unit of time represented on the x-axis is always presented progressing from lower to higher values.

The third important part of the graph is the performance curve itself. The curve is formed by marking the error score for each trial at the appropriate intersection point on the graph, then connecting each of these points with a line. Although the line that results rarely looks like a "curve," it nevertheless is called a performance curve.

For many experiments you will read about in this text graphs are presented with performance curves for groups of subjects rather than for just one individual. Figure 2.1–2 presents such a graph, which is based on performing the anticipation timing task used to produce Figure 2.1–1. Notice some differences between these two graphs. First, in Figure 2.1–2, there are two performance curves, one for each of two different experimental conditions used in the experiment. Each group is designated on the graph by its own symbol. In the experiment, one condition involved having subjects perform the anticipation timing task without verbal feedback about the accuracy of their responses. This verbal information is typically called knowledge of results, or KR. On the graph, this group is labeled "No KR." The other condition, labeled "KR" on the graph, involved providing verbal KR after every practice trial. The performance curves represent the mean, or average, performance of all subjects in each group. Second, note that the performance measure shown on the y-axis is absolute constant error (|CE|). |CE| was discussed in Concept 1.2 as being a more appropriate group performance measure of response bias than is constant error (CE), which was presented for the individual subject in Figure 2.1–1. Third, notice that the x-axis unit of measurement has changed in this graph to "blocks of trials." You will see this terminology in many experiments. It simply means that each unit is the average of a block or series of trials. In Figure 2.1–2, each block is the average of 5 trials, thus performance for only 15 blocks is represented. Blocking trials is a useful means of providing a less variable representation of performance.

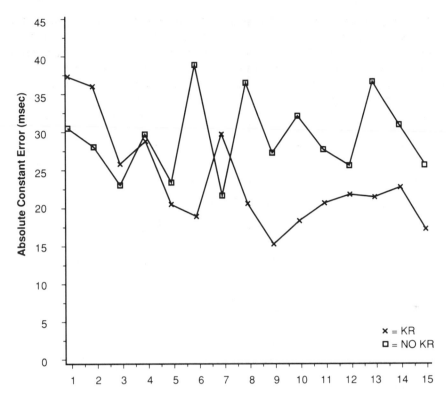

Figure 2.1-2
An example of
performance curves
for two groups of
subjects performing
an anticipation
timing task. One
group performed
with knowledge of
results (KR) after
each trial whereas
the other group
performed without
KR. Notice that
although the two
groups appear to
differ from each
other after seven
blocks of trials,
there is no
statistical difference
between the two
groups.

Blocks of 5 Trials

Interpreting the performance curve. Now that you have in mind the basic elements that make up a curve, the next step is to consider how to interpret it. In any performance curve an important characteristic that should be considered in order to make any inference about learning is that the curve should show an *improvement in the performance score* over the practice trials. Statistically, a significant improvement in the score should be expected. To more easily see this, it will be helpful to understand the types of curves typically presented. Four performance curve types are common to the research literature. Examples of these curves are presented in Figure 2.1–3.

Curve A is a *linear curve* or a straight line. This indicates proportional performance increases over time; that is, each unit of increase on the horizontal axis (e.g., one trial) results in a proportional increase on the vertical axis (e.g., one second). Curve B is a *negatively accelerated curve,* which indicates that a large amount of improvement occurred early in practice and then leveled off to some extent. Although improvement is usually still occurring in the latter part of the curve, it is very slight. Curve C is the inverse of curve B and is called a *positively accelerated curve.* This curve indicates slight

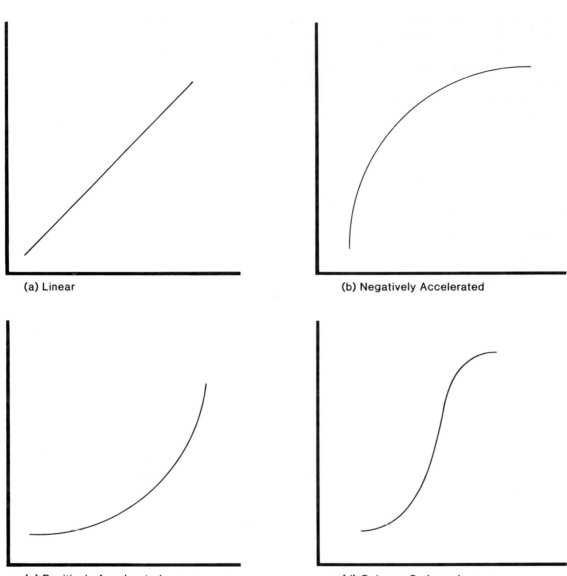

(a) Linear

(b) Negatively Accelerated

(c) Positively Accelerated

(d) Ogive or S-shaped

Figure 2.1-3
Four general types
of performance
curves.

performance gain early in practice but a substantial increase later in practice. Curve D is a combination of all three curves, and is called an *ogive* or *S-shaped curve.*

Each of these curves shows better performance as the curve slopes upward. There are, however, instances in which improvement in performance is indicated when the slope of the curve is in a downward direction. That occurs when the performance, or dependent, measure is some aspect like errors or

time, where a decrease in the performance measure means better performance. Some examples would be absolute error, reaction time, and running the mile. Performance improvement is noted when the amount of error or time for the performances decreases. In these cases, the performance curves would be in the direction opposite to those just described, although the types of curves would be the same.

One further point needs to be clarified concerning performance curves. The four curves presented in Figure 2.1–3 are termed smooth curves. Typical curves found in research studies are not smooth but erratic, as can be seen in Figure 2.1–3. However, when the curves are hypothetically smoothed, they appear as presented in this discussion of types of curves.

Although improvement in trial-to-trial consistency is an important characteristic of learning, this is not typically readily observable in most performance curves in most research articles. There are two reasons for this. First, the performance curves you typically see are for groups of subjects, such as the one in Figure 2.1–2. The individual subjects' scores have been averaged together to present a general picture of the group's performance. When this is done, the individual's trial-to-trial performances cannot be determined. Second, the trial performance scores are often grouped into blocks of trials, as in Figure 2.1–2 where they are in a block of three trials. The results of this is to reduce the actual trial-to-trial variability, although it presents a more realistic picture of performance.

Graphically representing kinematic measures. Another means of judging improvement in performance and a decrease in trial-to-trial variability can be seen in the graphs of movement displacement in Figure 2.1–4. These graphs are from the experiment by Marteniuk and Romanow (1983) that you were introduced to in the discussion of kinematic measures in Concept 1.2. Because of the complexity of the performance measures used in that experiment, it is not possible to develop a performance curve where the measure for every trial is represented by a point on a graph. The graphs in Figure 2.1–4 illustrate one way that these types of measures can be graphically presented for a series of practice trials, which in the Marteniuk and Romanow experiment involved 800 trials.

The graphs in Figure 2.1–4 represent the performance for one subject practicing a task that required the horizontal movement of a handle in such a way as to produce the criterion pattern of movement that was shown as the displacement curve in Figure 1.2–6 in Concept 1.2. This criterion movement was shown to the subject on a computer monitor. The subject was required to move the handle in the proper direction and speed to produce the pattern. Each graph to the right of the criterion represents the subject's average pattern drawn for a series of 10 trials, indicated by the solid line (mean) and the variability of the patterns drawn for those same 10 trials, as indicated by the dashed lines (S.D.). Notice two things about these graphs. First, the average

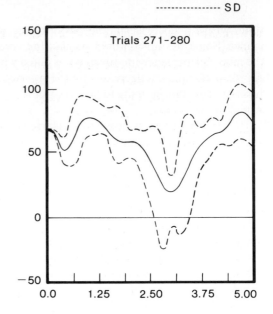

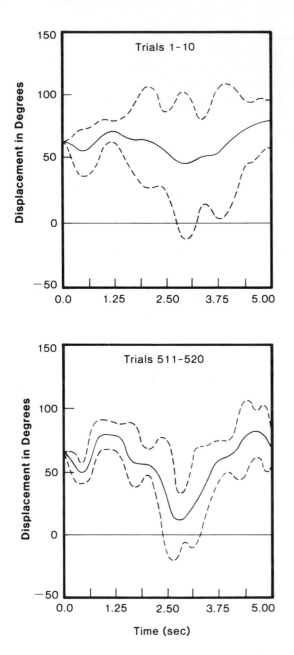

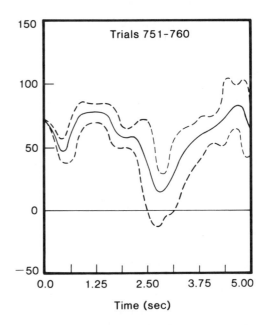

Figure 2.1-4
Results of an experiment by Marteniuk and Romanow showing changes in performance accuracy (displacement) on a tracking task at different practice trial blocks for one subject.

pattern drawn becomes more like the criterion pattern as the subject has more practice. In fact, by trials 751 through 760, the pattern made by the subject is almost identical to the criterion pattern in Figure 1.2–6. Second, notice how far from the mean pattern drawn are the lines for the standard deviation in trials 1 through 10. This shows a large amount of trial-to-trial variability. However, notice how close to the mean the standard deviation lines are during trials 751 through 760. The subject has become more consistent in producing the same pattern on each practice trial.

Another means of inferring learning from performance is to administer a re-tention test. You have experienced this approach to assessing learning since you began school. Teachers are always giving tests covering units of instruc-tion. As you are well aware, these are to determine how much you know, or have retained from your study. However, what is more important is that the teacher then makes an inference concerning how much you have learned about the particular unit of study on the basis of your test performance.

Retention Tests

The usual way of administering a retention test in a motor skill situation is to develop an appropriate test of the skill that you were teaching to your students. Administer the test to the students on their first day of practice. After a period of time for practice, administer the test again. The difference between these two scores will be an indicator of performance increase. How-ever, if you are interested in learning, you should administer the test once again some time later, after no actual practice of the skill has occurred. If there is a statistically significant difference between that score and the score on the first practice day, you can be certain that learning has occurred. Thus, the inference of learning from performance can be made on the basis of a retention test. The decision concerning how much learning has occurred is a real measurement problem. However, our concern will be only to determine that learning has occurred and that such conclusion as to learning is an in-ference that can have an objective basis. The inference based on retention test results that learning has occurred provides a very practical and useful tool for the teacher, who must objectively and quickly assess the learning that has occurred in students.

In the motor learning experiments you will read about in this text, re-tention tests are used rather frequently. The most common use of the retention test is to have the subjects perform the same skill they have been practicing some time after the practice period has been completed. This time interval may be any length. Usually, the retention test involves subjects performing the skill without receiving any verbal knowledge of results after each trial. The reason for this is that the experimenter wants to determine how well the subjects can perform the practiced skill on their own, without relying on any assistance from the experimenter.

Transfer Tests   The third means of inferring learning is by using what are known as *transfer tests*. This involves establishing a test situation where the subjects or students must use the skill they have been practicing but in a new situation. In the tennis serve example presented earlier, the transfer test was serving in a game situation. If the students were learning the tennis serve during practice, then there should be an increase in the number of good serves in the games compared to good serves before they actually began practicing. In this example, the teacher uses the transfer test as a *pretest,* a test given before practice begins, and as a *posttest,* a test given after practice ends. The inference about learning is made on the basis of an observed, or statistical, increase in serving performance from the pretest to the posttest.

Transfer tests are especially important when the skill being learned will have to be performed under a variety of test conditions. Recall that open skills have this characteristic. For example, although you can practice receiving a variety of tennis serves, it is highly unlikely that in a game you will receive a serve that has every characteristic of a serve you practiced. These types of skills require the individual to adapt to the demands of each response situation. Closed skills may also require the person to be adaptable. For these skills, rather than having to adapt to new variations of the skill, the person must be able to perform the practiced skill in a variety of contexts. Shooting a free throw in basketball is such an example because during a game a variety of context factors will differ both from practice and on each shot. One way to test how capable a person is at adapting to these unique situations is to use a transfer test. Learning can be inferred on the basis of how successful the person is at performing the skill in this new situation. An example of using a transfer test is when students are evaluated on their performances using the skill they have been practicing.

In motor learning experiments, transfer tests usually involve changing the context in which the practical skill must be performed, or changing the skill to be a new variation of the practiced skill. The performance context can be anything related to the condition of the subjects when they perform, such as being fatigued or stressed, or it can be related to the environment in which the skill is performed, such as in front of an audience, or in a game situation. Performing a new variation of the practiced skill involves performing the skill but under conditions where some characteristics of the skill are different. An example of variation of a skill that involves striking a moving object would be an object that moves at a faster rate of speed or that moves in a different spatial plane.

In experiments where transfer tests are used there usually is a control group. When the transfer test is used to assess performance of the practiced skill in a new context, the control group is typically one that has engaged subjects in practicing the skill, but only in the context of the transfer test. Learning is assessed by observing how well the practiced group adapts to the new context compared with a group that has already experienced that context. In the

next section you will read about an example of using this type of transfer test where the performance context of interest is whether or not the subjects perform the skill when fatigued. When the transfer test is used to assess how adaptable the subjects are at performing a new variation of the practiced skill, the control group consists of subjects who have not practiced the skill previously and only perform the skill during the transfer test. If the skill was learned, the practiced subjects would be expected to perform the new variation better than subjects who have never practiced the skill.

One of the benefits of using retention tests or transfer tests to assess learning, rather than relying solely on practice performance observations, is that these tests can often lead to more reliable inferences about learning. To see this, consider an example from motor learning research where an incorrect learning inference would have resulted if a transfer test had *not* been used.

Practice Observations Can Be Misleading

In an experiment by Godwin and Schmidt (1971), subjects were required to learn an arm-movement task called a sigma task. This task required subjects to move a handle as rapidly as possible in a complete circle in one direction, then reverse direction making another circle, let go of the handle, and knock down a small barrier a few inches from the handle. The performance measure was movement time, the amount of time it took to begin moving the handle before the barrier was contacted. One group of subjects (the fatigued group) was required to engage in arm-cranking activity for 20 seconds between trials, while the other group (the nonfatigued group) rested for 20 seconds. Results of the 20 practice trials are presented in the left portion of the graph in Figure 2.1–5. From these results, it appears that the fatigued group did much worse than the nonfatigued group.

Before drawing any conclusions about the influence of fatigue on learning, notice the right-hand portion of the graph. This portion represents the results from a transfer test of 10 trials. In this test, all subjects performed the sigma task again, but with a 20-second rest between trials. Consider the nonfatigued group as a control condition and the fatigued group as an experimental condition. As such, the control, nonfatigued group continue under the same performance conditions during the transfer trials as they did during the practice trials. However, the experimental, fatigued group are transferred to a new situation, rest between trials. The logic here is that if fatigue influences learning, then removing the fatiguing situation during the transfer trials should lead to performance similar to that during the trials with fatiguing exercise between trials. However, the results in this experiment showed that there was no difference between the groups' performance during the common situation of the transfer trials. The conclusion, then, is that the between-trials exercise influenced practice performance but *not* learning.

The Godwin and Schmidt (1971) experiment illustrates how an incorrect inference about learning can be made if a transfer test is not used. Without this transfer test, the inference would have been that fatigue influences learning.

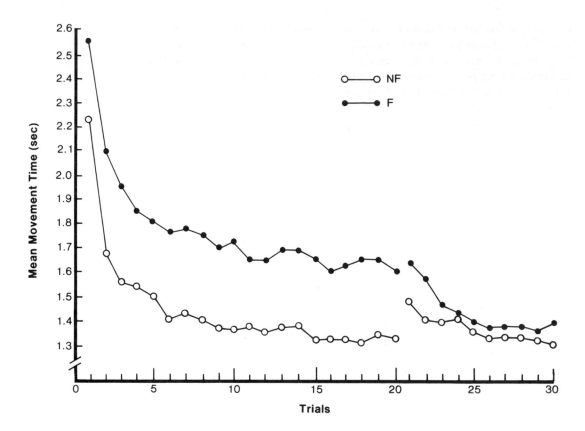

Figure 2.1-5
Results of the experiment by Godwin and Schmidt showing the performance curves for the fatigued (closed circles) and the nonfatigued (open circles) groups for the sigma task.

However, when the transfer trials are taken into consideration, it becomes apparent that the fatigue influence was not on learning but on practice performance.

This example of the use of transfer tests is just one of many you will find in this book. You will also see retention tests used in similar ways. The important point is that you be aware of the problems that can arise when making inferences about learning. Retention and transfer tests are important for looking at the "performance" part of the learning definition. As such they are critical for making accurate inferences.

Performance Plateaus

Another point in support of the need for using retention and transfer tests for making inferences about learning can be seen in practice situations where *plateaus* in performance seem to occur. During these plateaus, performance that had been steadily improving suddenly seems to reach a steady state where there appears to be little or no further improvement. Then, after further practice, performance begins to show improvement again.

The idea that plateaus exist as a normal phase of the learning experience has been debated since the end of last century. Plateaus seem to be something

that people frequently experience in real life; but researchers have had difficulty finding plateaus in an experimental setting. The question that develops from the conflict is this: Are plateaus normal in learning, or are they merely concomitants of performance? As performance concomitants, plateaus may not be typical of learning but can be observed on occasion in practice performance.

The first research evidence that brought about discussion of the possible existence of plateaus appeared in 1897 in a classic article by Bryan and Harter. Telegraphers were learning Morse code over a period of 40 weeks. Steady improvement in the telegrapher's letters-per-minute speed was observed for the first 20 weeks. But then performance leveled off for the next 6 weeks before any improvement was again noted. The final 12 weeks were characterized by performance similar to that observed over the first 20 weeks. Those 6 weeks of no improvement were labeled a plateau. Whether this plateau was a real learning phenomenon or merely a temporary performance artifact was discussed with little resolve until 1958, when Keller wrote an article entitled "The Phantom Plateau," which attempted to clarify some problems concerning the interpretation of plateaus. (See Adams, 1987, for an excellent review of plateau research.) Keller maintained that plateaus are not general characteristics of learning but of performance. This interpretation takes us back to the learning inference. Plateaus may appear during the course of practice, but it appears that learning is still going on; performance has plateaued, but learning continues.

An example of a performance plateau. It is difficult to see evidence of performance plateaus in the motor learning research literature because experimenters rarely report performance curves for individual subjects. Because plateaus are individual performance characteristics, performance curves for individual subjects are necessary if plateaus are to be observed. An exception to this situation, and one that provides a good illustration of a performance plateau, is an experiment reported by Ian Franks and Robert Wilberg (1982). One of the subjects in their experiment practiced a complex tracking task for 10 days, with 105 trials each day. The task involved moving a lever that was mounted on a tabletop in such a way to follow the movement of a target cursor on the computer screen. The lever was a mechanical arm the length of the subject's forearm and was pivoted on the table at the elbow location so that the subject could move the lever away from or toward his or her body through a 90-degree range. Moving the lever controlled a response cursor on a computer screen so that a lever movement away from the body moved the cursor up on the screen whereas a lever movement toward the body moved the cursor down on the screen. The speed of the cursor movement was controlled by the speed of the lever movement. The subject's task was to move this lever movement to follow (or track) the movement of a target cursor across the computer screen. The pattern made by the target cursor can be seen in Figure 1.2–7 in the discussion of the root mean squared error (RMSE) performance measure

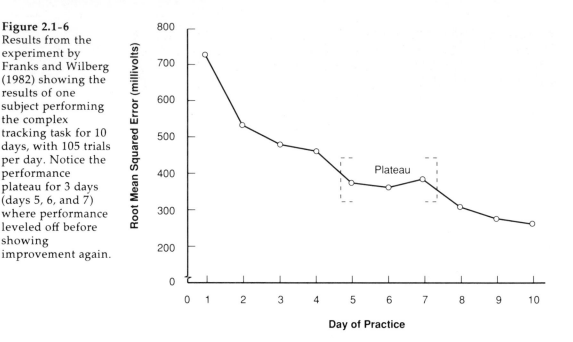

Figure 2.1-6
Results from the experiment by Franks and Wilberg (1982) showing the results of one subject performing the complex tracking task for 10 days, with 105 trials per day. Notice the performance plateau for 3 days (days 5, 6, and 7) where performance leveled off before showing improvement again.

(Concept 1.2). Only the moving target cursor, not the pattern, was seen by the subject. The subject was instructed to try to follow the target cursor as accurately as possible. One trial, which meant the pattern was presented one time, lasted just over 2.5 seconds.

Results of the ten days of practice on this tracking task for one subject are presented in Figure 2.1–6. Notice that the trials along the x-axis are presented in blocks of 105 trials each, or one day of practice. As you can see from the performance curve for this subject, she showed consistent improvement in accurate tracking (as measured by RMSE) for the first four days of practice. Then, days 5 through 7 show a period when performance improvement stopped, and actually worsened slightly on one day. These days of practice are a good example of a performance plateau. However, as is typical of most plateaus, the steady-state performance was temporary as the subject again showed improvement on day 8 and continued to improve each of the next two days of practice. If you removed the plateau section from this graph, and only plotted days 1 through 5 and 8 through 10, it would appear as if the subject showed steady improvement throughout practice. But, this was not the case as there was a distinct period of no improvement that lasted several days.

The cause of plateaus. Now that we have described and illustrated performance plateaus, we will consider their causes. One of the most plausible explanations has been proposed by Singer (1980), who postulated that when a

complex skill is learned a "hierarchy of habits" must be mastered by the learner. This means that when you are learning some skill, you first learn the fundamental phases of the skill and then begin to concentrate on learning the more advanced aspects of that skill. For example, you should learn to stroke the tennis ball while you are in a stationary position before you learn to hit the ball on the run. Singer's point is that between these two steps of learning the skill, you begin to try to apply what you already know to a new situation. It is during this time the plateau in performance may occur.

Other possible explanations for performance plateaus may be a period of poor motivation, or a time of fatigue, or a lack of attention directed to an important aspect of the skill. Furthermore, plateaus may also be the result of the performance measure that is being used. This would be the case when the performance measure involves what is known as *ceiling or floor effects*. These effects occur when, because of the nature of the performance measure, it will not permit the score to go above or below a certain point. For example, if a performance score is a certain number of correct responses out of a possible total number of responses, then improvement in performance can only be recorded up to a certain point. If tennis serves are being scored on a number of good serves out of 20 each day, as soon as the person reaches 20 out of 20, no further improvement can be observed. It is possible, however, that improvement was in fact occurring, though the performance measure included a ceiling effect that limited the amount of improvement which could be observed. The term *floor effect* would be applicable when a decrease in the performance score indicated improvement.

Plateaus seem to be common in motor skills practice. While there is limited information on which to base any conclusion about *why* they occur, it seems safe to conclude that they do not appear to be related to a lack of increase in learning. Plateaus should more accurately be considered performance "artifacts" that are caused by variables influencing performance. Teachers of motor skills would do well to determine what that cause is. The students may be tired or bored, or attending to the wrong cues in trying to learn a more complex part of the skill. Assessment of the cause of a performance plateau is often possible, and such investigation can aid the student in learning any motor skill.

From the preceding discussion, it is possible to conclude that in any learning situation, some conditions, or variables, influence practice performance but not learning. Learning seemingly continues even though practice performance does not reveal it. These kinds of variables are considered to be *performance variables*. Such things as fatigue, boredom, certain practice organization routines, etc., are good candidates for this type of variable. You will confront more performance variables as you continue to study motor learning.

On the other hand, there are variables that when involved in practice conditions will influence both the observed practice performance and learning.

Learning and Performance Variables

These variables, called *learning variables,* yield transfer or retention performance that may be either similar to or different from performance at the end of the practice sessions. Again, you will become more acquainted with these variables as you study this text. For now, it is important that you realize the difference between performance and learning variables and prepare yourself to see them in a variety of topics covered in this text.

Summary

Three methods have been discussed that can be used to infer that learning has occurred. The first is the use of practice observations, typically seen in the form of performance curves plotted over practice trials or trial blocks and series of kinematic measures that are recorded for each trial. Since practice observations can sometimes be misleading, other methods are often necessary. One of these is the second method of making a learning inference. This is by using retention tests. Such are tests given after a specified time of no practice and are usually given under the same conditions in which the skill was practiced. Third, transfer tests also provide a powerful means of assessing the amount of learning that has occurred. These tests require the learners either to perform the skill that has been practiced in a new situation or to perform a new variation of the practiced skill. For both retention tests and transfer tests, learning can be inferred when performance is better than if no practice on the skill had occurred. Since learning must be inferred from performance, the use of these three methods can be valuable tools in developing appropriate conclusions about learning, a task that is required of all teachers.

Finally, an intriguing performance phenomenon known as a performance plateau was discussed. A plateau is actually a performance artifact, as it appears to represent a period of practice when, although performance seems to have stabilized, learning still occurs. Several causes of performance plateaus were considered.

Related Readings

Carron, A. V., & Marteniuk, R. G. (1970). An examination of the selection of criterion scores for the study of motor learning and retention. *Journal of Motor Behavior, 2,* 239–244.

Davis, F. B. (1964). *Educational measurements and their interpretations.* Belmont, Calif.: Wadsworth.

Dunham, P. (1971). Learning and performance. *Research Quarterly, 42,* 334–337.

Keller, F. S. (1958). The phantom plateau. *Journal of the Experimental Analysis of Behavior, 1,* 1–13.

The learning of a motor skill occurs in stages   Concept 2.2

Have you noticed when you are first learning a skill, such as the serve in tennis, the hook in bowling, or a jump in ballet, that you must think about some very specific aspects of the skill, which differ from what you think about after you have become rather proficient at performing that skill? When you are first learning the tennis serve, you are very concerned with how you are holding the racket, how high you are tossing the ball, whether you are transferring your weight properly at contact, and so on. These fundamental elements of the serve are very important when you are first learning the serve. However, when you practice the serve and improve, these concerns seem less important; you become more familiar with serving and you improve your own serving skill. After much practice, you notice that you concentrate on other aspects of serving. Although you still concentrate on looking at the ball while tossing it and during contact, you also find that you are thinking about where you are going to place this serve in your opponent's service court.

Consider novice basketball players. If you put them in a one-on-one situation, you will observe that most of what they are thinking about are the basic mechanics of the fundamental skills involved. They are probably very concerned with dribbling the ball properly because they do not want to lose it to the opponent. Or they attend to the basic mechanics of shooting a lay-up. These concerns predominate. This is quite different from highly skilled basketball players. Highly skilled performers do not direct attention to the mechanics of dribbling or shooting, since these skills are already mastered. Rather, concentration is centered on how to maneuver around the opponent. They may be watching for specific cues from the opponent's movements that will let them know exactly how to move to make a shot. Since skilled players do not have to concentrate on the dribbling or shooting mechanics of the task, they are free to direct attention to other concerns.

Both these situations typify phases that occur during the process of learning a motor skill. As practice continues, under proper conditions, certain changes take place in the learner. These modifications can be noted in terms of what the learner thinks about or concentrates on during the performance of the skill. These changes will also be evident in certain characteristics of the individual's performance. In the discussion that follows we will consider these developments more specifically by discussing the stages or phases of learning that have been identified by certain theorists to describe the learning process.

Discussion

One characteristic of motor skill learning is that it is possible to identify distinct stages or phases that all learners seem to experience as they learn skills through practice. Several attempts have been made by researchers to identify

these stages to assist us in better understanding the learning process. Three of these proposals to identify the stages of learning will be presented here. Each view purports that the earliest stage of learning is predominated by cognitive concerns about a skill although later the focus shifts to more automatic performance of the skill. The first approach we will consider was developed by Paul Fitts and Michael Posner in 1967 and is traditionally accepted as the classic stage of learning model. This model is commonly referred to in the motor learning literature when stages of learning are being addressed. The other two learning stages proposals have been published since the Fitts and Posner model was proposed and have some unique features that are interesting to consider. One model was developed by Jack Adams as a part of his theory of motor learning, which will be discussed in Concept 2.3. The other model was proposed by Ann Gentile in a monograph in *Quest* in 1972 and, of the three, is the most closely related to motor skill instruction applications.

Fitts and Posner's Three-Stage Model

When learners begin to acquire a new skill, they are generally confronted with some very specific, cognitively oriented problems. What is the basic task? How do you score in this game? How do you know who wins? What is out of bounds? What is the best way to hold this racket, or bat, or club, etc.? Each of these questions indicates the basic and cognitive level at which the new learner is operating in the early part of learning a motor skill. To account for this cognitive activity, Fitts and Posner labeled the first stage of learning the *cognitive stage*. This stage is marked by a large number of errors in performance, and the nature of the errors being committed tends to be gross. For example, the beginning golf student gets the ball in the air sometimes, while dribbling it on the ground at other times. These results are due to some very gross errors made by the student during the golf swing itself. The cognitive stage is also marked by performance that is highly variable. Although beginners may know that they are doing something wrong, they are generally not aware of exactly what should be done differently the next time to improve. As a result, they need specific information that will assist them in correcting what they have done wrong.

The second stage of learning in the Fitts and Posner model is called the *associative stage*. The nature of the cognitive activity that characterized the cognitive stage changes during the associative stage. Many of the basic fundamentals or mechanics of the skill have to some extent been learned. The errors are fewer and less gross in nature. The learners are now concentrating on refining the skill. They have developed an ability to detect some of their own errors in performing the task. While this ability to locate their errors is not perfect, they are able to identify some of the errors. This provides the learners with some specific guidelines about how to continue practice. The golfer may be getting the ball in the air rather consistently now, but often he or she still slices the ball. He or she does not always get maximum distance or height out of the shot. However, the student can notice that he or she did not transfer weight properly, grip the club correctly, and so on. Such types of detections

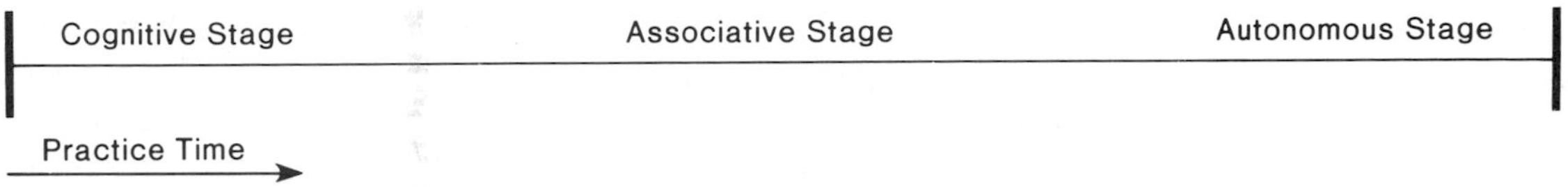

| Cognitive Stage | Associative Stage | Autonomous Stage |

Practice Time →

are rather gross in nature but represent a definite change in the course of the learning process. At this stage variability of performance from one attempt to another also begins to decrease.

After much practice and experience with the skill, the learner moves into the final stage of learning, the *autonomous stage*. Here the skill has become almost automatic or habitual. The individual does not have to attend to the entire production of the skill but has learned to perform most of the skill without thinking about it at all. Highly skilled golfers concentrate on the ball and some of the specific adjustments that they must make in their normal swing to produce a particular shot. Highly skilled dancers do not think about the individual steps of the routine, for they have become automatic. Instead, they have learned to concentrate on some of the more critical phases of the routine that are particularly difficult or that indicate that some major change in the routine is to begin.

In this autonomous phase skilled performers are now able to not only detect their own errors but also make the proper adjustments to correct them. In this stage the variability of the day-to-day performance has become very small. The autonomous stage is the result of a tremendous amount of practice; it allows performers to produce a response without having to concentrate on the entire movement. Therefore, they are able to attend to other aspects that will permit optimal performance.

Fitts and Posner state that "there is a good deal of similarity between highly practiced skills and reflexes" (p. 15). This does not mean that learning stops or that the individual ceases to make errors but rather that there ceases to be the need for conscious attention to the motor act itself. Thus, the highly skilled tennis player is able to serve without having to concentrate on the particular fundamentals of the serve, on how to hold the racket, toss the ball, and so on, but can concentrate on what is needed to produce a serve that will land in a particular part of the service court.

It will help you to think of the three stages of the Fitts and Posner model as parts of a continuum of practice time, as depicted in Figure 2.2–1. The cognitive stage represents the first portion of this continuum. This is followed by the associative stage and then the autonomous stage. It is important to realize that learners do not make abrupt moves from one stage to the next. There is a gradual changing of the learner's characteristics from stage to stage. It is often difficult to detect which stage best represents an individual at a particular moment, especially when that individual is in a transitional state, moving out of one stage and into the next. However, as we will discuss in more detail, the beginner and the skilled performer have distinct characteristics that need to be understood.

Figure 2.2-1
The stages of learning from the Fitts and Posner model placed on a time continuum.

Adams' Two-Stage Model

In contrast to Fitts and Posner's three-stage model, Adams (1971) proposed a model of the stages of learning where there are only two stages. The first stage of learning is the *verbal-motor stage*. This stage is essentially the same as Fitts and Posner's cognitive and associative stages. Adams' second stage incorporates the autonomous stage and is called the *motor stage*. Adams' terminology implies that the first stage of learning a motor skill is not entirely cognitive, as might be erroneously concluded if one uses the Fitts and Posner label for this stage. However, the same connotation problem that Adams avoided with his label for the first stage of learning is not eliminated by his second stage label. There is also a cognitive component to the response even though this response can be produced almost automatically. Chapter 4 will deal with this problem more specifically. At this point, it will suffice to realize that learning does progress in stages that can be differentiated on the basis of the amount and nature of the cognitive activity associated with the production of the response.

Gentile's Two-Stage Model

Another model that proposes two stages of learning is one proposed by Gentile (1972). The first stage is identified by what Gentile sees as the goal of the learner in this stage, which is *getting the idea of the movement*. The "idea" of the movement can be thought of as the general concept of what must be done in order to accomplish the goal of the skill. Gentile proposes that the learner must do two things during this stage of learning. First, the learner must establish the *relevant* and the *irrelevant* stimuli related to the skill. Relevant stimuli are those pieces of information in the environment that will regulate the movements that will be produced as the skill is performed. For example, if the goal of the skill is to hit a pitched ball with a bat, the relevant stimuli include such information as the spin of the ball, the speed of the ball, the spatial trajectory of the ball, and so on. These pieces of information will determine specific characteristics of the batter's swing. If the person is to learn to hit the ball, these relevant stimuli must be given attention. On the other hand, there are other available pieces of information that also can attract the individual's attention but are in fact distracting. To give attention to these stimuli would not help the person accomplish the goal of the skill. For example, the motion used by the pitcher in the delivery is usually irrelevant information in helping the batter know what the pitch will be like. Other irrelevant stimuli can be such things as the pitcher's eyes, which tend to attract the attention of novice batters, or talk by other players in the field during the pitch, such as "swing batter."

The second important thing the learner must do during this first stage is establish the most appropriate movement pattern for effectively attaining the goal of the skill. This aspect of learning involves coordinating the limbs

correctly so that they work together properly. For example, hitting a baseball is a complex skill that requires much coordination among the limbs. It is during this first stage of learning that the individual concentrates on developing coordination by practicing the skill so that the coordinated movement pattern becomes characteristic of the response.

The second stage of learning in Gentile's model is called *fixation/diversification*. The learner must focus on accomplishing two things during this stage as well. First, he or she must develop the capability of doing what is needed to accomplish the goal of the skill, regardless of the situation. Second, the learner must increase his or her consistency in achieving the goal of the skill. The two terms used to label this stage relate to what the learner must do with respect to whether the skill being learned is an open or a closed skill. The terms fixation and diversification are related specifically to what each of these types of skills requires in terms of the movement patterns that must be produced to accomplish the goals of these skills. *Fixation* refers to what is required of closed skills. That is, to be successful in performing a closed skill, the person must refine the movement pattern developed in the first stage of learning so that this pattern can be correctly produced at will. Practice during this stage must enable the learner to refine the movement pattern learned in the first stage so that the required movement pattern can be produced correctly, consistently, and efficiently from response to response. *Diversification*, on the other hand, relates to the needs of performing open skills. Because a critical characteristic of open skills is that the exact same movement pattern will not be required on successive responses, the movement pattern learned in the first stage must be practiced but with the goal to diversify the variations of the pattern that can be produced. The focus in this stage, then, is on developing the capability of successfully adapting to the changing environmental demands that characterize open skills. To accomplish this, Gentile states that the learner must develop a larger repetoire of motor patterns that will provide the basis for adapting to the demands of open skill performance situations.

An important feature of Gentile's two-stage model is its suggested application to instruction. The goal of practice in the first stage is to develop the basic movement pattern that will achieve the goal of the skill, regardless of whether the skill is open or closed. But, different conditions of practice must be established in the second stage according to the type of skill being practiced. Practice conditions for closed skills must involve structuring practice so that the learner will practice as closely as possible under the conditions as they will be experienced on a test or in a game. For open skills the teacher must systematically vary the possible conditions under which the skill being learned is to be performed. These are some of the practice-related suggestions Gentile made in connection with her learning stages model. We will consider these as well as other suggestions, in more detail, in the chapter on practice.

Research
Evidence
Related to the
Stages of
Learning

One way to better understand the learning process is to look at what characterizes learners' performance at different points in time along the learning stages continuum. Different stages of learning become recognizable and some insight can be gained into understanding why these stages occur. An additional benefit of studying learners in this way is that it can provide a basis for determining what teaching strategies will be optimally beneficial for students during the different learning stages. As you will see, teaching strategies that are effective for beginners are likely not to be successful in helping skilled students, and vice versa. Because an important goal of motor skill instructors is to help students move along the learning continuum from beginner to highly skilled performer, understanding what characterizes the points along the continuum will enable the teacher to more effectively assist the student progress through the stages.

The remainder of this discussion, then, is a look at some of the characteristics that differentiate learners at different points along the learning stages continuum. We will look at five different performer- or performance-related changes that have been identified related to progression through the learning stages. Some research examples will be described for each change to illustrate how we know that the changes actually occur. Specifically, the five changes to be discussed are (1) changes in achieving the goal of the skill, (2) changes in detecting and correcting errors, (3) changes in movement efficiency, (4) changes in coordination, and (5) changes in EMG patterns. In the final section of this discussion we will look at an interesting, popular approach to investigating the question of what changes occur across the learning continuum. This approach involves the use of an experimental paradigm where a direct comparison is made between novices and experts in a particular skill.

Changes in achieving the goal of the skill. Because any motor skill has a goal that must be achieved to successfully perform that skill, one means of investigating changes that occur during learning is to look at how individuals change in terms of goal attainment characteristics. That is, how do their movements differ early in practice compared with later in practice as they become more successful at achieving the goal of the skill? A good example of an experiment that investigated this question was published by Marteniuk and Romanow (1983), and was briefly introduced in Concepts 1.2 and 2.1.

Subjects in this experiment practiced producing the complex waveform pattern shown in Figure 1.2–6 by moving a horizontal lever back and forth. The goal of this skill was to reproduce the waveform pattern as closely as possible, both spatially and temporally. To achieve this goal, subjects had to learn how often to move the lever back and forth, where to make each reversal of the lever, and how fast to move the lever at different times throughout the entire pattern. As you saw in Figure 2.1–3, the subjects became increasingly accurate and consistent at achieving the goal of the skill during 800 trials of

practice. On the basis of the kinematic performance measures that were analyzed, Marteniuk and Romanow concluded that early in practice subjects focused primarily on the spatial components of this task. This conclusion was based on results that showed that displacement characteristics became more accurate and consistent before acceleration and velocity characteristics, which are time-based features of the skill. Only after a significant amount of practice did the subjects show evidence that they were refining their skills by increasing the accuracy and consistency of the acceleration and velocity components of this complex task. Also, even though this was a very complex task, subjects always worked on improving the entire skill as a unit. Their performance characteristics during practice showed that they did not divide the task into smaller parts and try to improve each part independently and then put them together into larger and larger units until the entire pattern was performed correctly. Thus, the goal of this complex skill was achieved by systematically improving specific kinematic features of the movements required for this skill.

Changes in error detection and correction capability. One of the characteristics commonly cited for people in the final stage of learning is the ability to identify and correct their own movement errors. In slow movements, this correction process may occur during the performance of the skill itself, as when a gymnast moving into a handstand must make some adjustments to get the alignment correct or to hold it steady. However, in rapid movements, such as initiating and carrying out a swing at a baseball, the correction cannot usually be made in time during the execution of that swing. The awareness of what correction should be made will have to be used to correct future swings. However, regardless of when the correction of errors must be done, the important point is that the ability to make these corrections develops as the individual progresses along the learning stages continuum.

An experiment that demonstrates the development of this capability to detect and correct errors was published by Schmidt and White (1972). Subjects were required to learn to move a lever along a linear trackway a distance of 9 inches in 150 msec. The goal was to move the lever so that it passed a marker at the 9-inch mark at exactly 150 msec. After each attempt, or trial, subjects were asked to estimate how accurate they thought their responses were and were then told their actual accuracy score. Following 140 practice trials, they were no longer told their accuracy score but were still required to estimate their error. If learners increase their capability to detect and correct errors as they learn a skill, they should become increasingly able to match their estimates of their own responses (called subjective error) with the actual error score for that response (called objective error). The relationship between the subjective and objective error measures is shown correlated in Figure 2.2–2. A low correlation indicates the subjects demonstrated poor error estimation capability whereas a high correlation indicates they demonstrated good error

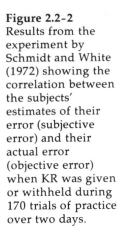

Figure 2.2-2
Results from the experiment by Schmidt and White (1972) showing the correlation between the subjects' estimates of their error (subjective error) and their actual error (objective error) when KR was given or withheld during 170 trials of practice over two days.

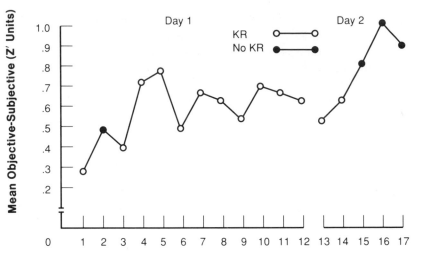

Blocks of 10 Trials

estimation capability. As you can see from trial block 16, this correlation had risen from .30 on the first trial block to above .90. Even more convincing is that they continued to demonstrate this high degree of error estimation capability even after they were no longer told their actual error after each trial.

Changes in movement efficiency. Efficiency of movement refers to the amount of energy expended while producing a movement. It is a commonly accepted characteristic of skilled performers that skills are performed efficiently, that is, with a minimum expenditure of energy.[1] Skilled performers appear to perform effortlessly. A problem with this view, however, was brought to light by Sparrow (1983), who showed that although this view is commonly accepted, there is little empirical evidence to support it. As a result, he (Sparrow & Irizarry-Lopez, 1987) developed an experiment to look specifically at movement efficiency changes that occur as a person practices and learns a complex motor skill. Subjects were required to learn to crawl on their hands and feet on a motor-driven treadmill that was moving at a rate of .76 m/sec. They practiced this skill for 3 minutes a day for 20 days. Two common exercise physiology measures were used to determine if efficiency increased during practice. One measure was mechanical efficiency, which is the mechanical work rate divided by the metabolic rate of the individual. The other measure was caloric cost. Subjects showed a 13.7% improvement in mechanical efficiency from the beginning to the end of the practice period, along with a significant improvement in caloric cost. Thus, evidence appears to demonstrate that as we learn a skill, our performance efficiency increases so that the energy cost becomes more economical.

[1]It should be noted that there are many who prefer the term "economy" rather than "efficiency"; see Cavanagh & Kram, 1985.

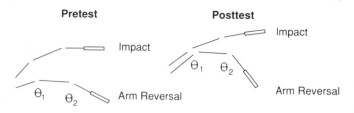

Figure 2.2-3
The pretest and posttest configurations of the arm segments at arm reversal and impact for hitting a racquetball forehand shot. From the experiment by Southard and Higgins (1987). Note: θ_1 = joint angle at the elbow; θ_2 = joint angle at the wrist.

Changes in coordination. One reason why skilled performers move more efficiently in terms of energy expenditure while performing is that they have increased the coordination among the various limbs used to produce the movement. An excellent demonstration of this change in coordination that occurs during practice was presented by Southard and Higgins (1987). Subjects practiced a racquetball forehand shot 10 minutes a day for 10 days. The investigation of coordination was limited in this experiment to three segments of the arm holding the racquet. One segment was the upper arm between the shoulder and elbow joints; the second segment was the forearm between the elbow and wrist joints; the third segment was the hand from the wrist joint to and including the racquet. The interrelationship of these segments was evaluated during the arm reversal part of hitting the ball and during the actual impact when the ball was hit. Figure 2.2–3 compares these interrelationships before practice began and after 10 days of practice, during which subjects were able to observe the appropriate swing action.

Before practice began, there was no significant change in elbow and wrist joint angles from the arm reversal to impact with the ball. This result shows that the arm was being controlled as a single unit. However, with practice, this unitary control changed in that the elbow and wrist joints functioned much differently during the arm reversal than they did at impact. The wrist joint angle during arm reversal at the pretest was 205° (with 180° being a straight line). After the 10 days of practice, this wrist joint angle was 232°. The elbow joint angle also changed with practice as it went from 190° at the pretest to 225° after 10 days of practice. For the impact phase, the elbow and wrist angles did not appreciably change as a result of practice. Another measure from this study that can also be used to show an increase in coordination of the segments of the limb, as well as of the entire body, is the velocity of each segment in relation to each of the other segments as the arm moved through space to hit the ball. These velocities increased dramatically during the practice period. Before practice, the forearm segment moved at a velocity of 23.5 degrees/sec relative to the upper arm, whereas after 10 days of practice this segment velocity increased to 320.7 degrees/sec. The velocity of the hand-racquet segment relative to the forearm was 34.5 degrees/sec and increased to 596.5 degrees/sec after 10 days of practice.

These results demonstrate how arm control in hitting a racquetball changes as a function of practice. At the beginning of practice, the approach

was to control the entire arm and hand as if it were a single unit. Hence, elbow and wrist joint angles were similar at both the arm reversal and impact phases of the swing. However, with practice, a more segment-specific control approach developed so that the goal of the action could more effectively be accomplished. Then, the elbow and wrist joint angles were distinctly different during the arm reversal phase than they were at impact.

Changes in EMG patterns. If efficiency of movement in terms of energy expenditure improves with practice and if coordination of the various body parts involved in producing a movement improves with practice, then we should see evidence of these changes at the muscular level. One way to see this is to look at changes in EMG patterns as a person practices a skill. The increases in movement efficiency and coordination imply that more muscles than necessary are involved in performing the skill early in practice and that as practice progresses, the amount of muscle involvement decreases.

Some research evidence illustrating this change in EMG patterns was provided by Vorro, Wilson, and Dainis (1978). In this experiment, the subjects' task was to learn to accurately throw a ball at a target. Two arm muscle groups, the biceps brachii and the coracobrachialis, were of interest in terms of their involvement in the throwing action and how their involvement changed during practice. EMG recordings of these muscles were made for 103 practice trials. Results indicated that as practice progressed, the two muscle groups began to respond differently. For example, early in practice, the biceps began contracting 15 msec before the throwing movement began, and the coracobrachialis began contracting just 1 msec before the movement began. By trial 103, both muscles were contracting almost simultaneously, 40 msec after the movement began. Obviously, with practice, the functions of these muscles in the total throwing movement change. The article did not discuss precisely what those functions were and how other muscles involved in the movement changed. However, these results do illustrate how EMG measures can be used to observe performance-related changes across the stages of learning.

In an experiment comparing the actions of an agonist and antagonist pair of muscles as a function of practicing a movement, Moore and Marteniuk (1986) found two distinct characteristics that changed with practice. For this movement, subjects were required to make a 45° horizontal forearm extension to a target in either 200 or 500 msec. One distinct change noted for both the 200- and 500-msec movements was a very inconsistent pattern of EMG activity for the triceps (the agonist for this movement) and biceps (antagonist) from trial to trial. However, with practice, a consistent trial-to-trial pattern emerged, especially for the faster 200-msec response. The second distinct change was that subjects moved from showing a regular pattern of co-contraction of the two muscles early in practice to a more efficient pattern of distinct bursts of activity for each muscle that were separate in time.

A feature of the experiments described in the preceding section was that learners were observed throughout a specified practice period. Observations were made about changes that occurred during that time. Although this is a useful means of investigating changes that occur either in the performance of the skill or in the performer, there are some limitations to this approach. Perhaps the most limiting factor is that it is virtually impossible to see changes in individuals or their performance for a complex skill as they move from being a beginner, or novice, to being a highly skilled, or expert, performer. The limitation is the result of the time demanded by a complex skill to become a highly skilled performer. For example, in the experiment by Southard and Higgins (1987), it was noted that the forearm and racquet relationship after 10 days of practice was still not like it would have been for an expert racquetball player. Thus, this approach can provide only a limited look into changes over specified periods of practice and cannot provide the full account of changes that occur across the entire learning continuum.

One way to overcome this problem is to compare persons easily classified as beginners with those who are highly skilled. Although this approach allows comparison of performance and performer characteristics across the full learning continuum, it too is limited in that comparisons must be made among individuals rather than within one individual. Nonetheless, this approach to studying the learning process is a valuable one and has become increasingly popular over the past few years. In this section, we will look at the novice vs. expert paradigm and identify what this approach tells us about learning motor skills.

The novice-expert paradigm has been successful in identifying a number of characteristics that differentiate the beginner and the advanced performer in a number of skills, such as chess playing (Chase & Simon, 1973), computer programming (McKeithern, Reitman, Reuther, & Hirtle, 1981), bridge playing (Engle & Bukstel, 1978), and badminton (Housner, 1981). An interesting feature of this work is that there are some distinct commonalities among these varied activities for experts. For example, experts have more concepts about the activity than do novices and these concepts are more interrelated for the expert. Experts also have more decision rules that they use for knowing how to perform a response in specific situations. Experts also take in important information faster and in larger amounts than novices. These characteristics lead experts to be able to make faster and more accurate decisions and to make quicker responses that require anticipation.

Most of the research using the novice vs. expert paradigm has been done using cognitive skills. However, there has been an increase in the use of this paradigm to look at motor skills. Consult Starkes and Deakin (1984) and Thomas, French, and Humphries (1986) for good reviews of this work. Here we will consider two examples of the use of this paradigm to gain insight into the skill learning process.

In an experiment reported by Housner (1981), a novice and an expert badminton player were asked to respond to a detailed set of questions related to the strategies they use in a game. Questions included "What do you think about during a game?", "Why do you choose to respond in a particular way in this situation?", and so on. After completing this questionnaire, the two subjects were put into actual badminton games against opponents of similar skill levels. The subjects were interviewed before, during, and after the games to determine what they planned to do, what they actually did and why, and how well they followed their game plans. Results showed that the expert player had more strategy concepts than did the novice and that the expert used these concepts in ways that resembled problem-solving approaches. The novice tended to operate on very specific rules that were not very adaptable to the changing conditions of the game.

Another example of the novice vs. expert paradigm demonstrates its usefulness to better understand developmental processes that interact with learning a sports skill. In an experiment by French and Thomas (1987), experts and novices were limited to 8 to 10-year-olds and 11 to 12-year-olds playing in youth basketball leagues. Players were assessed in terms of basketball skills and knowledge of the game. As expected, the child experts possessed more skill and knowledge than the novice players. Even more interesting was that children who possessed greater basketball knowledge about such things as rules of the game and positions of players exhibited greater decision-making capabilities during games. This finding has important implications for teaching sport skills. An interesting additional feature of this study was the observation of changes that resulted from an entire season of practices and games. Again the results have important implications for instruction. The children in these basketball programs demonstrated a greater increase in their cognitive knowledge than in their motor skills. In particular, the players learned what to do in certain basketball situations faster than they learned the motor skills required to carry out these actions.

Although we would clearly expect novices and experts to differ both in cognitive knowledge of activities and in skills required to perform the activities, we need to know more about what these differences actually are. The continued use of the novice vs. expert paradigm has great potential to provide this information. With this information, we can not only gain more insight into the skill learning process but we can also more appropriately design instruction to fit the needs of individuals at the various points along the learning stages continuum.

Summary

Learning is a process that involves time and practice. As an individual progresses from being a beginner in an activity to being a highly skilled performer, he or she progresses through several distinct stages. These stages have been described in three different models. Fitts and Posner proposed that the

learner progresses through three stages, which they identify as the cognitive, the associative, and the autonomous stages. Adams proposed only two stages, called the verbal-motor and the motor stages. Gentile also proposed two stages. These were identified on the basis of the goal of the learner in each stage, hence the first stage is known as getting the idea of the movement whereas the second stage is known as the fixation/diversification stage. The goals of the second stage are related specifically to closed and open skills. Evidence that learners show distinct characteristics as they progress through the different learning stages has been shown in numerous ways. Some of these characteristics relate to changes in achieving the goal of the skill, changes in the capability to detect and correct one's errors, changes in movement efficiency as seen by increased economy of energy expenditure, changes in coordination, and changes in the EMG patterns associated with producing the movements required by the skills. An additional approach to the study of changes that occur as a result of progressing through the learning stages is to compare novices and experts in the same activity. This research has successfully demonstrated distinct cognitive and motor skill differences that can be useful in better understanding the learning process and in designing more effective skill instruction.

Related Readings

Adams, J. A. (1971). A closed-loop theory of motor learning. *Journal of Motor Behavior, 3,* 111–150.

Adler, J. (1981). Stages of skill acquisition: A guide for teachers. *Motor Skills: Theory into Practice, 5,* 75–80.

Fitts, P. M., & Posner, M. I. (1967). *Human performance* (pp. 243–285). Belmont, Calif.: Brooks/Cole. (Read chapter 2.)

Starkes, J. L., & Deakin, J. (1984). Perception in sport: A cognitive approach to skilled performance. In W. Straub & J. Williams (Eds.). *Cognitive sport psychology* (pp. 115–128). Lansing, NY: Sport Science Associates.

Thomas, J. R., French, K. E., & Humphries, C. A. (1986). Knowledge development and sport skill performance: Directions for motor behavior research. *Journal of Sport Psychology, 8,* 259–272.

Concept 2.3 A theoretical basis is necessary for the advancement of knowledge about how we learn and control motor skills

Application

If we are to increase our understanding of how we learn or control motor skills as well as how we can effectively improve instructional methods for teaching motor skills, a theoretical base is essential. Accordingly, this need for a viable motor learning theory is as important for researchers in motor skills who may not teach as it is for teachers of motor skills who may not be involved in research.

Any theory of motor learning is the result of a synthesis of many experiments. The theory is presented as a basis from which predictions can be made in related situations in which the conditions addressed by the theory have not yet been specifically tested. Additionally, a good theory establishes ways in which it can be tested in order to be further substantiated by new situations or revised to accommodate these new situations.

The need for a solid base for understanding how we control and learn motor skills has been emphasized by several theorists. Consider some views expressed by the two individuals who developed the motor learning theories that will be presented in the next section. Jack Adams (1971) stated that in order for scientific productivity to develop, researchers must begin with laws and theory about movement and then find situations in which to test these laws and theories. The most productive means of accomplishing the development of a viable theory of motor learning is by research that will allow the steady building of scientific knowledge to enable us to "some day have power to answer all the problems" (p. 112). Whether this actually happens is secondary to the importance of developing research that provides the greatest potential for it to happen.

Another perspective has been presented by Richard Schmidt (1975b). He argued that without adequate theory to provide explanations for motor learning, a loss of interest in motor learning as a viable area for research could result. Interestingly, from a historical perspective, this is what occurred with motor learning research in the late 1950s and most of the 1960s. Immediately prior to that time, during and after World War II, there was a flurry of motor learning research activity. However, that research was not based on learning theory specific to motor skills learning, although Hull's popular theory of learning made several predictions about factors that influence the learning of motor skills. Nonetheless, the primary incentive for conducting motor learning

research at that time was from the immediate needs of the military for developing effective methods for teaching military personnel various jobs involving motor skills, such as gunnery or piloting an airplane. In fact, it was not until the publication of the motor learning theory by Adams in 1971 that motor learning research once again increased.

The need for a solid theoretical base for teaching motor skills can be seen in statements made by theorists concerned with the process of effective teaching. It is interesting to note that these statements are similar to those made by motor learning theorists about the need for a theoretical base. For example, N. L. Gage (1972) published a book presenting the view that teaching is both a science and an art. The art aspect of teaching, he says, calls for "intuition, creativity, improvisation, and expressiveness" (p. 15). The science part of teaching involves the application of laws and theories on which teaching methods can be based. Along these same lines, Siedentop (1983) stated that teaching is not just applying the right method at the right time because you have been told to do so. Rather, the effective teacher must be able to *construct* the use of the right method to use according to the demands of the specific teaching situation, which may or may not have been confronted before.

In the following discussion, an important objective is to help you begin to establish a theoretical basis for your needs as a teacher of motor skills by presenting two significant theories related to how we learn and control motor skills. As you discover how people learn and control motor skills, you will be better able to develop effective teaching methods to accommodate these characteristics.

Discussion

Although the beginning of research related to the learning and control of motor skills can be traced back to the 1850s, it was not until 1971 that a comprehensive, testable theory of motor learning was presented. The impact of that theory was to spark renewed interest in studying motor learning. Perhaps even more importantly, it increased an interest in developing research questions, or hypotheses, on the basis of understanding the "processes" involved in learning and controlling motor skills rather than hypotheses concerning what might be the effect of some situation on this or that task. This increase in what has been referred to as a process-oriented approach has led to the testing and refinement of the 1971 theory, the development of new theoretical approaches, and an increased amount of research on how we learn and control motor skills.

In this discussion, you will be introduced to two influential theories of motor learning. The first is the closed-loop theory presented by Jack Adams in 1971. The second is the schema theory published by Richard Schmidt in 1975. These two theories, while not the only existing theories related to motor learning, will introduce you to some of the significant factors that shape current views of how we learn and control motor skills. The discussion of these

theories will provide you with the beginnings of an essential theoretical base on which you can build your knowledge of motor learning and how to develop effective methods for teaching motor skills.

Adams' Closed-Loop Theory

The motivation behind Adams' development of a theory of motor learning was what he considered to be an unfortunate lack of a well-defined subject matter and a paradigm on which to base and pursue the study of motor learning. To overcome this problem, he presented his "closed-loop theory" of motor learning (Adams, 1971).

The term *closed-loop* relates to the use of information in controlling a movement and comes from an engineering term that describes what is called a servomechanism device, such as a thermostat for an air-conditioning unit. The desired room temperature is set on the thermostat. This setting then becomes a reference against which varying room temperatures can be compared. If the temperature is higher than this reference, then a command is sent to the air-conditioning unit to turn on and begin cooling the room. If the temperature is lower than this reference, the unit stays off. Thus, continuous "information" is sent from the room, to the thermostat, to the air-conditioning unit, to the room, and back to the thermostat, thereby establishing a constant "loop" of information flow to control the room's temperature in accordance to the specified thermostat temperature. (You will study more about closed-loop control systems in Chapter 3.)

Adams' frame of reference for his theory was simple, limb-positioning movements such as those described in Concept 1.3. Although Adams felt that this theory could be generalized to include more complex movements, he argued that it was essential to begin the process of theory development for motor learning by focusing on simple skills. In addition, he also wanted to develop a theory around existing research literature, which primarily involved the use of simple, limb-positioning movements.

The perceptual trace. The basis for any closed-loop theory is a reference mechanism, or referent of correctness that can be used to compare a movement being made. In Adams' theory, this reference mechanism is called the *perceptual trace*. This trace involves the memory of past movements and is responsible for determining the extent of a movement in progress. It is used by the performer to know where to stop the limb as well as how to adjust another attempt at the same movement. An important characteristic of this trace is that it must be developed by appropriate practice of the movement being learned.

As we considered earlier, the reference mechanism in any closed-loop system uses information that is fed back into the mechanism from some source. For the perceptual trace, this information is fed back by means of sensory

pathways from the muscles, joints, eyes, ears, and so on. (These will be discussed in Chapter 3.) The perceptual trace uses this information to compare what the movement is currently like with what it is supposed to be like. If there is a perfect match, the command is issued to stop the movement. If error is detected in this comparison, then commands are sent to make some adjustments in the movement. How well this comparison and correction process can be accomplished depends on how accurate and well-developed the perceptual trace is at the time.

Essential to our understanding of the perceptual trace is that it gets stronger, or better developed, as practice of the movement occurs. Adams' view was that an essential part of this development is the availability of knowledge of results (KR), or information about the correctness of a response provided by some external source, such as an experimenter, a teacher, or coach. (KR will be discussed in Chapter 7.) As a part of practice, the individual combines this KR information with the feedback information received through his or her own sensory system. Eventually, the perceptual trace becomes strong enough for the individual to be able to detect and correct his or her own error when making the movement. When this occurs, Adams indicates that the individual has moved from the verbal-motor stage of learning into the motor stage of learning, where the movement can be made "automatically."

The memory trace. While Adams considered the perceptual trace as the reference mechanism used to establish how far a limb movement should go, he needed to specify a mechanism for getting the limb moving in the first place and in the proper direction. To accommodate this need, Adams proposed the *memory trace*. The role of the memory trace is to "select and initiate a response, preceding the use of the perceptual trace" (p. 125). This trace is also developed as a result of practice. However, different from the perceptual trace, the memory trace was described by Adams as a "modest motor program." That is, this trace does not operate as a closed-loop system but as an open-loop system that sends out all the necessary information to *initiate* the movement. No feedback information is needed to accomplish this task. (A more complete discussion of motor programs will be presented in Chapter 3.)

The closed-loop theory proposed by Adams had some limitations. Richard Schmidt (1975b) sought to overcome these by presenting an alternative theory of motor learning. Although Schmidt specified several limitations, we will consider two of them here. The first concerned the closed-loop theory's being too limited to generalize to motor skills other than those related to simple, slow, limb-positioning movements. Second, there did not seem to be a logical way to establish how people could make a correct response for a movement they had not previously performed in exactly that way, such as is common in the open classification of motor skills discussed in Concept 1.1.

Schmidt's
Schema Theory

The motor response schema. To accommodate these limitations and to establish what Schmidt considered to be a more appropriate view of how we learn and control motor skills, Schmidt presented his schema theory. Rather than considering the memory and perceptual traces as the controlling mechanisms of a movement, this theory presented schemas. A *schema* can be defined as a rule or set of rules that serves to provide the basis for a decision. An important characteristic of a schema is that it is developed from abstracting important pieces of information from related experiences and combining them into a type of rule. For example, your concept of "dog" is the result of many experiences with seeing many different types of dogs. As a result of these experiences, you have developed a set of rules that will allow you to produce the response "dog" when you are asked what this animal is that is being shown to you. You may never have seen that type of dog before but yet you still can identify it as a dog.

Schmidt stated that we learn and control movements on a similar basis. That is, for a given class of movements, such as the overhand throwing pattern, we abstract different pieces of information about each throwing response made where an overarm throwing pattern is used. Throughout these experiences, we construct a schema that will enable us to successfully carry out a variety of movements where the overhand throwing pattern is involved. What is abstracted are four pieces of information from each movement experience.

The first is information concerning the *initial conditions* related to the response. This involves such things as the position of the limbs and body, the environmental conditions in which the response is made, etc., which are related to the response before it is made. Second, the performer stores information about the *response specifications.* These are the specific demands of the movement, such as the direction, speed, force, etc., that are involved in carrying out the movement. Third, the *sensory consequences* of the movement are determined. These involve information based on sensory feedback received through the various sensory systems during and after the movement is actually made. Finally, information is abstracted on the *response outcome.* This information is related to the comparison of the actual outcome with the intended outcome. KR information is an important element here. These four sources of information, then, get stored together after the movement is made. When many movements are made, these abstracted pieces of information are synthesized to form a general rule (schema) about the movements.

The motor response schema is actually made up of two schemas, each with different responsibilities. First is the *recall schema,* which is responsible for determining the desired response. This schema adds specific response instructions to the motor program and initiates the movement execution. The second schema is the *recognition schema,* which enables the performer to evaluate the correctness of the initiated movement by comparing actual sensory feedback information against the expected sensory feedback and then to make movement corrections. Exactly how these schemas are involved in the control of movement will be discussed in Chapter 3.

Success in novel response situations. One of the features of the schema theory that generated a great deal of research interest was related to the problem of accounting for success in performing a novel response within a movement class. That is, how can a person make a response that had not been made in exactly the same way before? Since the motor response schema is an abstract set of response rules, Schmidt predicted that the performer can be successful in a novel situation by generating the appropriate response by synthesizing the response requirements of the novel situation with the general rules for performing that type of movement already available in the motor response schema. The probability of making a correct response in the novel response situation can be increased, according to Schmidt, by increased amounts of practice and variety of practice experiences in the response situation. This practice prediction will be considered in more detail in Chapter 9.

As you compare these two theories, do not try to determine if one is good and the other is not. Each has strong and weak points. As you continue your study of motor learning, you will be better able to determine these characteristics for yourself.

Comparing Adams' and Schmidt's Theories

However, certain immediately noteworthy similarities in these theories can be pointed out. First, both are based on the important role of feedback information from the senses. Second, both incorporate a role for motor programs. Third, both suggest two memory-related constructs in which information is stored and which are directly involved in the initiation and carrying out of a response. Fourth, both theories assign an important role to KR information during the learning of a motor skill. Fifth, both theories indicate that as a result of the appropriate amount and type of practice, learners can produce correct responses without the aid of KR. Sixth, each theory establishes a means for the performer both to detect and correct a movement, either while the movement is being executed or before another movement response is made.

There are some specific differences between these two theories as well. First, Adams' theory suggests that each movement response is represented in memory. Schmidt's, on the other hand, states that each movement remains in memory only long enough for certain pieces of information about each movement to be abstracted and get represented in memory as parts of a movement schema. Second, Adams' theory is primarily limited to slow, limb-positioning movements whereas Schmidt's theory accommodates the demands of other types of movements, such as rapid, ballistic movements. Third, success in performing a novel response cannot be accounted for by Adams' theory whereas Schmidt's schema theory specifically addresses this situation. Fourth, Schmidt's theory provides a more central and elaborate role for the motor program than does Adams' approach.

While there are other similarities and differences between these two theories of motor learning, these few will suffice for our present needs. Each point made in the presentation of these comparisons and contrasts will be discussed

more extensively in the following chapters of this book. For now, it is important for you to understand the essential features of each theory and how they are related to each other, and it is important that you see the significance of these theories for present and future understanding of how we learn and control movements. The increase in interest in motor learning and in motor learning research owes a great deal to these two theories.

One final point is worth considering. You probably noticed in this discussion of Adams' and Schmidt's theories that certain specific points in each theory were criticized. You will also see evidence that certain predictions made by each theorist cannot be supported. It is important to view these criticisms and research findings in a positive way as they reflect important processes in the advancement of scientific knowledge. These theories have been and continue to be important. They provide a basis for research so that we can better understand how we learn and perform skills. New theories will emerge from this increased research activity. This continuing process of theory development and prediction testing is a critical step in uncovering the mysteries of how we learn skills.

Summary

Two influential theories of motor learning have been presented to introduce you to how a theoretical basis has been established for the advancement of our knowledge about how we learn and control motor skills. The first theory was presented by Adams as the closed-loop theory of motor learning. Two essential features of this theory are the perceptual trace and the memory trace. The perceptual trace is the reference mechanism of the correct movement and is used when a movement is in progress to determine when to stop the movement. The perceptual trace is strengthened by practice and the appropriate use of knowledge of results. The memory trace is responsible for initiating the movement.

According to Schmidt's theory, which is known as the schema theory, the performer of a motor skill abstracts four important pieces of information from each movement experience. These are information about the initial conditions related to the response, the response specifications needed to produce that response, the sensory consequences of the response, and the response outcome itself. As the response is practiced, these abstracted pieces of information get synthesized into a schema that is used to control the response. One of the benefits of the schema theory is that it presented a means of predicting success in a novel response situation.

These two theories have some similarities and some differences. However, it is important that you understand and use both as the basis for what you will be studying in the remainder of this book and for developing effective methods for teaching motor skills.

Adams, J. A. (1976). Issues for a closed-loop theory of motor learning. In G. E. Stelmach (Ed.), *Motor control: Issues and trends* (pp. 87–107). New York: Academic Press.

Schmidt, R. A. (1976). The schema as a solution to some persistent problems in motor learning theory. In G. E. Stelmach (Ed.), *Motor control: Issues and trends* (pp. 41–65). New York: Academic Press.

Schmidt, R. A. (1977). Schema theory: Implications for movement education. *Motor Skills: Theory into Practice, 2,* 36–48.

Related Readings

1. Explain how the terms *performance* and *learning* differ.
2. Name two important performance characteristics that should change during learning a motor skill and how they should change. Give an example of these changes in a motor skill situation with which you are familiar.
3. Why must we *infer* learning?
4. What are the advantages of using retention tests and transfer tests compared with observing practice performance for making a valid assessment of learning? Give an example of how an incorrect inference about learning a skill could be made from only observing practice performance and how the use of a retention or transfer test would permit a more appropriate inference.
5. What is a performance plateau? What seems to be the most likely reason why a performance plateau occurs in motor skill learning?
6. What are some characteristics of learners as they progress through the three stages of learning proposed by Fitts and Posner?
7. How does Gentile's stages of learning model differ from the Fitts and Posner model? How does her model relate specifically to differences in learning open and closed skills?
8. Name three specific changes that research has shown occur as a person progresses through the stages of learning a motor skill.
9. How has research shown novices to differ from experts in motor skill performance?
10. How do the perceptual trace and the memory trace differ according to Adams' closed-loop theory of motor learning?
11. What does Schmidt mean by the term *schema* in his schema theory of motor learning? How does this schema view account for why we can be successful at performing a skill that we have never practiced in the way that the performance situation requires?
12. What are three similarities between Adams' closed-loop theory and Schmidt's schema theory? What are three differences?

Study Questions for Chapter 2 (Introduction to Motor Learning)

Unit 2

The Learner

Controlling Movement

3

Concept 3.1
The control of movement is dependent on the structure and function of the neuromuscular system.

Concept 3.2
Coordinated voluntary movement is controlled by both open-loop and closed-loop systems in the nervous system.

Concept 3.3
Proprioception and vision play important roles in the control of voluntary movement.

Concept 3.4
Certain types of motor skills and well-learned skills appear to be controlled by motor programs.

Concept 3.5
Anticipation timing is an essential element for successful performance of skills requiring the precise coordination of an external event with a motor response.

Concept 3.1 The control of movement is dependent on the structure and function of the neuromuscular system

Application

Suppose you are sitting at your desk and you want to make a few notes about what you are reading. What is the first thing you must do? Well, first you must pick up your pen so that you can begin writing. Have you ever thought about what is going on in your nervous system and your muscular system that enables you to accomplish this relatively simple action of reaching and grasping a pen? As simple as these movements are, there is a rather complex array of activity going on in both the nervous and muscular systems of the body. Consider, for example, some of the questions that could be asked in attempting to describe what occurred in these systems before, during, and after this action was carried out.

What muscles in the body were activated during this action? How did your intention to pick up the pen get translated into commands that caused these muscles to be activated? What parts of the nervous system were involved in this action? How did the limb know where to go and how far to go? How did the fingers know when to begin grasping the pen and how much pressure to apply to hold the pen so it wouldn't slip from your grasp? How did the limb know when the pen was grasped so that it could be lifted? The list of questions could go on and on. These few reveal the complexities involved in even a relatively simple movement. An important part of understanding how voluntary, coordinated movement is controlled is determining answers to these questions.

How the body is involved in controlling its own movement is indeed an intriguing problem. In this concept, we will look briefly into the various complexities of what we call the motor control system. This comprises an intricate network of nerves, nerve endings, and musculature, as well as the central nervous system itself. Each component of this control system can be considered as a distinct structural and functional unit. Each part can also be considered in terms of its role in a complex network charged with responsibility for initiating and controlling movement. Whether the actual movement is a simple one, such as squeezing the trigger of a rifle, or a complex one, like performing a routine on a balance beam, this control system is operating.

Discussion

Study of the learning and performance of motor skills would be incomplete if the underlying neuromuscular system were ignored. Throughout the other chapters in this book, the discussion centers around the behavioral aspects of learning and performance. While these aspects reflect the focus of this book, in themselves they do not explain fully the processes involved. Therefore, it is

necessary to consider the neuromuscular system, which is involved in the control of movement. Thus, in order to provide an important foundation for what you will study in the remainder of this book, we shall examine the components of that system and discuss how they work together to produce and control movement.

Our study of the structure and function of the neuromuscular system will include the central and peripheral nervous systems as well as the innervation of these systems with the sensory receptors and musculature involved in movement. No attempt will be made to describe the entire neural and muscular systems; rather, the focus will be the parts of those systems that are the primary components functioning in the control of movement.

General structure. The most basic component of the neuromuscular system is the *neuron,* or nerve cell. The nerve cells in the nervous systems number in the billions. Every phase of the movement control system that we discuss in this chapter has the neuron as its primary foundation block. These functional units of the nervous system, varying in size from 4 to 100 microns, provide the means for receiving and sending information throughout the entire system. Although there are several different types of neurons, most share a relatively identical structure. This includes the three parts known as (1) the cell body, (2) dendrites, and (3) the axon (Figure 3.1–1).

The *cell body* contains the all-important nucleus. The nucleus regulates the homeostasis of the neuron. *Dendrites* are nerve fibers that extend from the cell body and are primarily responsible for receiving information from other neurons. A neuron may have none or as many as thousands of dendrites. The *axon* is also a nerve fiber, but it is responsible only for sending information from the neuron. Unlike dendrites, there is only one axon per neuron, although most axons branch into many-sided axons, or collateral fibers. The ends of the axonal fibers are called boutons or knobs that provide a signal transmission relay station as nerve impulses are passed on to other neurons or muscles.

Types and functions of neurons. The most convenient means of classifying neurons is according to their function in sending and receiving information to and from the central nervous system (CNS), that is, the brain and spinal cord. (See Figure 3.1–2 for examples of neuron types.) Neurons that send signals to the CNS are called *sensory neurons.* These neurons are also referred to as receptor neurons or *afferent neurons* (the prefix *a-* means "to"), because they receive sensory information and send information to the CNS. Sensory neurons receive information from the various sensory receptors and transmit that information to the CNS. In a sense, the sensory receptor is much like a transducer in electronics, because it converts the information it receives into an electrical signal that can then be transmitted along the neural pathways and received by the CNS. Structurally, the sensory neurons are unipolar; that is, they have no dendrites and only one axon connecting them with the cell body.

The Neuron

Figure 3.1-1
A neuron or nerve cell.

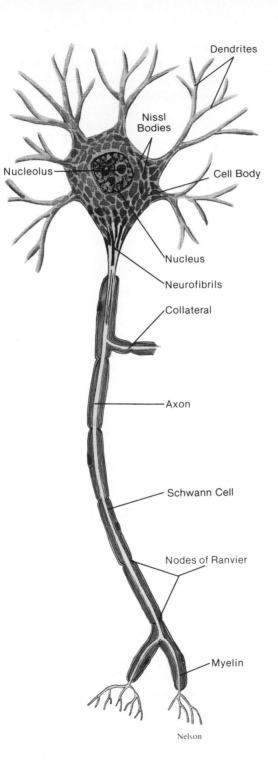

Dendrites

Nissl Bodies

Nucleolus

Cell Body

Nucleus

Neurofibrils

Collateral

Axon

Schwann Cell

Nodes of Ranvier

Myelin

Nelson

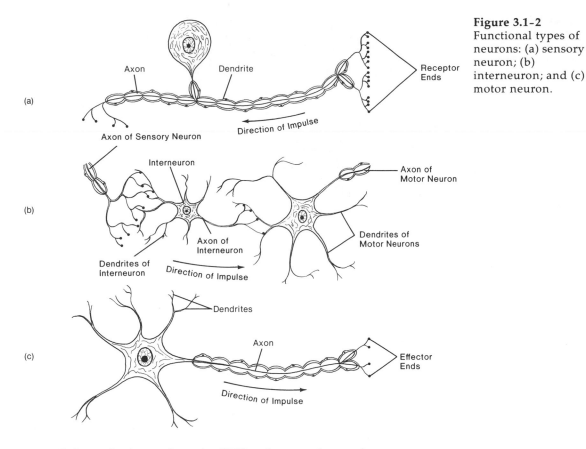

(a)

Axon   Dendrite

Receptor Ends

Direction of Impulse

Axon of Sensory Neuron

(b)

Axon of Sensory Neuron

Interneuron

Axon of Motor Neuron

Axon of Interneuron

Dendrites of Motor Neurons

Dendrites of Interneuron

Direction of Impulse

(c)

Dendrites

Axon

Effector Ends

Direction of Impulse

Figure 3.1-2
Functional types of
neurons: (a) sensory
neuron; (b)
interneuron; and (c)
motor neuron.

Information is sent from the CNS to the musculature via *motor neurons,* or *efferent neurons* (the prefix *e-* means "from"). While there are several types of motor neurons, only four need be considered for this discussion. *Alpha motor neurons,* or motor horn cells, are found predominately in the spinal cord. They have many branching dendrites and a long axon that extends out in many branches to connect with the skeletal muscle fibers. *Pyramidal cells* are found in the motor cortex and cerebellum of the brain. These pyramid-shaped cells are believed to be long-distance transmitters and may have axons as long as three feet. *Purkinje cells* are motor neurons found almost exclusively in the cerebellum of the brain. *Gamma motor neurons* supply a portion of the skeletal muscle called intrafusal fibers. These neurons are fast conducting (10–50 m/sec) and are intricately involved in the control of skeletal muscle contraction. The nature of the role of these motor neurons in the control of movement will be considered more fully later in this discussion.

One final type of neuron needs to be mentioned. The *interneurons* are those found in the CNS. They originate and terminate in the brain or spinal cord. Their function will be considered later in this discussion.

Figure 3.1-3
Structural components of the central nervous system (CNS).

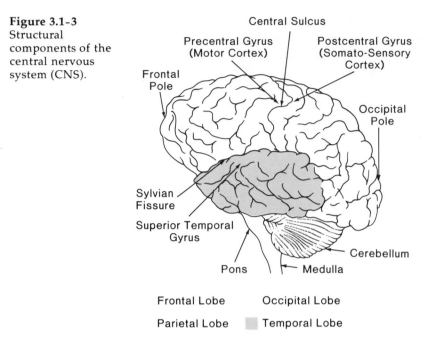

Central Sulcus

Precentral Gyrus (Motor Cortex)

Postcentral Gyrus (Somato-Sensory Cortex)

Frontal Pole

Occipital Pole

Sylvian Fissure

Superior Temporal Gyrus

Pons

Medulla

Cerebellum

Frontal Lobe   Occipital Lobe

Parietal Lobe   Temporal Lobe

The Central Nervous System (CNS)

The CNS is the command center for human behavior; it is an incredibly complex system. Volumes have been written in attempts to describe its structure and function. This system is made up of two essential components, the *brain* and *spinal cord*. These two structures form the basis of the control system that is the center of activity in the integration and organization of sensory and motor information in movement control. Rather than present a complete anatomical and physiological picture of the components of the CNS, this discussion will concentrate on those primary portions of the CNS that are most directly related to the control of movement. In the brain, these important sections are the *cerebral cortex, basal ganglia, cerebellum,* and *brain stem.* The spinal cord is a structural and functional unit of the CNS that need not here be considered in terms of any further subdivisions. As you follow this discussion, you will find it helpful to refer to Figure 3.1–3, where the structural components of the brain and spinal cord are illustrated.

The cerebral cortex. The part of the brain that is generally pictured in photographs is the undulating, wrinkly gray-colored covering of the brain itself; this is called the cerebral cortex. It is a thin tissue of nerve cells that is about 2- to 5-mm thick and, if unfolded, would cover an area of about 20 square feet. The cortex is divided into two halves, the left and right hemispheres. The hemispheres are connected by a sheet of nerve fibers known as the corpus callosum.

In terms of movement control, several parts of the cerebral cortex are noteworthy. The primary motor area of the cortex is on the precentral gyrus, which is located just to the front of the central fissure. Just to the back of the central fissure, on the postcentral gyrus, is the sensory cortex, where sensory neurons terminate.

The primary function of the cerebral cortex in the control of movement is both complex and comprehensive. The cortex is charged with the responsibility of receiving and interpreting sensory signals, sending the interpreted signals to the appropriate effectors via the appropriate neural pathways, as well as storing and organizing information.

The basal ganglia. Buried within the cerebral hemispheres are three large nuclei known as the basal ganglia. These nuclei, called the caudate nucleus, the putamen, and the globus pallidus, receive inputs from the cerebral cortex and the brain stem. Outputs from the basal ganglia are sent to the brain stem. In particular, there is a loop of information flow that involves the basal ganglia, thalamus, and motor cortex, which is receiving increasing consideration as important for controlling movement.

Insight into the function of the basal ganglia has come from work with Parkinson's disease patients. This disorder is primarily a disease of the basal ganglia. The disease is typically characterized by physically observable characteristics, such as involuntary shaking movements of the limbs (known as tremor), stiffness of the muscles (rigidity), and slowness of movement (bradykinesia). These symptoms vary in the degree to which they characterize an individual. One reason motor control researchers are investigating Parkinson's patients is because, as a disease of the basal ganglia, a comparison of capabilities and performance characteristics of both diseased and nondiseased persons can provide insight into better understanding Parkinson's disease and the function of the basal ganglia in controlling movement.

As a result of work with Parkinson's patients, researchers have identified an important role of the basal ganglia in controlling coordinated movement. Basal ganglia have been found to be important for response selection and response organization processes. When Parkinson's patients are compared with normal subjects (e.g., Glencross & Tsouvallas, 1984) the former typically show slower reaction times (RT) and slower movement times (MT) when a response to a signal requires them to make a specified movement as quickly as possible. In fact, when a rapid, complex response must be made to the signal, the normal subject will typically plan the entire response, whereas the Parkinson's patient will plan the sequence one segment at a time. You will study the use of these types of movement both later in this chapter and in other chapters in this book.

In research based not on Parkinson's disease but rather on basal ganglia lesion research with monkeys, Hore and Vilas (1980) provided evidence that basal ganglia disorders lead to a failure to achieve the correct balance of activity between the agonists and antagonists that must occur for a particular

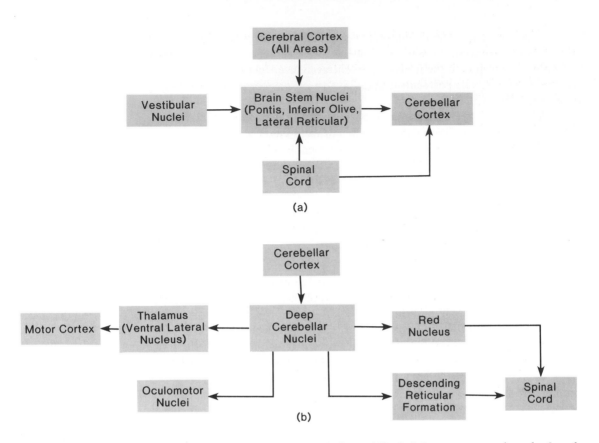

Figure 3.1-4
(a) Block diagram of the principal cerebellar afferents (inputs). (b) Block diagram showing the principal cerebellar efferents (outputs).

motor act. Research such as this is rapidly helping us to see that the basal ganglia are critical for movement control. Only further research will provide us with the exact nature of this role.

The cerebellum. As you can see in Figure 3.1–3, the cerebellum is located behind the cerebral hemispheres and is attached to the pons. The cerebellum has distinct parts, each of which appears to have specific functions. The cerebellar cortex covers the cerebellum, which, like the cerebrum, is divided into two hemispheres. Under this cortex lies white matter in which are embedded the deep cerebellar nuclei.

The major inputs into the cerebellum arise from three principal regions: the spinal cord; the cerebral cortex; and the brain stem. The outputs from the cerebellum connect to the spinal cord via the red nucleus and the descending reticular formation. Also, output goes to the motor cortex by way of the central lateral nuclei of the thalamus. Finally, there is output to the oculomotor nuclei, which are involved in the control of eye movement. These inputs and outputs of the cerebellum are illustrated in a block diagram in Figure 3.1–4.

The function of the cerebellum has traditionally been thought to relate primarily to balance, postural adjustments, locomotion, and reflex activity. However, there is some current speculation that the cerebellum is also the vital center of control for programmed movements, a theory which will be discussed more fully in other concepts in this chapter.

Eccles (Popper & Eccles, 1977) has stated that while the cerebral cortex has all the neural circuits for initiating and controlling voluntary movements, these movements are crude and irregular if damage to some other part of the brain occurs. In particular, damage to the cerebellum results in severe movement disruption, especially to those movements that have been well-learned and are produced automatically. Losses in equilibrium, timing, and coordination have been noted in individuals with cerebellar damage. This critical role of the cerebellum in movement control has been further reinforced in a review of cerebellum research by Llinas and Simpson (1981), who refer to the cerebellum as "the seat of motor coordination" (p. 281).

The brain stem. Four main areas of the brain stem are significantly involved in movement control. At the top of the brain stem, which is directly underneath the cerebral hemispheres, is the *thalamus*. This collection of nuclei is divided into left and right sections. The nuclei are connected to various areas of the cerebral cortex, including the sensory cortex and motor cortex. Essentially, the thalamus functions as a type of relay center, transmitting sensory information from lower brain centers to the cortex. However, some of the cortex connections are actually information loops that provide the basis for speculation for additional roles played by the thalamus.

The *pons* serves primarily as a bridge through which various neural tracts either pass from the cortex on their way to the spinal cord or terminate as they come from the cortex. The *medulla,* which is like an extension of the spinal cord, serves as a regulatory agent for various vital internal processes such as respiration and heartbeat. In voluntary movement control, the medulla functions as a site where the corticospinal tracts of the sensory and motor pathways cross over the body midline and merge on their way to the cerebellum and cerebral cortex.

The fourth area of the brain stem involved in movement control is called the *reticular formation.* This composite of nuclei and nerve fibers has been determined to be one of the most vital links in the chain of neural structures that lie between the sensory receptors and the movement command centers in the cerebellum and cerebral cortex. Its primary role in movement control is that of an integrator of sensory and motor impulses. The reticular formation appears to have access to all sensory information and can exert direct influence on the CNS to modify the activity of the CNS either by inhibiting or by increasing that activity, which in turn influences the activity of the skeletal muscles.

Figure 3.1-5
Cross-section of the
spinal cord showing
the butterfly-shaped
gray matter, with
the dorsal and
ventral horns, and
the white matter,
with the ascending
and descending
tracts.

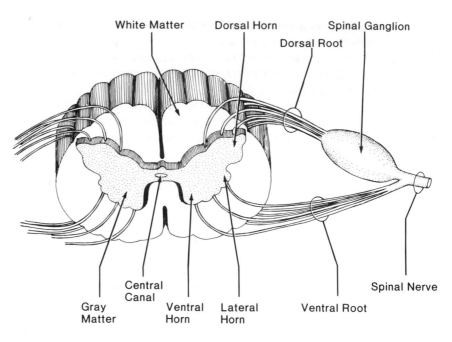

The spinal cord. The traditional view that the spinal cord is like a telephone cable that simply relays messages from the brain to the muscles is no longer given much credibility. Instead, the spinal cord is currently viewed as a complex system that interacts with a variety of systems and may itself be critically involved in the movement control process. A review of the components of the spinal cord will provide a basis for this view.

The spinal cord consists of 31 segments, from which the spinal nerves emanate. The two major portions of the spinal cord are called the *gray matter* and the *white matter*. The gray matter is the butterfly- or H-shaped central portion of the spinal cord (note Figure 3.1–5). This gray matter consists primarily of the cell bodies and axons of neurons that reside in the spinal cord. Two pairs of "horns" protrude from the gray matter, and these are vital to movement control. The top pair of horns are known as the *dorsal horns;* they contain cells related to the transmission of sensory information. The bottom pair of horns are called *ventral horns;* these horns contain cells from which motor or efferent fibers arise and terminate on skeletal muscles. Sensory information from the various sense receptors in the musculature synapse on neurons in the dorsal horn. Neurons from the brain that contain motor information synapse on motor neurons in the ventral horns and exit to their respective effectors.

In addition to the presence of alpha motor neurons and the sensory neurons, the spinal cord also contains *interneurons*, which are located primarily in the ventral horn. Many of the descending fibers from the brain terminate

on these rather than on motor neurons. While the traditional view of the function of these interneurons is that they are merely a relay station (e.g., Hole, 1984), there is growing speculation that they have a specific unique function in the control of voluntary movement (e.g., Kots, 1977).

The nerve fibers in the spinal cord are in the white matter that surrounds the gray matter. The various ascending tracts (fibers going to the brain) and descending tracts (fibers coming from the brain) can be found in different locations in the white matter. These tracts will be elaborated on later in this discussion, when we consider efferent transmission.

Throughout the body various sensory receptors are involved in the control of movement. However, we will concentrate primarily on the sensory receptors of the joints, tendons, and skeletal muscles. It must be acknowledged that the sensory receptors of the visual system and the auditory or vestibular system (the inner ears) are also involved with movement control. We will not elaborate on those systems, in order that we can direct attention to the peripheral receptors of the joints, tendons, and muscles. These receptors, sometimes referred to as *proprioceptors,* include the *muscle spindles* and the *joint receptors.*

Sensory Receptors

Muscle spindles. The primary proprioceptor mechanism in the skeletal muscles is the muscle spindle. Spindles, located in the muscle (extrafusal) fibers of the skeletal muscles, as shown in Figure 3.1–6, are specialized muscle fibers that contain a capsule which consists of both sensory receptors and muscle fibers, known as intrafusal muscle fibers. The sensory receptor portions of the muscle spindle are the *annulospiral* and the *flower-spray endings.* Annulospiral endings (also termed Ia or primary endings), the primary receptors, are in the middle portion of the spindle capsule. These receptors are generally associated with large, low-threshold, fast conducting afferent neurons. Flower-spray endings are also called II or secondary endings.

The sensory receptors of the muscle spindles are mechanical in nature; that is, they respond to the stretching of the muscle that causes a mechanical deformation of the receptors resulting in an impulse. Thus, the length of the extrafusal muscle fiber is the critical consideration in determining whether or not the muscle spindle receptors will "fire." When these receptors do "fire," the afferent information is fed into the dorsal root of the spinal cord, where it is either carried up the cord to the cerebellum or to an alpha motor neuron in the ventral horn, as would be the case in a simple reflex movement.

The relative importance of the muscle spindles in the control of voluntary rather than reflexive movement is not well understood. The muscle receptors are believed by some to be important as feedback mechanisms in movement (a point we will consider further in the description of sensorimotor integration later in this discussion). Others consider their role to be important in providing the individual with information as to where a positioning-type movement has stopped. Investigation of this problem is the object of many

Figure 3.1-6
Schematic representation of a muscle spindle showing the annulospiral ending. The flower-spray endings are not shown in this diagram but are also in the intrafusal muscle fiber.

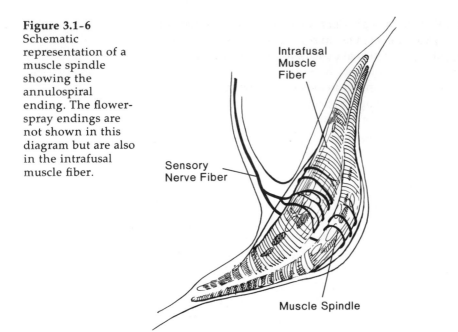

current research projects. Until the time when such research indicates the precise roles of these receptors, we must accept a more general conclusion that the muscle spindle receptors contribute to voluntary movement control, as do the sensory receptors. This contribution is in the form of (1) providing the CNS with information that the muscle has stretched and (2) participating in the neural feedback system that is an important part of movement control.

Joint receptors. There are three major types of proprioceptors, or sensory receptors, associated with the joints. These receptors, the *Golgi-tendon organs,* the *Ruffini endings,* and the *Pacinian corpuscles,* are important to voluntary movement control because of the information that they provide concerning limb movement and position. Golgi-tendon organs are found in two locations. They are in the tendons near the insertion of the tendons into the muscle, and more significant for movement information, they are located in the ligaments that tie joints together. Ruffini endings and Pacinian corpuscles are found in the connective tissue of the joint capsule itself.

The function of these joint receptors in movement control has been more extensively documented than the roles of muscle receptors. A summary of this documentation was provided by Kelso and Stelmach (1976). They indicated that their review of the research showed that "the major types of receptors and their mode of operation are as follows:

1. The Golgi-tendon organs in the ligaments, which are unaffected by the muscles inserting at the joint and thus may signal exact joint position as well as direction.

2. The highly sensitive Ruffini endings which signal speed and direction of movements. Since these are affected by muscle tension at the joints, they may also signal resistance to movement and perhaps discriminate active from passive movement.
3. The Pacinian corpuscles, which may be capable of detecting very small movements as well as movement acceleration . . ." (p. 9).

In the preceding section, attention was directed to the afferent transmission of information from the sensory receptors to the CNS. In this section, the concern will be the efferent transmission of information from the CNS to the musculature. Of primary importance here are the motor pathways; these are the means by which information moves from the brain to the musculature, and the motor unit, which is the basic effector structure in the musculature.

Motor pathways. Voluntary movements are primarily under cortical and cerebellar control. Movement information from these control centers reaches the musculature by pathways of axons that originate primarily in the cortex. These pathways can be considered as two systems, the *pyramidal* and *extrapyramidal* systems, which are also commonly referred to as the direct and indirect motor pathways. These two systems represent pathways or tracts along which movement information is carried from the cerebral cortex to an appropriate location, either for integration with other information or to command the appropriate musculature to move.

The pyramidal system is responsible for the efferent transmission of information that controls fine voluntary movements. For example, Evarts (1980) reported that destroying the pyramidal tract will eliminate fine hand movements while allowing coarser movements involving the same muscles. The origin of this system is primarily in the premotor and motor areas of the cortex, the precentral gyrus. This small strip of the brain is located just in front of the central fissure in the cortex (Figure 3.1–3). Axons from the pyramidal tract neurons in the motor area of the cortex travel to the spinal cord, where they synapse on alpha motor neurons or on interneurons, which in turn synapse on alpha motor neurons. These alpha motor neurons send axons to the musculature where the efferent transmission of the movement information is completed.

The axons of the pyramidal system activate motor neurons on the opposite side of the body from their point of origin in the cortex. That is, pyramidal tract neurons in the right hemisphere of the cortex activate movement in the left side of the body. The crossover of the majority of the axons (generally considered to be between 80% and 90%) takes place in the brain stem at an area called the *motor decussation*. Either all or almost all (there is some debate here) of the remaining axons cross over in the spinal cord. This process is illustrated in Figure 3.1–7.

Traditionally, all other motor areas of the brain not related to the pyramidal system have been called the *extrapyramidal system*. However, the

Figure 3.1-7
Motor fibers of the
pyramidal tract
begin in the
cerebral cortex,
cross over in the
medulla, and
descend in the
spinal cord. There
they synapse with
neurons whose
fibers lead to spinal
nerves supplying
skeletal muscles.

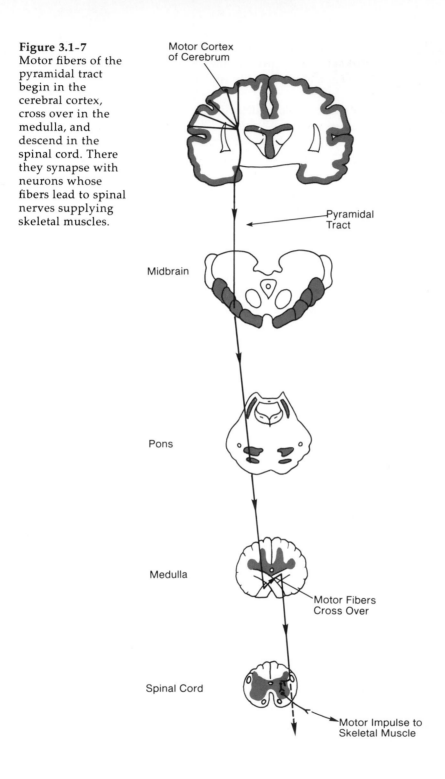

Motor Cortex
of Cerebrum

Pyramidal
Tract

Midbrain

Pons

Medulla

Motor Fibers
Cross Over

Spinal Cord

Motor Impulse to
Skeletal Muscle

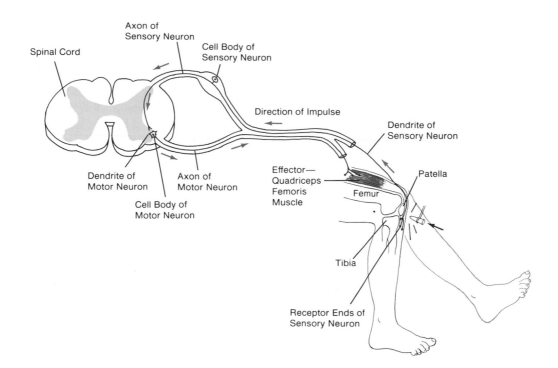

Spinal Cord

Axon of
Sensory Neuron

Cell Body of
Sensory Neuron

Direction of Impulse

Dendrite of
Sensory Neuron

Dendrite of
Motor Neuron

Axon of
Motor Neuron

Cell Body of
Motor Neuron

Effector—
Quadriceps
Femoris
Muscle

Femur

Patella

Tibia

Receptor Ends of
Sensory Neuron

current approach is to more specifically define this extrapyramidal system as brain stem efferent systems and the basal ganglia (Schwindt, 1981). These systems are comprised of the vestibulospinal tract, the rubrospinal tract, the tectospinal tract, and reticulospinal tract, which are named according to the particular part of the brain stem they include in their interaction with the spinal cord. Additionally, these tracts receive direct and/or indirect connections with the cerebral cortex. According to Schwindt (1981), each brain stem system can serve as a center for integration of information from the cerebellum, as well as a simple relay of neural information from the motor cortex. These systems are extensively interconnected, and for this reason it has been difficult to specifically determine the role of each structure of the extrapyramidal system in the control of movement. More about this later in this section in the discussion of some current thinking about brain function processes in controlling voluntary movement.

The motor unit. The ultimate end of efferent transmission is the motor unit (Figure 3.1–8), a concept introduced by Sherrington (1906). The motor unit is the alpha motor neuron and all of the muscle fibers that it innervates. Eccles (1973) has indicated that there are about 200,000 motor neurons with their dependent motor units in the human spinal cord. The alpha motor neuron connection with the muscle fibers occurs at the motor end plate. Motor end plates

Figure 3.1-8
The knee-jerk reflex involves only two neurons: a sensory neuron and a motor neuron. Note the synapse of the axon of the motor neuron on the quadriceps femoris. This is an example of a motor unit.

are located near the middle of muscle fibers. This special type of synapse allows nerve impulses to be transmitted from the nerve fiber to the muscle fibers so that the appropriate contraction can occur.

The number of muscle fibers served by one alpha motor neuron axon varies greatly. In general, muscles involved in controlling fine movements, e.g., the muscles of the eye or larynx, have the smallest number of muscle fibers for each motor unit even to one per fiber. Large skeletal muscles have the largest number of muscle fibers per unit (Basmajian, 1967). This number may be as large as 700. What occurs, then, is that groups of muscle fibers contract when an alpha motor neuron fires. The number that contract depends on the number of fibers innervated by that particular motor neuron.

It is interesting to note that individuals can learn to control the firing of a single motor unit. In fact Basmajian (1967) reported several experiments showing that with appropriate EMG biofeedback procedures, subjects need only general instructions and about 15 minutes of practice to be able to contract muscle fibers served by a single motor unit. One of the practical benefits of this type of training can be the development of training to more effectively control a prosthetic device or to provide a basis for training that will allow a person with a motor dysfunction to use a disabled muscle (Clamann, 1981).

Sensorimotor Integration

We have discussed the structures and processes involved in the reception of sensory information and in the transmission of efferent information. What is left to consider is how the CNS integrates these two kinds of information in the process of coordinating and controlling movement. The most elementary integration process involves simple reflex movements. More complicated is the integration of information for voluntary movement.

Reflex movements. The reflexive response of the "knee jerk" when the physician hits the patellar tendon is an example of a movement that falls into the simple reflex movement category (see Figure 3.1–8). Such nongoal-directed movements involve both the sensory transmission of information from the appropriate receptors and the efferent transmission of information to the appropriate musculature. However, the integration phase of this system is distinctly different from more complex, voluntary movements. The difference lies in where the integration occurs. For simple reflex movements, the integration of the sensorimotor information occurs at the level of the spinal cord. The appropriate stretch receptor in the muscle receives the stimulus. The afferent nerve fiber transmits the impulse to the spinal cord, where the fiber synapses on an alpha motor neuron that carries the efferent impulse to the appropriate skeletal muscle.

Voluntary movements. The integration of sensory and motor information for voluntary movements occurs in the brain, with the cerebral cortex, basal ganglia, thalamus, and cerebellum as the primary integration sites. Sensory information is ultimately received by the cortex in the sensory area, or the

postcentral gyrus, which is the area behind the central fissue (note Figure 3.1–3). Efferent information transmission originates in the motor or premotor cortex or in the cerebellum.

The exact role of the cerebral cortex in movement control continues to be debated. Some argue that voluntary movement is initiated in the cortex, while others consider the cortex as primarily responsible for the refining of movement and as a relay station for movement information. There is considerable agreement, however, that the cerebral cortex is deeply involved in the organization of information.

The cerebellum is of primary importance in the control of movement. The primary roles of the cerebellum appear to be as initiator of movement as well as monitor of ongoing movement. The only pathway out of the cerebellum is by way of Purkinje cells, which exert an excitatory influence. Through a complex system of afferent fibers, known as mossy fibers and climbing fibers, both excitatory and inhibitory effects are imposed on the Purkinje cells, thus controlling efferent transmission from the cerebellum. Axons from the Purkinje cells proceed either to the cerebral cortex or to the spinal cord. Thus, a small feedback loop is located between the cerebral cortex and the cerebellum. This feedback loop appears to enable both the cortex and the cerebellum to monitor and provide ongoing control of movement that has been initiated by the other structure.

When the control of voluntary movement is considered, there is a need to account for the intention or goal of the movement, its planning, and its execution. This point has been emphasized by various researchers. For example, Evarts (1980) argued that voluntary movement differs from reflexive movement in that voluntary movement is directed toward a goal whereas reflexive movement is not. Putting this in terms of the movement control system, Llinas and Simpson (1981) stated that motor coordination must be thought of as the transformation of the intent to move in a particular way into the actual execution of the movement.

Eccles (Popper & Eccles, 1977) has presented a scheme integrating the various nervous system parts related to movement with these considerations (Figure 3.1–9). Note that there are several feedback loops in this model, such as has been suggested throughout this discussion. These loops show that the CNS can be continually updated during the planning and execution of a movement. Additionally, note that the motor cortex does not enter the picture until quite late in the process. This approach follows current research findings that oppose the traditional view that movement is initiated in the motor cortex. The roles of the basal ganglia and cerebellum are seen in this model as being important early in the planning and initiating process. It will be useful to keep this model in mind as you study the remaining concepts in this chapter.

An interesting hypothesis has been proposed by Ito (1970) concerning the interaction between the cerebellum and the cerebral cortex in terms of movement control. Ito proposed that the cerebral cortex is responsible for response initiation commands for voluntary unskilled movements, that is, the

Figure 3.1-9
Diagram showing the pathways concerned in the execution and control of voluntary movement; *Assn CX,* association cortex; *Lateral CMB,* cerebellar hemisphere; *Intermed CMB,* parts intermedia of cerebellum; *VL Thal,* ventrilateral thalamus; *Motor CX,* motor cortex.

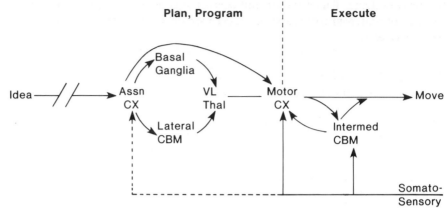

early learning stage of skill acquisition. As a result of experience, the site of control of these movements becomes the cerebellum. Thus, as the individual moves from the early or cognitive stage of learning to the late or autonomic stage, the center for the control of the movement shifts from the cerebral cortex to the cerebellum. In support of this view, Eccles (Popper & Eccles, 1977) stated his view that "throughout life, particularly in the earlier years, we are engaged in an incessant teaching program for the cerebellum. As a consequence, it can carry out all of these remarkable tasks . . . in the whole repertoire of our skilled movements" (p. 287).

This seems consistent with the stages of learning hypothesis suggested by Fitts and Posner, as the type of activity involved in each stage is considered. A large amount of cognitive or verbal activity is necessary in the early stage of learning, hence the need for cerebral cortex involvement. However, as the automation of movement results from practice, the role of the cortex becomes less important. However, feed-forward pathways from the cerebellum to the cortex keep the cortex informed of the messages simultaneously sent to the musculature. In this way, the cortex continues to be involved as a monitoring device to provide necessary adjustments of movement as needed.

Summary

The control of movement involves a highly complex system of peripheral and central nervous system structures. Movement control involves the sensory reception of information from the environment, the efferent transmission of information concerning the movement to be produced, and the integration of the sensory and motor information in order to produce coordinated movement. Sensory information involved in the control of movement comes from a variety of sources. Of primary importance to this discussion are the proprioceptors, which are the peripheral sensory receptors in the muscles, the joints, ligaments and tendons. Efferent transmission of movement information from the motor cortex travels to the musculature by way of the pyramidal and extrapyramidal

pathway systems. The initiation and control of movement appears to be centered in the cerebral cortex and in the cerebellum, in an intricate and complex control system.

Evarts, E. (1980). Brain mechanisms in voluntary movement. In D. M. McFadden (Ed.), *Neural mechanisms in behavior* (pp. 223–259). New York: Springer-Verlag.

Groves, P. M., & Schlesinger, K. (1982). *Introduction to biological psychology* (2nd ed.). Dubuque, IA: Wm. C. Brown Publishers. (Read chapter 9.)

Jokl, E. (1978). Sherrington on movement. In E. Jokl (Ed.), *Medicine and sport* (Vol. 12, pp. 1–5). Basel, Switzerland: S. Karger.

Popper, K. R., & Eccles, J. C. (1977). *The self and its brain.* New York: Springer-Verlag. (Read chapter E3.)

Related Readings

Concept 3.2 Coordinated voluntary movement is controlled by both open-loop and closed-loop systems in the nervous system

Application

Consider the wide variety of motor skills that we perform. Some involve relatively slow movements, such as positioning a bow prior to releasing an arrow; others require fast, ballistic movements, such as throwing a ball. Some motor skills are relatively simple, such as moving a gearshift from first to second gear; others are very complex, as in the tennis serve. Each of these motor skills involves voluntary, coordinated movement that is oriented toward achieving a particular goal. Even though the ways in which the movements are carried out are different in these situations, the movements required must be controlled by the nervous system in such a manner as to allow the intended goal of the action to be achieved. In the discussion of this concept, you will be introduced to how this control process is viewed by motor control theorists. We will look at two general models of control that provide basic descriptions of how coordinated movement is considered to be regulated by the nervous system. As you will see later in this chapter, these two control systems form the basis for discussion of more specific control processes that relate to the performance of various types of motor skills.

Discussion

You have already been introduced to some of the important neuromuscular features critical to the control of voluntary movement. Here we will take another step in the process of understanding how movement is controlled by considering two systems of control that form the basis of most current theories of motor control. These two control systems, termed *open-loop* and *closed-loop* systems, are based on mechanical engineering models of control. Therefore, it will be helpful to view these two control models as elementary descriptions of how the nervous systems actually function in producing movement. How these models relate to actual control functions will be considered later in this discussion and in the remaining concepts in this chapter.

Open-Loop and
Closed-Loop
Control Systems

Diagrams illustrating simple open-loop and closed-loop control systems are presented in Figure 3.2–1. Notice that in each of these systems there is a *control center*. The control center is sometimes referred to as an *executive*. An important part of its role is to issue movement commands to the *effectors,* which are the muscles and joints involved in producing the desired movement. Also, each control system contains *movement commands* coming from the control center and going to the effectors.

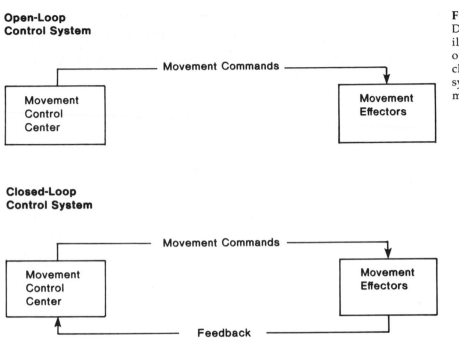

Open-Loop Control System

Movement Commands

Movement Control Center

Movement Effectors

Closed-Loop Control System

Movement Commands

Movement Control Center

Movement Effectors

Feedback

Figure 3.2-1
Diagrams illustrating the open-loop and closed-loop control systems for movement control.

These systems differ, however, in two essential characteristics. The first is evident in the diagrams: a closed-loop control system involves *feedback* while an open-loop system does not. In human movement, this feedback is afferent information sent by the various sensory receptors to the control center. While the diagram of the closed-loop system in Figure 3.2–1 shows that feedback comes only from the movement effectors, which would be from the proprioceptors, there is also feedback information from other sensory systems, such as the visual and auditory systems. The purpose of this feedback is to update the control center about the correctness of the movement while it is in progress.

The second important difference between these two control systems relates to the nature of the movement commands issued by the control center. In the open-loop system, these commands contain all the information necessary for the effectors to carry out the planned movement. While feedback is produced and available, it is not used to control the ongoing movement, although it may be used to help plan the next response after the completion of the present one. In the closed-loop system, the movement commands are quite different. First, there is an initial command to the effectors that is sufficient only to initiate the movement. The actual execution and completion of the movement are dependent on feedback information reaching the control center. In this case, then, feedback is used to help control the ongoing movement as well as to help plan the next response using this same movement.

As was indicated in the discussion of Concept 2.3, any closed-loop system must include in the control center a reference mechanism that contains the representation of the desired movement. The feedback information is compared to this reference standard, and further movement commands are sent to the effectors. If this comparison indicates that the ongoing movement is different from the planned movement, corrective movement commands are sent to the effectors. If the feedback indicates that movement is being carried out as planned, then movement commands are sent to the effectors to continue as they are. In this way, a continuous "loop" of information is involved in controlling movement until the command to stop is sent, which would be based on a match between the planned end of the movement and where the movement was actually located.

In summary, each of these control systems begins with a movement plan. In the open-loop system, this plan is complete enough so that all the movement commands sent from the control center will initiate and execute the intended movement. In the closed-loop system, the execution of this plan is dependent on feedback information provided from the sensory system. Without this feedback information, the movement cannot be executed as planned.

Examples of open- and closed-loop control. There are many machine-type examples of open-loop and closed-loop control all around us. For example, open-loop systems control traffic lights. Each light is programmed to go on at specific time intervals. Traffic conditions will not affect these intervals as the signals are impervious to this type of feedback. The alarm on your clock radio will turn on your radio at the preset time regardless of whether or not you are asleep, want the radio to turn on, or are gone from the house. The only way you can stop this from occurring is by turning off the alarm. Similarly, you can program a videocassette recorder to tape certain programs from your television set even when you are not present. What is common in each of these examples is that commands are programmed in advance. These commands will be carried out as specified without regard to environmental conditions.

In the discussion of Concept 2.3, a good example of a closed-loop control system was presented. The example was a thermostat that controls the air-conditioning system in a house. Other examples include such things as speed-control sensors included in many stereo turntables and cruise-control systems in automobiles. In each of these examples, feedback is necessary for the mechanism to carry out the desired action. The thermostat uses the room temperature as feedback and compares it against its reference mechanism, which is the preset temperature. The turntable uses feedback received by a strobe-light arrangement that senses the speed of the revolving turntable and compares it to the preset speed. The cruise control compares the car speed against the desired speed and adjusts the speed accordingly.

Since current theories of movement control include either one or both of these two control systems, it will be helpful to consider some examples of how these systems have been incorporated into models or theories of movement control. In this section, we will briefly consider some current theories of movement control that emphasize either open-loop or closed-loop control. Research evidence supporting each of these control systems will be considered in the next two concepts in this chapter.

Closed-loop control theories. You have already been introduced to two of the prominent models of movement control that emphasize the closed-loop nature of this control, Adams' closed-loop theory and Schmidt's schema theory. These theories were presented in Concept 2.3 to indicate how they describe the way we learn motor skills. In this discussion, they are considered in terms of how they describe the control of a planned movement.

In both theories, feedback is essential although both include an open-loop controlled component. According to Adams, when a person produces a learned movement that involves positioning an arm at a certain point in space, the *memory trace,* an open-loop control mechanism, initiates the movement. However, sensory feedback is then used to provide information to continue and terminate the movement. To accomplish this, the feedback is continually matched against the *perceptual trace,* the representation of the movement, or reference mechanism, stored in the control center. When feedback concerning the location of the limb matches the location specified by the perceptual trace, the movement is stopped. If there is a mismatch, that is, the comparison of the feedback and perceptual trace indicates error, then information to correct the movement is sent to the limb.

Schmidt (1975b) argued that Adams' theory was essentially appropriate for slow, limb-positioning movement. Schmidt proposed that the executive be considered as a response *schema* (see Figure 3.2–2). As was discussed in Concept 2.3, a schema is an abstract rule or generalization that can be used to guide behavior. According to Schmidt's conceptualization, two schemas are important in controlling a movement. The *recall schema* is involved in the production of a desired movement. It acts together with the generalized motor program, which Schmidt views as an abstract memory structure, to initiate a desired movement in accordance with the demands of the situation. The recall schema sets the specific parameters or rules that the program must follow in order to produce the required response. The recall schema is developed on the basis of abstracting and storing information about responses that have been made in the past. Three sources of information are necessary to develop the recall schema. Information must be obtained about the initial conditions of the response situation, such as the position of the body and limbs. Information indicating the parameters that were set for past responses requiring similar movements must also be stored. Finally, information about the outcome of the previous responses that were made must also be included in the recall schema.

Controlling Movement   111

Figure 3.2-2
Schmidt's schema
theory view of the
motor response
schema in relation
to events occurring
within a response.
The recall and
recognition schemas
are combined
within the motor
response schema.
(KR = knowledge
of results, EXP PFB
= expected
proprioceptive
feedback, EXP EFB
= expected
exteroceptive
feedback.)

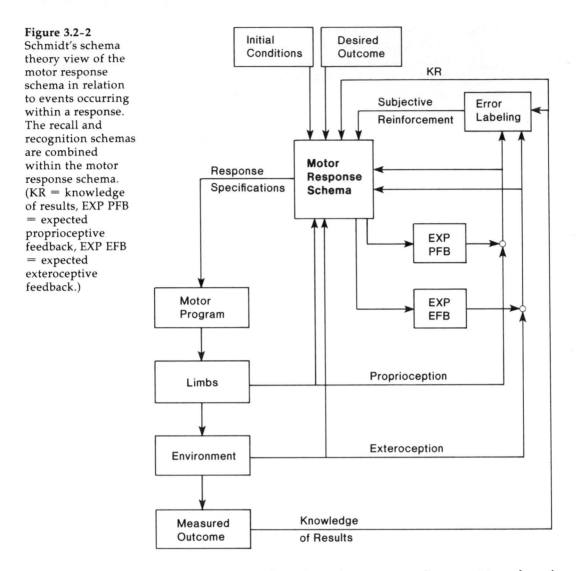

To continue and terminate the movement, the *recognition schema* is proposed. This schema is the reference mechanism used as a comparator for sensory feedback about a particular movement. It is developed as the recall schema is by abstracting information from past experiences. In particular, the information abstracted and stored is comprised of the initial conditions of each response, past response outcomes, and the actual sensory feedback (sensory consequences) related to those past responses. Schmidt's theory, then, emphasizes the abstract or general nature of what is stored in the control center as opposed to Adams' more specific view of what is represented.

While Schmidt's theory emphasizes the essential role of feedback to control an ongoing slow, positioning movement, it portrays the role of feedback quite differently for controlling a rapid, ballistic movement, such as swinging a bat at a ball or throwing a ball. In tasks such as these, there is not sufficient time for feedback information to be used to make necessary movement corrections while the movement is being executed. The movement is simply completed too quickly for the feedback-correction command loop to operate effectively. In such cases, Schmidt indicated that sensory information is used in the preparation of a movement (information about initial conditions and response specifications) and after the completion of a movement (as sensory consequences) rather than during the execution of a movement.

Rather than get involved in developing this control situation further at this point, it will more appropriately be discussed in the next two concepts of this chapter. For the present, it is important to understand that Schmidt's schema theory is essentially a feedback-based theory, as is Adams' closed-loop theory. However, to generalize to motor skills other than slow, positioning movements, Schmidt places a stronger emphasis on the role of open-loop control in certain situations. Additionally, Schmidt's theory advocates a more generalized, abstract schema representation of a learned movement, while Adams' traces emphasize more specific representations of all movement experiences involved in learning a movement.

While other closed-loop oriented views of movement control exist (e.g., Bernstein, 1967; Smith, 1969), these two will serve to provide you with an understanding of how a closed-loop, feedback-based control system has been incorporated and emphasized in theories of how we control movement.

Open-loop control theories. Open-loop control is involved in both the Adams and Schmidt theories. Each theory proposes open-loop control to initiate slow-positioning movements. Schmidt's theory proposes open-loop rather than closed-loop control to execute fast ballistic movements. However, in both theories, feedback is emphasized as important to movement control. In the theory considered in this section, open-loop control is the emphasis for executing even slow-positioning movements.

One example of a control view that emphasizes open-loop control is the *mass-spring model*. This view of movement control looks at muscles and joints involved in a limb-positioning movement as a lever and spring device. For example, as depicted in Figure 3.2–3, the forearm can be thought of as a lever that is attached to a pivot, the elbow. The agonist and antagonist muscles involved in flexion and extension of the forearm, the biceps and triceps, are represented as springs, attached at one end to the forearm lever (a mass) and fixed at the other end to the shoulder. If the lever is pulled or pushed and let go, the mechanical properties of the springs will cause the springs to oscillate and then finally stop at the point where they began, their equilibrium point. This equilibrium point is determined by the stiffness, or length-tension ratio, of the springs.

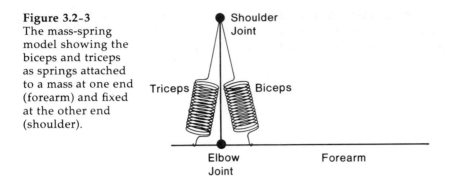

Figure 3.2-3
The mass-spring model showing the biceps and triceps as springs attached to a mass at one end (forearm) and fixed at the other end (shoulder).

When this view is applied to the control of limb positioning, the stiffness characteristic of the mass-spring system becomes very important. In fact, according to proponents of this view (e.g., Fel'dman & Latash, 1982; Kelso & Holt, 1980; Polit & Bizzi, 1979), it is this "stiffness" characteristic that is an important part of the movement command sent to the limb when a specific limb position must be achieved. Thus, regardless of from where the limb begins its movement or how much "mass" is attached to it, the limb will stop at the desired location. This occurs because the stiffness of the springs, preset by the movement commands, dictates the final equilibrium, or stopping point for the springs. In this way, the limb moves to its prescribed location in space without the need for sensory feedback to indicate where it should stop.

Movement Control Involves Both Systems

An important point to keep in mind about the control of complex, coordinated, voluntary movement is that it cannot be viewed as being related to either a closed-loop or an open-loop system. To take such an either/or approach is too simplistic a viewpoint. As you will see in the discussion of the concepts in the remainder of this chapter, *both* systems are involved in the control of human movement. While there may be some types of movements where one system predominates, complex voluntary movement typically exhibits characteristics of both systems.

What is important to watch for in the upcoming discussion, then, will be answers to such questions as these: Under what circumstances is feedback essential to movement? What feedback is important in these circumstances? What are the commands from the movement control center actually like? What generates these commands? Where do these commands actually go? Is it possible to have a movement under open-loop control and still have it modified by feedback? These and other questions can be generated from our discussion about open-loop and closed-loop systems of control as applied to controlling human movement. You should be able to find how researchers have attempted to answer these questions in the remainder of this chapter.

Two simple systems of control, the open-loop and closed-loop systems, form the basis of most current theories of movement control. Both of these systems involve a command center, commands, and effectors. However, the closed-loop system operates on the basis of feedback from the effectors, and the open-loop system contains sufficient information to control an entire movement without the need for feedback. In the closed-loop system, the commands initiate the movement and then must be continually updated by feedback as the movement continues. In this system, the execution and termination of a movement are dependent on sensory feedback.

When applied to the control of voluntary movement, these systems are emphasized in different theories of movement control. Both the Adams closed-loop theory and the Schmidt schema theory are feedback-based theories. As such, they are examples of control theories that emphasize a closed-loop system of control. However, it is important to remember that each theory also includes an open-loop control component. An example of a view of motor control emphasizing open-loop control is the mass-spring model where the muscles, joints, and limbs are seen as mass-spring devices that move the limbs without the need for sensory feedback. When applied to voluntary movements in general, it is necessary to consider both control systems. As will be seen in further discussions in this book, some types of movements operate under closed-loop control while others operate under open-loop control. Some are controlled by both systems for different parts of the same skill.

Adams, J. A. (1976). Issues for a closed-loop theory of motor learning. In G. E. Stelmach (Ed.), *Motor control: Issues and trends* (pp. 87–107). New York: Academic Press.
Schmidt, R. A. (1982). The schema concept. In J. A. S. Kelso (Ed.), *Human motor behavior* (pp. 219–235). Hillsdale, NJ: Erlbaum.
Tuller, B., Turvey, M. T., & Fitch, H. L. (1982). The Bernstein perspective: II. The concept of muscle linkage or coordinative structure. In J. A. S. Kelso (Ed.), *Human motor behavior* (pp. 253–270). Hillsdale, NJ: Erlbaum.

Summary

Related Readings

Concept 3.3 Proprioception and vision play important roles in the control of voluntary movement

Application

Have you ever considered how you make the appropriate movements to successfully hit a ball, whether it is in baseball, softball, tennis, or racquetball? In this skill, very rapid decisions must be made and movements must be executed quickly and precisely if the ball is to be successfully hit. However, it is very unlikely that you make many conscious body or limb adjustments in carrying out this task. In fact, you undoubtedly concentrate heavily on watching the ball. The needed adjustments seem to occur automatically.

Compare this situation to situations that do not require such rapid adjustments. For example, if you are shooting an arrow, your bow needs to be steady and accurately positioned before you release the arrow. You can wait to shoot until the needed adjustments have been made. Similarly, in many gymnastics stunts and weight-lifting events, the body and limbs can be adjusted while the movements are being executed.

In these situations, what information do you use to make the necessary adjustments? In the discussion that follows, you will see how that sensory information from the proprioceptors and vision is important for this function. The question that arises concerns how this information gets used to control the movements involved in the response. Do the different types of tasks described here use this sensory feedback differently? These and other questions form the basis for the discussion of this concept.

Discussion

In the discussion of Concept 3.2, you were introduced to how sensory feedback is seen as a component of movement control. You saw that some theories of movement control emphasize sensory feedback as essential to controlling movement while other views do not. In this discussion, you will take another step in uncovering the underlying processes involved in movement control by considering examples of research that have examined the question of exactly what role sensory feedback plays in controlling voluntary movement. To do this, we will focus on two sensory feedback systems, proprioception and vision. These two have been singled out not only because they account for a major part of the feedback involved in movement control but also because they have been primary targets of a great deal of research. Because of this, an examination of evidence and views of the roles of proprioception and vision in the control of movement will provide a sufficient basis for introducing you to the roles played by sensory feedback in movement control.

In Concept 3.1, the proprioceptors were presented as the sensory receptors for limb and body movement information. Similarly, the eyes contain sensory receptors for visual information. As such, these receptors are responsible for picking up and transmitting information to the CNS. This process is typically termed *sensation*. However, when the use, or interpretation, of that information by the CNS is considered, then we are involved in the process known as *perception*. When the terms *proprioception* and *vision* are used, both sensation and perception are implied as these terms denote both the reception and interpretation of sensory information. Because of this interaction between sensation and perception, we will refer to systems such as vision or proprioception as *sensory-perceptual systems*.

Before discussing how vision and proprioception are involved in controlling movement, it will be helpful to investigate an important characteristic of any sensory-perceptual system. This characteristic, which we will call the sensitivity of the system, must be taken into account when consideration is given to establishing how voluntary movements are controlled.

The sensitivity of proprioception and vision. An important characteristic of any sensory-perceptual system is how easily that system can discriminate one level of intensity of sensory information from another. For example, how sensitive, or keen, is vision for judging if two lights are different in their luminance intensity? In perceptual terms, the question becomes, Is one light brighter than the other? Another example is, how well can the proprioceptive system judge whether two limb positions in space are the same or different?

In the study of perception, these questions are investigated by researchers involved in *psychophysics,* the study of the relationship between our objective world and our perception of it. In the example of comparing the two lights, the objective part is the measured intensity of the luminance of the two lights; the perception, or subjective part, is how we perceive that brightness. While two lights may be measurably different in terms of their luminance intensity, it is possible that we may not judge them as different. In this case, the concern is how accurately we can make these types of comparison judgments when perceiving sensory information.

Of particular interest for this discussion is how precisely our proprioceptive and visual systems can discriminate differences. The measure that has been developed to indicate the sensitivity of a perceptual system to make these discrimination judgments is called the *just noticeable difference (j.n.d.).* The j.n.d. is also referred to by some as the difference limen or difference threshold. The j.n.d. can be generally defined as the least amount of change in the intensity of a stimulus that can be correctly detected by the individual. For example, suppose you were given a tennis racket that was strung with 50 lbs.

pressure. How much of an increase or decrease in that string weight would it take for you to detect that the new string weight was actually different from the 50 lb. one? Or, how much heavier or lighter does a baseball bat need to be before you can tell that it is different from the one you just used?

Research has shown that we have rather keen senses of vision and proprioception. For example, if a light has a luminance intensity level of 1,000 photons, we can usually detect a change in intensity with only a $\pm$ 16 photon change in actual brightness (Woodworth & Schlosberg, 1954). For any luminance intensity level within that range, we would typically indicate that the two lights were the same. For proprioception, evidence indicates that people can discriminate between two arm positions if they are greater than $\pm$ 1.25 cm apart (Magill & Parks, 1983). Conversely, if the two positions are within 1.25 cm, it is unlikely that they will be detected as different.

Implications of the perceptual j.n.d. Understanding the characteristics and limitations of the sensory systems when used for making perceptual judgments has implications for both movement control and motor skills instruction. For example, the fact that each sensory system has certain perceptual limitations suggests that any understanding of the roles of sensory feedback systems in the control of movement must take these limitations into account. In the Magill and Parks (1983) study, for example, it was demonstrated that we can more precisely discriminate differences between two limb positions in space than we can differences between two movement distances made by the same limb. A conclusion from these results was that either different proprioceptors account for our perception of limb position and movement distance, or the proprioceptors may not be directly involved in providing movement information such as this. While further research is needed to resolve this issue, the fact remains that our understanding of the roles of physiological mechanisms in movement control cannot be developed independently of knowledge concerning perceptual characteristics and limitations of those mechanisms.

Information concerning the perceptual limits of the sensory systems also has implications for motor skill instruction. This can most readily be seen in a situation where you, as the teacher, must help students correct a movement error. For example, as the students are working on a gymnastics or dance routine you notice an error in the arm placement of a student in a critical part of the routine. After repeated efforts to correct this problem, the student states that he or she can't seem to correct the problem because it feels like the arm is exactly where you indicated it should be. The problem here may well be an inability to discriminate between the arm position you have shown the student and the actual position of the student's arm during the routine. In this case, your awareness of this possible perceptual limitation can help you realize that correcting the problem will simply require more time than you had thought. Continued practice in making the correction will alleviate the problem.

In the 1970s, a controversy occurred concerning whether voluntary movements were under open-loop or closed-loop control. While that controversy has calmed on the basis of sufficient evidence indicating this is not an either/or issue, the research generated to address the question has provided us with insights into the role played by proprioception in controlling movement. As you will see, this research has taken a variety of approaches and has provided examples of where proprioceptive information is necessary for a movement to be accurately performed and where this information is not needed for performance.

Deafferentation studies. One approach to determining whether proprioceptive feedback is important in controlling movement has been to compare a movement performed under normal conditions with the same movement performed when the proprioceptive feedback is not available. One way to make proprioceptive feedback unavailable is to surgically sever or remove the afferent pathways involved in the movement, a process called *deafferentation.* Typically, this procedure has been followed in experiments using monkeys to perform movements.

An early example of using this deafferentation procedure was provided in several experiments by Taub and Berman (1963, 1968). In these experiments, the researcher observed monkeys performing well-developed motor skills, such as climbing, reaching, and grasping, before and after deafferentation of the afferent pathways from the limbs to the CNS. Results of these experiments were consistent in showing that the deafferented monkeys were still capable of performing these skills.

The studies of Taub and Berman considered skills that were well developed in the animals. What would happen if the same deafferentation procedure were used with relatively new-learned skills? This approach was taken by Emilio Bizzi and his colleagues at M.I.T. (e.g., Bizzi & Polit, 1979; Polit & Bizzi, 1978). In these experiments, monkeys were placed in an apparatus as shown in Figure 3.3–1 and trained to point an arm at one of a series of lights when it came on. The lights were arranged in a semicircle in front of the monkey, who could see the lights but not the arm making the pointing movement. Following training, that is, after the monkeys had learned to accurately point to each light when required, the monkeys were deafferented so that no proprioceptive feedback information from the pointing arm was available during the movement. The monkeys were then again placed in the positioning apparatus. Results from these experiments showed that the monkeys were able to accurately position their limbs in the deafferented state. In fact, they were even able to make these accurate movements from starting positions that were different from the starting positions used during training. As you may recall, this was one of the predictions made by the mass-spring model discussed in Concept 3.2.

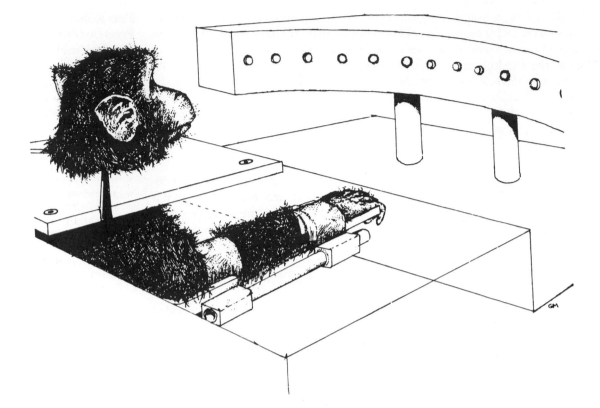

Figure 3.3-1
Monkey in the experimental apparatus used in the experiment by Polit and Bizzi. The monkey's arm is strapped to the splint that pivots at the elbow. Target lights are mounted at 5° intervals. During experimental sessions, the monkey could not see its arm and the room was darkened.

Deafferenting human subjects for experimental purposes is not possible for obvious reasons. However, Kelso, Holt, and Flatt (1980) reported an experiment that used humans who had no joint receptors available. The subjects in these experiments were rheumatoid arthritis patients who had recently had the metacarpophalangeal joints removed from the fingers of their hands. The joints were replaced with flexible silicone rubber implants to hold the bones of those joints together. As a result, joint receptors were not available as a source of proprioceptive information during movement. These patients performed positioning responses using a device that allowed only finger movement of a pointer over a protractor graduated in degrees. On each trial, the subjects moved to a specified finger position (the criterion location) or moved through a specified distance (the criterion distance), returned to a new starting point, and then attempted to reproduce the criterion location or distance. Results, as shown in Figure 3.3–2, indicated the subjects had little difficulty in accurately reproducing the criterion location from a starting point that was either − 5° or − 15° from the original starting point. However, for reproduction of the movement distance, accuracy was severely influenced by how far the new starting point was from the original starting point.

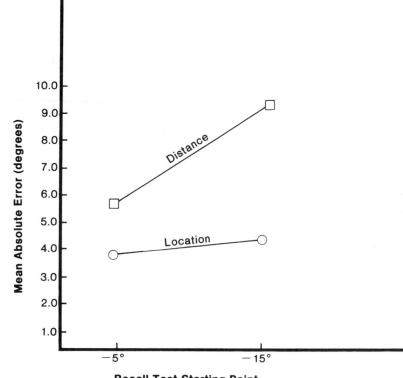

Figure 3.3-2
Absolute error
results from the
experiment by
Kelso, Holt, and
Flatt where finger-
joint-replacement
patients were asked
to reproduce
location and
distance
movements. Recall
movements were
begun either 5°
beyond (−5°) or
15° beyond (−15°)
the starting point
used for the
presentation of the
criterion movement.

Results of these studies suggest that limb movements, especially limb-positioning movements, *can* be carried out in the absence of proprioceptive feedback. The control of these movements must therefore be considered to follow an open-loop rather than a closed-loop system, since the lack of proprioceptive feedback did not disrupt the movements. However, a word of caution is needed here. Before completely accepting an open-loop control conclusion, the degree of accuracy exhibited in these studies when proprioceptive feedback was not available must be considered. In the Taub and Berman studies, the monkeys, while portraying climbing, grasping, and reaching responses, were clumsier than they had been before deafferentation. In fact, it was difficult for them to grasp food with their hands in this condition. In the Bizzi experiments, a relatively wide target area was used to indicate a correct pointing response for the monkeys. It is difficult, then, to compare the *precision* of the accuracy responses under the normal and deafferented conditions. In the Kelso, Holt, and Flatt experiments, while a comparison was not made of positioning accuracy before and after joint-capsule replacement, distance movements were severely disrupted by changing starting positions. These points should be kept in mind as we look at other research investigating these same issues.

Nerve-block studies. An interesting approach was developed by Judith Laszlo and her associates in Australia to try to replicate the animal deafferentation studies using humans but without having to surgically deafferent them. In this procedure, known as a nerve block, a blood pressure cuff is placed just above the subject's elbow and then inflated until the subject can no longer feel anything with the fingers. Thus, afferent pathways are assumed to be blocked. However, it is important to note that while afferent pathways are inoperable, the efferent pathways remain unaffected. Following the nerve block, subjects were required to produce finger-tapping responses.

Results of several studies by Laszlo (e.g., 1966, 1967) indicated that motor skills could be performed in the absence of afferent sensory information from the muscles and joints of the fingers, hand, and forearm. However, some work by Scott Kelso and others (e.g., Kelso, Stelmach, & Wanamaker, 1974; Kelso, Wallace, Stelmach, & Weitz, 1975) have questioned the efficacy of Laszlo's procedures. A particular question has been the validity of the assumption concerning the unaffected condition of efferent pathways using these procedures. To overcome this problem, Kelso (1977) modified Laszlo's procedure by placing a child's blood pressure cuff on the subjects' wrists after the subjects felt no sensation in the fingers. The arm cuff was then removed and the positioning task was performed. Results of these experiments and others (Kelso & Holt, 1980) showed that subjects were able to position their fingers as accurately after the nerve block as they could prior to it.

Again, evidence has been provided to show that certain kinds of voluntary movement can accurately be performed without proprioceptive feedback. Problems remain, however, concerning the validity of several assumptions important for the use of the nerve-block technique. Critical among these is whether or not all afferent information that could be used to carry out the required movement has been blocked.

Switched-limb studies. Another way to examine the accuracy of limb movement and the involvement of proprioception is to have subjects reproduce a criterion location with the arm that was not used originally to experience or learn the movement. While the rationale behind this procedure was actually developed to test a question related to how we represent movement information in memory (to be considered in Chapter 5), the switched-limb procedure can provide some insights into the role of proprioception in movement control.

An example of a study using this approach is one reported by Wallace (1977). Subjects were blindfolded and required to move a lever to a specific location. The subjects were then required to reproduce the movement with either the same or opposite (switched) arm. If the same proprioceptive feedback available when the movement was first produced is not important, then the switched-arm movement should be as accurate as the same-arm movement reproduction. Wallace's results indicated that this was indeed the case as there was no difference between switched- and same-arm movement reproduction.

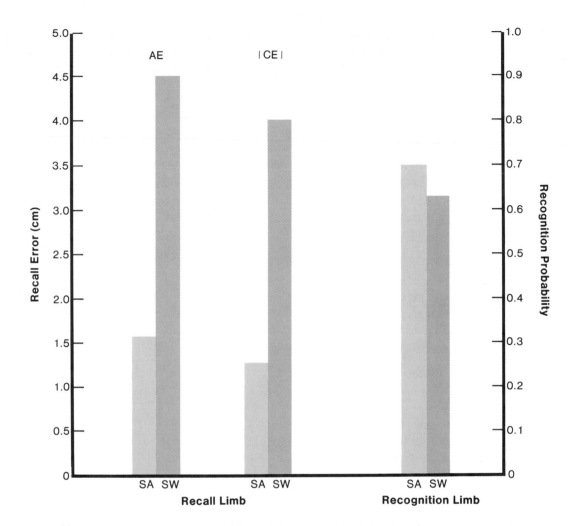

Recently, however, attempts to replicate Wallace's (1977) findings have not been very successful. Reeve and Stelmach (1982), for example, found that reproduction of a series of six limb positions was more accurate when the subjects used the same rather than the opposite arm that was used for presentation of the movements. Magill and Goode (1982) found similar accuracy results when subjects were required to learn to position their arm to within ± 0.5 cm for three consecutive trials and then reproduce that position with either the practiced (same) or nonpracticed (switched) arm (see Figure 3.3–3). However, when all subjects were then asked to move to specified positions and respond whether this position was or was not the learned position, they responded equally well with either limb, as shown in the bar graph on the right of Figure 3.3–3. These results suggest that reasonable or "ball park" accuracy

Figure 3.3-3
Results of the experiment by Magill and Goode showing absolute error (AE), absolute constant error (CE), and recognition probability for same (SA) and switched (SW) limb for the recall and recognition tests for a practiced limb-positioning movement.

of a learned limb position can be obtained without the same sensory feedback that was available during practice. However, limb-positioning accuracy can be increased when that feedback is available.

The Role of
Vision and
Movement
Control

In each of the experimental procedures described in the preceding section, vision was not available to the subjects to aid their movement. They were either blindfolded or kept from seeing their arms by some type of opaque screen. The purpose of this was to limit the type of useful feedback to proprioceptive feedback. In the studies to be considered in this section, vision is the primary sensory source of interest. In particular, our interest is in determining how vision interacts with proprioception in the control of movement.

Vision predominates the sensory feedback systems. When all sensory systems are available to us, we tend to use, and trust, vision the most. For example, when you first learned to type or play the piano, you undoubtedly felt that if you could not see your fingers hit each key, you could not perform accurately. Beginning dancers have a similar problem. Many times they feel that they cannot perform accurately if they cannot watch their feet. In many other motor skills like these, we only feel comfortable when we can see the limbs carry out the required movement.

Research evidence demonstrates our tendency to allow vision to predominate over the other sensory systems. For example, in a study by Reeve, Mackey, and Fober (1986), blindfolded subjects practiced positioning a handle of a linear-positioning apparatus along a trackway at a specific location. All subjects had 21 trials of practice with KR provided about the error for each trial. Following these trials, the subjects performed 9 trials without KR in one of three transfer conditions. One group, the kinesthetic feedback-only condition, continued to perform the positioning response without vision, just as they had during the practice trials. The second group, the kinesthetic plus visual feedback condition, performed the positioning response with vision available. The third group, the visual feedback-only condition, did not move the handle but watched the experimenter move the handle and verbally indicated where the experimenter should stop the handle as he moved it along the trackway. The results (see Figure 3.3–4) indicated that when vision was available in addition to kinesthetic feedback, subjects greatly overshot the target. Also, transfer of the limb-position location from a kinesthetically based code to a visual code, which was required by the vision-only transfer condition, was not performed very well. This group also did much worse on the transfer trials than they had done at the end of the practice trials when they moved the handle themselves without vision available. These results extend previous work by Reeve and colleagues (Reeve & Cone, 1980; Reeve & Mainor, 1983) that are consistent in showing that vision will predominate as the sensory system to which a person will direct attention, even if vision is not involved in practicing the skill being tested.

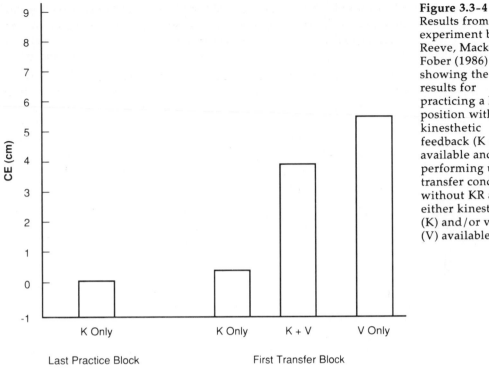

Figure 3.3-4
Results from the
experiment by
Reeve, Mackey, and
Fober (1986)
showing the CE
results for
practicing a limb
position with
kinesthetic
feedback (K only)
available and then
performing under
transfer conditions
without KR and
either kinesthetic
(K) and/or vision
(V) available.

These results fit very well with the dominant role given vision by Posner, Nissen, and Klein (1976) in a general review of research concerned with vision and its role in processing information. There seems to be little doubt that we assign vision a very special place in our daily activities. Unless we have learned to do otherwise, such as in touch typing or playing the piano, we will attend to visual information whenever possible to guide our movements.

The knowledge that vision tends to dominate the other sensory feedback systems does little to help us understand the role of vision in movement control, however. In the next section, we will look specifically at some examples of research directed at uncovering that role.

A two-component model of visual control. When vision interacts with proprioceptive information to provide movement-related information, David Lee (1980) has suggested it be called *exproprioceptive* information. Although this term has not found widespread use, it does point to the conditions involved when considering the role of vision in controlling movement. Vision must be seen as *interacting* with proprioceptive information.

To study this interaction of systems, it will be helpful to consider a two-component model of visual feedback presented by Paillard (1980), a French neuropsychologist. The *initial phase* of an action involves a ballistic or programmed phase that controls the direction of the movement and brings the moving limb in the general vicinity of the target. The second phase involves a closed-loop type of process in which vision provides the needed information for the accurate "homing in" on the target. Paillard states that two components of vision are responsible for these pieces of information. Central vision provides the final homing-in information, whereas peripheral vision provides the movement trajectory guidance information.

In the remaining sections of this discussion, keep this two-stage model in mind as we consider how researchers have examined the role of vision in the control of a variety of different types of motor skills. As you will see, this model seems to describe very well the role of vision for some tasks but needs to be modified somewhat to handle other tasks.

Vision and aiming tasks. An aiming task requires rapid movement of an arm over a prescribed distance to a target. In a task such as this, it would appear that the two-stage model of visual control would apply very well. For example, Keele and Posner (1968) had subjects move a stylus from a starting point to one of two targets one-quarter inch in diameter and 6 inches away. Subjects were trained to make their movements in as close as possible to 150, 250, 350, and 450 msec. On half of the trials, the lights were turned off as soon as the subjects left the starting point. On the other half of the trials, the lights remained on throughout. If visual feedback is needed to perform the final homing in on the target, then having the lights turned off should seriously affect accuracy. The results of this experiment showed that the lights-off condition did not affect movements that took approximately 190 msec or less to execute. However, accuracy was impaired for movements lasting longer than 260 msec. These results suggest that the aiming movements of short duration, those lasting less than 190 msec, appeared to have been controlled entirely on an open-loop basis, and movements of longer duration were completed by using visual feedback. From this, Keele and Posner speculated that the processing of visual information takes between 190 and 260 msec. This amount of time has more recently been questioned, however, because a series of experiments by Zelaznik, Hawkins, and Kisselburgh (1983) showed evidence that there were beneficial effects of vision for movements lasting less than 200 msec.

Other studies have also supported the view that the role of visual feedback in controlling aiming movements is dependent on the duration of the movement. For example, Klapp (1975) had subjects move a stylus as rapidly as possible to very small targets (2 mm) that were either 2 or 336 mm from the start position. Half of the trials were conducted with the lights on, and the other half were conducted with the lights turned off after the movement began.

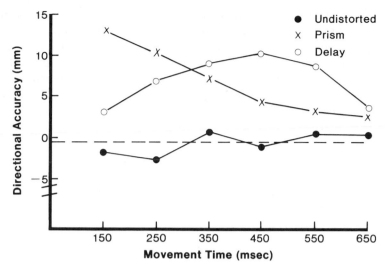

Figure 3.3-5
Directional accuracy (CE) results from the Smith and Bowen experiment where subjects practiced aiming movements of different movement times under three different vision conditions.

For the longer 336 mm movements, accuracy decreased from 4.4% misses with the lights on to 93.0% misses with the lights off. Accuracy was affected very little, however, for the shorter 2 mm distance as subjects had only 1.6% misses with the lights on and only 10.0% misses with the lights off.

Another approach to the role of visual feedback in the control of aiming movements was reported by Smith and Bowen (1980). By using cameras and mirrors, they either distorted visual information about the movement to the right by 10° or delayed the visual information by 66 msec. This was accomplished by having the subjects see their hand movements only by watching a monitor. As can be seen in Figure 3.3–5, both forms of distortion decreased aiming accuracy. However, as in the studies we considered earlier, the distance moved or the length of time required to complete the movement had different effects on accuracy.

Thus, visual information is used in different ways for aiming tasks depending on the length and duration of the movement. If the movement is to be a rapid one, where MT will be less than 150–200 msec, vision is used to preset the aiming response. If vision is not available while this response is underway, the aiming accuracy is not disrupted since it was not dependent on visual information that could enable corrections to be made during the movement to the target. However, for longer duration movements, the availability of vision during the movement is important as corrections to the ongoing movement are dependent on visual information about the limb and the target being available during the movement.

These results suggest then, that for longer duration movements, vision may not be important during the early part of the movement but may be critical during the latter parts. If this is so, then eliminating vision during the first half of an aiming response should not alter accuracy, whereas eliminating it

during the latter half should lead to increased inaccuracy. This hypothesis was tested by Carlton (1981) by varying the availability of visual feedback during the initial segments of an aiming task. He found that when the response lasted between 364 and 440 msec, seeing the initial 50% of the limb movement was not important for target accuracy. These results have been further supported in research by Moore (1984). Moore had subjects make a 400-msec aiming response during which she systematically varied the availability of vision during the initial 25%, 50%, 55%, 60%, 65%, and 100% of the movement. Results showed that aiming error did not increase when vision was not available for the first 50% of the response. For all other conditions, accuracy decreased dramatically.

One further test of Carlton's findings can be seen in some work by Beaubaton and Hay (1986). In this experiment, as opposed to those by Carlton and Moore, there was a condition in which visual information about the termination of the response was blocked, in addition to conditions in which vision was blocked for the initial portion of the response. Again, vision of the initial phase of the movement was not crucial for aiming accuracy, whereas vision of the final phase was strongly related to accuracy.

In our discussion so far, the view of the role of vision in aiming tasks has been limited to being dependent on the movement time of the response. A series of experiments by Elliott and Allard (1985) demonstrated that additional variables can also influence the use of vision in aiming tasks. One such variable was whether or not the individual had prior knowledge that vision would or would not be available during the course of the aiming movement. From the results of the experiment by Zelaznik, Hawkins, and Kisselburgh (1983) mentioned earlier, it appeared that rapid visual processing time was most pronounced when subjects knew in advance that the lights would be on during the response. Elliott and Allard replicated this effect in their first experiment and showed that when subjects knew before a trial began that the lights would be on, movements of 225 msec benefited from having vision available. However, when they did not know if the lights would be on or off, their error increased with the lights on and decreased with the lights off, compared with when they knew in advance that the lights would be on or off. Thus, certainty about what the vision conditions will be during the aiming response influences the use of vision. If there is uncertainty, fast movements will typically be programmed in advance and performed in an open-loop manner, whereas slower movements will require visual feedback to terminate the response.

Finally, a finding about the role of vision in the control of an aiming movement that deserves some consideration is the fact that there is a performance advantage for the preferred hand (Flowers, 1975; Roy, 1983). The important motor control question here is, Why does this hand advantage occur? With respect to our discussion on vision, one possible reason is that visual information during movement is processed more efficiently for the preferred hand.

To test this possibility, Roy and Elliott (1986) had subjects perform rapid aiming movements (100–400 msec) with the lights on or off. For movements that were made very rapidly, that is, in less than 200 msec, there was no difference between the condition of lights on or off, although there was a preferred hand accuracy advantage. Because the presence or absence of visual information during movement did not influence the hand advantage, it seems likely that the handedness advantage explanation in these aiming tasks is inappropriate. However, a vision-based explanation is still a possibility. Turning the lights off after a movement has been initiated does not remove the possibility that visual information about the required response can be obtained *before* the response is initiated. Thus, the hand advantage could be due to more efficient processing of visual information related to that hand, but the processing may occur before movement initiation rather than during. However, research is needed in this area as the cause for the preferred hand advantage in aiming movements remains undetermined.

Vision and locomotion. Although the study of locomotion has been popular in a variety of areas of science, only recently has the role of vision in the control of locomotion been seriously considered. One of the first attempts to show that locomotion is controlled by information picked up by the visual system was made by David Lee at Edinburgh University in Scotland. Lee (1974, 1976) argued that locomotion is visually guided by what he called "time-to-contact" information on the retina of the eye. More specifically, Lee meant that as a person walks or runs closer to an object, that object becomes a larger image on the retina. When this retinal image reaches a certain size, it triggers specific action to produce the appropriate locomotor response so that the person can either avoid the object or step on the object. In fact, Lee showed that an optic variable could be described mathematically by a function he termed *tau,* which specifies time to contact with an object (see Lee, 1980, for a further description of the derivation of tau). More specifically, Lee argued that the optic variable tau modifies one parameter of the gait action, the vertical impulse, to cause the appropriate locomotor response. This means that vision provides *time-based,* rather than distance-based, information to the motor control system to establish when an action should occur and thus allows accomplishment of the task goal. We will consider two interesting experiments that support this hypothesis.

In one experiment, Lee, Lishman, and Thomson (1984) investigated long jumpers because they clearly require regulated step lengths to be successful. In long jumping, the athlete runs down a long trackway and must accurately strike a takeoff board. The more accurate they are, the better jumping distance they can attain. In this study, step length characteristics of three world-class female long jumpers were observed throughout their approaches to the takeoff board. These athletes used an 18-stride takeoff, a 19-stride takeoff, and a 21-stride takeoff. By filming and analyzing stride-length changes as each

athlete approached and contacted the takeoff board, certain observable characteristics suggested how the gait patterns required for the approach and takeoff were controlled. All the athletes increased stride length for the first nine or ten strides, at which time the stride lengths began to become similar. Then, on the final three to five strides, something interesting began to occur. The athletes made definite stride length adjustments during these last strides so they could accurately hit the board. In fact, over 50% of these adjustments were made on the last stride. It was evident that these stride length adjustments were being made by the athletes' adjustment of the vertical component of their stride lengths to effect error corrections. And, this correction process was based on visual information obtained in advance of these strides. That is, step length error began to accumulate as the athlete ran down the trackway. If no step length corrections were made, the athletes would have missed the takeoff board. To accommodate for this correction need, the visual system picked up time-to-contact takeoff board information and directed the final adjustments needed to contact the board as accurately as possible.

One final interesting point is how nonconsciously these corrections were made by the athletes. When questioned, none of the athletes was aware of making these adjustments. In fact, both the athletes and their coaches were quite surprised when shown the results of this experiment.

Another experiment that demonstrates that a single gait parameter can be adjusted on the basis of time-to-contact visual information was reported by Warren, Young, and Lee (1986). They investigated a time-to-contact problem in locomotion different than is experienced by the long jumper. This situation involves walking or running through a cluttered environment where the subject must step very precisely, as when crossing a creek on rocks or navigating along a wooded, rocky path. Here again, step lengths must be adjusted so that each step can be correctly made. To simulate this situation in a controlled setting, Warren, Young, and Lee had subjects walk on a treadmill that was modified to be similar to what one might encounter in irregular terrain. They attached a 5-meter long sheet of plywood to the front of the treadmill. Then, they attached a pulley under the far end of the plywood sheet so that three parallel nylon tapes, 2-cm wide, could run over the plywood and the treadmill belt and form a continuous loop while the treadmill was running. On these tapes, yellow targets, 2-cm wide by 30-cm long, were attached at various intervals. As the treadmill belt moved, the tapes with the targets also moved. The subjects were told to run so that they would hit each target as accurately as possible. Because of the treadmill and target arrangement, subjects could see the targets moving towards them 5 meters in front of them. In this way, it was possible to simulate running forward with the goal of stepping on a series of targets that were irregularly spaced.

Analysis of each subject's stepping actions was done by using a Selspot movement analysis system (described in Concept 1.2) and by digitizing specific lower limb landmarks at different phases of the step cycle. Each subject stepped on over 50 targets while running during the testing period. Step length

adjustments occurred in the manner Lee had predicted they would. That is, subjects altered step length to hit each target by altering only the vertical component of the step length. Again, this adjustment was done on the basis of advance time-to-contact target information detected by the visual system.

Other research has suggested additional evidence that vision provides important information to direct specific actions required during locomotion. Meeuwsen and Magill (1987), for example, showed that the time-to-contact conclusions by Lee, Lishman, and Thomson (1984) could be applied to performing a gymnastics vault, where accuracy is required for hitting the spring board with the feet and for hitting the horse with the hands. Mark (1987) showed that visual information guides the required actions for stair climbing and Warren (1987) reported evidence that vision guides walking through aperatures, such as different-sized doorways. In these last two cases, rather than a time-to-contact variable guiding action, an optic variable related to the ratio between the size of the door opening or the stair step height and the shoulder width or the leg length of the individual was shown to be the basis for guiding the appropriate movement response to successfully go through the door or climb the stairs.

Another issue related to the role of vision in locomotion concerns the question of whether or not visual information must be continuous during locomotion to achieve accurate contact with a target. You saw earlier in this discussion that for rapid aiming tasks performed with the arm, continuous visual information was not necessary, as the task could be performed just as accurately with the lights on as with the lights off. A similar conclusion was made by Thomson (1983) with regard to walking to specific target locations in the environment. As in the arm-aiming tasks, Thomson showed that there is a time limit for which continuous visual information is not needed. In his experiments, subjects first observed and walked to a target point on a path. These target points were located 3, 6, 9, and 12 meters from the subject's starting point. The subjects were then asked to close their eyes and walk to the target point. Results showed that subjects were able to do this with little difficulty for distances as far away as 21 meters as long as fewer than 8 seconds were required to reach the target. When more than 8 seconds elapsed, target accuracy diminished.

More recently, concern has been raised about the time limit established by Thomson's results. For example, Elliott (1986) reported two experiments that were designed to replicate Thomson's and failed to find evidence for the existence of a critical 8-second time limit. Elliott found that walking error increased as a function of distance walked and had little to do with how long it took to reach the target. Thus, Elliott concluded that continuous visual information is required during locomotion when the goal is to make contact with a specific target a certain distance away. Clearly, more research is needed to resolve this question. However, this question is important in that it relates well to the work of David Lee discussed earlier and it provides information about the interaction of visually detected information and memory.

Vision and catching. Although researchers have investigated a number of questions concerning the role of vision when the action goal is to catch an object, such as a ball, we will consider only two. (See von Hofsten, 1987, for a discussion of other questions that have been considered.) The two questions that our discussion will focus on will provide you with a good foundation for understanding the involvement of vision in the coordination and control necessary to catch an object. These questions are: How long must a person watch the object to be caught in order to successfully catch it? Must the person be able to see his or her hands in addition to the object in order to successfully catch the object? As you can readily see, these questions are similar to those asked in regard to the role of vision in the control of other actions.

A good example of research related to how long a person must watch an object if it is to be successfully caught can be seen in work done by H. T. A. Whiting and colleagues. For example, Whiting, Gill, and Stephenson (1970) reported an experiment that specifically addressed this question. They designed a special ball that could be illuminated for specific lengths of time during its flight. The subjects sat in a dark room and were required to catch this ball as often as possible. The ball was illuminated for 0.1, 0.15, 0.2, 0.25, 0.3, and 0.4 sec during its flight. As you can see from the results (Figure 3.3–6), the longer the ball was illuminated, the more catches were made. However, a closer look at these results indicates that there was little difference in the number of catches made between the 0.3- and 0.4-sec conditions. This finding suggests that after an initial period, which lasts for at least 0.3 sec (or 300 msec), visual information that can be obtained from the ball is no longer critical for catching it. This, of course, only relates to a ball that will not unexpectedly change its course of flight after that period.

The issue of how long the object must be seen is related not only to catching an object but also to striking an oncoming object. As you will see in the discussion that follows concerning vision and batting, it is suggested that the most important part of observing the ball in flight is the beginning or the middle part of the flight. Because this issue has not been investigated using a catching action, we will defer discussion about this topic until the skill of batting is considered.

An interesting debate regarding our second question of interest related to vision and catching concerns the issue of whether or not the subject's hands must be seen throughout the flight of a ball. Of particular interest here is to determine, if the hands are not observed, can the ball be caught as successfully as if the hands can be seen? And, if the ball cannot be caught as successfully, why not?

One of the first experiments developed to look at this question was reported by Smyth and Marriott (1982). They hypothesized that if the eyes are occupied with tracking the moving ball, then preventing subjects from seeing their hands, while being able to see the ball, should not affect ball-catching

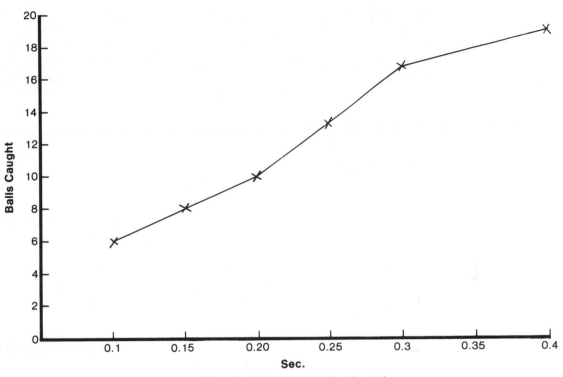

Balls Caught (y-axis)

Sec.
Time for Which Ball Is Illuminated (x-axis)

accuracy. In their experiment, a screen was designed and attached to the subjects so they could see the oncoming ball but not their hands. The results showed that when the subjects could see their hands, they averaged 17.5 catches out of 20 balls thrown. However, when they could *not* see their hands, subjects were able to catch an average of 9.2 balls out of 20. What characterized the differences in these two situations? When the hands could *not* be seen, the typical error was in positioning; that is, the subjects could not get their hands into the correct spatial position, which led to no contact between the hands and the ball. But, when subjects could see their hands, the typical errors involved grasping, rather than not getting the hands into the correct spatial position. Grasping errors occurred when subjects initiated the flexion of the fingers to grasp the ball too early and the ball hit the fingers after they had already begun to close.

Although there has been additional support for the conclusion that catching accuracy diminishes when a person cannot see his or her hands during the flight of a ball, controversy exists concerning why this outcome occurs. For example, Fischman and Schneider (1985) argued that two reasons why the subjects in the Smyth and Marriott experiment showed different types of errors when they could or could not see their hands could be related to the experience

Figure 3.3-6
Results from the experiment by Whiting, Gill, and Stephenson showing the number of balls caught (out of 20) under different periods of illumination.

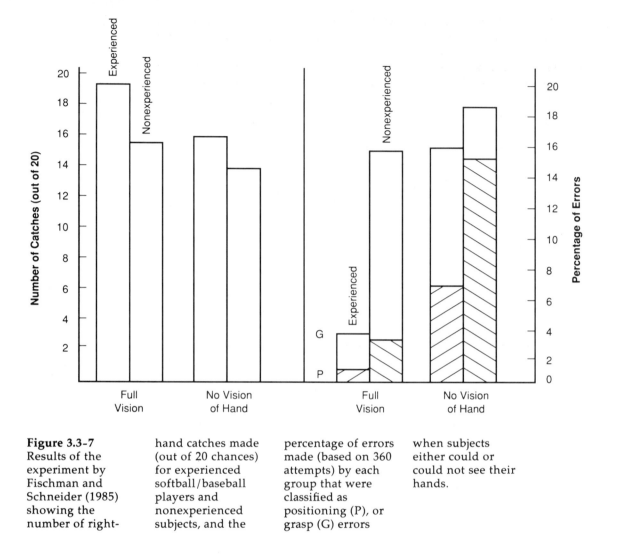

Figure 3.3-7
Results of the experiment by Fischman and Schneider (1985) showing the number of right-hand catches made (out of 20 chances) for experienced softball/baseball players and nonexperienced subjects, and the percentage of errors made (based on 360 attempts) by each group that were classified as positioning (P), or grasp (G) errors when subjects either could or could not see their hands.

level of the subjects. Persons with more ball-catching experience could have more accurately predicted ball arrival location and time and therefore not exhibited different types of errors under the two conditions. They also hypothesized that the more experienced subjects would not show diminished catching success under the condition where they could not see their hands. Their experiment followed procedures similar to those of Smyth and Marriott except that all subjects had at least 5 years experience in varsity baseball or softball. The results of this experiment can be seen in Figure 3.3–7. As you can see, while the number of catches decreased when the hands could not be seen, there was no interaction between the type of error and whether or not the hands could be seen. However, with the inexperienced subjects, positioning errors increased much more than grasp errors when the hands could not be seen.

The results of these experiments reveal some important features about the role of vision in the control of catching. First, there is evidence to support the two-stage model of visual control discussed earlier. That is, there is an initial arm-and-hand-positioning stage and a final fine-tuning action required to catch the ball. A minimum amount of object observation time appears necessary if these two stages are to be carried out successfully. According to Whiting, Gill, and Stephenson, this amount of time is about 300 msec. However, further research by Whiting (Sharp & Whiting, 1974, 1975) has shown that the minimum duration needed to gain required information for successful catching is about 240 msec preceding the final 125 msec of object flight. Thus, the initial time in flight is not as critical as the time just prior to the end. The ball must be seen for about 240 msec, but that time does not coincide with the final 240 msec. The critical viewing time is the segment of ball flight just prior to the final 125 msec.

One final point about vision and the control of catching is worth noting. Research based on high-speed cinemagraphic analysis by Alderson, Sully, and Sully (1974) has shown that the fine-tuning, or homing-in, phase of hand position begins about 150 to 200 msec before the ball contacts the palm of the hand, and about 32 to 50 msec before this contact the fingers begin to get into their final grasping positions. These time limits not only indicate positioning and grasping phases for catching a ball, they also indicate that the act of catching involves very precise timing. Also, these results show that vision provides advance information to enable the motor control system to spatially and temporally set the arms, hands, and fingers *before* the ball arrives so that the ball can be caught. This is especially interesting with regard to the grasp phase as it shows that grasping a ball occurs on the basis of information obtained before the ball actually makes contact with the hand, rather than on the basis of feedback obtained after the ball has hit the hand.

Vision and batting. Just as precise time constraints are related to successful catching, so are there similar limits for successful batting. One of the best examples of evidence of the role of vision in successful batting was provided by Hubbard and Seng (1954). Using photographic techniques, they found that their subjects, including 25 professional baseball players, were able to track the ball only to a point at which the swing was made. This point did not seem to coincide with where contact of the ball was made. Hubbard and Seng also found that the batters tended to synchronize the start of their step forward with the release of the ball from the pitcher's hand. Additionally, the duration of the subjects' swings were remarkably consistent from swing to swing. These results were taken to indicate that all of the adjusting to the oncoming pitch was made during the 500 msec between the release of the ball from the pitcher's hand and the initiation of the swing. In this situation, then, vision provides the needed information to initiate and execute the correct bat swing. This information appears to be provided during the first one-half second of the pitch.

In some research reported since the Hubbard and Seng study, some of their findings have been either verified or extended. For example, Bahill and LaRitz (1984) closely monitored eye and head movements of a major league baseball player and several college baseball players in a laboratory situation that simulated the player responding to a fastball. These researchers threaded a fishing line through a white plastic ball and stretched the line between two supports that allowed a 60.5-ft distance to simulate the distance between the pitcher's mound and home plate. A string was attached to the ball and wrapped around a pulley attached to a motor so that the ball could be pulled down the line at speeds between 60 mph and 100 mph. The line was set to simulate a high-and-outside fastball thrown by a left-handed pitcher to a right-handed batter.

The major league player visually tracked the ball longer than the college players. The college players tracked the ball to a point about 9 ft in front of the plate at which point their visual tracking began to fall behind the ball. The major league player kept up with the ball to a point about 5.5 ft in front of the plate before falling behind. Also, regardless of the pitch speed, the major league player followed the same visual tracking pattern and was very consistent in every stance taken to prepare for the pitch. His head position was within 1 degree on all pitches. Interestingly, he had slight head movements while tracking the ball but never moved his body.

These results indicate that batters probably never see the bat hit the ball. If they do, it is because they jumped their visual focus from some point in the ball flight to the bat contact point. Tracking the ball from pitcher's hand to bat contact is apparently physically impossible. However, it is worth noting that the professional batter watched the ball for a longer time than did the college players. Thus, the instruction to "watch the ball all the way from the pitcher's hand to your bat" is a good one even though it really can't be done. This instruction directs the individual's attention to visually tracking the ball for as long as physically possible. Better batters do this tracking for longer lengths of time. Also, moving the body is more of a problem than moving the head. If the head can be moved during ball tracking without the body position being altered, then there should be no problem. However, for young players, this is difficult because head movement typically results in body movement.

Another important point regarding vision and batting is determining when during the flight of the ball the most critical information is extracted. An experiment by De Lucia and Cochran (1985) indicates that the last two-thirds of the flight contain the most important information related to batting success. They had experienced baseball and softball batters hit tennis balls from a tennis ball server located on the pitcher's mound of a softball field. All subjects initially hit 20 balls so that baseline hitting success could be obtained. Then, subjects hit balls that they were unable to see during the first third, the middle third, or the final third of the ball flight. Results showed that the least ball contact was made when the final part of the flight was screened from view,

as contact percentage dropped from a baseline of 78% to 69% when the first third was screened, 65% when the middle third was screened, and 57% when the last third was screened. It was also interesting to see how the accuracy of the contact was affected by blocking the different portions of the ball flight. During baseline trials, fair balls were hit to left field 33% of the time, to center field 39% of the time, and to right field 28% of the time. When the first third of the flight was screened, subjects only hit 25% to center field with the rest of the hits equally distributed between left field and right field. When the middle third was blocked, only 22% were hit to center and 50% were hit to right. When the final third was blocked, 34% were hit to center and 45% were hit to right. Thus, blocking vision of any portion of the ball flight influenced the timing of the swing so that even though contact was made and fair balls were hit, the swing was typically swung late when the middle or final third of the ball flight was screened. It is important to keep in mind that the pitched balls were all straight balls and were travelling at 60 mph. However, even for this limited set of conditions, it is clear that being able to see the ball for as long as possible is important for successful batting.

In the discussions concerning the roles of proprioception and vision in the control of movement, some important points were made. *First,* although it is possible to carry out certain movements in the absence of either proprioception or vision, movement precision is typically degraded in these cases. Rough accuracy seems possible without these sensory feedback sources, but the degree of accuracy loss is noticeable. *Second,* the amount of accuracy decrement without these sources of feedback seems to be related to the time duration of the movement. Very fast, or ballistic, movements are affected less by feedback loss than are movements of longer duration. *Third,* both proprioceptive and visual feedback appear to have two important functions in controlling movement. The first is a guidance of limb or body trajectory. Here initial positioning movements are adjusted according to the demands of the task. Then a final homing-in or refining of the movement is made to complete the task. Again, depending on the length of time available, these two functions may be carried out in an open-loop fashion, where visual and proprioceptive information is used in a feedforward rather than in a feedback role. Here the visual and proprioceptive information is sent by the sensory receptors to the central control center before the movement is initiated and is used to develop the appropriate set of commands to be issued to the effectors to carry out the necessary response. In cases where sufficient time is available, these sources of feedback will provide feedback information and these guidance and homing-in functions will be carried out in some open-loop, closed-loop combination.

In the next concept, you will see how these control events can be carried out. The motor program will be considered as the principal mechanism involved in the control of movements such as we have been discussing. The role played by the motor program fits very nicely into the interaction view for the

The Interaction of Proprioception and Vision

operation of open-loop and closed-loop control systems, a view that has been the prevalent control condition involved in the discussion of the present concept.

Summary

Both proprioception and vision play significant roles in the control of coordinated, voluntary movement. These sensory-perceptual systems are characterized like any sensory-perceptual system by being able to discriminate one level of intensity of sensory information from another. Debate continues concerning the roles played by these systems in the control of movement. The importance of proprioception and movement control has been investigated primarily by research involving deafferentation, nerve-block, and switched-limb procedures. These studies have shown that although movements can be performed accurately in the absence of proprioception, the degree of accuracy can be increased by having this sensory information available. Vision consistently has been shown to predominate the sensory system. Visual information plays an important role in the control of movement. For skills requiring accurate limb movement, vision is involved in controlling movements in two phases of the response. First, it is involved in initiating appropriate movement of the limb. Second, vision helps ensure that the response is made accurately and that it provides information to get the limb to the correct target. Vision has been shown to be an important part of the control of a wide variety of skills, such as aiming tasks, locomotion, catching, and batting. Important control-related questions have been considered by investigating the involvement of vision in these skills. Questions such as, How long does it take to process visual feedback? How much information must vision take in before an accurate response can be made? and How does visual information help adjust movements so that accurate responses can be made? are all important for better understanding how vision functions in the control of complex motor skills.

Related Readings

Glencross, D. J. (1977). Control of skilled movements. *Psychological Bulletin, 84,* 14–29.

Lee, D. N. (1980). Visuo-motor coordination in space-time. In G. E. Stelmach & J. Requin (Eds.), *Tutorials in motor behavior* (pp. 281–295). Amsterdam: North-Holland.

Magill, R. A., & Parks, P. F. (1983). The psychophysics of kinesthesis for positioning responses. The physical stimulus-psychological response relationship. *Research Quarterly for Exercise and Sport, 54,* 346–351.

Paillard, J. (1980). The multichanneling of visual cues and the organization of a visually guided response. In G. E. Stelmach & J. Requin (Eds.), *Tutorials in motor behavior* (pp. 259–279). Amsterdam: North-Holland.

von Hofsten, C. (1987). Catching. In H. Heuer & A. F. Sanders (Eds.), *Perspectives on perception and action* (pp. 33–46). Hillsdale, NJ: Erlbaum.

Certain types of motor skills and well-learned skills appear to be controlled by motor programs

Concept 3.4

Application

We seem able to perform many motor skills that require little if any conscious thought to what we are doing during the performance of the skill. For example, if you have learned a dance step very well, you really do not give any "thought" or attention to the step after you decide to do it. The step may have eight counts to it, but you perform it as if it had only one count. You may give some attention to the beginning of the step, but beyond that you do not really think about what you are doing. In fact, you can even carry on a conversation while you are doing it. If the music were cut off in the middle of the step, you would probably keep dancing until you finally realized the music had stopped.

Let's consider a similar situation in tennis. If you have learned the forehand stroke to a high degree of proficiency, you rarely give much thought to the actual mechanics of carrying out that stroke after you have made the decision to hit the forehand. More than likely you are more concerned with the placement of your shot than you are with the mechanics of how to hit a forehand. This skill has been so well learned that you can concentrate on aspects of the skill other than the basic fundamentals of how to perform the skill. This does not mean that you should not concentrate on what you are doing. What we are interested in here is what you are concentrating on during the performance of a skill. This is of utmost importance for our understanding of how we control complex movements.

Running is a relatively simple skill that most of us have performed for years. Do you really think about what you are doing as you run? In this connection is not one of the suggestions for helping in long-distance running or jogging to run with a friend so that you can converse with that person and keep your mind off your running? Even in the midst of intense conversation, you can keep on running until it is time to stop or until you notice something in your path that you think you must respond to by altering your running.

Each of these three examples points to a basic concept in current motor learning theory, that is, the motor program. Like the computer program, once the motor program is put into operation it seems to "run off" until the command to stop is given. What we will be discussing here is an extension of the preceding two concepts. We will expand our discussion of how open-loop and closed-loop control systems seem to operate in controlling movement by examining the motor program. Exactly what the motor program is like, what kinds of commands it gives, and how these commands can be altered will be at the heart of our discussion.

Controlling Movement   139

Discussion

The motor program is by no means a new idea; in fact, it has been known for many years. Indeed, it has appeared in various types of research literature since 1917, when Lashley used the motor program concept to describe the control of movement of one of his patients. This individual had suffered a gunshot wound in the back that destroyed the afferent neural pathways from his legs, although the efferent pathways were apparently intact. Lashley found that the patient could still position his legs with "surprising accuracy" when commanded to do so, even though he could not receive any kinesthetic feedback from his legs. Previously it was thought that this peripheral feedback would be essential to control such a positioning task. However, the apparent ability to control movement in the absence of peripheral feedback led Lashley to conclude that the movement was being controlled centrally.

From Lashley's demonstration, we find some anecdotal evidence to support the claims that open-loop movement control is indeed possible. While we discussed this control system in Concept 3.2, we did not consider the means by which the movement was centrally organized so as to be controlled in an open-loop manner. In the present concept, we shall consider that organization to be in the form of a motor program.

Defining the Motor Program

The motor program seems to be much easier to define than it is to support on the basis of empirical evidence. Rather than spend time trying to examine the theoretical arguments for and against the existence of the motor program, we shall take a less devious path, simply assume its existence, and work from there. However, such an assumption is not unfounded. As we shall see, there is evidence to support the motor program notion; it is on this evidence that we acknowledge the validity of accepting the existence of the motor program, and it is from that point that we shall move by defining it and providing some evidence for it. In doing so, we shall also try to describe how the motor program is put to use in motor skill performance.

Earlier views. An interesting way to trace the history of the concept of the motor program is to consider the definitions and alternative terms that have been used to describe it. The motor program concept can be traced back as far as William James (1890) when he argued that in order for an action to occur, all a person has to do is form a clear "image" of that action. James called this an "idea-motor" action. Sir Frederick Bartlett (1932) alluded to a motor program concept when he used the term *schema* to describe internal representations and organizations of movements. K. S. Lashley (1951), who had presented some empirical support for the motor program concept in 1917, stated that it is the "intention to act" that determines the sequence of events to produce a well-learned motor act. Miller, Galanter, and Pribram (1960) presented a well-developed argument centering on the notion of a "Plan" as being responsible for controlling the sequence of events of an action. This Plan, they stated is "essentially the same as a program for a computer" (p. 16).

These examples indicate that the concept of the "programmed" control of voluntary movement has been with us for some time. However, it was not until Franklin Henry and his students at Berkeley developed a series of experiments directly related to exploring motor skill programming that the motor program concept gained a needed conceptual and empirical boost. Henry hypothesized that the "neural pattern for a specific and well-coordinated motor act is controlled by a stored program that is used to direct the neuromotor details of its performance" (Henry & Rogers, 1960, p. 449). Henry's concept of the motor program was that of a computer program, which when initiated, controls the exact movement details with essentially no modifications possible during the execution of the movement. What is significant here is not only the further development of the notion of a motor program but the development of the concept of what the motor program is like and what it controls.

As research and theorizing about motor programs continued, the primary point of change was how people viewed its structure. Again, this issue was not a new one as Lashley had discussed the structure controversy in his 1951 article. However, the development of the structure concept since the Henry and Rogers (1960) article marks the intensity of the formalized pursuit of coming to grips with an old problem. Perhaps the most formalized theorizing about the motor program following the Henry and Rogers article was by Steven Keele (1968). While his definition of the motor program did not significantly alter the view expressed by Henry, it did present a more formal version of that view which led to increased research activity directed at identifying the characteristics and operation of motor programs. Keele defined the motor program as "a set of muscle commands that are structured before a movement sequence begins, and that allows the entire sequence to be carried out uninfluenced by peripheral feedback" (p. 387).

Keele emphasized in his discussion of this definition that the motor program is *not* a movement but rather it acts to *control* movements. It should also be emphasized that the definition asserts that the movement will be *uninfluenced* by peripheral feedback. This does not mean that there is no peripheral feedback during the movement; it means that even in the presence of sensory feedback, the movement is carried out in accordance with the predetermined commands. The peripheral sensory feedback is not attended to by the performer and thus does not influence the movement sequence.

The current view. The current view of the motor program is best expressed by Richard Schmidt (1987). He described a *generalized motor program* that is a memory representation of a class of actions and that is responsible for producing a unique pattern of activity when it is executed. The program has certain features, called invariant characteristics, that provide the essential elements of the class of actions under its control. The program requires that other features, called parameters, be added to enable an action to be controlled. These parameters are considered to provide the basis for the program involved

in controlling a number of different movement responses from the same movement class. We will discuss invariant characteristics and parameters in more detail later. For now it is important to be aware that this view of the motor program differs in several ways from earlier views. We will consider some of these differences to emphasize the uniqueness of the present view of the motor program.

The first important distinction of the current view of the motor program is that it is presented as an *abstract representation of action.* That is, the motor program is not stored in memory with the specific details of a specific movement. Instead, it is stored in an abstract form of a class of actions having certain common characteristics. This means that instead of having a motor program for every possible variation of an overhand throw to a target, the program contains certain characteristics of this action that provide the basis for one motor program to control both a very fast throw or a very slow one. This feature of the motor program gives it a very flexible quality that allows the same program to control a wide variety of movements.

Second, because the motor program is only an abstract representation of action, specific *muscles involved in a movement are not part of the motor program.* The specific muscles that are to be used to produce an intended action are specified at the time of the action and are not a part of what is permanently stored in memory as the motor program. This means that an action can be carried out in a variety of ways and still be under the control of the same motor program. For example, you can write your name on a check, or on a blackboard, or in the sand with your foot. The current view of the motor program argues that underlying control of these actions is attributable to one program. What differs about these situations are the muscles that must be used to accomplish the goal of the action, which is to write your name.

A third important distinctive feature of the current view of the motor program has not yet been discussed. That is, this view of the motor program indicates that *feedback can influence the ongoing program.* This is a marked departure from the more restrictive views of Henry and Keele, which presented the motor program as controlling movement in a completely open-loop fashion so that the course of the movement was unaffected by sensory feedback. As you shall see later in this discussion, an ongoing movement can be amended. However, such modification to the planned movement appears to be possible only after a certain amount of time has elapsed in the progress of the movement. Also, such modification can only be carried out successfully if there is sufficient time remaining in the course of the movement for it to be amended.

Given this starting place, then, we can begin our investigation of what the motor program is like and how it operates to control movement. Before doing this, however, it will be instructive to backtrack somewhat and consider the kinds of research evidence that led to establishing the need for a concept such as the motor program.

As you may have already concluded from the discussion in the previous two concepts, the research findings that goal-oriented movement can be accomplished in the absence of sensory feedback led to the need for proposing a mechanism that can control movement in this situation. While the open-loop control system model provided an elementary description of what is happening during the movement, it did not accommodate the need for indicating what is responsible for this control. With the advent of the computer and because the open-loop control situation seemed analogous to the running of a computer program, the motor program metaphor seemed appropriate to handle this void. While it appears that the idea of motor programs came about primarily as a default argument, the point remains that there was a need to propose a mechanism that would accommodate the results of a wide range of movement control research. We will consider some of this research next.

Evidence of movement accuracy without feedback. The most obvious research findings indicating the need for a control mechanism such as the motor program came from studies such as those we considered in Concept 3.3, that showed accurate limb control in the absence of sensory feedback. As you may recall, those studies compared performance of motor skills with and without sensory feedback. In general, it was demonstrated that certain movements can be accurately carried out in the absence of peripheral feedback. Those findings, however, were not the sole reason for proposing the motor program concept. We will consider those additional findings next.

Evidence that we preplan movements. The motor program concept proposed by Franklin Henry was based on a number of experiments that provided evidence that we plan movements *before* we physically initiate them. This evidence of preplanning seemed especially pertinent for rapid, ballistic movements. The results from the experiments reported in the Henry and Rogers (1960) study will serve to show how Henry reached his conclusion.

Henry reasoned that if preplanning occurs, a complicated movement should take longer to plan than a simple one because there is a larger amount of stored information for the complicated movement. This increased planning time should be reflected in a change in the amount of time from the signal to move until the person physically begins the response, which is reaction time (RT). To test this prediction, Henry and Rogers (1960) compared subjects' RTs associated with three situations.

One group of subjects was required simply to release a telegraph key as quickly as possible after a gong. This was movement A. A second group was required to also release the key at the sound of the gong but then to move their arm forward 30 cm as rapidly as possible and grasp a tennis ball hanging from a string. This was called movement B. The most complex movement was movement C. Here subjects were required to release the key at the gong, reach

forward and strike a hanging tennis ball with the back of the hand, reverse directions and push a button, and then finally reverse directions again and grasp another tennis ball. All of these movements were to be done as quickly as possible. If movements are preplanned, then the RTs associated with each of these three movements should be increasingly larger, because each is more complex and requires more stored information to put into operation. The results of this study supported this prediction (see Figure 3.4–1). The average RT for movement A was 165 msec, for movement B the average RT was 199 msec, for movement C the average RT was 212 msec.

Since the RTs increased as the complexity of the rapid movement increased, Henry reasoned that preplanning of the movement must be going on during that time. The increase in RT was due to the increase in the amount of information that had to be planned to control the movement so that it could occur as rapidly as possible. The motor program seemed to be the most likely candidate to explain this situation.

Evidence from characteristics of unexpectedly blocked movements. An impressive type of evidence showing the need for a mechanism such as the motor program comes from research where a subject preparing to make a practiced response is unexpectedly blocked from moving. Based on characteristics of the EMG patterns related to the movement, or the lack of a movement, it becomes apparent that the movement was planned and commands were sent to the muscles in advance and that these commands were not amended until a minimum amount of time had elapsed. An example of this research evidence can be seen in an experiment by Wadman, Dernier van der Gon, Geuze, and Moll (1979). Subjects practiced a rapid linear flexion movement, that of moving a handle along a trackway 7.5, 15, 22.5, or 30 cm. After 20 trials of practice, they performed 20 in which, on some trials, they were unexpectedly mechanically blocked from making the movement. The EMG recordings from the biceps and the triceps indicated that for the first 100 msec after the signal to move occurred, there was tremendous EMG similarity between responses in which movement actually occurred and in which no movement occurred. These results indicate that for the first 100 msec, the motor system does not make use of proprioceptive information for controlling movement. The muscle commands are executed as planned.

More recently, Magill, Young, Schmidt, and Shapiro (1986) replicated the results of Wadman et al. with a more complex response. The task required subjects to make an initial flexion response of a lever to a target area and then to make a quick reversal back to the starting area. Rather than using different movement distances in this experiment, the same distance was used but different total movement times were compared. Figure 3.4–2 presents the results of the EMG characteristics for the biceps and triceps for one subject performing this response at a 150-msec goal. As you can see, there is very little difference between EMG patterns for either muscle group when a normal,

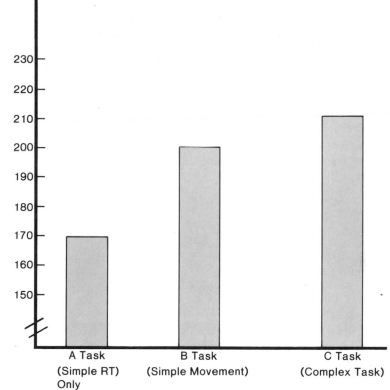

Figure 3.4-1
Results of the experiment by Henry and Rogers showing the changes in RT associated with performing rapid movements of different complexities.

unblocked movement was carried out and when the planned response was unexpectedly blocked. It is important to keep in mind that the EMG patterns for the blocked movement occur even though no movement is made. As in the experiment by Wadman et al., the first 100 msec showed very similar EMG patterns for blocked and normal movements.

These types of results, then, indicate that some mechanism is needed to prepare a response in advance and execute that response as planned until sensory feedback indicates that the planned response cannot be made. The current view of the motor program provides such a mechanism to accommodate this situation.

Evidence from the time needed to inhibit a preplanned response. If a central open-loop mechanism controls the initiation of a rapid movement, then once planned, that movement will be initiated even if the movement *should not* be made. Many of you may experience this effect when you are typing. For example, you see the word *there,* but for some reason you plan, unconsciously, to type *their.* Even though you catch yourself by the time you type the *e* and

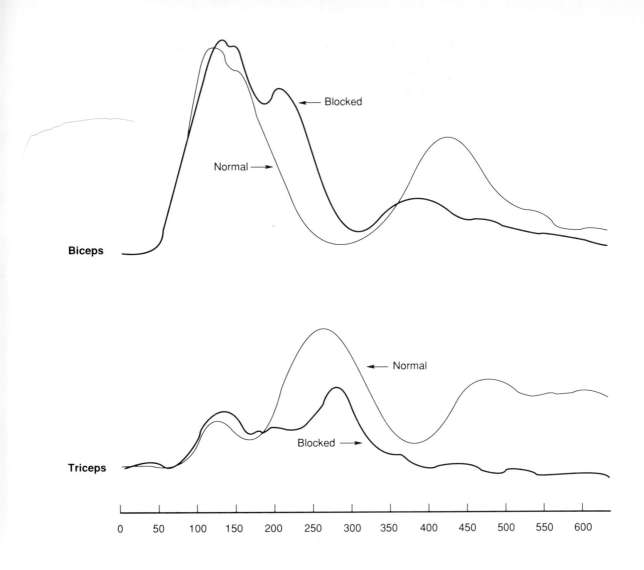

Biceps

Blocked

Normal

Triceps

Normal

Blocked

| 0 | 50 | 100 | 150 | 200 | 250 | 300 | 350 | 400 | 450 | 500 | 550 | 600 |

Time (msec)

Figure 3.4-2 EMG results from one subject performing an arm flexion-extension reversal movement with a goal movement time of 150 msec to the reversal point. On some trials, the movement was unexpectedly blocked (the darker line on the figure). The 150-msec movement time to reversal occurred at the 350-msec point in time in the figure, as the horizontal axis marks time from the signal to begin the movement.

begin the *i*, you probably type both the *i* and *r*. You are not able to inhibit your planned response in the short period of time it takes to type these last two letters.

Support for the typing example was provided by the results of a series of experiments by Logan (1982). Skilled typists were given a "stop" signal at different times after they had begun to type words or sentences. Results of the procedure indicated that the typists continued typing for at least one or two more letters before stopping. In some cases, as for a short word such as *the*, the entire word was typed before typing stopped. These results suggest that the typists preplanned typing movements in such a way that the planned response could only be inhibited after the preplanned action had taken place to the extent that the feedback system could intervene and stop the plan.

Another example of response inhibition was provided many years earlier in the laboratory by A. T. Slater-Hammel (1960), one of the early physical educators involved in motor behavior research. Slater-Hammel had subjects observe the sweep hand of a clock on which one revolution took one second. The subjects' task was to lift a finger from a response key so that it coincided with the sweep hand reaching a target at the place where the *8* is on a clock face (i.e., 800 msec after the hand started). Obviously, in order to do this accurately, subjects would have to initiate the lifting movement *before* the hand reached the target. On some trials Slater-Hammel had the hand stopped before it reached the target. On these trials, the subjects were told to do nothing and to keep the finger on the key. By having the hand stop unexpectedly at points between 200 and 750 msec (i.e., 600 to 50 msec before the target), Slater-Hammel could observe the length of time it took to inhibit a planned response. Figure 3.4–3 shows the results of this experiment. Subjects were correctly able *not* to move from the key only half of the time if the clock stopped approximately 140 msec before the target. If it stopped with less time than that before the target, not moving became increasingly difficult. At 50 or 100 msec before the target, subjects almost always lifted the finger. It was not unless the hand stopped unexpectedly 180 to 200 msec before the target that subjects could almost always inhibit the lifting response.

These results are interesting in that they suggest the need to describe a mechanism that initiates a planned movement even after the individual realizes the plan should not be put into effect. The motor program concept accommodates this situation by establishing a mechanism that initiates a preplanned response that is unaffected by sensory feedback until the feedback can be used, which, according to the Slater-Hammel results is approximately one RT.

Evidence from rapid serial movements. Many piano pieces contain sections that require a very rapid series of finger movements. This point was used by Lashley (1951) as an important part of his proposal for the need for a central

Figure 3.4-3
Results of the Slater-Hammel experiment showing the probability of subjects actually making a response when they were given a signal at different time intervals not to respond. The time intervals indicate when the clock hand stopped unexpectedly before it reached the target location on the clockface.

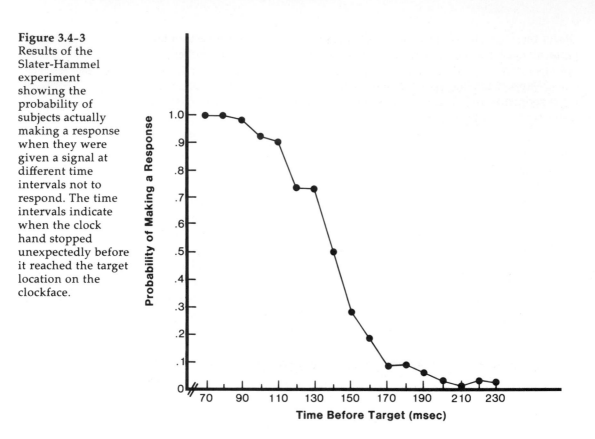

mechanism to control the correct organization and movement of these responses. The alternative view, which states that sensory feedback from the response of one finger is the stimulus for the next finger's response, argues for the importance of feedback in the control of such movements. The problem with this response-chaining view is that many piano passages require faster finger movements than can be controlled by a feedback-dependent control system.

Support for the use of motor programming by highly skilled pianists has been provided by Shaffer (1976, 1980, 1981). Based primarily on the timing involved between key strokes, Shaffer argues that only a motor program view can accommodate these results. Similar arguments have been made on the basis of the rapid serial response skills exhibited by skilled typists (e.g., Rumelhart & Norman, 1982; Shaffer, 1978).

The evidence taken together. On the basis of the evidence just considered from experiments concerned with the deafferentation and nerve-block techniques, the preplanning of movements, the characteristics of unexpectedly blocked movements, the time needed to inhibit a preplanned response, and the timing

constraints on rapid, serial movements, there is obviously a need for a mechanism such as the motor program. Fortunately, this point is rarely debated any more.[1] The motor program concept, after many years of debate, seems to have achieved a high degree of acceptance from motor behavior theorists. What is debated, however, is what a motor program is like and how it operates movement. We will consider these two issues next.

1. See Kelso, Tuller, & Harris, 1983, as an example of an alternative viewpoint.

Characteristics of a Motor Program

An essential characteristic of a motor program is its *flexibility*. Because of this flexibility Schmidt (1982) argued that a motor program should actually be thought of as a *generalized* motor program. That is, the motor program contains only a general representation of a class of actions. The specific requirements demanded by a particular action must be added as *parameters* by the movement control system before that movement can be successfully carried out. For example, there are many ways to throw an object. If we consider only the overarm throw, it appears that we represent only an abstract, general representation of the overarm throw in the motor program. Now, suppose you have to use the overarm throw to pitch a baseball to a batter. Since that type of throw will be different from throwing a football to a receiver and since each pitch has its own unique requirements and situations, more specific requirements must be added to that representation to effectively produce the correct pitch. Such parameters as the speed of the pitch, placement, type of spin put on the ball, etc., all must be added to this general representation known as the motor program.

This example raises several questions that continue to be sources of investigation for motor behavior researchers. One of these questions concerns how general the motor program is. In the example of the overarm throw, a question of interest to researchers is whether one motor program represents all possible actions using an overarm throw pattern or whether each type of overarm throw, such as pitching a baseball, throwing a football, or passing a basketball, is represented by a separate motor program. A second question from the example relates to what specific parameters must be added to the motor program. Finally, if the specific parameters can be identified, what in the movement control system is responsible for these being added and how is this accomplished? Each of these research questions presents a challenge for motor behavior researchers.

Invariant characteristics. To answer the question of what parameters must be specified for a given motor program, we must consider first what characteristics of the motor program remain consistent from one response to the next. We will call these *invariant characteristics* of an existing motor program. These differ from the characteristics that must be specified for each response that will be made.

From research using such diverse tasks as handwriting, piano playing, typing, walking, running, rapid arm movements to targets, and tracking, there

seems to be some general agreement about the invariant characteristics of a motor program. These include the *relative force* used to produce the movement, the *relative timing* (or phasing) among the components of the movement, and the *order* of the movement components (Schmidt, 1987).

These characteristics can be better understood by applying them to an example. Consider how you produce a tennis serve. This complex skill has several identifiable components, such as the ball toss, the backswing, the forward swing, ball contact, follow through, etc. To produce a serve, there is a specific order for these events. If that order is disrupted, the serve will not be executed correctly. In carrying out this order of events, the body and limbs must be in relatively similar positions at relatively the same time from one serve to the next. If this does not occur, you will be very inconsistent in your serving. Similarly, when one serve is compared to another, one may have been hit harder than another. However, a comparison of the two would reveal that the amount of force generated by each of the muscle groups producing each component of the serve remained similar between the two serves.

Changeable parameters. While the relative force and timing characteristics between the various components of a task seem to be rather fixed characteristics of a motor program, there are certain characteristics of a response that seem to vary from one attempt to the next. For example, the *overall* force and timing characteristics of a response seem to be easily changed from one response to another, depending on the needs of the response situation. This can most easily be seen in the tennis serve example. To hit one serve harder than another, the overall force applied must be greater and the overall time taken to carry out the events of the serve must be faster. Speeding up the overall response and increasing the overall force can seemingly be done without altering the invariant characteristics of the motor program controlling the response.

Evidence for invariant characteristics and parameters. An interesting research example of how parameters can be changed while the invariant characteristics of the motor program are maintained can be seen in a study published by Shapiro, Zernicke, Gregor, and Diestal (1981). They examined subjects walking and running at different speeds on a treadmill. While subjects had no difficulty in speeding up or slowing down their pace, as you would expect, the relative amounts of time for each of the four components or phases of a walking step remained the same (see Figure 3.4–4). Thus the program governing walking could be speeded up (at least to 6 km/hr) or slowed down overall while the relative timing among the components of the walk step was maintained. Running (speeds greater than 8 km/hr) appears to be controlled by a different motor program than walking, according to the Shapiro et al. results. This conclusion is based on the differences evident in the between-component percentages for each running step as compared to the walking step.

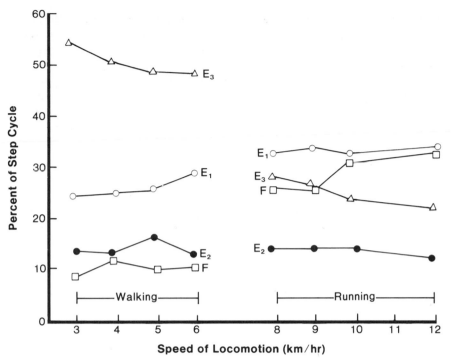

Figure 3.4-4
Results of the experiment by Shapiro, et al. showing the relative timing of the four step-cycle phases (mean values), determined by comparing percentages at the different locomotion speeds.

The issue of determining invariant characteristics of motor programs and what parameters can be applied to a motor program is important for additional research. Much research effort is currently directed toward this issue with the goal of better understanding how we represent in memory the skills we learn and what mechanisms underlie the control of these skills. Excellent reviews of this work are available (e.g., Gentner, 1987; Schmidt, 1985) and should be consulted for further information about the continuing search for the characteristics of motor programs.

We have seen what appear to be some of the characteristics of a motor program that are relatively fixed and remain consistent from one response to the next and characteristics that can be changed from one response to the next. What remains to be seen is how the features are incorporated in the actual control of a movement. While this has already been alluded to, we can gain a more critical view of this situation by considering how the motor program concept applies to the control of simple and complex movement skills.

How a Motor Program Functions to Control Movement

Motor programs and simple movement control. The most common "simple" movement used in the movement control research literature is a rapid aiming task. To perform this task, the subject moves a stylus from a starting point to

a target as rapidly as possible. What makes this task interesting is that performance on it follows a specific law of movement known as *Fitts' Law*. This law, based on the work of Paul Fitts (1954), indicates how the two essential components of the task, the distance to move and the size of the target, are related to how fast the movement will be. Essentially Fitts' Law describes this relationship as MT $= \log_2 (2D/W)$, where MT is movement time, D is the distance moved, and W is the width, or size, of the target. That is, movement time will be equal to the $\log_2$ of two times the distance to move divided by the width of the target. As the target size gets smaller or as the distance gets greater, the movement speed will slow down in order to allow for an accurate movement. In other words, in these aiming tasks, there is a *speed-accuracy trade-off* where we will slow down if greater accuracy is required or we will speed up if we do not have stringent accuracy requirements. Because of this relationship, Fitts indicated that the Fitts' Law formula actually presents an index of difficulty (ID) where the higher the ID, the more difficult the task. This index has become a convenient means of cataloging aiming tasks as well as sport skills for practice purposes.

From a movement control perspective, the interesting question here is how the control system operates in this movement situation. For our purposes, an advantage of considering this question will be to provide an opportunity to see how what we have been discussing so far in this chapter applies to an actual movement control situation.

Current views of this control problem appear to fall into one of two general approaches (Keele, 1982). One of these approaches argues that the distance to move is determined before the movement begins. This information is then used to establish specific force and duration information to the motor program, which is able to initiate the movement. An example of this approach is the *impulse-timing model* (Schmidt, Zelaznik, Hawkins, Frank, & Quinn, 1979). The second approach is the *mass-spring model* presented in Concept 3.3. Here the end location is programmed independently of the distance to move by setting the appropriate length-tension characteristics of the muscles responsible for executing the movement.

Both of these views regard the motor program as important. What is different is what they suggest the motor program does. According to the impulse-timing view, the force and duration of the movement are the movement commands sent by the motor program. These requirements are based specifically on the distance to move. The mass-spring view, on the other hand, argues that the distance to move has nothing to do with what commands will be sent from the motor program. In this view, the end location is the critical information that is used in the preplanning stage of preparing the motor program.

Visual feedback can be involved in either approach as the source of information responsible for the accurate termination of movements that last longer than 250 msec. Support for this was demonstrated in an experiment by Wallace and Newell (1983). Subjects had to perform an aiming task with the lights on for some trials and with the lights off for other trials. However, different from the Keele and Posner (1968) experiment discussed in Concept 2.3, Wallace and Newell observed subjects' performance for aiming tasks having different IDs. Results showed that the two situations made little difference for tasks with IDs of less than 4.58. However, for tasks with IDs of from 4.58 to 6.58, no vision always resulted in more errors. Interestingly, the movement time to perform the tasks with a 4.58 ID was approximately 250 msec.

For aiming tasks lasting longer than 250 msec, it appears that the motor program initiates the movement in an open-loop manner while visual feedback provides information to enable an accurate termination of the movement, following a closed-loop system. Exactly how this interaction between the motor program and the use of visual feedback occurs is not known. Much more research is needed to answer this intriguing question. However, research presently available provides sufficient evidence to demonstrate how motor programs interact with feedback to provide the needed control for a voluntary movement.

Motor programs and complex movement control. A complex movement is one that has many component parts, such as serving a tennis ball or playing a piano. While the primary problem of control for the rapid aiming movement concerned how distance and accuracy are determined, the control problems related to the complex task include many additional concerns. Among these are accounting for the organization of the many parts, the role of feedback in controlling the movement, and so on. While these problems have been considered in earlier discussions, we will look at them here as a means of seeing how the motor program concept is related to the specific movement problems involved in a common movement task.

Some of the more interesting research investigations of how we control complex movements have been conducted on the skills of piano playing and typing. Any investigation of motor programming and these skills must be done with skilled individuals (Shaffer, 1980). The reasoning behind this is based on a point made at the end of the discussion in Concept 3.1. That is, the beginner is very dependent on feedback in performing a complex skill. It is not until the skill has reached the autonomous stage that performance exhibits features that suggest a high degree of programmed control.

One reason piano playing and typing have attracted so much attention is because they can be so readily controlled for research purposes. Piano strings and typewriter keys can be interfaced with a computer to record time and force information. Information can be presented to subjects in a variety of

ways to enable researchers to manipulate events. By observing the effects of these manipulations, researchers can then make inferences concerning the characteristics of the control processes operating. Much of the piano playing and typing research has addressed the issue of *timing*. For example, how is the timing of the various events in playing a piano piece represented in the motor program? Timing is critical in this task as each hand has specifically timed responsibilities and the hands must work together to produce the notes at appropriate times.

Shaffer (1980, 1981, 1982) argues that an abstract timing schedule for movements is represented in the motor program. For a complex piano piece, a timing pattern is represented for a group of notes containing a rhythmic figure. The pianist adds certain specifications to this abstract plan that allow for variations in such things as tempo, rhythm, and intensity from one performance to another. For the skilled pianist, these specifications can be made differently for each hand as well as for the two hands together. In this view the motor program sends timing-based commands to the musculature to control the movements. These commands are based on abstract timing requirements for the task. These abstract requirements are made specific by the performer's adding specifications related to the needs of the performance being executed.

Coordinative Structures

[1]See also, Whiting, 1984, for a reprinting of Bernstein's book along with added commentaries by present-day motor control scholars.

Another interesting question concerning the complex skill control situation concerns what the motor program actually controls. The traditional view of this has been that the individual muscles are given instructions by the commands generated by the motor program. This view, however, is being seriously challenged on the basis of work originally published in the Soviet Union by Nicolai Bernstein in the 1950s but not available in English until 1967.[1] Bernstein argued that rather than individual muscles being controlled by the motor program, groupings of muscles were controlled. These groupings, later called *coordinative structures,* are collectives of muscles and joints that are involved in the control of a specific act. The motor program commands are directed toward the particular coordinative structure, which then signals all the muscles within its group to act accordingly.

Coordinative structures and limb control. Results from a study by Kelso, Southard, and Goodman (1979) provide some support not only for the existence of coordinative structures but for the fact that they are under a timing-based control system. In a series of experiments, subjects performed simple, rapid-aiming movements with the right, left, and both hands. One hand moved to a target that was different in size and distance from that of the other hand. According to the Fitts Law, the hand moving to the target with the smaller ID should move faster. As can be seen in Figure 3.4–5, when each hand moved alone to a target, the Fitts prediction was upheld. However, when the two hands moved together to the two targets, the movement times became similar for

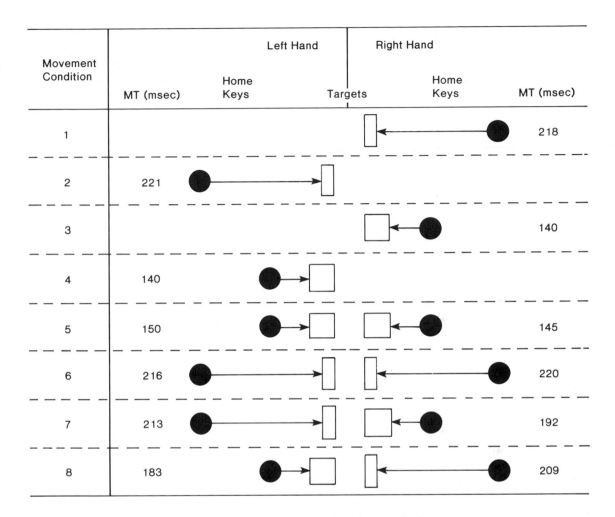

Movement Condition	MT (msec)	Left Hand		Right Hand		MT (msec)
		Home Keys	Targets		Home Keys	
1						218
2	221					
3						140
4	140					
5	150					145
6	216					220
7	213					192
8	183					209

the two hands. In this type of movement situation, the Fitts prediction was not upheld. Obviously, something was acting to constrain the two hands to act together as one. Kelso, Southard, and Goodman argued that this was due to the two limbs being considered by the control system as a coordinative structure. As such, when the two hands were in a situation in which they had to act at the same time, even though their two tasks were different, the system controlled them as though they both had the same task to perform.

Obviously, we can learn to make our two arms or hands act independently. We see this every day in pianists, typists, guitarists, violinists, and a number of other skilled performers. However, to accomplish such independence takes work, a point worthy of note for teachers of skills requiring this type of hand movement independence. Early instruction and practice will need to focus on this important aspect of the task. What the Kelso, Southard, and Goodman results demonstrate, however, is that since innate coordinative

Figure 3.4-5
Movement time scores for one- and two-hand movements to targets of different distances and sizes reported in Kelso, Southard, and Goodman's second experiment.

structures can be shown to exist, it seems reasonable to expect that they can be developed as a result of practice. As a result of practice, then, muscles and joints become constrained to act together as a functional unit designed to carry out a specific task. Whether this structure controls movement on the basis of time commands or some other element, such as force, continues to be debated and awaits further research (note e.g., Corcos, 1984; Marteniuk & MacKenzie, 1980).

Coordinative structures and speech control. Another impressive form of evidence supporting the existence of coordinative structures comes from research done with speech control. For example, Kelso, Tuller, Vatikiotis-Bateson, and Fowler (1984) published a series of experiments in which they observed what occurred in the various components of the articulators when the jaw was perturbed during an utterance. In two experiments, subjects were asked to say the syllable "bab." On several utterances, an unexpected force load was applied to the jaw during the upward jaw motion for the final "b" sound of the syllable. According to the coordinative structure notion, such a perturbation should result in an immediate compensation by other parts of the articulation system involved in producing this sound, since all parts work as a functional unit to achieve the common goal of the intended sound. This is, in fact, what they found. As the jaw was forced upward, there was an almost immediate compensation in the upper and lower lips so that the sound was still produced in an understandable way. A similar perturbation was applied as the subjects uttered "baz." The result was an immediate tongue compensation. Thus, the articulators can be seen as working together as functional units to achieve specified goals. When one element of the unit is disturbed, other elements compensate in a way that allows the goal to be achieved. The elements involved in this compensation and how they achieve it depend on the goal of the action.

Summary

The control of movement appears to be under the direction of motor programs. Similar to computer programs, motor programs contain information that allows a movement to be executed smoothly, efficiently, and accurately. However, different from computer programs, motor programs seem to be modifiable by sensory feedback to some degree during the course of a movement. The only restriction here is that for feedback to have any immediate effect, the movement must last longer than 200 to 250 msec.

Essentially, the motor program is an abstract representation of the action. Certain characteristics of that action seem to be fixed characteristics in the motor program itself. These invariant characteristics include the order of events, relative time between events, and relative force for the musculature involved to produce the action. At the time a specific act must occur, certain

parameters are established for the motor program so that the action can occur as the situation demands. These parameters include such things as the overall duration and force of the movement.

The application of motor programming to the control of movement can be seen in research on the performance of tasks such as simple, rapid-aiming tasks and complex skills such as piano playing and typing. Results of this research indicate that motor programs interact with feedback to control these skills.

Bernstein, N. (1967). *The coordination and regulation of movements*. London: Pergamon Press. (Read chapter 2.)

Gentner, D. R. (1987). Timing of skilled motor performance: Tests of the proportional duration model. *Psychological Review, 94,* 255–276.

Keele, S. W. (1982). Behavioral analysis of movement. In V. B. Brooks (Ed.), *Handbook of physiology Sec. 1: The nervous system. Vol. II: Motor Control, part 2* (pp. 1391–1414). Baltimore: American Physiological Society.

Kelso, J. A. S., Southard, D. L., & Goodman, D. (1979). On the nature of human interlimb coordination. *Science, 203,* 1029–1031.

Miller, G. A., Galanter, E., & Pribram, K. H. (1960). *Plans and the structure of behavior*. New York: Holt, Rinehart & Winston. (Read chapters 1 and 6.)

Rosenbaum, D. A. (1985). Motor programming: A review and scheduling theory. In H. Heuer, U. Kleinbeck, & K.-H. Schmidt (Eds.), *Motor behavior: Programming, control, and acquisition* (pp. 1–34). Berlin: Springer-Verlag.

Schmidt, R. A. (1983). On the underlying structure of well-learned motor responses. In R. A. Magill (Ed.), *Memory and control of action* (pp. 145–165). Amsterdam: North-Holland.

Schmidt, R. A. (1985). The search for invariance in skilled motor behavior. *Research Quarterly for Exercise and Sport. 56,* 188–200.

Related Readings

Concept 3.5 Anticipation timing is an essential element for successful performance of skills requiring the precise coordination of an external event with a motor response

Application

Hitting a baseball, ground strokes in tennis, shots during a rally in handball or racquetball, and many situations in driving an automobile require a common ingredient we often refer to as "timing." A fastball pitcher who has a good change-up is effective because he is said to affect the batter's "timing" and usually makes the batter overswing at the change-up. A tennis player who hits an effective drop shot is usually credited with having "timed" his or her swing just right so as to make this difficult shot an effective one. An automobile driver who is able to avoid an accident by moving his or her car out of the way of an oncoming vehicle also is said to have timed that last-minute maneuver effectively to avoid the accident.

Each of these situations points out a different condition in motor behavior where timing is an essential ingredient of successful performance. Involved in timing is the ability to predict rather precisely *when* an external object, such as a baseball, will be at an exact location. Further involved here is the ability to coordinate with that prediction the required motor response necessary to accomplish the goal of the task, such as hitting the oncoming baseball. In the motor behavior literature, this concept of timing is referred to as *anticipation timing*. In the following discussion we will analyze the meaning of this term more specifically and consider how it is involved in motor behavior.

Discussion

Anticipation timing requires the performer to coordinate and synchronize a motor response with an external event. This specific type of perceptual situation has been studied by researchers for many years. One of the earliest discussions of anticipatory timing from a theoretical point of view appeared in an article in *Psychological Bulletin* in 1957 by a British psychologist, E. C. Poulton. Poulton hypothesized that there are actually two types of anticipation situations in motor skills where the target, or external stimulus, is moving. He termed these *receptor anticipation* tasks and *perceptual anticipation* tasks. Very simply, these two situations can be distinguished by the presence or absence of the external stimulus for viewing purposes. In receptor anticipation tasks, sometimes called coincidence anticipation, the stimulus events necessary to evoke motor responses are in full view of the performer before and during the response. The outfielder in baseball, for example, generally has the baseball in full view from the time the ball leaves the bat until it reaches its

final location. Here, during the entire flight of the ball, that is, while watching the ball throughout its course, the fielder is able to prepare himself or herself to catch it.

Perceptual anticipation tasks, on the other hand, are not performed with the external stimulus in view before the response can be initiated. The performer must predict where the external stimulus will be as when his or her response is completed. Thus the performer is required to learn the pattern of regularity of the stimulus so that he or she can make the necessary spatial and temporal predictions that are required to perform the task successfully. In these tasks events occur in a predictable fashion, so that it is possible for the performer to learn the required timing of the response in association with the external event. In motor behavior, an example of Poulton's perceptual anticipation task would be a person picking up an object from a conveyer belt when the object but not the moving belt can be seen.

While many references to anticipation timing refer to Poulton's dichotomy of anticipation tasks rather matter of factly, John Dickinson (1974) criticized such a view by stating that such a dichotomy is not needed. To distinguish the two tasks is to imply different perceptual demands for each of them, when in fact most research has shown that the basis for responding in both tasks is a proprioceptive-based timing mechanism. The only difference between these two situations, Dickinson argued, is the sensory modality that is primarily involved in receiving the external stimulus information. In many cases, both types of anticipation may be involved in the same task. This seems to be especially true in the course of learning. Preview of the stimuli may be necessary early in learning but becomes less essential at later stages.

For our purposes we will consider anticipatory timing as proposed by Robert Christina (1976, 1977). Both receptor anticipation and perceptual anticipation tasks are included when anticipatory timing is considered. Anticipation or coincidence timing, then, will be considered in this discussion as including any motor response situation that requires the performer to coordinate a movement in response to an external stimulus event.

Anticipation timing plays a significant role in the performance of many motor skills, especially open skills. Because of this, a consideration of some of the factors that influence anticipation timing should help us better understand anticipation timing performance as well as the development of effective instruction for these skills. You were already introduced to some of these factors when the role of vision in movement control was discussed in Concept 3.3. However, two points worth remembering provide a basis for looking at anticipation timing situations separately from the discussion of vision and motor control. First, all the skill situations considered in the vision and control discussion did not involve anticipation timing. Second, all anticipation timing tasks are not necessarily only under visual control. Thus, we will consider the anticipation timing situation separately to establish what factors influence response accuracy in these situations and how we control such actions.

Factors Influencing Anticipation Timing

Figure 3.5-1
The Bassin
anticipation timing
apparatus.

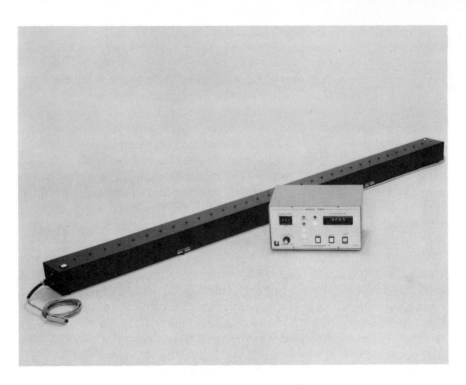

Before we consider some of these influencing factors, it will be helpful to know how anticipation timing experiments are typically conducted. Subjects are required to observe a moving stimulus and then make a response that coincides with the arrival of the stimulus at a target. You may recall the Slater-Hammel (1960) experiment discussed in Concept 3.4. The apparatus was a clock on which one revolution of the sweep hand was one second. The stimulus was the sweep hand on the clock. The target was where the *8* is on the clock. The subject's task was to release a telegraph key to try to stop the sweep hand at the target.

A more popular task has been to have a subject view a runway of lights that appear one after the other according to a preset time (see Figure 3.5–1). As each light goes on in rapid succession, there is a simulation of motion. The subject is seated at the end of the runway of lights and is required to depress a button at the time he or she thinks the final light of the runway will go on. A timer then records the difference between the time when the subject depressed the button and the time when the last runway light went on. The score for the response is the amount of timing error made by the subject. This error can be a negative anticipation error (the subject's response was early) or a positive anticipation error (the subject's response was late). Although the type of movement that must be made as the response may differ from experiment to experiment, the goal is always the same. That is, to make the required response as accurately as possible.

Predictability of the stimulus. One consistent factor that influences anticipation timing accuracy is how predictable the stimulus is. Research results
have typically shown that the more predictable characteristics are of the oncoming stimulus, the easier it is to make an accurate response (Christina, 1977).
When used in this context, the term *predictability* refers to the consistency of
the spatial and/or temporal pattern of the oncoming stimulus. A high degree
of *spatial* consistency occurs when the oncoming object travels in a path that
does not vary from the beginning of its flight until it reaches the target point,
e.g., the point at which a ball must be hit or caught. It is easier to respond in
a case such as this than when the object travels in an unpredictable flight pattern. In baseball, the batter has a much easier task when hitting a pitch that
doesn't "move," that is, a pitch that doesn't rise, curve, or drop, than hitting
a knuckleball, which is highly unpredictable in its flight pattern.

Temporal consistency of an oncoming object can be seen in any sport in
which a moving individual must be intercepted to stop a possible score, such
as in football, soccer, basketball, lacrosse, or hockey. The anticipation timing
aspect of this situation occurs when the defensive player must time his or her
movement to intercept the offensive player who is moving rapidly down the
field, court, or ice. If the offensive player maintains a consistent rate of speed,
he or she is easier to intercept than one whose speed varies, all other things
being equal, of course. The obvious reason is that the consistent speed allows
the defensive player to predict more easily where the offensive player will be
in a given amount of time. The defensive player can then simply focus on
getting to that position in the appropriate amount of time.

Another aspect of stimulus predictability concerns the situation in which
a number of different *stimulus events* occur in succession and the responding
individual must make a correct response to each one. In open skills, this situation is evident in baseball or softball where the batter must make a response
on every pitch. Remember, the decision not to swing at a pitch is a response.
If the pitcher is very predictable about his or her pitches, the batter will be
better able to time and prepare a response than if the pitcher mixes up the
pitches.

In the discussion of Concept 4.1, you will see that this "event predictability" leads to faster reaction times. That is, if an event has an 80% chance
of occurring, subjects have faster reaction times than if the event has only a
50% chance of occurring. When we specifically consider the anticipation timing
situation, the same effect can be seen. The more likely that an event will occur,
the greater the likelihood of making a correct timing response to intercept the
oncoming stimulus (e.g., Adams & Xhingesse, 1960).

Rate of speed of the stimulus. There appears to be somewhat of an inverted-
U relationship between the rate of speed of an oncoming object and the response accuracy associated with intercepting that object. That is, slower objects are more difficult to respond to accurately than are faster objects.

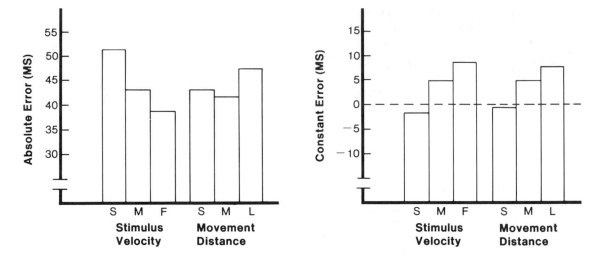

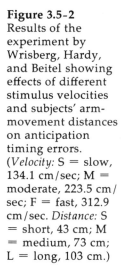

Figure 3.5-2
Results of the
experiment by
Wrisberg, Hardy,
and Beitel showing
effects of different
stimulus velocities
and subjects' arm-
movement distances
on anticipation
timing errors.
(*Velocity:* S = slow,
134.1 cm/sec; M =
moderate, 223.5 cm/
sec; F = fast, 312.9
cm/sec. *Distance:* S
= short, 43 cm; M
= medium, 73 cm;
L = long, 103 cm.)

However, there is a point at which oncoming objects are moving so fast that an accurate response to them is impossible. This is especially true when the object moves from its starting point to its target point in less than one reaction time.

While the "too fast" side of this relationship seems reasonable, the other side of the relationship seems almost paradoxical. However, in experiments that have compared different stimulus speeds, faster speeds consistently yield more accurate responses. For example, Wrisberg, Hardy, and Beitel (1982) had subjects respond to different runway light speeds on the Bassin anticipation timing apparatus. These speeds were 134.1 cm/sec, 223.5 cm/sec, and 312.9 cm/sec. These velocities translate into 2.2, 1.32, and 0.93 sec, respectively, of viewing time. Figure 3.5–2 shows the anticipation time errors for these speeds. As you can see, the error became larger as the stimulus speed became slower. A look at the constant error results shown in Figure 3.5–2 further illustrates this effect. The slower speeds were typically undershot, i.e., early anticipation, whereas the faster speeds showed late anticipations.

In many respects, these results are not surprising. You have undoubtedly experienced a similar effect in performing an open skill. For example, you have probably found you have more difficulty returning a soft lob or easy, slow bound in racquetball or tennis than you have in returning a hard driving shot. The paradox of this situation seems to relate to the expectation that a person would have more time to predict the arrival of the stimulus and therefore more opportunity to properly prepare a response for the slower moving stimulus than for the one moving more rapidly.

An experiment by Simon and Slaviero (1975) may provide some insight here. Subjects were required to make a simple key press response to a light stimulus. They were told that the foreperiod, the interval of time between the warning signal and the stimulus light would be a constant 2 seconds on every

trial. For half of the 144 trials, subjects were provided a series of six "count-down" lights during this interval. That is, a light went on every 0.28 seconds after the warning signal until the stimulus light appeared. For the other half of the trials, no such aid was provided. Results of this experiment showed that the RT for the "countdown" trials was faster than it was for the "empty fore-period" trials. These results illustrate that we do not seem to time a 2-second interval very accurately. If that is indeed the case, then slower stimuli give us trouble because they lead to problems in internal timing accuracy.

Another view of this situation can be related to the open-loop and closed-loop control of an anticipation timing response. For a rapidly moving stimulus, the tendency is to allow the response to be controlled by open-loop processes. That is, as soon as you determine that you have all the information necessary to make a correct response, you "let it happen." The motor program runs its course uninterrupted. However, when the stimulus is moving slowly, there is a tendency to attend to feedback information to carry out the movement. So rather than an open-loop controlled response being run, the response comes under more closed-loop control. From the results of the Simon and Slaviero study, it would seem that this is not a very effective means of control since our ability to time short intervals of time is not as accurate as the response situation may demand.

Amount of time to preview the stimulus. From the discussion in Concept 3.3, it seems that the longer we have to see a stimulus, the more accurate we are in making a response to it. The point to emphasize here, so that this discussion does not seem inconsistent with the preceding section, is that this conclusion is based on comparing amounts of preview time when the stimulus speeds are equal. In other words, for a given stimulus speed, the length of time we can see the stimulus will influence the accuracy of the response.

Based on the results of the experiments with ball catching (Whiting, 1969) and baseball batting (Hubbard & Seng, 1954) that were discussed in Concept 3.3, it appears that there is a point in time where further viewing of the stimulus is not necessary, or even possible. What does this mean for teaching such skills as batting or catching a ball? Is there any merit to the common instructions used by teachers and coaches to "Keep your eye on the ball until you see the ball hit the glove" or ". . . until you see the bat hit the ball"? Whiting (1969) provided some conclusions to his ball skill research that will prove instructive for answering this question.

First, *once he or she is familiar with the flight path,* a player does not need to keep his or her eye on the ball for the whole of its trajectory. It is extremely important to notice the italicized qualifying statement. If the path of the ball is highly unpredictable, or if the performer is unfamiliar with where the ball is going, then success will be closely related to the length of time the ball is watched. Therefore, while it may be physically or perceptually unnec-essary to view a ball during its entire path, it is emphatically advisable to

instruct beginners to "Keep your eye on the ball," for as long as possible, since they have no knowledge of when not to watch it. The accomplished player, on the other hand, should be encouraged to obtain as much information about the path of the ball as early in its course as possible. This will permit better as well as more "last-second" decisions, or a change of strategy. A highly skilled tennis player can tell quite early in the flight of a tennis ball whether or not the bounce of the ball will be high and long or spinning away and low, etc. The earlier such knowledge can be obtained by the performer, the greater are his or her chances of being able to determine and implement a successful response.

"Keep your eye on the ball" is a good instructional strategy. However, the quality of that instruction will be related to *what* the instructor tells the performer about keeping his or her eye on the ball. To the beginner, such instruction should be to watch the ball all the way to contact. Even if this is physically impossible, the performance gains derived from such a strategy, and the perceptual learning that result, will benefit the learner. Beginners should also be instructed to learn as much as they can about the flight of the ball, based on such information as how it was hit, its speed, etc. This will aid them in predicting the spatial and temporal characteristics of a ball, an estimate that is essential to successful performance in anticipatory timing situations. The more skilled performer, on the other hand, should be instructed to obtain as much information about how the ball will act, and as early as possible. These few instructional suggestions that are related to ball skills will be helpful in developing successful instructional strategies for all types of skills involving anticipation timing.

Complexity of the response. In most experiments considered so far, the movement response that subjects must make is rather simple. However, some research has shown that if the complexity of the required response is increased, anticipation timing accuracy decreases. The term "complexity" is being used here to differentiate responses in terms of the number of degrees of freedom that the motor control system must control as the response is being made. A simple response, same as a simple button press, has very few degrees of freedom to be controlled, whereas a more complex response, such as throwing a ball at a target, has many degrees of freedom to be controlled by virtue of the number of body and limb segments involved in performing the response.

An experiment by Michelle Fleury and Chantal Bard (1985) in Québec, Canada showed that the response complexity effect for anticipation timing accuracy held for age groups ranging from 9–11 years to 41–52 years and for stimulus velocities from 75 cm/sec to 300 cm/sec. In this experiment, subjects had to either depress a hand-held button when the target light on an anticipation timing trackway illuminated or they had to throw a ball to hit a target at the same time the target light illuminated. In the latter task, the throwing target had the target light as its center. All subjects performed their responses

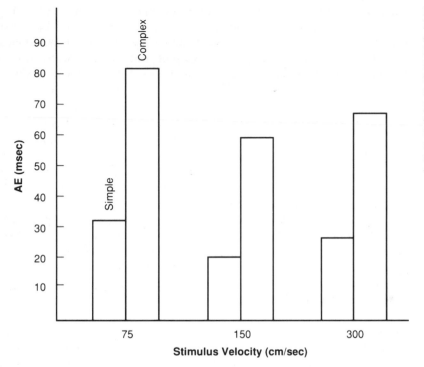

Figure 3.5-3
Results from the experiment by Fleury and Bard (1985) showing the timing error (AE) for a simple button press response and a complex ball-throwing response for three different trackway speed velocities.

for trackway speeds of 75, 150, and 300 cm/sec. The results (see Figure 3.5–3) showed that for each stimulus speed, the amount of timing error was greater for the more complex response. Also, as has been shown for simple responses, the very slow speed (75 cm/sec) led to poorer accuracy than the faster speeds for the complex response.

There appears to be no acceptable reason why such a complexity effect occurs for anticipation timing accuracy. As you saw in Concept 3.4, more complex tasks take longer to organize and initiate. However, in the anticipation timing situations in the Fleury and Bard experiment, the amount of preparation time did not differentially influence the complexity effect. In fact, the slower stimulus speed seemed to show a greater complexity effect than faster speeds. Probably the most plausible reason relates to the degrees of freedom that must be controlled in the complex response situation. As the degrees of freedom to be controlled increase, consistency in control from response to response becomes more difficult to achieve. Although not reported in the Fleury and Bard article, it is very likely that the absolute error difference between response types seen in Figure 3.5–3 was due largely to variable error, or response-to-response inconsistency. Although this explanation only partially explains the basis for the complexity effect, it directs future research to investigate why such increases in degrees of freedom control lead to greater anticipation timing inaccuracy.

Amount of practice. While it may seem reasonable to expect practice to help anticipation timing accuracy when the stimulus moves at the same rate of speed on every trial, it has also been demonstrated that practice also aids accuracy when the stimulus moves at different rates. These two points are illustrated in the following two studies. Christina and Buffan (1976) had subjects anticipate the arrival of a moving pointer on a V-belt at a target. The pointer moved at a consistent rate of 161.27 cm/sec on every trial. Absolute error averaged 63 msec on the first block of 10 trials. By the last block of trials of the 150 trials, that error had been reduced to only 30 msec. In the experiment by Wrisberg, Hardy, and Beitel (1982) discussed earlier, three different movement speeds were varied across the 180 practice trials. While the actual improvement scores were not reported, it was reported that subjects showed a significant improvement in accuracy during the practice trials.

Anticipation timing accuracy, then, can be improved by practice. For the instructor or performer, the point of emphasis in this practice appears to be on the visual-perceptual aspect of the skill rather than on the actual response (Wrisberg, Hardy, & Beitel, 1982). Based on our discussion of Schmidt's schema theory in Concept 2.3, the suggestion is that students should be provided with a variety of anticipation timing experiences. The emphasis in these experiences should be on providing a variety of stimulus movement characteristics for the students to respond to. That is, speeds and spatial patterns especially should be varied to allow students an opportunity to improve their anticipation timing skills. How early in the course of instruction this variety should be introduced is a question that will be addressed in Chapter 9.

The age of the performer. While there is not an abundance of research literature related to developmental aspects of anticipation timing, sufficient evidence has been reported to provide us with some insight into this matter. An example of such evidence can be seen in a study by Peter Dorfman (1977). Subjects in this experiment were 40 people in each of the following age groups: 6–7, 8–9, 10–11, 12–13, 14–15, and 18–19 years old. The task involved the subjects intercepting a moving target dot on an oscilloscope by moving a handle that controlled the cursor dot on the screen. The target dot moved at a constant 10.88 cm/sec on each of the 60 practice trials. An interesting feature of this experiment was that the target dot was not visible for the last 20 trials. This procedure permitted a test of the degree of learning resulting from the preceding 40 practice trials. From the results presented in Figure 3.5–4, you can see that age is an influencing factor in anticipation timing performance. The younger age groups were significantly different from one another until age 14–15. This age group and the 18–19 group were not different from each other. It is interesting to note that all age groups showed improvement during practice and demonstrated a relatively substantial degree of learning.

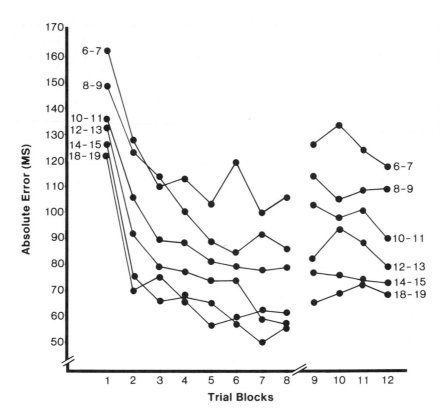

Figure 3.5-4
Results of the experiment by Dorfman showing anticipation timing performance by six different age groups across practice trial blocks (five trials per block). The first eight blocks were performed with a visible target; the last four blocks were performed without a visible target.

An interesting question arising from the results showing an age relationship to anticipation timing accuracy is, Why are children worse than adults in anticipation timing? Several reasons have been proposed. Some researchers (e.g., Gallagher & Thomas, 1980; Hay, 1979) have suggested that children are worse because they have a decreased capacity for processing the information that must be processed in these types of tasks. A related view, offered by Thomas (1980), argues that children are not able to process information as quickly as adults and so time-restricted response situations show adults to perform better than children. Another view presents the difference as due to motor control reasons. For example, Hay (1979) argued that children have decreased guidance control of movements compared with adults because they are not able to use motor programs and feedback control as effectively as adults.

An experiment designed to investigate this question was published by Christopher Ball and Denis Glencross (1985), two motor skills researchers in Australia. In this experiment, subjects moved a hand-held joystick so that it would move a cursor on a computer monitor. The subjects' goal was to move this cursor so that it would intercept a falling target at a prescribed location

at the bottom of the monitor screen. The anticipation timing task involved varying the velocity and visible duration of the falling target across four possible combinations: a slow velocity (6.6 cm/sec) and short duration (468 msec); a slow velocity and long duration (936 msec); a fast velocity (13.2 cm/sec) and short duration; and a fast velocity and long duration. The subjects for this experiment were children aged 5, 7, and 9, and adults.

That the children were limited by the time required to process information was shown by the fact that, although all age groups showed better accuracy for the slower velocity, the 5-, 6-, and 7-year-olds were equally inaccurate for both velocities at the short duration target. In fact, for the long duration targets, the age differences in accuracy performance tended to disappear. When all the results of this experiment were taken into account, it became apparent that children clearly needed more time to organize and execute their response than did adults. Also, evidence indicated that programming and feedback control were still developing in children. This experiment, then, provides support for two views described earlier concerning why children perform anticipation timing tasks less well than adults. Children appear to need more time to process information to organize and initiate a response, and their movement guidance processes are not as well developed as adults. Whether or not these are the only reasons why children differ from adults in anticipation timing tasks awaits further research.

Summary

Anticipation timing involves making a response that coincides with a moving stimulus. Skills such as catching a ball, hitting a ball, intercepting a soccer pass, and tackling a runner in football are all examples of motor skills requiring anticipation timing responses. Five factors that can influence anticipation timing performance have been discussed. These are the degree of predictability of the moving stimulus, the rate of speed of the stimulus, the amount of time available to the performer to preview the stimulus prior to making the response, the complexity of the response, the amount of practice experienced by the performer, and the age of the performer. Each of these factors can be seen by the instructor of motor skills as providing useful information for developing effective instruction for anticipation timing tasks.

Related Readings

Ball, C. T., & Glencross, D. (1985). Developmental differences in a coincident timing task under speed and time constraints. *Human Movement Science, 4,* 1–15.

Christina, R. W. (1976). Proprioception as a basis of anticipatory timing. In G. E. Stelmach (Ed.), *Motor control: Issues and trends* (pp. 187–199). New York: Academic Press.

Christina, R. W. (1977). Skilled motor performance: Anticipatory timing. In B. B. Wolman (Ed.), *International Encyclopedia of Psychiatry, Psychology, Psychoanalysis, and Neurology* (Vol. 10, pp. 241–245). New York: Van Nostrand Reinhold.

Hubbard, A. W., & Seng, C. N. (1954). Visual movements of batters. *Research Quarterly, 25,* 42–57.

Tyldesley, D. A. (1981). Motion prediction and movement control in fast ball games. In I. M. Cockerill & W. W. MacGillivary (Eds.), *Vision and sport* (pp. 91–115). Cheltenham, England: Stanley Thornes.

Whiting, H. T. A. (1969). *Acquiring ball skills.* Philadelphia: Lea & Febiger. (Read chapter 2.)

1. Identify by name and location four major areas of the brain involved in the control of voluntary movement.
2. What are proprioceptors and where are they located? What types of movement information do proprioceptors send to the CNS?
3. How does Eccles present how the different components of the CNS become involved in the process of controlling a voluntary movement?
4. Describe an open-loop and a closed-loop control system. Give a mechanical device example of each type of control system.
5. Describe how a movement would be controlled by a closed-loop system. Describe how a movement would be controlled by an open-loop system.
6. What is a j.n.d.? What implications does the j.n.d. have for aiding our understanding of how we control movement?
7. Describe three methods for investigating the role of proprioception in the control of movement. What conclusions can be made from the results of these investigations about the importance of proprioception for movement control?
8. How has a two-stage model of the role of vision in movement control been demonstrated in aiming movements?
9. What do we know about the length of time it takes to process visual information in performing a motor skill? How have researchers investigated this question?
10. What role does vision play in the control of locomotion? In the control of catching a ball? In the control of batting a ball?
11. Discuss the current view of the nature of the motor program. What is meant by invariant characteristics and parameters of the motor program?
12. What is Fitts' Law? What are the current views about how we control movements in which speed and accuracy are required?
13. What is a coordinative structure? How has the existence of these structures been demonstrated in limb control and in speech control?
14. Define the term *anticipation timing.* Give three examples of anticipation timing tasks that you have experienced.
15. Describe four factors that influence anticipation timing accuracy and indicate how each factor influences this accuracy.

Attention

4

Concept 4.1
An important aspect of attention involves alertness and preparation of the movement control system to produce a response.

Concept 4.2
Attention is related to the idea that we have a limited capacity to process information.

Concept 4.3
Successful motor skill performance requires the ability to select and attend to meaningful information.

Concept 4.1 An important aspect of attention involves alertness and preparation of the movement control system to produce a response

Application

Undoubtedly you have heard, or even said, following a poor shot in tennis or a bad swing at a good pitch in baseball, "I wasn't ready!" These words imply that if you had been "ready," the results would have been quite different. Why is that? What is so important about getting ready for a response that makes it an essential part of successfully performing any motor skill?

In the discussion of this concept, we shall see the role played by alertness and preparation in the outcome of a response. We are not talking here about the long-term preparation that occurs during the days prior to an event but to the final, specific preparation made by the movement control system that occurs immediately prior to a required response. This preparation includes the entire spectrum of motor responses: for example, when the sprinter in track gets into the blocks and prepares to explode out of them in order to get a good start; when the batter in baseball prepares for a pitch; when the golfer prepares to make a particular shot. In each case, preparation during the time immediately preceding the response is critical to the outcome of that response. In the discussion that follows, we will be primarily concerned with what occurs during preparation time that makes it such a critical part of any performance, and what influences alertness and the preparation of a response.

Discussion

Since the earliest days of experimental psychology, the study of attention has been an area of interest to people concerned with understanding human performance. In 1859, Sir William Hamilton conducted studies dealing with attention. Others, such as William Wundt, the "father of experimental psychology," were also interested in the concept of attention. William James provided an early definition of attention in 1890, describing attention as the "focalization, concentration, of consciousness." In 1908, Pillsbury wrote a classic work titled *Attention* in which he related attention to eight psychological concepts such as memory, perception, and the self. E. B. Titchener was also involved in this early investigation of attention, as noted by his book *Lectures on the Elementary Psychology of Feeling and Attention,* published in 1908.

This turn-of-the-century emphasis on attention was soon to wane as the influence of behaviorism became more insistent. The study of attention simply was considered no longer relevant to the understanding of human behavior. A renaissance of attention research occurred, however, when the practical requirements of World War II developed a need to understand human performance on such tasks as radar, where attention had to be maintained over long

periods of time. Other factors have also been attributed to the revival of attention study, such as interest in the reticular formation of the brain stem and the trend toward considering human performance from the standpoint of information processing.

During the renewed investigations of attention, interest was directed toward what occurred immediately prior to making a response. This aspect of the study of the concept of attention, sometimes referred to as the study of *alertness,* involves what is considered in much of the research dealing with this topic as *signal preparation.* This term developed from the typical experimental approach taken to study response preparation, which involved subjects' responding in a predetermined fashion to a visual or auditory signal. By manipulating conditions immediately prior to the signal or by manipulating the characteristics of the signal itself, researchers were able to investigate influences on a subject's preparation to respond to a signal.

Attention as Alertness and Response Preparation

In this discussion, the primary focus will be on preparing the motor response system to produce a required voluntary movement. An important element of this preparation is being alert to detect the signal indicating that the response should be initiated. Of particular interest in this discussion is what happens during the preparation time before and after the signal to respond occurs, just prior to the response. Also of interest will be the various factors that have been shown to influence alertness and the amount of time needed to prepare a response.

To study alertness and the preparation of a response, researchers have typically used reaction time, or RT, experimental paradigms in their investigations. Because RT is the amount of time between the onset of a signal to respond and the initiation of that response, RT seems a good measure on which to base inferences about response preparation. As you will see in various experiments considered in this discussion, the typical approach used by experimenters to investigate questions related to alertness and response preparation is to observe the effect on RT of manipulating some experimental variable, such as the complexity of the movement that must be made or the number of response choices possible. The logical inference made from these manipulations is that if RT is longer under one condition than under another, then the first condition requires more preparation. By skillfully manipulating appropriate experimental variables, researchers are able to determine not only what variables influence response preparation but also what occurs during that preparation. Thus, it is important to consider RT as a measure of response preparation. Note, however, that RT can be used as a measure of other processes involved in learning and performance, which you will see in other parts of this text. However, in the context of preparing a motor response, RT provides a useful means of investigating response preparation.

The Need for Alertness and Time to Prepare a Response

An important assumption regarding the investigation of response preparation is that preparation takes time. If more preparation is needed in certain circumstances than others, then more time will be required to make that preparation. Thus, RT is used as a measure of response preparation. An important question that you might ask is, On what basis is this assumption made? How do we know that preparing to make a response takes time and that this amount of time is influenced by the amount of preparation required?

You have already been introduced to some evidence supporting this assumption. In the discussion of Concept 3.4, the experiment by Henry and Rogers (1960) showed that RT increased as a function of the complexity of the rapid response. That is, when a simple response had to be made to a signal, in this case simply lifting the finger off a telegraph key, the RT was shorter than when a more complex response had to be made, such as making a three-component rapid movement. From these results, Henry and Rogers inferred that the preparation required for a rapid response to a signal is dependent on the complexity of the response that must be made.

However, two other, more basic, approaches provide a basis for the assumption that preparing for a response takes time. Each approach also manipulates a variable and observes the effect of manipulation on RT. In the first approach, the variables of interest are whether or not there is a warning signal before the "go" signal, and the length of time between the warning signal (if there is one) and the "go" signal. In the second approach, the variable of interest is what occurs between the "go" signal and the initiation of the required response.

The RT foreperiod. The time interval between a warning signal and the "go" signal is called the *foreperiod*. This time interval is of interest in the study of alertness and response preparation because it is when the individual initially prepares to respond. Two questions are of interest with regard to this interval. First, what happens to RT if there is no warning signal, thereby effectively eliminating a foreperiod? Second, what happens to RT if the length of the foreperiods vary? We will consider the evidence that exists to answer these questions and what these answers mean with respect to response preparation.

The influence on RT of the use of a warning signal was a popular topic in the first half of this century. By 1954, Teichner, in a review of RT research, concluded that the use of a warning, or "ready," signal prior to the onset of the "go" signal yields faster RTs than does the omission of such a preparatory signal. Also, for choice RT situations, the occurrence of a warning signal not only leads to faster RTs, it also leads to more accurate responses to the "go" signal.

What is the benefit of the warning signal? Primarily, it alerts the individual to prepare for the "go" signal. If the warning signal is not provided, then RT increases, indicating that the individual was not fully prepared to respond to the "go" signal. Thus, alertness of the individual is an important

part of the preparation to respond. Without sufficient alertness, preparation will not occur as effectively and efficiently as it would otherwise. Another important alertness issue will be considered later in this discussion. That issue concerns a focus contrary to our current one and involves the effect of alertness when attention must be maintained over long periods. For now, however, the focus is on alertness as an important factor in preparing to respond to an imminent signal, as in any RT task situation.

The second question related to the RT foreperiod concerns foreperiod length. Is there an optimal foreperiod length that relates to optimal RT performance? This question is particularly relevant to the assumption concerning the need for time to prepare a response. Changes in RT as a function of changes in the RT foreperiod would indicate that preparation time needed to respond to a signal is indeed important. This question is also particularly relevant in many sport situations where an athlete must hold a prepared response until a signal to respond occurs, such as in a swimming or track start.

Research investigating this question can be traced back to the early part of this century. For example, in 1914, Woodrow used foreperiods ranging from 1 to 24 seconds for three subjects in a simple RT situation. The results indicated that maximum preparation was not reached in much less than 2 seconds, and was not maintained much longer than 4 seconds. This 2- to 4-second range has been generally accepted as reflecting the minimum and optimal signal preparation time. There is other evidence which indicates a 1- to 2-second minimum.

The results of the study by Woodrow, as well as other similar investigations, indicate the need to regard the time required to prepare for a signal as a continuum. This continuum implies that there is a minimum amount of time necessary for signal preparation as well as a maximum period of time. Between those extremes is the optimal amount of time during which the signal should occur for the best response. This continuum is presented in Figure 4.1–1. Following a warning or ready signal, if the signal to respond occurs too early, that is, before the optimal range of time, then the individual will not have had sufficient time to prepare to respond. If the signal occurs after the optimal time range, then the individual has been waiting too long, and his or her ability to respond is less than it would have been during the optimal time range. Figure 4.1–1 represents a general time line.

The exact amounts of time that should be used on this time line will vary according to the motor task associated with it. For example, a simple RT response made with a hand can be made with a shorter foreperiod than if the response is made with the foot. Also, simple RT responses can be made with a shorter foreperiod than a choice RT response. In general, however, it appears that the minimum foreperiod length is between 0.5 and 2 seconds. The maximum time should be about 4 seconds. Thus the optimal range of time would be from approximately 0.5 to 4 seconds.

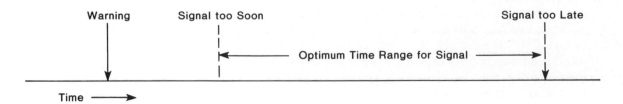

Warning   Signal too Soon   Signal too Late

|← ——— Optimum Time Range for Signal ——— →|

Time ——→

Figure 4.1-1
A time line
showing a
continuum of time
for the occurrence
of a response signal
to follow a warning
signal to ensure
optimal readiness to
respond. The actual
amounts of time
along this
continuum should
be considered as
task-specific.

A good example of the application of this optimal time for signal preparation principle can be seen in swimming- and track-start examples mentioned earlier. In these sports starters in the various events are instructed to adjust the time span between giving the ready signal and firing the gun to a range of between 1 and 3 or 4 seconds. This range fits very nicely into the RT signal preparation optimal time range that we have proposed based on the research literature.

The psychological refractory period (PRP). Another way to demonstrate that time is needed to prepare a response is by considering the *psychological refractory period* (*PRP*). The term *refractory* is synonymous with the term *delay*. The PRP can be thought of as a delay period during which a planned response seems to be "put on hold" while another response is being executed. Although there are different views of why the PRP occurs (see Gottsdanker, 1979, 1980, for a review of these), there is little disagreement that the PRP demonstrates that some minimal amount of time is needed to prepare a motor response.

Figure 4.1–2 illustrates the PRP in a situation where two different responses must be made to two different signals. However, rather than the signals' occurring simultaneously, one occurs just after the other. The subject in this situation is told to respond as quickly as possible to the first signal, press a button when the light goes on and also to respond as quickly as possible to the second signal (say "bop" into the microphone when the buzzer sounds). If the response to the buzzer in this situation is compared to the response to the buzzer when another preceding response has not been required, then the PRP can be seen. The RT for the buzzer signal will be longer when a response has to be made immediately prior to it than when no previous response is required. This extra time, or delay, is the PRP.

An interesting application of the value of the PRP in a sport situation involves faking. For example, suppose a basketball player is dribbling the ball and is confronted by a defensive player in a one-on-one situation. A common strategy to get around the defensive player is to use a head fake by moving the head in the opposite direction the body will go. If done properly, the defensive player will initiate a response to go in the direction the head indicates. However, upon seeing the offensive player's body actually going in the other direction, the defensive player must initiate a second response to go in the opposite direction. The advantage gained by the offensive player in this situation is the extra time, the PRP, required to initiate a second response after an initial one was already in progress.

176   **The Learner**

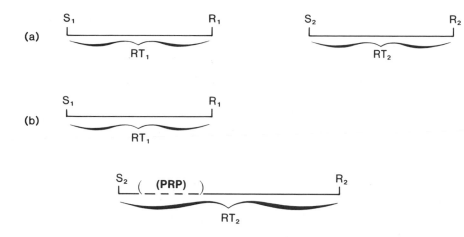

(a)

S_1 R_1

RT_1

S_2 R_2

RT_2

(b)

S_1 R_1

RT_1

S_2 (_ (PRP) _) R_2

RT_2

Figure 4.1-2
The psychological refractory period. (a) The RTs for the S_1 (light)-R_1 (button press) and the S_2 (buzzer)-R_2 (vocal response) conditions when performed separately. (b) The effect on RT for the S_2-R_2 condition when S_2 arrives during the RT interval for the S_1-R_1 condition. RT_2 is typically lengthened by the amount of time between the onset of S_2 and the completion of R_1. This extra time is shown by the dashed line and indicates the PRP.

Two important characteristics of the PRP provide some additional insight into the faking example. First, the PRP will not be demonstrated if the second stimulus occurs after a period of time that is the RT for the first stimulus. For the fake, this suggests that it is important that the "real" move be made quickly after the fake has been given. If it is not, the opponent can easily prepare and initiate the appropriate response to defend the real move.

Second, the PRP will not occur if the first signal is not considered important and the subject only pays attention to the second signal. The implication for the fake should be obvious here. If the fake is not viewed by the defender as being an indication of the real move, then the fake will not be effective. The defender will simply ignore the fake and wait to respond to the real move.

One way to realize that different events occur during the preparation of a response is to *fractionate* an EMG recording of the RT interval. (You were introduced to this in Concept 1.2.) As you can see in Figure 4.1–3, the EMG signal can be divided, or fractionated, into two distinct parts. The first part is called the *premotor time,* although it also has been referred to as electromechanical delay. Note that the EMG signal has not changed much from what it was like prior to the onset of the stimulus. However, shortly after the onset of the stimulus, the EMG signal shows a rapid increase in electrical activity. This indicates that the motor neurons are firing and the muscle is preparing to contract even though no observable, physical response has yet occurred. This period of time is called the *motor time.* It is the period of increased EMG activity preceding the observable response, which begins at the point marked response.

From this fractionation researchers have inferred that the premotor time indicates perceptual or cognitive processing of the stimulus information. It seems reasonable to consider that if motor program preparation is occurring during the RT interval, as discussed in Concept 3.2, this preparation would

Fractionating RT

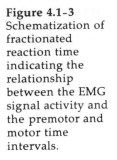
Figure 4.1-3
Schematization of fractionated reaction time indicating the relationship between the EMG signal activity and the premotor and motor time intervals.

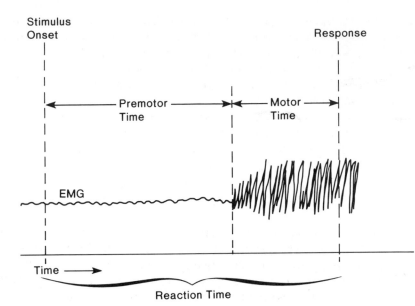

occur during this time. The motor time, on the other hand, begins the actual motor output phase of a response. During this time, the specific muscles involved in the action are firing and preparing to begin the observable movement.

Some researchers have attempted to determine if changes in RT that result as a function of various response characteristics are due primarily to changes in premotor time, motor time, or both. For example, Christina and Rose (1985) reported that the changes in RT due to increases in *response complexity,* such as those reported by Henry and Rogers (1960), were reflected in increases in premotor time. For a two-part arm movement, premotor time increased an average of 19 msec over that for a one-part arm movement, while motor time increased only 3 msec. In an experiment investigating movement *response durations,* Siegel (1986) found that while RT increased linearly as response durations increased from 150, 300, 600, to 1,200 msec, premotor time also increased linearly. Motor time, on the other hand, remained the same until the response duration became 1200 msec, then motor time showed a slight increase. Premotor time was also shown to be responsible for RT increases due to increases in the velocity of the required movement (Sheridan, 1984). However, Carlton, Carlton, and Newell (1987) found that both premotor and motor time changes resulted from altering *force-related characteristics* of the response. Thus, certain response characteristics primarily influence the more perceptual-cognitive component of RT whereas others affect this component as well as the more peripheral, motor component.

Thus, fractionating RT is a useful procedure for gaining insight into the locus of preparation activity. For example, for those who advocate that preparation of a response involves programming activity involving central processing, it is important to show that factors that should require more programming time influence premotor time during the RT interval. However, our current knowledge about the processes involved in response preparation is such that more research is needed, especially research involving RT fractionation so that more definitive conclusions can be made concerning what occurs during the RT interval. By developing appropriate manipulation of response and situation characteristics and then observing the influence of these manipulations on the components of RT, researchers will be able to provide more insight into response preparation activity.

As you are undoubtedly aware by now, numerous factors influence the amount of time required to prepare a response. This point has been alluded to in discussions of motor program preparation in Concept 3.2 and in the preceding section on fractionating RT. In this section, we will consider several of these factors in more detail. As you will see, factors related to characteristics of the individual, the task, and the response situation all influence the amount of time taken to prepare a response when that response must be made as rapidly as possible to a given signal. It is important to remember that although it can be demonstrated that various factors influence RT, we do not need to conclude that this influence necessarily reflects motor program preparation. Although such a conclusion has been made with regard to several of these factors, as discussed in Concept 3.2, there is some debate concerning whether or not motor program preparation must be inferred from changes in RT. (See Carlton, Carlton, & Newell, 1987, and Kelso, 1984, for discussions about these differing views.)

Factors Influencing Response Preparation Time

However, regardless of what the RT changes represent in terms of processes causing such changes, it is important to be aware of what factors alter the amount of time required to prepare a response. It should be apparent from the discussion thus far that knowledge of these factors has implications for theoretical issues related to the preparation of a motor response. However, such knowledge also has important implications for practical applications. For example, if you know that a particular factor can increase the RT associated with making a response, then it may be possible to appropriately alter the situation to enable the person to respond more quickly than he or she might if the situation had not been altered. What follows, then, is a discussion of several factors that influence the amount of time needed to prepare to make a motor response to a signal.

The arousal level of the performer. One of the most significant factors related to the individual that influences response preparation is his or her arousal level.

Figure 4.1-4
Diagram illustrating the inverted-U prediction of performance level for different levels of activation or arousal according to the Yerkes-Dodson Law.

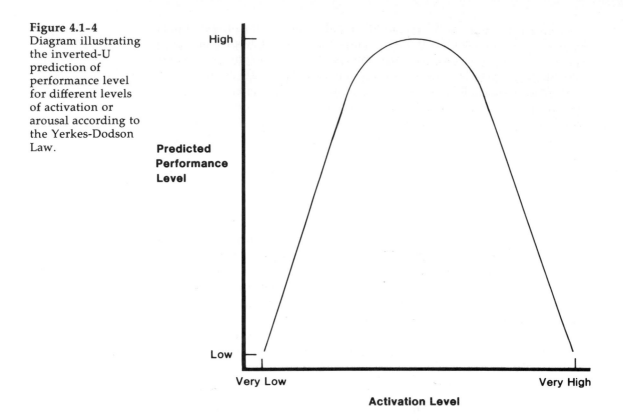

Arousal level can be thought of as the energy level of the individual at the time of the performance of a task. Terms such as *anxiety* or *activation* are often used synonymously with *arousal*. Levels of arousal can range from very low, as in sleep, to very high, as in an extremely energized or highly frenetic state.

The arousal level of the individual is related to the quality of his or her performance. This relationship, based on research by Yerkes and Dodson (1908), can be described by an inverted U, as seen in Figure 4.1–4. This inverted-U relationship, sometimes referred to as the Yerkes-Dodson Law, indicates that an individual's arousal level can be too low or too high to produce his or her best performance on a task. Each of these extremes yields negative performance results. We will consider this relationship more extensively in Chapter 10 where motivation is discussed. For the present, we will limit our interest in this relationship to how it relates to response preparation.

Because the specific details about an upcoming response are perceived and added to the generalized motor program during response preparation, the arousal state of the individual is a critical factor. Daniel Kahneman (1973) has indicated that levels of arousal that are too low or too high reduce the individual's capability to receive and effectively use information necessary to

perform a task as optimally as possible, a point that will be discussed more extensively in Concept 4.2. The actual optimal level of arousal for a given task varies according to the characteristics of the task. For tasks that are very complex, that is, that have many component parts, such as the quarterback's role in carrying out an option play, the optimal level of arousal is lower than for a less complex task, such as the defensive tackle's task in stopping a running back coming through the line. The important point for this discussion is that if the preparation of a response is to be effective, then the arousal level of the individual must be optimal for the task to be performed.

For the teacher or coach, the inverted-U relationship between the performer's arousal level and the effectiveness of response preparation can be a useful concept. Teachers are often confronted with situations in which a student does not seem to be able to perform a skill effectively because he or she is missing some detail of the performance. For example, when performing a forward roll, a student may not be tucking the chin next to the top of his or her chest. While this seems like a minor detail, it can have a major effect on the outcome of the forward roll. What may be occurring is that performing this stunt creates such an increased anxiety state in the student that this "detail" never gets prepared in the plan of action for performing the roll. If the teacher is attentive to this situation, he or she can take steps to reduce the anxiety and direct the student's attention to this detail of the skill.

Reaction time vs. movement time set. Throughout this discussion, many of the response situations involve a goal of moving as fast as possible when the signal to move occurs. In these situations, there are two important components of the total response, the RT and the movement time (MT). Because the amount of time taken to produce these two components is essentially independent (an important point that will be discussed in Concept 6.2), it is possible to influence RT by consciously attending either to reacting to the signal as fast as possible or to moving as fast as possible. These two different response strategies have been called a *sensory set* and a *motor set,* respectively.

The first evidence to show that having either a sensory or a motor set would differentially influence RT was offered by Henry (1961). However, because Henry's results were based on the subjects' opinions of what their set was for a particular trial, Christina (1973) sought to replicate these results by imposing on subjects a sensory or a motor set. The task required the subject to respond as quickly as possible to a buzzer by moving the index finger of the right hand to four different response keys that were positioned at different locations on a response panel. The sensory set group was told to focus attention on the sound of the buzzer but to move off the response key as fast as possible. The motor set group was told to focus on moving as fast as possible. Results showed that RT was affected; the sensory set group showed a 20-msec faster RT than the motor set group. Interestingly, MT for the two groups was not

statistically different. Thus, focusing attention on the reaction signal and allowing the movement to happen naturally shortened the preparation time required and did not penalize movement speed, as the overall response time was faster for the sensory set group.

An obvious application of Christina's results is in sport situations where a rapid movement must be made in response to a signal, as in track or swimming. But, do these results generalize to these nonlaboratory situations? To investigate this question, Jongsma, Elliott, and Lee (1987) compared sensory and motor set for a sprint start in track. They also considered the influence of experience. Half the subjects had at least 8 years of sprinting experience and half had only a 6-week track class at a university. To measure RT, a pressure-sensitive switch was embedded in the rear foot starting block. MT was measured as the time from release of this switch until a photo-electric light beam was broken 1.5 meters from the starting line. Subjects were given 10 trials on which they were to use their normal start, 10 trials with a sensory set, and 10 trials with a motor set.

Results of this experiment showed that for both novices and experienced sprinters, RT was fastest for the sensory set condition. The novices had a 292-msec RT for their preferred set, a 308-msec RT for the motor set, and a 285-msec RT for the sensory set. Thus, there was a 7-msec advantage for the sensory set over their preferred set, and a 23-msec advantage over the motor set. For the experienced sprinters, the preferred set yielded a 259-msec RT, while the motor set had a 261-msec RT and the sensory set had a 252-msec RT. Again, the advantage of the sensory set was small as it was only 7 msec and 9 msec faster than the motor and preferred set, respectively. Although these times were not statistically different, they are worth noting, however, as the set time differences for the novices are in line with those reported by Christina. The smaller differences observed for the experienced sprinters is a good example of the effect of practice on response preparation, which will be discussed later.

The number of stimulus-response choices. One of the characteristics of the task to be performed that will influence response preparation is the number of decision alternatives, or choices, that are possible before the required response is known. For example, a racquetball player must prepare to respond to a variety of possible serves while the swimmer must prepare to respond to only one signal to go. As these examples suggest, the preparation demands for motor skills vary as the number of possible responses that can be made in response to the stimulus varies.

In the discussion of Concept 1.2, you saw that RT increases according to the number of stimulus or response choices. The fastest RTs occur in a simple RT situation, where there is only one stimulus and one response. RT slows down when more than one stimulus and more than one response are

possible, as in the choice RT situation. This demonstrates how the response preparation demand increases as the amount of information that must be processed to make a response increases.

The RT increase in a choice situation is such a stable effect that a law, i.e., a reliable prediction, has been developed to predict the RT when the number of stimulus response choices is known. This law, known as *Hick's Law* (Hick, 1952), states that RT will increase logarithmically as the number of stimulus-response choices increases. The equation that describes this law is $RT = K \log_2 (N + 1)$, where K is a constant, which is simple RT in most cases, and N equals the number of possible choices. This means that RT increases linearly as the number of stimulus-choice alternatives increases. The magnitude of this increase can be mathematically predicted by applying Hick's equation.

in the information transmitted by the possible choices, rather than to only the number of choice alternatives. Log_2 is known as a *bit* in information theory and represents a choice between two equally likely alternatives. Thus, a 1-bit decision involves two alternatives, a 2-bit decision involves four alternatives, a 3-bit decision involves eight choices, and so on. The number of bits indicates the least number of "yes/no" decisions that could be made to solve the problem created by the number of choices involved. For example, if there were eight choices possible in a situation, the first decision would be based on the answer to "Is the correct choice in this half of the possible choices?" Regardless if the answer is yes or no, you now have reduced the possible choices to four. You would then ask the same question again in reference to one-half of these remaining possible choices to make the second decision. This answer reduces the possible choices to two. For the third decision, you ask the question that will give you the correct choice, "Is it this one?" Again, regardless of whether the answer is yes or no, you will know the correct choice. In this way, you have determined the correct choice out of a possible eight-choice set with only three yes/no questions, hence a 3-bit decision situation.

Relating the choice RT situation to information theory was an important part of Hick's work. Previously, the increase in RT was considered related only to the number of stimulus alternatives. By relating the choice situation to information theory, Hick expanded the application of this law to variables other than the number of choices. For example, the law also holds when the number of alternatives are held constant but probabilities of either response occurring on a given trial are varied. For example, in an experiment by Fitts, Peterson, and Wolpe (1963), a nine-choice RT situation was used in which one stimulus was designated as occurring more frequently (with a .94 probability) than the other eight. The results showed that for the frequently occurring stimulus, RT averaged 280 msec while the others averaged 450 msec. We will address this probability influence on RT later in this discussion.

One of the applications of Hick's Law to sport skills can be related to situations in which an individual has several options of what to do, depending

on what occurs in a situation. For example, suppose a football quarterback is running an option play and has the choice of handing off to a back, keeping the ball and running, or running and pitching out. In this situation, there are three response alternatives. How can the situation be structured to reduce the total possible stimulus conditions? If the quarterback is not given very specific "keys" to watch for in the defense, then there will be an extremely large number of possible choices on which he can base his response. This will result in the need for greatly increased preparation time, which will result in the play's having little chance for success. The implication for the coach is to tell the quarterback what specific information to look for and to make the response accordingly.

Stimulus-response compatibility. Another factor that will influence the amount of preparation time in a reaction time task concerns the relationship between the stimulus and response choices. In fact, this factor is so influential that it is related to how likely Hick's Law will apply to the situation. The rule of thumb here is that RT will be faster as the stimulus-response relationship becomes more compatible; conversely, RT will be slower as this relationship becomes less compatible. A highly compatible situation would be one where the stimulus indicator on a panel and the response mechanism are part of the same device. For example, if a button is to be depressed when it lights up, then the stimulus and response mechanisms are highly compatible and RTs will be faster than if the stimulus is a light in a different location than the response device.

The spatial arrangement relationship between the stimulus and response devices is the most typical way of considering stimulus-response compatibility. Here, for example, consider a three-choice situation in which illumination of one of three lights indicates that one of three buttons should be depressed. Now, if the lights and buttons are arranged horizontally, this situation is more compatible than if the lights are vertical and the buttons are horizontal. Also, if both lights and buttons are arranged horizontally and both relate to each other so that the first light to the left corresponds to a response for the left-most button, this situation is more compatible than if the far right button was the response for the far left light. In each of these situations, the more compatible relationship would lead to faster RTs than the less compatible situation. Also, as compatibility decreases, the number of choice errors will increase (see Fitts & Seeger, 1953).

In terms of the relationship between stimulus-response compatibility and Hick's Law, it has been shown that when the stimulus and response are highly compatible, such as being a part of the same mechanism, Hick's Law will not apply. In fact, Fitts and Posner (1967) reported after reviewing several studies concerning this issue, that anything tending to decrease the spatial compatibility between the stimulus and its corresponding response will increase the slope of the Hick's Law relationship between number of alternatives and RT. Hick, for example, used lights as stimuli and key presses for responses and

provided support for the lawful relationship, whereas Leonard (1959) had the response key vibrate as the stimulus and found no increase in RT as the number of choices increased.

The stimulus-response compatibility influence on response preparation is an important one when the design of equipment or presentation of instructions is provided. For example, when you give instructions, especially if you use visual aids or demonstration, consider how compatible what you show the student is with the required response. The more translation that must be made from what is seen to what must be done, the more preparation time will be required to make the response. And, in the process, especially with a beginner, there is an increased possibility of errors being made as the translation may be incorrect.

The predictability of the stimulus. Many times in sport we hear the comment that a player "telegraphed" a move. By this, the speaker means that the responding player had a lot of time to prepare an appropriate response because the other player let his or her response be known in advance of its actual occurrence. This often occurs in baseball when a pitcher "telegraphs" a pitch by only throwing a certain pitch with a unique motion. It can also occur in other sports where one player gains an advantage by increased preparation time and another has very little preparation time.

As you saw in the discussion of anticipation timing (Concept 3.5), the more predictable a stimulus, the faster and more accurately a person can make a response. This increase in accuracy is undoubtedly related to having more time to make fewer decisions about the response than would otherwise be possible. Our baseball example fits well here. If a ball is pitched at 90 mph, it will take approximately 0.4 second to reach the plate. To be successful, the batter typically has 0.15 second of this time to start a swing and get the bat to make contact with the ball. This allows only 0.25 second for decision making about whether or not to swing and, if the decision is to swing, what swing should be made. Of that 0.25 second, probably only 0.1 to 0.15 second can realistically be allotted to conscious decision making. The obvious advantage of being able early in the pitch to know what the ball will do during its flight is that the batter will have more time to make the appropriate decisions necessary to hit the ball.

Research that has demonstrated the relationship between the predictability of a stimulus and response preparation time and accuracy has typically followed a choice-RT arrangement in which the subjects are provided advance information about which stimulus will appear. This experimental procedure, popularized by the work of David Rosenbaum (1980), is called the *precuing technique*. One of the results of this procedure has been to demonstrate the benefit gained in RT by receiving any amount of advanced information about the upcoming response.

Figure 4.1-5
Response panel
used in the
Rosenbaum
precuing
experiments.

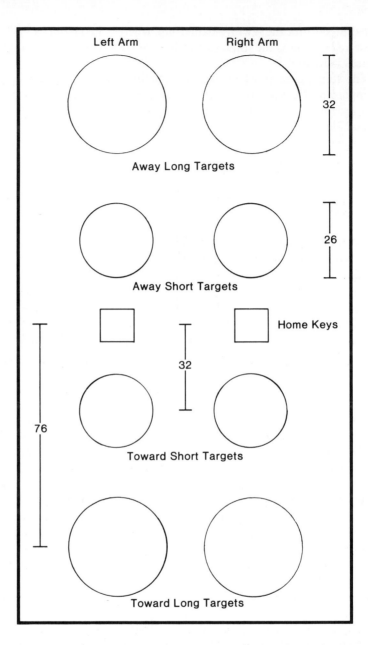

A discussion of the precuing technique by Rosenbaum (1983) reveals some of the history, rationale, procedures, and inferences that are possible using this experimental technique. We will concern ourselves only with the basic procedures used and how these procedures yield results that we can use to determine the role of advance information in aiding a response. Figure 4.1–5 illustrates the response panel used in the experiments by Rosenbaum. The

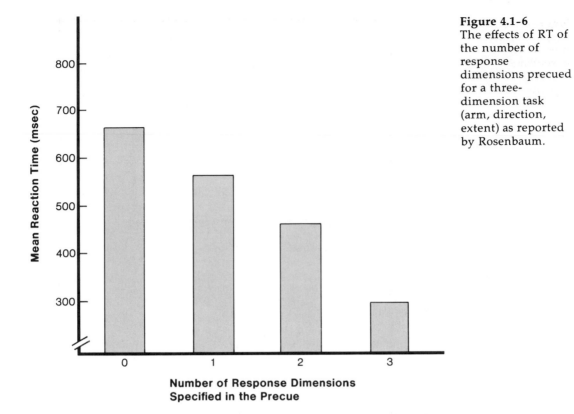

Figure 4.1-6
The effects of RT of the number of response dimensions precued for a three-dimension task (arm, direction, extent) as reported by Rosenbaum.

squares in the center are the "home" buttons for the subject's two index fingers. The circles represent the target buttons. The response to be made contained three dimensions: the *arm* to move (left or right); the *direction* to move (away or toward the body); and the *extent* of the movement (short or long). The subject observed a monitor. When a colored dot appeared, the subject was required to move the correct arm as rapidly as possible from the home button to the target that was marked with the corresponding colored dot shown on the monitor. Prior to the signal to move, that is, the appearance of the colored dot on the screen, the subject could receive advanced information (the precue) that indicated something about the upcoming response. The subject could receive a precue about none, one, two, or all three of the dimensions of the response.

The results of this precuing procedure are presented in Figure 4.1–6. As you might expect, the fastest RT occurred when all three dimensions were precued. This should be no surprise because the three-choice RT situation was reduced to a simple RT situation. Similarly, as the number of precued dimensions was decreased, the RT increased. The benefit of the precue information was to allow the subjects to prepare the precued dimension(s) in advance of the "go" signal and then only have to prepare the remaining dimensions after the "go" signal.

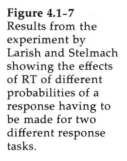

Figure 4.1-7
Results from the experiment by Larish and Stelmach showing the effects of RT of different probabilities of a response having to be made for two different response tasks.

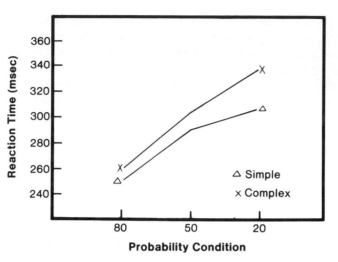

An interesting effect can be seen in research studies where advance information is provided but that information may not be accurate. If, for example, in the task used in the Rosenbaum study, the subject had been given the precue "right arm" and the response signal actually indicated "left arm," what would the result have been? Typically, the result will depend on the *probability* of the advance information's being correct. If the precue has only a 50–50 chance of being correct, the performer will ignore it and respond as if no precue had been given. However, if there is an 80% chance that the precue will be correct, the performer will *bias* his or her response to make the response indicated by the precue.

What will happen when the performer biases a response according to the precue and the response signal requires the opposite response? In other words, what is the price of preparing the wrong response? Figure 4.1–7 illustrates the answer to this question. What you see are the results from an experiment by Larish and Stelmach (1982) where subjects were required to make a rapid movement with the correct hand from a home key to one of two targets 40 cm away. Advance information was provided about which target would be the response target. However, this information was correct 20%, 50%, or 80% of the time. Figure 4.1–7 shows the *cost-benefit tradeoff* associated with this situation. When there was a 50–50 chance (50% correct condition) of the precue's being correct, subjects responded as if the task were a two-choice RT task. In other words, they basically ignored the advance information. However, in the 80–20 condition, subjects obviously biased their response to move in the direction of the precued direction. When they were correct, there was a benefit as their RTs were *faster* than if they had not biased their response. However, if they were wrong (the 20% case), there was a cost paid as now their RT was *slower* than in the 50–50 condition.

In many physical activities, we find ourselves biasing our responses by expecting to have to produce one particular response rather than some other possible one. For example, if a basketball player knows that the player he or she is defending goes to the right to make a shot only on rare occasions, the defensive player will undoubtedly bias his or her anticipated movement by "cheating" to defend moves to the left. In racquet sports, players who consistently hit to one side of the court will find their opponents "cheating" to that side. In these examples, the players have found that an advantage can be gained by "playing the percentages" and biasing their expectancies. If they are right, the appropriate response can be made faster than otherwise would be possible. However, this is done with the possibility of being wrong. In this case, the appropriate response will take longer to initiate than if no biasing had occurred.

Response complexity. You were introduced to the effect of movement response complexity in Concept 3.2 when the experiment by Henry and Rogers (1960) was discussed in connection with the motor program concept. Recall that in this experiment, Henry and Rogers showed that RT increased from 165 msec for a simple finger lift from a telegraph key response to 199 msec for a situation requiring a movement from the key to grab a ball, and to 212 msec for a three-part movement. Thus, as the response required more component parts, the RT, or amount of preparation time, increased. Numerous other experiments have confirmed these findings since that time (e.g., Anson, 1982; Christina & Rose, 1985; Fischman, 1984; Glencross, 1973).

Of particular interest in the results concerning the effect of movement complexity on RT has been determining if, in fact, the key factor is the number of parts involved in the movement response. This question bears consideration if you think about the characteristics of two different complex responses. The more complex response may have more component parts to it, but it will also require more time to carry out. Also, the more complex response may require the person to move a greater total distance, and there may be a host of other possible differences as well. To address this issue and to test the Henry and Rogers conclusion that complexity is based on the number of parts to the movement, Christina and colleagues at Penn State University (Christina, Fischman, Vercruyssen, & Anson, 1982; Christina, Fischman, Lambert, & Moore, 1985; Fischman, 1985) have carried out a series of experiments in which various parameters of the movement responses have been manipulated, in addition to the number of parts. As a result of these manipulations the key variable in the RT increase in the Henry and Rogers task was the number of parts to the movement, as Henry and Rogers contended.

Practice. One of the most effective means of reducing the amount of time required to prepare a motor response is by extended practice of the response. For example, Norrie (1967) had subjects practice a three-part rapid arm

movement response that involved two changes of direction. She found that only 50 trials of practice reduced the RT approximately 32 msec, from an average of 252 msec on the first 10 trials to an average of 220 msec on the last 10 trials.

Practice also can eliminate the effect of many factors discussed so far that affect response preparation time. For example, it has been consistently shown that the influence of the number of stimulus choices described by Hick's Law can be reduced by practice. Mowbray (Mowbray, 1960; Mowbray & Rhoades, 1959) has reported that the RT for a four-choice situation can be reduced to the RT for a two-choice situation after extensive practice. In fact, the effect of practice becomes even more pronounced as the number of choice alternatives increases (see Teichner & Krebs, 1974). Also, the effects of stimulus-response incompatibility on RT can be reduced by practicing the incompatible condition to the point that the RT becomes comparable to that of an unpracticed compatible situation (see Duncan, 1977).

Thus, it appears that practice is an important factor in influencing response preparation time. What does practice do that reduces this time demand? One possibility is that it reduces uncertainty in situations where much preparation time is due to translating unfamiliar stimuli or unfamiliar stimulus-response relationships. This possibility seems especially likely in the stimulus-response compatibility situation. By practicing, the person can overcome the preparation demands caused by the translation or confusion effects that were a part of the task initially. Another benefit of practice is that programming requirements are reduced as the response becomes better organized into larger coordinative structures. Because much of early practice involves developing the appropriate coordination of muscle, joint, and limb action, preparation time demands are greater than later in practice after coordination demands are reduced.

Maintaining Alertness

Earlier you saw that for a given response there is an amount of time between the "ready" signal and the "go" signal after which a person will not be at optimal readiness to respond to the "go" signal. Although this situation is a problem of maintaining response preparation, there is another preparation maintenance problem to consider. This problem concerns the situation in which a person must respond quickly and accurately to stimuli that occur very infrequently during extended periods. This specific preparation maintenance situation is called *vigilance* in the research literature and is probably more accurately a case of maintaining alertness to detect stimuli, rather than a case of maintaining the preparation of a response. In vigilance situations, the response is typically performed if the stimulus has been detected. The problem, however, is to detect the stimulus. Thus, the individual must maintain alertness to know when the required response must be made.

Examples of vigilance situations are relatively common in a variety of motor skill performance contexts. A common example involves monitoring a

radar scope and responding to a detected signal. Another is seen in a factory setting in which a worker must detect a defective product and remove it from the assembly line. Driving a car along an uncrowded freeway can become a vigilance task if a person drives for an extended time. Engaging in a repetitive motor skill drill can become a vigilance task, especially if the person has been instructed to detect and correct a specific error that occurs rather infrequently during the drill. Being a lifeguard at a pool or beach can be a vigilance problem as there are very infrequent situations requiring a response during a long shift on duty. Medical personnel are often required to work long hours and still be able to correctly identify symptoms of health problems. Sport settings involve a number of vigilance situations, such as a baseball outfielder who must maintain alertness throughout an inning in the field but who may have only one ball hit his or her way, despite the many pitches thrown. Given these many situations in which vigilance maintenance is essential for successful performance of a task, it is important to develop a better understanding of the factors that influence vigilance decrements and how these decrements can be reduced.

Evidence for vigilance decrements. Research concerned with vigilance developed during World War II and shortly thereafter. The need for this research became apparent when it was common practice to have radar observers working for several hours at a time. During this time, attention had to be maintained so that any important signal on the radar screen was reported. Researchers want to know how effectively these radar observers could perform their task over such an extended period of time. This research has not only provided practical information to aid in establishing productive working practices for jobs requiring long periods of attention maintenance, it has also provided useful information that helps us understand human information-processing characteristics.

Most of the vigilance experiments followed similar procedures. Subjects were required to watch something similar to a radar screen. At rare intervals, a certain designated signal appeared. The subject's task was to report when a signal was noticed. The first of these vigilance studies was conducted by a British psychologist, N. H. Mackworth, during World War II (see Mackworth, 1956). The British military was primarily interested in problems associated with detecting submarines by radar from an airplane. In this study, the task involved watching a pointer moving around a clock face in one-second jumps that would sometimes make double jumps, about 24 per hour. These double jumps were to be reported by the subjects. Mackworth's study determined that during a two-hour work interval, the subjects' ability to detect the jumps markedly decreased each half hour.

Other vigilance studies have tried to determine what factors affect the ability to maintain attention. One example is a study by Wilkinson (1963). A primary concern in this study was the effect of lack of sleep, or sleep deprivation, on a task requiring attention over a long period of time (see Figure 4.1–8). The assignment was a serial reaction time task, where the subject was

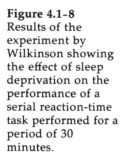

Figure 4.1-8
Results of the experiment by Wilkinson showing the effect of sleep deprivation on the performance of a serial reaction-time task performed for a period of 30 minutes.

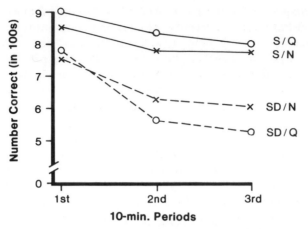

required to tap a series of targets in a certain order as specified by a series of lights. Five lights defined the series, and they were programmed to appear in various orders. This task was performed for 30 minutes by each subject. Subjects were either awake for 32 hours prior to the experiment, or they had normal sleep during that time. During the experiment, they were in conditions of either a low, constant "white" noise, like soft radio static, or quiet. Results showed that the most errors were committed by subjects who had been deprived of sleep and who performed the experiment in the quiet situation (SD/Q). Subjects who had had normal sleep and performed in the quiet situation S/Q had the fewest errors by the end of the 30-minute testing period. It is interesting to note in Figure 4.1–8 that the quiet experimental condition produced both the most and fewest errors by the end of the testing period. But with sleep deprivation, noise helped, whereas with normal sleep, the noise hindered performance.

Accounting for vigilance decrement. What do experiments like those we have just considered tell us about why people experience a loss in alertness over time? If that loss is a function of the amount of continuous time spent concentrating on a task, then perhaps we can suggest possible ways to increase our ability to maintain attention.

Several years ago, Donald Broadbent (1958) reviewed some theories that he called "theories of vigilance decrement." Some of these seem appropriate to our discussion. One theory suggests that attention loss occurs because the surroundings are monotonous. In such a setting, the person's entire level of nervous activity may be lower. The theory seems quite applicable to what happens in many instructional settings. The instructor may have set up a drill that after a short period of time becomes rather monotonous and boring to many students. Their attentiveness to instruction in the drill, or their application of such instruction to their own needs, is greatly reduced in this situation.

Another theory postulates that poor performance will occur when attention must be maintained in a setting where a signal is very infrequent, because the individual's general state of readiness has deteriorated over the time of inactivity. Such could be the case of the doubles partner in tennis who has had very few balls to return during the course of a point. What typically happens in this case is that when a ball does come toward this player, she is not as prepared to make the shot as she might otherwise have been had she been actively involved.

An interesting experiment by Eason, Beardshall, and Jaffee (1965) provided physiological evidence that an important part of vigilance decrement could be attributed to a reduction in the individual's state of readiness or arousal. Subjects were required to attend to a flashing light and report when it stayed on longer than its normal 0.5 second. The light flashed every 3 seconds and would stay on for 0.8 second 10% of the time. Subjects were given prior training to discriminate these two lengths of time. A session lasted for 1 hour, during which heart rate, neck muscle tension, and skin conductance were monitored. As expected, results indicated that vigilance performance decreased over the hour as correct detections declined from almost 90% during the first 10 minutes, to approximately 75% during the second 10 minutes, to nearly 60% over the next 30 minutes, and finally to approximately 50% during the final 10 minutes. Skin conductance followed a decrease that essentially mirrored the detection performance. Heart rate showed no change while neck tension showed a steady increase over the 1-hour session. The skin conductance decrease was considered indicative of an increased calming and drowsiness state over the session, for which the nervous system attempted to compensate by increasing muscle activity in the neck. Thus, these physiological data support the view that decline of vigilance is due to a reduction in the arousal or readiness state of the individual.

Suggestions to aid the maintenance of alertness. If we are aware that a task demands maintaining alertness for a rather long period of time, during which there will probably be infrequent opportunities for action, then we can begin to help the performer of that task. Since the baseball outfielder offers a good example of a maintenance of attention problem in sports, let's begin with that situation. What can be done to help the player maintain an optimum state of readiness during an entire inning when there is typically very little activity for the outfielder? One suggestion is to keep the player's mind active in observing each pitch by having the player think, "What will I do with the ball if it is hit to me?" Then, at each pitch, the fielder will prepare for the necessary response. Between pitches he or she should relax for a short time, then again prepare for the next pitch. In this way, the problem of maintaining attention is solved by making each pitch a signal preparation concern.

We also used the example of the soccer, field hockey, ice hockey, or lacrosse goalie who encounters attention maintenance problems. A good suggestion for this situation would be for the coach or players on the bench to periodically yell words of encouragement or instructions directed specifically to the goalie. These words should be clear and precise so that the goalie is aware of them, and thus is "rescued" from any attention wandering that he or she may have indulged in.

Another very real attention maintenance situation occurs with physical and occupational therapists. Their patients are required to perform rather repetitive exercises. These are often monotonous but must be done. A helpful suggestion applicable to this situation is based on an observation made by Mackworth in his early radar vigilance studies. He noticed that efficiency of performance could be maintained over a rather extended period of time when the subjects were given verbal knowledge of results after each of the signals to be detected had appeared. For the therapy situation, similar reports of results of the patient's performance could be furnished in such a way as to motivate the patient to keep on working. Also, frequent rest pauses and changes in the task being performed have also been shown to be effective in reducing attention decrements.

One additional suggestion is that the student's instructional environment should never be permitted to become monotonous or boring. Drills should be limited in time to such a degree that they do not cease to be effective. The handball student who is told only to "keep practicing that serve" for an entire period will probably lose attention rather rapidly. By the end of the class period, little will be learned by the constant repetition after the time when attention began to diminish.

Maintenance of attention is vital to good performance or for effective instruction in any motor skill. It is very important for the teacher to be aware of these situations and to attempt actively to use some procedure that may help students stay attentive to the task being performed. The suggestions made in this section are but a few that can be tried.

Summary

An important part of studying the concept of attention relates to alertness and response preparation. It is clear from research related to the benefit of a warning signal in a reaction time task and related to the RT foreperiod that a certain degree of alertness is required for optimal response performance, as is a minimum amount of time to prepare the response. The RT interval is an important measure of response preparation time. RT can be increased or decreased as a function of a number of factors related to the individual, the task, and the situation. Several of these factors have been discussed, such as the arousal level of the individual, the number of stimulus-response choices, the compatibility of the stimulus and the response, the predictability of the stimulus, the complexity of the response, and the amount of practice the individual has had

with the task. Another important aspect of attention as alertness is the maintenance of alertness to detect a signal to respond over an extended time, especially when there are infrequent signals. In these vigilance situations, alertness declines as a function of time, probably due to monotony and a reduction of appropriate levels of readiness or arousal.

Required Readings

Gottsdanker, R. (1980). The ubiquitous role of preparation. In G. E. Stelmach & J. Requin (Eds.), *Tutorials in motor behavior* (pp. 355–371). Amsterdam: North-Holland.

Kelso, J. A. S. (1984). Report of panel 3: Preparatory processes. Considerations from a theory of movement. In E. Donchin (Ed.), *Cognitive Psychophysiology* (pp. 201–214). Hillsdale, NJ: Erlbaum.

Koelega, H. S., & Brinkman, J. A. (1986). Noise and vigilance: An evaluative review. *Human Factors, 28,* 465–481.

Posner, M. I. (1978). *Chronometric explorations of mind.* Hillsdale, NJ: Erlbaum. (Read chapter 1.)

Rosenbaum, D. A. (1983). The movement precuing technique: Assumptions, applications, and extensions. In R. A. Magill (Ed.), *Memory and control of action* (pp. 231–274). Amsterdam: North-Holland.

Concept 4.2   Attention is related to the idea that we have a limited capacity to process information

Application

When you are driving your car on a road that has little traffic and few sharp curves, it is relatively easy to carry on a conversation with a passenger in the car at the same time even if you have to shift gears. But what happens when you are driving on a congested city street? It is much more difficult to carry on a conversation with your passenger while driving under these conditions.

Why is it easy to do several things at the same time in one situation but difficult to do these same things in another situation? One answer to this question is an important aspect of the present concept. That is, we can only consciously attend to, or think about, so much at one time. As long as what we are doing can be handled within the capacity limits of our information processing system, we can effectively carry out several activities at the same time. However, if what we are doing requires more of our attention than we can give to all the tasks being attempted at the same time, we either have to stop doing some things in order to do others well, or we will do all of them poorly. In the driving example, driving required little attention on the open road so you could converse relatively easily at the same time. However, when traffic became heavy, your conversation suffered because driving was requiring all your attention.

Consider some other examples that incorporate this concept of attention but in a slightly different way. Why, for example, is it easy for a skilled second baseman to effectively do all that is required in completing a double play when a beginner has so much difficulty in trying to complete all the parts of that skill at the same time? Or, why can a skilled typist carry on a conversation with someone while continuing to type? A skilled gymnast or dancer shows little difficulty in smoothly and effortlessly carrying out a complex routine whereas the beginner typically performs in a rough, inefficient way. These examples also relate to the concept of attention as our capacity to attend to what we are doing as we perform complex motor skills.

Discussion

Interest in the problem of doing more than one thing at a time successfully is not a new concern. In 1886, a French physiologist named Jacques Loeb showed that the maximum amount of pressure that can be exerted on a hand dynamometer actually decreases when the operator is engaged in mental work. Until the 1950s very little was done in developing the implications of this result, which was the notion that humans have a limited information processing capacity. Then, such theorists as A. T. Welford and Donald E. Broadbent, both British psychologists, advanced the idea that the human performer, or operator as they termed it, constitutes a single limited processing capacity channel.

This early perspective of the human as a single channel processor of information viewed the individual as having difficulty doing several things at one time because the information processing system took time to perform its functions. Added to this was the idea that in performing its functions, the system only did one thing at a time. That is, the system contained a *bottleneck* so that only one activity could be performed at a time. Other activities to be performed were "put on hold" until one was completed. Much of the rationale behind this single-channel, or bottleneck, view came from research related to the psychological refractory period (PRP) discussed in Concept 4.1. Examples of this view of attention can be seen in the works of Welford (1952, 1968) and Broadbent (1958).

It became apparent from further research, however, that because it is often possible to respond appropriately to more than one stimulus at the same time, this single-channel theory had to be modified. The most acceptable alternative proposed that not all mental operations require space in a single limited-capacity mechanism. This modification of the single-channel view was advanced by Posner and Boies (1969). They argued that the only time it was difficult to do more than one mental operation at a time was when the tasks required more information processing space than was available. Otherwise, the tasks could easily be performed at the same time. Here, then, the limit for doing more than one thing at a time was not related to time limits but to *space* limits. If the limited-capacity information-processing system could handle the tasks being simultaneously attempted, then there should be no interference between the two tasks and they should be performed with little difficulty.

One way of looking at this limited-capacity view is to represent our information-handling system as a large circle. The different tasks we try to do at one time are seen as small circles. As long as all the small circles can fit into the large circle, we can effectively carry out the tasks. Problems arise, however, when we try to fit more small circles into the large circle than will fit.

The emphasis of theories of attention has been that only a limited amount of information can be processed at one time. Since the earlier time-based, limited-capacity models, such as proposed by Broadbent and Welford, this limit was portrayed primarily as a space capacity. It is worth noting that there have been attempts to overcome use of the rather difficult-to-define term *capacity* by suggesting that there is a limit in *resources* available to appropriately process the information or by suggesting a limit in the amount of *effort,* or mental activity, that can be devoted to processing the information. Regardless of the terminology, the underlying theme is similar. That is, humans are characterized by a distinct limitation of being able to effectively process only so much information at one time. The continuing search by scholars is to ascertain *why* this limitation occurs. Limited-capacity theories reflect one approach to answering this question.

Limited-Capacity Theories

Three different types of limited-capacity theories have emerged over the years since general agreement was reached that a single-channel view could not acceptably account for attention limits. Two of these theories hold that the capacity limit is a global, central one. That is, all information that enters a person's processing system, regardless of its source, its characteristics, or its output requirements, must compete for space in a single processing mechanism. The first of these theories holds that this mechanism has a fixed capacity whereas the second holds that the capacity has flexible limits. The third theory of processing capacity argues against a single, central mechanism and proposes that there are multiple sources of attention, with each source having its own capacity limits. We will look briefly at each of these three types of limited-capacity theories.

Fixed-capacity theories. The first alternatives to the time-based models of attention proposed by Welford and Broadbent argued that there is a central mechanism of attention that has a fixed capacity for processing information and that the limits of this mechanism are based on how much information can be handled simultaneously. Most of the early theories of attention that proposed capacity limits based on the amount of available processing space were of this type (e.g., Deutsch & Deutsch, 1973; Moray, 1967; Norman, 1969). This approach predicts that if there is a fixed, limited capacity, it would not be possible to successfully perform simultaneously two difficult tasks, although two easy tasks would be possible. Whether an easy and a difficult task could be successfully performed together would depend on the demand on capacity of the difficult task (see Kantowitz & Knight, 1978, for more discussion of this point).

The most debated issue among the different fixed-capacity models has been *where* in the stages of processing the limit exists for incoming information. Because there is a large amount of information coming into the system from the environment before and during task performance, and because there is a fixed limit as to how much of that information can be processed at one time, the logical questions become, Where does the information that gets processed get selected? and How does this selection take place? These questions are difficult to answer and have led to a variety of differing views. We will discuss these questions in more depth in the next concept, which concerns selective attention.

Flexible-capacity theories. Some researchers have argued that a fixed-capacity view of attention capacity is not acceptable. Although these persons agree that the attention mechanism is a single, centrally located unit, they proposed that its capacity limits are flexible. This means that the capacity could be larger or smaller depending on certain conditions related to the individual and the situation. A good example of this type of theory was proposed

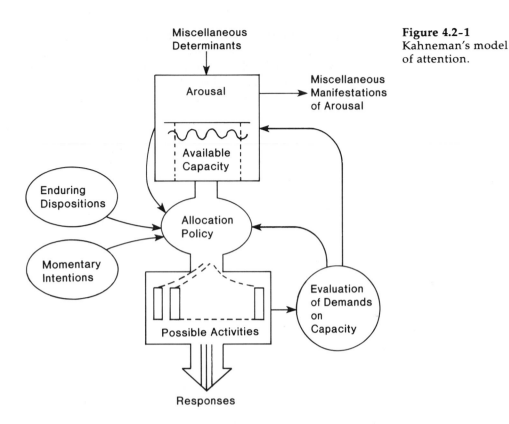

Figure 4.2-1
Kahneman's model
of attention.

by Daniel Kahneman (1973). We will consider this theory in some detail as it
has many interesting practical implications for motor skill learning and performance.

Kahneman stated that the *available* attention that could be given an
activity or activities should be thought of as a general *pool of effort.* This one
pool is distributed to activities on the basis of the characteristics of those activities and the allocation policy of the individual, which is influenced by situations internal and external to the individual. Figure 4.2–1 illustrates
Kahneman's capacity model by portraying the various conditions that influence the allocation of the individual's attention, which can also be thought of
as the mental resources necessary to carry out the activities.

Notice first that the box containing the wavy line represents the available attention capacity. This represents the single pool of limited resources
available for allocation to activities. The wavy line suggests that the arousal
level (discussed in Concept 4.1) of the individual influences the available capacity. Arousal levels that are too low or too high result in a decreased attention capacity. Kahneman further indicates that both the arousal level and the
available capacity will increase or decrease according to the demands of the
activities being performed.

The distribution or partitioning of the available capacity is dependent on the allocation policy. This policy is controlled by four kinds of factors. The first are called *enduring dispositions*. These are the basic rules of "involuntary" attention, such as, attention will be given to a novel signal, to a sudden noise, or to one's name being called in a crowded room. Second are the *momentary intentions*. These are the instructions given to the individual or the individual's specific intentions for the situation. They include such things as being directed to watch the ball or the intention to listen to the coach while performing. The third factor is the *evaluation of demands*. That is, the demands of the activities to be engaged in are evaluated in terms of whether sufficient attention capacity is available. Kahneman suggests that there is a type of rule operating in this situation where the system will be directed to complete one activity if more capacity is needed than is available to do two activities. Finally, the *effects of arousal* will have a systematic influence on the allocation policy.

The benefit of this model is that it demonstrates the various processes involved in allocating the available attention to activities. If the activities that it is possible to perform can be effectively handled within the available capacity, then the response should be the effective performance of all activities. On the other hand, if performing the possible activities will result in an "overload," this model indicates the basis on which the limited resources, or attention capacity, will be allocated.

Multiple-resource theories. Perhaps the most influential theories of attention currently in vogue are those proposing we have not just one central information-processing mechanism with a limited capacity, but rather several mechanisms, each of which is limited in how much information can be processed simultaneously. The most prevalent of these theories are those proposed by Navon and Gopher (1979), Allport (1980), and Wickens (1980, 1984). Wickens, for example, proposed that resources for processing information are available from three different sources. These are the input and output modalities (e.g., vision, limbs, speech system), the stages of information processing (e.g., perception, memory encoding, response output), and the codes of processing information (e.g., verbal codes, spatial codes). When two tasks must be performed simultaneously and they share a common resource, they will not be performed as well as when the two tasks must compete for the same resource. For example, performing a tracking task and a verbal memory task would be more effectively performed simultaneously than a tracking task and a verbal task requiring spatial decisions, because tracking and the spatial task would compete for the same resource as they each involve spatial coding of information. Further, when task difficulty is taken into account, two difficult tasks could be performed simultaneously if they require different resources, but could not if they competed for the same resources (see Wickens, Sandry, & Vidulich, 1983, for examples of experiments supporting the predictions of this model).

The current state of limited-capacity theories. Although limited-capacity theories have been the most predominant theories related to explaining why we have limits in performing multiple tasks simultaneously, there is considerable debate about the utility of such theories. Kantowitz (1985), for example, wrote an extensive review of the strengths and weaknesses of a capacity-based view of the limits of human information processing. He stated that what is particularly distressful is the lack of satisfactory empirical answers to such important questions as, What is capacity? How is capacity measured? Is capacity limited? and Where is capacity limited? He also presented arguments about the unsatisfactory state of the theoretical aspects of this issue. However, he did not suggest abandoning a capacity-based view, as he remains a strong advocate of such a view. But he did argue that there is a need for more carefully designed research and well-defined models to explain processing limitations.

Perhaps the strongest current advocate against a capacity-based view of information-processing limits is Odmar Neumann of Germany (see Neumann, 1987). He argues that the problem with capacity-based views of attention is that they have regarded the selection of information (to be discussed in the next concept) as a functional consequence of limited capacity. Neumann proposes the opposite approach. That is, limited capacity should be viewed as a necessary by-product of the solution to problems related to the selection of information to perform tasks. In this "functional" view of attention, he sees attention as a generic term for a number of different phenomena, each of which is related to different mechanisms involving problems with the selection of information. Some examples of what he considers selection problems include the selection of skills to attain an action goal, the recruitment of effectors to carry out an intended action, and the planning of specific response characteristics. Whether two tasks can be performed simultaneously, then, is not based on capacity limits of resources or effort, but on whether similar or different action rules must be selected to perform them. When the two tasks require different and complex action plans, it will be difficult to perform the tasks simultaneously. Thus, capacity limitations result from the selection problems involved, rather than the other way around. Although Neumann indicates that his functional view is not yet sufficiently developed to be considered a theory, it is worth noting that alternatives to traditional limited-capacity views of information-processing limitations are on the horizon.

Dual-Task Procedures

The typical experimental procedure used in investigations of limited-capacity models of attention is the *dual-task procedure*. The general purpose of experiments using this technique is to determine whether performance of a task, or its components, demands the performer's processing capacity, i.e., attention. The general approach is to determine the attention demands of an activity by noting the degree of interference caused on one task while being simultaneously performed with another task.

The dual-task procedure has been commonly used for research related to either single, central capacity or multiple resource models of attention. In

the dual-task procedure, the task of interest in terms of the attention demands to perform it is called the *primary task*. It is important that performance on this task be as constant as possible at all times. Performance on the primary task should be similar whether performed alone or simultaneously with the second task. The second task is called the *secondary task*. It is from the performance effects of doing this task together with the primary task that inferences are made about the attention demands required of the primary task. This should become clearer as we consider two different approaches to the use of the dual-task procedure.

Continuous secondary task technique. One approach to the use of the dual-task procedure is exemplified in a study by Kantowitz and Knight (1976). The primary task is a reciprocal tapping task in which subjects must maintain a specified rate of speed as they move a stylus back and forth between two targets. The tapping speed is indicated by a metronome. The secondary task involves the continuous performance of some type of mental task, such as adding columns of digits. The subject is told to perform both tasks at the same time but to be certain to maintain the proper tapping speed at all times. If the tapping task and the adding task can be done together, then the subject should be able to perform the secondary task as well while doing the primary task as when doing the secondary task alone. In other words, a type of "time-sharing" can go on in the processing system to enable both tasks to be done simultaneously.

Kantowitz and Knight have shown that the two tasks can be done together with little difficulty if the secondary task is an easy one, such as simply naming digits presented to the subject. However, as the secondary task becomes more difficult, as in subtracting 9 from a presented number, performance on the secondary task worsens. These results provide a clear demonstration of the limited-capacity concept. That is, whether two tasks can be performed simultaneously depends on the attention demanded by them. If both can be performed as well together as they can separately, then the attention capacity has not been exceeded. However, when performing the two tasks together leads to poor performance in one or both tasks, it seems reasonable to conclude that the available attention capacity has been exceeded.

In terms of the circle analogy used earlier, the small circle representing the attention needed to perform the primary task remained the same size because subjects were instructed to maintain constant performance on this task at all times. However, the size of the secondary task circle depended on the difficulty of that task. An easy secondary task was a small circle that allowed it and the primary task circle to fit inside the large, attention capacity circle. However, the circle representing the more difficult task was too large for both it and the primary task circle to fit into the larger one representing the total available information-processing capacity.

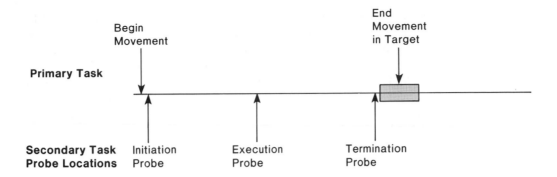

Figure 4.2-2
Diagram illustrating
one form of probe
technique to
determine attention
demands of primary
task at three
different phases of
the primary task
movement, which is
here depicted as a
rapid movement to
a target area. The
three probe
locations represent
points along the
primary task
movement where a
reaction time signal
occurs.

Probe technique. The second approach followed in using the dual-task procedure involves the use of a discrete secondary task and has been called the *probe technique.* This approach is especially popular when the researcher's interest is in the attention demands of the individual parts, or components, of a task. In the study of attention and motor skill performance, the typical primary task when this procedure is used is a type of discrete movement, such as an aiming task or moving a sliding handle along a trackway at a specified rate of speed to a target area. For example, the subject may be told to "move the handle 40 cm in 2 seconds." Here, as in the tapping time-sharing technique, it is important that the subject maintain consistent performance on the primary task at all times.

The secondary task in the probe technique differs markedly from what was used in the continuous secondary task technique. Since the primary interest is determining the attention demands required of certain components of the primary task, it is only necessary to "probe" that component with a secondary task. This is usually done by using a reaction time task where the subject is required to depress a response button when a signal sounds while the primary task is being performed. Figure 4.2–2 illustrates a typical probe technique situation.

The subject's job is to move the handle with one hand and respond to the RT stimulus, such as a buzzer, with the other hand. The buzzer is positioned so that it can be set to go off at different phases of the primary task movement, such as at the very beginning, in the middle, or at the end. The subject is told to concentrate on the primary task because it is the task of interest. But he or she is also instructed to respond to the buzzer as quickly as possible.

The rationale behind such a procedure is that any phase of the primary task that demands the performer's attention will diminish processing space required by the secondary task. Thus, performance of the secondary task should be much poorer than it would be if it were being carried out alone. Because of this, it is necessary first to determine the person's RT under normal conditions, that is, when no other task is being performed. The effect of performing the primary task on RT, which is equivalent to determining the

attention demands of the primary task, is calculated by comparing the subjects' RT score at any phase of the primary task movement to the normal or baseline RT score. If the scores are statistically distinct, then attention, or processing capacity, is required by the primary task. This inference is made since the subject was unable to respond normally in the secondary task. If the RT scores are not statistically different, then it would be inferred that processing capacity was not overloaded during that phase of the movement; thus the subject could perform both tasks at the same time quite satisfactorily.

Results of experiments using the probe technique have revealed that all components of a simple, discrete movement do not require the same degree of attention. There has been general agreement that movements require attention or processing capacity to *begin* them. This was shown rather vividly by Ells in 1973. Using the secondary task technique just described, he demonstrated that attention demands were highest at the initiation of the response of moving a sliding handle to a stop, but that these demands decreased as the movement continued. There also seems to be agreement that the *actual movement* or *execution phase* of a well-learned movement does not require processing capacity. However, the *termination* or completion of a movement may or may not demand processing capacity, depending on the requirements or limitations of the completion of the movement. When Ells' subjects completed their movement, they hit a stop, and processing capacity was not required. However, in an earlier experiment by Posner and Keele (1969), the subjects were to move to a target and to make a correction of the movement if they overshot the target. In this situation, attention demands were dependent on the characteristics of the target (see Figure 4.2–3). If the target was small and therefore required a precise termination, attention demand was high for this phase of the movement, a point more clearly substantiated by Salmoni, Sullivan, and Starkes (1976). When the target was large, however, the attention required to stop the movement was much less.

Thus, it seems that when the termination of a movement can be corrected, the attention demanded by that action will depend on how precise the final position must be. If there is a relatively minimal demand for precision to terminate a movement, such as at the completion of the follow-through in tennis or golf, little or no attention is demanded during the termination phase of the movement. However, attention is required if the termination of the movement requires a precise placement of the hands or feet, such as a wrestler placing his hand in a proper location to execute a maneuver or a long jumper hitting a precise spot on the take-off board.

An important point to emphasize at this stage of our discussion concerns the use of the term *attention demands*. As it is typically used, and as we have been using it, the term implies "conscious" attention. This can be seen in the examples presented in the application section of this concept. Another example occurs when a child is learning to bounce a ball with one hand and run at the same time. This is difficult to do since the bouncing of the ball requires

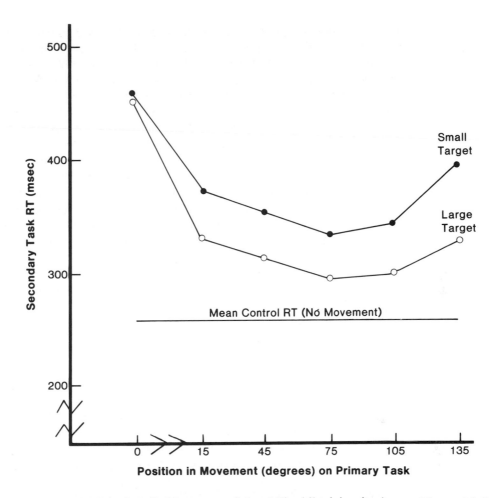

Position in Movement (degrees) on Primary Task

the child to be "thinking about" this aspect of the skill while doing it. As a result, there is little attention space left to think about running too. However, there do seem to be situations in which attention demand is not the same as "conscious" attention. An example of this was seen in the study of the long jumper by Lee, Lishman, and Thomson (1984), considered in Concept 3.3. Their results indicated that while visual attention was important for the precise hitting of the take-off board, skilled long jumpers and coaches were not aware of the corrections being made as the approach run was being completed. Here, then, attention is demanded of the visual system; however, it is not a conscious attention situation for the skilled athlete.

A word of caution about the probe technique. The conclusions and applications made thus far in this discussion have been generally based on studies using the probe technique. While this appears to be a valid approach, there is

Figure 4.2-3
Results of the experiment by Posner and Keele showing differences in secondary task performance (RT) as a function of where the response was made during the 135° rapid primary task. RT effects are shown for primary task movements to large and small targets.

need for a word of caution. This need stems from certain research findings presented by Peter McLeod (1978, 1980). He argued that if the secondary task probe actually permitted an inference about capacity demands of attention, then it should make little difference what physical structure was involved in performing the secondary task. However, if the typical probe technique was actually demonstrating a structural rather than a capacity interference, then using some other physical structure for the RT task, such as the voice, should lead to different results than were obtained when the other hand was used for the secondary task.

McLeod (1980) compared performance under conditions similar to those of Ells (1973). One group of subjects performed the secondary task using the hand RT probe used by Ells and other researchers. The other group performed the secondary task using a vocal RT, where speaking a word into a microphone stopped the RT clock. Results showed that the hand RT probe was higher than the vocal RT probe, indicating that the two probes were not assessing a central capacity of attention. Additionally, he reported that no one phase of the movement showed a demand for more attention capacity than any other phase of the movement.

An interesting follow-up to McLeod's experiment was reported by Girouard, Laurencelle, and Proteau (1984) at the University of Québec at Trois-Rivières. They identified several issues from the McLeod experiment that required further consideration. One was the voice vs. limb response mode for the probe RT task. Another concerned the analysis of the probe RT. The typical way to plot the RT in the dual-task situation is to consider it as occurring during the primary movement at the same time as the RT stimulus occurs. However, in rapid primary movements, the response to that probe may actually occur during a different phase of the movement than the one in which the stimulus probe occurs. In fact, when McLeod plotted vocal RT as a function of probe response during the primary task, he found that no one phase of the movement demanded more attention than any other.

The experiment by Girouard, Laurencelle, and Proteau required subjects to perform a primary task that involved either moving the right arm from a home base to a small target 11 cm to the right, then back to the home base, or moving from the home base to a target 11 cm to the left, and then back to the home base. The home base and targets were each 1×15-cm rectangular metal plates. The target to be moved to was indicated by the appropriate target lighting up. This task was performed for 50 continuous trials at a time. The secondary task was a two-choice RT task with a high or low tone as the stimulus. In experiment 1, a high tone indicated that the index finger should depress a key while the low tone signaled a middle finger response. In experiment 2, a high tone indicated that the word "quatre" should be said aloud while the low tone indicated that the word "quatorze" should be said aloud. (These are the French words for four and fourteen.) Five parts of the primary task were probed with the RT signal: (1) the interval between arrival at the home base

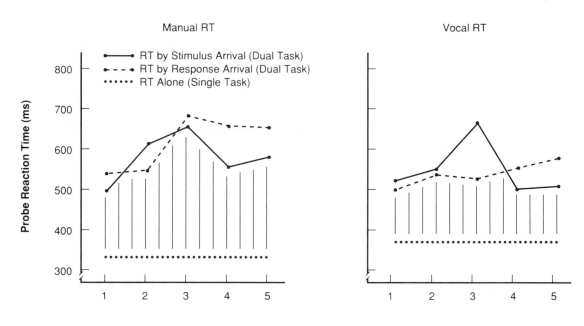

Manual RT

Vocal RT

● ●── RT by Stimulus Arrival (Dual Task)
● ─ ─ ● RT by Response Arrival (Dual Task)
● ● ● ● ● RT Alone (Single Task)

Probe Reaction Time (ms)

Phases of the Movement

and the onset of the next light signal; (2) the interval between the light onset and the departure from the home base; (3) during the movement to the target; (4) while on the target; and (5) during movement to return to the home base. The results of these experiments are presented in Figure 4.2–4. As you can see, probe RT was elevated in a different pattern for the manual response than for the vocal response and that plotting of RT on the basis of when the stimulus occurred versus when the response to that stimulus occurred also showed a different pattern of results for both the manual and vocal response.

What do these results mean? First, they indicate support for McLeod's findings regarding vocal RT as plotted for probe response that no particular phase of the primary task demands more attention than any other. However, these results also indicate that McLeod was not correct in contending that no central attention capacity is required by the primary movement. In the results shown in Figure 4.2–4 it is obvious that RT is elevated above its baseline level (which is determined by having the RT task performed alone) throughout the primary task for both RT response modes, regardless of when RT is plotted, although the manual response created more of an RT deterioration. In sum, these results suggest that we should be cautious in how strictly we interpret results of experiments using probe RT as the basis for determining *when* attention is demanded in the course of preparing or performing a movement. And, these results indicate that much research remains to be done to increase our knowledge of attention demands required by performing movements.

Figure 4.2–4
Vocal and manual RT results from the experiment by Girouard, Laurencelle, and Proteau (1984). RTs are plotted for each of five phases of the primary movement (described in the text) and are plotted according to when the stimulus occurred during the primary movement and when the RT response was made during the primary movement.

In the discussion of Concept 2.2, you saw that one of the changes that characterizes performance of a skill from the early to later stages of practice is the amount of attention demanded by the task. Fitts and Posner (1967) actually called the final stage of learning the autonomous or automatic stage. The implication here is that movements become more automated and therefore demand less attention as they are practiced over long periods of time. A similar view was expressed in the discussion in Concept 3.1 of neural mechanisms involved in movement control. The notion expressed in that discussion was that as a skill is practiced, the center of control shifts from the higher to the lower centers of the brain. The control of the skill becomes less and less closed-loop and more open-loop as a result of practice.

This shift in control resulting from practice was well presented in the Henry and Rogers (1960) article discussed earlier. These researchers stated that "an unlearned complicated task is carried out under conscious control, in an awkward, step-by-step, poorly coordinated manner" (p. 449). In other words, the beginner consciously attends to, or thinks about, each step of a complex skill. Sensory feedback is important throughout the task performance. As a result, the fluid, effortless motion characteristic of a skilled individual is not observed in the beginner.

An example may help clarify this point. Suppose you are learning the serve in tennis. This is a complex task that has several identifiable parts, such as the stance, racquet grip, ball toss, backswing, forward swing, ball contact, and follow-through. As a beginner it is likely that you will try to think about each of these individual parts as you perform a skill. As a result, you perform in a rather awkward manner, and your serve does not look like a skilled player's serve. However, as you practice, you stop "thinking about" the individual parts. You begin to put the individual parts together as larger parts so that the ball toss, backswing, etc., become one, fluid action. You find that you may attend only to the height of the ball toss, or its placement in relation to your body. You don't even think about the rest of the serve movements, you just "let them happen." Then as you become even more skilled, you may not think about any of the parts of the serve. Your conscious attention is directed to carrying out the type of serve you want to hit, while your visual attention is directed to the ball.

This example shows how attention demands change over extended periods of practice. The fine spatial-temporal relationships of each of the parts of the serve have become automatically controlled. In fact, if you "think about" what you are doing as you serve, you may find that you won't serve well. This occurs because directing conscious attention to the various parts of the skill disrupts the established motor program controlling this task by adding extra time to the intervals of time between the components of the task. This results from the reliance on feedback to provide you with information to control the task. As a result, you disrupt the programmed spatial-temporal relationships of the parts of the serve that you have developed through much practice.

The preceding section concerning the change in attention demands for skills as a function of practice emphasized an important assumption that has characterized views of motor skill learning for many years. That is, as skills become practiced, and therefore well learned, they can be performed "automatically." The implied notion here is that skills can be performed without conscious attention demands being required. However, there exists in current thinking some concern about this concept of automaticity and how it relates to motor skills. What exactly is automaticity and what does it have to do with motor skill performance?

Some insight into the issues surrounding the concept of automaticity and its relationship to motor skill performance can be gained by considering an important article by Gordon Logan (1985). He points out that the concept of skill, i.e., being a skilled performer of some activity, and the concept of automaticity are closely related, as we have alluded to in this text. Automaticity is an important component of skill in that skill consists of knowledge and procedures that can be called upon and carried out automatically. Both automaticity and skill can be acquired through practice. However, automaticity, like our concept of skill, should not be considered as a dichotomous category where some aspect of skill is or is not automatic. Automaticity should be thought of as a continuum of varying degrees. It is possible, for example, that some processing activity required in the performance of a skill may only be partially automatic. If this is so, then there is a need to restructure the dichotomous yes/no question that researchers have asked regarding attention demands when dual-task procedures are employed. One approach to addressing this need would be to assess dual-task performance at various stages of practice.

It is interesting to note in light of Logan's emphasis on the need to consider automaticity as a continuum, that in relation to motor skill performance there is little empirical evidence indicating that we perform skills absolutely attention free (see Stelmach & Hughes, 1983). However, people do perform skills in such a way that they are able to direct conscious attention to information that earlier in practice they were not capable of doing. For example, the young child learning to dribble a basketball while running must direct a great deal of visual attention to the ball and the dribbling. However, with practice, visual attention can be redirected to observing what is going on in the surrounding environment. The question that remains for researchers to address is, Does this change in attention demand reflect a decrease in attention capacity or can some other process account for the development of this characteristic?

How automated do complex skills become? Some skills are highly complex, such as a dance or gymnastics routine or playing a piano piece. Do these become automated all the way through the piece so that little, if any, attention is needed? The reasonable response to this question seems to be that the performer develops automated "chunks" of the entire piece (see Miller, 1956).

These chunks are parts of the piece that have been put together into groups and performed with little attention directed toward what is in the chunks. Attention is demanded, however, at the beginning or initiation of each chunk.

Anecdotal evidence for this view of attention demands for performing well-learned complex skills comes from discussions with skilled individuals. During performances, these individuals indicate that they perform many parts of the routine automatically, that is, without directing conscious attention toward these parts. However, they also indicate that there are also places in the routine to which they must direct conscious attention. These places seem to be identified by distinct characteristics. The dancer may attend to the place where the tempo changes or a partner must be contacted or lifted; the pianist may attend to tempo changes. The gymnast may direct attention to parts of the routine that are dangerous if missed. All of these individuals indicate that they give attention to parts of the routine that they have had difficulty with.

There is, unfortunately, almost no research evidence supporting this view of attention and the performance of complex skills. One reason for this is the difficulty to test this view. However, some studies concerned with simple movements have shown that attention demand changes as a result of practice. These studies (e.g., Reeve, 1976; Wrisberg & Shea, 1978) have shown that while attention may be reduced for some aspects of the movement, the movement does not reach what might be considered a completely automated state. Attention remains critical regardless of the amount of practice for some parts of the skill. What remains to be determined are the characteristics of the parts of a complex skill that will always demand the performer's conscious attention regardless of the stage of learning.

Attention Capacity and Instruction

While the portions of a movement demanding attention may vary according to the skill or action being performed and the stage of learning of the performer, it remains an important principle that the amount of attention demanded by a movement varies according to the critical nature or degree of importance of the part of the movement being performed.

For any task and at any level of performance, the initiation of the movement demands attention. We should give attention to how we begin to move in any skill. The golfer is taught to be sure to begin the movement properly by paying attention to body and hand position and to starting the club back properly. The tennis player attends to the initial phases of hitting a forehand by briefly attending to getting set properly in preparation to hit the ball. The archer attends to the beginning phases of drawing the arrow back. In each of these situations, attention, or processing capacity, is directed toward the initiation of the movement to be executed. Attention directed toward other aspects of the skill or game during this initiation phase will probably cause performance of the movement to be poorer than otherwise expected.

Another instructional point relates to the way in which a complex skill is sequenced in the instructional unit. Since one of the benefits of practice is to automate certain parts of a skill, it becomes an effective strategy to make certain that sufficient practice is given to those parts before adding additional parts of the skill. For example, suppose your goal is to teach a child to dribble a ball, one-handed, while running around a series of obstacles. For the beginner, this task demands more attention than is typically available. What must be done is to break the task into parts to allow each part to reduce its attention demands. Dribbling a ball while standing still may require all of a child's attention. If this is the case, provide sufficient instruction and practice for this part to allow it to decrease in attention demand before having the child dribble and run at the same time. Then allow sufficient practice with dribbling and running before having the child run an obstacle course.

A similar approach can be taken to teaching almost any complex skill. The skill must first be broken into parts. These parts should be meaningful ones and not just arbitrarily determined. Then determine the part that should be practiced first. This will usually be a part that needs to become automated so that it can be performed without thought. Build on this by adding the other parts of the skill until finally all that remains is the part that will essentially always be attention demanding. For open skills, this part will typically be the actual response to the moving object. Thus, it would seem reasonable to make sure a person had practiced the basics of the tennis stroke and had practiced hitting a ball that was predictable in terms of speed and where it would bounce before having the person rally with a partner.

If you go back to the discussion in Concept 1.1, you will find that this progression of practice follows the four parts of the Gentile 2×2 classification system. That is, the student first practices the skill as a completely closed, or category 1 skill, and then progressively opens it by practicing the skill as a category 3 then category 2, and finally as a completely open category 4 skill.

A research example. The point being emphasized here is that by changing certain characteristics of a skill, you can influence attention demands in such a way as to facilitate learning of the skill. Reducing attention demands for one aspect of the skill allows the student to give additional attention to another part of the skill. An example of how this can benefit the learner was provided in a study by Jack Leavitt (1979), which concerned the attention demands of skating and stick-handling in ice hockey. Subjects were from six age-group hockey programs, pre-novice through university varsity. (See Figure 4.2–5 for average age and prior experience for each age group.)

In the first experiment, the players were required to skate and/or stick-handle under four conditions: skating only, skating while identifying as many geometric figures shown on a screen as possible, skating while stickhandling

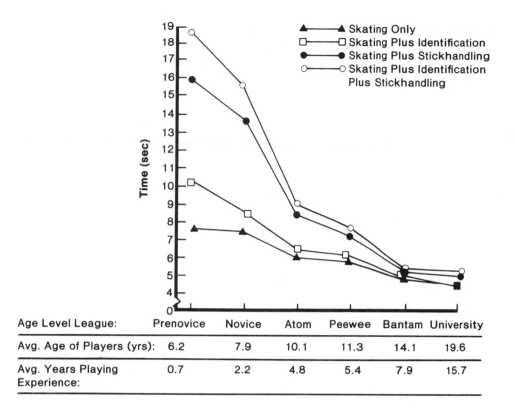

Age Level League:	Prenovice	Novice	Atom	Peewee	Bantam	University
Avg. Age of Players (yrs):	6.2	7.9	10.1	11.3	14.1	19.6
Avg. Years Playing Experience:	0.7	2.2	4.8	5.4	7.9	15.7

Figure 4.2-5
Skating speeds required by the different ice hockey players in the experiment by Leavitt.

a puck, and skating while stickhandling a puck and identifying geometric figures. Results for the skating speed times are shown in Figure 4.2–5 for these four conditions. Notice that it was not until the bantam group (age 14 with 8 years experience) that the skating and stickhandling or the skating while stickhandling and identifying figures could be done in such a way as to not slow down the skating speed. An obvious interpretation here is that skating was not "automated" enough prior to 8 years of experience to allow skating and stickhandling to be done simultaneously without negatively influencing skating speed.

To consider an attention demand interpretation, Leavitt conducted a second experiment, in which the players were given a larger than regulation-sized puck to use. The idea was that this larger puck would be less attention demanding for the stickhandling. The results indicated that the larger puck did in fact lead to skating and stickhandling speeds that were comparable to when the players were only skating.

These experiments by Leavitt provide support for the suggestion that instruction of a complex skill needs to consider the attention demands of the parts of the skill that must be performed simultaneously. In these situations, beginning instruction must emphasize those parts of the skill that must eventually become automated, such as skating in ice hockey. Additional tasks to

be done simultaneously should be added after there has been sufficient practice to demonstrate a reasonable degree of skill with the part of the task that should eventually become automated. When these additional tasks are added, they should be added in such a way that will allow the entire skill to be performed without exceeding attention capacity limits. This procedure was exemplified in the Leavitt study when the larger puck was used for stickhandling.

Summary

Attention has been considered as indicating information-processing space. The individual is portrayed as having a limited capacity to process information. As a result, it is often difficult to perform more than one attention demanding task at one time. The most popular theories of attention limits propose that we have a limited capacity to process information. Some theories consider this limitation to be a central, fixed capacity while others consider it to be a central, flexible capacity. An example of a flexible limited-capacity view was presented by Kahneman. According to this view, attention is allocated from a single, central pool of resources that is influenced by several factors related to the individual and to the activities to be performed. Other limited-capacity models include the multiple-resource models, which propose that rather than a central capacity limitation, we have several resources from which attention can be allocated. The typical experimental procedures used to support a limited-capacity view are called dual-task procedures. Two of these, the continuous secondary task technique and the probe technique were discussed. Attention demands are determined according to the ability of the individual to perform two tasks simultaneously. Results of these experiments indicate that different amounts of attention are required by different phases of a movement. Attention demands for performing a motor skill have been shown to decline as a result of practice. Implications based on an understanding of attention demands and motor performance were suggested for providing effective instruction for complex motor skills.

Related Readings

Allport, A. (1987). Selection for action: Some behavioral and neurophysiological considerations of attention and action. In H. Heuer & A. F. Sanders (Eds.), *Perspectives on perception and action* (pp. 395–419). Hillsdale, NJ: Erlbaum.

Kahneman, D. (1973). *Attention and effort.* Englewood Cliffs, NJ: Prentice-Hall. (Read chapter 1.)

Kantowitz, B. H. (1985). Channels and stages in human information processing: A limited analysis of theory and methodology. *Journal of Mathematical Psychology, 29,* 135–174.

Logan, G. D. (1985). Skill and automaticity: Relations, implications, and future directions. *Canadian Journal of Psychology, 39,* 367–386.

Posner, M. I. (1980). Attention and the control of movements. In G. E. Stelmach & J. Requin (Eds.), *Tutorials in motor behavior* (pp. 243–257). Amsterdam: North-Holland.

Stelmach, G. E., & Hughes, B. (1983). Does motor skill automation require a theory of attention? In R. A. Magill (Ed.), *Memory and control of action* (pp. 67–92). Amsterdam: North-Holland.

Concept 4.3 Successful motor skill performance requires the ability to select and attend to meaningful information

Application

As the tennis player prepares to return a ground stroke from an opponent, an obvious question comes to mind: What should the player be watching or concentrating on in order to provide the best opportunity for returning the ball? Consider the possibilities or choices that are available. The player could watch the opponent's eyes, or feet, or even body motions for the necessary information. The movements of the opponent's racquet or the ball could also be observed for needed indications. The list of possible cues could go on and on. However, the important fact is that a variety of cues are available to tennis players, clues that they should pay attention to in order to increase their chances of hitting a good return shot.

Consider this same tennis action situation from another perspective, also related to the problem of selecting information to attend to. To return the serve, you not only must select and attend to relevant cues from the environment, but you must also select and attend to relevant information within your own information-processing system. For example, information must be selected to determine the appropriate response to make and what muscles should be activated to make that response; specific kinematic and kinetic details of action must be applied to these muscles to carry out the response. These examples indicate the volume of information that must be dealt with from within your own motor control system to allow the intended response to occur. Because you know from your study of the preceding concept that you have a limited capacity to process information, it seems only logical then, that you will need some means of selecting the appropriate information to generate and carry out the ground stroke that will be successful in this situation.

The same problem occurs when a child is learning to catch a thrown ball. There are a number of possible choices of what to watch. While the skilled individual has learned to watch the ball, the child will watch any number of things, such as the thrower's eyes or hands or just about anything but the thrower and the ball. The child must also select and apply appropriate motor control-related information so that the ball can be caught. Even with the simple, fundamental skill of catching, then, the problem of selecting appropriate information from the environment to pay attention to is a significant one that must be addressed by the instructor in the process of teaching the child this skill.

These examples are critical problems for motor skill performance, especially since we realize that we have a limited capacity to process information. Because of this limitation, as well as a very short amount of time available

to us for selecting a proper response, before responding we are forced to select only certain cues or information from the environment and from within our own cognitive and motor control systems. We have already discussed why this is so, but a few questions remain relating specifically to what has been termed *selective attention*. How can we select certain information or cues and ignore others? What kinds of cues do we pay attention to, and what clues *should* we observe? How does the kind of cue we select to attend to change as a result of our becoming more proficient at the skill? These and other important questions will be considered in the following discussion. It should become apparent that selection of correct cues from those available in the environment may be one of the most important procedures that an instructor of motor skills can include in the teaching process.

The study of selective attention is the third area of concentration in our total discussion of attention. Thus far, attention has been considered as preparing for a response and as relating to processing capacity. Selective attention, while related to the other two concepts, has usually been used in a specific way that distinguishes it from these other uses. Specifically, *selective attention deals with the way in which we select certain information for processing and ignore other information*. Obviously, selective attention is important when more than one source of information is available and the performer must select some particular component of the sources available.

Discussion

One of the earliest generalizations about selective attention was given the rather intriguing label of the "cocktail party phenomenon." Very simply, this deals with something we have all experienced in any large crowd, such as at a cocktail party. Much talking is going on all around you, and yet you are able to attend quite specifically, or selectively, to one person with whom you are engaged in conversation. Furthermore, if during that conversation someone nearby mentions your name, your attention is immediately diverted to that person. Thus, in this cocktail party setting, these two common experiences lead to two interesting questions regarding selective attention. One concerns the ability we have to selectively attend to one message in the midst of many other competing messages. The second question concerns how we can be attending to one message and then suddenly be distracted by another message to which we were not specifically, or at least knowingly, attending.

Cocktail Party Phenomenon

In this discussion, the focus of interest in selective attention will be on selecting appropriate information from the environment so that appropriate response characteristics can be selected and applied by the motor control system. Issues related to the selection of information from within the cognitive and motor control systems are considered elsewhere in this text. For example, in Chapter 3, the process of selecting appropriate motor programs and program characteristics was discussed, and in Chapter 5, the selection of information stored in memory will be considered. What is important at this juncture,

then, is the consideration of selecting and attending to relevant cues from the environment that enable us to prepare and execute an intended movement response in a given situation. The examples considered earlier of the tennis player hitting a ground stroke and the child catching a ball illustrate the selection of appropriate visual cues from the environment so that a response can be successfully executed. As discussed in the previous two concepts in this chapter, these persons each have a limited amount of time to make the decisions necessary to prepare and execute the required response, as well as a limited capacity to process the large amount of information in the environment. These characteristics combine to establish the importance of selecting meaningful information so that the correct response can be made.

Some rather significant experiments have investigated this phenomenon. The earliest research was reported in 1953 by E. Colin Cherry, a British experimental psychologist. He introduced an experimental technique called *shadowing*. In these experiments, a subject was presented messages or sounds through one or both sides of a set of earphones. The experimental procedure required the subject to repeat the message of interest, or *shadow* the message. Thus, the subject was generally following or receiving one message and ignoring any others. In effect, this is the same situation that occurs at the cocktail party, but it is now present in a controlled, laboratory setting.

The first set of Cherry's experiments dealt specifically with how we recognize what one person is saying when others are speaking at the same time. The subject was presented with two mixed speeches that had been recorded on tape and was then asked to repeat one message, either word by word or phrase by phrase. The task was to separate one of the messages. While subjects often required the tape to be replayed many times, the task was always quite successfully accomplished. A further set of experiments fed one message into one ear while a different message was sent to the other. Again, the subjects experienced no difficulty in selecting one message and rejecting the other.

Other experiments involved changing the message or characteristics of the message that was being sent to the ear where the message was to be rejected. During transmission of the message to the "rejected" ear, certain changes occurred. These changes included such modifications as the message being presented in a different language, or a shift from a male to a female voice, or the speech being reversed, or the message becoming a pure tone. Following the test, subjects were asked if they could identify what had happened in the rejected ear during the test. In most cases, they could not report what had happened. However, the male to female voice change was always identified, as was the tone. Thus, it became obvious that subjects were able to attend to one message and completely reject another, unless the other message took on certain physical characteristics. In none of these cases could the subjects repeat the message that was sent to the "rejected" ear.

Other experiments, such as those of Moray (1959), showed that we are generally unaware of the content of a rejected message. Studies by Anne

Treisman (1969, 1971), however, indicated that subjects could repeat some content of a rejected message when that content was relevant to the subject. Thus, as in the cocktail party situation, we may be attending to only one message, but we can be directed to notice a different one if it contains information that is very relevant, such as our name or a topic of more interest than the one presently being discussed.

In Concept 4.2, we considered Kahneman's (1973) model of attention. In that model selective attention plays a very important role as the limited capacity must not be exceeded. As a result, certain activities must be selected for the available capacity to be allocated in such a way that the system is not overloaded. Accordingly, Kahneman indicated that certain factors will influence the allocation policy for distributing the available capacity to certain activities. In this section, we will consider two of those policies in more detail to see how Kahneman's model can help us better understand what influences our selection of the information to which we will direct attention in the performance of motor skills.

Selective Attention and Limited Capacity

Enduring disposition rules. The first factor presented by Kahneman as influencing the selection of information for the allocation of attention capacity is called *enduring dispositions*. Kahneman indicated that these are what can be considered as "rules of involuntary attention." That is, some things characteristically attract our attention regardless of our intentions.

There are several such "rules." The *first* is that *unexpected stimuli attract our attention*. You can see this in your own daily experiences. When concentrating on your professor during a lecture, haven't you been distracted by a classmate sneezing or dropping some books on the floor? You switched your attention from the professor to the noise, thus altering your attention capacity allocation policy. This rule helps explain why a golfer needs a quiet crowd when hitting a ball, whereas a baseball batter performs very well with a noisy crowd. To the golfer, noise in the crowd will attract his or her attention because it is uncharacteristic of the way in which golf is played. As a result the noise represents unexpected stimuli, which tends to be distracting. To the baseball player, crowd noise is a common experience, not a distraction.

A *second* enduring disposition rule is that *we tend "naturally" to direct attention to visual information* rather than to some other sensory modality. This point fits nicely with the discussion in Concept 3.3 that considered vision as the predominant sensory system. The typically observed predominance is an enduring disposition for attention allocation. As Posner (1978) has indicated, we really do not know why this attention bias toward vision exists.

The effect of this rule of visual attention bias is that in situations where performers should be allocating attention to sensory information from sources other than vision, the tendency will be to ignore those other sources unless instructed to do so. For example, beginning typists and pianists must practice

Figure 4.3-1
Information-flow
diagram illustrating
Norman's
"Pertinence
Theory" of selective
attention.

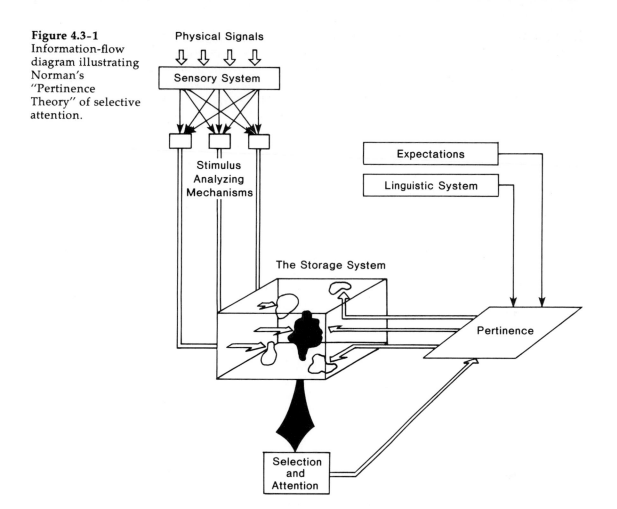

Physical Signals

Sensory System

Stimulus
Analyzing
Mechanisms

Expectations

Linguistic System

The Storage System

Pertinence

Selection
and
Attention

not watching their fingers while typing or playing. Children must be instructed not to watch their hands dribbling a ball if they are going to effectively move while dribbling. In each of these situations, the "natural" tendency is for the individuals to allocate attention capacity to visual information that comes from a source other than where it should for effective performance. Instruction and practice for doing otherwise becomes critical for overcoming this enduring disposition.

Third, we typically allocate attention to the most meaningful information when confronted with a choice of stimuli. An example of this was seen in the cocktail party phenomenon. A person's name is very meaningful to him or her. As a result, when his or her name is heard in a crowded room, attention will be directed to where the name was spoken.

Donald Norman (1968) actually developed a model of selective attention based on this notion of meaningfulness (see Figure 4.3–1). Rather than using the word *meaningfulness,* however, Norman used the term *pertinence.*

In his model, Norman maintains that all signals which arrive at the sensory receptors pass through a stage of analysis performed by the early physiological processes. Based on this analysis, certain information is stored concerning each signal. But all signals excite their stored representations in memory; that is, they activate what has been placed in memory from previous experiences. However, only the information that the system considers to be the most *pertinent,* based on expectations and perceptual processes, is selected for further processing. Thus, the pertinence model implies that we only select that information from the environment which we consider to be the most pertinent, or relevant, to the situation. Here the need to consider the meaning of the available information is critically important. If the pertinence model accurately describes how we selectively attend to information in the environment, then the importance of previous experience and instruction concerning essential cues becomes critical for instructors of motor skills.

While there are other enduring disposition rules that could be considered, these three provide sufficient support for the principle that attention capacity is allocated according to "natural" distractions. Because of this, it is essential that the second factor influencing allocation be given an important role in the attention allocation process.

Momentary intentions. Kahneman indicated that we allocate attention to those things we have been instructed to attend to or that we have, through practice or experience, learned to attend to. These are considered to be *momentary intentions.* That is, in a given situation, we allocate attention to sources of information that we might not otherwise consider. One way of viewing this allocation factor is that it takes into account our natural tendencies to attend to certain types of information and provides a means of overcoming those tendencies. As such, this factor provides the basis for establishing the need for effective instruction to beginning students in motor skills where they may be confused about the appropriate stimuli to which they should direct their attention.

An interesting point here is that we seem to be capable of very quickly redirecting our allocation of attention from one source of information to another. This process, known as *attention switching,* can be both an advantage and a disadvantage in different performance situations. The advantage occurs in activities that demand rapid decision making that must be made from a variety of sources of information. The quarterback in football must determine if a primary receiver is open; if not, he must find another receiver. In the meantime, the quarterback must be making certain that he is not about to be tackled or kept from delivering the pass. He uses both visual and auditory sensory modalities to receive this information. All of this activity must go in the course of a few seconds. To effectively carry out these activities, the player must rapidly switch attention from one source of information to another. This switching occurs within the same sensory modality as well as between different modalities.

Attention switching can be a disadvantage in activities requiring a rapid, accurate series of movements, as in closed skills like typing, piano playing, or dancing. In these situations, a certain degree of attention switching may be helpful, as we considered in the discussion of Concept 4.2. However, it will be to the advantage of the performer to maintain attention directed at a primary source of information for extended periods of time. If the pianist is constantly switching visual attention from the written music to the hands and keys, it will be difficult to maintain the precise timing structure required by the piece being played.

Selective
Attention and
Learning

In the discussion of Concept 4.2, the point was made that the term *attention* does not necessarily indicate that conscious awareness is characteristic of attention processes. This point is also an important one to consider in the present consideration of selecting information from the environment for processing to allow an appropriate response to be made. It is evident from research that we select information from the environment that enables us to make correct responses without being consciously aware of that information. A good example of this can be seen in an experiment reported by Richard Pew (1974) in which he showed that people improved in performing a tracking skill without being aware of an important characteristic of the stimulus pattern they were tracking.

In Pew's experiment, subjects sat before an oscilloscope and observed a target cursor move for 60 seconds in a very complex waveform pattern. The subject's task was to move a joystick in such a way to move his own cursor so that it stayed as close to the target cursor as possible. This task was practiced for 24 trials on each of 16 days. The interesting feature of the pattern produced by the target cursor was that the first and third 20-second segments of the pattern were randomly generated patterns on every trial. However, the middle 20-second segment was always the same on each trial. For learning purposes, you would expect that selecting this relevant feature of the waveform pattern would be related to improving performance on this portion of the task. In fact, you would probably expect that because this characteristic could be selected that subjects would do better on this segment of the task than on the other two segments. The results indicated that, in fact, the subjects did perform the middle segment better by the end of practice than the other two segments. But, what is important for our present discussion is that they were not consciously aware that this middle segment was the same on every trial. The relevant information was obviously selected by the processing system to enable performance on this segment of the task to be greater than that of the other two segments, but this selection was an unconscious process.

Another example of the unconscious selection of appropriate environmental stimuli was reported by Nissen and Bullemer (1987). In this experiment, subjects performed a serial RT task on a microcomputer. On each trial, an asterisk appeared on the computer monitor at one of four locations indicating that one of 3, 5, 7, and 9 digit keys on the keyboard should be depressed,

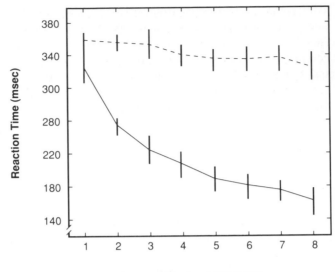

Figure 4.3-2
Results from experiment 1 by Nissen and Bullemer (1987) showing RT effects from practicing a serial RT task in 10-trial sequences that were either the same sequence (———) or random sequences (------) for sets of ten 10-trial sequences. The bars represent standard errors.

with the 3 key being for the left-most stimulus position, the 5 key for the next left-most position, and so on. The stimuli appeared one by one every 500 msec for a 10-trial sequence. Subjects performed a total of eight blocks of 100 trials each. One group of subjects received a repeating sequence on each set of their 10 trials in the 100-trial block. Thus, the sequence of asterisks might be for the response keys of 9–5–7–3–7–5–9–7–5–3 for each set of 10 trials. The second group of subjects received a 10-trial sequence that was randomly determined for the 100-trial block. Thus, on each set of 10 trials, a different sequence occurred. The results (see Figure 4.3–2) were as you might expect. The subjects who performed the repeated sequence for a block of ten 10-trial sequences improved RT much more than the group who received the random sequences. In fact, the randomly presented sequence group did not show much improvement at all over the 800 total trials. But, what is even more revealing with regard to selective attention is that when questioned, *none* of the subjects in the repeated sequence group said they noticed a sequence. What may be even more interesting is that in another experiment in this study (experiment 4), Nissen and Bullemer did essentially the same experiment but with persons who suffer from Korsakoff's syndrome, which is a memory disorder related to alcoholism. The pattern of results was the same for these patients as for the university students who participated in the first experiment. And, as would be expected, because of their memory disorder, they too were unaware of the repeating sequence.

Such experiments reveal an important characteristic of the selection process involved in attending to appropriate environmental information so that a correct response can be made. That is, this selection process can occur without conscious awareness. Does this mean that you should not direct people to attend

to important cues in the environment? To answer this, consider first the characteristics of the tasks used in the experiments just described. In both cases, the stimuli were very limited in terms of cues competing for attention. In the Pew experiment, subjects visually attended to the target cursor. In the Nissen and Bullemer experiments, subjects visually attended to the asterisks appearing on the monitor. These results indicate that when a person attends to the appropriate stimuli, the information from that stimuli that is relevant for performance of the response will be selected and appropriately used by the motor control system. Thus, the key is directing people to attend to the appropriate stimuli and to let the processing system take over from there. It does not appear necessary for people to be consciously aware of what features characterize that stimulus information.

Selective Attention and Instruction

From this discussion of factors that influence the allocation of attention capacity, we can draw several conclusions about how instruction can be effectively designed to incorporate what we know about selective attention and motor skill performance. We will consider three conclusions here. The first is that we have the ability to attend to only one cue in the midst of many competing cues. This should provide instructors of motor skills with a basis of support or confidence that learners can be taught to ignore the many irrelevant cues or distractions that will confront them in most motor skill situations.

Second, we conclude that the learner will attend to the cues that are most meaningful or pertinent to him or her in the particular situation. This conclusion should convince the instructor of motor skills that the learner needs instruction about *what* cues are important. For example, the child needs instruction concerning where to concentrate his or her visual attention with regard to the oncoming ball so it can be caught. The racquetball player should be told what cues to concentrate on when receiving a serve. To ignore this important aspect of instruction is to invite less than optimum performances by students.

Finally, while we know that distractions can and do occur, we do not completely understand why we are distracted by stimuli that we are not attending to. However, we can identify some possible reasons that may be applicable to motor skill situations. A primary reason for the influence of distractions appears to be related to the meaningfulness of the unattended to stimuli. This seems to indicate that the instructor must provide the learner with ample practice in concentrating on the cues that have been suggested by the instructor as the most pertinent or meaningful. What is hoped for here is that eventually the number of possible distractions should decrease as the most meaningful cues are more and more reinforced in the learner. Another reason for distractions seems to be the learner's lack of confidence that the cues he or she is attending to are the most pertinent. Again, the importance of practice while directing attention to the most relevant or important cues is essential to develop the learner's confidence in attending to those cues.

A problem often faced by instructors of motor skills is that they have difficulty getting students to "selectively attend" to them in a particular situation. Based on our discussion of factors influencing selective attention policies, certain attention gaining methods would seem to have a reasonable chance for success. Some effective methods for gaining attention were presented by Travers (1972) in his book *Essentials of Learning.*

One frequently used means of gaining attention is shouting. This works, Travers says, because it provides a strong stimulus that cannot generally be "blocked from entering the perceptual system" of the student. Coaches and physical education teachers use a whistle to accomplish the same result.

There are at least two other, more subtle ways of gaining a person's attention in an instructional setting. Travers refers to these as associated with the *novelty* and *complexity* of the stimulus characteristics of what is being presented to indicate to the learner that what is occurring is priority information.

Novelty of a situation seems to work because it attracts an "orienting response" by the individual. It arouses the curiosity of the learner in such a way as to direct him or her to this new stimulus. Travers suggests that a situation can be made novel, and therefore gain the learner's attention, by (1) not having been presented recently; (2) presenting the stimulus in a new or unfamiliar setting or context; or (3) presenting a stimulus that has never been used before. Prior to reading further in this section, it would be helpful if you would try to write down some examples of how you could employ these three methods.

Complexity as a means of gaining attention in the teaching of motor skills is not so easy to apply as was the novelty factor. Travers relates research which indicates that in terms of visual attention individuals are more likely to attend visually to an object that is more complex than to one that is less complex. Hence, more information is available in one location. For example, babies will fixate on a more complex diagram hanging above their head rather than on a simple one. Even in contemplating the human face, research has shown that an individual will visually attend more to a person's eyes and mouth than any other portion of the face. Evidently, this is because there is more information in a smaller space.

Applying this complexity factor to motor skills instruction, one generalization that can be offered is to try to plan demonstrations or visual aid materials of such a nature as will contain a maximum amount of information in any one demonstration or visual aid. This seems to have merit if initial attracting attention is desired. The students will be more prone to attend to that one aid than to let their eyes wander to seek more interesting objects to look at.

It is interesting to note that Travers' suggestions follow our discussion of factors that influence the attention allocation policy as presented in Kahneman's attention model in this and the preceding concept. The factor of enduring dispositions is applied in the shouting and novelty methods. Each of

these will attract a person's attention because the individual has a natural tendency to be attracted to this type of stimuli. Second, the complexity method can be related to the role Kahneman attributes to arousal in the attention allocation decision process (discussed in Concept 4.2). By increasing the amount of attention demanded by the task as suggested by Travers, the arousal level of the individual is increased to a higher, more optimal level. It is important to remember here, however, that the complexity method can be taken to an extreme. More is not necessarily always better. As you will recall from the discussion in Concept 4.2, there is a point at which arousal level is optimal for a given task. Beyond that level, increasing arousal will begin to yield less than maximum performance. And as you also saw in Concept 4.2, too much information can be provided with the result that the individual, who might be attentive, is also confused. The requirement for instructors, then, is to take these factors into consideration when developing attention gaining methods based on these ideas and implement them according to the unique demands of their own particular teaching situations.

Summary

An essential aspect of the process of producing a motor response is the selection of information from the environment on which the response can be based. The process of selecting certain information from the environment while ignoring other phenomena is known as selective attention. The "cocktail party phenomenon" illustrates our ability to attend to specific information in the midst of much noise or unwanted information. It also indicates how we can be distracted by information other than what we are attending to. Two of the factors influencing attention allocation policy presented in Kahneman's model of attention were developed in relation to how certain stimuli have a tendency to receive attention while others do not. Certain characteristics of stimuli attract attention because they receive our involuntary attention. These characteristics include being unexpected, visual, and meaningful to the individual. Attention is also directed to certain stimuli because the individual has been directed to do so or has learned to do so. It is also important to realize that learning skills are not dependent on all relevant stimuli being attended to consciously. These factors have been considered in terms of how to develop instruction based on our knowledge of selective attention principles. Finally, some examples of methods for gaining students' attention were considered.

Related Readings

Kahneman, D. (1973). *Attention and effort.* Englewood Cliffs, NJ: Prentice-Hall. (Read chapter 1.)

Keele, S. W. (1973). *Attention and human performance.* Pacific Palisades, CA: Goodyear. (Read pp. 147–151.)

Nissen, M. J., & Bullemer, P. (1987). Attentional requirements of learning: Evidence from performance measures. *Cognitive Psychology, 19,* 1–32.

Norman, D. A. (1976). *Memory and attention: An introduction to human information processing* (2nd ed.). New York: John Wiley. (Read chapter 2.)

Treisman, A. M. (1971). Shifting attention between ears. *Quarterly Journal of Experimental Psychology, 23,* 157–167.

1. Describe two ways that researchers have demonstrated that there is a need for alertness and time to prepare a motor response.
2. Identify three factors that can influence the amount of time taken to prepare a motor response. Indicate why each factor affects preparation time.
3. Why is Hick's Law known as a "law"? Describe how Hick's Law relates to the issue of response preparation.
4. What is the "cost-benefit trade-off" involved in the amount of time required to prepare a response when the probability of a specific signal occurring is 80–20? Describe a situation where under certain conditions it would be best to prepare for the 80% likely signal and under other conditions it would be better to prepare for a 50–50 likelihood of a signal occurring.
5. Describe a "vigilance" situation in motor skills. Why is this an important issue in the study of preparing a response?
6. What is meant by the use of the term *attention* to indicate we have a limited capacity to process information? What different types of theories have been proposed to account for this notion of limited processing capacity?
7. In Kahneman's model of attention, what four factors influence how we allocate attention in a performance situation? Give an example of how each factor can influence motor skill performance.
8. How are dual-task procedures used to investigate the role of attention in performing motor skills? What are some advantages and disadvantages of using this experimental approach?
9. Why do attention demands associated with performing skills decrease as a person practices and becomes more expert at performing the skill? Give an example of how this phenomenon can be illustrated.
10. How can your knowledge about attention as limited capacity be used to assist you in designing effective instructional procedures for teaching motor skills? Give an example.
11. What is meant by the term *selective attention*? How does the "cocktail party phenomenon" demonstrate two characteristics of selective attention?
12. Must the process of selective attention be conscious? Give an example where selective attention of appropriate information goes on nonconsciously. Indicate how we know that this information was attended to nonconsciously.
13. Describe two effective ways to gain students' attention when teaching motor skills. Indicate why you think these would be effective.

Memory

5

Concept 5.1
The structure of memory consists of two functional components
called working memory and long-term memory.

Concept 5.2
Forgetting can be related to trace decay, interference, or
inappropriate retrieval cues.

Concept 5.3
The retention of information in memory is related to control
processes involved in the storage and retrieval of information.

Concept 5.4
Recall of serially presented information follows a pattern in
which the earliest and most recent parts are recalled best, while
the middle parts are recalled most poorly.

Concept 5.1 The structure of memory consists of two functional components called working memory and long-term memory

Have you ever had the experience of calling an information operator to ask for a telephone number and then found out that you didn't have a pen? Hurriedly, you dialed the number as quickly as possible after the operator gave it to you. Why did you do this? "Obviously," you say, "because I would have forgotten it if I hadn't dialed right away." Do you need to do this with your home telephone number? You can quite readily recall your home number at almost any time, without any assistance.

Consider a few other memory situations. When you are at a party and you are introduced to someone, you often find it very difficult to recall that person's name, even a very short time later. Compare that to remembering a teacher's name from your elementary school. You can probably name most of your teachers with little difficulty. Consider also the situation when you are shown how to serve a tennis ball for the first time. When you try it, you find that you have considerable difficulty in remembering all the things that are to be done to produce a successful serve. That situation differs quite drastically from your ability to hop onto a bicycle, even after you have not been on one for many years, and ride it down the street successfully.

The situations described here point out one of the important characteristics of human memory; that is, its structure involves a distinction in how permanently information is stored in memory. Information may be only temporarily stored or it may be more permanently stored. The telephone number you received from the information operator was only kept in a temporary store, whereas your home number has been kept more permanently in a long-term store. The discussion section that follows will focus on these two memory storage systems, considering *what* distinguishes them and *how* we seem to be able to transfer information from one store to the other.

Discussion

Memory plays an important role in our processing of information in order to produce the desired response. As you have observed in the preceding section, we are involved in memory situations almost constantly. Whether in conversation with a friend, working mathematical problems, or playing tennis, we are confronted by situations that require the use of memory to produce action.

What is memory? We often think of memory as being synonymous with the words *retention* or *remembering*. Howe (1970), in a concise introduction to the subject of memory, stated that the word *memory* "is used to denote a capacity to remember; it is not an explanation of remembering" (p. 4). Tulving

(1985) stated that memory is the "capacity that permits organisms to benefit from their past experiences" (p. 385). The study of human memory involves a variety of topics, some of which you can see by looking at the list of concepts for this chapter.

Before considering some of the various topics related to the study of memory, it will be helpful to first clarify two issues concerning terminology that could cause confusion as you study this discussion of memory.

Some
Introductory
Issues

Motor memory and verbal memory. The first issue concerns the use of two terms used frequently in this text and in the research literature related to human memory: *motor memory* and *verbal memory*. These expressions seem to imply that motor and verbal memory are separate entities. Although this issue has yet to be resolved by memory theorists, it is important for the purposes of this text to postulate a resolution to this issue. Here we will consider the memory for motor skills and for verbal skills as representing one entity; that is, one memory system is adaptable to the specific or unique requirements of both verbal and motor skills. Thus, the terms *motor memory* and *verbal memory* should be more appropriately designated as *memory for movement* and *memory for verbal information.*

One of the advantages of considering motor and verbal memory as one entity is that the knowledge we have acquired about memory, derived from research dealing with motor skills and with verbal skills, can be considered together in the same context and be applied to memory in general. Specific differences between memory for movement and memory for verbal information, which have been pointed out in the research literature, can be considered in support of the adaptability of the memory system to unique demands of specific situations.

Retention and forgetting. The second issue concerns the meanings of two terms common to any discussion about memory. These terms, *retention* and *forgetting,* are closely related. In fact, it could be said that they are opposites. Ellis (1978) indicated that these terms are like two sides of the same coin, that each "process is defined in terms of the other. . . ." (p. 78). However, a potential problem exists with how we interpret forgetting, as this term can mean two different things. When we say that something has been forgotten, we can mean that the information is either lost from memory and therefore not in memory, or we can mean that the information is in memory but unretrievable at the moment. For example, suppose you were asked a question about some material you have been studying and were unable to answer it. Does this mean that you have forgotten the answer, i.e., that it is not in memory, or that you just can't retrieve it based on the way the test question is structured? Suppose the same question is posed in a multiple-choice format and you are now able

to select the correct answer. This would indicate that you just needed something to help you locate the information in your memory. Keep this problem about the definition of forgetting in mind as it will be a recurring theme in various discussions in this chapter and in other parts of this book.

Memory
Structure

Although the structure of memory is debated, the notion that we have a memory oriented toward events that have just occurred as well as a memory that retains information about events in the past has been generally accepted for many years. For example, in 1890, William James wrote of an "elementary" or "primary" memory that makes us aware of the "just past." He distinguished this from a "secondary memory" that is for "properly recollected objects." To primary memory, James allocated items that are lost and never brought back into consciousness, while to secondary memory, he allocated ideas or data that are never lost; although they may have been "absent from consciousness," they are capable of being recalled.

The debate about the structure of memory has centered around the concept of how the distinction between memory for immediate things and for things in a more distant past fits into a structural arrangement in memory. Is the memory for the immediate or "just past" a special function of memory, or is it a separate, functional component of memory? The answer to this question is no simple matter. However, there have been many attempts to provide theoretical explanations of this structural arrangement. These hypothetical clarifications have come primarily from two perspectives. One of these is proposed by the experimental or cognitive psychologist. According to this view, the structure of memory is considered as comprising the functions of memory that are observed in the behavior of individuals in memory situations. The other perspective is that of the neuropsychologist or neurophysiologist, who is interested in explaining the structure of memory in terms of what is occurring in the nervous system during behavioral changes that are related to memory.

In this discussion we will limit our consideration of the structure of memory to the theories or approaches that have been developed from the perspective of the experimental or cognitive psychologist. Since this direction reflects the general nature of the approach presented in this book, it would be beyond the scope of this work to become involved in the discussion of the neurophysiological bases of memory. However, if you would like to study the neurophysiological view of human memory more closely, consider some of the important works that have been published by Hebb (1949), Penfield (1954), and Pribram (1969).

It should be noted that the term *kinesthetic* appears throughout this chapter. *Kinesthetic* as generally used in the memory literature is synonymous with *motor* or *movement*. To be consistent with the research literature's use of the term, it will be used here in this sense.

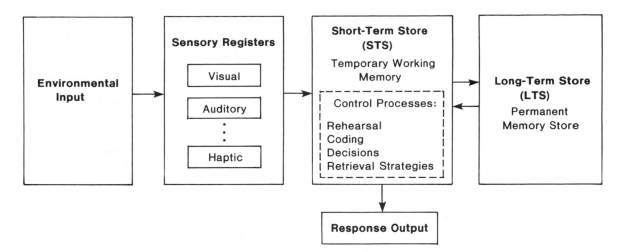

The Atkinson and Shiffrin Model. An important contribution to our understanding of memory structure was made in an article by Atkinson and Shiffrin in 1968. In that essay they argued that memory must be considered in terms of its structure and control processes. Structure, they contended, involves fixed, permanent features that maintain their characteristics or traits regardless of the task. Control processes, on the other hand, refer to those processes of memory that are under the direct control of the individual, such as storage of information, rehearsal, or retrieval of information. Using a computer analogy, Atkinson and Shiffrin conjectured that structure is similar to computer hardware, while control processes are like software. The structural components, they concluded, consist of a sensory register, short-term store, and long-term store. These components are presented in schematic flowchart form in Figure 5.1–1.

Since the time of Atkinson and Shiffrin's presentation of their theory of memory structures, the primary theoretical problem has been to determine the exact nature of these structures. Some theorists claim that the structures are separate and distinct storage systems that are controlled by different laws or principles. Others visualize the structures as lying along a continuum, with each store representing a phase or stage of memory.

Levels of processing. A view of memory that argues against the Atkinson and Shiffrin "boxes" model of memory is called the *levels of processing* approach to memory. This view of memory was first presented by Craik and Lockhart (1972), who considered levels of processing as a new "framework for memory research." Their view was to deemphasize the argument about memory structures by stressing the functional aspects of memory. What is most important for remembering information, acccording to this view, is what the individual

does with that information and how much time the person has to do it. Craik and Lockhart proposed a "hierarchy of processing stages" that would predict the strength of information in memory by determining how "deeply" the information was processed by the individual. As such, this view argues that memory is actually a "by-product" of information-processing activity.

If the subject briefly views information, or if he or she directs attention only to the physical characteristics of the information, then the depth or level of processing is very shallow. This would be the case if you look at a word and make no attempt to determine its meaning; you simply acknowledge what it looks like. On the other hand, if the individual processes the information to the extent that he associates the new information with what he already knows, then the depth or level of processing is very deep. Shallow processing would yield storage and retention effects similar to the sensory or short-term stores in the Atkinson and Shiffrin model, whereas deep processing would be related to long-term storage. We will be referring to this view of levels of processing throughout this chapter.

A component functional model of memory. One of the primary objections to the stage approach to the structure of memory represented by the Atkinson and Shiffrin model has been that too much emphasis is placed on *where* information resides rather than on what a person actively does with the information. According to the stage model, information is lost or forgotten according to the memory store in which it happens to be. Even though Atkinson and Shiffrin made provision for the individual's active transfer of information from one store to another, the ultimate fate of the information is dependent on the store in which it resides. In contrast, the Craik and Lockhart view emphasized what the individual does with the information. Nevertheless, a close inspection of the Craik and Lockhart view reveals that they saw their levels of framework as fitting within a model structure similar to the one by Atkinson and Shiffrin.

The need, then, is to see the structure of memory as accommodating a necessity for different memory storage systems while at the same time emphasizing the role of what the individual does with the information. Such a view not only bases forgetting on which stage of memory the information resides in but also on the characteristics of the information in each stage and on what the individual does with that information.

One approach that accommodates these needs was proposed by Baddely and Hitch (1974; Baddely, 1986). Rather than establishing a sensory register and a short-term store to handle the needs posed by immediate experiences, they suggested a component called *working memory*. In many ways, working memory is similar to the sensory and short-term stores. For example, information seems to have a relatively short life in working memory. However, the important differences is that this short life is not only due to the information's being in working memory but also to the information's not having been adequately processed by the individual to make it more resistant to being lost from

memory. (We will discuss this notion of what causes forgetting and what helps maintain information in memory in the next two concepts of this chapter.)

Thus, in addition to being a passive place where information is stored, which was the view of short-term memory, working memory is also seen as an active structure where critical information-processing activity occurs, enabling people to respond according to the demands of a "right now" situation. One of these activities is to serve as an interactive "workspace" for integrating information in working memory with information that has been retrieved from the more permanent, long-term memory. This is an especially critical process that allows problem-solving and decision-making activity to occur. Also, essential processing activity needed for the adequate transfer of information into long-term memory is an important part of working memory activity.

Memory, then, consists of two functional components, *working memory* and *long-term memory*. As functional components, each component of memory has its own distinct characteristics related to memory function. For our purposes, we will focus particularly on those functions related to the storing of information and to the processing of information that resides in that component, which will be considered in the following sections.

Because working memory involves both storing and processing information, it is important to consider each function separately. In terms of storing information, two characteristics of working memory are essential to understand: the length of time information will remain in working memory, which is called *duration,* and the amount of information that will reside in working memory at any one time, which is called *capacity.* In terms of processing information that resides in working memory, the primary processing activity of interest here is working memory serving as an interactive workspace with long-term memory. Other processing activities will be considered in Concept 5.3 in the discussion of control processes in memory.

Working Memory

Duration. Our understanding of the duration of information in working memory is of relatively recent vintage. Peterson and Peterson (1959) were the earliest to report research on this problem; their findings were simple and straightforward. They showed that we tend to lose information (forget) from working memory after only about 20 to 30 seconds. Other research followed shortly, supporting the notion of brief duration of information in working memory.

The first, perhaps one of the most significant experiments ever published concerning working memory and motor skills, was by Adams and Dijkstra in 1966. Their experiment was quite simple in its conception. Basically, the idea was that if verbal information in working memory has a short duration, then should not motor information at this stage of memory have a similar fate? Results of their experiment indicated that motor or kinesthetic information is also lost quite rapidly in working memory.

For many years the procedures followed by Adams and Dijkstra became the standard pattern for what was termed motor short-term memory research. Subjects were blindfolded and seated in front of a linear positioning task, which is simply a free-moving handle that slides along a metal rod. The subject holds the handle and moves it to a stop and then returns the handle to the starting point. Following a specified interval of time (the retention interval) the subject's task is to move the handle along the bar to a place that he or she estimates is the location of where he or she moved to the stop. For this phase of the procedure, the stop is removed. To score the accuracy of the subject's response, the experimenter simply records how far the subject's estimate is from the criterion location (where the stop actually was).

Though many other studies followed the Adams and Dijkstra investigation, the results of those experiments generally supported the notion that the duration of kinesthetic information in working memory is about 20 to 30 seconds. Information that we do not process further or rehearse is lost. We will discuss later why such information is lost as well as how we can transfer the information from working memory to the more permanent long-term memory. For the present, it is essential to understand that information in the short-term storage stage of memory remains there for a rather brief time, approximately 20–30 seconds, before it begins to be lost from memory.

Capacity. We are not only concerned with *how long* information will remain in short-term storage but also *how much* information we can accommodate there. The issue of capacity in working memory was originally presented by George Miller in 1956, in an article that has become a classic in experimental psychology literature. Miller provided evidence to indicate that we have the capacity to hold about seven items (plus or minus two items) such as words or digits, in short-term storage. To increase the "size" of an item in memory involves a control process termed *organization,* which we will discuss in Concept 5.3. The larger item, or "chunk" as Miller called it, that results from the additional processing activity enables people to recall far more than five to nine individual items at a time. However, with no practice or rehearsal of newly presented information, the capacity limit of working memory is five to nine individual items. It is worth noting that this generally accepted working memory capacity limit has been challenged. Chase and Ericsson (1982) have argued that Miller's limits actually exceed the working capacity. They provide evidence that the capacity is actually only three to four items when no practice or rehearsal has been permitted. Regardless of which view is correct, the principle of a very limited working memory capacity remains. In an immediate recall situation, we can accurately recall somewhere in the range of three to nine items. Beyond this limit, errors in recall increase.

The translation of this capacity limit notion for working memory into motor terms is not an easy task. The most immediate problem is to translate an "item" into motor terms. We do not know if an item is an entire skill, a

component of a skill, or a simple movement of one limb. However, in terms of looking at this capacity issue when an item is defined as a simple limb position, we do have some research evidence that fits very well with the capacity limits just discussed. In an experiment by Robert Wilberg and John Salmela (1973), subjects were presented with a sequence of two, four, six, or eight limb-positioning movements using a two-dimensional joystick. Immediately following the presentation of these movements, the subjects were asked to move through the sequence just presented. Results indicated that subjects could handle eight movements, although that was clearly at the upper limits of capacity.

Processing activities. Information presented in the immediate past is processed in working memory so that it can be used to accomplish the goal of the problem at hand. The goal may be to remember what you have just been told to do or it may be to use this information to solve a specific problem. In each case, you will undoubtedly integrate this newly presented information with information already stored in long-term memory.

An example of the first goal would be when you have been given a specific instruction to concentrate on your hand position as you swing a golf club. You must not only remember this instruction as you swing, but you must also retrieve from long-term memory the correct hand position and evaluate your present hand swing compared with the ideal. Of course, how successfully you make this comparison on your own depends on your stage of learning.

An example of the second goal would be a situation where you have been receiving instruction about how to throw a curveball. You already know how to throw a fastball so to throw a curve you must alter certain features of how you throw. You use working memory as a workspace to integrate new information about how to throw a curve with information you retrieve from long-term memory about how to throw a fastball. In this way, you solve the problem at hand, which is to throw a curveball, by using working memory as an essential component in this problem-solving situation.

Other information-processing activities are also the function of working memory, such as preparing the information for storage in the more permanent long-term memory. These activities will be described in more detail in Concept 5.3. For now it is important to be aware that working memory is more than a storage depository for newly presented information. It also serves a critical function as a workspace so that the information in working memory can be processed so that a problem can be solved, a decision can be made, or the information can be transferred to long-term memory.

We are calling the second component of the structure of memory *long-term memory*. As indicated earlier, this is a more permanent storage repository of information. It is what we typically think of when the term *memory* is mentioned. William James (1890) considered long-term memory as "memory

Long-Term Memory

proper." This is the component of memory that contains information about specific past events as well as our general knowledge about the world. In terms of the duration of information in long-term memory, it is generally accepted that the information resides in a relatively permanent state in long-term memory. (Note however a discussion of this by Loftus, 1980; Loftus & Loftus, 1980.) We will come back to this point in the discussion of Concept 5.2. With regard to the capacity of long-term memory, it is generally agreed that there is a relatively unlimited capacity for information in long-term memory (e.g., Chase & Ericsson, 1982). In terms of information duration and capacity characteristics, it becomes obvious that long-term memory is distinct from working memory.

Procedural, episodic, and semantic memory. Although several proposed models describe the structure of long-term memory (see, for example, Chase, & Ericsson, 1982), a model that is interesting to consider is one proposed by Endel Tulving (1985). He argues that there are at least three "systems" in long-term memory, which he termed *procedural, episodic,* and *semantic* memories. Each system differs in terms of how information is acquired in the system, what information is included, how information is represented, how knowledge is expressed, and the kind of conscious awareness that characterizes the operations of the system. We will briefly consider each of these systems and how they function and differ.

Procedural memory is best described as the memory system that enables us to know "how to do" something, as opposed to enabling us to know "what to do." This system enables us to respond adaptively to the environment by carrying out learned procedures in such a way that specific action goals can be successfully achieved in various environmental circumstances. For the performance of motor skills, procedural memory is a critical memory system, as motor skill is evaluated on the basis of producing a correct response, rather than simply verbalizing it. According to Tulving, an important characteristic of procedural memory is that procedural knowledge can only be acquired through overt behavioral responses, a point commonly accepted from motor skills perspective. Information stored in procedural memory serves as a "blueprint for future action."

Semantic memory is, according to Tulving (1985), characterized by "representing states of the world that are not perceptually present" (p. 387). This means that we store in this memory system our general knowledge about the world that has developed from our many experiences. This includes specific factual knowledge, such as when Columbus discovered America or the name of the tallest building in America, as well as conceptual knowledge, such as our concepts of "dog" and "love." How information is represented in semantic memory is currently the source of much debate. The debate ranges from suggestions that all experiences are represented in some fashion in memory to suggestions that individual experiences are not represented in semantic

memory, but rather, only abstractions, such as prototypes or schemas, are represented. However, to discuss this debate in any detail is beyond the scope of this text. The knowledge stored in semantic memory can be expressed various ways. You may verbally express this knowledge, or you may use typewriting or handwriting. There is no one way that semantic knowledge must be expressed.

Episodic memory consists of knowledge about personally experienced events, along with their temporal associations, in subjective time. It is this memory system that Tulving (1985) believes enables us to "mentally 'travel back' in time" (p. 387). An example here would be your memory of an important life event. You are very likely to recall this event in terms of both time and space. If you are asked a question like, "Do you remember where you were when you heard about the space shuttle explosion that killed seven astronauts just after takeoff?", you would retrieve that information from episodic memory. Thus, episodic memory is usually expressed in terms of remembering some experience, or episode. If you are an eyewitness to a crime, episodic memory becomes a very critical memory system if you are called to be a witness in court.

Relating the three LTM memory systems to motor skills. The question of primary interest is, How do these three systems of long-term memory relate to motor skills? This question can best be answered by considering what you must do to achieve the goal of the skill in a specific performance situation. For example, if your goal is to return a tennis serve down the line by using a forehand drive, how are these memory systems involved in accomplishing this goal? It seems likely that all three memory systems are involved.

To see how these systems are involved, consider first how you establish the goal of the action. You obviously see certain cues from the server and his or her action, as well as from the ball as it is served, and use these cues to help you determine that goal. You also establish your action goal, to some degree, on the basis of situational information even before the server hits the ball. For example, you may know what the server tends to do given the present score of the game and match. Although this type of specific information is available from the server, the serve, and the situation, how do you translate that information into a specific action goal for returning the serve? This is where your use of the three memory systems becomes integral. Before you set your action goal, you must retrieve information from long-term memory to interact with this currently available information to enable you to make an appropriate decision.

Episodic memory undoubtedly comes into play as you retrieve information related to past similar experiences that will provide guidance in the current situation. Semantic memory provides you with the important information about what you have learned to do in this type of situation, thus allowing you to retrieve information that enables you to determine "what to do"

in this situation. Then, procedural memory becomes the vital source for putting this action goal into motion. Now that you have determined what to do, you need to know "how to do" it if you are to succeed.

When we consider the underlying control processes that enable you to carry out a plan to return a serve, it seems that procedural memory is the primary source of this information, although information is undoubtedly retrieved from the semantic and episodic memory systems as well before the action is finally determined and set into motion. Unfortunately, there has been no theoretical effort to relate the concept of the generalized motor programs and schemas to these three memory systems. But, if we consider how the generalized motor program and schemas are proposed to function (as discussed in Concepts 2.3 and 3.4), it is possible to relate these control mechanisms to the three memory systems.

Because the generalized motor program is essentially a type of blueprint for action, it fits very well with what Tulving describes as characteristic of procedural memory. The motor program is the memory representation of carrying out an action. However, it cannot function to allow a goal-directed response to occur without additional response-specific information (parameters). This additional information must come from the recall schema. According to Schmidt (1975), this schema is a general rule that has been developed after much practice. The schema is formed from abstracting certain pieces of information from past episodes and then synthesizing that information so that the episode-specific information is no longer represented in the schema. This suggests that the schema is stored in semantic memory and is called upon to provide parameter values for this response to the motor program that has been retrieved from procedural memory. Since we know that specific episodes are also stored in long-tem memory, it is also likely that past personal experiences similar to the present one will be retrieved and used as a source of information for determining what parameter values should be attached to the generalized motor program. Although this scenario seems quite plausible, there are some who would argue that the parameter information related to the motor program is stored along with the program itself, thus suggesting a procedural memory storage for both program and parameter values (e.g., see Rosenbaum, 1988).

Distinguishing between knowing "what to do" and doing it. An important part of relating the three memory systems of long-term memory with processes underlying motor control is the distinction between knowing "what to do" and being able to successfully perform the action to accomplish that goal. If evidence was available that these are independent concepts, then an empirical basis could be established to support the distinction between the procedural knowledge stored in procedural memory and what has been labeled "declarative knowledge" that is stored in episodic and semantic memory.

One of the only experiments that has investigated this issue was done by McPherson (1987) as part of her doctoral dissertation at Louisiana State University. She classified 9 to 12-year-old children as "expert" or "novice" tennis players based on length of playing experience and tournament play. Novices had never played in tournaments and had only 3 to 6 months playing experience. The "experts," on the other hand, had at least two years experience and had played in junior tournaments. These subjects were clearly in an elite group for their age. McPherson involved these players in games in which she interviewed them after each point (something she had previously established did not disrupt the quality of performance). Players were asked to state what they had attempted to do on the previous point. When this information was later compared with what they had actually done (which was analyzed from a video tape recording), some interesting results were obtained. First, in terms of having an effective strategy or action goal, the "experts" knew "what to do" nearly all the time, whereas the novices generally never knew "what to do." Second, although the "experts" were quite capable of demonstrating they knew what action goal to establish in a specific situation, they were not always able to accomplish it in their performance of the action. This suggests that the appropriate goal was established but there were problems in attaching the appropriate parameter values to the selected motor program. This "what to do" and "how to do it" distinction may be unique to complex motor skills as opposed to most verbal skills, where knowing what to do is all that is needed to be able to do what is intended.

It is important to be aware that we are not certain how the motor control system and the memory systems interact in order to produce an action in a specific situation. Much theory development needs to be done. Part of the problem has been the hesitancy of cognitive skill and motor skill theorists and researchers to see the commonalities between the underlying processes related to the learning and the control of these skills. The tradition has been to consider these skills distinct, the result being theories that make little or no attempt to establish relationships between these skills and their control mechanisms. If this relationship was carefully considered, it is quite likely that what has been previously considered the separate areas of motor control research and memory research will come to be seen as more closely related than will distinct areas of motor behavior research (note, for example, the introduction in Magill, 1983).

Summary

Memory is best viewed as consisting of two functional components, working memory and long-term memory. Working memory briefly stores information presented in the immediate past as well as information that has been retrieved from long-term memory. It has a limited capacity for storing this information. It also serves an active information-processing role as working memory processing activities integrate recently presented information with information retrieved from long-term memory so that a specific problem can be solved.

Long-term memory is our "memory proper" and stores different types of information on a more permanent basis. It appears to have no real limits in terms of how much information can be stored or the length of time the information will remain there. There are three memory systems in long-term memory: procedural memory, semantic memory, and episodic memory. Each system stores a different type of information and has certain unique characteristics that distinguish it from the other systems. These memory systems can be related to motor skill performance by relating their functions to the characteristics and functions of the generalized motor program and the recall schema proposed by Schmidt. The relationship between what has been called memory research and motor control research has also been discussed.

Related Readings

Adams, J. A. (1983). On integration of the verbal and motor domains. In R. A. Magill (Ed.), *Memory and control of action* (pp. 3–15). Amsterdam: North-Holland.

Craik, F. I. M., & Lockhart, R. (1972) Levels of processing: A framework for memory research. *Journal of Verbal Learning and Verbal Behavior, 11,* 671–676.

Ellis, H. C., & Hunt, R. R. (1983). *Fundamentals of human memory and cognition* (3rd ed.). Dubuque, IA: Wm. C. Brown. (Read chapters 4 and 5.)

Ericsson, K. A. (1985). Memory skill. *Canadian Journal of Psychology, 39,* 188–231.

Magill, R. A. (1983). Preface/Introduction. In R. A. Magill (Ed.), *Memory and control of action* (pp. xi–xvi). Amsterdam: North-Holland.

Tulving, E. (1985). How many systems of memory are there? *American Psychologist, 40,* 385–398.

Forgetting can be related to trace decay, interference, or inappropriate retrieval cues

When we use the term *forget,* we usually indicate that we are unable to remember something. If you are asked to throw a curveball, you may respond, "I forget how to hold the ball." In this case, why can't you remember this information? Has it been permanently lost from your memory or are you only temporarily unable to retrieve it? We use the term *forget* to imply both situations. As you will see in the discussion of the present concept, the distinction between information being permanently gone versus its being temporarily lost is an important one for understanding the causes of forgetting.

Our problem, then, is to consider how and why information is forgotten. Examples of forgetting in the motor domain are many, as we have already pointed out. What is perplexing, however, are the causes of forgetting. In some situations we seem to forget information when no other activity follows our receiving the information. In other situations, we forget only when some activity occurs before or after we acquire the information, regardless of the amount of time that has elapsed. Sometimes either condition can exist, and we still fail to remember all the information that has been presented.

You have probably been in the situation where someone showed you how to perform a movement skill. Let us consider the approach and release of the ball in bowling as an example. The instructor told you to follow her through the steps so that you could see how to coordinate your steps with the arm movements necessary to release the ball properly. The intent of the instruction was for you to begin to get the "feel" of these movements as you practiced them with the aid of a model to observe. After you went through this procedure, the instructor had you perform the whole skill on your own. But, for some reason, you had to wait before trying it. Perhaps some in the class had questions for the instructor. Finally, you tried the skill on your own. For the most part you are able to do the steps and release quite well, but there were a few components of the entire movement that you did not remember exactly. As a result, you performed those according to what you thought they should be. But a small error caused the ball to be off target and not as effective as it could have been. Why did you forget the exact movement? Was it because of the time you had to wait between performing the skill with the instructor and doing it yourself? Was it the interference caused by the questions from other members of the class? Although there are a number of other possible reasons to explain why you did not perform well, we will concentrate on the factor of forgetting as it is related to time and interference.

According to our discussion in the first concept of this chapter, the example we have just considered relates to working memory. However, we may

also consider forgetting in the long-term storage stage of memory. For example, you go to a party and someone says, "Can anyone here do a jitterbug?" You haven't done a jitterbug since you were in a dance class in high school several years ago. You say to yourself that you are not going to be the one to demonstrate it to the others. You may remember parts of the steps, but you just cannot seem to get the feel of putting the whole thing together. Finally, someone in the group gets out on the floor and shows the group how to do the jitterbug. Now you remember, and immediately you go through the steps with little difficulty.

This dance example points to a very real problem in the study of human memory, especially in long-term storage situations. Do we ever really forget, or permanently lose, information in long-term storage? Or do we merely misplace it? If it is the latter, then recall from long-term storage becomes a retrieval problem, since the assumption is that the information is there and we just have to locate it.

These few examples of forgetting information in the motor domain should provide you with some understanding of the aspect of memory that we are dealing with in this concept. Forgetting is not only a very important theoretical issue in the study of human memory but also a critical, practical phenomenon. If we can determine the cause or causes of forgetting, then it seems reasonable that this would be a tremendous aid in the development of instructional procedures. If we can anticipate not only *what* but *why* students forget in the process of learning motor skills, we can begin to arrange the presentation of instructional information to take advantage of this knowledge.

Discussion

In our discussion of the structure of memory in the first concept in this chapter we indicated that information in working memory seems to remain there for a very limited amount of time. On the other hand, information in long-term storage seems to be there indefinitely. Thus, it would appear that time alone can cause forgetting information in working memory; but an inability to retrieve, or gain access to the stored information, accounts for forgetting in long-term storage. While these two conclusions seem to have empirical support, they cannot be presented as unequivocal conclusions to explain forgetting. In this discussion, some evidence will be considered relative to both working memory and the long-term storage system implying that a variety of viewpoints exist to explain memory loss.

Measuring Forgetting

Before we discuss the causes of forgetting, it will be helpful to consider how we generally determine whether or not forgetting has occurred. Bear in mind that when we make statements about forgetting, we are making an inference based on observable behavior. We are in a very similar measurement situation as the one we discussed concerning learning and performance; we make an inference about an internal event on the basis of external observations.

Recall and recognition tests. Measuring how much a person has forgotten, or conversely, remembered, typically involves administering one of two types of tests. A *recall test* requires the person to produce a required response with few, if any, available cues or aids. In the verbal domain, recall tests typically take the form of fill-in-the-blank tests or essay tests. In motor skills, a recall test asks the subject to produce a certain movement, such as "move your arm the correct distance." A *recognition test* provides the individual with some cues or information on which to base a response. In the verbal domain, multiple-choice or matching tests are recognition tests. In movement situations, recognition tests can be administered by having a subject produce several different movements and then asking which of these is the one just practiced. Another form of recognition test found in the motor skills literature involves having the subject move to a given location, as on a linear positioning apparatus, and asking whether this is the "same" or "different" location as compared to the one just practiced. Other types of recognition tests have had subjects move a handle or cursor through a prescribed pattern of movement and then indicate if they had practiced that pattern before.

In terms of motor skill performance situations, we are often confronted with both recall and recognition "tests," sometimes in the same situation. An example of a recall test is when a basketball player must shoot a free throw. He or she must recall what must be done and how it should be done in order to make the shot. An example of a recognition test is when a football quarterback must visually inspect the defense to determine if their alignment is as it should be if he is to use the offensive play that has been called. Both recall and recognition tests are relevant to a baseball batter when deciding whether or not to swing at the pitch (Is the ball in the strike zone?) and then when swinging appropriately to hit the pitch where it is thrown.

Although there are other types of memory tests that can be used to determine what is remembered or forgotten, recall and recognition tests are the most common and provide a sufficient introduction into the methods used to test memory performance. The benefit of recall and recognition tests is that each provides different information about what has been remembered or forgotten. It is possible not to be able to produce a correct response on a recall test and yet to be able to produce that response when it is one among several alternatives in a recognition test. The value of the recognition test, then, is that it enables the researcher to determine if information is actually stored in memory, but the individual requires retrieval cues or aids in order to gain access to that information.

Memory experiment paradigms. In the sections that follow in this discussion, you will consider examples of memory research. Common among these are the experimental paradigms used to carry out this research. These paradigms can be used for both working memory and long-term memory investigations. Figure 5.2–1 illustrates these paradigms in simple line diagrams. Typically,

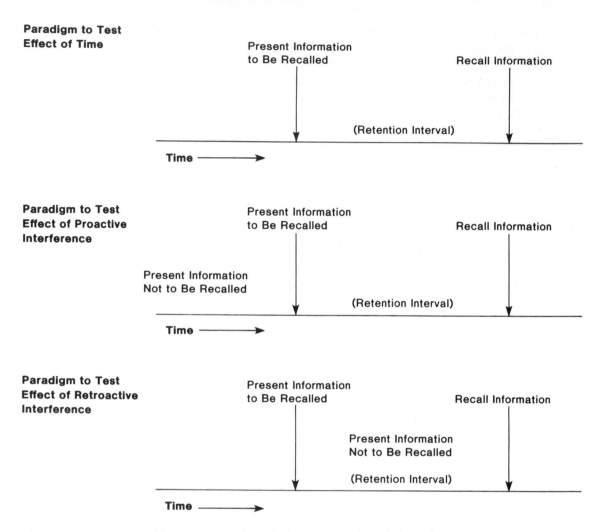

Paradigm to Test Effect of Time

Present Information to Be Recalled

Recall Information

(Retention Interval)

Time ⟶

Paradigm to Test Effect of Proactive Interference

Present Information to Be Recalled

Recall Information

Present Information Not to Be Recalled

(Retention Interval)

Time ⟶

Paradigm to Test Effect of Retroactive Interference

Present Information to Be Recalled

Recall Information

Present Information Not to Be Recalled

(Retention Interval)

Time ⟶

Figure 5.2-1
Time-line diagrams illustrating typical experimental paradigms used to investigate some causes of forgetting from memory.

this system consists of the presentation of the information to be recalled, a retention interval, and the recall of the information. The purpose of the experiment will dictate more specific procedures. For example, if the hypothesis to be tested indicates that time is a cause of forgetting, then the experimenter will vary the length of the retention interval. The Adams and Dijkstra (1966) study discussed in Concept 5.1 is a good example of such a paradigm. If the experiment is investigating interference as a cause for forgetting, then some activity, either cognitive or motor, is inserted either before the information to be recalled is presented or during the retention interval. When the interference occurs before the presentation of the information, we are setting up a *proactive interference* situation. If the interfering activity occurs during the retention interval, that is, after the presentation of the information, the paradigm

is one investigating *retroactive interference*. Each of these experimental situations will be used in the examples of research studies that we will discuss shortly.

The procedures of the Adams and Dijkstra (1966) experiment provide a good model to help understand the paradigm for measuring forgetting. Since memory for movement information rather than verbal information is the primary concern, there is a need to ensure that only motor or kinesthetic information is being used as the information to be recalled. The linear slide apparatus is typical of equipment used for motor memory research. When the subject is blindfolded, no information other than kinesthetic is available or reliably useful to him or her. The response of the subject is easily measured by noting the number of centimeters, millimeters, or degrees of arc that the subject moved. Thus, the indicator of how well the movement is remembered, is the error score obtained by subtracting the subject's estimate of the movement from the criterion, or actual, movement. Since the subject moved or was moved to the criterion location, the accuracy with which he or she estimates that same movement can be considered a valid indicator of retention. (It will be helpful at this point to review the various error-related measures discussed in Concept 1.3 as those measures are extensively used in the motor memory literature.)

To make an inference about the influence of time or interference on forgetting, the researcher compares the various experimental time or interference conditions in terms of the amount of error associated with each condition in relation to reproducing the criterion location. If one condition shows more retention test error than another condition, we infer that the condition producing more error caused more forgetting.

Trace Decay

One of the earliest investigations of time as a possible cause of forgetting in motor memory was the Adams and Dijkstra (1966) study. Subjects were asked to move to a stop on a linear positioning task and then estimate the location without a stop. Seven different retention intervals were used: 5, 10, 20, 50, 80, and 120 seconds. While there were other procedures for this experiment, the one presented here is sufficient for our needs. Figure 5.2–2 indicates the results of this experiment. You can readily see that the amount of error the subjects made increased steadily as the length of the retention interval increased, with 20 seconds appearing as the point in time when the amount of error was appreciably different from almost immediate recall, that is, 5 seconds. Since nothing occurred during the retention interval except the passage of time, the conclusion drawn by Adams and Dijkstra was that memory for movements is subject to rapid forgetting. In the memory literature this cause of forgetting is generally termed *trace decay*.

In a review of research investigating the retention of motor skills, Stelmach (1974) indicated that few researchers other than Adams and Dijkstra have directly studied trace decay as the primary cause of forgetting. Most of

Figure 5.2-2
Results from the
experiment by
Adams and Dijkstra
showing the mean
absolute error for
the recall of a
positioning task
following different
lengths of retention
intervals.

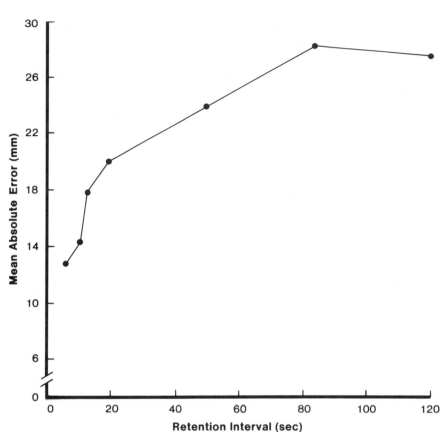

the evidence showing that trace decay is an important cause of forgetting comes from experiments that investigated interference but also included a trace-decay component. We will indicate those situations when we discuss interference theory.

As a result of the Adams and Dijkstra (1966) study, as well as several other studies, we can be rather certain that when kinesthetic information is in working memory, it is very susceptible to the effects of time. Following a period of 20 to 30 seconds, that information begins to be lost rather rapidly.

Only in working memory does trace decay appear to be a cause of forgetting. Long-term storage of information appears to be influenced primarily by interfering activity, which of course interacts with time. For example, if you try to recall a gymnastic routine after several years of not having performed it, you will have some initial difficulty remembering all the varied aspects of the routine. While it is obvious that time is a factor here, we must consider the possible interfering influences of the many verbal and motor tasks

you have performed since you last performed the routine you wish to recall. Hence, we observe the interaction of interference and time in the long-term storage situation. However, it is important to remember that long-term storage is not a temporary depository of information but rather a relatively permanent storage, where information seems to be misplaced rather than to decay. A major problem here is the practical impossibility of investigating the time factor in forgetting from long-term storage, since it would not be possible to maintain a no-interference situation. As a result, we know very little about the effects of time on information in long-term storage.

It is generally accepted that interference is a cause of forgetting. However, there seems to be only limited agreement concerning the nature of the activity that interferes with memory or when the interfering activity occurs. For our purposes, we will consider the evidence that seems to support the interference theory for both working memory and long-term storage.

Interference

Proactive interference. Relatively convincing evidence suggests that proactive interference is a reason for the forgetting of kinesthetic information in working memory. George Stelmach (1969) presented some early evidence for proactive interference effects. In his experiment, subjects were required to move to either zero, two, or four locations on a curvilinear positioning task before moving to the location to be recalled. Following a retention interval of 5, 15, or 50 seconds, the subjects were asked to estimate in reverse order each of the locations they had moved to. Thus, the first location recalled was the criterion location, or the location of interest for this study. Results of this experiment are presented in Figure 5.2–3. Proactive interference effects can be seen rather markedly when there were four prior movements and a retention interval of at least 15 seconds. It should also be noted that some supporting evidence for trace-decay theory can be seen here, since error increased as the retention interval lengthened when there were no movements preceding the criterion movement.

Several attempts have been made to explain why proactive interference affects remembering movement information. One plausible suggestion is that when the proactive interference takes the form of other movements, especially those that are similar to the criterion activity, *confusion* occurs. The individual is unable to make precisely the criterion movement because of the influence of the prior activities on the distinctiveness of the criterion movement. Whether or not verbal activity is an effective proactive interference agent does not seem to be known at this time. What evidence is available indicates that if we store the movement to be recalled as a verbal symbol, such as when we count and use a number to help recall the movement, then verbal activity can be a cause of forgetting. However, we will have to wait for more research to be published in order better to understand why proactive interference causes forgetting in working memory.

Figure 5.2-3
Results of an
experiment by
Stelmach showing
proactive
interference effects
as a function of the
amount of proactive
interference activity
and the length of
the retention
interval.

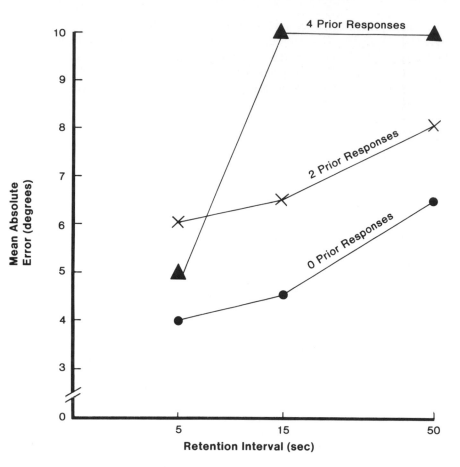

For movement information that has been transferred into long-term storage, the role of proactive interfering activities is virtually unknown. It appears that we can quite readily overcome proactive interference effects by actively rehearsing the information. This means that by active practice of a movement, we strengthen the trace for the movement in memory and thus notice few, if any, effects of proactive interference.

The appropriate view of proactive interference is that it occurs only when there is similarity in what is to be remembered and the interfering activity. This similarity seems to relate to "attribute" similarity. That is, if the information to be remembered and the interfering activity relate to the same movement attribute or characteristic, then proactive interference will build up as the number of similar movements preceding the movements to be remembered increases.

To support this viewpoint, a technique called release from proactive interference (developed by Wickens, 1970) has been used with some success. An example is a study by Leavitt, Lee, and Romanow (1980). On each trial,

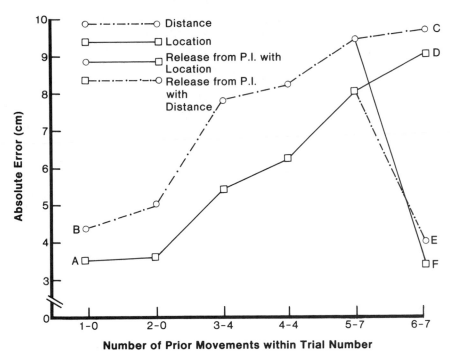

Figure 5.2-4
Results from the
experiment by
Leavitt, Lee, and
Romanow showing
the buildup and
release from
proactive
interference (P.I.) as
a function of the
number of
movements made
prior to the
criterion movement
(second number of
pair of numbers on
horizontal axis) and
the number of trials
(first number of
pair) for location
and distance
criterion
movements. Release
from P.I. occurs
when a new
criterion movement
is experienced
(points E and F on
trial 6).

subjects were presented a criterion location or distance movement on a linear positioning apparatus. On the first two trials, only the criterion movement was presented and recalled. On the third and fourth trials, four additional locations or distances were presented before the criterion movement was presented. Then on the fifth trial, seven additional movements were presented prior to the criterion. If proactive interference builds up as a function of the number of preceding movements and experiences, error in recalling the criterion movement should increase accordingly. As you can see from Figure 5.2–4, proactive interference effects were in fact greater when the criterion movement was preceded by more movements. Notice, however, what happened on trial 6. On this trial, some of the subjects had their criterion movement switched to the opposite type of movement, i.e., from a distance to a location movement or vice versa. When this occurred, there was a dramatic reduction in recall error (points E and F). Proactive interference effects were still noted for those subjects who did not have the criterion movement switched on this final trial. The important point here is that proactive interference is a specific type of interfering effect from which a person can be quickly "released."

Retroactive interference. If an interfering activity occurs during the retention interval, we will generally observe poorer recall than if no activity had occurred. Although some conflicting research evidence exists concerning the influence of retroactive interference on movements in working memory, several

studies indicate the effect of this type of interfering activity. Four experiments that clearly illustrate retroactive interference effects were presented in a study by Williams, Beaver, Spence, and Rundell (1969). These experiments involved combinations of retention of digits and movements, with both digit manipulation and movements as interfering activities. For the recall of a series of six digits, the accuracy of recall decreased as the difficulty of the interfering digital manipulation task increased. In other words, retention of the series of digits was poorer when they simply recorded a list of digits during the retention interval. However, for the recall of movements, the degree of difficulty of these digit manipulation interfering tasks did not produce any differential effects on recall accuracy. When subjects were required to perform simple movements of a lever during the retention interval, the opposite effects were observed. Movements interfered with the recall accuracy of movements but not with the recall of digits. Thus, retroactive interference effects were noted for kinesthetic memory as well as for verbal memory, although the type of activity that produced interference effects was specific to the memory involved.

Another study that reported retroactive interference effects for working memory was published by Roy and Davenport (1972). Using a linear positioning task, they showed that retroactive interference effects were evident when subjects were required to make four movements during the retention interval but not when they had to make no movements or two movements. It would appear, then, that while retroactive interference effects are observed in motor memory, the activity that causes the interference must be relatively demanding for the subject. Perhaps another way of expressing this would be to state that the activity must be "attention demanding" for the subject. If the activity does not require processing capacity, as we discussed in Concept 4.2, then it seems likely that the interfering activity will have a minimal influence on the recall of the criterion movement. The subject is still able to rehearse mentally the movement to be recalled while performing the activity during the retention interval.

A useful approach to the study of retroactive interference effects has been the investigation of what influence this interference actually has on the movement to be recalled. One effect that has had some experimental support is that retroactive interference makes the subject inclined to either overshoot or undershoot the criterion. The evidence indicates that the bias occurs in the direction of the interfering activity. Thus, if the subject moved to various locations that were beyond the criterion location during the retention interval, then the tendency for the response at recall was to overshoot the criterion location. A study by Stelmach and Kelso (1975) found that this response biasing could be either increased or decreased by varying the amount of time the subject remained at the criterion location during the presentation of the movement or by varying the number of repetitions of the interfering movements. Increasing both of these variables caused a reduction in the amount of response biasing.

What do these studies tell us about retroactive interference and memory? In general, they provide evidence that we are susceptible to retroactive interference effects in motor memory. Certain types of interfering activities seem to produce more interference than others. Another motor activity, especially if it is relatively similar to the one you are trying to remember, will produce more interference than verbal activity. This appears to imply that if you are making a movement by following a model, such as going through a dance step or swinging the golf club as the instructor demonstrates, then the accuracy of your attempt to reproduce that movement will be greater if you do not perform some other related movement between the demonstration and the practice attempt. As an instructor, you should try to make certain when you are going through a series of movements, that you have your students practice the movements you are emphasizing as close in time to the demonstration as possible. Try not to have them swing the club along with you and then introduce some variations before they practice the swing that they did with you. If you are teaching a wrestling maneuver and having the students watch your demonstration or do it along with your demonstration, do not show them some alternate ways of doing the maneuver before they have had an opportunity to practice the basic move on their own. They can practice the alternate ways after they feel confident performing the basic maneuver.

Retroactive interference and long-term memory. The memory situations we have described to this point have primarily involved working memory. Retroactive interference effects have also been found for kinesthetic information in long-term storage. While research findings on this have been scant, there is some evidence that retroactive interference effects do occur. Methodological difficulties seem to limit the number of research studies of this problem. It is difficult to control a subject's activities between the learning practice trials of a task that places the information in long-term storage and the recall test when it is a week, or month or even a year later.

A notable phenomenon in long-term memory is that motor skills seem to be remembered better over long periods than are verbal skills. Your own experiences may provide some support for this. You probably had very little trouble remembering how to ride a bicycle, even after not having been on one for several years. However, you did experience some difficulty in remembering a poem you learned in school around the same time you learned to ride a bicycle.

A few research studies have supported this long-term memory effect for motor skills. Bell (1950) had subjects practice for 20 one-minute trials on the pursuit rotor, then return after one year for a retention test. Scores dropped only 29% after the one-year layoff. In fact, after only 8 trials, the subjects' scores returned to where they had been a year earlier.

Ryan (1965) found similar results with the stabilometer. After 11 trials of practice, the subjects had a 3-, 6-, or 12-month retention interval. Figure

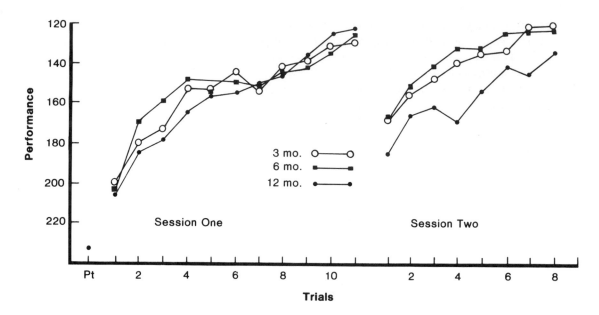

Figure 5.2-5
Results of the
experiment by Ryan
showing the
performance curves
for learning trials
on the stabilometer
(session one) and
for relearning trials
(session two)
following either 3,
6, or 12 months of
no practice.

5.2–5 shows the results. On trial 1 of the retention test, all groups' performance dropped significantly. However, after just a very few trials, their performance increased to a level similar to previous performance. Although these results differ markedly from some other findings, they serve to show how resistant to time the learning of motor skills can be.

Several reasons have been proposed over the years to account for this apparent motor vs. verbal skill long-term retention difference. We will consider only two of the more plausible reasons. First, it is likely that more verbal skills have been "overlearned" to a greater extent than have motor skills. We will consider the concept of overlearning in Chapter 9, but for now it can be best understood as practice over and above what was needed to learn the skill. If you compare the bicycle riding and the poem recitation examples presented earlier, it is very likely that there was a much higher degree of practice beyond what was needed to learn to ride a bike than there was with the poem. The second proposed reason for the motor skills retention longevity is that motor skills are typically more inherently meaningful than are verbal skills. In fact, verbal skills that are highly meaningful to people have a remarkable longevity in memory.

Inappropriate Retrieval Cues

One of the things we can learn from the results of memory tests is that the availability of retrieval cues can be important for remembering. Retrieval cues should be thought of as aids or hints that provide a useful means for finding a particular piece of information stored in memory. For example, you may be asked to recall the name of the world's tallest building, and you respond, "I forget." The implication is that you have the correct information stored in

memory but you cannot gain access to it. The questioner then says that the building belongs to a large department store chain. You now have received a cue that can aid your search through memory for the information and you find that you can correctly answer the question.

In movement situations, we often are unable to produce the required response because we "forget" how it should be done. However, a closer inspection of this situation indicates that we simply cannot retrieve the needed information on the basis of the available cues. For example, you have been asked to throw a curveball and you find that you cannot do it. You may have "forgotten" how to correctly release the ball when you throw it, although you have remembered how to do everything else. If someone helps you remember that one aspect of the pitch, you find that you can successfully throw a curve. The problem was not that you did not have the information in memory; it was that you were unable to retrieve the stored information until you were provided a useful retrieval cue.

One of the important sources of retrieval cue information for producing a movement is the context of the movement. The term *context* refers to all the conditions surrounding the performance of a movement. A consideration of the movement context is particularly helpful for investigating the role of the availability of appropriate retrieval cues for remembering movement information. For certain movements, the availability of the same context during the test that was available during practice is essential to the accurate recall of a movement. In such situations, requiring individuals to produce a practiced movement in a new context will lead to poorer performance because of the unavailability of appropriate retrieval cues.

An experiment demonstrating this was reported by Lee and Hirota (1980). Subjects were required to move the handle of a linear positioning apparatus to a physical stop defining the movement distance to be remembered. On some trials, the subjects actively moved the handle to the stop and were then asked to recall that movement by either again actively moving the handle to where they thought the criterion movement ended or they were moved passively by the experimenter. On the passive recall trials, the subject would tell the experimenter when to stop moving his or her arm. On other trials, the subjects passively moved the criterion movement distance. The recall was again either active or passive. According to the role played by context in this situation, a specific prediction of the results can be made. If the retrieval cues that were available during the presentation phase are important for recall of the criterion movement, then the results of this experiment should show that the active presentation with active recall and the passive presentation with passive recall conditions should have better recall performance than the two situations in which the recall conditions were different from the presentation conditions. Figure 5.2–6 illustrates the results. As you can see, the availability of appropriate retrieval cues during the recall test was important. When the recall test

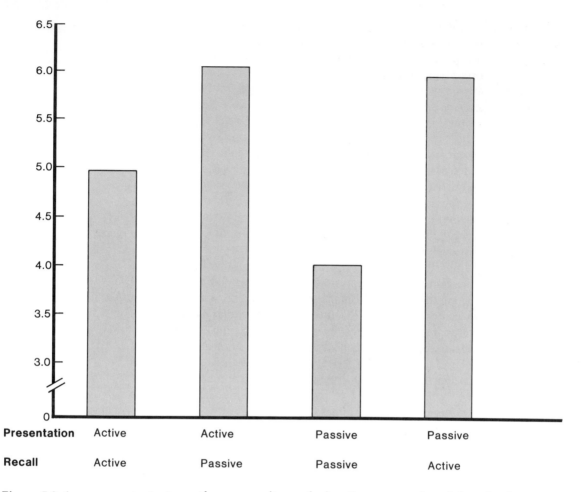

Presentation	Active	Active	Passive	Passive
Recall	Active	Passive	Passive	Active

Figure 5.2-6
Results of the experiment by Lee and Hirota showing absolute error for recalling arm-position movements presented as either active or passive and recalled in either the same or opposite conditions.

context was the same as it was during the presentation of the criterion movement, the recall error was less than when the presentation and recall contexts were different.

This experiment illustrates that inferior recall performance from which we infer forgetting can be due to the unavailability of important retrieval cues. When these cues are available, recall performance is improved. The question that remains, however, concerns how far this principle can be extended and under what condition it holds. We will consider this question more specifically in the discussion of the next concept. For the present, the important feature to understand is that forgetting is often the result of the unavailability of appropriate retrieval cues. When those cues are available, remembering is enhanced.

Summary

Forgetting or loss of information is a very real problem in the study of memory. Forgetting is typically measured by determining the amount of information that a person can recall or recognize following a certain interval of time after the presentation of the data to the individual. Both trace decay, or time, and interference seem to be primary causes of forgetting. Interference must be considered in terms of interfering activities occurring either before (proactive interference) or after (retroactive interference) the presentation of the information. Another cause of forgetting is the unavailability of appropriate retrieval cues. Here information cannot be remembered because the individual is not able to gain access to the information stored in memory. When appropriate cues are made available, an appropriate response can be made.

Related Readings

Adams, J. A. (1987). Historical review and appraisal of research on the learning, retention, and transfer of human motor skills. *Psychological Bulletin, 101,* 41–74.

Adams, J. A., & Dijkstra, S. (1966). Short-term memory for motor responses. *Journal of Experimental Psychology, 71,* 314–318.

Fischman, M. G., Christina, R. W., & Vercruyssen, M. J. (1981). Retention and transfer of motor skills: A review for the practitioner. *Quest, 33,* 181–194.

Lee, T. D., & Hirota, T. T. (1980). Encoding specificity principle in motor short-term memory for movement extent. *Journal of Motor Behavior, 12,* 63–67.

Loftus, E. F., & Loftus, G. R. (1980). On the permanence of stored information in the human brain. *American Psychologist, 35,* 409–420.

Stelmach, G. E. (1974). Retention of motor skills. In J. R. Wilmore (Ed.), *Exercise and sport science reviews* (Vol. 2, pp. 1–26). New York: Academic Press.

Concept 5.3 The retention of information in memory is related to control processes involved in the storage and retrieval of information

Application

When you are given instruction on how to serve a racquetball or how to release the ball in bowling, what aspects of the movement do you remember or try to remember? How do you make yourself remember what is important for the proper execution of such skills? Do you select certain phases of each skill and in some way concentrate on remembering these? Do you try to combine the new instruction with past instruction and past practice experiences you have had? Each of these questions points to an important aspect of the study of human memory, that is, the control processes. As we will later discuss, control in memory relates to those actions or reactions over which you have some direct control. Such components as what information you store in memory, how you rehearse or use the information, how you organize the information, and how you retrieve the stored information are examples of control processes.

In sports skills, we are required to learn rather complex movement patterns and sequences. This learning requires memory. We will discuss some of the factors that influence our remembering movement information. Rather than focusing on what causes us to forget, as we did in the previous concept, we will consider how those influences can be overcome. The result should be a more durable and accessible memory for the information being learned. To accomplish this, we will discuss some of the problems that arise in attempting to determine how the learner of movement skills stores, organizes, and uses information. Understanding these control processes will enable us better to explain how memory functions, as well as to make pertinent suggestions concerning how better to utilize the control processes that are at our command.

Discussion

Control processes are important in the study of human memory, for they represent the means by which we use our memories. Primarily, control processes are employed to enable us to remember information. Some of these processes are under our direct control while other control processes are automatic and not under our direct control.

Control processes involve such functions as selecting particular aspects of presented information to place in working memory, the retrieval of appropriate information from long-term storage to interact with the information in working memory, and rehearsal processes used to transfer and organize information from the working memory to the long-term store. While there are other control processes (see, for example, Hasher & Zacks, 1979; Shiffrin & Schneider, 1977), these few identify the type of operations that will be the focus of this discussion.

Rather than study these control processes directly, we will consider various factors that influence the remembering of movement information. From this study, the control factors involved in these influences can be addressed and considered more specifically in terms of how they relate to memory processes. We will consider three general influences on remembering. First is the influence of the type of movement or movement characteristic that must be remembered. Second is certain strategies that can be employed by the learner or incorporated into the learning situation by the instructor to enhance remembering. Third is the relationship of the context characteristics between when a movement is practiced and when it is performed in some type of test.

Certain terms involved in the discussion of these influences need to be identified and defined. *Encoding* refers to the transformation of information to be remembered into a form that can be stored in memory. *Storage* of information is the process of placing information in long-term memory. *Rehearsal* is a process that enables the individual to transfer information from the working memory to long-term memory. *Retrieval* involves the search through long-term memory for information that must be accessed in order to respond to the task at hand and the assessment of that information.

Discrete vs. continuous skills. One of the several classification systems discussed in Concept 1.1 was a system that distinguished skills in terms of the distinctness or arbitrariness of the beginning and end point of the required response. Discrete skills are those skills whose response has a defined, distinct beginning and end, such as hitting a typewriter key. Continuous skills have rather arbitrary beginning and end points, such as would be characteristic of a tracking task. When these two classifications of skills are compared in terms of how well they are remembered over an extended time, discrete skills are more susceptible to long-term forgetting than are continuous skills.

This retention difference seems to be especially characteristic when the continuous skills are compared with a series of discrete responses that must be performed in a specific order if the goal of the task is to be achieved. This type of serial discrete skill has been commonly referred to as a *procedural skill*. Examples of how well continuous skills are retained over a long-term retention interval were discussed in Concept 5.1 when motor and verbal skills were compared in their retention longevity. A number of examples of the retention loss associated with procedural skills exist in the motor skills research literature. For example, Adams and Hufford (1962) trained military personnel to perform a complex bomb-toss maneuver. When these soldiers were tested on this skill 10 months later, during which they had not performed this skill, a 95% loss in performance proficiency was found.

More recently, Schendel and Hagman (1982) trained soldiers to disassemble and assemble an M60 machine gun, a procedure that includes 35 distinct responses. One trial was counted when a soldier completed both the disassembly and assembly of the gun. The soldiers continued to practice this

The Type of
Movement or
Movement
Characteristic

skill until they were able to perform one errorless trial. Four weeks later, during which the soldiers did not perform this skill, one group of soldiers had a refresher training session during which they practiced the skill as they had previously. Then, four weeks later (eight weeks later for the group that had no refresher training) a test of disassembly/assembly performance was given. The group that had the refresher training session in the middle of the retention interval showed a 57% advantage over the other group in terms of the amount of errors made on the first trial on the retention test. Thus, much forgetting occurred in this skill over an eight-week retention interval.

Several reasons have been suggested to explain why this discrete, procedural skill vs. continuous skill retention difference occurs. Adams (1987), for example, suggests that the difference is related to procedural skills having a large verbal component. If you recall the discussion in Concept 5.1 with regard to the motor vs. verbal skill retention characteristic, the large verbal component characteristic of procedural skills indicates that they would not be expected to be retained well over an extended time without additional practice. As evidence that procedural skills have a large verbal component, Adams cites a study by Neumann and Ammons (1957) in which subjects had to learn a complex sequence of manipulating switches. Almost half of these subjects reported that they had used verbal cues to designate the locations of the switches.

What are the implications for motor skill instruction of this continuous skill vs. discrete, procedural skill retention difference? One implication is that when students are taught skills in which they must learn a complex sequence of movements, such as a dance or gymnastics routine, it is important to provide additional practice on the sequence after the original learning has occurred if a test is to be given. It should not be assumed that because the student can perform the sequence correctly that he or she will remember it well enough to be tested on it at some later time. Compare this sequence to the machine gun disassembly/assembly experiment discussed earlier.

Another implication for developing effective practice is to require additional practice at the time of original practice. This extra practice should be beyond what is needed to achieve one correct performance of the sequence. The additional practice, called "overpractice" or "overlearning," appears to be very beneficial in diminishing the amount of forgetting that occurs in procedural skills over long-term retention intervals, and will be more thoroughly considered in Concept 9.2.

Location and distance characteristics. Movement has many characteristics that we could code in memory. We might consider the spatial position of various points of a movement, such as the beginning and the end point of a golf swing. We could also code the distance of the movement, its velocity, its force, or the direction of the movement. These characteristics represent specific spatial and temporal features of movement. Two of these, *location* and *distance,*

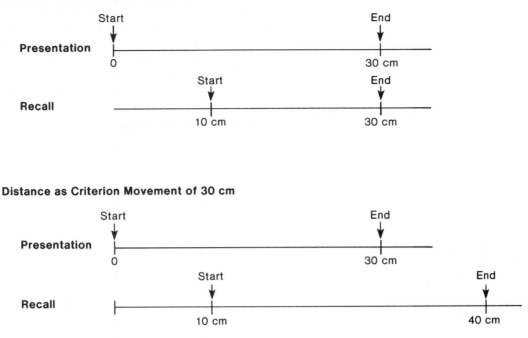

Location as Criterion Movement of 30 cm

Presentation

Start | End
0 | 30 cm

Recall

Start | End
10 cm | 30 cm

Distance as Criterion Movement of 30 cm

Presentation

Start | End
0 | 30 cm

Recall

Start | End
10 cm | 40 cm

have been extensively examined with regard to their codability. The logic here is that the more codable a movement characteristic is, the more easily it can be remembered. As a result, those movement characteristics that are more readily encoded are more durable and more easily accessed in memory.

Most of the research comparing location and distance characteristics of movement have used the working memory paradigms described in Figure 5.2–1. These experiments have typically used some form of limb-positioning task. To distinguish a movement's end location from its distance so that these two characteristics can be compared, the starting and/or end positions of the criterion movement must be changed for the subject's recall movement. These changes are diagramed in Figure 5.3–1. If the end location characteristic is of interest in the experiment, the recall starting position is changed. The criterion end location remains the same, thereby making the movement's distance an unreliable cue to aid recall. If the distance of the movement is of primary interest, the recall starting and end positions must be changed. This procedure requires the subject to remember how far the movement was and makes the location where the presentation movement ended an unreliable cue to aid recall.

Early research concerned with memory for movement information did not separate location and distance characteristics of positioning movements (e.g., Adams & Dijkstra, 1966; Stelmach, 1969). The problem with this was made apparent primarily by Laabs (1973) when he demonstrated that when

Figure 5.3-1
Diagrams illustrating method of making location and distance characteristics of a 30-cm limb movement distinct for experimental purposes.

location and distance characteristics are separated, memory effects are markedly different. Location characteristics were found to decay very little during an empty retention interval of 20 seconds, whereas extent characteristics were influenced by decay. Activity during the retention interval was also found to have different influences on location and distance characteristics. Location was influenced by verbal counting during the retention interval, whereas distance characteristics showed no more effect for activity than for no activity during the 20-second retention interval.

Much of the research that followed essentially confirmed Laabs' findings (e.g., Diewert, 1975; Hagman, 1978), although there were conflicting findings concerning the remembering of distance information. An important breakthrough in this research was provided by Diewert and Roy (1978). They showed that when location information is a relatively reliable recall cue, subjects will use a location-type strategy to recall the movement. However, when location information is totally unreliable and only distance information will aid recall, subjects will use some nonkinesthetic strategy, such as counting, to help remember the distance of the criterion movement. Interestingly, spontaneous use of this dual strategy to aid the remembering of location and distance information has been demonstrated with children only after age nine (Thomas, Thomas, Lee, Testerman, & Ashy, 1983).

Another interesting aspect of remembering location information has been pointed out by Larish and Stelmach (1982; Stelmach & Larish, 1980). They showed that subjects can more easily remember end locations of movements when they are within their own body space. For positioning movements, subjects typically use a body part cue to associate with the end location of the criterion movement. Other research that will be considered later suggests that subjects will also associate end locations with well-known objects, such as a clock face, to aid recall.

In practical terms, when you are teaching a beginner a golf swing, the important phases of the swing that he or she should concentrate on are critical location points in the swing. The keys would be the beginning point of the backswing, the location point of the top of the backswing, and some location cue about the finish of the swing. A common practice is to use the clock-face hours as cues for these important locations. Thus the learner will be better able to use that information in learning the golf swing because he or she can code location information rather effectively.

The meaningfulness of the movement. Another characteristic of movement information that influences remembering movements is the *meaningfulness* of the movement. A movement can be considered meaningful to an individual if that person can readily relate the movement to something already known. For example, a movement that forms the shape of a triangle is considered more meaningful than one that makes an unfamiliar, abstract pattern.

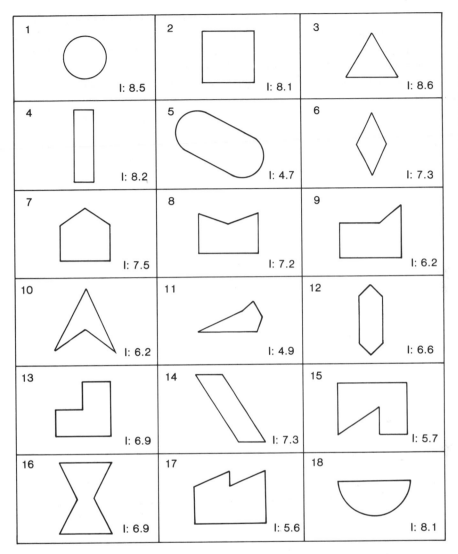

Figure 5.3-2
Movement patterns used in memory experiment by Hall. Number in each top left corner is the pattern number. Number in each bottom right corner is the imagery value of the pattern. Higher numbers indicate the pattern is easier to image.

1 — I: 8.5	2 — I: 8.1	3 — I: 8.6
4 — I: 8.2	5 — I: 4.7	6 — I: 7.3
7 — I: 7.5	8 — I: 7.2	9 — I: 6.2
10 — I: 6.2	11 — I: 4.9	12 — I: 6.6
13 — I: 6.9	14 — I: 7.3	15 — I: 5.7
16 — I: 6.9	17 — I: 5.6	18 — I: 8.1

An example of how movement meaningfulness influences remembering has been provided by Hall (1980). Subjects were presented closed multidimensional movements (as seen in Figure 5.3–2) by means of a pantograph, a movement device that allows the subject to make the exact same arm movements as the experimenter. The memory test in this experiment was a recognition test where subjects were moved through a series of patterns and asked to indicate whether or not each pattern was the one just practiced. Results, shown in Figure 5.3–2, indicated that recognition was highest when the presented pattern was a common geometric figure and lowest when it was an abstract pattern. These results led Hall to develop an imagery scale for the 48

different movement patterns. On this scale, the highest values are the easiest to recognize, and the lowest values are the most difficult to recognize.

Hall's experiments, among others, suggest that certain movements have more inherent meaningfulness to people than other movements. This seems especially to be the case when the imagery value of a movement is considered. The more meaningful a movement is to a person, the easier it is to remember that movement. This point is an important one to consider when providing instructions to students to help them remember how to perform a skill. We will come back to it later in this discussion when we consider strategies that influence remembering.

Strategy Employed

In addition to the type of movement or movement characteristic that must be remembered, individual strategy influences how well movements are remembered. The strategy may be one generated by the person who must remember the movement or it may be one imposed by the experimenter or teacher. In either case, different remembering strategies can have different influences on how well a movement is remembered or how much is forgotten. In this section, we will consider five strategies that could be used in a movement memory situation. The first strategy involves making the movement more meaningful to the subject or student. The second involves allowing the individual to select his or her own movement to remember, rather than requiring that a particular movement be remembered. The third strategy involves rote repetition of the movement to be remembered. Fourth is a strategy involving the influence on remembering of intentionally trying to remember a movement versus not intentionally trying to remember. And the last strategy involves what is known as subjective organization.

Knowledge about effective remembering strategies is important for students and teachers alike. Students need to know about the benefit of certain strategies over others to enhance their own learning performance. Teachers need to be aware of the effectiveness of different remembering strategies so that they can incorporate effective strategies into the instructional process to aid student learning. Thus, this discussion of strategies will not only help you gain a better understanding of memory processes, it will also provide you with useful information to aid your own learning and teaching of motor skills.

Increasing the movement's meaningfulness. Most movements that you learn require the coordination of the body and limbs in a new way. In this respect, we could say that when you are first presented with a new motor skill, you are confronted with a movement that is more abstract than it is concrete. That is, the skill typically has little inherent "meaningfulness" to you in terms of the required organizational structure of the spatial and temporal characteristics of the limb coordination needed to perform the skill. Here we will consider some ways in which you can increase the meaningfulness of the movements

you are trying to learn. By doing this, you will find that it becomes easier to learn the skill as you practice it. This increased ease in learning the skill occurs to a large extent because more meaningful movements are remembered better than less meaningful movements, a point discussed in the preceding section. We are attempting to relate (a) the concept that more meaningful movements are better remembered with (b) a remembering strategy application.

The more commonly used strategies to increase the meaningfulness of a movement involve the use of *imagery*. Imagery as a remembering strategy involves developing in your mind a picture of what the movement is like. It is best to use an image of something that is very familiar. Before considering the application of using imagery as a remembering strategy, we will consider some research that indicates the benefit of such a strategy.

An example of a research study that showed the benefits of having subjects image to aid in the recall of movement patterns was by Hall and Buckolz (1982–83). Subjects were given 18 movement patterns from the list shown earlier in Figure 5.3–2. One group of subjects was given specific instructions to develop mental images of the patterns as they were presented. Another group was simply presented with the patterns and given no instructions to image. Although the results of this experiment showed no recall difference between these two groups, it is interesting to note that postexperiment interviews with subjects revealed that *all* subjects in the no-instructions group spontaneously imaged when the movement patterns were presented.

We will consider other procedures related to imagery strategy in Chapter 9 in the discussion of mental practice. For the present, it is important to see that the use of mental imagery appears to be a powerful rehearsal strategy. As such, it can also be an effective instructional strategy for teachers. For example, rather than provide the complex instructions for how to coordinate the arm movements to perform a sidestroke in swimming, the instructor can provide the students with a useful image to use while practicing the stroke. The image is that the students should see themselves picking an apple from a tree with one hand, bringing the apple down, and putting the apple in a basket. In this way, the remembering of this complex movement is enhanced by changing the abstract, complex components involved in this skill into a concrete, meaningful movement.

Another effective strategy that increases the meaningfulness of a movement so that the movement is more accurately remembered is to attach a useful or meaningful *verbal label* to the movement, then using that label-movement association to aid the recall of the movement. One of the earliest demonstrations of the beneficial influence of attaching verbal labels to simple movements was by John Shea (1977). He had subjects move to a stop on a semicircular positioning apparatus. When the subjects arrived at the criterion location, one group was provided with a number that corresponded to the clock-face location of the criterion location; another group received an irrelevant verbal label such as a nonsense three-letter syllable; another group received no verbal label

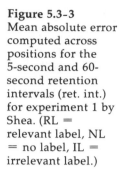

Figure 5.3-3
Mean absolute error computed across positions for the 5-second and 60-second retention intervals (ret. int.) for experiment 1 by Shea. (RL = relevant label, NL = no label, IL = irrelevant label.)

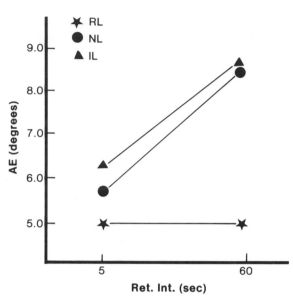

about the criterion location. Results, as seen in Figure 5.3–3, indicated that the group given a clock-face label showed no increase in error over a 60-second unfilled retention interval, whereas the other two groups showed a large increase in recall error.

In a subsequent experiment (Ho & Shea, 1978), the subjects provided with a clock-face label recalled the criterion movement better than the no-label group even after interfering activity occurred during the retention interval. Additionally, Winther and Thomas (1981) showed that when useful verbal labels are attached to positioning movements, young children's retention performance (age 7) can become equivalent to that of adults.

More recently, Magill and Lee (1987) reported the results of a series of experiments in which the meaningfulness of the movements to be remembered was manipulated for a task requiring subjects to learn a series of end-location movements on a linear-positioning apparatus. On each trial of these experiments, subjects were presented with twelve (experiment 1) or seven (experiments 2 and 3) locations. After these were presented, the subjects were asked to move to as many of the criterion locations as they could in any order they desired. One group of subjects was always provided with a verbal label for each location (which were called spatial labels) that designated its exact location on the apparatus, although the subjects did not know of this association. The other group of subjects was provided a verbal label, a number from 1 to 12 or from 1 to 7, for each location depending on the number of locations presented (these labels were called number labels). In all three experiments, the subjects who had received the more meaningful spatial labels more accurately recalled the locations, even though they were never told what the

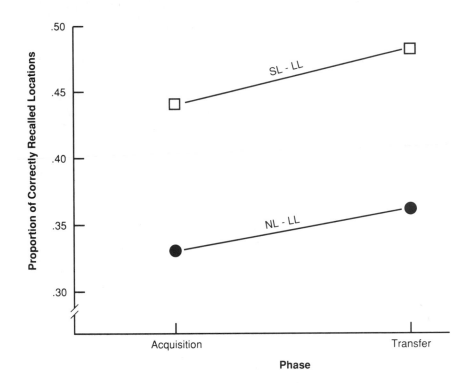

Figure 5.3-4
Results of experiment 3 by Magill and Lee (1987) showing the proportion of 7 location movements recalled on each of 10 acquisition trials and the proportion of 5 location movements recalled on each trial on a transfer test. Locations were labeled as spatial (SL) or number (NL) labels during acquisition. During transfer both label condition groups performed new locations having letter labels (LL).

locations were or that the labels were related to these locations. The results of the third experiment (Figure 5.3–4) were particularly striking. In this experiment, after practicing the series of criterion limb locations for 10 trials, subjects were given a series of transfer trials on which both practice groups were given a series of five new locations, each with a letter label (from A to E). As you can see in Figure 5.3–4, the subjects who had practiced in the condition where the more meaningful spatial labels had been provided during practice were able to perform better on the transfer test where new locations had new labels.

From a theoretical perspective, the use of images and verbal labels to aid the learning and control of movements poses interesting questions about the interaction of processes subserving the control of verbal and motor skills. For example, why do these strategies benefit memory for motor skills? The most probable answer is that images and labels, which are well known to us, are beneficial in that they speed up the retrieval process required to pull together the requisite information to perform the movement. In this way, images and labels serve as mnemonics, which are simply techniques that aid remembering. Mnemonics are commonly used to remember lists of words, such as a grocery list or the bones of the hand. Chase and Ericsson (1982) argued that mnemonics derive their power from their ability to narrow the search in long-term memory to just the information needed. If you will recall the discussion

at the end of Concept 5.2 concerning the structure of long-term memory and how those structures interact to perform a goal direction movement, this view of images and verbal labels as useful mnemonics seems quite appropriate.

Preselecting movements. In most of the memory and learning situations described thus far in this chapter, subjects were required to remember or learn movements selected by the experimenter. Would it make any difference if the movements to be remembered or learned were selected instead by the subjects? Results of investigations into this question have yielded some interesting implications for both memory theory and instructional applications.

When subjects are allowed to select their own criterion movements on which they will be tested, we call these *preselected* movements. This term is in contrast to the term *constrained* movements, which describes movements to be remembered that have been selected by the experimenter. Results of experiments comparing the recall of preselected and constrained movements have consistently shown that preselected movements are recalled more accurately. (See an excellent review of this research in an article by Kelso & Wallace, 1978.) Interestingly, this same type of effect is common in memory for words, in what is called the "self-generation benefit." In these experiments, subjects are provided with a list of words to remember. Some subjects see the list in which all the words are complete whereas other subjects see the same word list but with blanks where certain letters should be (e.g., "broom" compared with "bro_m"). A similar effect occurs. That is, the self-generated study condition promotes better retention of the word list. (See an article by Lee & Gallagher, 1981, for more information about the comparison between the preselected movement and self-generation effects.)

What causes the recall accuracy difference that has been consistently found between preselected and constrained movements? One possibility is that a preselected movement requires more attention, or central processing, by the subject than is required by the constrained movement. If the subject must select the movement that will later be recalled, the subject cannot just produce the criterion movement without giving it a great deal of attention. However, this is not true for the constrained movement. Thus, Kelso (1981) argued that the difference lies in the degree to which the preselected movement requires preparation. Another possibility is that preselecting a movement allows the subject to more accurately encode the movement. Also, from a retrieval perspective, it can be argued that the preselected movement has been selected on the basis of some long-term memory-based association that will make the preselected movement easier to recall, being inherently more meaningful to the individual.

What does the preselection effect mean in terms of application to motor skill instruction? One application can be made to teaching basic movement skills to elementary children. An effective technique is to allow the children to select their own movements that will accomplish the teacher's movement

goal. The goal, "Can you jump over this bar in different ways?" allows the children to select their own movements to accomplish the goal, rather than trying to imitate specific movements that the teacher may have selected for them. Also, the preselection technique may be useful for aiding initial learning of a complex skill for which the person must eventually learn to perform a number of variations. For example, when teaching the volleyball serve, the student will eventually want to be able to serve to any given place on the opposite court. Why not let initial practice of the serve be done by allowing the student to select his or her own target area. In doing this, the student can devote more attention resources to learning the skill without having to also try to put the ball where the teacher wants it. These are just a couple of suggestions, but they suffice in showing that the preselection effect can be translated into a potentially useful instructional technique.

Rote repetition. One effective rehearsal strategy that positively influences remembering movement information is drill-like repetition of the movement to be learned. This form of rehearsal, often referred to as rote repetition, involves repeating the same movements over and over again. The benefit of this type of rehearsal has been demonstrated many times in the research literature. In fact, in the study by Adams and Dijkstra (1966) referred to earlier in this chapter, it was demonstrated that rapidly increasing recall error observed in 20 seconds was dramatically reduced by increasing the number of practice repetitions of the criterion movement. Gentile and Nemetz (1978) also demonstrated this effect by showing that as the number of repetitions of a positioning movement increased, the amount of recall error decreased.

The use of rote repetition seems especially practical and effective for closed skills. Since the test and practice conditions can be duplicated for these skills, repetition of the exact movement to be learned is an effective rehearsal strategy. Storage of the movement as it will be performed under test conditions seems to be a primary benefit of this form of rehearsal for closed skills.

The intention to remember. In all the memory experiments considered so far, subjects have always known in advance that the movements they were presented or had to practice would be later subject to a recall test. But, suppose the subjects were not told in advance? Suppose they were told that the goal of the experiment was to see how well they could move their arm to a specified location. If an unexpected recall test was given later, how well would they recall the movements made earlier? The two situations just described are known in the memory research literature as intentional vs. incidental memory situations. In addition to investigating the influence of intention to remember as an effective remembering strategy, the comparison of these two situations provides insight into the encoding of movement information processes. That is, do we only store information to which we give conscious attention, as in the

case of the intentional memory situation, or do we store more information, as would be shown by good memory performance in the incidental memory situation?

This question has received little research interest in the study of memory for movements. However, the research that has been done indicates that, in general, intention to remember leads to better remembering than no intention to remember. (See Crocker & Dickinson, 1984, for a review of this research.) Yet, retention test performance in the incidental situation is typically better than if no previous experience with the test movements had occurred. In fact, some reports show incidental memory test performance to be as good as it was for the intentional situation. For example, Dickinson (1978) presented subjects with four end-locations on a linear-positioning apparatus. Then "intentional" group was told that they were to learn these four positions and that there would be a recall test later. The "incidental" group was told that this experiment was examining how well people could visually estimate a movement of their own hands. The experiment contained retention intervals, one immediately after the four locations had been presented to the subjects, and a 30-second, a 60-second, and a 600-second retention interval. The results showed that for recall tests given following the 0-second, 30-second, and 60-second retention intervals, there were no differences between the two groups. However, after a 5-minute (600-second) retention interval, the intentional group's performance showed little forgetting whereas the incidental group's showed much. Thus, more information was encoded during the practice phase of this experiment than was given conscious attention. However, the information that was incidentally encoded did not resist the effects of time as well as did the intentionally attended information.

For more complex tasks, the intention to remember benefit is even more striking, although the performance of an incidental condition is rather striking also. For example, in a series of experiments by Crocker and Dickinson (1984), subjects performed a movement task in which they moved from a home response key to a target response key as rapidly as possible. To increase the complexity of this task, a series of six target keys were to be struck in response to a signal. In some cases there was a series of four, seven, or eleven target keys that had to be struck in a specified sequence, which was indicated by a light near the key to be struck next. In the incidental condition, subjects were told to react and to move as quickly as possible to each designated target key in the sequence. In the intentional condition, subjects were told not only to move as quickly as possible to each designated key in the sequence but also that they would be tested later on how well they had learned the sequence. The results consistently showed that, regardless of sequence length, subjects who had been told of the impending recall test performed better when tested than the subjects who had not been told (the incidental group). In a follow-up experiment, Crocker and Dickinson had subjects practice a 15-target key sequence for either 2 or 10 trials to determine if practice would eliminate the

benefit of intention to learn instructions. Again, the intention-to-remember strategy resulted in superior performance.

Another type of experiment done with more complex tasks that is relevant to intentional and incidental remembering or learning was seen in Concept 4.3 when we discussed the experiment by Richard Pew (1974). Subjects practiced a very complex tracking task that involved moving a joystick to move a cursor on an oscilloscope screen to track a target cursor that moved in a series of randomly generated wave patterns for 60 seconds. The unique characteristic of this target pathway was that the first and third 20 seconds of it were random on every practice trial but the middle 20-second portion remained the same on every trial. At the end of the practice period, tracking performance measures indicated the subjects had improved their tracking skill and had improved in the middle portion more than in either of the other two portions. What is important here, however, is that the performance improvement in the middle portion occurred incidentally as none of the subjects reported any awareness that this portion was the same for every trial.

The investigation of intentional vs. incidental memory strategies is an important one to increase our understanding of memory processes, especially those processes related to encoding and storing information. Research indicates that we encode and store much more information than we are consciously aware. You will see another example supporting this conclusion in the discussion concerning the effect of practice and test contexts on memory.

One implication the intentional vs. incidental memory research provides for instructional situations is that memory performance and skill learning can be enhanced by telling students when they begin to practice a skill that they will be tested on the skill later. Also, this research indicates that when the same actions are embedded in a complex series of actions, learning will occur even if the students are not aware of this situation.

Subjective organization. A strategy frequently used when learning a large amount of information is grouping or organizing the information into units. For example, a child learning the alphabet will generally group letters into two- to four-letter units and recite an alphabet rhyme to aid learning. If you need to learn a dialogue or a list of terms, you often will divide these long sequences into shorter, more manageable groups. In the course of practice, you find that it becomes helpful to combine these smaller groups into larger ones.

These examples of verbal organization have been well established in the research literature as effective remembering and learning strategies. For example, Tulving (1962) reported that a typical strategy when learning a long list of works was to organize the words into groupings meaningful to the subject. This process of grouping has been termed *subjective organization,* indicating that a large amount of information has been organized in a way that is meaningful to the individual. Other terms that have been used to describe this process are chunking, clustering, categorizing, unitizing, and grouping.

The relationship between organization and motor skill learning has not been considered to any great extent. In 1978 Diewert and Stelmach published a review of organization and memory with their potential application to motor learning. However, research demonstrating how the organization of movement occurs and its effect on performance is practically nonexistent. The importance of organization in motor learning appears to relate to enabling the learner more effectively and efficiently to acquire a complex movement skill as well as more effectively to produce the response required for a complex skill.

Insight into the benefit of organizing information to help learn it can be seen in a recent study by Magill and Lee (1987) that was described earlier. In the first experiment, subjects were presented a series of 12 criterion locations on a linear-positioning apparatus on each of 12 trials of practice. The same 12 locations were presented on every trial but in a different order. The subjects were required to recall as many of the locations as they could in any order they wished. What was important here was to determine whether the subjects began to ignore the presentation order of the movements and develop a consistently organized order of recall on each trial. The results showed that the subjects typically did develop some subjective organizational structure to the series of movements. Further, the subjects who demonstrated higher degrees of organization tended to have more accurate recall of the criterion movements.

The beginner tends to consider complex motor skills as comprised of many parts. As the beginner develops his or her ability to execute the skill, the number of components of the skill seems to decrease. This does not mean the structure of the skill itself has changed. Rather, the learner's view of the skill has changed. A good example is a dance or gymnastic floor exercise routine; here each of the routines is made up of many individual parts. To the beginner, a dance routine is thought of step-by-step and movement-by-movement. Beginning gymnasts think of a floor exercise as so many individual stunts. Notice, however, that as these performers practice, their approach to the skills changes. They have begun to organize the routines into units or groups of movements. Three or four component parts are now being considered as one. The result will eventually be to be able to perform the entire routine with the requisite timing, rhythm, and coordination necessary. Together with that result, moreover, will be the added effect of developing a more efficient means of storing the complex routine in memory.

It is interesting that skilled individuals organize information to such an extent that it appears they have an increased working memory capacity. However, it has been shown that experts have organized what they have learned so well that, in effect, they do not need to recall every item in the organizational scheme. For example, Chase & Simon (1973) showed that an expert's memory for chess piece location was superior to a novice's only when the pieces were organized in a typical game structure situation. When the expert and novice players were compared on remembering chess piece positions that were

randomly arranged on the board, their recall success was equivalent. A similar effect was shown in motor skills with dancers when Starkes, Deakin, Lindley, & Crisp (1987) compared skilled and novice 11-year-old ballet dancers at the Canadian National Ballet School. These dancers were presented sequences of eight elements. Some sequences were organized as would occur in a ballet routine while other sequences were random arrangements of these elements. The results showed that the skilled dancers recalled significantly more elements when the elements resembled part of a structured routine. However, when the same number of elements was presented in an unstructured sequence, there was no difference between the skilled and novice dancers in terms of the number of elements they correctly recalled.

Since most complex motor skills have a specified organizational structure, there are a variety of ways to break up that structure for teaching or practicing the skills. Skills should not be arbitrarily broken into parts for practice. Better and more efficient learning will result from keeping together those components of a movement sequence that are interrelated and dependent on each other. For example, the motion for pitching a softball is often initially practiced by using only the underhand backswing and forward motion of the pitch. A better organizational approach would be to incorporate the forward swing of the initial part of the windup to allow the student the opportunity to understand the full structure of the movement.

An important influence on the retention of motor skills is the relationship between the context of practice and the context at the time of the test. As was discussed briefly in Concept 5.2, the context of a movement relates to both the environmental conditions in which the movement is performed as well as to characteristics related to the person performing the movement. For example, if a memory experiment is performed in a laboratory, the environmental context includes such things as the room in which the experiment is done, the experimenter, the time of day, the noise the subject can hear, the lighting, and so on. Personal context involves such things as the mood of the individual, the limb used to make the movement, the sitting or standing position of the subject, and the sensory feedback sources that are available to the subject. As you will see in this section, differences in these conditions during the time the movement to be remembered or learned is presented or practiced and during the time the movement must be recalled can influence the success of the recall performance.

Practice-Test Context Effects

The encoding specificity principle. An important point that must be raised in regard to the influence of the movement context on remembering or learning a motor skill is how the practice and test contexts are related (Bransford, Franks, Morris, & Stein, 1979). In some situations, the test goal is essentially the same as the practice goal. This is especially so for closed skills. That is, to shoot a free throw, you must stand in essentially the same place and shoot

the ball through a hoop that is the same distance from you as it was when you practiced it. In such closed skill situations, what is known as the *encoding specificity principle* applies.

The encoding specificity principle was introduced by Tulving and Thomson (1973). According to this principle, the more the test context resembles the practice context, the better the retention performance will be. We already considered some support for this principle in the motor domain when we discussed the experiment by Lee and Hirota (1980) in Concept 5.2. Briefly, they showed that when subjects were presented limb-positioning movements, recall accuracy of the movements was greater when the recall test was performed under the same active or passive movement mode as was the presentation condition. Recall error increased when subjects were required to perform the recall test in the opposite movement mode. Thus, having the same movement context available at recall was beneficial for remembering the criterion movements.

More recently, Lee and Magill (1985) addressed this similarity of context issue by using a learning paradigm but with the same active and passive conditions as reported by Lee and Hirota (1980) and also added a condition involving the limb used for practice and for testing. The subjects were required to learn a 30-cm blind-limb positioning response on a linear-positioning apparatus. Following 16 trials of practice on which the subjects received knowledge of results about their accuracy on each trial, they were required to perform 20 additional trials without any knowledge of results. In the first experiment, two practice conditions were compared. Similar to the Lee and Hirota (1980) experiment, subjects either actively moved their own limb on each trial or were passively moved and told the experimenter where to stop. On the test trials, half the subjects in each practice condition were transferred to perform under the opposite active or passive response mode. The results confirmed those reported by Lee and Hirota, that maintaining the same mode of action, active or passive, during the test trials yielded better performance than switching to the other mode. In the second experiment, the same procedures were followed except that the subjects practiced with either their right or left arms. During the test trials, half the subjects in each practice condition were required to perform the movement with the same arm used in practice or with the opposite arm. As you can see in Figure 5.3–5, maintaining the same movement context between the practice and the test trials led to a maintenance of performance, even without KR being given. However, when the movement context was altered so that the opposite limb had to be used on the test trials, the error increased significantly and remained high for the remainder of the test trials.

One additional feature of this experiment emphasizes the relationship this experiment has with the encoding specificity principle. Notice the set of results for block 9 at the far end of Figure 5.3–5. On this final test block, all subjects were tested using the same arm used during practice. Notice what happened when the practice context was reinstated. The opposite limb transfer

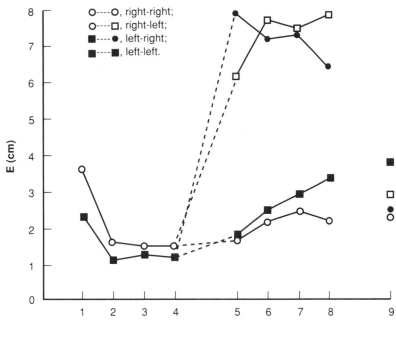

Figure 5.3-5
Results from
experiment 2 by
Lee and Magill
(1985) showing the
accuracy (as
measured by E) for
performing a 30-cm
distance movement
during practice
with KR (blocks 1–
4) and during a no-
KR retention test
(blocks 5–8).
Practice was with
either the right or
left arm; the
retention test was
with either the
same or opposite
arm used during
practice. Block 9
shows performance
when the same arm
used in practice
performed the
movement after the
retention test was
completed.

Blocks of 4 Trials

group showed an immediate improvement in performance and performed the movement more like they had at the end of practice.

The encoding specificity principle is important for increasing our understanding of memory processes. An essential finding has been that the memory representation for a movement, such as a limb position or a movement distance, has stored with it important sensory feedback information that is specific to the context conditions in which the movement was practiced. If the movement was practiced passively, then different feedback information is stored with the representation of the criterion response than if the movement had been practiced actively. The same can be said for the limb used to practice the movement. Recall that this issue was discussed in Concept 3.2 when the role of proprioceptive feedback in movement production was considered. Evidence also supports a memorial representation for movements that have specific movement context information associated with it. Thus, the more the test, or recall, conditions match the practice, or encoding, conditions, the more accurate the test performance will be expected.

The practical implications of the encoding specificity principle seem especially relevant to remembering and learning closed skills. In a closed skill, the test context is typically stable and predictable. Because of this, practice conditions can be established that will closely mimic the test conditions. In these cases, then, the more similar the practice setting is to the test setting, the higher the probability or successful performance during the test. Consider,

for example, practice for shooting free throws in a basketball game. The encoding specificity principle would apply as we consider the context of shooting free throws in the game. Free throws are always either one, two, or one-and-one situations. According to the encoding specificity principle, it is essential that players have practice experiences in which these gamelike conditions prevail. This does not say that this is the only way that free throws can be practiced. However, if game performance is the test of interest, it is essential that gamelike practice be provided.

This basketball free throw example can be related to any number of closed skills, such as bowling, tennis serving, etc. Increased performance during the game, or the test, will be seen if practice that mimics game conditions has been provided. From a memory processes perspective, this type of practice helps store in memory the appropriate information that can be easily accessed and retrieved when necessary.

Novel response test conditions. The encoding specificity principle holds very well for closed-skill situations where the test conditions are stable and predictable. However, when the test conditions are unpredictable and novel, as in open skills, the encoding principle falls short as a basis for specifying the relationship between practice and test conditions. The type of practice context important for success in open skills was addressed by Schmidt (1975b) in his schema theory (Concept 2.3), where he stated that both the amount and the variability of practice are important for success in open-skill performance test situations. Here again the relationship between practice and test contexts is seen as important. However, rather than the emphasis being on the similarity between the practice and test contexts, the emphasis is on the variability of the practice contexts to yield maximum performance during the test. We will consider the practice context more specifically in Chapter 9. For the present, keep in mind that remembering or learning movement information is influenced by the nature of the relationship between the practice and test contexts.

Summary

Control processes are those aspects of memory that enable a person to store and retrieve information in memory. Some of these processes are under direct control of the individual and some are not. Controversy continues concerning which processes the individual can and cannot control. Several different control processes were discussed in the context of considering a number of variables that influence the remembering of motor skills. These were presented and discussed in three categories. The first category of influences on remembering was the type of movement or movement characteristic that must be remembered or learned. Research is rather consistent in showing that continuous skills are remembered better than discrete skills, and that location information is remembered better than distance information, although some qualifications are made with each of these conclusions. Also, movements that

are more inherently meaningful to the individual are remembered better than those that are not meaningful. The second category concerned the strategy employed by either the student or the teacher. Movements can be made more meaningful if imagery or verbal labeling is properly used. Also, preselected movements are remembered better than constrained movements. Rote repetition and subjective organization were also discussed as useful remembering strategies. Finally, the influence of the practice and test context characteristics were considered. The encoding specificity principle indicates that the more these context characteristics are similar during practice and during the test, the better the practiced movements will be recalled during the test. Also, variable practice conditions for open skills can enhance success in remembering during a test situation.

Related Readings

Adams, J. A. (1987). Historical review and appraisal of research on the learning, retention, and transfer of human skills. *Psychological Bulletin, 101,* 41–74.

Crocker, P. R. E., & Dickinson, J. (1984). Incidental psychomotor learning: The effects of number of movements, practice, and rehearsal. *Journal of Motor Behavior, 16,* 61–75.

Davies, G. (1986). Context effects in episodic memory: A review. *Cahiers de Psychologie Cognitive, 6,* 157–174.

Diewert, G. L., & Stelmach, G. E. (1978). Perceptual organization in motor learning. In G. E. Stelmach (Ed.), *Information processing in motor control and motor learning* (pp. 241–265). New York: Academic Press.

Magill, R. A. (1984). Influences on remembering movement information. In W. F. Straub & J. M. Williams (Eds.), *Cognitive sport psychology* (pp. 175–188). Lansing, NY: Sport Science Associates.

Concept 5.4

Recall of serially presented information follows a pattern in which the earliest and most recent parts are recalled best, while the middle parts are recalled most poorly

Application

When a dancer is first presented with a routine to learn, he or she is confronted with a series of individual movements that are to be performed in a very specific order. The same challenge faces an assembly-line worker who must assemble parts of a piece of equipment by combining the components in a precise order so that the desired finished product will result. Any person who is learning a new sport skill faces a similar assignment. Learning to hit a golf ball, serve a tennis ball, deliver a bowling ball, or perform a gymnastic routine are all examples of sport skills that require the performer to combine several movements in a specified arrangement. In any of these situations, if the correct order of performing the component actions is not followed, or if certain phases are forgotten or performed improperly, the final outcome will not be the desired product.

These situations describe very common, practical problems that involve memory processes. Whether the task is merely to recall a series of movements for a test or to learn a series of movements for some performance requirement, the role of memory is a most important one. We are seldom confronted with single-movement reproduction situations in real world settings. Thus, for our understanding of memory processes to be complete, we must include the investigation of memory for information that has a specified serial organization. We are not denying the importance of investigating situations involving single-movement reproduction, such as were encountered in our discussions in the preceding concepts in this chapter. Those investigations have added greatly to our knowledge of memory processes for movements. However, we are now seeking to expand some of that research and thus to broaden our own understanding to include situations that involve more direct application to everyday motor skill experiences.

Discussion

In the discussion of forgetting, we considered a few examples of research from the verbal domain, using serially presented information as a means of distinguishing between forgetting in working memory and long-term memory. Thus, we observed experimental procedures that involved the presentation of a list of items to be recalled by each subject. Those items may have been numbers, letters, words, etc. Each item was presented individually for a brief moment at a constant rate of speed, usually about one every two seconds. Following a specified retention interval, the subject was asked to recall as many of the

items on the list as possible. The manner in which those items were recalled depended on the study and its purposes. The subject may have been required to recall all the items in the same order as they were presented, that is, in *serial recall.* When the study was concerned with *free recall,* the subject was asked to recall as many items as possible in any order. Sometimes the experiment might be directed to recognition memory. In this case, the subject was presented with another list, with the task of indicating whether or not each item on the new list was on the original list.

Procedures in experiments investigating serial memory in the motor domain have followed similar patterns. A typical task has involved linear arm positioning. The subject has either moved actively, or has been passively moved, to a series of locations or movement distances. Following a specified retention interval, the subject has been asked to move to those same locations, or distances, either in an indicated order or in any order.

There is an obvious difference between these procedures and those used in the memory research we have discussed in the past few concepts. Here we are concerned with memory for a series of movements. Previously, most discussion was limited to memory for single movements. This shift is a necessary and important one. As discussed in the application section of this concept, most of the motor skills that we perform in everyday life, whether they are sport, industrial, dance, or military skills, tend to be serial in nature. Thus, it seems only reasonable that in the discussion of human memory for motor skills, we include a consideration of what we know about our memory for series of movements.

One of the most consistent results obtained in the study of human verbal behavior is termed the *primacy-recency effect.* This is seen when a person recalls verbal items in series, such as words or numbers. Those items that were first presented to the person, that is, the early portion of the list, and those that were presented last, the end portion of the list, are usually recalled better than items in the middle of the list. Accordingly, this typical experimental result has come to be known as the primacy (early items on the list)-recency (end items on the list) effect.

This effect can be clearly seen in the graphs in Figure 5.4–1. These results represent an experiment by F. I. M. Craik (1970). In this experiment, subjects were presented lists of 15 two-syllable nouns. The presentation was either spoken (auditory) or visual, and the recall was either spoken or written. Regardless of the method of presentation or of recall, the characteristic primacy-recency U-shaped curves resulted. The dependent measure on the graphs is the proportion of words that the subjects had correct. By far, the best recall was for words at the end of the 15-word lists, with proportions ranging from 70% to almost 100% for words that were in positions 12 through 15. Words at the beginning of the list, positions 1 and 2, were recalled better than 50% of the time. Words in the middle of the list were recalled the poorest. These

Primacy-
Recency Effect

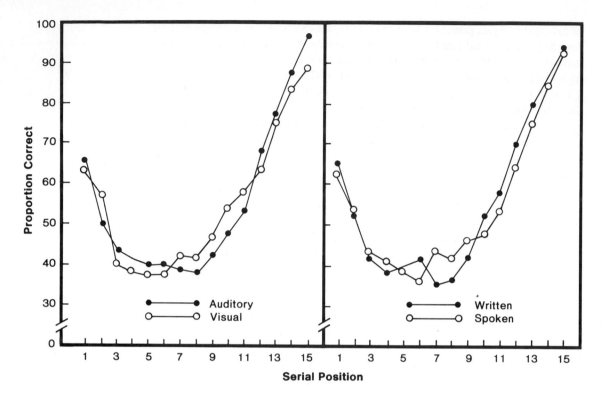

Figure 5.4-1
Results of the
experiment by
Craik showing the
serial position
curves for the recall
of 15 words in a list.
The graphs show
results for mode of
presentation of the
lists (auditory or
visual) and for the
method of response
for recalling the
lists (written or
spoken).

results not only demonstrate quite clearly the primacy-recency effect, but also typify the general characteristic of results in verbal behavior involving the recall of series of words, letters, or numbers.

One very important point should be noted, however. The Craik experiment used word lists that were 15 words long. This length was chosen quite purposefully. The explanation can be traced both to the results of a relevant study by John Jahnke in 1963 and to memory capacity theory, which was discussed previously.

Jahnke was concerned with the relationship between the length of the list of items to be recalled and the primacy-recency effect. Subjects were presented a list of 5, 6, 7, 8, or 9 English consonants. Following a short retention interval, the subjects were asked to recall all the consonants in the order in which they were presented. Results show that the bowing of the serial position curve is related to the number of consonants in the list to be recalled. In fact, no bowed curve was noted for the list of 5 consonants, while the recency portion of the curve became more pronounced as the length of the list to be recalled increased.

The Jahnke experiment provides very convincing evidence that the primacy-recency effect is significantly related to the length of the list to be recalled. Other evidence for this relationship can be inferred from what we know

about memory capacity for working memory, as discussed in Concept 4.1. As you may recall, in that discussion, we indicated that the capacity was between 5 and 9 items. Thus, it would be reasonable to expect that you could retain 5 to 9 items in memory with relative ease. When the task required you to recall a list of 12 or 15 items, you would probably have to do something with the items on the list to help you remember them. Some memory theorists postulate that one of the things we apparently do is to rehearse actively the items on the list. To quite an extent this assumption helps to explain the primacy-recency effect. We have more time to rehearse the items presented first, hence they are recalled better. But why are the final items recalled better than the middle ones? The rehearsal explanation does not seem to predict that result. The last items on the list appear to be recalled well because of what has been termed "temporal distinctiveness." That is, the final items are distinct to us because of their location at the end of the list. Thus, we have a dual-process explanation of the primacy-recency effect. Whether or not this explains the primacy-recency effect remains to be proved. However, it seems to be a reasonable hypothesis that can be supported.

The results of Jahnke's experiment led to the finding that the primacy-recency effect exists in the motor domain as well as in the verbal domain. Several studies had reported that recall of a series of movements did not follow the same laws as did the recall of a series of words. Instead, it appeared that movement series were recalled with a primacy effect only; that is, early movements were recalled best and end movements were recalled most poorly. However, in a study reported by Magill and Dowell in 1977, Jahnke's length-of-list effects were repeated, with application to the motor domain.

In the Magill and Dowell study, subjects were blindfolded and asked to move a handle on a linear slide to a series of stops along a steel rod. The movement series consisted of either three, six, or nine movements. The recall of these movements was indicated in the same order in which they had been presented to the subjects. The results can be seen in Figure 5.4–2. Motor behavior researchers had surmised that a series of movements would be recalled in a linear pattern; that is, the bowed serial position curve would not be evidenced. The Magill and Dowell study revealed that this linear pattern was only evident for the three-movement series. For both the six- and nine-movement series, a bowed serial position curve indicating the classic primacy-recency effect began to appear. Remember, as you look at Figure 5.4–2, the curves are inverted when compared to the curves in the verbal studies. This is because error is the dependent measure; thus, the better recall scores are lower on this graph.

Other studies in the motor domain have supported the primacy-recency effect for movement series and the belief that this effect is related to the length of the movement series. While the Magill and Dowell study involved serial recall, a study by Wilberg and Girard (1977) showed the bowed-shaped curve with free recall. They demonstrated that when the length of the movement series was beyond "memory span," i.e., greater than five to nine movements, the primacy-recency effect is readily noted.

Figure 5.4-2
Results from the experiment by Magill and Dowell showing the serial position curves for the recall of a series of three, six, or nine movements on a linear positioning task. The triangles equal the three-movement series, the squares equal the six-movement series, and the circles equal the nine-movement series.

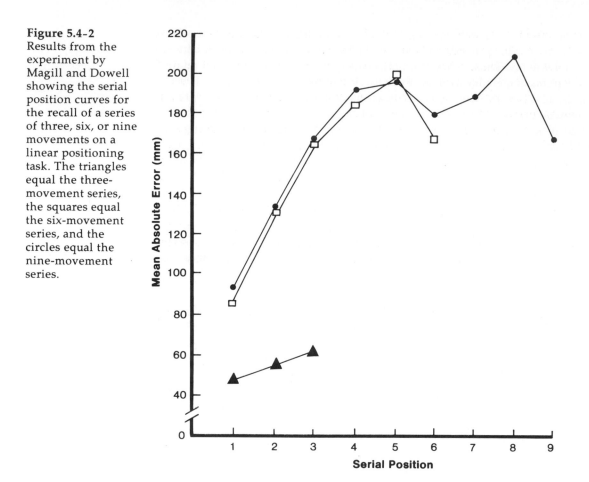

Implications for Motor Skill Instructions

We have been discussing a very theoretical problem in this concept. A reasonable question is, What does all of this have to tell us about the instruction in motor skills? In answer to that question we shall consider several direct implications of the study of serial memory as applied to motor skill instruction.

If your task as a physical education teacher is to teach a routine of floor exercises to a gymnastic class, you are in a serial memory situation. You are immediately confronted with questions relating to the order of presentation of each of the movements or components of the routine that needs to be emphasized. It could be predicted, based on our discussion of serial memory research, that your class will have the most difficulty remembering what to do in the middle portions of the routine. If you demonstrate the entire routine to them, they will probably recall most readily the first and last portions of the routine. Thus, you should be prepared to reemphasize middle portions of the routine or to encourage practice of these movements first. Another possibility is to break down the routine into smaller units, especially if the routine has several

parts. Divide the routine into segments. If these consist of three or four movements each, then the segments can be practiced as individual units, and all units can be combined when the units are well learned. Such a procedure will help you in solving the problem posed by the primacy-recency effect. You effectively break down the whole routine into units of movements that contain a number of components well within a student's memory span. In other words, you do not overload the memory span. Dancers or pianists apply this by initially practicing segments or units to assist them in learning a new routine or piece. The entire score is broken down into manageable units for practice. As these are learned thoroughly or memorized, they are combined as larger units until the entire score is learned as one unit.

These instructional suggestions are applicable to many other motor skills. You can supply some further examples; simply consider any complex motor skill that requires combining a series of individual movements. Some examples are a tennis serve, putting together the parts to a rifle, or an assembly-line task.

Summary

Most sport or dance skills tend to be serial in nature. That is, they consist of a series of movements that must be performed in a certain order. The study of memory to determine the characteristics of serial information indicates that recall occurs in the form of a bow-shaped curve. Information in the beginning and the end of a series is recalled better than information in the middle of the sequence. Better recall of information at the beginning of the list is termed the primacy effect, while the end-of-the-list recall superiority is described as the recency effect. Attempts at explaining why the primacy-recency effects occur have proposed a variety of reasons. Most notable among these explanations are the ability to rehearse earlier presented information for a longer time than other information, the primacy effect, and the temporal distinctiveness of the end information.

Related Readings

Jahnke, J. (1963). Serial position effects in immediate serial recall. *Journal of Verbal Learning and Verbal Behavior, 2,* 284–287.

Magill, R. A., & Dowell, M. N. (1977). Serial position effects in motor short-term memory. *Journal of Motor Behavior, 9,* 319–323.

Murdock, B. B., Jr. (1974). *Human memory: Theory and data.* Potomac, MD: Erlbaum.

Wrisberg, C. A. (1975). The serial position effect in short-term motor retention. *Journal of Motor Behavior, 7,* 289–295.

Study Questions for Chapter 5 (Memory)

1. How are the terms *retention* and *forgetting* similar yet different in respect to memory issues?
2. Describe how working memory and long-term memory differ in terms of the duration and capacity of information of each of these functional components of memory.

3. Name three types of information stored in long-term memory. Identify examples of these types of information as related to motor skills.
4. What are the typical experimental paradigms used to test the causes of forgetting? How does each paradigm permit the researcher to draw conclusions about a cause of forgetting?
5. Explain how trace decay, interference, and inappropriate retrieval cues can be considered causes for forgetting. Give a motor skill example of how each cause can be related to forgetting.
6. Why do motor skills seem to be remembered longer than verbal skills?
7. Certain types of motor skills have been shown to be remembered better than others. Indicate what these are and why they may be better remembered.
8. Name three effective strategies that can be used to help a person more effectively remember movement information. Give an example of how each of these strategies can be used in a motor skill learning situation.
9. What is meant by the "practice-test context"? How is this related to influencing how well movement information will be remembered? Give a practical example of taking advantage of the "encoding specificity principle" when teaching motor skills.
10. How does the primacy-recency effect relate to recalling a series of movements? What does this effect suggest in terms of teaching skills?

Individual Differences

6

Concept 6.1
The study of individual differences has identified various motor abilities that characterize individuals.

Concept 6.2
Individual difference research does not support the notion of a "general motor ability."

Concept 6.3
Knowledge about an individual's motor abilities can be used to help predict potential for success in a motor skill.

Concept 6.1 The study of individual differences has identified various motor abilities that characterize individuals

Application

People obviously differ in how they learn and perform motor skills. One way of seeing these differences is by observing a class in which a physical activity is being taught to beginners. While most beginners' classes usually include students with some previous experience in the activity, the diversity of initial skill levels is apparent even if those individuals are not considered in the comparison. Consider for example a beginning golf class. As you observe the members of that class on the first day they are permitted to hit the ball, you will see various degrees of success and failure. Some students will spend an inordinate amount of time simply trying to make contact with the ball. At the other extreme, there will be those who seem to hit the ball rather consistently. The remainder of the class will usually be distributed somewhere along the continuum of success between those two extremes.

Parallel differences can be observed in any physical activity class. Students enter dance, gymnastics, bowling, fencing, soccer, etc., classes with a wide variety of what is referred to in some education literature as "entry behaviors." These entry behaviors reflect the very real behavioral phenomenon that individuals differ in their performance of motor skills. These differences will also be seen as the students continue in these classes; they will learn in different ways and at different rates. The impact of certain instructional techniques will not always be the same for every student or during all stages of learning for any one student.

Several questions associated with a better understanding of the role of individual differences in motor learning arise from these examples. One important question is concerned with why students exhibit such a wide range of initial skill levels in a physical activity. In the discussion that follows, this question will be addressed by attributing a large part of the differences in initial skill to differences in motor abilities. To accomplish this, we will consider what abilities are, how they have been identified, and how they relate to motor skill performance.

Discussion

In each of the preceding chapters, we have concentrated on what can be called the average learner. In each of the concepts, the focus of the conclusions was on how people in general are characterized by certain information-processing limitations, or motor control limits, or are influenced by certain environmental features. For example, we saw that individuals can be characterized by a limited ability to store information in memory for a short period of time. In this connection, it was suggested that this capacity can be quantified as 7 ± 2

items. However, it is important to keep in mind that this generalization is made in terms of a population average; that is, on the average, people seem to have this memory capacity.

But, what happens when we select a certain individual and try to determine how that general "rule" of memory capacity applies to him or her? This one individual may actually have a greater or lesser capacity. Does this mean the conclusion is in error? No. It simply indicates that the rule is a statement of average behavior. When it is applied at the individual level, the rule may be exactly accurate, or it may deviate somewhat. In effect, then, the rule represents a norm for behavior. In the present chapter, rather than being concerned with "average behavior," we will examine individual conduct, that is, how individuals differ.

The study of individual differences in psychology has been termed *differential psychology*. This term has been used to distinguish the study of individual differences from the study of normative or average behavior. This distinction was made in a rather straightforward manner by Lee Cronbach in 1957 in his address as president of the American Psychological Association, delivered before the national convention of that organization. He entitled his presentation "The two disciplines of scientific psychology." In his talk, he proceeded to outline the apparent differences between the two approaches to the scientific investigation of human behavior, that is, experimental psychology and differential psychology. An illustrative chart highlighting these differences is presented in Figure 6.1–1. The essential points of Cronbach's statements are (1) experimental psychology is concerned with examining individuals in terms of average behavior, whereas differential psychology examines individuals in terms of how they deviate or differ from the average; (2) experimental psychology investigates behavior by experiments that impose some manipulation of behavior and then observe group differences, whereas differential psychologists investigate behavior by observing behavior without experimental manipulations; (3) experimental psychologists attempt to minimize individual differences in their experiments, while differential psychologists seek to maximize individual differences, as these are of central interest.

Characteristically, the study of individual differences has been concerned with identifying and measuring individual abilities or traits. The study of intelligence is a prime example of this type of investigation. Study of intelligence, in turn, led to the development of the identification of the components of intelligence. This was followed by the formulation of tests to quantify an individual's level of these components, or of a general intelligence. Thus, the concept of I.Q. (intelligence quotient) emerged as a quantified indicator of the intelligence of an individual. In this way, a rather abstract concept like intelligence is made somewhat concrete by putting it in the form of a meaningful number. Individuals can then be compared with some degree of objectivity.

Differential
Psychology

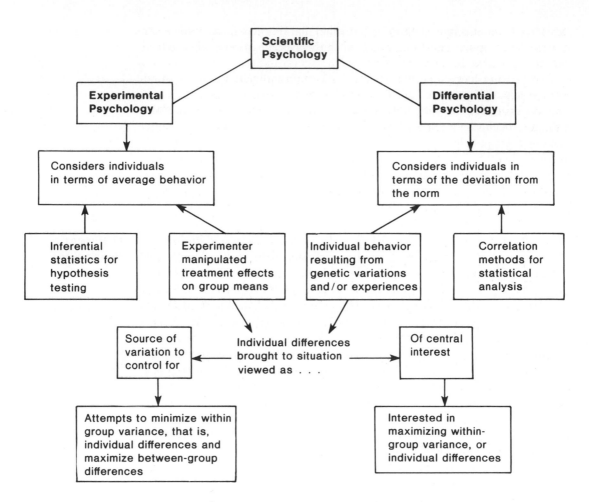

Figure 6.1-1
Diagram depicting
the essential
differences between
the research
approaches taken
by experimental
and differential
psychologists.

In motor behavior, the study of individual differences has followed a similar pattern. Here the identification and measurement of motor abilities has been a primary focal point for investigation. Identification of motor abilities has not been an easy task; as a result, very few researchers have ventured into this area of study. Of those who have investigated human motor abilities, one of the most successful has been Edwin Fleishman. His work on the identification and measurement of motor abilities has been going on for many years and must be considered as the major source of information for any scientific discussion of motor abilities.

As you may recall from the definition presented in Concept 1.1, the term *ability* refers to *a capacity of the individual that is related to the performance of a variety of tasks* (Fleishman, 1978, 1982). As a capacity, an ability should be seen as a relatively enduring attribute of the individual. Fleishman found, for example, that the ability called spatial visualization is related to the performance of such diverse tasks as aerial navigation, blueprint reading, and

dentistry. The assumption here is that the skills involved in complex motor activities can be described in terms of the abilities that underlie their performance. An important step in understanding how abilities and skill performance are related is identifying these abilities and matching them with the skills involved. The approach taken by Fleishman to accomplish this has not been to identify as many abilities as possible but to identify the fewest ability categories that relate to performing the widest variety of tasks.

In 1972, Fleishman published the results of some of his research concerned with developing a "taxonomy of human perceptual-motor abilities." To develop this taxonomy, Fleishman administered an extensive battery of perceptual-motor tests to many people. The results of this testing led him to propose that there seem to be 11 identifiable and measurable *perceptual-motor abilities*. He identified these abilities as follows: (1) *multilimb coordination,* the ability to coordinate the movement of a number of limbs simultaneously; (2) *control precision,* the ability to make highly controlled and precise muscular adjustments where larger muscle groups are involved, as in the pursuit rotor task; (3) *response orientation,* the ability to select rapidly where a response should be made, as in a choice reaction time situation; (4) *reaction time,* the ability to respond rapidly to a stimulus when it appears; (5) *speed of arm movement,* the ability to make a gross, rapid arm movement; (6) *rate control,* the ability to change speed and direction of responses with precise timing, as in following a continuously moving target; (7) *manual dexterity,* the ability to make skillful, well-directed arm-hand movements that are involved in manipulating objects under speed conditions; (8) *finger dexterity,* the ability to perform skillful, controlled manipulations of tiny objects involving primarily the fingers; (9) *arm-hand steadiness,* the ability to make precise arm-hand positioning movements where strength and speed are minimally involved; (10) *wrist, finger speed,* the ability to move the wrist and fingers rapidly, as in a tapping task; (11) *aiming,* the ability to aim precisely at a small object in space.

In addition to perceptual-motor abilities, Fleishman also identified nine abilities that he designated as *physical proficiency abilities*. These abilities differ from the perceptual-motor abilities in that they are more generally related to athletic and gross physical performance. Typically, these abilities would be considered physical fitness abilities. The "physical proficiency abilities" identified by Fleishman are as follows: (1) *static strength,* maximum force that can be exerted against external objects; (2) *dynamic strength,* muscular endurance in exerting force repeatedly, as in a series of pull-ups; (3) *explosive strength,* the ability to mobilize energy effectively for bursts of muscular effort, as in a high jump; (4) *trunk strength,* strength of the trunk muscles; (5) *extent flexibility,* the ability to flex or stretch the trunk and back muscles; (6) *dynamic flexibility,* the ability to make repeated, rapid trunk flexing movements, as in a series of toe touches; (7) *gross body coordination,* the ability to coordinate the action of several parts of the body while the body is in motion; (8) *gross*

Identifying
Motor Abilities

Individual Differences 289

body equilibrium, the ability to maintain balance without visual cues; (9) *stamina,* the capacity to sustain maximum effort requiring cardiovascular effort, as in a distance run.

As indicated earlier, these lists cannot be considered as exhaustive inventories of all the abilities related to motor skill performance. Remember that Fleishman wanted to identify the fewest number of abilities that would describe the tasks performed in the test battery. While he used hundreds of tasks to identify those abilities, additional types of tasks could lead to the identification of other motor abilities. For example, abilities not included in the two lists just considered include the following: *static balance,* the ability to balance on a stable surface when no locomotor movement is required; *dynamic balance,* the ability to balance on a moving surface or to balance while involved in locomotion; *visual acuity,* the ability to see clearly and precisely; *visual tracking,* the ability to visually follow a moving object; and *eye-hand* or *eye-foot coordination,* the ability to perform skills requiring vision and the precise use of the hands or feet. These are just a few of the motor abilities that were not on Fleishman's two lists. In other parts of this chapter, additional abilities will be identified.

It is important to understand that all individuals are characterized by these motor abilities. Because it is possible to measure these motor abilities, a quantifiable measure of an individual's level of each ability can be determined. People differ in the *amount of each ability* they possess. For this reason, motor abilities, as capacities, indicate limits that influence the person's potential for performance achievement in skills. This notion will be explored more extensively in the next section and in the remaining concepts of this chapter.

Relating Abilities to Motor Skills

We have been viewing motor abilities as underlying, foundational components of motor skill performance. As is illustrated in Figure 6.1–2, complex motor skills can be analyzed by a process known as *task analysis* in order to identify the abilities that underlie any motor skill. For example, to serve a tennis ball successfully, certain components of that skill must be properly performed. These components are identified in the first level of analysis of the tennis serve and are represented in Figure 6.1–2 in the middle tier of the diagram. By identifying these components, it is possible to more readily identify the underlying motor abilities that are related to the successful performance of this task. These abilities are identified in the bottom tier of the diagram. Based on Fleishman's lists, these include such abilities as multilimb coordination, control precision, speed of arm movement, rate control, aiming, static strength, etc. You could undoubtedly add others. However, these few examples should serve to illustrate the foundational role played by perceptual-motor and physical proficiency abilities in the performance of motor skills.

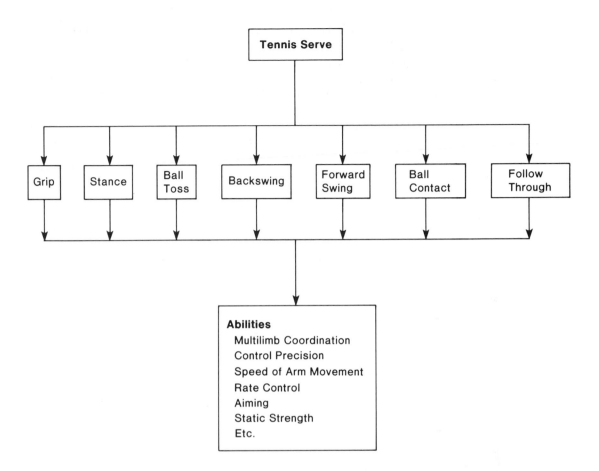

The value of identifying abilities. An important question at this point concerns the value of being able to identify these underlying, foundational abilities. *One benefit* is that this knowledge can be useful in the construction of effective elementary physical education curricula. If you were to compare the abilities underlying a large number of motor skills, you would find some very interesting similarities. For example, speed of arm movement is important for performing a wide range of throwing and batting skills. Balance is likewise a foundational ability to many different skills. From this type of information, it is possible to identify those abilities that should be the basis for establishing what foundational movement experiences should be provided for preschool and elementary school children. For example, since balance is an essential component ability required in a variety of complex skills, movement experiences must be provided that will allow the children the opportunity to develop their balance ability in a variety of movement situations.

Figure 6.1-2
A task analysis for the tennis serve indicating the component parts of the serve and some examples of perceptual-motor abilities underlying performance of the serve.

A *second benefit* of identifying foundational motor abilities is that this process can allow the teacher more specifically to identify the source of problems or difficulties in students' performances. Often an individual has difficulty learning a new skill because he or she lacks adequate experiences involving the motor ability essential to the performance of that particular skill. For example, a child may be having difficulty hitting a pitched ball. In addition to the probable lack of experience with this skill, the child may also have a poorly developed ability to visually track a moving object or to time a movement response to an oncoming object. An important step for the teacher here is to provide specific practice experiences that emphasize these abilities related to the successful performance of a batting skill.

A *third benefit* of understanding the relationship between motor abilities and the performance of motor skills relates to predicting the potential for an individual to succeed in a particular skill. Since this issue will be the basis for the discussion in Concept 6.3, it will not be discussed here. At this point, know that the identification and measurement of underlying motor abilities can be a useful component in a test battery designed to determine which individuals may be best suited for certain motor activities.

The Cause of Motor Abilities

One question that is important to consider concerns why individuals differ from each other in terms of motor abilities. This is by no means an easy question to answer. Attempts at responding to such questions have led to some of the most heated professional controversies of our time, such as the debate concerning the causes of intelligence, which raged during the late 1960s and early 1970s. We may assume, however, that the answer to this question can be related to one or both of two factors. One explanation postulates that the abilities are *genetically determined;* that is, individuals are born with these characteristics. The second explanation maintains that individuals develop abilities through *nongenetic factors,* such as *experience,* which appears to be the most predominant of the nongenetic factors.

It seems that the most satisfactory means of resolving this issue is to view the response as not being an either/or issue. Rather, the limited literature available seems to indicate that both genetics and experience are involved in the level of ability an individual possesses. The point to be investigated, then, is the relative contribution of each factor to abilities. For example, what proportion of an individual's manual dexterity ability is due to genetics and what proportion is due to experiences?

Unfortunately, there is very little empirical evidence on which to base unequivocal conclusions to this issue. Instead, we must rely on authority as the basis for our decision making. Most motor behavior theorists maintain that motor abilities are more genetically than experience determined; that is, the ultimate ability level of an individual is controlled primarily by genetic factors. However, you must be careful in what you conclude from such a statement.

Do not assume from this that two individuals cannot achieve similar levels of proficiency in a physical skill because of genetically determined ability differences. Experience, or training and practice, can often compensate for a lack of certain levels of specific abilities in an activity.

Summary

Individual difference research in motor behavior is concerned with the study of perceptual-motor abilities. The first problem encountered in this study is the identification of these abilities. One approach to this identification process is to consider Fleishman's lists of perceptual-motor and physical proficiency abilities. The value of identifying foundational motor abilities was discussed and was seen as being related to elementary school physical education curriculum development, aiding problem identification in motor skill learning, and predicting the potential for success that an individual may have in a motor skill. Most motor behavior theorists seem to agree that motor ability levels have a higher proportion of genetic determination than experiential.

Related Readings

Cronbach, L. (1957). The two disciplines of scientific psychology. *American Psychologist, 12,* 671–684.

Fleishman, E. A. (1978). Relating individual differences to the dimensions of human tasks. *Ergonomics, 21,* 1007–1019.

Fleishman, E. A. (1982). Systems for describing human tasks. *American Psychologist, 37,* 821–834.

Thomas, J. R., & Halliwell, W. (1976). Individual differences in motor skill acquisition. *Journal of Motor Behavior, 8,* 89–99.

Concept 6.2   Individual difference research does not support the notion of a "general motor ability"

Application

Have you ever been puzzled by the person who appears to be an "all-around athlete?" This person seems to be proficient at whatever athletic endeavor he or she is involved in. The image of the all-around athlete is kept alive with stories and news features about the wide range of athletic skills possessed by a variety of professional athletes like Bo Jackson, Tony Gwynn, Dave Winfield, or Danny Ainge. It has been reported that Wilt Chamberlain, an outstanding former professional basketball player, could have been a world-class boxer, bowler, and volleyball player had he chosen to do so rather than to play professional basketball. We do not even have to look to these highly successful professional athletes for examples of the all-around athlete. Most of us have known certain individuals with whom we went to school or whom we knew by reputation in the community in which we grew up. These individuals seemed to have little difficulty in achieving a high level of success in every sport they were involved in.

A perplexing question concerning these all-around athletes is why they are so good in so many different activities. Are they born with some special motor ability that enables them to be successful at all they do? Have they had an abundance of good training and practice in a wide variety of sports? Are they really good at everything or only at certain sports? Do they learn more quickly than others, or are they "naturally" better at the sports in which they participate?

Discussion

A common way to explain the individual who seems to excel in a wide variety of motor skills, or the all-around athlete, is to say that he or she has a high level of athletic or motor ability. Note that the word *ability* is used in the singular. This is done deliberately, for the notion that individuals possess a singular motor ability has been popular for a long time. Such a conclusion seems to be quite contrary to the multimotor abilities view that we discussed in Concept 6.1. If you thought that you detected such a difference of views, you were right, because for many years there has existed a continuing controversy about the existence of a general motor ability or a multitude of specific motor abilities.

In terms of the discussion of Concept 6.1, the question of a general motor ability versus specific motor abilities has important relevance. There is little doubt from the results of research considered in that discussion that people are characterized by a variety of abilities. The question being addressed here is how these abilities relate to one another in the same individual. If they are highly related, then the general motor ability view represents the nature of

these abilities in an individual. If, on the other hand, these abilities are relatively independent of one another, then the specificity view of motor abilities is the more valid representation.

This controversy over general motor ability versus specific motor abilities was very evident in the research literature during the 1950s and 1960s. Although the controversy has diminished in intensity since that time, the question of which view is correct has been kept alive in many tests used to evaluate motor ability and in physical education textbooks. McCloy's General Motor Ability Tests, Cozen's Athletic Ability Test, and the Barrow Motor Ability Test are examples of tests intended to determine the motor ability of an individual. They are so constructed that the end result of the test battery is the calculation of one score that will reflect an individual's "motor ability." Teachers are encouraged to use these tests as a device for the homogeneous ability grouping of students in physical education classes, where grouping on the basis of individual activities would be cumbersome.

Before any test is administered, the test user should determine the theoretical basis on which that test was developed. If that basis is strong, then the test has merit. However, if the theoretical foundation for the test is questionable, then the merit of the test is likewise impugned. In order to help prepare you to make such a decision, as well as better to understand the nature of the performer of motor skills, we will consider the controversy over the existence of a general motor ability or specific motor abilities. As you will see, the controversy has been resolved in the research literature. However, there are segments of the physical education profession and of society in general that fail to pay attention to that resolution. As we progress through the discussion of these two views, judge for yourself how effectively the research evidence has resolved the issue.

The general motor ability hypothesis maintains that there exists in individuals a singular, global motor ability. The level of that ability for an individual is purported to influence the ultimate success which that person can expect in any athletic endeavor or motor skill. This notion has been in existence for quite some time. The prediction of this hypothesis is that if a person is good at one motor skill, then he or she has the potential to be good at all motor skills. The reasoning behind this prediction is based on the idea that there is *one* general motor ability.

The General Motor Ability Hypothesis

Some well-known figures in physical education such as C. H. McCloy, David Brace, and Harold Barrow were proponents of the existence of such an ability. The tests they developed purported to be of value in assessing a person's present motor ability as well as predicting the success of the individual in athletic endeavors.

McCloy (1934; McCloy & Young, 1954), for example, developed the General Motor Capacity Test as one of his general motor ability tests. He considered *motor capacity* to comprise a person's inborn, hereditary potentialities for general motor performance. The purpose of this test is to predict

potential levels that an individual may be expected to attain. The application of this test, however, is not as broad as these last few statements may suggest. McCloy noted that the test is not a measure of specific skill such as football or basketball because of the specialized abilities required in those sports. The activities in which the motor capacity test can be used for predictive purposes are those requiring "motor ability of a general nature," such as track and field. Thus, the "general" nature of the test may certainly be questioned.

There has been very little evidence reported in the research literature to support the General Motor Ability Hypothesis. An excellent review of many of the studies that have been published to investigate the validity of the tests assessing such general motor ability can be found in the tests and measurements text by Johnson and Nelson (1985). One suspects that the basis for the continued existence of this hypothesis is its intuitive appeal; tests of general motor ability are appealing because they are convenient. The fact that they are unable to predict specific sport skill ability apparently has not diminished their appeal. However, the point that must not be overlooked is that the theoretical basis on which tests rest is indeed tenuous.

The Specificity of Motor Abilities Hypothesis

Since there seems to be little direct support for the general motor ability hypothesis, an alternative hypothesis has been proposed. This suggests that there are many motor abilities and that these abilities are relatively independent. This implies that given the level of ability in one motor ability, it would be impossible to state with any confidence what a person's ability level might be in a different motor ability. Thus, if a person exhibited a high degree of balancing ability, it would not be possible to predict what the person's reaction time might be.

Support for this specificity hypothesis was developed by designing experiments based on a common assumption. That assumption was that if motor abilities are specific and independent, then the relationship between any two abilities will be very low. Thus, in the simplest of cases, the relationship between two abilities such as balance and reaction time, or between reaction time and speed of movement, or even between static balance and dynamic balance would be very low. On the basis of this hypothesis, many experiments that followed such a rationale were published during the 1960s.

By far the bulk of the research that was based on this rationale was published by Franklin Henry and many of his students at the University of California at Berkeley. An example of this investigation is a study published by Henry in 1961. Subjects were tested on two motor abilities, reaction time (RT) and speed of movement, called movement time (MT). A subject's task was to react as quickly as possible to an auditory tone by lifting his or her finger from a telegraph key and then to continue moving as rapidly as possible through a target made of a piece of string that was 30 inches away from the telegraph key. The time between the onset of the stimulus tone and the release of the telegraph key was called RT, while the time between the release of the

Table 6.2-1.
Results from the experiment by Drowatzky and Zuccato (1967) showing the correlations among six different tests of static and dynamic balance.

Test	1 Stork Stand	2 Diver's Stand	3 Stick Stand	4 Sideward Stand	5 Bass Stand	6 Balance Stand
1	—	0.14	−0.12	0.26	0.20	0.03
2		—	−0.12	−0.03	−0.07	−0.14
3			—	−0.04	0.22	−0.19
4				—	0.31	0.19
5					—	0.18
6						—

telegraph key and moving through the string target was termed MT. If the specificity of motor abilities hypothesis was valid, then the relationship between these two simple motor abilities, RT and MT, should be very low. The results of this experiment yielded a correlation coefficient of 0.02, thus supporting the specificity notion.

Other studies have produced similar results that support the specificity of motor abilities theory. Bachman (1961) and Drowatzky and Zucatto (1967) reported experiments which showed that we cannot even consider balancing to be a single, comprehensive ability but rather that there are several specific types of balance. The Drowatzky and Zucatto study is particularly interesting because the researchers had subjects perform six different balancing tasks that have been generally regarded as measures of either static or dynamic balancing ability. The results of the correlations among all the tests are reported in Table 6.2–1. Note that the highest correlation is between the sideward stand and the bass stand (0.31). Most of the correlations range between 0.12 and 0.19. On the basis of these results, it would be difficult to conclude that there exists one test that can be considered a valid measure of balancing ability. Obviously, even the ability we generally label as "balance" should be considered more specifically in terms of certain types of balance.

So far in this discussion, we have considered experiments comparing what we have designated as perceptual-motor abilities. A study by Singer (1966a) examined the relationship between two basic or fundamental motor skills, throwing and kicking. The results of this comparison indicated that even for skills such as these, the relationship between an individual's performance on one test compared to his or her performance on the other is very low.

On the basis of the few experiments that we have considered in this section, it appears that the only justified conclusion is that motor abilities are specific in nature. There seem to be many different motor abilities that are quite independent of each other.

Although theoretical arguments continue concerning precisely how "specific" motor abilities are, there seems to be very little controversy about the statement that people possess many motor abilities. The evidence by Fleishman, referred to in Concept 6.1, as well as that produced by Henry and his colleagues, is strongly indicative of this fact. Ironically, even McCloy admitted that sport skill abilities are numerous. Thus, the exact nature and scope of so-called "general motor ability" can be seriously questioned. The value of determining a person's general motor ability or capacity seems to be so limited that the use of such tests appears meaningless and of negligible value.

Explaining the "All-Around Athlete"

Accepting the hypothesis supporting the specificity of motor skills or abilities does little to resolve questions about the "all-around athlete" that were raised in the application section of this concept. If motor abilities are numerous and independent, then how does one person become so proficient at such a variety of sports? The answer appears to be twofold. First, we must consider the athlete and, second, the sports or activities in which he or she is successful.

According to the specificity hypothesis, a person is characterized by a large number of abilities. Each of these abilities can be described as being somewhere along a range of low, average, and high in terms of the amount of each that characterizes the individual. Because people differ, it seems reasonable to expect that some people have a large number of abilities at an average level and other people are characterized by a majority of abilities at the high or low end of the scale. For example, one person may be at the high end of the scale for the abilities speed of movement, balance, and manual dexterity, while another person may be at the high end of the scale for several other abilities. Therefore, it is to be expected that a person will do very well in those activities in which the underlying abilities required for successful performance match the abilities in which he or she is at the high end of the scale.

The second point to consider in explaining the all-around athlete relates to the sports skills in which this person shows prowess. It is reasonable to assume that the all-around athlete possesses high levels of the abilities that underlie the sports or activities in which that person exhibits high levels of performance. Where this person differs from the "average" individual is in the number of abilities in which he or she can be characterized as being at the high end of the scale. As a result, there are more activities in which this individual can achieve success.

In actual fact, the true all-around athlete is a rare individual. Typically, when a person shows high performance levels in a variety of sport skills, a close inspection of those skills reveals many foundational motor abilities in common. Thus it is to be expected that a person exhibiting high levels of such

abilities as speed of movement, speed of reaction, agility, dynamic balance, and visual acuity will do well in activities in which those abilities are foundational to performance. If this person engages in activities in which these abilities are not as important and in which he or she possesses only average levels of the abilities that are important, then we would expect average performance. It should also be noted that people who perform a variety of activities well are people who had a wide range of movement and sport experiences as children. Thus, early movement experiences may be an important feature of many "all-around" athletes.

One further issue related to the study of motor abilities is a concept that in the past has been referred to as *motor educability*. This term was developed by Brace (1927) and popularized by McCloy (1937). These men used the expression *motor educability* to refer to the "ease with which an individual learns new motor skills." The intent of the tests developed to measure motor educability is not to assess current ability or to predict future success but rather to indicate how quickly an individual will learn motor skills. Notice that here again the general motor ability notion is apparent, as the purpose is to predict ease of learning for motor skills in general.

Motor Educability

Some tests and measurements textbooks in physical education maintain that motor educability tests are useful for the homogeneous grouping of physical education classes and as screening devices for selecting candidates to become physical education majors at the college or university level (for example, note Mathews, 1978, p. 153). In contrast, other texts (e.g., Baumgartner & Jackson, 1982) question both the validity and utility of such tests. Which of these opinions is correct? Perhaps an investigation of some of the research evidence concerning the validity of motor educability will reveal the correct answer to this question.

Two experiments that investigated the validity of motor educability tests were published by Gire and Espenschade (1942) and by Gross, Griessel, and Stull (1956). Gire and Espenschade evaluated the ability of the Brace, Iowa-Brace, and Johnson tests of motor educability[1] on the basis of their ability to predict the ease with which students learned basketball, volleyball, and baseball. In all cases, the correlations were low, indicating little relationship between a student's motor educability score and the ease with which he or she learned a sport skill. Gross, Griessel, and Stull (1956) compared scores on the Iowa-Brace and the Metheny revision of the Johnson tests with students' ability to learn wrestling skills. Again, correlations were quite low.

More recently, Gallagher (1970) developed his own motor educability battery for use in determining the utility of such a test to indicate how quickly college men could learn novel motor tasks. Subjects were divided into high-skilled and low-skilled groups on the basis of the test battery scores. Results indicated that those men classified as high-skilled learned only two of six novel motor tasks more quickly than did the low-skilled group.

1. Complete descriptions of these motor educability tests may be found in most tests and measurements in physical education textbooks.

Experiments such as these attest to the lack of validity of motor educability tests. Thus, the use of such tests would appear to be extremely questionable. The tests are not only founded on a theoretical basis that has little empirical support, they likewise appear to have very little justifiable use in a physical education setting.

Summary

The popular notion of the "all-around athlete" leads to a conclusion that individuals possess or exhibit different levels of a general motor ability. Thus, a person possessing a high degree of such ability would be successful at whatever motor skill he or she attempted. A low level of this ability would predict just the opposite. Although there are people who are highly skilled and successful in a wide variety of sports, the general motor ability hypothesis does not appear to be a satisfactory means of explaining the causes of that success, since this hypothesis has almost no empirical support. An alternative explanation is the specificity of motor skills hypothesis, which postulates that individuals possess many different and relatively independent motor abilities. Each person has different levels of these abilities. Thus, the all-around athlete is a person who has higher levels of the motor abilities that are most important for performance in the sports in which he or she is successful.

Motor educability is a concept that relates to the "ease" with which a person will learn motor skills. Validity studies of tests of motor educability militate against the use of motor educability as a reliable concept in physical activities.

Related Readings

Drowatzky, J. N., & Zuccato, F. C. (1967). Interrelationships between selected measures of static and dynamic balance. *Research Quarterly, 38,* 509–510.

Gallagher, J. D. (1970). Motor learning characteristics of low-skilled college men. *Research Quarterly, 41,* 59–67.

Henry, F. M. (1961). Reaction time-movement time correlations. *Perceptual and Motor skills, 12,* 63–66.

Johnson, B., & Nelson, J. K. (1985). *Practical measurement for evaluation in physical education* (4th ed.). Minneapolis: Burgess.

Magill, R. A., & Powell, F. M. (1975). Is the reaction time-movement time relationship "essentially zero"? *Perceptual and Motor Skills, 41,* 720–722.

The Learner

Knowledge about an individual's motor abilities can be used to help predict potential for success in a motor skill

Concept 6.3

A major task of a coach of any athletic team is to select a team. When members of a team are selected, the coach has indicated that he or she is *predicting* that each individual selected will perform better than those not selected. Unfortunately, the accuracy of this prediction can seldom be known because the coach rarely has a chance to see how well those not selected might have performed.

Every four years at Olympics time, the question of the selection and development of the best athletes in the country becomes a major issue. Certain countries appear to have well-developed selection processes while other countries appear to have less than desirable selection processes. At issue here again is the prediction of future success. The common view is that the country that can more accurately predict, at the earliest possible age, those who will be world-class athletes will have an advantage in competitions such as the Olympics.

This selection problem is not unique to sports. Industry is also involved in the selection process. The desire of any company is to select those individuals for specific jobs who have the greatest potential to perform those jobs well. If the wrong people are chosen, the company stands to lose money. As a result, many companies have developed sophisticated procedures for matching individuals with the jobs that they should be able to perform successfully.

Another prediction situation occurs in many beginning physical education activity classes. If the class is a large one, the teacher may wish to subdivide it into smaller, more homogeneous groups. What is typically done is to place individuals who exhibit high initial performance levels into one group, individuals who exhibit poor initial performance levels into another group, and so on. A question that emerges from this practice concerns the relationship between the initial performance level and later success in the activity. Do individuals who begin an activity by performing poorly have any chance for later success?

In each of these situations, the issue of predicting the *potential* for success in a motor skill is important. In the following discussion, this issue will be considered as it relates to how a knowledge of motor abilities can *aid* in the prediction process. However, first it is important to realize that information about motor abilities is only one type of information that is or should be

used to predict the potential for success. You should use additional information to increase your chances for accurate prediction. This additional information comes from tests of other characteristics besides motor abilities, observing a person's performance over time, and by regularly testing performance of the skill.

Motor abilities testing can provide a useful part of advance information about future performance potential before an individual begins an activity. The caution here is that prediction based on motor abilities testing alone may not be accurate enough. When necessary, or possible, it should be used in conjunction with additional sources of information to provide a more accurate basis for predicting potential for success in a skill.

Discussion

In the discussions of the preceding concepts in this chapter, you have seen that individuals are characterized by a variety of motor abilities and that each of these abilities can be described, if the appropriate tests are available, as being at a certain level. You have also seen that motor skills can be described in terms of the motor abilities that are required for the successful performance of the skills. In this discussion, these two points will provide the basis for establishing how information about motor abilities can be used to predict potential for success in motor skills.

It is important to be aware that what is being considered here is the prediction of a person's *potential* for future success rather than a person's actual future success. Whether or not an individual actually achieves his or her potential will depend on many factors, such as motivation, training, opportunities, etc. Thus, the use of motor abilities for prediction must be limited to making predictive evaluations about what a person's potential for success might be given the availability of the appropriate conditions to develop that potential.

Prediction Accuracy

Before considering how motor abilities information can be used for prediction purposes, it is essential to consider some of the limitations related to how accurately this prediction can be made. While the accuracy of the prediction for a particular situation will be dependent on several factors, two are particularly critical.

First, predicting the potential for success in a motor skill depends on an accurate identification and assessment of the essential abilities required to successfully perform the skill in question. We will refer to this skill as the target skill. The first step here is to develop a task analysis for the target skill, as was discussed in Concept 6.1. Within this analysis should be the identification of the abilities that seem to underlie the successful performance of this skill. The next step is to administer a battery of abilities tests that have been validated as tests of the abilities identified in the task analysis to a large sample of people. Finally, the scores on these tests must be compared to the actual

performance of the target skill by your sample of people. An appropriate performance measure must be used. You can use various statistical techniques to provide the information you are seeking. We will not discuss these as that is not the purpose here.

Given an appropriate statistical analysis, the statistic of interest is what is known as the *variance accounted for*. This simply means that the amount, as designated by a percentage, of the statistical variance of the performance scores of the target skill is accounted for by the scores on the abilities tests. If the target skill performance variance accounted for by the tests used is high (i.e., 70% or better), then you can be confident that you have identified the essential abilities underlying performance of the target skill. If, on the other hand, the variance accounted for is below that percentage, then other abilities remain to be identified.

The *second* factor critical in the accuracy of the success prediction is the validity and reliability of the abilities tests used to measure the identified abilities. If these tests are not valid and reliable measures, then there is little basis on which to expect reasonable prediction accuracy of motor skill performance.

At the present time, these two factors are at the heart of problems related to accurately predicting a person's potential for future success in a motor skill. There is much work to be done in both identifying the important abilities underlying successful performance of skills and in developing valid and reliable ability tests. However, as you will see, there has been sufficient success in many situations to warrant the consideration of the use of motor abilities testing to predict future success potential.

One of the essential points to understand when attempting to predict potential for future skill performance achievement from levels of abilities is the relationship between performance of a skill at the early stage of practice and performance later in practice. This is important because a low relationship between early and late stages of learning indicates that the abilities underlying performance at each stage of learning may be different. On the other hand, a high relationship between stages of learning simplifies matters by allowing the identification of abilities to be made without regard for the stage of learning.

An experiment by Ella Trussell (1965) provides some insight into this issue. In her experiment, Trussell had 40 college women learn to juggle three tennis balls. Each of the 27 practice sessions included 75 tosses, and the subjects practiced during three sessions per week for nine weeks. Final success in juggling was operationally defined as the average score, which was the number of errors or dropped balls, for the last four practice periods. Figure 6.3–1 shows the performance curve for the practice sessions. Notice that the subjects improved over practice. Error scores dropped from 50 errors per 75 tosses in the first practice period to 20 errors per 75 tosses in the final session. The second

Relating Initial and Later Achievement

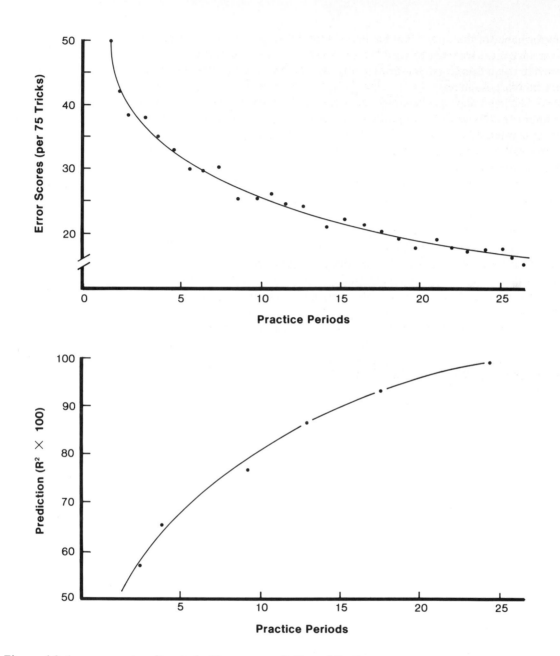

Figure 6.3-1
The top graph shows the performance curve from the experiment by Trussell for a juggling task. The numbers of errors are indicated for the practice periods. The bottom graph indicates the accuracy of prediction of final performance in the juggling task as a function of the amount of practice used for prediction.

graph shows to what extent the final scores for the subjects could be predicted on the basis of the error scores for each practice period. The measure on the vertical axis is to be interpreted as indicating the probability of being correct in predicting the final score. During the first five practice sessions, we would be correct only 50% to 60% of the time in predicting final scores. This is about as good as we could do by flipping a coin. We would like to have a more meaningful prediction than this if we wish to predict ultimate performance in the learning of a motor skill. The ability to predict final scores increased as more practice sessions are observed. After 15 sessions, or 1,025 tosses, we could predict with about 85% accuracy. Performance early in practice, then, does not lead to a very accurate indication of future performance.

Another way of looking at this same issue of the relationship of early to later practice performance is to consider the relationship of performance scores between any two trials. The common finding here has been that trials that are close to each other in time are more highly correlated than trials that are further from each other. That is, trials 2 and 3 will show a higher correlation than will trials 2 and 20. This characteristic of the relationship between trials follows what has been called a *superdiagonal form*. This term refers to the way the trial-to-trial correlations appear on a correlation matrix where all trials are compared against each other, with the same trials located on both the vertical and the horizontal axes of the matrix. The correlation of a trial with the trial that succeeds it, such as trials 2 and 3, will be found just above the diagonal of the matrix where a trial would be correlated with itself. According to the superdiagonal form, the highest correlations in the matrix should be found along the diagonal that is just above the main diagonal of the matrix.

An example of the superdiagonal form for learning a motor skill was reported by Thomas and Halliwell (1976) for the pursuit rotor, the stabilometer, and a rhythmic arm movement task. The correlation matrix in Table 6.3–1 is from the results of subjects' initial 15 trials of practice on the rhythmic arm movement task. This task involved learning to move a lever held at the side of the body to a visual target in time with a metronome. Performance was scored in terms of both spatial and temporal error. As you can see in Table 6.3–1, the highest between-trial correlations for spatial error performance on the practice trials for this task are typically found along the diagonal located just above the main diagonal of the correlation matrix. (Note that if the correlations were presented on the main diagonal, they would be 1.0, because a trial would be correlated with itself.) Then, as you move to your right to compare a particular trial to other trials, the correlation between trials is generally less. For example, the correlation between trials 4 and 5 is 0.73 while the correlation between trials 4 and 12 drops to 0.15. It should be noted that although performance on the stabilometer in this study did not follow the superdiagonal form as precisely as might have been predicted, the general character of the correlations between trials fits the expected form. As such, these results provide additional evidence that performance early in practice is a poor predictor of performance later in practice.

Table 6.3–1.

The intertrial correlation matrix from performance on a rhythmic arm movement task reported by Thomas and Halliwell (1976). The correlations are based on the spatial error scores from the task.

Trial	1	2	3	4	5	6	7	8	9	10	11	12	13	14	15
1	—	27	−.05	.33	.23	.08	.27	.15	.00	−.04	−.09	.11	−.05	.13	−.12
2		—	.63	.71	.57	.57	.64	.54	.57	.38	.54	.29	.15	.67	.25
3			—	.60	.46	.18	.56	.50	.45	.53	.48	.12	.09	.37	.24
4				—	.73	.45	.61	.62	.45	.29	.51	.15	.17	.49	.12
5					—	.37	.67	.57	.59	.32	.52	.22	.28	.52	.21
6						—	.53	.54	.50	.39	.68	.52	.41	.61	.35
7							—	.71	.67	.70	.65	.51	.57	.80	.50
8								—	.67	.67	.65	.52	.43	.59	.48
9									—	.47	.73	.54	.61	.78	.41
10										—	.56	.59	.63	.62	.64
11											—	.49	.57	.72	.62
12												—	.63	.58	.47
13													—	.71	.63
14														—	.53
15															—

Accounting for this poor prediction. An important question concerning the common finding that early practice performance is a poor predictor of later performance achievement is, What accounts for this poor prediction? Why does it occur? Although there is some debate among individual difference psychologists (see Henry & Hulin, 1987, for a good discussion of both sides of this debate), we will consider a prevalent view that has been promoted by Fleishman. He argues that the repertoire of abilities needed to perform a skill changes as a skill has been practiced so that the abilities related to performance early in practice are not the same abilities related to performance later in practice.

Support for Fleishman's "changing-task" view is found in the research by Fleishman and colleagues. In one experiment (Fleishman & Hempel, 1955), 264 subjects were given a battery of nine motor abilities tests and then practiced a complex motor skill. The task was a complex discrimination test that required the subjects to push toggle switches as quickly as possible in response to a pattern of signal lights. The complexity of this task was established by requiring a certain movement response to different patterns of signal lights. The subjects had to learn the appropriate signal light pattern and response combination as they practiced the task. It was reported that subjects were able

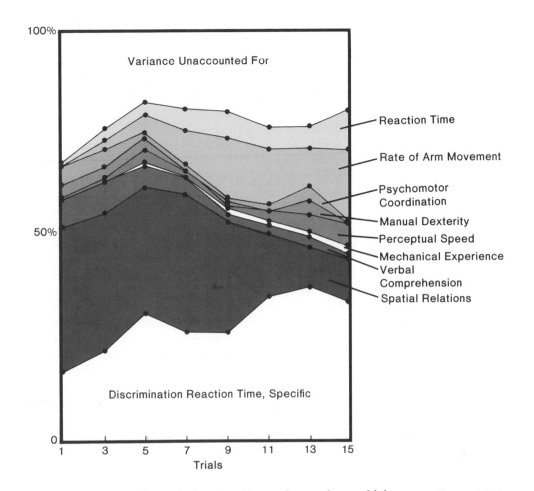

100%

Variance Unaccounted For

Reaction Time

Rate of Arm Movement

Psychomotor Coordination

Manual Dexterity

Perceptual Speed

Mechanical Experience

Verbal Comprehension

Spatial Relations

50%

Discrimination Reaction Time, Specific

0

1   3   5   7   9   11   13   15

Trials

to improve their response times during the 16 practice sessions, which consisted of 20 trials each. The average response times of the subjects improved from almost 500 msec during the first practice session to under 250 msec during the final practice session.

Of interest to this discussion are the results indicating the relationship between the nine abilities and the performance levels across the practice sessions. These results are presented in Figure 6.3–2. This graph shows the percentage of variance accounted for by each of the nine abilities. In this graph the amount of variance is represented by a marked area that indicates the percentage of the total variance accounted for by the particular ability. The greater the percentage of the total variance accounted for by an ability, the more important that ability is to performance of the task.

As you can see, the relationship between each ability and performance of the task is plotted across the practice sessions. During the first practice session, the abilities spatial relations (36%), discrimination reaction time (17%),

Figure 6.3–2
Results of the experiment by Fleishman and Hempel showing the percentage of variance accounted for by different abilities at different stages of practice on a complex discrimination reaction-time task. Percentage of variance is represented by the size of the shaded areas for each ability.

verbal comprehension (6%), and psychomotor coordination (5%) accounted for 64% of the variance for the performance on the complex task. Now look at the right-hand side of the graph where performance during the last session of practice is considered. As you can see, the relative importance of the various abilities to task performance has changed in many cases from what it was earlier in practice. Here the most significant abilities related to task performance were discrimination reaction time (35%), rate of arm movement (17%), spatial relations (11%), reaction time (9%), and perceptual speed (5%).

Early in practice, spatial relations was a very important factor in accounting for performance on the task. However, by the last practice session, its level of importance had decreased significantly (from 36% to 11%). On the other hand, reaction time and rate of arm movement were of negligible importance early in practice. However, later in practice, these abilities accounted for over 30% of the variance of the task performance. Discrimination reaction time increased from 17% to 35% over the practice sessions.

From this experiment, you can see that abilities contributing to performance change in importance from the early stage of practice to later stages. Those abilities that are important in accounting for a person's performance score early in practice are typically not as important later in practice.

It is interesting to note in this regard that the types of abilities important to performance at each stage of learning are rather closely related to the terms used by Fitts and Posner (discussed in Concept 2.2) to identify the stages of learning. Those abilities important early in learning are typically perceptual or cognitive in nature, e.g., spatial relations and verbal comprehension. However, later in practice, during the autonomous stage, abilities more related to controlling movement increase in importance.

The key point here is that it is very difficult to predict future achievement in learning a motor skill when the prediction is based on early performance only. The prediction seems to improve, however, if there is an awareness of the specific abilities that are essential to performance in the different stages of learning and if there is also an awareness of the corresponding abilities within the learner.

To the instructor of motor skills, this concept is very important. The instructor must be aware that a person may eventually perform better than initial performance indicates. To "give up" on a person because of such undependable evidence as early performance alone would be doing that person a grave injustice. Also, to cut players from a team solely on the basis of their performance during early practice sessions would likewise be inadvisable. Keep in mind here that we are referring to inexperienced participants.

Predicting Success Potential from Abilities Tests

Thus far in this discussion we have considered some of the problems involved in using motor abilities tests to predict an individual's potential for success in a motor skill. While it is obvious that there are problems, there has been some success in using abilities tests for prediction purposes. The primary source of

information about the successful use of ability testing for future success prediction comes from research in industry. We will consider one study from an industrial application to exemplify how this performance prediction can be accomplished.

Reilly, Zedeck, and Tenopyr (1979) used a battery of 14 physical and motor ability measures to predict pole-climbing performance for telephone company trainees. These measures included such things as height, weight, body density, leg strength reaction time, arm strength, balance, and static strength. From this battery, three measures were found to successfully predict pole-climbing performance. These three measures were body density, balance, and static strength. As a result, these three tests could be given to training course applicants as an initial screening device to determine who should be permitted to enroll in the course. That is, a person achieving above a specified score on this test battery would have a 90% chance of passing the training course.

The benefit of early prediction of success potential in an industrial setting is obvious. People can be screened and placed into jobs for which they are best suited before the company invests a lot of time and money in training them. This same logic has been applied to the sport setting as a means of identifying people who have the greatest potential to be successful competitors in specific sports. If this could be done, individuals could be more accurately channeled into those sports in which they had the greatest likelihood of being world-class performers.

For example, in a study of individuals involved in training programs in archery, Landers, Boutcher, and Wang (1986) found that certain physical, perceptual-motor and psychological characteristics accurately predicted archery performance. After administering several batteries of physical and psychological tests to 188 amateur archers, they found that individuals with greater relative leg strength, lower percentage of body fat, faster reaction times, better depth perception, greater imagery ability, more confidence, and better use of past mistakes had higher archery performance scores than other archers. In fact, the leg strength, percentage of body fat, reaction time, depth perception, and past mistakes characteristics together correctly predicted how 81% of these archers would be classified, average or above average, as archers. Thus, on the basis of these few physical, perceptual-motor, and psychological characteristics, it was possible to correctly predict how most of these archers would be categorized as archers. Clearly, certain abilities and characteristics are required for people to achieve different levels of sport performance.

Perhaps the most vocal call in the sport world for developing accurate prediction instruments is from those who see this approach benefiting the selection of world-class competitors. The appeal of such a selection process for athletes goes beyond the savings in training time and money that this process represents, it also would help ensure a greater degree of success for a country in world-class competitions. Although some success has been reported using predictive-type testing for this purpose in many countries, particularly in

eastern Europe, the process of testing and selection is complex and lengthy. The testing process involves much more than just motor ability tests. This process also includes a wide range of physiological and psychological test batteries that must be carefully developed. Also, coaches and researchers must be trained not only to administer these tests, but also to carefully observe athletes at all stages of their development.

An additional important point must be interjected here. It is essential that developmental characteristics be taken into account in any attempts to predict potential for future success in sport. This is especially critical for preadolescents and adolescents. Attempts to make such predictions for these children are tenuous at best. The primary reason for this is that *children mature at different rates.* That is, a child of 12 may be physically more like an 8- or 9-year-old or more like a 12- or 13-year-old. (See Malina, 1984, for a good discussion of this topic.) Early maturers, those who are physically advanced for their age, may be successful because of their physical advantage rather than their skill advantage. When the late maturers, those who are physically behind for their age, catch up, the once apparent difference in skill levels often disappears. The message here, then, is never to give up on a young athlete because you think he or she has no chance to ever experience success. In your role as a teacher or coach of children and youth, it is essential to provide optimum experiences and opportunities for all, not just for those who look like they will be successful because of current success.

Summary

Information about an individual's motor abilities can be useful in predicting his or her potential for success in various motor skills. While this information cannot be expected to lead to absolutely perfect prediction, it can be used with other information to aid in the prediction process. Predicting the potential for success depends on the accuracy of the identification of the essential abilities related to successfully performing the motor skill of interest. Also critical to the prediction process is the development and use of valid and reliable tests of motor abilities. Abilities related to performance of a skill in the early stages of learning are often different from those that are important for performance of the skill later in learning. Predicting future success depends on identifying levels of abilities within the individual that are essential to successful task performance and on identifying those abilities within the task that relate to successful performance of the task.

Related Readings

Fleishman, E. A. (1969). Abilities at different stages of practice in rotary pursuit performance. *Journal of Experimental psychology, 60,* 162–171.

Fleishman, E. A. (1982). Systems for describing human tasks. *American Psychologist, 37,* 821–824.

Henry, R. A. & Hulin, C. L. (1987). Stability of skilled performance across time: Some generalizations and limitations on utilities. *Journal of Applied Psychology, 72,* 457–462.

Malina, R. M. (1984). Physical growth and maturation. In J. R. Thomas (Ed.), *Motor development during childhood and adolescence* (pp. 2–26). Minneapolis: Burgess.

1. How does the study of individual differences differ from the study of normative or average behavior?
2. What motor abilities has Fleishman identified? What other motor abilities can you identify?
3. Describe two ways in which knowledge about minor abilities can be of value to a teacher of motor skills.
4. What seems to be the most generally accepted position concerning the cause or origin of motor abilities?
5. What is the difference between the general motor ability hypothesis and the specificity of motor abilities hypothesis? Give an example of some research that indicates which of these hypotheses is more valid.
6. How can a specificity view of motor abilities explain how a person can be an "all-around athlete"?
7. What is meant by the term *motor educability?* Is it a valid notion?
8. Why can knowledge of an individual's motor abilities only help in predicting that person's potential for success in a particular motor skill?
9. How successfully can eventual success in motor skill performance be predicted from how well a person performs the same skill in early practice?
10. What is the "superdiagonal form" that is characteristic of the between-practice trial relationship for many motor skills? What does this correlation pattern tell us about the relationship of early to later practice performance?
11. According to the Fleishman and Hempel study, what is important to know concerning predicting success in motor skills?
12. Why is cutting a 10-year-old from a sports team because of poor performance a bad policy? Consider this in terms of maturation rate differences in children and how that relates to motor skill performance success.

Unit 3

The Learning Environment

Knowledge of Results

7

Concept 7.1
Knowledge of results (KR) facilitates skill learning by being a source of error correction information, motivation, and reinforcement.

Concept 7.2
KR must provide adequate information to facilitate learning.

Concept 7.3
Three time intervals are associated with the use of KR during a practice trial: the KR-delay interval, the post-KR interval, and the interresponse interval.

Concept 7.1   Knowledge of results (KR) facilitates skill learning by being a source of error correction information, motivation, and reinforcement

Application

When you are starting out to learn a new activity, such as golf, tennis, racquetball, or dance, how do you generally feel after the first few attempts at performing some part of that activity? Probably you feel somewhat frustrated in that you have so many questions that you need to have answered before beginning the next few attempts. Remember, you are in the early phase of the cognitive stage of learning. You should have many questions about what you are doing right and what you are doing wrong.

One of the important roles played by a teacher of motor skills involves providing this type of information to a student. When a novice golfer is hitting balls on the practice range, what the instructor tells that individual about each hit or series of hits is very important to the development of that person's skill in playing golf. This information can be valuable to the learner in a number of ways. First, it can provide specific information about what he or she has been doing incorrectly. This information then becomes a basis for trying to make some adjustments on the next practice attempt. Second, the information provided can be a valuable form of reinforcement. This is especially noticeable when the learner has done something correctly or nearly correctly. When the instructor informs him or her about that correct performance, this becomes a reinforcement. As a result, the learner will try to duplicate that performance on the next attempt. Finally, what the instructor tells the novice golfer can be valuable as a form of motivation. Learners need to know that they are improving, yet many times they are unable to detect improvement by watching their own performance. In this case the instructor becomes a vital source of motivation to help learners continue practicing.

In the following discussion, we will be considering the information that the instructor gives to the learner following a practice attempt. Providing this information, which we are referring to as knowledge of results (KR), will thus appear as one of the most important functions that an instructor of motor skills performs for the learner.

Discussion

When a person performs a motor skill, there are several sources from which information can be obtained about the outcome of the response or about what caused the outcome. One of these sources of information, discussed in Chapter 3, is the person's own sensory feedback system. This information source comes into play, for example, when the person sees where the golf ball he or she just hit has landed or feels what the swing was like that produced that outcome.

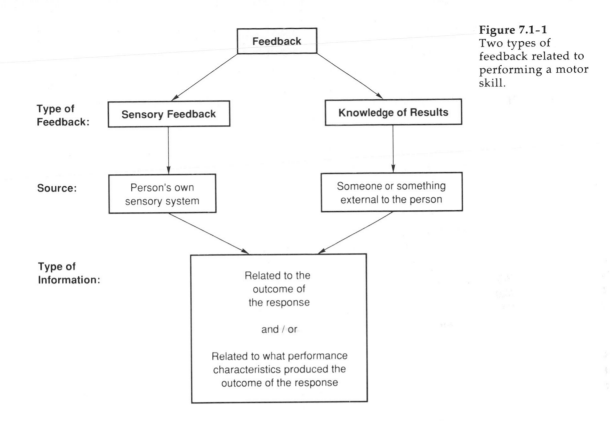

Figure 7.1-1
Two types of
feedback related to
performing a motor
skill.

The second source of information is when another person observes the skill and the observer provides information about the outcome of the response or its cause. For beginning learners of a motor skill, the observer is often the instructor. These two sources of information, one internal and one external to the person performing the skill, are important for skill learning to occur.

In Figure 7.1–1, these two sources of information about a response are represented as parts of the feedback family. The key feature that distinguishes these two types of feedback is the source. For *sensory feedback,* the source is within the individual in the form of the sensory system. Useful feedback about a response can be provided by the visual, auditory, tactile, and proprioceptive systems. The other source of information is outside the individual and is generally known as *knowledge of results, or KR.* This form of information can come from a teacher, coach, videotape, computer, or any external source capable of providing information about an individual's performance.

Although the terms *feedback* and *KR* are often used interchangeably, in this text we will keep their meanings distinct, as the source of information provided to or available to the individual differs for each. The advantage of this designation of sources is that it provides a useful means of establishing how each source of information influences skill learning. This designation has

merit for relating the roles of these sources of information in the skill learning process. It also has merit in identifying the type of information that is most likely to be under the direct control of the instructor.

Defining KR

Although the terms *feedback,* or *sensory feedback,* and *KR* will be kept distinct in these discussions, there remains an additional terminology problem for the term *KR.* Feedback information that is provided to an individual from an external source can be either about the response outcome or about what caused the response outcome. These two types of externally presented feedback information have caused some concern among motor learning scholars as to whether or not the term KR should refer to both types of information. The most prevalent alternative to using KR for both is to use KR only when referring to response outcome information and to use the term *knowledge of performance,* or *KP,* when referring to information about the actual performance characteristics that produced or caused the outcome. Thus, according to this distinction, KR about a golf shot that sliced into the woods would be, "The ball went off to the right into the woods," whereas KP would be something like, "Your hands are leading the club head at contact so that the clubface is open when it contacts the ball." (See Gentile, 1972, and Salmoni, Schmidt, & Walter, 1984, for more discussion of this KR-KP distinction.)

As you can see, it is important not only to distinguish the source of feedback information, but also to distinguish the type of information provided if the feedback is from an external source. The question that remains is, Should separate terms be used to designate the two types of external feedback? For our purposes, the term *KR* will encompass *both* types of information. Thus, KR is defined in this text as *information provided to an individual after the completion of a response that is related to either the outcome of the response or the performance characteristics that produced that outcome.*

Although the controversy about the appropriate terminology will continue, it seems unnecessary to use both KR and KP. As you can see in Figure 7.1–1, both information about the response outcome and about what caused the response outcome can be provided by either sensory feedback or by an external source. Thus, it seems rather inconsistent to argue for a distinction between these two types of feedback when from an external source but not when the source is the individual's sensory system. What is most important then, is to specify what type of information is being referred to when using the term KR. In some instances, KR will refer to response outcome information whereas in others it will refer to information about what caused the outcome. The context in which the term KR is used will typically specify which type of information. However, if you find it helpful to use the terms KR and KP in this regard, feel free to do so.

There seems little doubt that KR plays a critical role in the process of learning motor skills. As a learning variable that the instructor can directly manipulate, it becomes especially important to understand KR in terms of

how and why it influences skill learning. The first point to understand about KR is that it plays several different roles or functions in the skill-learning process. Sometimes these roles are independent of one another whereas in other situations KR functions overlap. Functionally, then, KR provides information about performance that serves to guide error correction, to motivate the individual, and to reinforce correct performance. As you will see in the next three sections, each of these functions is intricately involved in establishing KR's prominent position in the skill-learning process.

Adams (1971) stated that learning a motor skill is best viewed as a problem-solving situation. Accordingly, there is a need to establish what is essential or necessary for this problem solving to succeed. One of the most obvious factors that has been recommended by learning theorists is information about a response. In the motor skills situation, it is important that the information about a response be of such a nature that it will help the person make some necessary adjustments before attempting the skill again. Eventually, when the learner has made the appropriate types of adjustment, in the proper "amount," the responses will become quite satisfactory and proper.

Information to Guide Error Correction

It appears, then, that information about a response is essential to the learner. One way to illustrate this is to look at the learner in the beginning stage of acquiring a new skill. As an example, suppose you have never before had a golf club in your hand and you are beginning to take golf lessons. As you first begin to learn the golf swing, you find that you do not understand clearly what the swing is supposed to look like and how it should feel. You have some idea from watching your instructor, but you are not quite sure what your own swing looks and feels like as compared to what it should be. This is where KR as information plays a vital role. Your instructor will tell you after each swing or after several swings what errors you have been making in your practice. What you must then do is to use that information to make necessary changes in your swing so that your next practice swing will be more like what it should be. In this way, learning the golf swing is seen as a continuous process of practice attempt, having error information presented, developing changes in what you have been doing, and swinging again.

From this example, it should be obvious that KR is a primary source of information that can be used to correct performance errors made during any given practice attempt. These corrections eventually should lead to a correct performance. Theoretically, the learner is *using KR as information to form hypotheses and strategies* about a performance, then testing the effectiveness of those hypotheses and strategies in each succeeding practice attempt.

How essential is KR for error correction? An important consideration on which to base any further discussion of KR concerns the importance of KR for directing error correction by the learner. Early evidence for KR being an essential part of the learning process can be traced to a study published in Britain

in 1938 by Elwell and Grindley. These researchers were attempting to show that KR for humans in a motor learning situation is much more than a reward that merely strengthens the learner's tendency to repeat a movement. The reward idea, which was quite prevalent then and still is today, is based on some work done by the famous Edward Thorndike. What Elwell and Grindley demonstrated was that subjects actually used the error information that was in KR to correct errors in each trial of a two-hand coordination task that required the lining up of a light in a bull's-eye. Their experiment showed rather convincingly that, for humans, KR is more than a reward for a correct response. KR is actually information that can be used by the learner to learn motor skills.

A study that has come to be considered a classic statement for demonstrating the importance of KR for learning was made by Bilodeau, Bilodeau, and Schumsky (1959). The logic behind their experiment was that if KR is necessary for learning a motor skill, then withdrawing KR during different trials of a task should indicate different levels of improvement. While blindfolded, subjects were required to learn to move a handle of a linear slide-type apparatus to a specific location. They did not know beforehand where the correct location was but had to learn it. KR was furnished in the form of the direction and amount of error made on a trial. For example, if the correct response was to move to 50 cm and the subject's response was 40 cm, KR was given as 10 units short. The term *units* was used so that subjects who might have a better knowledge of the size of a cm would not prejudice or predispose the results. The results of this study can be seen in Figure 7.1–2. Notice that the group who received no KR did not perform very accurately in the 20 trials. Subjects who had KR withdrawn after 2 or 6 trials began to perform rather poorly after that point. However, the subjects who received KR for every trial improved their accuracy to about 2 mm of error on trial 8 and then performed with that level of accuracy for the remainder of the 20 trials.

A more recent study was reported by George Stelmach (1970), in which he had two groups of subjects either receiving KR or not receiving KR. All subjects were to learn a complex arm response. Each subject sat in front of a table with an index finger on a reaction key. When a stimulus light appeared, the subject had to release the reaction key, move his or her arm forward 11 inches to make contact with a flexible piece of rubber tubing 10 inches long, then move his or her hand back to touch a sensitive dummy switch, and then finally move forward 11 inches again to depress the movement time key. Each subject was scored on the amount of time elapsed between the appearance of the stimulus light and the depressing of the final key. Results are graphed in Figure 7.1–3 and show that those subjects who received KR performed better during the trials than those who received no KR (the control group).

Based on studies such as these, many learning theorists and researchers argued that there was sufficient evidence to indicate the importance of KR

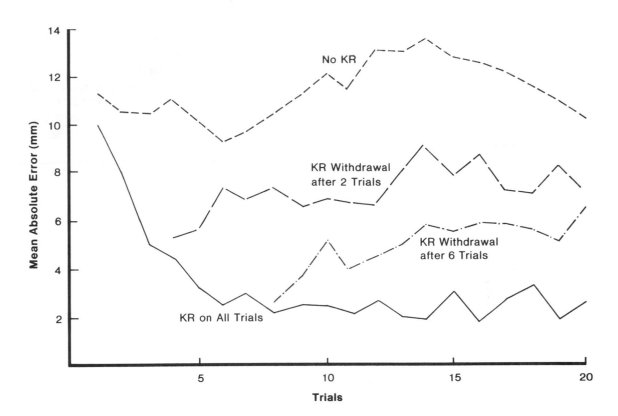

for learning. In fact, by the 1960s, KR research had been sufficient for Bilodeau and Bilodeau (1961) and Fitts (1964) to consider KR as the strongest and most important variable involved in learning and performance. Dennis Holding (1965), in his book *The Principles of Training*, amplified this line of thought by indicating that the manipulation of KR is one of the most effective ways to influence the course of learning. Adams (1971) stated that "performance improvement in acquisition depends on knowledge of results" (p. 130).

Does all of this mean that learning a motor skill *requires* the presence of KR? One way to address this question is to take a closer look at the Stelmach (1970) results presented in Figure 7.1–3. Notice that the subjects who did not receive KR were able to improve their performance with practice. Obviously, KR was not absolutely essential for learning the task. Further support for learning without KR has been provided by other researchers (e.g., Zelaznik, Shapiro, & Newell, 1978). What appears to be the case is that certain tasks absolutely require KR as response outcome information, as in the case of the line-drawing or blind-positioning tasks. Other tasks, however, can be learned without KR, as evidenced by the movement-speed task in the Stelmach experiment.

Figure 7.1-2
Results of the experiment by Bilodeau, Bilodeau, and Schumsky showing the effect of KR on the learning of a simple positioning task.

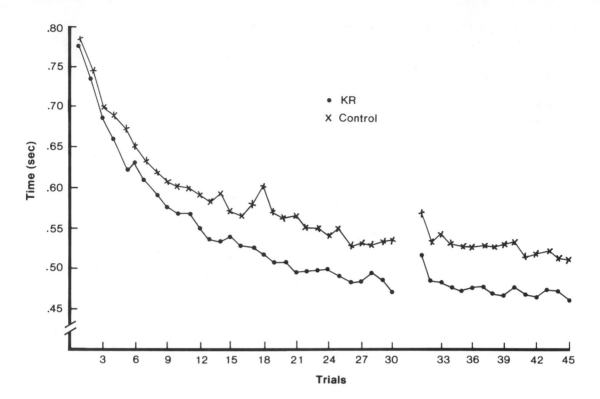

Figure 7.1-3
Results of the
experiment by
Stelmach showing
mean performance
times for groups
with or without KR
as a function of
practice.

Therefore, although KR may not be absolutely essential for learning all motor skills, it does appear to play a critical role in guiding error correction for most skills during the course of learning. This role is established by two important benefits provided to the learning process.

First, KR leads to *more efficient error correction.* That is, error correction typically occurs faster with KR than without it. Notice in Figure 7.1–3 that subjects in the KR group were performing the task in less than 0.55 second after 12 trials whereas the no-KR group did not achieve that level of performance until after 24 trials. *Second,* KR leads to *better eventual performance.* Notice again in Figure 7.1–3 that even after 45 trials of practice, the no-KR group was not performing as well as the KR group. While performance improved during practice without KR, there appeared to be a limit to the level of performance achieved with that amount of practice.

Practice with KR can lead to error correction capabilities without KR. In the motor skill learning situations described in the preceding section, learning was either impossible or hindered without KR. But, recall the discussion in Concept 2.3 about the theories of motor learning by Adams (1971) and by Schmidt (1975b). An important part of both theories was that a person should be able to eventually perform a skill without KR. Each theory proposed that when

KR functions to guide the error correction process early in learning, a model of correct performance is developed, which becomes the basis for successful performance in later learning stages. Thus, if the model of correct performance, called the *perceptual trace* by Adams (1971) and the *recognition schema* by Schmidt (1975b) is developed well enough, then correct performance is possible, even without KR.

In this discussion, then, we are concerned with how the individual develops a model of correct performance for a motor skill. It will become apparent that KR is an important ingredient in the development of this model for any motor skill. KR contains the information that the learner needs in order to develop his or her own model of correct performance for the skill being learned. The KR is used to evaluate both what the individual thinks the correct performance should be and the information received from his or her own sensory feedback system. The learner can then use the discrepancy that is apparent from this comparison evaluation to make some adjustments not only on the next response but also in the internal reference system. As we discussed in Chapter 2, while the learner amends his or her own reference system during the course of practice and on the basis of the KR and sensory feedback matches, he or she can develop a very adequate internal model of correct performance. A well-developed model is something that characterizes the highly skilled performer. This individual is then able to make a response not only pinpointing errors he or she had made but also how to determine a way to correct those errors.

One way to investigate the role of KR in developing this model of correct performance was reported in an experiment by Karl Newell (1974). In this experiment, he followed the KR withdrawal paradigm used by Bilodeau, Bilodeau, and Schumsky (1959) discussed earlier. Newell, however, increased the amount of practice used in that experiment, reasoning that if a certain amount of practice with KR is critical for the development of a model of correct performance, then the experiment by Bilodeau et al. couldn't support this idea because subjects practiced so little. Thus, Newell's goal was to show that with sufficient practice with KR, withdrawing KR would not lead to poor performance of the practiced skill.

Subjects in Newell's experiment were required to learn to make a rapid, ballistic movement of a sliding handle on a trackway. The correct response was a movement of 24 cm in 150 msec, i.e., 0.150 seconds. The subjects knew the distance to move but did not know the correct speed of movement. They were to learn this through their practice trials and the KR they received, this latter in the form of milliseconds fast or slow. There were six groups of subjects, each having KR withdrawn after a given number of trials, 2, 7, 17, 32, 52, or not withdrawn at all. The results of withdrawing KR at these various trials are depicted in the graph in Figure 7.1–4. You should notice that the best performance occurred when KR was withdrawn later in the practice trials. It is also relevant to note that subjects who had KR withdrawn after 52 trials

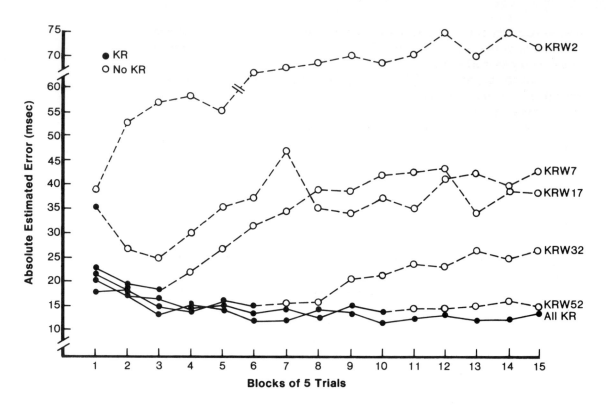

Figure 7.1-4
Results of the experiment by Newell showing the performance curves for groups who had KR withdrawn at various points of the 75 trials to learn to make a linear movement in 150 msec. The open circles indicate blocks of trials during which no KR was given; the closed circles show blocks of trials with KR. The numbers following the KRW indicate the trial on which KR was withdrawn.

maintained their performance for the remaining 25 trials. All the other groups showed decreasing performance following the KR withdrawal. Thus, the need for KR early in the practice of even a simple motor task is quite clearly indicated in this experiment.

The benefit of KR as error correction guidance information. It is quite possible that a person could learn a motor skill without the benefit of KR. Skills such as shooting a basketball, serving a tennis ball or racquetball, or relearning to walk could very likely be acquired by an individual on the basis of his or her own trial-and-error practice. However, KR becomes an essential ingredient in the instructional setting when its role in the development of an internalized model of correct performance by the learner is considered in two ways. First, KR helps to ensure the proper development of the model of correct performance by the individual. Learning without the benefit of KR would be a random hit-and-miss process where the likelihood of adequately learning the skill could not be predicted very well. Second, the use of KR in the instructional setting enhances the acquisition of the skill by facilitating the learning process. Since the efficiency of instruction is such an important consideration in the typical time-limited schedules in which a skill must be taught, methods

that increase the teacher's ability to accomplish the most in the least amount of time are highly desirable. Thus, KR is seen to add an important element in increasing that efficiency.

Many questions about KR as error correction guidance information still exist that have yet to be satisfactorily answered. For example, when during the course of learning is KR most important? What kind of information should KR provide? That is, how much and what should be the nature of the information? When should KR be provided? When should the next practice attempt occur after KR has been provided? In connection with each of these questions, others develop. We will consider these in more detail in the other concepts in this chapter.

To many people, KR is the equivalent of a form of reinforcement or reward. **Reinforcement**
This use of the term KR was brought about by the usual use of food as a reward for animals following a correct or nearly correct response. However, the work that we discussed by Elwell and Grindley (1938) showed that KR was more than a reward. While KR can be more than reward, this does not eliminate the fact that KR can also serve as a reward or reinforcement.

The use of any reward following a correct response has as its purpose the strengthening of the response or increasing of the probability that this same, or a similar, response will occur again. Applying this to the situation of learning the golf swing, let us suppose that on a particular practice attempt you make a correct swing. Your instructor tells you that it was correct. This form of KR, then, serves not only as information to let you know that what you did was correct, but it also serves as a reinforcement. The hope is that you will perform that same swing on the next trial. It should be obvious here that some portions of the swing will be correct and others will be incorrect. We should not conclude that KR as reinforcement is only applicable when a response is totally correct, as the whole golf swing. The instructor may well use KR in a reinforcing way to reinforce a certain part of the swing that you did correctly. He or she may even provide you with error information about another part of your swing to help you to do that part better the next time.

Is there any research evidence to support the notion that KR serves a reinforcement function? Actually, the evidence is quite abundant, especially in the literature pertaining to animal learning. In fact, most of the work dealing with animal learning by the famous B. F. Skinner has been based on this reinforcement principle. The early study of human learning by Lorge and Thorndike in 1935 referred to KR as reward or punishment; their reasoning was based on KR as a means of strengthening the prior response by the learner.

The third function that KR can perform in a learning situation is to provide **Motivation**
a source of motivation for the learner. Motivation is defined as anything that impels a person to start or keeps a person moving toward a goal. In the context of our KR discussion, the goal is the successful performance of the skill being

learned. In the example of learning the golf swing, it should be quite apparent that there is a definite motivational factor involved in continuing to practice the skill enough times to learn it correctly. You obviously need something to motivate you to maintain your interest and desire to keep practicing. Significantly, KR has been shown to have a definite influence in this regard.

In an excellent review of the research literature related to the motivation effects of KR, Locke, Cartledge, and Koeppel (1968) indicated that research evidence has shown rather consistently that KR relates to an individual's goals, while this, in turn, relates to the individual's performance. A problem exists when considering KR simply as a form of information to enhance performance. In many of the situations where KR functions as information to direct the learner's error correction, KR is also fulfilling a valuable motivational role. This seems especially evident where the learner has set a specific goal of performance for himself or herself. In this situation KR is viewed as information not only to correct errors on the next trial or practice attempt but also to provide information about the performance in relation to goal attainment.

Some useful research evidence of KR as motivation in motor skill learning was provided several years ago by Edwin Locke (1968). In this study, seven groups of subjects were given 40 trials on a visual reaction time task. The seven groups were distinguished by the amount of KR each received and by the performance goal they set or were assigned. The significant result of this study was that while KR was definitely related to better reaction time performance, it was discovered that the subject's goal levels rather than the amount of KR he or she received governed performance.

Since goal setting as a form of motivation will be discussed in detail in Chapter 10, we will not develop this section any further. It is important to note, however, that KR is a potent source of motivation in the goal-setting situation.

Summary

Knowledge of results, or KR, refers to information provided to the performer from some external source about a performed response. KR is distinct from sensory feedback, which is information about a response from the performer's own sensory system. Both types of information, KR and sensory feedback, can provide information about the outcome of the response or about the performance characteristics that led to that outcome. KR is an important source of information that functions to guide error correction, to reinforce correct performance, and to motivate the individual to continue toward achieving a performance goal. The primary focus of the discussion of KR in this concept was on KR as information guiding the error correction process during learning. In certain skills, learning cannot occur without KR; however, in other skills, although not essential for learning, KR facilitates the learning process by shortening the time needed to achieve a certain level of performance and by leading

to better eventual performance. After sufficient practice with KR, an adequate model of correct performance has been developed by the individual so that successful performance can continue, even in the absence of KR.

Related Readings

Adams, J. A. (1987). Historical review and appraisal of research on the learning, retention, and transfer of human motor skills. *Psychological Bulletin, 101,* 41–74. (Read the sections on KR: pp. 43–44, 48–49, 61–62.)

Bilodeau, I. M. (1966). Information feedback. In E. A. Bilodeau (Ed.), *Acquisition of Skill* (pp. 295–296). New York: Academic Press.

Holding, D. H. (1965). *Principles of training.* Oxford: Pergamon. (Read chapter 2.)

Salmoni, A. W., Schmidt, R. A., & Walter, C. B. (1984). Knowledge of results and motor learning: A review and critical reappraisal. *Psychological Bulletin, 95,* 355–386.

Zelaznik, H. N., Shapiro, D. C., & Newell, K. M. (1978). On the structure of motor recognition memory. *Journal of Motor Behavior, 10,* 313–323.

Concept 7.2 KR must provide adequate information to facilitate learning

Application

Suppose that you are learning the golf swing and it is the second or third day of your lessons. After you have made a few practice swings, your instructor says, "You are not hitting the ball correctly." What would be your reaction? And how much help would that comment be in improving your swing? Let us carry this example one step further. This time your instructor tells you, "You are not keeping your head down long enough, your grip is too tight, your right hand is under the club too much, your backswing is too fast, you are not shifting your weight properly, and your follow through is too short." What would be your reaction this time? Obviously both examples are extremes, but they lead to a discussion of how much KR or error information should be presented to the learner. At one end of the continuum, you have the problem of not enough information, while at the other end you have an equally perplexing problem of too much information. Are these "problems" real for the learner in terms of acquiring a skill? How should the characteristics as well as the amount of KR change as performance becomes more skilled?

Now suppose your instructor provides just the right amount of information each time he or she gives you KR. But the teacher insists on giving KR after *every* swing you make. The question here is whether this provides an optimal learning situation. Could it be that too much KR is provided if it is given too often? Suppose that it is. Then the question becomes, how often should KR be given to lead to the best possible learning of the skill?

When these questions are considered, another related concern must be addressed. Is having the teacher give verbal KR the best means of providing the information needed by the learner to improve his or her performance and to learn the skill being practiced? What about other methods of giving KR, such as videotape or kinematic graphic representations of a performance? How effective are these methods of providing KR?

Each of the questions raised in this section concerns a basic issue that confronts every teacher, that is, the need to provide adequate information to benefit the learner. As these questions are addressed in the following discussion, compare the answers provided with your own experiences and intuitive responses. The answers to these questions not only help us better understand motor skill learning processes but also provide useful practical information for the teacher.

Discussion

Up to this point we have considered two very important concepts or principles relating to the role of KR in learning motor skills: the need for KR and the functions of KR. However, a fundamental question which develops from that discussion is, What KR is adequate?

The precision of KR An important part of determining what KR information provides for optimal learning comes from the study of *KR precision,* which concerns the amount of specific response outcome information that is given a subject. For example, if a subject is practicing a task where the goal is to make a 30-cm arm movement in 200 msec, very precise KR would be response error information as to the number of msec too fast or too slow. Very imprecise information would be KR as simply "too fast" or "too slow," with no numbers provided. This latter form of KR is typically labeled *qualitative,* whereas KR that includes numbers related to the amount of error is called *quantitative.* Most KR precision research has involved manipulating qualitative and quantitative KR and observing the influence of these manipulations on task performance over a number of practice trials.

As pointed out in an excellent review of KR research by Salmoni, Schmidt, and Walter (1984), KR precision effects in motor learning are not well understood. This lack of understanding is undoubtedly due to the lack of consistency in the results of KR precision experiments. In this section, we will consider a few of these experiments and then attempt to draw some useful conclusions. From these, we can better understand what KR precision research tells us about the problem of how much KR is appropriate for a learner.

An interesting study investigating KR precision was reported by Smoll (1972). In this investigation, subjects were required to learn to roll a duckpin bowling ball at 70% of each subject's maximum velocity. KR in one of three forms was given after every trial: (1)quantitative, or accurate to hundredths of a second; (2) quantitative, or accurate to tenths of a second; and (3) qualitative, or "too slow," "too fast," and "correct." Smoll's results are presented in the graph in Figure 7.2–1. They show rather well the better performance of the quantitative groups over the qualitative group. However, Smoll's results revealed something else: there was no difference between the tenth-of-a-second and the hundredth-of-a-second groups. Thus, it would seem that the more precise information did not add to the ability of the subjects to learn the task.

A study by Rogers (1974) revealed that too precise KR not only may be of limited, if any, help to the learner; it may actually be detrimental to learning. Rogers had subjects learn to turn the knob of a micrometer to a certain setting. The subjects could not see the micrometer and had to rely on KR to learn the task. KR was provided in one of four ways: (1) direction of error only, that is zero digits; (2) direction and error to the nearest whole unit, or one digit; (3) direction and error to the nearest tenth unit, or two digits; and (4) direction and error to the nearest thousandth unit, or four digits. Results of this experiment showed that one and two digits of KR were better than zero digits, as expected, but that four digits produced just as poor response as did zero digits. Rogers conducted one further experiment which showed that when the subjects in the four-digit group were given more time following the giving of KR, they were then able to perform as well as the other two quantitative groups. While the time provided a learner the opportunity to

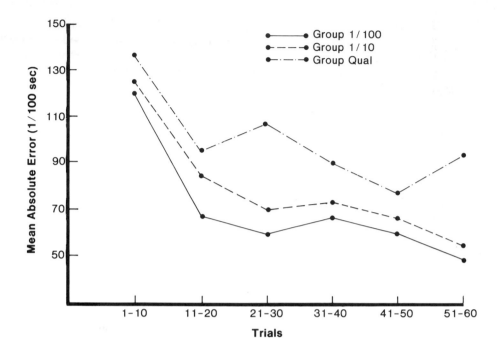

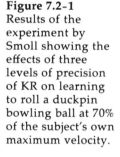

Figure 7.2-1
Results of the
experiment by
Smoll showing the
effects of three
levels of precision
of KR on learning
to roll a duckpin
bowling ball at 70%
of the subject's own
maximum velocity.

use the information given following a response is shown to be important here, the more important finding for our discussion seems to be that KR can be too precise for the learner and can actually produce poor learning. It would seem that the amount of time that the learner has available to use the information in KR is only one part of the precision problem. We will discuss the time to use KR problem in greater detail in the next concept.

Finally an experiment from our lab at LSU by Magill and Wood, (1986) presented some evidence suggesting that the question of KR precision cannot be satisfactorily answered without taking into account the stage of learning of the individual. Based on a suggestion from the results of a previous experiment by Reeve and Magill (1981), the need was to consider that more general, i.e., less precise, information may be more important to the learner early in practice while more precise information becomes important later in practice. Also, because neither the Smoll (1972) nor the Rogers (1974) experiment included retention tests, it is important to determine if the influence of KR precision will endure and be evident at some time after practice. To test these concerns, Magill and Wood had subjects learn to move an arm through a series of wooden barriers to produce a six-segment movement pattern. Each segment had its own criterion movement time that the subjects were required to learn as they practiced the entire pattern. Subjects were given either quantitative KR (the number of msec too fast or too slow) or qualitative KR ("too fast," "too slow," or "correct") about their movement time error for each segment of the pattern. The results, as presented in Figure 7.2-2, indicated that during

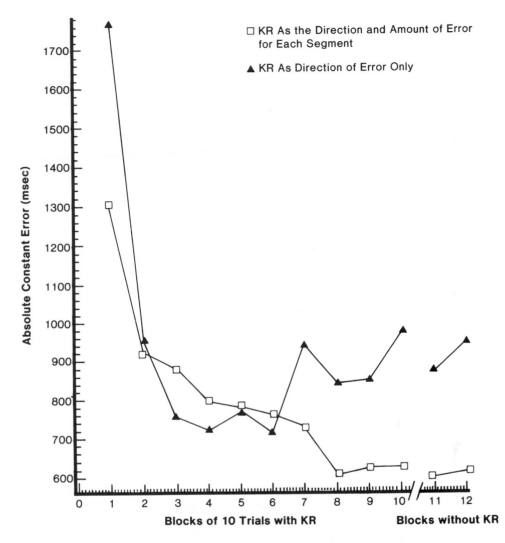

Figure 7.2-2
Absolute constant
error scores during
practice with KR
(blocks 1–10) and
without KR (blocks
11–12) on a six-
segment timing
pattern in the
experiment by
Magill and Wood.

the first 60 trials of practice, the two KR precision conditions resulted in similar performance. However, following that amount of practice, the quantitative group began to perform better than the qualitative KR group. The superiority of the quantitative KR group's performance was maintained on retention trials where no KR was provided (trials 100 to 120).

These three experiments reveal some important points concerning the amount of KR given to aid learners. *First,* more specific information is beneficial only after sufficient practice when the learner can effectively use that information. For example, in the Magill and Wood experiment, subjects were apparently first concerned with establishing some boundary limits for themselves related to each criterion movement. Their first concern was to determine

a general understanding of what was meant by "too fast" or "too slow." After this was established, the amount of movement time error began to take on meaning and could effectively be used to improve performance.

Second, more precise information is not necessarily better. The experiment by Smoll (1972) showed that KR in hundredths of a second was no better than KR in tenths of a second. In the Rogers (1974) study, evidence showed that too precise KR can actually result in poorer acquisition performance than less precise information.

Third, the level of precision of the KR is related to the amount of time available to process or use that information. As the Rogers (1974) experiment showed, very precise information can be as difficult to use by the learner as KR that is too imprecise. This becomes apparent especially when there is not sufficient time to make sense of the very precise KR and to use it to help develop the next response.

These three points concerning KR precision represent some of the issues that must be considered before developing broad generalizations about KR precision and motor skill acquisition. It should be apparent, then, that the amount of information about the learner's response contained in KR does influence the degree of skill acquisition attainable by the learner. However, the amount of information provided must take into account the individual's stage of learning, the task being learned, and the amount of time available to process KR.

The content of KR. In addition to determining how general or how specific the KR should be, it is important to determine the content of that information. Two points should be strongly considered when making this decision. The *first* point is to understand that when KR is given about a specific part of a response, the *KR serves to direct the person's attention* to that part. Recall in our discussion of Kahneman's model of attention in Concept 4.2 that an important feature of attention is the need to appropriately allocate attention capacity so that a skill can be performed correctly. One factor Kahneman proposed as influential in determining how attention capacity is allocated was what he called "momentary intentions." In many respects, KR serves as a type of momentary intention as the information contained in KR directs, or allocates, the individual's attention to a particular feature of the movement. Sometimes the KR is so general that the allocation of attention is not very useful. However, when KR provides specific information about a performance characteristic that needs to be corrected or performed again as it had just been performed, or if the KR is sufficiently meaningful to indicate to the individual what must be done on the next attempt, then KR serves an important attention-directing function. As KR guides error correction or as it reinforces correct performance, it helps the person allocate attention capacity in an appropriate way.

A *second* point that must be considered in determining the content of KR is to *establish what part or parts of the performance should receive directed attention.* If KR serves to direct attention to certain aspects of performing a skill, then it is important to direct the attention to the parts that, if improved, will significantly improve performance of the entire skill. For example, suppose you are teaching a child to throw a ball at a target. Also suppose this child is making a lot of errors, which is typical of beginners. The child may be looking at his or her hand, stepping with the wrong foot, releasing the ball awkwardly, not rotating the trunk, and so on. Probably the most fundamental error here is not looking at the target. So, this becomes the error about which you should provide KR, as it is the part of the skill to which you want the child to direct his or her attention; it is the part of the skill that, if corrected, will have an immediate, significant, positive influence on performance. By correcting this error, the child will undoubtedly also correct many of the other errors that may have characterized his or her performance.

Interesting experimental support for these two points about determining appropriate content of KR comes from an article by den Brinker, Stabler, Whiting, and van Wieringen, (1986) from Free University in Amsterdam. Subjects in this experiment were required to learn to perform on a slalom skiing simulator. The device (Figure 7.2-3) consists of two rigid, convex, parallel tracks on which sets a movable platform. The subject stands on the platform with both feet and is required to move the platform right and left as far as possible (55 cm to either side) with rhythmic slalom ski-like movements. Coordination and effort are required to perform this skill as the platform has rigid springs on either side that ensure the platform always returns to the center (normal) position. Thus, the subject had to learn to control moving the platform from side to side as far as possible using smooth ski-like movements, just as one would when actually skiing.

In this experiment, subjects were provided one of three types of KR. The amplitude group received KR in terms of the amplitude, or distance, of platform movement. The frequency group received KR about the frequency, or tempo, of their movement of the platform. (They were told there was an optimum frequency [0.67 Hz] for performing this skill.) The fluency group was given KR about the fluency of their movements, which was to be interpreted in terms of smoothness, or absence of jerk. Fluency KR was the difference between their achieved fluency and what was considered perfect fluency. Subjects practiced the ski simulation task for four days, with six 1.5-minute trials each day. A test trial was given daily before and after the practice trials, during which the subjects were filmed.

The results indicated that early in practice, the KR type provided influenced the performance measure related to that type of KR more than any of the other types. For example, early in practice the frequency KR group performed best on the frequency measure of performance. Thus, KR served to direct attention to that feature of the skill relevant to the KR. This directed

Figure 7.2-3
A person
performing on the
slalom ski simulator
used in the
experiment by den
Brinker, Stabler,
Whiting, and van
Wieringen (1986).

attention led to more initial improvement of that feature than of any other feature. However, another important result showed that the different types of KR were related to performance in different ways as practice proceeded over the four days. In the last day of practice, the fluency KR group reached amplitudes that were similar to those achieved by the amplitude KR group, while the amplitude KR group achieved as close to the perfect value as did the fluency KR group. Also, the amplitude and frequency KR groups performed with more fluency on the fourth day than did the fluency KR group. Thus, it was apparent that from the third day until the end of training, the amplitude KR group achieved the best performance on all three measures.

Therefore, both points about determining the content of KR are supported by the results of this experiment. First, when KR is given about specific performance characteristics early in practice, you can expect the person's attention to be directed toward that characteristic. You can also expect that characteristic to show the greatest improvment early in practice. Second, there are certain performance characteristics about which KR should be given preference over others, because attention directed to that feature will allow development of performance of that feature, as well as of certain other features.

The Learning Environment

Two guidelines for determining what KR to give. Based on the discussion in the preceding two sections, it appears two very general guidelines can help you determine how much KR to give and what kind is adequate to facilitate skill learning.

First, *KR should not provide too much information*. When too much information is given, it is likely that the recipient will be overwhelmed or confused. As a result, the teacher has little control over what the student will attempt to correct during the next practice attempts. Keep in mind that when KR is given about correcting an error, KR becomes a "momentary intention" attention allocation factor. A goal of the instructor is to have KR direct the student's attention to the specific error needing correction. If the KR contains too much information, it is difficult to know where the student's attention will be directed when trying to improve the next trial.

Also remember that our capacity to attend to and to remember information is limited. When KR is given, it not only must be attended to, but it must also be remembered and used to guide performance on the next trial. If the capacity for attention and remembering is exceeded by the amount of KR given, it will only be by chance that what should be altered on the next trial will be.

Probably the best rule of thumb here is to select what you consider the most important error being made and use that to provide KR to the student. The most important error is the one that is foundational to the other errors being made. If the most important error isn't corrected, it will be difficult to attain correct performance with any degree of consistency. Remember the example given earlier about which error to correct first for the child learning to throw a ball at a target. It is essential for the instructor to know what errors are important to correct and in what priority order they should be corrected. Then, the instructor should follow that priority order and select only one error at a time to be the basis for the KR given to the student.

The second guideline is that *KR should not provide too little information*. This statement may sound trite but it is one that many motor skills teachers violate repeatedly. The problem is that the KR provided must be *meaningful* to the individual. As was discussed in Chapter 5, meaningful information is information that is useful to an individual; it makes sense and can be more readily remembered and applied to the needs at hand. For the novice learner, KR must provide information that will direct his or her attention to the part of the skill that must be corrected *and* it must provide information that will enable the learner to make an appropriate correction.

The stage of learning of the individual is important here. As a teacher, you could tell a relatively skilled golfer that his or her elbow was not right during the swing. That would be meaningful information to this person, and he or she could make an appropriate correction. However, that same statement given to a novice golfer would be of little value. It is too little information. The novice needs more specific information about what was wrong with the elbow and what can be done to correct it.

How Often Should KR Be Given?

A question closely related to how much information to give as KR is the question of *how often* to give KR. In many ways these two questions are interrelated because giving KR too often could be a form of giving too much information and not giving KR often enough could be a form of giving too little information. In the KR research literature, the question of how often to give KR is considered with the issue of *absolute and relative frequency* of KR. *Absolute frequency* refers to giving KR a specific number of trials during a practice period, whereas *relative frequency* refers to giving KR a specified percentage of the practice trials. Although there has been some debate about whether absolute frequency schedules of KR help or hinder learning compared with relative frequency schedules, this issue has not been resolved. Rather than getting involved in this debate, it will be more beneficial to focus on the question of KR frequency. Thus, the question of interest to us is, Does KR frequency influence how well students learn the skill?

The most commonly cited study of KR frequency was reported by Bilodeau and Bilodeau (1958). In this experiment, subjects practiced an arm-positioning task in which the goal was to move a lever attached to a protractor device a distance of 33.57° arc. KR was given after every trial, every third trial, or every fourth trial. All groups received ten KRs, therefore, the number of practice trials differed for each group (10, 30, or 40 trials). However, regardless of the number of practice trials, the group that received KR on all trials, which practiced for only ten trials, performed best.

A problem with the Bilodeau and Bilodeau (1958) experiment is that there was no retention or transfer test, an important learning inference issue discussed in Chapter 2. Thus, it is difficult to determine if the results were temporary practice effects that would have changed on a retention test, or if they represented actual learning effects. It appears that the results were more likely temporary practice, or performance, effects, as more recent research using retention or transfer tests has supported different results.

Ho and Shea (1978) conducted an experiment investigating the KR frequency issue using a retention test; their findings differed from those of Bilodeau and Bilodeau (1958). In this experiment, subjects also practiced an arm-positioning task and were provided KR after every trial, after every third trial, or after every sixth trial. At the end of the practice trials, the results were similar to those found by the Bilodeaus. The group that received KR after every trial was performing with less error than the other KR frequency groups. However, following a 5-minute rest, all subjects were required to perform the response without KR. This test indicated that the group that had received KR on every trial now performed with the *most* error, while the performances of the other two groups were similar to each other.

In each of these experiments, KR frequency was varied according to an absolute frequency schedule. Recent research by Carolee Winstein (1987) (doctoral dissertation, UCLA) reports an example of KR frequency being

varied according to a relative frequency schedule. Winstein used an interesting and unique approach to the KR frequency question in the second experiment of this study. Two groups of subjects practiced moving a horizontal lever in a specified space and time pattern of movement. The lever was attached to an axle at the end closest to the subject. The subject rested a forearm on the lever holding a vertical handle at the far end of the lever. On a computer screen, subjects were shown a pattern resembling a sine-wave and were told that the goal was to produce the same pattern by moving the lever toward and away from the body an appropriate number of times, with each movement performed according to a required distance and time. This task was similar to the tracking tasks described in Concepts 1.2 and 2.1. A subject received KR by viewing on the computer screen the pattern he or she produced in relation to the criterion pattern. Subjects practiced this task for 200 trials and received KR in one of three relative frequency conditions. One group received KR after every trial (100% frequency). A second group received KR on 5 randomly selected trials out of each set of 10 trials (50% frequency). The third group, called the 50% fading-frequency group, received KR like the second group, but then on the second 100 trials of practice had KR frequency systematically reduced for each set of 10 trials until no KR was given. The results of a 2-day no-KR retention test showed that this fading group performed with less error than either of the other groups.

KR as a summary of performance on several trials. One way in which KR can be provided combines issues about both the content and frequency of KR. This method of KR involves giving the individual a summary of performance outcome or performance characteristics after a certain number of trials have been completed. This approach to giving KR provides no information about a specific performance and is not given after every trial. Although little research has examined the effectiveness of using summary KR, some evidence suggests that summary KR leads to better learning than when KR is given after every trial.

An example of evidence supporting the benefit of summary KR over KR provided after every trial was reported by Lavery (1962). Subjects practiced 3 different motor skills. The first was a "pinball" task where subjects shot a ball up an inclined trackway to a target by releasing a spring-loaded plunger. The second task required the subjects to move the ball up this same trackway by hitting the ball with a hand-held hammer. Finally, subjects practiced a "puff-ball" task, where they were required to move a table tennis ball up a tube to a target by blowing a puff of air through a pipe held in their mouths. The score for these tasks was the percentage of balls reaching the target, that is, the percent correct. Three KR conditions were used. One group received KR after each trial; a second group received a summary of performance for 20 trials; the third group received KR after every trial and the summary after

20 trials. Subjects practiced 20 trials daily for 6 days. Then, on the next 4 days, and 37 and 93 days later, a no-KR retention test was given. Results showed that during the practice trials, the summary KR group performed poorest, and the other two groups performed similar to each other. However, on the no-KR retention test, the opposite results occurred. The summary KR group was not performing the tasks better than the groups with the other two KR conditions, which again were performing similarly. Here again, then, KR given after every trial, as opposed to a less frequent interval, did not lead to better learning, even when that less frequent use was a summary score of 20 trials of practice.

The case for less than 100% KR frequency during practice. Although much more research is needed to satisfactorily investigate the KR frequency question, there is sufficient evidence to argue that KR given on every trial may not lead to an optimal learning situation. Even in experiments where less than 100% KR frequency has not been better than 100% frequency, the typical result has been for the less frequent conditions to be no worse than those with KR on every trial. These results, in addition to those that showed less than 100% frequency conditions to be superior to KR on every trial, suggest that to give KR after every practice attempt is either potentially detrimental to learning or is a waste of time.

Why would KR frequency of less than 100% be better for learning than KR after every trial? One very likely reason is that KR given after ever trial eventually leads to an attention or working memory capacity "overload." After several trials, the cumulative effect of the information received by the individual establishes a condition where there is more information available than the person can handle.

Another possibility is that giving KR on every trial leads to dependence on the KR, rather than dependence on the internal sensory feedback system for error detection and correction information. Eventually the individual will be tested in the absence of KR, therefore, it would seem logical that the practice conditions provide a situation in which the individual can successfully perform the skill without KR. If the student begins to depend on KR for error detection and connection information performance will deteriorate when KR is no longer available. Schmidt (1987) referred to KR as a "crutch" for the learner during practice. When the crutch is removed on the test, performance suffers because it was dependent on the crutch. The Winstein (1987) experiment showed a good example of how this crutch can be systematically removed so that a person is, in effect, "weaned" from dependence on KR.

Finally, receiving KR after every trial does not allow the learner an opportunity to work on correcting the errors that the KR has directed him or her to correct. There appears to be a need for a learner to do some trial-and-error problem solving on his or her own as a part of the practice routine. KR becomes important as a *guide* to help direct this problem-solving activity to

keep it from getting too far afield. This suggests that KR serves not only to guide the individual but also establishes some boundaries within which the learner should operate. As a result, the need is to administer KR only as frequently as necessary to permit the learner an opportunity to receive maximum benefit from his or her own problem-solving activity.

It should be remembered that according to both Adams' (1971) closed-loop theory and Schmidt's (1975) schema theory, discussed in Concept 2.3, KR plays an important function in learning motor skills. That function is to aid in the development of a sufficiently strong perceptual trace or recognition schema that can eventually be called upon to control the movement without the need for KR. From this perspective, it follows that how often KR is given must provide for an optimal condition for the use of KR by the learner. It appears that relative frequency is superior for this purpose. Ironically, this conclusion is in direct opposition to what Adams' and Schmidt's theories predict about the frequency question. (A close inspection of these theories indicates that they both predict that the more often KR is provided, the better the learning that will result.) This does not mean that these theories are therefore wrong as theories. It simply indicates that based on the currently available evidence, this one aspect of these theories needs to be modified.

The approach thus far in this discussion has been to limit KR to information about response errors and how to correct them. When the question of how often KR should be provided is asked, it is important not to ignore the roles of KR as a source of motivation to achieve a goal and as reinforcement about the correctness of a response. What we have seen in this discussion is that KR as error correction information is not needed after every trial. However, this is not to say that KR, when it serves a different purpose, cannot play important parts when given during the intervening trials. As Mosston (1981) has indicated in his text on teaching effectiveness, it is important that the teacher provide KR in the forms of "corrective statements," which identify error and how to correct it; "value statements," which project a value or feeling about the previous performance; and, "neutral statements," which provide factual information about the performance but do not correct or judge. Taken from this perspective, the question of absolute vs. relative frequency KR becomes one of effectively integrating the use of the various forms of information KR provides.

One concern an instructor has when providing KR is whether or not the information given will be useful to the student. Consider the possibility that what the instructor gives as KR may be information the student had already obtained through his or her own sensory feedback system. For example, if a golf instructor tells the student after a shot that he just hit a slice, this would seemingly repeat what the student could see for himself. If KR is redundant with sensory feedback, is the KR necessary?

First, we must establish if KR can be redundant with sensory feedback. Although the answer seems intuitively obvious, is there any research evidence

Can KR Be
Redundant
Information?

that demonstrates this effect? If you remember the experiment by Stelmach (1970) discussed in Concept 7.1, you will recall a situation where KR was not absolutely required for learning the skill, but it did lead to better eventual performance. Thus, KR in that experiment had a degree of redundancy with available sensory feedback. But, the demonstration of complete redundancy has not been characteristic of the KR research literature, as tasks used in most KR research are designed to require KR so that the effects of experimentally manipulating variables related to KR can be investigated. Another reason has been that most motor learning scholars have been rather quick to accept the conclusions from earlier assessments on the need for KR (e.g., Adams, 1971), that KR is needed for motor learning to occur. Even when research was reported showing learning of a motor skill without KR, there had been training of one part of the sensory system so that a model of correct performance was established through augmenting sensory feedback (e.g., Newell, 1976).

In a recent experiment at the LSU lab, we (Magill & Chamberlin, 1987) reasoned that if KR could be redundant with sensory feedback and, therefore, was not needed for learning, then this would most likely be demonstrated in a task where the learner has sensory feedback available that could be effectively used to improve performance. The task selected was the Bassin anticipation timing task, described in Concept 3.5. To increase the simulation characteristics of a common complex skill, subjects were required to sit facing the target light of the trackway and hold a short "bat" in their right hand on a start switch. Parallel with the target light and 40 cm from the start switch was a small wooden barrier that the subjects were required to knock over with the "bat" at the same time the target light illuminated. The trackway was mounted on the wall and was at the subject's eye level. A moderate trackway speed was used (7 mph) and subjects received 75 practice trials. The two conditions in this experiment were no KR and KR on every trial. The results showed that those who received KR performed no better during training or during a transfer test to a new trackway speed than the group that received KR on every practice trial. Thus, KR was not only redundant with sensory feedback, it was not needed for learning this task.

More research is needed to investigate questions related to this KR redundancy issue. For example, it is possible that some other form of KR, especially if it is in the form of information about some performance characteristic that led to the outcome (or KP as some call this form of KR), will lead to better learning. Also, what principles could be developed that would establish when KR would not only be redundant, but it would also be unnecessary? Is it possible that although KR may be redundant as error correction guidance information that it would still be useful to help motivate the learner to work toward achieving a performance goal? These are just some of the questions that need to be addressed to advance our understanding of the role of KR in motor skill learning when the KR seems to repeat sensory feedback.

For the motor skill instructor, the important point of this redundancy question is to be aware that sometimes what is given as KR does not help the student at all. That same information was already obtained by the student through his or her sensory system. This is an especially critical point when the student's stage of learning is taken into consideration. If you will recall the discussion earlier about what effective KR should be like, you will remember it was stressed that KR should be *meaningful* to the student. And, what may be meaningful to the skilled person may not be very meaningful to the beginner. This same principle relates to the KR redundancy question. With beginners, you can never be certain that they have attended to their internal sensory feedback. Thus, giving KR that seems redundant may in fact be useful, as it would serve to direct their attention to that information. Or, the KR could serve to reinforce their internal sensory feedback.

When the general question of what KR to give is considered, the question of how the KR can be given becomes an important related issue. So far in this discussion, KR presentation has been limited primarily to the verbal presentation of KR by the instructor or experimenter. The question of interest now becomes, how effective are alternative forms of KR? To address this question, we will look at three different methods of giving KR, videotape, graphic kinematic representation, and the use of augmented feedback as KR. While there are other means for providing KR, these will serve to illustrate the problems and potential associated with alternate methods.

Alternative Methods of Giving KR

Videotape. A popular alternate form of KR is the replaying of an individual's performance by means of videotape. The general and relatively inexpensive accessibility of videotape equipment has made this form of KR highly popular. One of the most extensive reviews of the research literature concerning the effectiveness of using videotape was conducted by Rothstein and Arnold (1976). In this review, over 50 studies were considered. These studies involved using videotape for 18 different sport activities, including archery, badminton, bowling, gymnastics, skiing, swimming, and volleyball. Students were typically at a beginner level, although some were at the intermediate or advanced level. While there were generally mixed results concerning the effectiveness of videotape as a form of KR, two points were clear and emphasized. *First,* while the type of activity was not a critical factor in determining videotape effectiveness, the skill level of the student was a critical factor. Beginners need the aid of an instructor to point out information from the replay. Advanced beginners or intermediates did not seem to require the teacher's assistance as much as did the beginners. *Second,* for videotape replays to be effective, it is important that the replays be used for periods of at least five weeks. Studies in which videotape was used for less time typically found the use of replays ineffective.

This synthesis of research on the use of videotape as a form of KR for teaching motor skills really does not lead to many surprises. The use of videotape as KR involves the same problems as the use of verbal KR. That is, meaningful information must be presented. Beginners are no more able to view a videotape replay and detect and correct errors than they are able to detect and correct errors from their own performance when videotape is not used. The teacher still plays an important role in helping the student. With videotape, the teacher must direct the student's attention to where errors are being made and how they should be corrected. The problems related to giving too much or too little information still apply.

Support for these guidelines for the effective use of videotape replay was provided in an experiment by Selder and Del Rolan (1979). In this study, videotape replay was used to provide KR to a group of 12- to 13-year-old girls learning to perform a beginning balance beam routine. A control group of girls the same age received only verbal KR about their performance. Each girl was given a checklist to use for critically analyzing her own performances. The girls in the videotape group were instructed to use the checklist of critical points in the routine to evaluate their performances while watching the videotape replay. Those in the control group were instructed to use this checklist to evaluate their own performances on the basis of the verbal KR they received and on their own judgment.

At the end of four weeks of practice in their regular physical education classes, all subjects were judged by three United States Federation of Gymnastics judges. The judging was based on the standard 10-point rating system used to judge gymnastic events. This system consists of eight standard factors, which are presented in Figure 7.2–4. At the end of four weeks, each group was judged as performing similarly, with the overall point values for each group averaging 3.4. However, a dramatic difference was seen in the next two weeks. At the end of six weeks, the girls were again judged. This time the videotape group (with an average score of 5.6) performed at a higher level than the control group (with an average score of 4.9).

As you can see in Figure 7.2-4, the greatest percentage of improvement *difference* between the two groups was for the scoring factors of precision, execution, amplitude, and orientation and direction. The other four factors show similar improvement by both groups. Based on the four factors that benefited from the videotape experience, it appears that the use of videotape will benefit those aspects of a performance that can be most easily observed and corrected on the basis of visual information. Such things as rhythm, elegance, and lightness, while observable, are difficult to translate from visual information into information that will result in a change in these factors, at least for individuals with the amount of experience the students in this experiment had.

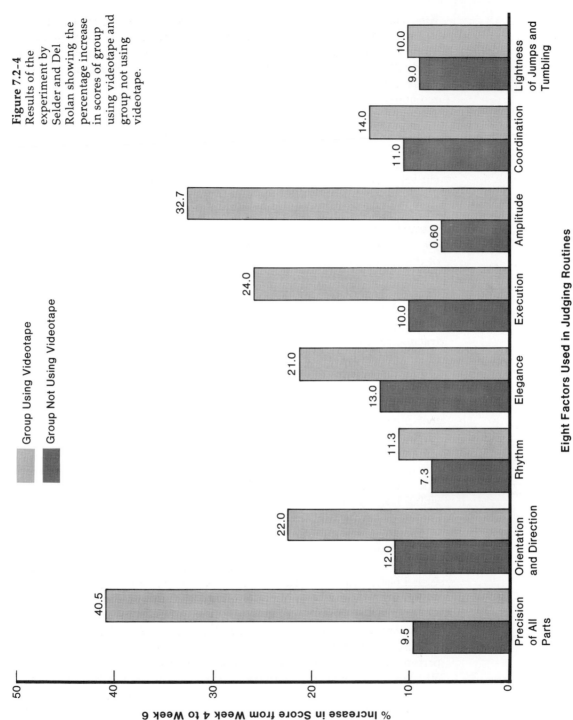

Figure 7.2-4
Results of the experiment by Selder and Del Rolan showing the percentage increase in scores of group using videotape and group not using videotape.

Group Using Videotape

Group Not Using Videotape

Eight Factors Used in Judging Routines

% Increase in Score from Week 4 to Week 6

Lightness of Jumps and Tumbling — 10.0, 9.0

Coordination — 14.0, 11.0

Amplitude — 32.7, 0.60

Execution — 24.0, 10.0

Elegance — 21.0, 13.0

Rhythm — 11.3, 7.3

Orientation and Direction — 22.0, 12.0

Precision of All Parts — 40.5, 9.5

Kinematic representations. It is becoming more and more common, especially at high levels of skill performance, to use some form of computer graphic representations of an individual's performance. Examples of this have been popularly presented in golf, running, tennis, and dance magazines, among others. Two examples of experiments investigating the effectiveness of kinematic representations will help illustrate the potential for using this method of giving KR.

A study in 1945 by Lindahl reported the effective use of providing kinematic graphic representations of performance for training machine operators in an industrial setting. Workers had to be trained to precisely and quickly cut very thin discs of tungsten with a machine that required fast, accurate, and rhythmic coordination of the hands and feet. Typical training for this job was by trial and error. As an alternative to this approach, Lindahl developed a training procedure based on presenting trainees with tracings made on a paper recorder of the pattern made by the foot movement during the cutting of the discs. The foot movement pattern was used because it had been identified as the most critical component of this complex task. An example of recordings for the correct foot action for 11 cuttings is presented at the top of Figure 7.2–5. The trainees were presented charts illustrating this correct foot action and were periodically shown the results of their own foot movement tracings made on the paper tape.

The bottom portion of Figure 7.2–5 shows the production performance of the trainees compared to the average production performance of workers trained by the plant's traditional trial-and-error method. Note that the trainees achieved a performance level in 11 weeks that was equivalent to what typically took 5 months with the traditional training method. Additionally, it was reported that the trainees reduced their percentage of broken cutting wheels on the machine to almost zero in 12 weeks, a level not achieved by the traditionally trained workers in less than 9 months. These results not only support the value of kinematic representations of movement as an effective means of providing KR, they also support the view expressed in Concept 7.1 that an important role played by KR in motor skill learning is to increase the speed of skill learning.

Further support for the beneficial use of certain types of kinematic information has more recently been presented by Newell, Quinn, Sparrow, and Walter (1983). In the second experiment of the study, subjects practiced moving a lever as fast as possible from its start position through a target point. KR was provided as the subject's movement time (MT), a graphic display on the computer monitor of the movement velocity time trace, or no KR. All subjects initially practiced for 25 trials with no KR to minimize the amount of initial performance difference among the three groups. Subjects then practiced for 50 trials on the same day with one of the three forms of KR provided after each trial. The subjects then returned a second day for 50 additional trials with KR. The results, presented in Figure 7.2–6, show that the group receiving

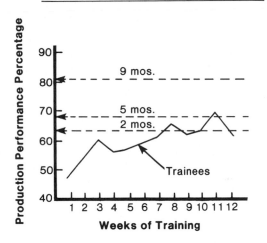

Figure 7.2-5
The upper panel illustrates the foot action required by the machine operator to produce an acceptable disc cut in the experiment by Lindahl. The graph at the bottom indicates the production performance achieved by the trainees using graphic information during 12 weeks of training. The dashed lines indicate the levels of performance achieved by other workers after 2, 5, and 9 months of experience.

the kinematic representation of the movement velocity consistently performed better during the 100 trials of practice with KR than either the verbal KR group or the no-KR group.

Two points about this experiment should be noted. First, performance improved without the KR during the initial 25 practice trials. This result offers support for the point made in Concept 7.1 that performance improvement *can* occur without KR. However, it is also worth noting here that the eventual level of performance achieved without KR was limited. Subjects without KR did not move the lever faster than 140 msec, even after 100 practice trials. On the other hand, both forms of KR, verbal and kinematic representation, led to performance levels beyond those obtained when no KR was provided.

The second point of interest to be noted in this experiment is that the kinematic form of KR led to better performance than receiving verbal movement time as KR. Here, then, is additional support for the value of this form of KR as an aid to improving motor skill performance. An important consideration here, however, is that in the first experiment reported in this study, where a variety of forms of kinematic KR were used, not all forms led to better performance than did verbal KR. For kinematic information to be beneficial, it must be meaningful to the student.

The study of the use and benefit of kinematic representations as KR needs more attention. As the use of computers becomes commonplace, rather than characteristic only of exclusive athletic clubs or organizations working

Knowledge of Results   345

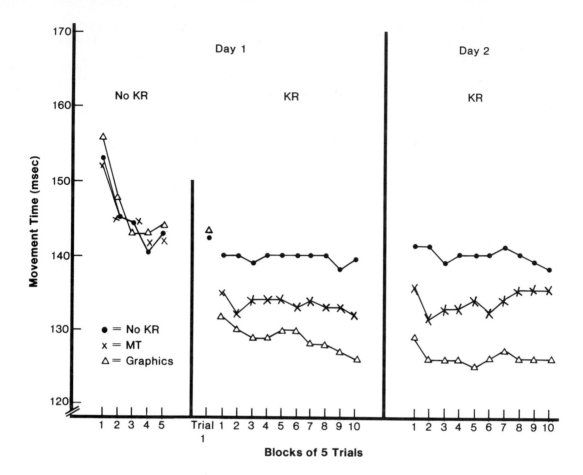

Day 1

No KR

KR

Day 2

KR

● = No KR
x = MT
△ = Graphics

Movement Time (msec)

Trial 1

Blocks of 5 Trials

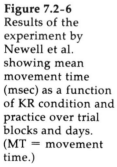

Figure 7.2-6
Results of the
experiment by
Newell et al.
showing mean
movement time
(msec) as a function
of KR condition and
practice over trial
blocks and days.
(MT = movement
time.)

with elite athletes, the availability of providing KR in graphic form representing various kinematic features of performance will increase. Thus, we need to better understand both how to present kinematics as KR to best promote learning and skilled performance, and why this use of KR is effective. Some initial steps have been taken by Newell and McGinnis (1985), who proposed a framework for advancing our understanding of the use of kinematic representations as KR. They suggest that this form of KR can be used effectively if it is provided in terms of the "control space" that defines the skill being performed in relation to an established biomechanical performance criterion objective for the skill. This performance objective may be to maximize clubhead velocity of the golf swing, or to minimize muscular effort in running. The "control space" is defined as consisting of a number of components, such as the spatial coordinates of the limbs in performing a skill, the space-time description of the limbs or body while performing a skill, or the velocity of the limb at particular positions during a performance. When these "control space" features can be identified and related to characteristics needed to achieve the

The Learning Environment

performance objective, then appropriate kinematic representations can be developed and effectively provided to aid the performer. Although this proposal by Newell and McGinnis is a good beginning, much research is needed to establish how successfully their ideas can be translated into providing a basis for using kinematic representations as KR for aiding beginners as well as experts.

Augmented feedback as KR. In the preceding discussions of different forms of KR, the focus has been on forms of response outcome or performance characteristics that are presented to the individual *after* a practice trial or performance is complete. Another method of providing KR does not follow these characteristics; it is given while the person is performing. This form of KR is generally called *augmented feedback* because it is sensory feedback information, that is increased or magnified. An example of augmenting visual information about a tennis ball's spin action would be to mark it in such a way that the spin can be more readily detected. Other ways of providing augmented feedback are to sound an audible tone when a particular muscle is contracting or to show a person a visual display of his or her EMG signal as a movement is performed. The potential for using this form of KR is especially relevant for physical therapy situations and has been explored to some extent. (For more information about this research, see Inglis, Campbell, & Donald, 1976; Keefe & Surwit, 1978; Wolf, 1983.) Its potential for training sport skills or dance remains to be explored.

Theo Mulder and colleagues at the University of Nijmegen in The Netherlands have worked with augmenting different forms of sensory feedback for several years. It is interesting to note that they refer to augmented feedback as "artificial feedback." An example of this research is seen in an experiment by Mulder and Hulstijn (1985). Subjects practiced a movement that required abduction of the big toe while keeping the other toes of the foot from moving. None of the 50 subjects could abduct their big toe before the experiment began. This is a difficult but possible skill to learn and one that requires the isolation and control of specific muscle groups, which is a common goal in therapy. There were five different KR conditions, three involving the availability of the normal sources of feedback that would be involved in performing this action: proprioceptive, tactile, and visual. In the proprioceptive feedback group, subjects could not see their foot and were given no verbal results of each trial's outcome. The proprioceptive and visual feedback group was able to see their foot during practice, but was not given verbal outcome information. The proprioceptive, visual, and tactile feedback group pressed their toe against a force meter as they moved the toe and was not given verbal outcome information. Two other conditions allowed all three sources of feedback plus provided augmented feedback during each movement trial (either for EMG for the abductor hallucis or for force, which involved showing the output of the force meter display). Results showed that providing more sensory feedback systematically increased performance on each of the two days of training and that

the groups with the two augmented feedback conditions performed better than the groups with nonaugmented conditions on days. Unfortunately, there was no retention or transfer test in this experiment. However, the results do show the benefit of using augmented KR as a training procedure for helping persons improve performance of a skill involving the control of a specific muscle group.

More research is needed so that results concerning the effectiveness of augmented feedback can be extended more confidently to the physical therapy and even sport skill training settings. We need to know more about which skills will benefit more from this form of information as opposed to forms of KR presented to the learner after completing a response. We need to know more about the boundaries that must be established for determining what and how much feedback to augment. We also need to know why this form of KR is an effective facilitator of skill learning. However, even though these and other issues about augmented feedback are not completely understood, there is little question that this form of KR can be an effective means of providing information about the performance of a skill that will facilitate learning that skill.

Summary

Because KR is such an important part of skill learning, it is important to understand what information should be provided to facilitate learning and how often that information should be given. Three points are important for determining what KR information should be given. First, the precision of the information should be determined. KR can be either too precise or too general to aid learning. Second, the content of the KR should be determined. To determine the content of KR, it is essential to understand that KR serves to direct attention to certain parts of the skill and that it is important to use KR to direct attention to the most important part of the skill that is to be improved on the next trial. Third, the form of presenting KR should be established. While verbal KR is the most common means, alternative methods, such as videotape replay, graphic representations of movement kinematics, or augmenting sensory feedback can be used effectively. With regard to KR frequency, it seems that KR should not be provided on every trial. Thus, there are many questions that the instructor of motor skills must answer before KR can be confidently provided to students to most effectively facilitate learning.

Related Readings

Keefe, F. J., & Surwit, R. S. (1978). Electromyographic feedback: Behavioral treatment of neuromuscular disorders. *Journal of Behavioral Medicine, 1,* 13–25.

Lindahl, L. G. (1945). Movement analysis as in industrial training method. *Journal of Applied Psychology, 29,* 420–436.

Newell, K. M., & McGinnis, P. M. (1985). Kinematic information feedback for skilled performance. *Human Learning, 4,* 39–56.

Newell, K. M., Quinn, J. T., Sparrow, W. A., & Walter, C. B. (1983). Kinematic information feedback for learning a rapid arm movement. *Human Movement Science, 2,* 255–269.

Rothstein, A. L., & Arnold, R. K. (1976). Bridging the gap: Application of research on videotape feedback and bowling. *Motor Skills: Theory into Practice, 1,* 36–61.

Salmoni, A. W., Schmidt, R. A., & Walter, C. B. (1984). Knowledge of results and motor learning: A review and critical reappraisal. *Psychological Bulletin, 95,* 355–386. (Read the section on precision of KR.)

Concept 7.3 Three time intervals are associated with the use of KR during a practice trial: the KR-delay interval, the post-KR interval, and the interresponse interval

Application

Each time you hit a golf ball during a practice session, three time intervals become important to you, if your instructor is there and is providing you with KR. First, there is the time interval from when you have finished hitting the ball until your instructor tells you what you did wrong or right: this is the KR-delay interval. The second is the time that elapses from the instructor's giving you that information until you are allowed or able to hit another ball: the post-KR interval. Finally, there is the entire time period between your hitting one practice ball and your hitting another ball: the interresponse interval. These three periods of time are important to you because it is during these intervals that you have the opportunity to use the information you have received both from your own feedback systems and from KR. Essentially, these intervals are the periods of time you process information about your performance. Some very important practical questions must be considered in relation to these intervals of time. How important is the amount of time or length of each interval? What will be the effect of doing something else during one of those intervals in your learning of the skill? These two questions in particular will provide the basis for the discussion in the following section.

Discussion

The three time intervals surrounding the presentation of KR are illustrated in Figure 7.3–1. In that figure, a series of practice trials is indicated with R being a response. The subscript behind the R, as R_1, indicates response number one, or the first practice attempt. The subscript behind the KR, as KR_1, indicates that the KR is for R_1. The KR-delay, post-KR, and interresponse intervals are seen as falling along a time line associated with a particular practice trial.

So far in this chapter, rather general agreement has been noted about the need for KR, when KR is important in the learning process, and that KR needs to be sufficiently precise to aid learning. However, when we come to discuss the time intervals associated with KR, there is very little agreement as to their respective relation to the acquisition of a skill. Specifically, the disagreement seems to relate to the two questions presented in the Application section. Those two questions, one related to the effect on learning of the length of each interval and the other related to the effect on learning of activity during each interval, have been the bases for research investigating the KR intervals for many years. In this section we will consider each of these questions for

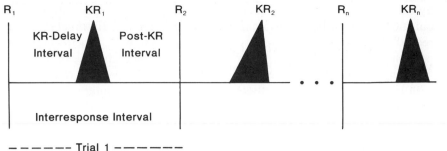

Figure 7.3-1
Intervals of time
related to KR
during the
acquisition of a
skill.

R_1 KR_1 R_2 KR_2 R_n KR_n

KR-Delay   Post-KR
Interval   Interval

Interresponse Interval

— — — — — Trial 1 — — — — —

each interval. What should become apparent to you as you consider these questions is the relationship that exists between these questions and what we previously discussed concerning memory. In effect, to consider the KR intervals is to apply memory research to the learning situation. That is an important consideration to bear in mind, for it may well be one reason for conflicting evidence that appears in the research literature relating to the KR intervals.[1]

One reason for some of the disagreement concerning the influence of the KR intervals on motor skill learning can be related to an experimental design problem. In Concept 7.2, it was pointed out that research dealing with the question of KR frequency was difficult to interpret because some experiments used retention or transfer trials following practice with KR while others did not. The same problem exists in the research literature related to the study of the KR time intervals. It is difficult to make appropriate inferences with a strong degree of confidence. When no retention or transfer trials are included, it is difficult to determine if the effects observed during practice trials with KR represent actual learning influence or only temporary performance effects.

Regardless of these concerns, the questions concerning the KR intervals are important for anyone interested in understanding processes underlying skill learning, as well as anyone involved in teaching motor skills. Thus, in the following discussion of each interval, the object will be to consider briefly some of the more significant and important research relating to each interval and then to synthesize that information to accommodate the needs of those seeking to better understand motor skill learning and control processes and of those who provide motor skill instruction.

The interval of time between the completion of a response and the presentation of KR is termed the KR-delay interval. This time interval has led to much confusion with regard to its relationship to learning. For example, Robert Ammons (1958) proposed the following generalization concerning KR: "The longer the delay in giving knowledge of performance, the less effect the given information has." Note that Ammons used the term "knowledge of performance" as synonymous with KR. Now compare Ammons' statement with one

1. For a further
discussion of the
memory learning
problem, see Harcum,
E. R. *Serial learning
and paralearning.* New
York: Wiley, 1975.

The KR-Delay
Interval

by Adams (1971) who stated that "delay of KR has little or no effect on acquisition." Obviously, both statements cannot be correct. If Ammons is correct, then as a teacher, you need to give KR as soon after the performance as possible. However, if Adams is correct, then *when* you give the information following a response is of little importance. Similar disagreements can be found with regard to the effect of activity during the KR-delay interval on skill acquisition. Let us attempt to draw some satisfactory resolution to these conflicts by considering each question individually for this KR-delay interval.

Effect of the length of the KR-delay interval. It appears that much of the confusion relating to the length of the interval or amount of delay of KR arises from failure to distinguish between animal and human learning studies. In animal studies, it has been shown rather convincingly that delaying reward following a response will definitely affect the acquisition of the task being learned by the animal. However, in human learning studies, quite the opposite has been found.

For example, some of the early studies concerning the effect of delay of reward in learning were published in 1929 by Hamilton and 1930 by Roberts. Using rats and reward delays of 2, 4, and 6 seconds, these researchers found that delays of the reward, or "satisfying after-effects" as they called it, affected performance. This means that learning took longer when reward delays were longer. As a general rule these results were accepted. Such thinking has been furthered by the direct application of these results from animal learning studies to human learning, such as by B. F. Skinner (1953), who has had a major impact on the instructional application of learning theory based on animal reinforcement research.

However, when delay of "reward" is viewed in connection with human learning, quite different results have been consistently found. One of the earliest reported findings that contradicted the animal learning results was by Lorge and Thorndike in 1935. They had subjects toss balls over their heads toward an unseen target. What Lorge and Thorndike termed "reward" was actually the information given to a subject following a toss, i.e., KR. Specifically, KR was a number that indicated whether the toss was beyond or short of the target, as well as how far. KR was either delayed or not delayed. Delays were 1, 2, 4, and 6 seconds, as well as one throw later. Results indicated no performance effects of any of these delay techniques.

More recent studies have also been carried out. Without question, the majority of these studies have come from the laboratory of Edward and Ina Bilodeau at Tulane University. A classic example of their studies was published in 1958 when they presented a series of five experiments in a *Journal of Experimental Psychology* article. Using motor tests such as a lever positioning task and a micrometer dial turning task, the Bilodeaus varied KR from a few seconds to seven days. The consistent results in these experiments were that KR delays, even up to one week, did not affect acquisition of the tasks.

However, since no retention or transfer trials were included in any of these experiments, it is difficult to determine if the empty KR-delay interval effects were performance or learning effects.

Some insight into this learning vs. performance issue and the empty KR-delay interval is provided by a review of research studies by Salmoni, Schmidt, and Walter (1984). In their review, experiments that included and did not include retention trials were considered. The researchers concluded that in those including retention trials there were hints of a too short KR-delay interval negatively affecting learning while there appeared to be *no* evidence showing any effect of delaying the presentation of KR.

The door is not closed on this issue. Although the overwhelming evidence has demonstrated that KR delay is not critically important to learning a motor skill, some recent research has shown that while KR delay does not affect performance, it may affect other factors that are not revealed by performance scores. For example, the confidence people have in what they think their error is on a particular trial seems to be related to KR delay. Also, the direction that the error consistently follows seems to be related to KR delay. While these findings may not make the effect of KR delay on skill acquisition any clearer, they indicate the complexity of the learning process and the fact that everything that affects us during learning is not always immediately apparent from our performance scores.

Effects of activity during the KR-delay interval. Research investigating the influence of activity during the KR-delay interval has provided us with a variety of results. In some cases, activity during this interval does not influence learning any differently than an empty interval, that is one in which the subject does not engage in activity and simply waits quietly for the KR to be given. In other cases, activity during the KR-delay interval has been more detrimental to learning than an empty interval. In still other cases, learning has actually been shown to improve due to the activity subjects engaged in during the KR-delay interval. Although this state of affairs may seem confusing, a closer look at the three types of results can reveal a better understanding of the learning processes in which the learner is involved during this interval. Also, these differing results have useful instructional strategy implications.

Most commonly, activity during the KR-delay interval has no influence on learning. This conclusion was reached by the Bilodeaus (Bilodeau, 1969) and has been supported by other investigations of KR (e.g., Boulter, 1964). More recently, Marteniuk (1986) has reported further evidence showing this same effect.

In the first experiment of this study, subjects practiced a complex task involving the movement of a horizontal level attached to a table top by a vertical axle at one end. Subjects placed their forearm on the lever with their elbow at the axle end and held a vertical handle that was located at the far end of the lever. The goal of the task was to move the lever back and forth

five times and to learn to make each of the five continuous movements a specified distance in a certain criterion movement in time. The total response took 3 seconds. KR was provided as RMS error for the entire movement for 51 practice trials. The KR-delay interval groups were used. One group received KR immediately after completing the response on each trial. Another group received KR 40 seconds after completing the response but rested during this empty KR-delay interval. The third group engaged in additional motor activity during a 40 second KR-delay interval. This activity consisted of the experimenter moving the lever through a different five-component pattern, followed by the subject attempting to reproduce the pattern. Results showed that during both the acquisition trials and then later on 10 trials of a no-KR retention test, the groups did not statistically differ in their performance of the criterion movement. These results were replicated in the second experiment for a less complex criterion response for the immediate KR condition and the condition involving subjects attempting to reproduce another movement during the KR-delay interval. The empty 40-second KR-delay interval was not included in the second experiment.

Several experiments, however, have been reported showing that learning is *hindered* because of KR-delay activity. We will consider two of these studies. Shea and Upton (1976) required subjects to learn two limb positions on a linear-positioning apparatus. On each practice trial, subjects moved to their estimate of each of the criterion locations. During the KR-delay interval, one group of subjects was required to make two different positioning movements, each to a physical stop on the trackway, then recall each position without the stop in place. A second group of subjects rested during the KR-delay interval. Results are shown in Figure 7.3–2. The circles and dots on this graph represent the two KR-delay groups and the solid and broken lines connecting these symbols represent the performance on the two criterion locations each group practiced for 20 trials. Notice that during the practice trials, the KR-delay activity group performed worse on both criterion locations than did the empty interval group. The pattern was the same for the no-KR retention trials. Thus, the KR-delay activity negatively influenced both acquisition performance as well as learning, as measured by performance on the retention test.

Another study by Marteniuk (1986), discussed earlier in this section, provides additional insight into the KR-delay interval activity question. In this study, two experiments reported evidence of a negative influence on learning by engaging in activity during the KR-delay interval. In the second experiment, subjects practiced a task in which they moved the horizontal lever device described earlier. The criterion movement for this task was a two-component lever movement, with each component having its own criterion movement distance and time. The total movement took 1.3 seconds to complete when done correctly. Three experimental groups were formed based on type of activity during the KR-delay interval. The immediate KR group received KR immediately after completing the response on each trial. A second group performed another two-component response (similar to the one described earlier

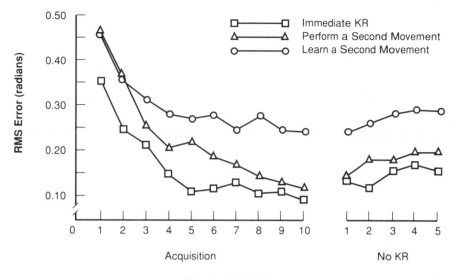

RMS Error (radians)

Legend:
□——□ Immediate KR
△——△ Perform a Second Movement
○——○ Learn a Second Movement

Acquisition   No KR

Blocks of 2 Trials

Figure 7.3-3
Results from the experiment by Marteniuk (1986) showing the interference effects of learning another complex movement during the KR-delay interval.

An important theoretical question that arises from these experiments showing negative learning effects of engaging in KR-delay interval activity is, With what learning process does this activity interfere during learning? Stephan Swinnen (1987), as a part of his doctoral dissertation at Catholic University in Belgium, provides some insight into the answer. Motor learning theorists have speculated that an important learning process involved in the KR-delay interval was error estimation based on sensory feedback. To test this hypothesis, Swinnen had subjects learn a rapid limb-reversal movement on a linear-positioning apparatus where the subject moved the handle along the trackway to a designated target area 65 cm from the starting point, then immediately reversed the movement to go to a second target area 20 cm from the first target, and then reversed the movement again to move through the first target. The total distance traveled was 85 cm; the goal time subjects were attempting to learn was 1 second for the entire movement. One group of subjects was engaged in a KR-delay activity in which they observed the experimenter making movements similar to the criterion movement. The subjects' task was to estimate the movement time for this task. Another group of subjects estimated their own error before beginning an empty KR-delay interval. A third group of subjects rested during the KR-delay interval.

As you can see in Figure 7.3–4, the group who performed the estimation of the experimenter's movement during the KR-delay interval performed poorest during the no-KR retention trials 2 days later. Also, note that the group required to estimate their own error before KR was given did not suffer any performance deterioration during the no-KR retention trials and performed

The Learning Environment

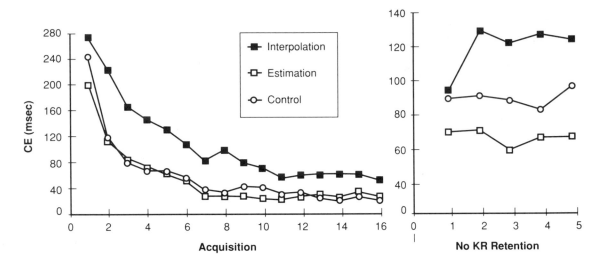

the best of the three groups on these trials, thus replicating the beneficial effects of subjective error estimation reported by Hogan and Yanowitz (1978). These results, then, support the view that during the KR-delay interval, the learner is engaged in important error estimation processes that must not be subjected to interference. When this processing activity is interfered with, learning will not be as effective as when this processing can be carried out without interference.

Finally, let's consider a situation where KR-delay activity has been found to *benefit* learning a motor skill. In the experiment by Hogan and Yanowitz (1978), one group of subjects was required to guess what they thought their error was on each practice trial before receiving KR. A second group of subjects did not have to guess their error. The task was to learn to move the handle on a trackway a distance of 47 cm in 200 msec.

As a point of interest here, this experiment, in addition to providing an investigation that is useful for better understanding learning processes, also has an applied feature. This can be seen if you consider the relatively common practice of instructors asking students, "What do you think you did wrong?" before providing the students with KR. The Hogan and Yanowitz experiment established that instructional situation under laboratory conditions.

KR and the guesses were given in msec of error based on the criterion movement time. As you can see in Figure 7.3–5, both groups performed similarly during the 50 practice trials when KR was given. However, when KR was withdrawn, the group that had not been required to guess their error showed a dramatic increase in error.

An explanation of these results can be found by going back to a view presented in Concept 7.2 of how subjects use KR. It was suggested that when KR is presented on every trial, it becomes a crutch for the learner. In fact,

Figure 7.3-4
Results from the experiment by Swinnen (1987) showing the influence of estimating the experimenter's movement error (interpolation group) and of estimating the subject's own error (estimation group) during the KR-delay interval compared with no activity during the interval. Note that the no-KR retention trials, performed 2 days later, are on a different y-axis scale.

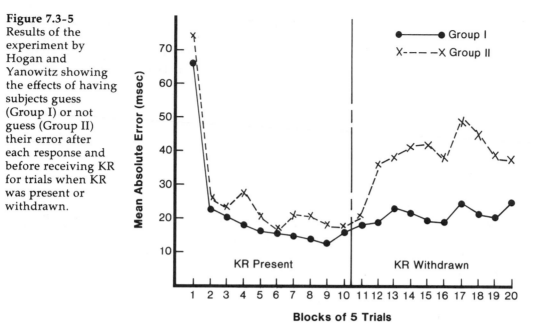

Figure 7.3-5
Results of the experiment by Hogan and Yanowitz showing the effects of having subjects guess (Group I) or not guess (Group II) their error after each response and before receiving KR for trials when KR was present or withdrawn.

the individual is probably learning more about the KR than about the task. What appears to be the benefit of having subjects guess their error before receiving KR is that this procedure forces them to focus their attention on the task and on the features of the task that are critical in effectively learning the task. Additionally subjects who are forced to guess their errors must be attentive to sensory feedback information, which is essential when KR is not provided.

What can be concluded about the effect of activity on motor skill learning during the KR-delay interval? The research indicates fairly clearly that the effect will depend on the type of activity engaged in during this interval. If the activity is not attention demanding, or at least does not interfere with critical learning processes during the KR-delay interval, then the activity will not influence learning of the criterion skill. However, if attention is demanded by the activity during the KR-delay interval such that it interferes with the learner's error estimation processes, then learning of the criterion skill will be hindered and it will not be learned as well as if the person has not engaged in that activity during the KR-delay interval. Finally, activity during this interval can benefit learning if it is the type that directs the learner's attention to critical features of the criterion task that must be learned for successful performance on a retention or transfer task. A good example of a beneficial activity is if, before KR is given, the learner is required to respond with what he or she thinks was done wrong on a response.

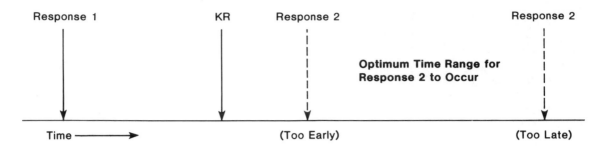

Time ———▶   (Too Early)   (Too Late)

The post-KR interval appears to be an interval that should be especially vital to the learning of a skill. This inference is based on the fact that it is during this period of time, after KR has been presented, that the learner must decide what to do about his or her next response, based on the KR he or she has received. If KR is vital to learning, as we established in Concept 7.1, then it would seem logical that the post-KR interval would be an exceptionally important period of time for the learner. However, results of research that have attempted to manipulate the length of the post-KR interval, or the activity that occurs during the interval, have had varying degrees of success in showing what really happens during that interval so far as the learner is concerned.

Figure 7.3-6
Time line indicating the optimal range of time for a response to follow the presentation of KR.

The Post-KR Interval

Effect of post-KR interval length. The logical expectations of how the length of the post-KR interval would influence learning seems to be based on the idea of a continuum for this interval, as presented in Figure 7.3–6. The continuum is based on when the next response occurs. If the next response occurs too soon, then one would expect poor performance, since the learner did not have time to use KR to his or her advantage. At the other extreme of the continuum is the situation where the next response occurs too long after the previous response, so that the learner will probably forget the KR, or parts of it, and perhaps some of the correction plans he or she had made. Certainly this reasoning is logical and it has been stated as such by several authors, including Adams (1971).

Unfortunately, the only success in confirming the existence of such a continuum has been with the minimum time to use the KR end of the continuum. In a study by Weinberg, Guy, and Tupper (1964), evidence was provided to show that poorer performance for a 1-second post-KR interval was noted on a 10-inch positioning movement than for a 5-, 10-, or 20-second interval. Studies that have considered the forgetting end of the continuum have not shown any effects at all on acquisition. For example, Magill (1977) reported that subjects were given either 10- or 60-second post-KR intervals during the learning of three positions using a lever. No differences between these two interval lengths were observed. The obviously perplexing feature of these findings is that the 60-second interval is well beyond the time when forgetting has been shown to occur in working memory. Recall, for example, the discussion of this in Chapter 5 where we discussed memory and retention.

The implication of these results about the effect of post-KR interval length on learning motor skills is that important information-processing activities occur during this interval and require a minimum amount of time to be carried out effectively. Also, it appears that these activities are not influenced by extended lengths of time during which the individual is not required to engage in additional activity. One reason for this could be that the learner engages in some form of rehearsal during this empty time, thus making increased interval lengths beneficial. However, this is only speculation and will require empirical support. At least, this additional rehearsal is some form of maintenance rehearsal since a longer interval does not lead to better learning than a shorter interval. In terms of instruction, the implication of the results about the influence of post-KR interval length suggest that it is important to give students an opportunity to "think about" the KR you have just given them. After KR has been given, the next attempt to perform the skill should occur after some time has passed, during which the student can act on the information you have just provided. Just how long that time should be is open for question and will clearly depend on the activity and the complexity of the KR given.

Effect of activity during the post-KR interval The influence of engaging in activity during the post-KR interval on motor skill learning appears similar to the influence of activity during the KR-delay interval. It seems engaging in post-KR activity sometimes does not influence learning at all, whereas other times it may hinder learning or perhaps help.

If you read the earlier reviews of research concerning KR (e.g., Adams, 1971; Bilodeau, 1969; Newell, 1976), you may have noted that apparent paradox of the motor learning literature is that essentially no reports provide evidence that post-KR interval activity interferes with learning. This is especially perplexing because it has been generally accepted that the post-KR interval was such an important time for information-processing activity to occur and therefore, it was believed logical to expect beneficial effects. One problem was thought to be that most of the research investigating this issue did not include a retention or transfer test (see the review by Salmoni, Schmidt, & Walter, 1984). For example, two experiments by Magill (1973, 1977) both reported no post-KR interval activity effects, but neither experiment tested subjects after their practice trials with KR. However, an experiment by Lee and Magill (1983a) added a retention test and still found that post-KR activity did not influence learning a skill.

In their experiment, Lee and Magill had subjects learn to make an arm movement through a series of three small wooden barriers in 1050 msec during the post-KR interval, the "motor" group was required to learn to make the same movement in 1350 msec; the "non-motor group" was required to guess

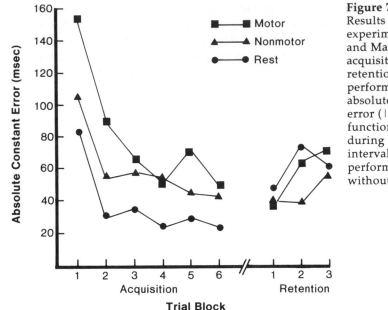

Figure 7.3-7
Results of the experiment by Lee and Magill showing acquisition and retention performance for absolute constant error (|CE|) as a function of activity during the post-KR interval. Retention performance is without KR.

a three-digit number, for which each subject received KR as to each guessed digit being too low, too high, or correct; the "rest" group did nothing for the 15-second interval. Results, as seen in Figure 7.3–7, indicated that both the motor and nonmotor groups performed with greater error during the practice trials with KR. However, on the no-KR retention trials, there were no differences among groups. Activity during the post-KR interval, even activity that demanded cognitive, problem-solving activity, did not influence the learning of the criterion task.

An experiment that found a *detrimental effect* of post-KR activity was reported by Boucher (1974). He had subjects read polysyllables as they were presented on a screen during the post-KR interval while learning a limb-positioning movement. Results showed that during the first two blocks of practice, the post-KR activity condition performed worse than the empty interval conditions. Hardy (1983) also reported detrimental effects of post-KR interval activity, but again, this was only during practice trials with KR. However, no retention tests were given and the only noticeable influence of the verbal activity was during the early trials of practicing the task. As such, these results are similar to those reported by Lee and Magill (1983a) considered earlier.

However, a recent experiment by Benedetti and McCullagh (1987) showed a detrimental effect on learning as measured by a no-KR retention test. In this experiment, subjects learned to perform a ballistic timing response of moving their hand from a starting button to knock down a small wooden barrier that was 24 cm away in exactly 150 msec. KR was provided after each

of the 30 practice trials. Post-KR interval characteristics were manipulated such that two groups had a 5-second interval with either no activity or with solving addition problems, and two groups had a 10-second interval with either no activity or with the additional solving activity. The results showed that during the practice trials, there was no difference among the groups. However, on the no-KR retention test, the group subjected to math problem-solving during the 10-second post-KR interval performed significantly worse than did subjects of the other three conditions.

However, the finding that post-KR interval activity hinders learning of a motor skill is the exception in the post-KR interval literature. Magill (1988) speculated that perhaps one reason why empirical evidence has not been particularly successful in showing that post-KR interval activity interferes with learning is that this expectation is not correct. The prediction of learning being hindered by post-KR interval activity comes from the notion that activity in a retention-type interval, which is what the post-KR interval is to some degree, interferes with retention. The logic continues here by expecting that if retention is interfered with, even during the course of many practice trials, then learning will not be as good as if no interference had occurred. But, if we consider an important classic effect found in the verbal learning literature, then it is possible that what appears to be interference activity can actually *benefit* learning in the long run. This effect, known as the *spacing of repetitions* effect (see Hintzman, 1974, for a good review of this work), has shown that if a list of words is presented to a subject where each word is on the list two times, the words that have the most separation between them by other words will be remembered better. Thus, increasing time between repetition activity benefits remembering the words, rather than hindering it.

Partial support for the hypothesis post-KR interval activity could *benefit* learning was reported by Magill (1988). In this experiment, subjects were required to perform a two-component movement in which each component had its own criterion movement time. In this experiment, there were two post-KR interval activity conditions and one no-activity condition. In the two activity conditions, which had 20-second post-KR intervals, subjects in one group were required to perform a mirror-tracing task, while subjects in the other activity group were required to learn two more two-component movements. The no-activity group had a 5-second, empty post-KR interval. Results showed that these three groups did not differ on a 24-hour no-KR retention test but that the two post-KR activity groups performed better on a new two-component task with different criterion movement times than did the no-activity group. Thus, post-KR activity did not have an effect on retention of a practiced skill, but it significantly benefited transfer to a novel variation of the practiced skill.

A possible explanation of these results comes from the work of Larry Jacoby and his colleagues (Cuddy & Jacoby, 1982; Jacoby, 1978). That is, activity that intervenes between practice trials of the criterion task may cause

the learner to forget much of what was done on the previous trial. As a result, he or she must re-solve the problem of the criterion task on the next trial. While this additional effortful problem-solving activity may lead to relatively slower skill acquisition performance, the long-term benefit is a more durable memory representation of the practiced task.

It is interesting to speculate about the finding that activity during the KR-delay interval can hinder learning, as reported by Marteniuk (1986) and by Shea and Upton (1976), although similar types of activity during the post-KR interval can benefit learning, as reported by Magill (1988). Although these effects require more empirical investigation, they provide evidence that different learning processes are occurring before and after KR is given. Based on the work by Swinnen (1986), there is evidence that essential error correction processing occurs during the KR-delay interval and not during the post-KR interval. According to the hypothesis forwarded by Magill (1988) and Lee and Magill (1985), critical action plan construction for the next trial occurs during the post-KR interval. Further research is needed to test these speculations and to provide more information about the nature of the learner's processing activities during the KR-delay and post-KR intervals.

Results and interpretations of results such as these have important implications for instructors of motor skills. Practice conditions that lead to the best practice performance may not necessarily lead to the best learning of the task. An example of this has been provided in the KR research we have just considered. Subjects who receive KR on every trial and have no activity during the post-KR interval will probably show very good practice performance but will not have learned the task as well as they could if more demanding practice conditions had been provided. We will come back to this point in Chapter 9.

The role of the interresponse interval is very intriguing for the study of skill acquisition. Part of this interest stems from a procedural problem that most researchers looking at the KR intervals have failed to take into account. This problem is that when one of the KR intervals is held constant, such as is typical in post-KR studies that kept the KR-delay interval the same length for all groups, the third interval varies also. For example, if you were considering the effect of the post-KR interval on skill acquisition, you might use two groups. These would be defined by the length of the post-KR interval, such as 2 and 30 seconds. To exclude any influence of the KR-delay interval, you would keep the length of that interval the same for both groups, such as 5 seconds each. Notice however, that you now have two different interresponse interval lengths to contend with, 7 and 35 seconds. Suppose your results indicated that the 30-second post-KR interval group was poorer in performance than the 2-second group. Would your conclusions indicate this was due to the longer post-KR interval or to the differences in the interresponse interval? Obviously, this is a perplexing problem but one that must be dealt with. Unfortunately, few people have confronted this question; and we are left with a rather ambiguous situation in studying the interresponse interval.

The
Interresponse
Interval

However, some proposals have been made about the interresponse interval. The Bilodeaus (1958) indicated that while they found the pre- and post-KR intervals had little to no effect on skill acquisition, the interresponse interval appeared to be a "critical" variable for learning motor skills. On the other hand, studies by Magill (1973, 1977) and Shea (1975) have not supported the interresponse interval role in learning. Thus, the inquiry and controversy go on. It has even been suggested that investigating the interresponse interval by varying its length is somewhat confused by the massed vs. distributed practice situation.

It is always difficult to conclude that nothing can be concluded! Unfortunately, for the interresponse interval, this is the case. We simply do not know its real role in the process of learning a motor skill. For the purposes of instruction, it would seem logical that if we properly present error information after a practice attempt, give the learner enough time to use that information, and then have him or her execute another trial in a reasonable amount of time, then the interresponse interval should be of little concern for the teacher. However, it should be noted that the influence of the interresponse interval may be important when we look at a related issue, known as massed vs. distributed practice, in Chapter 9.

Summary

Three time intervals are associated with KR. These intervals include the KR-delay, the post-KR, and the interresponse intervals. Each represents a period of time following a response and preceding another response. The KR-delay interval follows the completion of a response and precedes the presentation of KR. The post-KR interval follows the presentation of KR and precedes the next response. The interresponse interval is the total time between the two responses. Two concerns have determined the interest in these intervals in relation to motor skill acquisition. One concern is the relationship between the length of each interval to learning. The second concern has been the influence of activity during these intervals on learning. While much controversy still is centered on these two questions, it can be generally concluded that each interval can influence skill acquisition. We have considered some of the research that has somewhat clarified the nature of that influence.

Related Readings

Adams, J. A. (1971). A closed-loop theory of motor learning. *Journal of Motor Behavior, 3,* 111–149. (Read pp. 132–136.)

Bilodeau, E. A., & Bilodeau, I. M. (1958). Variation of temporal intervals among critical events in five studies of knowledge of results. *Journal of Experimental Psychology, 55,* 603–612.

Lee, T. D., & Magill, R. A. (1983). Activity during the post-KR interval: Effects upon performance or learning? *Research Quarterly for Exercise and Sport, 54,* 340–345.

Salmoni, A. W., Schmidt, R. A., & Walter, C. B. (1984). Knowledge of results and motor learning: A review and critical reappraisal. *Psychological Bulletin, 95,* 355–386. (Read section on the Temporal Locus of KR, pp. 364–372.)

1. What is the difference between sensory feedback and KR? Why is it beneficial to distinguish between these two?
2. What are the two types of information referred to by the terms KR and KP? Why is the term KR used in this text to refer to either of these types of information? How are these two types of information kept distinct using this approach?
3. How do we know that KR is useful for guiding error correction while learning or performing a motor skill? Give an example of how KR can be used this way. Under what conditions do you think KR is most likely to serve the learner in this way?
4. Explain how a skill that was dependent of the availability of KR early in learning can be performed later in learning without KR.
5. How could you differentiate when KR is being used to guide error correction from when it is being used primarily as a source of motivation? Give an example of a situation that would illustrate this different use of KR.
6. What is meant by the "precision" of KR? What do we know about the precision of KR and learning of motor skills?
7. What two important points must be strongly considered when deciding on KR content? Give an example of a motor skill situation that illustrates these two points.
8. Why is KR frequency an important issue to consider when it refers to providing KR in a practice situation? What seems to be the most appropriate conclusion to draw regarding the frequency with which KR should be given during learning?
9. How could KR be redundant information to a person practicing a motor skill? Give an example of how this could occur.
10. What are two important guidelines for the effective use of videotape as a form of KR?
11. What do we currently know about the use and benefit of kinematic information as KR to help learn a motor skill? When do you think this type of information would be most helpful?
12. What is meant by "augmented feedback"? How can this be an effective form of KR to aid motor skill learning?
13. What are the three time intervals associated with KR and practicing a skill? Why are researchers interested in investigating these intervals?
14. What can we conclude about the effect of time and activity during the KR-delay interval? During the post-KR interval? What do these conclusions tell us about the role played by KR in learning motor skills?

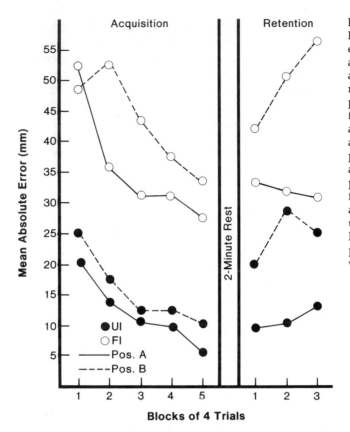

Figure 7.3-2
Results of the experiment by Shea and Upton showing acquisition and retention performance (AE) for learning two arm positions (A and B) on a linear positioning apparatus with the pre-KR interval filled with motor activity (FI) or unfilled (UI). Retention performance is without KR.

for the first experiment) during a 40-second KR-delay interval. The third group was required to learn a new two-component response, similar to the criterion movement they were practicing, during the 40-second KR-delay interval. KR was provided immediately after completing this new KR-delay task. As you can see (Figure 7.3–3), by the end of the 20 acquisition trials, the group that had to *learn* a second movement during the KR-delay interval performed worse than the other two groups. And, as noted previously, the group that *performed*, rather than learned, a second movement, was performing just like the immediate-KR group by the end of acquisition. These results also characterized performance on the 10 no-KR retention trials.

These experiments by Shea and Upton (1976) and by Marteniuk (1986) indicate that certain types of activity during the KR-delay interval do not interfere with learning whereas other types hinder learning. Characteristically, learning is hindered during the KR-delay interval if the activity diverts adequate attention from the essential underlying learning processes in which the person is engaged during this interval. If the activity during the KR-delay interval does not interfere with the attention demanded by the learning processes during this interval, the person is quite capable of performing that activity.

Knowledge of Results   355

Transfer of Learning

8

Concept 8.1
Transfer of learning is the influence of a previously practiced skill on the learning of a new skill.

Concept 8.2
Transfer of learning can be expected to occur between the same limbs when only one limb has been actively involved in practice.

Concept 8.3
Transfer of learning potential in teaching can be maximized by the instructor of motor skills.

Concept 8.1

Transfer of learning is the influence of a previously practiced skill on the learning of a new skill

If you have never played squash before but have had much experience playing handball, do you think that you would learn to play squash more easily than someone who has not played handball before? Undoubtedly, you would. Why? Primarily because many aspects of both games are very similar, even though the games themselves are quite distinct. Both games are played in a similar-sized four-wall court. Both require that the ball hit the front wall prior to hitting the floor. Both games involve moving and positioning in order to hit a moving ball. We could easily expand this list of similarities. However, there are some definite differences between the two games. For example, the most obvious is that squash involves a racquet while handball does not. Another major difference is that the ball in squash must strike the front wall at least 17 inches from the floor while in handball the ball may hit the front wall at any location. The balls are different in size and consistency in the two games; the squash ball is smaller and harder than the handball. Even though these differences exist, it seems reasonable to expect that a person with handball experience would learn to play squash more readily than a person with no previous handball experience.

In the elementary school, much time is often devoted to the game of kickball. The intent of this game, other than providing fun, is to function as a good lead-up game for baseball. The important question is whether the child who has had previous experience playing kickball will more easily adapt to learning to play baseball than the child who has not had previous kickball experience.

When you learned to play tennis, undoubtedly your teacher required you to spend a lot of time hitting the ball off a back wall. You also probably practiced hitting balls thrown to you either by another person or by a ball machine. The purpose of this practice was to help you learn a particular stroke without having to deal with the added requirements of rallying with another player. As in the kickball-baseball example, the important instructional question here is whether this type of practice is beneficial in helping a person to successfully perform the stroke in a rallying or a game situation.

In each of these three situations, a similar learning and instructional concern is highlighted. That is, what is the relationship between previous experiences and learning a new motor skill? In the squash-handball and kickball-baseball examples, the interest is in a general relationship between experiences in one sport activity and another new one. In the tennis example,

the concern is with the relationship between practice procedures and the eventual goal of that practice, to be able to successfully perform the practiced skill in a game. In all three situations, the learning phenomenon of interest is what is called transfer of learning. The intent is to transfer what is learned in one experience to a new experience in order to facilitate learning the new skill. Although you have become acquainted with the concept of transfer of learning in various previous chapters in this book, the discussion that follows will help you better understand what transfer of learning is and why it is an important learning phenomenon.

One of the most universally applied principles of learning in our educational systems is the principle termed *transfer of learning*. This principle is the foundation of curriculum development, for it provides the basis for arranging in sequence the skills to be learned. This concept is also extensively used by instructors in the classroom, playground, gymnasium, or dance studio, as they develop and implement their teaching methods. Thus, it is virtually impossible to disregard the influence of this learning phenomenon.

In this discussion, the goal will be to develop your knowledge of this critical learning principle. To achieve that goal, four questions will be presented and answered. These questions will be related to (1) defining transfer of learning, (2) determining why the understanding of transfer of learning is important, (3) discussing how we know transfer has occurred, and (4) presenting some of the various conditions that influence the transfer of learning phenomenon; this includes considering some of the reasons why transfer occurs.

A generally accepted definition of transfer of learning is that it is *the influence of having previously practiced a skill or skills on the learning of a new skill.* It appears that this influence may be either positive, negative, or neutral (zero).

Positive transfer occurs when experience with a previous skill *aids or facilitates* the learning of a new skill. The handball-squash and the kickball-baseball examples are positive transfer situations. In fact, each of the four examples of transfer that were suggested in the application section shows some positive transfer.

Negative transfer occurs when the experience with a previous skill *hinders or interferes with* the learning of a new skill. We must examine specific components of skills to find negative effects. For example, having learned the forehand in tennis before learning the forehand in badminton will generally result in negative transfer, since the badminton forehand is a wrist snap, whereas the tennis forehand requires a relatively firm wrist. It must be emphasized that negative transfer effects will generally be seen only in specific aspects of an activity. This is because when we consider the overall transfer effects of the two activities, there is most likely a positive transfer effect from previous experience with tennis to the learning of badminton. Thus, in the handball-squash example considered earlier, the overall transfer effects are

Discussion

What Is
Transfer?

positive. However, certain aspects of one game would be negatively transferred to the other game, such as the distance you stand from the ball to hit it, since squash uses a long-handled racquet, but handball uses no racquet. Negative transfer effects are typically temporary. They are usually overcome rather quickly with practice.

Zero transfer occurs when experience with a previous skill has *no effect* or influence on the learning of a new skill. Obviously, there is no transfer effect from learning to swim to learning to drive a car. Nor can it be assumed that experience with some motor skills will always have an influence on the learning of new motor skills.

Why Is Transfer of Learning Important?

Perhaps the answer to the question of the importance of transfer of learning as a learning principle is obvious by now. We have already pointed out that this principle forms the basis for educational curriculum development as well as for instructional methodology. Actually, these two roles of the transfer principle are at the very core of the practical significance of transfer. The transfer principle also has theoretical significance for understanding processes underlying the learning and control of motor skills. In Chapter 2, the need for using transfer tests to determine the degree of learning that resulted from practice was strongly emphasized. Implicit in the need for such tests is the view that if learning has occurred, positive transfer should be observable when the practiced skill must be performed in a new context or when a variation of the practiced skill is performed. However, although this transfer expectation plays an important part in making the learning inference, there is much to be learned about control and learning processes by understanding *why* the transfer occurs. In the following sections, we will discuss the practical and theoretical significance of the transfer principle in more detail to better illustrate these points.

Curriculum development. Mathematics provides a very useful example of how the transfer principle is applied in educational curriculum development. The curriculum from grades 1 through 12 is based on a simple to complex arrangement. Numeral identification, numeral writing, numeral value identification, addition, subtraction, multiplication, and division must be presented in this specific sequence, as each is based on the preceding concept. If a person were presented with a division problem before having learned addition, subtraction, or multiplication, he or she would have to learn those skills before completing the problem. Algebra is not taught before basic arithmetic. Trigonometry is not taught before geometry. We could go on, but the role played by transfer of learning in the development of mathematics curriculum should be apparent at this point.

The physical education curriculum, for example, should also be based on a transfer of learning foundation. It is difficult to understand why baseball would be taught before students have had ample experiences in learning to throw, catch, or bat. To do so would be like having a person do a division problem before learning addition, subtraction, and multiplication.

The same point can be made about any subject curriculum involving the training of motor skills. The curriculum should be designed to take advantage of the transfer of learning principle. Basic or foundational skills should be included in the curriculum *before* more complex skills that require mastery of certain basic skills are introduced. This means that any curriculum involving the teaching of motor skills should be based on a logical progression of skill experiences where skills introduced early in the curriculum provide a basis for transfer to the succeeding skills. If this approach is not used, time is wasted while students "go back" and learn prerequisite basic skills.

Teaching methodology. The second important application of the transfer of learning principle to motor skill instruction is in the area of teaching methodology. When an instructor teaches students the basic swimming strokes by using dry land drills before letting students try the strokes in the water, that instructor is assuming that there will be a positive transfer effect from the dry land drills to performing the strokes in water. That is, the assumption is that the students will learn the strokes more effectively and more efficiently because of their dry land drill experience.

John Brady (1979) published an interesting illustration of the positive transfer that results from employing the teaching methodology of using dry land training for skills that must be performed in the water. Certified SCUBA divers were used in this experiment in which the goal was to assemble under water as fast as possible a complex mechanical device. Eight subtasks were involved in this assembly task, which required the use of a box-end wrench. One group of subjects, the low-practice condition, only watched and participated in a demonstration of how the assembly task should be performed. They then practiced assembling the device one time on dry land before attempting to perform the task under water. The second group of subjects, the high-practice condition, not only viewed the demonstration of assembling the device, they also practiced assembling it eight times on dry land before entering the water. If the dry land training was not beneficial, that is, if it did not positively transfer to underwater performance, then both groups would be expected to perform the skill similarly under water. However, the results indicated that the high-practice group performed the task under water significantly faster than the low-practice group. Thus, dry land practice facilitated, or positively transferred to, the underwater performance of assembling the complex mechanical device. This finding has important implications for those who instruct persons who must perform skills under water because it suggests that the generally safer and less expensive dry land practice will facilitate performance of the skill under water, thus requiring less underwater training time.

The transfer principle is invaluable when the skill to be learned has a strong element of danger in it such as in diving or gymnastics. In these activities, body harnesses are used in practicing certain skills so as to aid the learner in developing confidence in his or her ability to perform the skill without having fear of injury slow down the learning process.

Other examples of instruction methodology that use the transfer principle are such activities as using a pitching machine to teach hitting in baseball, hitting tennis balls from a ball machine, and rebounding basketballs from a rebounder. Each of these instructional procedures is based on the assumption that practice with the machines will positively transfer to the "real" situation. Batting practice with a pitching machine, for example, will aid batting performance when a live pitcher is throwing the ball. The batter can concentrate on his or her swing and on making consistent contact with the ball when the pitching machine is being used rather than being concerned with where the ball will be, how fast it will be pitched, etc.

Learning inferences. In Chapter 2, you were introduced to the use of experimental designs incorporating the transfer of learning principle. These designs are structured to include a series of performance trials on a new task or under new performance conditions after practice trials have been performed under other conditions. The purpose of the transfer trials is to provide a means for observing performance in these new conditions so that a valid inference can be made about the influence of the experimental conditions on learning. The use of this type of transfer design is especially important for making inferences concerning the influence of certain practice procedures and instructional techniques on learning a motor skill.

In an article by Bransford, Franks, Morris, and Stein (1979), an impressive argument is made for *only* considering the effectiveness of any acquisition activity on the basis of how the skill being practiced is performed in a "test" context. That is, if our interest is in knowing whether one form of practice procedure is superior to another for learning a motor skill, no conclusion should be made until the skill of interest is observed in a test performance situation. The test may be a game, a specific test, or any condition that involves the expressed goal of the practice experience. Since this point has been emphasized in many portions of this text, it should be apparent that we cannot ignore it if we are to make valid inferences in motor learning research.

How Do We Know Transfer Has Occurred?

Transfer designs in learning research usually involve one of three different types of transfer situations. One situation involves performing the same skill that has been practiced in a novel situation. For example, you have seen many instances in this text where the transfer test involved performing the practiced skill without knowledge of results (KR). The dry land practice and underwater test experiment by Brady (1979) discussed earlier in this concept is a good example of using this type of transfer test situation. Another transfer test situation involves performing a novel variation of the skill that has been practiced, such as performing the skill more rapidly or more slowly than practiced. You may recall from the discussion of schema theory in Concept 2.3 that this was an especially important transfer situation to test the practice variability prediction of that theory. This prediction will be considered in more

detail in Concept 9.1. Third, the transfer test may involve performing a different, although somewhat related, skill than was practiced. This approach is especially common when the researcher is interested in knowing how well a particular practice drill transfers to a particular skill, such as determining how well hitting a baseball off a batting tee transfers to hitting a ball thrown by a pitcher. This approach is also useful for researchers investigating the usefulness of a simulator to train individuals to perform some skill. For example, a researcher may want to determine how effective a particular automobile simulator is for training people to drive cars.

There are various ways of designing experiments to implement these transfer situations and to make desired inferences about learning and learning conditions. However, consideration of all these designs is beyond the scope of this discussion. We will consider two common uses of transfer designs that encompass the transfer situations just discussed. Most transfer situations you will encounter in the motor learning research will involve one of these basic designs or a slight variation of them.

The two designs to be considered here differ on the basis of whether the transfer is between two different tasks or between two different practice or performance conditions for the same task. The term *task* is being used here in the same way that we have used the term *skill* throughout this text. Because the term *task* has traditionally been used in the transfer of learning literature when reference is made to these experimental designs, this term will be used here as well. Thus, when two different tasks is the issue being considered, the interest may be related to the transfer between two completely different skills or between different variations of the same skill. Although there are theoretical reasons for keeping distinct the issue of transfer between different skills versus variations of the same skill, the experimental designs investigating these issues generally follow a similar approach.

The first experimental design to be considered is typically labeled an *intertask transfer* design. Here the interest is on the influence of experience with one skill on a new one, with the new one being either a different skill or a variation of the first one. Examples of situations when this type of design (or a variation of it) would be used were discussed in the second and third transfer situations described at the beginning of this section. The second experimental design common in the transfer of learning research literature is called an *intratask transfer* design. The first transfer test situation described at the beginning of this section would utilize this design. This design is typically related to comparing how different types of practice conditions affect learning a particular skill.

Intertask transfer. The simplest and most frequently used experimental design for testing intertask transfer effects is the following:

Experimental Group	Practice Task A	Perform Task B
Control Group	Nothing	Perform Task B

For analysis purposes, the primary interest in the results of this experimental paradigm is in the performance by both groups on task B. If the experience with task A facilitated the learning of task B, then the experimental group would show more rapid improvement on task B than would the control group. On the other hand, if the learning of task A interfered with the learning of task B, then the experimental group would take longer to learn task B than would the control group.

A variation of this design will be presented in Concept 9.1 in the discussion of practice conditions that will lead to success in performing a novel response. To test this question, researchers have varied the experimental design seen here by having the experimental group practice several different tasks, such as task A, B, and C, while the control group practices only task A. The transfer test condition is conducted as the design illustrated above indicates in that both groups transfer to the same novel task, which in this case could be labeled task D.

Various *methods of quantifying the amount of transfer* have been proposed for intertask transfer. Two of the more frequently used quantifications of transfer have been percentage of transfer and savings score. *Percentage of transfer* is simply the percent of improvement on task B that would be attributable to having learned task A. A high percentage of transfer would indicate a strong influence of task A on task B, while a low percentage would suggest a much lesser, though positive, influence.

Percentage of transfer can be calculated very simply by subtracting the control group task B score from the experimental group task B score and then dividing that difference by the total of the task B scores for both groups. To obtain a percentage, multiply the result by 100. Note that the "task score" used in this calculation should be based on initial performance on task B. Expressed as a formula, this calculation is as follows:

$$\frac{\text{Percentage}}{\text{of Transfer}} = \frac{\text{Experimental Group} - \text{Control Group}}{\text{Experimental Group} + \text{Control Group}} \times 100$$

Although many different formulas have been proposed in order to determine percentage of transfer, this formula, suggested by Murdock (1957), appears to avoid the theoretical problems of other formulas.

The *savings score* is the amount of practice time saved in learning task B because of having had prior experience on task A. By using this score, it would be possible to show that the task A experience saved so many practice trials on task B. Thus, if the experimental group reached a criterion of 100 points on task B in 20 trials while the control group took 30 trials, the savings score would be 10 trials. A question here is whether or not the savings score is actually a real savings. Remember, the experimental group practiced task A while the control group did nothing. If the experimental group practiced 20 trials on task A, we would have to question the "savings score," since this score refers only to the amount of practice time "saved" on task B.

For practical applications, use of the savings scores has particular merit. This is especially true when the question being investigated is whether or not a particular drill effectively aids the learning of a skill. The savings score would indicate how much practice time on the skill itself could be saved by using the particular drill. If no practice time is saved, then there could be some concern about the continued use of the drill.

Intratask transfer research. To consider the transfer effects for intratask transfer conditions, it is necessary to reiterate some of what was presented in Concept 2.1 concerning how transfer tests are used to make inferences in research concerned with effective practice conditions and skill learning. The typical research paradigm used for this purpose is as follows:

Group A	Practice Condition A	Perform Under Condition C
Group B	Practice Condition B	Perform Under Condition C

Various examples of the use of this paradigm have been provided in several chapters of this book. For example, in Chapter 7, a discussion of the influence of KR precision on motor skill learning indicated how this experimental paradigm is used. In the KR precision situation, practice condition A could be practice with quantitative KR being given; practice condition B could be practice with qualitative KR being given. The transfer test, condition C, would be to perform a series of trials where no KR is given.

For analysis purposes, three points are of interest when this type of experimental design is used. First, how did performance under practice conditions A and B compare? Second, how did the two groups compare when performing under condition C? Third, what characterized each group's performance when comparing the last practice trial with the first transfer trial? Did the group improve, get worse, or show no change in performance? This last point of analysis is often overlooked. Its importance becomes apparent when groups show different performance level results during the transfer trials than they did during the practice trials.

In terms of quantifying the amount of transfer in an intratask transfer experimental situation, both the percentage of transfer and savings score measures can be calculated. The savings score can be calculated in the same way it is calculated for intertask transfer. To calculate the percentage of transfer, use the same principle as expressed in the formula presented in the discussion of intertask transfer. To apply this formula to the intratask transfer situation, use the task scores for performance trials under condition C. This score should be based on initial performance trials under condition C. Two separate calculations will be required, one to determine the percentage of transfer from practicing under condition A and one from practicing under condition B. To calculate the percentage of transfer to condition C due to condition A practice, subtract the transfer condition score of the condition B group from the transfer condition score of the condition A group. Then, divide this difference by the

total of the conditions A and B scores. Again, remember to multiply by 100 to obtain a percentage value. To determine the percentage transfer due to practice under condition B, simply reverse the numerator of the formula and subtract the condition A score from the condition B score, and follow the same steps as before.

It is important to keep in mind the use of the transfer design for motor learning research. In the next chapter, we will consider various practice-related issues in which the primary concern is the effectiveness of certain practice procedures for learning motor skills. The performance characteristics on transfer trials become an essential element in making valid conclusions concerning practice conditions.

Transfer and memory paradigms compared. You may have noticed that the experimental paradigms that have been presented in this discussion are similar to the paradigm presented in Concept 5.2, where proactive interference was discussed as a cause of forgetting. In the memory situation, we were concerned with how much forgetting was caused by previous task experience. In this transfer of learning situation, however, we are concerned with the general nature of the influence of the previous experience on the *learning* of the criterion task. That is, did the previous experience help, hinder, or have no effect on learning the criterion task? Thus, although the paradigms for determining proactive influences are similar for the memory and the transfer of learning situations, the primary goal of each is different. Factors that influence forgetting in the memory situation, however, can be thought of as having generalized application to the learning setting.

One other point to note here is that while the focus of the present discussion is proactive transfer effects, it is also possible to consider retroactive transfer effects, as in the memory situation. Here the concern would be the influence that experiencing task B has on the performance of task A when task B is experienced between the learning or performance of task A and another performance of task A. If you learn tennis and then learn to play badminton, what will be the effect of that badminton experience on your next tennis playing experience? This is a retroactive transfer question.

Keep the proactive-retroactive interference situations in mind as you study this section. It can be expected that the influences in the learning setting will be similar. Because of this similarity, we will focus on the proactive situation since it is the most common concern for those involved with teaching motor skills.

What Conditions Affect Transfer of Learning?

We will consider only three of the many conditions that seem to affect both the amount and the direction of the transfer of learning that can occur in motor learning. These conditions are the similarities of the components of the skills and/or the context in which skills are performed, the complexity and organization of the skills, and the amount and type of previous experiences. These

three conditions are especially important because the influence they exert on transfer situations is such that the amount and direction of transfer can be greatly affected by any of them. Each of these conditions will be discussed briefly here. They will be discussed in more detail in several of the concepts in Chapter 9. The introduction of these conditions here should help you to better understand some of the theoretical bases for many of the practical suggestions made in the next chapter.

One additional transfer situation to be considered in this section will be negative transfer. Because the negative transfer situation is somewhat unique, it will be helpful to consider separately those conditions that influence negative transfer and those that influence positive transfer, which is the focus of the three conditions discussed first in this section.

Motor skill and context components. Practically all of the motor skills that you will be teaching will be rather complex; that is, they will have many component parts. If you consider the constituents of a complex motor skill, such as a tennis serve, you will find that there are about seven component parts. These are usually considered to be the stance, grip, ball toss, backswing, forward swing, ball contact, and follow-through. Each of these can be further subdivided into several component structures. When two skills are compared in terms of the amount of transfer that will occur, the similarity of the components of the two skills plays a vital role. Likewise, based on the discussion in Concept 5.3 of context effects on memory performance, we can expect that the similarity beween two different performance situations will also influence the degree of transfer that can be expected. That is, *the higher the degree of similarity between the component parts of two skills or two performance situations, the greater the amount of positive transfer that can be expected between them.* Thus, we would expect that the amount of transfer between the tennis serve and volleyball serve would be greater than between the tennis serve and racquetball serve. We would likewise expect that practice conditions that emphasized performance characteristics similar to those that are required in a game would lead to a high degree of transfer. Hitting a tennis ball from a ball machine should lead to a high degree of transfer to rallying with another player because the skills required to be successful in these two performance situations have many components in common. Keep this latter point in mind as it will be very relevant to the discussion of the practicing of motor skills in Concept 9.4.

Complexity and organization of a motor skill. The complexity of a motor skill or task can be operationally defined as the number of component parts of the task and the information-processing demands of the task. *Complexity* of the task increases as the number of task components and the information-processing demands increase. *Organization* of a motor task is concerned with the interrelations of the parts of a skill. These two characteristics of motor

skills combine to be very influential in the amount of transfer that can be expected to occur between two tasks. In the research literature, the influence of the motor skill characteristics on transfer of learning has been considered in experiments concerned with *task difficulty* and transfer. That is, does more transfer occur when practicing a difficult task first and then a simple one or vice versa? This question seems especially important when we consider the transfer question in terms of intratask transfer.

Intratask transfer is involved when two variations of the same task or skill are involved. A *difficult-to-easy transfer situation,* for example, would be shooting a basketball at a goal that has a smaller than normal rim size and then determining the effects of that type of practice on shooting at a normal size goal. An example of an *easy-to-difficult transfer situation* would be when students in archery begin to learn archery at a target only 10 yards from the shooting line and then move back to a target 40 yards away. How much transfer can be expected in these types of common practice situations?

Both of the situations just cited have been used as bases of a research investigation into this very question. Singer (1966b), for example, found positive transfer effects in archery when students began at a short distance and moved to a longer distance. However, he also found positive transfer effects moving from a longer to a shorter distance in practice. In fact, no difference was found in ultimate archery success between these two practice methods.

Predictions about the facilitating effect of an easy-to-difficult or a difficult-to-easy practice condition on the learning of a motor skill can be made rather confidently when the organization and complexity characteristics of the skill to be learned are taken into consideration. A skill that is relatively high in complexity and relatively low in organization will benefit from prior practice that is based on a variation of the skill that is easier than that skill itself. In other words, the easy-to-difficult order will be most beneficial in that maximum transfer can be expected. Besides the short-to-long distance practice in archery, the lead-up game examples in the application section also can be considered a means of applying the easy-to-difficult transfer situation. On the other hand, a skill that is relatively low in complexity but high in organization can be expected to benefit from the difficult-to-easy order of practice, as in the example of the basketball rim size and basketball shooting. In a different context in Concept 9.4, we will consider the complexity and organization of a motor skill as it relates to practice.

Previous experiences. The concept of previous experiences as it relates to influencing transfer must be thought of as involving experiences prior to exposure to the task currently being learned as well as experiences involved in practicing the skill being learned. It should be obvious that the basis of movement education is the expectation that experiences with a wide variety of basic movement patterns will positively transfer to learning more specific physical

activities. Similarly, practice conditions are structured on the basis of providing the essential experiences necessary to being able to perform the skill in a test situation. Since both of these points are related to important practice concerns, we will not discuss them further at this point but will consider them in detail in the next chapter. However, as a preliminary step to studying the next chapter, it is important to consider the effectiveness of any practice condition in terms of the positive transfer that can be observed between the practice and the eventual test situation.

Negative transfer. We must qualify the generalization that the larger the number of similar components between two tasks or two performance situations, the more positive the transfer. This qualification is important to account for the negative transfer situation. While it has been argued that negative transfer effects are rare in motor learning (e.g., Annett & Sparrow, 1985; Schmidt, 1987), it is important to keep in mind what the negative transfer experience involves. The essential argument that negative transfer is rare refers to the actual movement control parameters involved in motor performance. That is, it is argued that what are typically observed as negative transfer effects are essentially cognitive rather than motor. The influence is not on the actual control parameters directing the movement. While this may be the case, and most research seems to support such a view, it does not diminish the need to consider negative transfer effects in motor learning situations. For the person who must teach motor skills, the need is to be aware of what may influence their occurrence as well as to determine how to deal with them in the instructional setting.

How, then, do we account for negative transfer effects? The most plausible explanation appears to be that *negative transfer effects occur when a new response is required for an old stimulus.* Two response conditions seem to be especially susceptible to negative transfer effects. These are involved when the *spatial locations* of a response must change in responding to the same stimulus and when the *timing* characteristics of the response must change when responding to the same stimulus. Two experiments illustrate these conditions.

In an experiment reported many years ago by Siipola (1941), subjects were required to learn to move a lever into one of 10 slots in response to a numbered stimulus, with the numbers 1 through 10. After learning this task as criterion, the subjects were required to learn a new but similar task. The second task required the same type of response as the first, except that the response to stimulus number 3 was now to move the lever to the slot that had been the response to number 7 in the first task. Also, the response to number 4 was to be the response that had been to number 8 in the first task. As expected, considerable negative transfer effects were noted in the learning of the second task. Thus, requiring a new spatial location response to an old stimulus produced negative transfer effects.

In an experiment demonstrating negative transfer effects for timing characteristics of a response, Summers (1975) required subjects to learn a sequential finger-tapping task. Subjects learned to execute a particular sequence of nine key presses. Each key press-to-key press interval required a specified criterion time. Following many practice trials, subjects were able to produce the correct sequence and timing structure from memory. Then subjects were told to produce the same sequential response but to do it as quickly as possible, thus ignoring the just-learned timing structure. While subjects were able to perform the entire sequence more rapidly, they were not able to overcome the learned timing structure. That is, they could speed up the entire task but the key press-to-key press intervals showed a similar relationship structure as had been characteristic of the learned sequence. While these results have important implications for what motor programs are like (discussed in Concept 3.4), they also show how timing components of a learned skill influence the performance of a modification of the response of that skill.

These experiments illustrate the essential point that if you must produce a new response to a familiar stimulus, you will probably experience negative transfer effects in teaching motor skills. First, negative transfer effects can be caused by *confusion*. In the Siipola experiment, the transfer task conditions undoubtedly led to subjects' confusion concerning which lever response went with which stimulus number. This is similar to the experience of having to type on a typewriter that is different from the one with which you are familiar. Typewriters often vary in their placement of certain keys, such as the backspace or margin release. When you first begin typing on the new machine, you have difficulty with these keys. The problem is not with your limb control but with the confusion created by the novel position of the keys.

The second point is that negative transfer effects are typically *temporary*. Depending on the task itself, the negative transfer effects can be overcome rather quickly. In the typewriter example, you find that after just a little practice, you are no longer bothered by the different key locations.

Teachers of motor skills need to be aware that when students are required to make new responses to old stimuli, they will have some initial difficulty in performing the skill. In such cases, it is important for the teacher to direct the students' attention to the parts of the skill where the negative transfer effects are occurring. With their attention directed specifically at those parts of the skill and with practice, students can overcome the negative transfer effects.

Why Does Transfer Occur?

Throughout the discussion of this concept, you have seen evidence that transfer occurs in motor skill learning and performance. The question that remains to be addressed is, Why does transfer occur? The conditions affecting transfer considered in the previous section do not provide an answer to this question, rather only provide important circumstances that give us insight into why transfer occurs. Perhaps the most disturbing aspect of answering this question

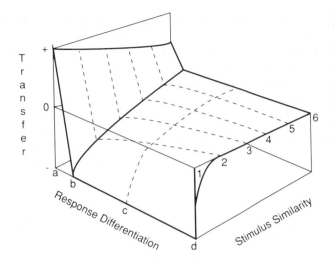

Figure 8.1-1
The transfer surface
proposed by
Holding (1976)
showing the
expected transfer
between two tasks
in terms of the
similarity or
difference of
characteristics of
stimulus and
response aspects of
the skills. Maximum
positive transfer is
predicted when the
stimulus and
response
characteristics are
identical, whereas
negative transfer is
predicted when the
stimuli for the two
tasks are identical
but the two
responses are
completely different
from each other.

is that general agreement is lacking among motor learning scholars. However, two possible answers seem to be the most prominently presented in the current motor learning literature. Both of these views emphasize the similarity of conditions between the previous experience and the new response situation, although they differ in terms of what about this similarity is critical to explain transfer.

Similarity of skill and context components. The first view, and the more traditional of the two, argues that transfer is due to the similarity of components between two skills or between two performance situations. This explanation has its roots in the early work of Thorndike (1914), who proposed his *identical elements theory* to account for transfer effects. To Thorndike, identical elements had a very broad meaning. "Elements" could refer to such general characteristics as the purpose of the response or the attitude related to the performance, or to such specific characteristics as particular components of the skill being performed. In fact, Thorndike considered identical elements to be mental processes that shared the same brain cell action as the physical action correlate.

   Later work by Osgood (1949) modified the Thorndike view by proposing that the amount and direction of transfer is related to the similarity of the stimulus and the response aspects of two tasks. To formalize this relationship, Osgood developed a "transfer surface" that provided a means for determining what type and amount of transfer to expect given the stimulus and response characteristics of two verbal tasks. Thus, the more similar both the stimuli and responses are, the more transfer will occur between the tasks. This "transfer surface" approach was extended to motor skills by Holding (1976) and is illustrated in Figure 8.1–1. Holding viewed this "surface" as a "loose predictive device" that could be suitably applied to instructional needs if it was

broadly interpreted. Notice that maximum positive transfer is predicted when the stimulus (S) and the response (R) for one task is the same as for the second task, and that as the stimuli decrease in similarity, transfer progresses toward 0.

More recently, this view of transfer focusing on the similarity of components of the skill or performance context has surfaced in the literature explaining memory effects. As you may recall from the discussion in Concept 5.3, Tulving's *encoding specificity* view of retention effects for episodic memory emphasizes the relationship between the encoding context and the retrieval context. That is, when the context at the presentation of the to-be-remembered item is reinstated at the retention test for that item, retention will be better than when these two contexts are less similar.

Similarity of processing requirements. The alternative view to the similarity of skill or context components view argues that rather than focusing on the similarity of these components, the focus should be on the similarity of cognitive processing characteristics required by the two skills or two performance situations. Work by John Bransford and colleagues (Morris, Bransford, & Franks, 1977; Bransford, Franks, Morris, & Stein, 1979) has promoted what they have termed the *transfer-appropriate-processing* view of explaining transfer effects. They argued that although similarity of skill and context components may explain some transfer effects, many transfer effects cannot be explained by such a view. For example, if a novel response must be performed in a new context, a similarity view is weak in handling this situation since similarity is minimal; yet, certain previous experiences can yield better novel response transfer performance than other previous experiences. These previous beneficial experiences do not require that the skills involved be more similar to the transfer skill, but, more important, that the cognitive processes required by the two skills be similar. More recently, Kolers & Roediger (1984) have argued a similar view that what accounts for transfer between practice and test or between two skills is the similarity of the "procedures" required by the two situations or skills. In fact, they argued that many transfer effects in motor learning could be accounted for by invoking this "procedures" explanation.

An experiment by Damos and Wickens (1980) provides an example of this view. Two different cognitive training tasks were used. One was a classification task in which subjects were presented with two digits simultaneously that could differ in either size or name. Subjects were required to determine the number of dimensions on which the two stimuli were alike. The second training task was a short-term memory task in which subjects were presented between one and four digits in a sequence. Subjects had to respond by recalling the next to the last digit in the sequence, thus they were required to hold the next to the last digit in memory and respond when the last digit appeared. Subjects never knew which digit was the next to the last or last until the last

digit appeared. The transfer task was a motor task called a compensatory tracking task. Subjects saw a moving circle on the video screen. Their task was to keep this circle centered in a horizontal bar that was also on the screen by making left to right movements with a control stick. At the same time on the screen there was a moving vertical bar that had to be moved up and down on the screen to keep it in contact with a constant horizontal line. This task was also controlled by a control stick. One control stick for each task was in each hand of the subjects.

Three groups of subjects were used in this experiment. One group received training with both the cognitive dual tasks. A second group received training on only one of the cognitive dual tasks, while a third group received no training on either cognitive dual task. All three groups performed the compensatory tracking task. Notice that in terms of task or context components, there is minimal to no similarity between the training and test tasks. The commonality of these situations is that both require attention-capacity time-sharing, which can be considered a cognitive process. Thus, if the similarity of skill and context components view more accurately explains transfer, then the group that had no practice on the cognitive tasks should not be at a disadvantage when they begin performing the tracking task and further, should do as well at tracking as the other groups. On the other hand, if the similarity of processing view more adequately explains transfer, then the group that had training with two of the cognitive dual tasks should do the best when transferred to the tracking task. The results supported this second view as the group that practiced both cognitive dual tasks performed the tracking task better than the other two training groups. The transfer benefit in this experiment was due to the transfer of the timesharing cognitive process.

Much is still unknown about what causes transfer of learning. There is evidence to support both currently held views of why transfer occurs. More than likely, the processing view may be an extension of the components view and may come into play only when skill components and context similarities are minimal, while processing activities are highly similar. But, as Schmidt and Young (1987) concluded in their extensive review of transfer in motor skills, we do not know very much about what accounts for the transfer phenomenon. Much more work is needed to answer the question of *why* transfer occurs.

Summary

Transfer of learning is a concept of learning that involves the influence of previous experiences on the learning of a new skill. The influence of the previous experience may either facilitate, hinder, or have no effect on the learning of the new skill. The transfer of learning concept is especially important in education as the basis for curriculum development and instructional methodology decisions and as the basis for making inferences in motor learning research about the influence of practice conditions on learning motor skills. The amount and direction of transfer can be influenced by many factors, of

which three were discussed. The similarities and differences in the components of motor skills will influence transfer. Generally, the greater the component similarity between two skills or between two performance situations, the greater the positive transfer from one skill to another. However, negative transfer effects can occur when a new response is required for a familiar stimulus. These effects are typically cognitively based and are relatively temporary. The complexity and organization of a skill can influence transfer of learning especially in terms of practice conditions related to intratask transfer. Finally, previous experiences influence transfer. These experiences include those prior to initiating practice of a new skill as well as those related to practice conditions involved in learning a new skill.

Related Readings

Annett, J., & Sparrow, J. (1985). Transfer of training: A review of research and practical implications. *Programmed Learning and Educational Technology, 22,* 116–124.

Ellis, H. C. (1965). *The transfer of training.* New York: Macmillan.

Fischman, M. G., Christina, R. W., & Vercruyssen, M. J. (1981). Retention and transfer of motor skills: A review for the practitioner. *Quest, 33,* 181–194.

Livesey, J. P., & Laszlo, J. I. (1979). Effect of task similarity on transfer performance. *Journal of Motor Behavior, 11,* 11–21.

Schmidt, R. A., & Young, D. E. (1987). Transfer of movement control in motor skill learning. In S. M. Cormier & J. D. Hagman (Eds.), *Transfer of learning,* pp. 47–49. Orlando, FL: Academic Press.

Singer, R. N. (1966). Transfer effects and ultimate success in archery due to degree of difficulty of the initial learning. *Research Quarterly, 37,* 532–539.

Transfer of learning can be expected to occur between the same limbs when only one limb has been actively involved in practice

Beginning basketball players are told that it will be an advantage to them to learn to dribble the ball with either hand. Similarly, young soccer players are encouraged to learn to shoot or kick the ball with either foot. These examples seem to indicate that in many sport activities, bilateral skill development is an important aspect of the training process. However, our own experiences tell us that we seldom use both limbs in practice with equal emphasis. More often than not, the young basketball player becomes very adept at dribbling with his or her right or left hand and remains relatively poor at dribbling with the other hand. The same is too often the case with the beginning soccer player.

Perhaps there are some reasons for this situation. The learning of sport skills is very often restricted by the amount of time available for instruction or practice. Add to that the often strong feeling by the young learner of wanting to be successful at the skill. Such factors combine to suggest that the novice, when given a choice, will emphasize the limb with which he or she feels most comfortable. Generally, that limb will be the one that will provide the greatest opportunity for quick success. The other limb remains largely ignored until the player becomes involved in situations where a lack of bilateral competence becomes a distinct liability.

Obviously, the most reasonable way to solve the problem would be to provide equal practice with both limbs. But some practical problems often overlooked intervene to make this solution less than desirable or possible. One problem is the availability of time for instruction and practice. If time is limited, the student will generally attempt to attain as high a level of success as possible during the time available. Since success is usually not measured by a criterion emphasizing skill with both arms and feet, emphasis on practicing with only one limb seems quite logical to the student. A second problem relates to an unavoidable dilemma that is too often created by the student: quite simply, he or she does not want to devote an equal amount of time to practice with each limb.

In the following discussion, we will consider a possible alternative solution to situations such as these by discussing an intriguing phenomenon known as bilateral transfer. We will consider evidence which shows that improvement is possible in a limb even though it has had little if any practice. The intent will be to provide a rational basis on which to make a decision about how to design instruction to promote optimal bilateral skill development when equal practice of each limb does not seem to be a practical alternative.

Discussion   The ability to learn a particular skill more easily with one hand or foot after the skill has been learned with the opposite hand or foot is related to what is known as *bilateral transfer.* Bilateral transfer is based on the principle discussed in Concept 8.1: learning transfers in some degree from previously learned skills to new skills so that the new skill is in reality not totally new to the learner. When we consider bilateral transfer, the focus is on the transfer of learning *between limbs rather than between tasks.* Here we will be generally involved with learning the same task but with different limbs, that is from arm to arm and from leg to leg.

It has been well documented in physiology that there can be a gain in strength in an unpracticed extremity or limb as a result of training of that limb's contralateral muscle group. Such evidence has existed as far back as the late nineteenth century. We want to know whether similar effects are found in the area of skill acquisition. Do these bilateral transfer effects that are so well documented in physiological situations occur also in motor skill learning situations? To answer that question, we will discuss some evidence which indicates that bilateral transfer does indeed occur in the motor skill learning situation. Then, we will consider some of the reasons why the bilateral transfer phenomenon occurs. Finally, in order to give this discussion practical significance, we will suggest how this information gives us a basis for providing instruction to promote bilateral skill development.

Evidence for Bilateral Transfer   Experiments that have been designed to determine whether bilateral transfer does indeed occur have followed similar experimental designs. The most typical design has been the following:

	Pretest	Practice Trials	Posttest
Preferred Limb	X	X	X
Nonpreferred Limb	X		X

This design allows the experimenter to determine whether bilateral transfer occurred from practice with the preferred limb to the nonpreferred limb, which had not practiced the task. If the question of interest is the amount of bilateral transfer from practice with the nonpreferred limb to the preferred limb, then the preferred limb/nonpreferred limb arrangement in this design would be reversed. Thus, the analyses of interest are to determine the pretest to posttest gains for each limb, then to compare these gains. It would be expected that the practiced limb should show the greatest gain or improvement. However, it should also be expected that a significant improvement in performance was made by the limb not used in practice. In that case, the obvious conclusion would be that bilateral transfer had occurred.

Research support for bilateral transfer. Investigation of the bilateral transfer phenomenon was very widespread during the 1930s through the 1950s. In fact, the bulk of evidence supporting the bilateral transfer of motor skills can be

found in the psychology journals of that period. One of the more prominent investigators of the bilateral transfer phenomenon during the early part of that era was T. W. Cook. From 1933 to 1936, Cook published a series of five articles relating to the various concerns of bilateral transfer, or cross education as he called it. He terminated this work by indicating that the evidence was sufficiently conclusive to support the notion that bilateral transfer does indeed occur for motor skills. Very few experiments published since those by Cook have investigated the question of the occurrence of the bilateral transfer phenomenon. That fact seems to be well accepted. The literature since the 1930s has been directed more toward other issues related to bilateral transfer, such as reminiscence, practice distribution, the overload principle, fatigue, the direction of the most transfer, as well as determining why bilateral transfer occurs and what this means in terms of underlying processes involved in the learning and control of skills.

Symmetry vs. asymmetry of bilateral transfer. One of the more intriguing questions concerning the bilateral transfer effect concerns the direction of this type of transfer. The question here is whether a greater amount of bilateral transfer occurs from one limb to the other (termed *asymmetric transfer*), or whether the amount of transfer is similar from one limb to the other (termed *symmetric transfer*). Reasons for investigating this question are theoretical as well as practical. From a theoretical perspective, knowing if bilateral transfer is symmetric or asymmetric would provide insight into the role of how the two cerebral hemispheres control movement. That is, do the two hemispheres play similar or different roles in movement control? A more practical reason for investigating this question relates to the issue of designing practice to facilitate optimal skill performance with either limb. If asymmetric transfer predominates, then this would suggest that training with one limb should always be done before training with the other, whereas if symmetric transfer predominates, it would not make any difference which limb was trained first.

The generally accepted view about the direction of bilateral transfer is that it is *asymmetric*. But, there seems to be some controversy concerning whether this asymmetry favors initial preferred or nonpreferred limb practice. Ammons (1958), in a comprehensive review of the bilateral transfer research completed prior to 1958, concluded that greater transfer can be expected to occur from the preferred limb to the nonpreferred limb. However, more recently, evidence appears to favor the opposite direction for greater transfer. For example, Taylor and Heilman (1980) showed that for a complex finger-sequencing task, initial training with the nonpreferred hand (the left hand for subjects in this experiment) led to greater transfer to the preferred hand than did the opposite practice and transfer schedule. Interestingly, subjects in this experiment were not permitted to see their hands while performing. When subjects were able to see their hands, the transfer was symmetric. Support for the asymmetric transfer direction of nonpreferred to preferred limb, even with

vision available, was provided more recently by Elliott (1985) using a sequential finger-tapping task similar to the one used by Taylor and Heilman.

It seems clear, then, that the direction of bilateral transfer is asymmetric. What is not clear is whether more transfer occurs following initial practice with the preferred or the nonpreferred limb. Perhaps one way of rectifying this issue is to consider the types of tasks used when one direction was supported over the other. The one clear distinction here is that when nonpreferred to preferred limb transfer showed a greater amount of transfer, the tasks required a complex sequencing of events, or parts of a complex skill. In terms of applying this result to designing effective instruction, the suggestion is that if the skill being taught is a complex one that has several parts that must be sequenced in a specific order, more bilateral transfer will occur if initial training is with the nonpreferred limb. However, it would appear that when other factors are taken into account, such as motivation related to initial process, this direction of transfer conclusion may not be as critical from a practical perspective as it is from a theoretical one.

The Cause of Bilateral Transfer

While the cause of bilateral transfer remains unknown, two possible reasons of why bilateral transfer occurs are noteworthy. The first, a *cognitive* explanation, postulates that the common elements of the tasks that must be performed by the two limbs underlie the transfer phenomenon (Ammons, 1958). This explanation must be considered as being based on the "identical elements" theory suggested by Thorndike, which was discussed earlier. A skill being performed with one limb and then the other can be considered to be almost two distinct skills. Throwing a ball at a target with the right hand is a different task from throwing a ball with the left hand. However, elements of these skills are common to both regardless of the hand being used. For example, the arm-leg opposition principle is similar to the need to keep your eyes focused on the target and to follow through. If you achieve proficiency at the task with the right hand, then these common elements do not need to be relearned when you begin practicing with the left hand. You should begin at a higher level of proficiency with the left hand than you would have if there had been no practice with the right hand. Thus, the cognitive components of the task being learned, which involve much of the beginning learner's attention (recall the stages of learning discussion in Concept 2.2) have been adequately learned *before* practice with the opposite limb begins.

A cognitive explanation. Some support for a cognitive basis for bilateral transfer was provided in a series of experiments by Kohl and Roenker (1980). In the second experiment, which is representative of the overall findings, subjects were divided into three groups. The physical practice group practiced a pursuit rotor task (60 rpm's for 30 seconds) with their right hand for 18 trials. The mental imagery group held the stylus with their right hand and, with eyes

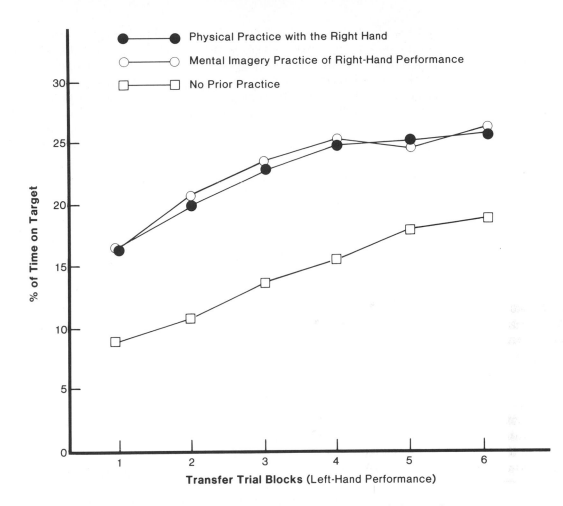

Figure 8.2-1
Transfer trial results from the experiments by Kohl and Roenker. Shown here are the performances of three groups experiencing different practice conditions during the preceding 18 trials.

closed, imaged themselves tracking the target for 18 trials (they had observed the experimenter perform one trial prior to these imagery trials). The third group, the control group, had no right-hand practice or imagery practice and did not see the apparatus until the transfer trials. Following these practice conditions, all three groups practiced on the pursuit rotor with their left hand for 18 trials. As can be seen in Figure 8.2–1, the physical practice and mental imagery practice groups performed similarly on the transfer trials. Both groups performed better than the control group. These results indicate the cognitive nature of bilateral transfer.

A motor control explanation. The second possible basis for bilateral transfer is a *motor control* explanation. Hicks, Gualtieri, and Schroeder (1983) argue that at least some bilateral transfer of skill is meditated by interhemispheric

transfer of the motor components of the task. One way of demonstrating this is by measuring the EMG activity in all four limbs when one limb makes a response. Results from earlier research by Davis (1942) indicated that the greatest amount of EMG activity is for the contralateral limbs (i.e., the two arms), a lesser amount for the ipsilateral limbs (i.e., arm and leg on the same side), and the least amount for the diagonal limbs.

Additionally, Hicks, Frank, and Kinsbourne (1982) showed that when subjects practiced a typing task with one hand, there was bilateral transfer only when the other hand was free. When the nontyping hand grasped the table leg during typing, no bilateral transfer effects were observed. These results were interpreted to indicate that when the control centers for the muscles that will be involved in the test trials are otherwise engaged, as they were when the fingers were flexed to grasp the table leg, those centers are unavailable for the "central overflow of programming" that goes on during an action.

One additional way of considering the bilateral transfer effect from a motor control perspective is to relate the effect to the concept of the generalized motor program discussed in Concept 3.4. The generalized motor program is characterized as a memory representation responsible for the control of a class of movements or actions. A key feature of the program is that the muscles required to produce an action are *not* represented in the motor program. Muscles are a *parameter* of the program that get added to the program according to what muscles are required to achieve the goal of the intended action. You may recall from the discussion in Concept 3.4 that such a program and parameter view provided a way to explain our capability to write our name with a pen in our preferred hand as well as with some other limb or even with a pen held between our teeth. It seems reasonable, therefore, to expect that the bilateral transfer should occur given this view of a generalized motor program. Because the program develops for a skill as a result of practice, and because the program does not include muscle information, it would be expected that after sufficient program development has occurred, performance with a nonpracticed limb would be possible. Due to other factors, such as perceptual, biomechanical, and specificity of training problems, initial performance with the nonpracticed limb would not be expected to be as good as performance with the practiced limb. However, this initial performance can be expected to be better than if there had been no practice at all with the other limb.

It appears, then, that bilateral transfer effects are the results of *both* cognitive and motor factors. For the teacher of motor skills, the next important question concerns how to take advantage of the bilateral transfer phenomenon and implement it into the instructional setting. This question is considered next.

Facilitating bilateral skill development for many motor skills is an important responsibility of the instructor. We discussed earlier several situations in which this type of development is essential. We concluded that consideration with the recommendation that equal amounts of practice with both limbs in a particular skill is not a practical means of achieving bilateral skill development. Furthermore, the evidence we have just discussed indicates that this equal practice approach is not a necessary solution.

Two key points based on our earlier discussions of motor learning and control theory can be used to provide a defensible approach to take for organizing an effective practice schedule to enhance bilateral training in motor skills. First, we established early in this text that the first stage of learning a motor skill is cognitively oriented. Second, it is generally agreed that motor skills are controlled by a generalized motor program that represents actions without including muscle information. When these two points are taken together and applied to the question of what is an appropriate practice schedule to develop effective bilateral training, a very specific conclusion results. That is, early practice sessions should concentrate on the development of a reasonable degree of skill performance proficiency with one limb before practice begins with the other limb. By achieving some level of proficiency, the individual will have answered most of the cognitive questions that need to be answered in early practice and will have developed a motor program for the practiced action to a point where skill refinement becomes the goal of practice.

Although there is some controversy about which limb should be practiced first, it seems that a reasonable argument can be made for initiating practice with the student's preferred limb. The basis for this argument comes from the importance of initial success in motivating the student to continue trying to learn the skill (a point to be discussed further in Chapter 10), the benefit of establishing practice conditions in which the student can attain a degree of confidence in his or her capability of learning the skill, and the need to provide a practice environment where perceptual and cognitive confusion will be minimal. Each of these characteristics can be enhanced by initiating practice with the student's preferred limb. By adopting this approach to bilateral skill development, an effective as well as efficient means of learning should result.

There is, in fact, research evidence to support the practice schedule organizaton recommended here for bilateral skill training. For example, in an experiment by Dunham (1977), subjects practiced a pursuit rotor task (20 rpm for 20 seconds) according to either a "sequence" order of right and left hand practice, or a "serial" order of practice. In the sequence order, subjects practiced with the preferred hand until a score of 70% on target (14 seconds out of 20) for two consecutive trials was achieved. When this criterion was

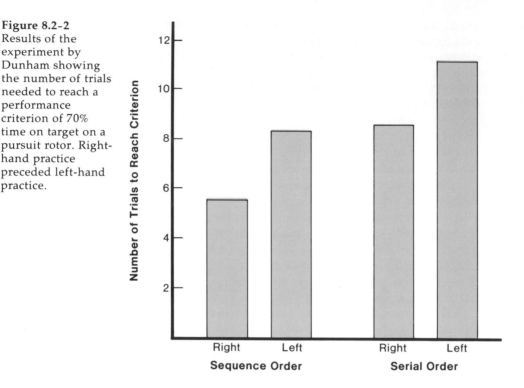

Figure 8.2-2
Results of the experiment by Dunham showing the number of trials needed to reach a performance criterion of 70% time on target on a pursuit rotor. Right-hand practice preceded left-hand practice.

reached, the subjects transferred to the opposite hand and practiced until they achieved the same 70% criterion with that hand. The serial order group alternated hands until each 70% criterion was achieved by each hand. The results, seen in Figure 8.2–2, show that the sequential order group achieved criterion performance with both hands in fewer trials than the serial order group. These results indicate that bilateral transfer occurs faster when one limb is practiced to a reasonable degree of proficiency before practice is begun with the opposite limb.

Summary

Bilateral transfer of learning involves the improvement in performance of one limb as a result of practice with the opposite limb. Many motor skills, such as dribbling a basketball or kicking a soccer ball, require bilateral skill development. This can be facilitated by combining what we have previously discussed about the stages of learning with the evidence that has been reported about bilateral transfer. Early practice should be oriented toward development of proficiency with the preferred limb. After a degree of proficiency has been developed with that limb, practice with the nonpreferred limb can be included in the practice sessions.

The Learning Environment

Ammons, R. B. (1958). Le mouvement. In G. H. Steward and J. P. Steward (Eds.), *Current psychological issues.* New York: Holt, Rinehart & Winston.

Dunham, P., Jr. (1977). Effect of practice order on the efficiency of bilateral skill acquisition. *Research Quarterly, 48,* 254–287.

Elliott, D. (1985). Manual asymmetrics in the performance of sequential movements by adolescents and adults with Down's Syndrome. *American Journal of Mental Deficiency, 90,* 90–97.

Hicks, R. E., Gualtieri, C. T., & Schroeder, S. R. (1983). Cognitive and motor components of bilateral transfer. *American Journal of Psychology, 96,* 223–228.

Kohl, R. M., & Roenker, D. L. (1980). Bilateral transfer as a function of mental imagery. *Journal of Motor Behavior, 12,* 197–206.

Laszlo, J. I., & Baguley, R. A. (1971). Motor memory and bilateral transfer. *Journal of Motor Behavior, 3,* 235–240.

Related Readings

Concept 8.3 Transfer of learning potential in teaching can be maximized by the instructor of motor skills

Application

It has been emphasized in the two preceding concepts that the principle of transfer of learning is vitally important in education. Both curriculum development and instructional methodologies have been shown to be based on the transfer principle. It seems rather apparent that the teacher of motor skills would be greatly remiss if he or she neglected to apply this principle. Attention must be given to applying the transfer of learning principle to teaching methods and course development since such principles may be neglected and not used in their maximum potential. The instructor who involves children in playing baseball before having adequately developed such fundamental motor skills as throwing, catching, running, or striking is doing the child a grave injustice. Similarly, an instructor of racquet sports would be remiss in ignoring transfer principles when teaching a new activity like squash to a group who has had considerable experience playing racquet ball. A great deal of time would be poorly spent if the instructor failed to emphasize to the students the similarities and differences of the two activities, since this emphasis would greatly facilitate the learning of the new activity.

While it is relatively easy to emphasize the need to apply the concepts or principles of transfer of learning to the instructional process, it may be more difficult for the person who needs to apply the principles to actually do so. A common complaint among students in education is that their textbooks do not give them enough specifics about *how* to apply the concepts and principles that the books have been recommending. This complaint can be avoided here by devoting discussion to some specific suggestions about how to maximize the potential of the transfer of learning principles in the teaching of motor skills.

Discussion

An excellent work entitled *The Transfer of Training* was written by Henry C. Ellis and published in 1965. A major contribution of that book was the concise and understandable presentation of the many facets of the study of transfer of learning. One of these aspects was the application of the principle of transfer to teaching. In a section of the book that Ellis titled "Teaching for Transfer," he presented several "guidelines for teaching so that what is taught is more likely to transfer to new learning situations" (p. 70). Since Ellis illustrated these guidelines with examples from classroom instruction situations, we will consider these rules here by applying them more directly to the teaching of motor skills. It would be beneficial to you, as you read these guidelines and examples, to add some examples of your own. In this way, you can expand the use of this list to fit the motor skill teaching situation in which you will most likely be involved.

1. *Maximize the similarity between teaching and the ultimate testing situation.* The "ultimate testing situation" statement may need some clarification. What is meant here is the situation in which the learner will eventually or ultimately use what has been learned. It may be in an actual test, such as a skill test, or the eventual use may be in a game situation or in a working situation. Thus, this guideline recommends that teachers provide for similarity between the practice and the ultimate testing situations.

Let's consider some specific examples. A basketball player will be shooting free throws in a game situation where he or she will only be permitted one or two shots, or two if the first one is made. Thus, the basketball coach should provide conditions in practice where this situation will be confronted. To assume that because a player can make 8 out of 10 free throws in a practice drill that player will have little difficulty in making a one-and-one situation in a game may be an ill-founded assumption. Please note that the "how many can you make out of 10" type drill is not being criticized or discredited. It may be very valuable in teaching and reinforcing the free-throw shooting skill. However, practice that is similar to a game situation should *also* be included to maximize the transfer potential of that practice. Another example would be the use of recorded crowd noise to add to the reality of the practice situation.

A common usage in methods of teaching physical education classes is to have students teach a lesson plan to a group of their peers. Because these groups often are small in number, this presentation, while it may help a student to practice the implementation of a lesson plan, is only remotely related to what the student will confront in a real teaching situation in an elementary or secondary school. The obvious alternative would be to practice with elementary or secondary students. However, this is usually not a practical or possible solution. What is recommended is that the student teach a lesson plan to a large group and encourage the members to role-play at a certain grade level. Within practical limits this situation maximizes the similarity between the practice and what the student will be ultimately confronted with.

2. *Provide adequate experience with the original task.* Lead-up games are popular in most elementary school physical education curricula. Such preparatory games are very useful in teaching important skills that will eventually be used in a more complex physical activity. For example, Newcomb is a lead-up activity for volleyball, kickball is a lead-up game for baseball, and line soccer is a lead-up game for soccer. Each of these preliminary activities modifies some elements of the activity for which it is a lead-up. What the teacher should be aware of is that maximizing practice on the original task is directly related to the likelihood of positive transfer to a subsequent task.

Drills that are devoted to teaching fundamentals of activities should not be allotted too little time in practice. The more experience the tennis player has in practicing a single movement like the serve or the backhand, the greater the likelihood of realizing maximum performance with those skills in a full

game situation. Similarly, a ballet teacher cannot overemphasize the amount of practice time that is required at the barre, for it is there that the fundamentals are learned, fundamentals that will be applied to a variety of ballet routines.

3. *Provide for a variety of examples when teaching concepts and principles.* There are certain concepts or principles inherent in every sport or motor activity with which participants need to be familiar. It is essential for the outfielder to know the principle of always throwing ahead of the base runner. Concepts related to receiving service strategies are important in all racquet sports. Basketball players need some guiding principles to follow to help them know when to pass the basketball and when to keep it while driving for a basket. In each of these situations, the instructor can facilitate understanding of these principles or concepts by providing as many concrete examples as possible in a practice situation. Not only should the instructor arrange practice that involves examples of the principles, but practice should also include examples of situations where the concept should not be applied. For instance, there are situations in baseball where the outfielder should not throw ahead of the base runner.

Movement education is based on teaching "movement concepts." These have been very adequately presented in a book by Gallahue, Werner, and Luedke (1975). In this book, the fundamental motor skills of throwing, catching, striking, jumping, etc., are presented as movement concepts because they are the basic movements that are so generally applied in all complex motor skills. Likewise, such notions as space, time, and force are considered to be movement concepts because they too are involved in all complex motor skills. To maximize the transfer potential of these movement concepts to complex motor skills is a critical instructional problem for the movement education teacher. The guideline that we are considering would encourage movement education teachers to provide students with the maximum number of practice situations in which concrete examples of these movement concepts are used.

4. *Label or identify important features of a task.* This guideline indicates that when an activity is being taught for its transfer potential to a subsequent activity (such as a lead-up game or skill drill), the instructor should direct the students' attention to those elements of the activity that will most directly transfer to the subsequent activity. Thus, the tennis instructor who has a student hitting backhands from a ball machine should direct the student's attention to those elements of hitting the backhand that will be critical to the effective use of that skill in a game situation.

This guideline can also apply to identifying features of a new task that is being learned that are similar and therefore transferable from a previously learned skill. The dance student's progress in learning a contemporary dance can be facilitated if that individual is given instructions that indicate how this new dance is actually an adaptation of a dance that he or she has learned and performed previously.

5. *Make sure that general principles are understood before expecting much transfer.* In developing a gymnastics routine, certain guiding principles must be followed. These principles not only include certain regulations about the types of stunts that the routine should include but also involve the components related to the types of stunts that fit together in an orderly and coherent sequence. The gymnast who does not fully understand these guiding principles will encounter much difficulty and will need more coaching time than will the student who fully comprehends these principles.

Perhaps you can see a relationship between this guideline and guideline 3 which dealt with providing as many specific examples of a principle or concept as possible. Application of guideline 3 will be a very useful means of ensuring that guideline 5 is followed. The understanding of a concept or principle will be greatly enhanced by the presentation of a variety of examples where the concept can be applied. It is hoped that this guideline has been followed adequately in this presentation, for the basis of this textbook is the development of concepts or principles related to motor learning. The examples that have been provided with each concept have been purposely included to assist you in better understanding the meaning of each concept. It is intended, however, that through your study and comprehension of these motor learning concepts you will be capable of providing your own applications of these concepts when the need arises in a specific teaching or performing situation.

Summary

A series of guidelines for teaching that emphasize the use of transfer of learning principles has been presented and discussed in this concept. These guidelines, adapted from *The Transfer of Training* by Ellis (1965), have been generalized to apply to the motor skills instructional setting. The implementation of these guidelines for the instruction of motor skills should enhance the effectiveness and efficiency of that instruction.

Related Readings

Ellis, H. C. (1978). *Fundamentals of human learning, memory, and cognition.* Dubuque, IA: Wm. C. Brown Publishers. (Read pp. 246–276.)
Ellis, H. C. (1965). *The transfer of training.* New York: Macmillan. (Read pp. 70–72.)

Study Questions for Chapter 8 (Transfer of Learning)

1. Define transfer of learning. What are three types of transfer effects possible in motor skills? Give an example of each.
2. How can the transfer of learning principle be implemented in the development of curriculum for any subject matter and in instructional strategies used to teach motor skills?
3. Why is the use of transfer tests important for designing experiments investigating factors that influence motor skill learning?
4. How can *percentage of transfer* and *savings score* be used to determine the amount of (1) intertask transfer that has occurred and (b) intratask transfer that has occurred?

5. In what kind of motor skill situation can you expect negative transfer effects to occur? Identify two important points to remember about negative transfer effects as they relate to motor skills.

6. How are task complexity and task organization interrelated to be influential in the amount of transfer that can be expected between two tasks?

7. What are two reasons why positive transfer occurs? For each reason, describe an experiment that would test what each reason would predict for transfer in motor skills.

8. What is meant by the term "bilateral transfer"? What is an example of an experiment that could be designed to demonstrate bilateral transfer?

9. What is the issue involved in the question of symmetry vs. asymmetry of bilateral transfer? Why is this transfer issue important to address?

10. Discuss two explanations that have been proposed to explain why bilateral transfer occurs.

11. Give an example of when bilateral transfer is a concern in teaching motor skills. What seems to be the best approach to optimize the occurrence of bilateral transfer in these situations?

12. Give some examples of ways that teachers can help ensure that positive transfer will occur between the practice and a test of a skill being learned.

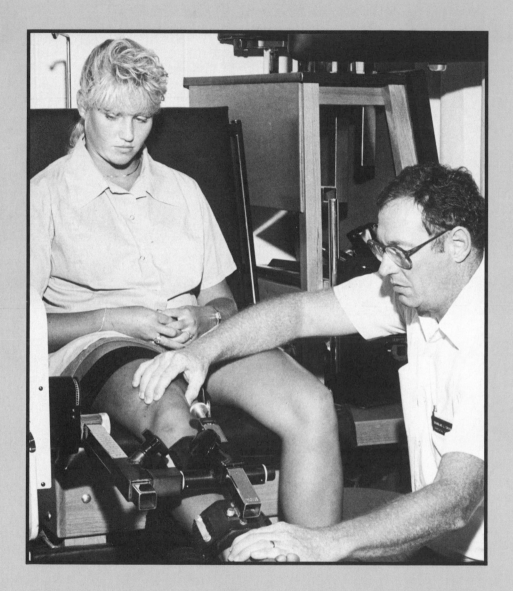

Practice

9

Concept 9.1
A variety of practice experiences is essential for learning both closed and open skills.

Concept 9.2
The amount of practice affects learning although the effect is not always proportional.

Concept 9.3
The spacing or distribution of practice can affect both practice performance and learning.

Concept 9.4
The decision to practice a motor skill as a whole or by parts should be made on the basis of the complexity and organization of the skill.

Concept 9.5
Modeling is an effective form of instruction for teaching motor skills.

Concept 9.6
Practice that occurs mentally can be beneficial for learning new motor skills and for preparing to perform a skill.

Concept 9.7
Practicing while being physically fatigued appears to affect performance to a greater degree than learning, although learning can be affected.

Concept 9.1 A variety of practice experiences is essential for learning both closed and open skills

Application

An important task for any instructor of motor skills is designing and establishing practice conditions that will lead to maximum test performance, whether the test be a game, a skill test, or any evaluation situation in which the practiced skill must be performed. One of the conditions of practice discussed earlier in this text was the need for variable practice experiences. Recall from the discussion of Schmidt's schema theory in Concept 2.3 that along with the amount of practice, a variety of practice experiences involving variations of the skill being learned is an essential condition for developing a motor response schema that can be successfully called upon in a variety of performance situations. One of the questions that can be asked here concerns *how* this needed variety in practice conditions can be effectively established to lead to the greatest potential for maximal test performance.

An immediate need is to determine how this variability of practice should be implemented for open and closed skills. This becomes apparent as you consider that open and closed skills are different with respect to how the performance conditions in practice relate to the conditions at the test. Closed skills, such as bowling or archery, can be practiced under conditions that are identical, or very similar, to those that will be faced in a test situation. On the other hand, open skills, such as hitting a pitched baseball or throwing a ball to a moving target, are always performed under conditions that are different from what has been experienced before. As a result, it is not possible to establish practice conditions that will be exactly like those confronted in a test situation. However, learning both closed and open skills will benefit from experiencing practice conditions that allow the learner to perform the skill in a variety of movement conditions. It seems, then, that because of the differences between open and closed skills, the way in which variability of practice experiences should be developed will require different approaches. In the discussion that follows, this issue will be addressed with the intent of providing some guidelines that you can use to establish effective practice conditions to take advantage of the benefit that variable experiences can provide.

Discussion

Some insight can be gained into the practice structure issue by considering a theoretical model of skill acquisition applied to teaching that was developed by Gentile (1972). An important concept in that presentation was the distinction between *regulatory* and *nonregulatory* stimuli or conditions. These terms refer to the conditions related to performing a skill that are either relevant or not relevant in establishing how the movement must be performed to achieve the desired goal of the movement. The idea behind the use of these

terms should not be new to you as you studied this situation in Concept 4.3 in the discussion about selective attention. Regulatory stimuli can be considered as movement-related information that must be attended to or taken into account if the goal of the movement is to be achieved. Nonregulatory stimuli include all other nonrelated environmental information.

To hit a racquetball in a rally, the regulatory information may include the opponent's position on the court, the speed of the ball, the angle and location of the rebound from the front wall, etc. If these pieces of information are not taken into account, chances of successfully returning the ball are greatly reduced. Nonregulatory information, on the other hand, includes information related to who is watching, what the opponent is wearing, type of racquet the opponent is using, etc. These factors, while they may be indirectly related to the response you will make, have little to do with setting the response output requirements that will enable you to produce the intended shot.

To develop appropriate practice conditions, it is first of all important to understand how the regulatory stimuli differ between closed and open skills. As you should recall from the discussion of Concept 1.1, closed skills require similar responses each time a response is required. In Gentile's terms, the "likelihood of change for the regulatory stimuli is close to zero" (p. 11). The performer can predict well in advance what the conditions will be like during the execution of the response. In contrast, open skills are performed under regulatory conditions that change during the movement execution and may vary from one attempt to the next. The performer is required to make rapid modifications in the plan of action in order to match the demands of the situation.

Variable practice and closed skills. Since the test conditions for a closed skill are stable and relatively predictable, Gentile indicates that the teacher should establish two conditions for practice. First, the students should practice under the same conditions as will prevail under the test situation. Second, the regulatory stimuli should be held constant while the nonregulatory stimuli should be varied in the practice conditions.

The Benefit of Variable Practice

These two points are supported by what you have already studied in this book. In the discussion of the practice-test relationship in Concept 5.3, you saw that increased remembering can be expected when the practice and test conditions are as similar as possible. At that time, it was stated that in terms of motor skills, this similarity situation seems especially pertinent to closed skills. Also, in the discussion in Concept 8.1, you saw that increased transfer from practice to test can be expected when the conditions are similar. Again, this holds especially for closed skills. Finally, Schmidt's schema theory established the need for variability of experiences. What Gentile's model provides is a guideline for establishing *what* needs to be varied in the practice conditions. That is, nonregulatory conditions rather than regulatory stimuli need to be varied in practice. Other conditions need to be as similar as possible to the test conditions to maximize the transfer effects.

The basketball free throw will serve as a good example here. Let's establish that there are two goals for the learner in this example. One, the learner needs to become proficient at successfully shooting a free throw. Two, the learner must learn to successfully shoot free throws in a game situation. These two goals suggest the type of practice conditions that should be established. On the one hand, there is a need to practice the free throw time after time in as constant a manner as possible. This holds constant the regulatory stimuli, such as hand placement, body position, etc. The goal is to learn the appropriate movement pattern that will consistently put the ball through the basket. On the other hand, to accomplish the game-related goal, it is important to incorporate game conditions into the practice routine. Two-shot free throws, one-and-one situations, and one-shot only situations must be practiced often. Similarly, the nonregulatory conditions, such as crowd noise, game score, time of game, etc., must be experienced and must be varied as much as possible to match the conditions that may be confronted in a game.

From this example, it is possible to see how variability of practice can be incorporated into practice conditions for closed skills. The variety of experiences must be developed around the nonregulatory conditions related to performing the skill under test conditions. For the regulatory conditions, similarity rather than variety of trial-to-trial experiences is the key.

Variable practice and open skills. The unique characteristic of open skills is that each response that must be produced is a novel one. That is, the response has probably not been produced in exactly the same way before. Something about the response conditions is unique and leads to the need to make some modification of previous responses. Examples of this were considered in the discussion of both Gentile's skill acquisition model and Schmidt's schema theory. That is, it is essential to vary the regulatory conditions related to the skill. As Gentile (1972) explained it, providing this variability of practice enables the performer to acquire the repertoire of motor patterns that match the possible responses that may be required.

Following the publication of Schmidt's schema theory in 1975, a number of studies were published that investigated the theory's variability of practice prediction as it relates to novel response production. While these studies typically were not conducted with open skills, they relate to the problem under consideration because they required subjects to produce a movement that had not been previously experienced. For this reason, a consideration of some of these studies will help provide some insight into the practice structure requirements for producing a novel response.

One study that did use an open skill task to test the variability of practice prediction was reported by Wrisberg and Ragsdale (1979). In their experiment, subjects practiced an anticipation timing task in which they were to depress a button to be coincident with the lighting of the last of a series of

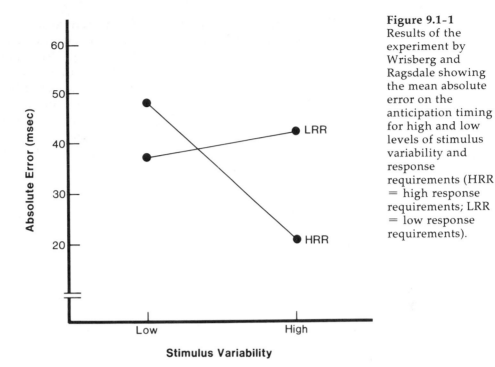

Figure 9.1-1
Results of the experiment by Wrisberg and Ragsdale showing the mean absolute error on the anticipation timing for high and low levels of stimulus variability and response requirements (HRR = high response requirements; LRR = low response requirements).

lights on a runway 29.5 cm long. Variability of practice conditions was developed for both stimulus and response characteristics of the task. The high stimulus-high response variability group practiced for 40 trials with velocities of 22.35, 31.29, 49.17, and 58.12 cm/sec. The high stimulus-low response variability group observed the same four speeds for 40 trials but did not make an overt response. The low stimulus-high response subjects overtly responded to a constant stimulus speed of one of the four speeds used for the high stimulus variability group. Finally, the low stimulus-low response group only observed a constant speed for 40 trials. All subjects were then required to respond to a novel speed of 40.23 cm/sec. Results are presented in Figure 9.1–1 and show that on the novel speed task, the subjects who were required to make an overt response and who had practiced the four different stimulus speeds were more accurate in responding to the novel speed.

The experiment by Wrisberg and Ragsdale (1979) is typical of the experiments supporting the variability of practice prediction concerning novel response performance. However, a different approach was taken in a study by Husak and Reeve (1979). They considered not only the variability of practice portion of the prediction, but they also tested an often forgotten part of the prediction, the amount of practice. Variability of previous practice experiences was manipulated by having subjects practice either one or three criterion locations on a linear positioning apparatus. Additionally, subjects in these two

variability of practice groups practiced for a total of 6, 18, or 36 trials. For the practice groups with three criterion locations, either 2, 6, or 12 trials of practice with KR were provided for each location. Subjects with one criterion location practiced 6, 18, or 36 trials at the one location. Following these practice trials, all subjects were required to move to a new location, that is, one they had not previously practiced. Results of this transfer task showed that the group that had experienced more variability of movement experiences along with the greatest number of practice trials performed better than the group in the other condition. These results indicate that while variability of practice is important for novel response success, the amount of practice given each experience during practice is also important.

Although some studies have not found that variable practice leads to superior novel response performance (e.g., Johnson & McCabe, 1982; Zelaznik, 1977), sufficient evidence exists to give us confidence in the variability of practice prediction. When a person is practicing a skill in which the test will be a novel response, an important requirement of the practice is that it provide a variety of experiences related to the skill being learned. As a result, a wide range of the varying regulatory stimuli will be experienced; this will enable the individual to develop a strong recall schema. From this schema, he or she can more accurately select the appropriate response required to execute a novel movement.

An education application of the variable practice benefit. An interesting application of the variability of practice component of Schmidt's (1975b) schema theory was made by Schmidt himself in an article published in 1977. He indicated that the approach taken in the typical movement education experience is well supported by the schema theory view of the benefit of practice variability. In a movement education class, students are encouraged to explore and experience a variety of ways to perform a skill. For example, students may be asked to find as many ways as possible to jump across two ropes lying on the floor as a means of allowing them to experience a variety of jumping movements. Or, they may experience throwing a variety of objects at different targets and use several different throwing patterns. The benefit of these types of experiences is that they serve to help develop a strong motor recall schema that can be called upon when the students must eventually produce a novel response. As such, these movement exploration experiences provide a foundation that will serve the students well when they must learn more specific skills, such as pitching a baseball.

Organizing Variable Practice

You have seen that variability is beneficial as a characteristic for practicing both closed and open skills. For closed skill practice, the need for variability is with the nonregulatory factors related to the movement. For open skills

		Class Day					
		1	2	3	4	5	6
Blocked Practice	10 min 10 min 10 min	All Overhand	All Overhand	All Underhand	All Underhand	All Sidearm	All Sidearm
Random Practice	10 min 10 min 10 min	Underhand Overhand Underhand	Sidearm Underhand Overhand	Overhand Sidearm Sidearm	Underhand Overhand Overhand	Sidearm Overhand Sidearm	Underhand Underhand Sidearm
Serial Practice	10 min 10 min 10 min	Overhand Underhand Sidearm	Overhand Underhand Sidearm	Overhand Underhand Sidearm	Overhand Underhand Sidearm	Overhand Underhand Sidearm	Overhand Underhand Sidearm

practice, just the opposite is required. Open skills require practice in which the regulatory factors are varied. But how should variability be organized within a teaching unit?

Suppose you have organized a teaching unit on throwing for your elementary school classes. You have determined that you will devote six classes to this unit and want the students to experience three variations of the throwing pattern, the overhand, underhand, and sidearm throws. How should these three different throws be arranged for practice during the six classes? Figure 9.1–2 shows three possible arrangements. One is to practice each throw in blocks of two days each (blocked practice). Another possibility is to practice each throw in some random arrangement with 10-minute blocks devoted to each particular pattern (random practice). Thus, each day three 10-minute blocks are experienced, although there is no specified order of occurrence for the three patterns; the only stipulation is that all three be practiced an equal amount over the course of the unit. The third arrangement, serial practice, also suggests a 10-minute block for each pattern. However, in this approach, each pattern is practiced every day in the same order.

Figure 9.1-2
A six-day unit plan demonstrating three different practice structures (blocked, random, and serial) for teaching three different throwing patterns (overhand, underhand, and sidearm). All classes are 30 minutes long and are divided into 10-minute segments. Each practice condition provides an equal amount of practice for each throwing pattern.

The contextual interference approach to the scheduling question. A shortcoming of Schmidt's schema theory is that it did not provide a way to determine the best schedule of practice variability. However, there is a way to address this scheduling question by considering what has been called the *contextual interference effect*. The term *contextual interference* was introduced by Battig (1979) to indicate the interference that results from practicing a task within the context of the practice situation. In some practice situations, a high degree of contextual interference can be established by having students practice several different but related skills during the same practice session. On the other hand, practicing only one skill during a practice session leads to a low contextual interference condition. Based on what you studied in Concept 5.2 about

the role of interference as an agent that induces forgetting, you might expect that a low contextual interference situation would lead to superior learning. However, Battig proposed that while the low contextual interference practice situation leads to superior practice performance it results in much poorer retention performance than the high contextual interference situation. Thus, based on our continuing emphasis on the role of retention tests in making inferences about learning, high contextual interference practice conditions are predicted to lead to better skill acquisition.

The first test of Battig's prediction using motor skills was reported by Shea and Morgan (1979). They had subjects practice three movement patterns in which the goal was to move one arm through a series of small wooden barriers as rapidly as possible. Practice conditions were arranged so that one group practiced the three patterns following the blocked arrangement of each pattern in 18 trial blocks. A second group practiced the patterns in random arrangement so that the 18 trials of practice for each pattern were randomly distributed over the 54 total practice trials. Results supported Battig's prediction. The blocked practice group performed better during practice trials with KR while the random practice group showed superior performance during retention trials and transfer trials where a new arrangement of barriers was introduced.

In an attempt to uncover possible reasons for these contextual interference results, Lee and Magill (1983b) added a third group to the two used by Shea and Morgan. The new group was called a serial practice condition. Here the 54 total practice trials were arranged so that movement pattern 1 was always followed by pattern 2, which was always followed by pattern 3. This group combined features of the blocked practice condition (perfect predictability of the upcoming pattern to be practiced) and of the random practice condition (high degree of interference between repetitions of any one pattern). The intent was to see which group the serial practice condition was more like, the blocked or the random practice.

Results, shown in Figure 9.1–3, indicated almost exact similarity between the random and serial practice conditions during both practice performance and retention. Based on these results, Lee and Magill developed the argument that the contextual interference effect is essentially a cognitively based effect that creates a difficult practice condition in which subjects must engage in problem-solving activity each time the same pattern is practiced. As they viewed it, blocked practice allows the individual to devise and test action strategies to solve the problem of performing a movement without any interfering activity involved where action strategies for other movements would have to be developed and tested. For the random and blocked conditions, the situation is just the opposite. Thus, the end result is poorer practice performance under random and blocked practice conditions but superior retention performance.

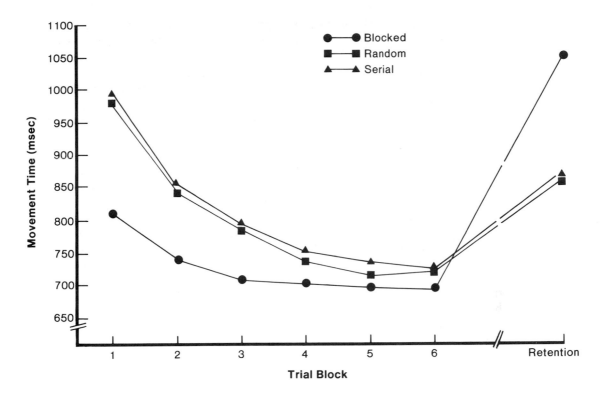

Figure 9.1-3
Results from the experiment by Lee and Magill showing mean movement time for completing three movement patterns using three different practice structures (blocked, random, and serial). Trial blocks (3 trials per block) 1 through 6 were with KR. The retention block was without KR.

High contextual interference schedule benefit outside the laboratory. Since the experiments by Shea and Morgan (1979) and by Lee and Magill (1983b), other experiments have been reported which demonstrate the benefit of practice schedules involving high levels of contextual interference for laboratory tasks other than those where the goal is to learn to move as fast as possible through different movement patterns or to move in specific criterion times through these patterns. An example has been reported by Del Rey, Wughalter, and Whitehurst (1982). They found that the random practice schedule was better than a blocked schedule for learning to respond to different stimulus speed variations for an anticipation timing task. Although evidence based on laboratory tasks is important for supporting the benefit of high contextual interference as a practice schedule characteristic, it does not generate the desired confidence that these results can be effectively generalized to skills learned outside the laboratory.

One of the more encouraging experiments that demonstrates the high contextual interference benefit in this regard is one reported by Goode and Magill (1986). In this experiment, they provided evidence that a random practice schedule is better than blocked practice for learning variations of a skill that likely would be taught in a physical education or recreation setting. College-aged women with no prior experience in badminton were required to

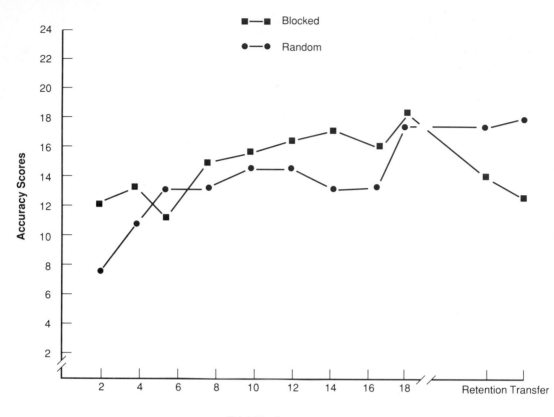

Accuracy Scores

Trial Block

Figure 9.1-4
Results from the experiment by Goode and Magill (1986) showing the effects of blocked and random structured practice for three types of badminton serves on acquisition, one-day retention, and transfer.

practice the short, long, and drive badminton serves from the right service court. They practiced the serves three days a week for three weeks, with 36 trials each practice session for a total of 324 trials (108 trials per serve) during the practice period. The blocked practice schedule group practiced one serve each day of each week. Thus, this schedule was actually a modification of the blocked condition used in previous studies. The random practice schedule group practiced each serve randomly in every practice session. In this condition, the experimenter told the subject what serve should be done next. On the day following these 9 days of practice, all subjects were given a retention test and then a transfer test on which they were required to perform all three serves from the left service court.

As you can see from the results (Figure 9.1–4), the group that practiced with the random schedule did worse during the practice sessions, but did better on the retention and transfer tests. What is especially remarkable here is that on the transfer test, the random group showed no deterioration of performance. On the other hand, the group that had practiced in a blocked schedule was not able to adapt well to performing these serves from the left court and performed at about the same level at which they had when they had begun

practicing the serves from the right court 3 weeks earlier. Thus, even in a non-laboratory setting, a practice schedule involving high contextual interference can be seen as leading to better learning than a schedule involving low contextual interference.

Contextual interference and experience. An interesting finding from experiments using anticipation timing tasks to investigate the contextual interference effect has been that the effect is typically observed for subjects who have a strong background with open skills but not for those with a poor or no background with open skills. For example, Del Rey, Wughalter, and Whitehurst (1982) compared women with experience in varsity or city league competition in tennis, volleyball, rugby, or softball with women with no previous competitive involvement in open skills. These subjects were required to practice a task that involved pressing a button coincident with the arrival of the moving lights at the last light on a Bassin anticipation timer. The blocked and random practice schedule groups practiced this response with four different stimulus speeds: 5, 7, 11, and 13 mph. Each speed was practiced for 16 trials. The blocked group practiced 16 trials of one speed, then practiced 16 trials of a second speed and so on until all four speeds had been practiced. The random group practiced 16 trials of each of the four speeds in a random order distributed throughout the 64 total trials. After the practice session was completed, all subjects were given 6 transfer trials at each of two new stimulus speeds, 6 and 12 mph. The results of the transfer performance showed that the experienced subjects who had practiced in a random schedule did better than experienced subjects who had practiced in a blocked schedule. However, for the nonexperienced subjects, there was no transfer performance difference for the two practice schedule conditions.

These results have been recently replicated in a comparison of open skill experienced and nonexperienced women (Del Rey, Wughalter, & Carnes, 1987) and for nonexperienced women only (Goode, 1986). It appears that for individuals without a significant amount of open skill experience, high levels of contextual interference during practice of anticipation-timing tasks are not more beneficial to learning than low levels. However, the high contextual interference practice schedule does benefit those who have had a past history of open skill sport experience.

Another important experience-related concern here is *when* during the stages of learning a skill should higher or lower levels of contextual interference be interjected. In the experiments discussed earlier, random practice, for example, was always initiated at the beginning of practice. However, for the most part, the skills being learned were relatively simple ones, except for the badminton serves. An interesting question is whether beginning the introduction of variations of a skill at the beginning of practice is the best approach to use for more complex skills. An alternative might be to introduce the variations in a blocked form for a short time and then introduce a practice schedule that would increase the contextual interference during practice.

According to Gentile's (1972) model for skill acquisition, variability should be increased only after practice that has emphasized the achievement of the basic goal of the skill (e.g., hitting the ball with a forehand) under relatively constant practice conditions. Then, as the person moves into the second stage of learning, the systematic introduction of variability is recommended. For example, practicing a tennis forehand from a ball machine where the ball is moving at the same speed and direction should precede varying the speed and direction of the ball. This approach is undoubtedly the most prevalent in physical activity instructional situations. Whether it leads to better learning than introducing the student to variability as soon as possible, as many of the contextual interference experiments have indicated, awaits much needed research. However, those experiments that have shown the contextual interference benefit only for more experienced individuals rather than for beginners indicate that there may be certain skills that would benefit more by introducing a high contextual interference schedule later in the practice schedule.

Implementing high contextual interference practice schedules. A close observation of the different experiments considered in this discussion about the scheduling of variable practice indicates that different forms of schedules have been compared. For example, Lee and Magill (1983) showed that a serial form of practice, where each of the variations as practiced in a 1-2-3 arrangement of trials, was better than blocked practice. Goode and Magill (1986) showed that a modified blocked form, where one variation was practiced for an entire day, although experienced again a week later, was not as good as random practice. These results indicate that it is possible to invoke low and high levels of contextual interference in different ways. Random practice is not the only form of high contextual interference, and blocked practice is not the only form for invoking low contextual interference.

A practical conclusion that seems to evolve from the research is that practice conditions that allow students to experience all variations each day are superior to those that allow students to only experience one variation each day. One way of implementing practice schedules that avoid this characteristic and provide more desirable variable schedules is to engage students in practicing different variations of a skill being taught in different stations. Students are scheduled to spend a certain amount of time at each station, where one specific variation is practiced, and then move on to another station. During one class period, or practice session, all variations are experienced. Another method is to practice different variations at different times during the practice session. Again, the goal is to experience all variations each session.

Although there have been numerous experiments showing that higher levels of contextual interference lead to better learning than lower levels, a question that remains unsolved is, *why* does this effect occur? At present, two hypotheses have been proposed to account for the contextual interference effect. One, the elaboration view, has been promoted by John Shea and colleagues (Shea & Morgan, 1979; Shea & Zimny, 1983). The other, the action plan reconstruction view, has been promoted by Tim Lee and Richard Magill (Lee & Magill, 1983b, 1985). Although we will not debate these two hypotheses at length, it will be instructive to briefly consider each.

Accounting for the Contextual Interference Effect

The elaboration view. In their experiment that first demonstrated that the contextual interference effect could be demonstrated in motor skill learning situations, Shea and Morgan (1979) argued that the reason for the effect could be found in the elaboration of the memory representation of the criterion skill variations that resulted from random practice. They stated that during random practice, the individual engages in more strategies as well as more different strategies than do those who practice in a blocked schedule. Also, since in a random practice schedule all three variations being practiced are in working memory together, the person can compare and contrast each variation so that each becomes distinct from the other. The result of engaging in more and more different strategies during practice and being able to develop more distinct representations of each variation leads to the development of a memory representation for these skills that can be more readily accessed during a recall or transfer test.

The action plan reconstruction view. The alternative view from the one offered by Shea and colleagues is one forwarded by Lee and Magill that argues that the high contextual interference benefit does not necessarily enhance the elaboration of the memory trace. Rather, the key is that the benefit results from individuals being required to engage in more active processing during practice. This active processing is primarily involved in the person needing to reconstruct an action plan on the next trial for a particular variation, since the action plan developed for the previous trial of that skill has been partially or completely forgotten due to the interference created by the intervening practice trials of the other skills. This is in contrast to the blocked practice condition where the person can essentially use the same or slightly modified action plan used on the previous trial. An example from the work of Jacoby (1978), in which this view has its roots, is seen when you must add a long set of numbers. If you do this addition problem and then are asked to promptly do the same problem again, it is likely that you will not re-add the numbers but remember and repeat the answer. In contrast, if you were required to add several

additional lists of numbers and then were given the first list again, you would probably perform the addition again since you forgot the solution to the problem. Thus, you were required to re-solve the problem, rather than merely remember the solution.

Lee and Magill argued that the random practice condition is like the addition situation where you have forgotten much of the action plan developed for the previous trial of the task and, therefore, must re-solve the problem on the next trial on which that problem appears. On the other hand, the blocked practice schedule is like the addition problem where the next trial follows immediately and it is easy to remember the solution to be successful on the next trial. In the motor learning context, high contextual interference conditions require subjects to more actively engage in problem solving activity during practice. While this activity typically leads to poorer performance during practice than would be found for a low contextual interference schedule, this short-term performance deficit becomes a long-term benefit since it leads to better retention and transfer test performance.

Comparing the two views. There is much work to be done to determine which of the two hypotheses proposed to account for the contextual interference effect is correct. Currently, evidence has been generated that indicates more support for the action plan reconstruction view than for the elaboration view. This evidence comes from two different approaches, each based on varying the spacing between practice and test of the criterion response. One approach involved using a modified version of the classic short-term memory experimental paradigm that was considered in Chapter 5. The second approach has used a learning paradigm in which the lengths and the activity of the intertrial intervals are varied.

An example of an experiment following the memory paradigm approach was reported by Lee and Weeks (1987). In this experiment, subjects were required to move a linear positioning device to a stop designating a criterion limb position to remember. Following a retention interval, they were asked to repeat the criterion movement to the stop. Then, there was a second retention interval followed by a recall estimate of the criterion position. Two conditions were compared based on characteristics of the interval between the first and the second repetition of the criterion movement. One group of subjects repeated the criterion movement immediately after they had returned to the starting position following the first criterion movement. The second group of subjects were given a 20-second interval between the first and second repetition of the criterion movement during which they had to count backwards by 7s from a 3-digit number the experimenter gave them. This second retention interval was different from two groups of subjects. The results showed that subjects who had the 20-second filled interval between criterion movement repetitions had better recall accuracy for the criterion position than those who had the criterion position repeated immediately. Thus, the presentation of the second

repetition of the criterion movement after some "forgetting" of the first repetition had occurred actually led to better recall test performance. These results, then, are in line with what would be expected from the action plan reconstruction view of the contextual interference effect.

The second approach favoring the action plan reconstruction view involved experiments where subjects practice a skill for several trials but with different intertrial interval characteristics compared. An example of this approach is seen in a series of experiments by Magill, Meeuwsen, Lee, and Mathews (1987). In the second experiment, for example, subjects were required to learn to move their hand through a two-segment pattern of push-button switches in criterion times of 300 and 600 msec, respectively. One group of subjects practiced this movement for 30 trials with each trial occurring 5 seconds after KR was given. A second group of subjects waited for 20 seconds after KR was given to perform another trial. A third group of subjects had to practice two additional movement patterns that were similar to the criterion patterns, with movement time goals of 500 and 800 msec and of 700 and 1000 msec. According to the elaboration view, this condition should provide an opportunity for elaboration experiences that should be beneficial for learning the criterion movement. Finally, a fourth group also engaged in activity between trials but this activity involved practicing a mirror tracing task for the 20-second interval. According to the action plan reconstruction view, individuals who experience between-trial intervals that should invoke more forgetting of the action plan developed for the preceding trial should do better on a retention or transfer test than those who experience intertrial intervals that should invoke less forgetting. However, according to the elaboration view, conditions that provide for greater elaboration should lead to the best retention and transfer. Results of this experiment showed that the groups did not differ on a 10-minute and a 24-hour no-KR retention test and that the group that had short intertrial intervals did worse on a transfer task, which had criterion movement times of 900 and 1200 msec for the two segments, than the other groups. Thus, the elaboration view cannot account for these results while these results are according to the expectations of the action plan reconstruction view.

Obviously there is much more research that needs to be done if we are to understand why the contextual interference effect occurs. This is an important issue to further our understanding of learning processes since the contextual interference effect shows a situation in which conditions that lead to better practice performance do not lead to better retention and transfer performance.

An important theoretical issue related to the contextual interference effect concerns its relationship to Schmidt's schema theory in regard to what each says about practice characteristics and novel response transfer success. As you will recall, Schmidt's schema theory said nothing about the scheduling of variable practice and its effect on novel response performance. Also, numerous

Contextual Interference and Schema Theory

experiments show no support for the amount of variability prediction made in that theory (see Lee, Magill, & Weeks, 1985, and Shapiro & Schmidt, 1982, for good reviews of this literature). In the review of the research showing support or lack of support for the variability of practice prediction of schema theory, Lee, Magill, and Weeks (1985) noted that there was an interesting scheduling of the variable practice that might have influenced those differing results. In studies that found no support for the variability of practice prediction, the variable practice condition was typically organized in a blocked schedule. On the other hand, when support for this prediction was found, the variable practice condition was usually a random schedule. Lee, Magill, and Weeks then presented two experiments that tested this observation and found that indeed, when variable practice was in a blocked schedule, it led to no better novel transfer performance than a nonvariable, or constant, practice condition. However, when the variable practice condition was organized in a random schedule, novel transfer performance followed the variability of practice prediction. Thus, the key to novel transfer success may not be in the amount of variable practice experience only, but in the scheduling of that variability as well. The resolution of this issue awaits further research.

Errors Can Benefit Learning

When variable practice involves practicing different goal variations of a skill, such as three different movement time goals for the same movement pattern, it is easy to see that this is a more variable practice condition than when only one movement time goal is practiced. However, there is another means of manipulating the variability in practice even when only one response goal is practiced. This approach to practice variability is based on the use of different practice methods that increase or decrease the amount of error that a person will experience while practicing a skill. At present, there seems to be two differing views about the influence of experiencing errors during practice. One view argues that errors should be kept to a minimum so that the correct response can be experienced as often as possible. Programmed instruction approaches to learning are good examples of this view. The other view argues that errors made during practice are beneficial for the learner and, although increasing errors during practice may lead to decreased practice performance, there will be a long-term benefit seen in retention and transfer performance. Clearly, Schmidt's schema theory, as well as contextual interference results, favor this approach. Discovery learning or problem-solving techniques are good instructional strategy examples of the view that sees making errors in early practice as an important part of learning.

The typical experimental approach to investigating this question has been to compare practice methods that will lead to different amounts of error during practice. A good example of this can be seen in an experiment reported by Edwards and Lee (1985). Two groups of subjects were required to learn to knock down a specified pattern of three small wooden barriers in a goal movement time of 1200 msec. One group, called the prompted group, was given

extensive instructions about the task by means of verbal cues, tape recordings, and demonstrations. These subjects were told that if they moved according to a "ready, and, 1,2,3,4,5" count on a tape, they would complete the movement in the criterion time of 1200 msec. Each subject practiced saying this count aloud and clapping it to establish the appropriate rhythm and length of time. They practiced this until they could correctly do three trials in a row at 1200 msec. Thus, as much as could be done to have the practicing of the actual task with as little error as possible was done for these subjects. The second group, called the trial-and-error group, was told that the goal movement time was 1200 msec and that after each trial they would receive KR in the form of how many msec their response was early or late of the 1200-msec goal time. All subjects practiced the task for 26 trials. Following this practice, there was a no-KR retention test and a transfer test. The transfer test involved performing the task in 1800 msec.

The results of this experiment for the practice trials and the transfer test can be seen in Figure 9.1–5. As you can see, the prompted group performed as expected with very little error during practice. The trial-and-error group experienced a lot of error during the first 15 trials and then became more similar to the prompted group by the end of the practice trials. The two groups were not different from each other on the retention test. However, what is quite revealing is that on the novel transfer test, the group that had experienced the greatest amount of error during practice, the trial-and-error group, performed the novel transfer task more accurately than the group that had experienced much less error during practice. Thus, experiencing less error during practice was no more beneficial for a retention test of the practiced response than was experiencing a great deal of error. And, experiencing less error during practice was detrimental for transfer to a novel variation of the practiced response.

The results of the experiment by Edwards and Lee (1985) indicate that when a practice condition is used in which the likelihood of errors being made early in practice is relatively high, the long-term effect is a benefit for learning the skill. Another way to look at these results is that they show when practice conditions limit the amount of error that occurs; then this condition is detrimental to learning. These results fit very well with the expectations of schema theory that proposes the benefit of practice variability for learning skills. The unique characteristic here is that the variability is created by the type of practice strategy in which the individual engages, rather than by having different response goals practiced.

Much more research needs to be done concerning this question of the influence of errors during practice on learning of motor skills. This question has had a sketchy history of research (see Singer, 1977, for a good review) and has generated divergent conclusions. The Edwards and Lee (1985) experiment is just one example of an investigation into this issue. Because research concerning this issue has potential to provide important direction for

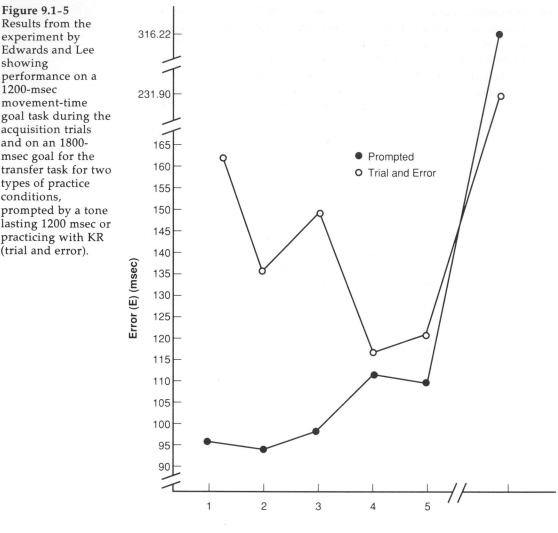

Figure 9.1-5
Results from the experiment by Edwards and Lee showing performance on a 1200-msec movement-time goal task during the acquisition trials and on an 1800-msec goal for the transfer task for two types of practice conditions, prompted by a tone lasting 1200 msec or practicing with KR (trial and error).

both instructional strategy implementation as well as for motor skill learning theory, there is an obvious need for a more concerted effort to better understand how and why errors during practice influence learning.

Summary

A variety of experiences is an essential ingredient for practice conditions that will lead to maximal test performance. This variety should be established on the basis of regulatory factors for open skills and nonregulatory conditions for closed skills. That is, for open skills, it is important to provide learners with a variety of experiences that require them to produce as many variations or

modifications of the basic movement pattern as possible. On the other hand, closed skills practice should emphasize producing movement patterns that are as similar as possible on each response. However, variety should be introduced by requiring that patterns be produced in all possible test conditions. An important part of designing variable practice experiences is organizing those experiences within the practice sessions. Insight into the best type of organization has been provided by considering research on the contextual interference effect. This research has shown that increasing the variability within each practice session is preferred to practicing one variation during one session, another variation another session, and so on.

Two different views exist concerning why the contextual interference effect occurs. One view suggests that higher levels of contextual interference increase the elaborateness of the memory representation of the skills being practiced. The other view argues that the effect occurs because the action plan construction for a preceding trial for a skill must be more actively reconstructed when there have been intervening trials of a different skill. Contextual interference and schema theory differ to some degree regarding their expectations of what type of practice will lead to better novel transfer performance. Finally, the influence of different practice conditions on the amount of errors made during practice was considered as another way of looking at how variability could be manipulated during practice. Results indicate that making more errors during early practice trials benefits transfer performance.

Related Readings

Gentile, A. M. (1972). A working model of skill acquisition with application to teaching. *Quest,* Monograph XVII, 3–23.

Lee, T. D., & Magill, R. A. (1983). The locus of contextual interference in motor-skill acquisition. *Journal of Experimental Psychology: Learning, Memory and Cognition, 9,* 730–746.

Schmidt, R. A. (1977). Schema theory: Implications for movement education. *Motor Skills: Theory into Practice, 2,* 36–38.

Shapiro, D. C., & Schmidt, R. A. (1982). The schema theory: Recent evidence and developmental implications. In J. A. S. Kelso & J. E. Clark (Eds.), *The development of movement control and co-ordination* (pp. 113–150). New York: Wiley.

Singer, R. N. (1977). To err or not to err: A question for the instruction of psychomotor skills. *Review of Educational Research, 47,* 479–498.

Concept 9.2 The amount of practice affects learning although the effect is not always proportional

Application

It seems reasonable to assume that the more practice a person has, the better the eventual performance will be. If a golfer wants to become a better putter, it seems only reasonable that he or she should be encouraged to spend as much time as possible on the practice putting green. The dancer who is a bit tentative in certain parts of a routine should be encouraged to spend as much time as possible going over the routines repeatedly in practice. The rehabilitation patient should be encouraged to practice the skill he or she is relearning as often as possible. Thus, when we consider the needs in each situation, it seems reasonable to accept the "more practice" approach that has been suggested. But while such an approach seems logical and will undoubtedly work, is that approach necessarily the best alternative?

When a person practices a motor skill, is it possible that he or she reaches a point of "diminishing returns" in terms of the benefits derived from the practice in proportion to the amount of time put into the practice? This "benefits vs. time" question is an important consideration that instructors of motor skills should not overlook when designing instruction. The amount of practice time devoted to a skill is a critical variable in any motor skill teaching situation. This is especially true because of the time limitations that are a part of all instructional settings. For example, a physical education teacher has only so many minutes per day to teach and a unit of instruction can only last for so many weeks. Or, the dancer has only so long to rehearse before opening night. Or, the therapy patient may have limited financial resources so the maximum benefit must be achieved in a minimum amount of time.

It is paramount for all who teach motor skills to consider the time constraints that exist for their instruction. Thus, the need to consider the efficiency of instruction is critically important to the instructional process. The goal of the available instruction and practice time should include not only the most effective means of instruction or practice but also the most efficient procedure. In other words, what form of instruction or practice will yield the greatest returns for the least expenditure of time?

The efficiency of instruction and practice methods is a principle that should not be overlooked or underestimated by instructors of motor skills. In the following discussion we will consider an important concept that can be directly applied to the development of efficient instruction.

Discussion

The problem of how much practice is beneficial to assure the optimum amount of learning while considering the question of time spent for benefits received has been the focus of an area of study in learning that traditionally has been

termed *overlearning,* although the term should be "overpractice" or "overtraining" to be more accurately descriptive. Overlearning can be defined as the *practice time spent beyond the amount of practice time needed to achieve some performance criterion.* The implementation of overlearning in an instructional situation would be to establish a performance criterion, determine the amount of practice time spent in attaining that criterion, and then require extra practice time. The intent of the extra practice time is to help develop a memory representation of the skill that is as durable and as accessible as possible. Consider this point in relation to our earlier discussion of the storage and retrieval of information in long-term memory in chapter 5 and of motor programs in chapter 3. Based on this view, it could be said that the intent of the extra practice is to strengthen the generalized motor program and response schema for the skill being learned so that it can more readily be called into action when required.

The study of overlearning for motor skills has not been a popular area in recent years for motor learning research. However, there has been sufficient investigation through the years to determine that overlearning is an effective means of aiding skill learning. To help illustrate what we presently know about the benefits and implementation of the overlearning strategy as a practice procedure, two experiments will be briefly discussed. These two experiments are useful to consider as they show the effectiveness for the overlearning practice strategy for two different types of motor skill situations.

One type of motor skill that was discussed in Chapter 5 as being particularly susceptible to forgetting is what are termed *procedural skills.* These skills typically require performing a series of discrete responses which by themselves are relatively easy to execute. However, the total task involves knowing what discrete responses to make and in what order. These types of skills are especially common in industrial and military settings. An article by Schendel and Hagman (1982) proposes that using an overlearning, or overtraining as they call it, practice strategy could be an effective way to decrease the amount of forgetting associated with procedural skills. As researchers for the U.S. Army Research Institute, they were particularly interested in improving retention following training of soldiers to assemble and disassemble an Army machine gun. This skill was of interest because it is typically taught in a short training period and is usually characterized by a large amount of retention loss soon thereafter.

Two forms of overtraining were compared with a no overtraining situation. The first overtraining condition required the soldiers to perform 100% more trials than were necessary to achieve a performance criterion of one correct assembly/disassembly trial. The second overtraining condition also involved an additional 100% more practice trials, but these trials were administered as "refresher" training midway through the 8-week retention interval used for all subjects. Results showed that both of these overtraining groups performed better than the no overtraining control group on the retention test, which required the soldiers to practice until they were again able to

assemble and disassemble the gun correctly on a trial. However, the two overtraining groups did not differ from each other in the number of trials it took to retrain to the one correct trial criterion. The recommendation by Schendel and Hagman was to use the immediate overtraining situation because it was the more cost and time effective means of increasing the durability of what was learned during the original practice session. Since the trainees were already in the training session, it would save time and be less expensive to have them engage in additional practice there rather than bring them back several weeks later for a refresher training session.

In an experiment that involved learning a skill that could be considered more "motor" than the gun disassembly/assembly skill, Melnick (1971) investigated the use of overlearning for learning a dynamic balance skill. Two questions were of primary interest in this experiment. The first question concerned whether practice beyond what was needed to achieve a performance criterion was better than no further practice, which was a question also addressed in the Schendel and Hagman (1982) experiment. Assuming that there would be such a benefit, the second question addressed whether there was an optimum amount of extra practice that was beneficial. To investigate these questions, Melnick had subjects practice balancing on a stabilometer until they were able to achieve a performance criterion of 28 seconds out of 50 seconds. Following the achievement of this criterion, the subjects were then required to perform either no further trials, 50%, 100%, or 200% extra trials of practice. Then, a retention test was administered to all subjects one week and one month later.

The results of this experiment (Table 9.2–1) indicated that the answer to the first question was as expected: the groups that had been required to engage in practice beyond what was required to achieve the 28-second performance criterion performed better on the retention tests than the group that only practiced until the criterion had been achieved. The answer to the second question was somewhat more interesting. There appeared to be a point of "diminishing returns" in terms of the amount of retention benefit gained in relation to the amount of extra practice required by the different overlearning conditions. That is, the 50% additional practice group did as well on the retention tests as the 100% and 200% groups. So, although additional practice was beneficial, increasing the amount of additional practice beyond a certain amount was not proportionally more beneficial for improving retention performance.

Implementing the overlearning practice strategy. Three points are especially worth noting with regard to the use of overlearning as a practice strategy. *First,* the effective implementation of this strategy can be achieved only when you know how much practice the students need to achieve a certain performance level. Thus, for skills that are practiced until a criterion level of performance must be achieved, requiring additional practice beyond the achievement of that criterion can effectively aid learning.

Table 9.2-1.
Results of the experiment by Melnick showing the mean scores and standard deviations at the end of practice to criterion (criterion trial) and at the end of the overlearning practice (last pretest trial) for the four overlearning groups for the 1-week and 1-month retention intervals.

Groups (N = 10)		Trials to Criterion	Criterion Trial Time on Balance (sec)	Last Pretest Trial Time on Balance (sec)
0% 1-wk.	M	7.7	28.72	28.72
	SD	3.80	.57	.57
0% 1-mo.	M	6.4	28.45	28.45
	SD	3.58	.30	.30
50% 1-wk.	M	7.6	28.83	29.04
	SD	2.94	.36	.83
50% 1-mo.	M	7.3	28.59	28.64
	SD	4.43	.50	.89
100% 1-wk.	M	7.5	28.81	28.18
	SD	3.38	.43	1.19
100% 1-mo.	M	6.8	28.59	28.80
	SD	3.34	.41	.92
200% 1-wk.	M	7.3	28.92	29.11
	SD	1.19	.59	.70
200% 1-mo.	M	7.1	28.80	28.60
	SD	3.15	.45	1.32

Second, the amount of extra practice required should not be based on the notion that "more is better." Remember that there seems to be a point of diminishing returns; the amount of retention benefit gained for the extra time required to practice is not worth the extra time. Although this point has to be determined for your own particular situation, the experiments we considered

in this discussion showed that a "safe bet" can be around 100% additional practice trials beyond the number required to achieve your specified performance criterion.

Third, the use of requiring additional practice beyond what was needed to achieve a performance criterion seems to be a particularly useful strategy for skills that will be practiced during a specified period and will then not be performed for some time after that. For example, in the Schendel and Hagman (1982) experiment, the Army wanted the soldiers to know how to disassemble and assemble the machine gun in case a situation would arise where these procedures would be required. This skill was not something the soldiers would use every day but they still needed to be capable of performing the skill. Thus, the goal was to provide a practice situation that would help insure as much as possible the durability of the capability of successfully performing this skill. This goal was achieved by requiring the soldiers to engage in 100% more practice trials than they required to correctly perform the skill one time.

The overlearning practice strategy and learning. An important aspect of the results of overlearning research is that they help to support the effectiveness of what was called in chapter 4 "rote rehearsal" as a learning strategy. As you may have noted in the two overlearning experiments considered here, the conditions of practice were simply a rote repetition of practice trials. Thus it would appear that practicing a skill over and over, even though it can be performed correctly, is a valuable form of practice to increase the permanence of the capability to perform the skill at some future time.

Finally, you should be aware that a consistent conclusion from the overlearning research with motor skills is that the amount of practice is not *the* critical variable influencing motor skill acquisition. As you have seen in many portions of this book, amount of practice invariably interacts with some other variable to influence learning. You have seen this interaction with such variables as the type of KR or the variability of practice. From this perspective, then, the typical overlearning research study indicates that a particular condition of practice is beneficial to a point. However, for continued performance improvement that is more proportionate to the time and effort given to the practice, a change must be made. Some new approach to practice must be developed by incorporating a new learning variable into the practice routine. For example, some new form of KR could be provided, such as the use of videotape replay, or performance goals could be established.

The topic of overlearning has a long history in motor learning research. Today, however, it is seldom investigated by itself. This does not mean that the question of the amount of practice is unimportant. It does mean that current views of motor learning are aware that this issue cannot be studied in isolation but must be considered as it interacts with other important instructional variables.

Summary

The question of the time spent in practicing a motor skill versus the benefits derived from the amount of time spent in practice has been considered. While the amount of practice is an important concern for the instructor, it is more important to consider how the amount of practice interacts with other variables influencing motor skill learning. As the amount of time spent in practicing a skill increases, the value of certain conditions of practice decreases. However, the need increases for incorporating other variables into the practice routines.

Related Readings

Melnick, M. J. (1971). Effects of overlearning on the retention of a gross motor skill. *Research Quarterly, 42,* 60–69.

Rubin-Rabson, G. (1941). Studies in the psychology of memorizing piano music. VIII: A comparison of three degrees of overlearning. *Journal of Experimental Psychology, 32,* 688–698.

Schmidt, R. A. (1971). Retroactive interference and level of original learning in verbal and motor tasks. *Research Quarterly, 42,* 314–326.

Concept 9.3   The spacing or distribution of practice can affect both practice performance and learning

Application

Suppose you are a physical education teacher teaching a volleyball unit. In this unit, you must schedule time to practice basic skills of volleyball, such as the serve, pass, set, spike, receiving serve, and so on. In addition to the practicing scheduling concerns addressed in the previous two concepts in this chapter, you are also faced with how to distribute the practice of these various skills throughout the unit. For example, should you spend entire class periods having the students practicing these skills and then devote the remaining class periods of the unit to playing actual games of volleyball? Or, would it be better to more widely distribute the practice time for these skills by devoting only a portion of each class period to practicing these skills and then allow them to play some games each period? Although both of these schedules would devote the same amount of practice to each skill, the difference between the two schedules is how that practice is distributed within and between the class periods. The second schedule would spread out the instruction and practice time devoted to teaching these skills over a greater number of class periods than the first schedule. Then, even if you make this decision, you must consider another scheduling problem that concerns the distribution of practice within a class period itself. The question here is, Is there an optimum amount of time that your students should rest between practice trials or can they simply begin another trial as soon as possible after they complete the previous trial?

This example, although taken from a physical education context, points out important decisions that must be made by anyone involved in motor skill instruction. These decisions concern how to distribute the practice required to learn a skill. The volleyball unit example illustrates two scheduling concerns that must be taken into account before making these decisions. The first is related to how much practice time should be spent on a particular skill in a given practice session. In order to address this problem, you must first decide whether it is best to practice the skill for a relatively short period each day, which will mean practicing it for several days, versus practicing the skill for a longer period each day, which will mean that the amount of practice time you have allocated to that skill could be accomplished in fewer days. The second scheduling concern relates to the amount of rest given between practice trials. Here the scheduling concern shifts from distributing practice sessions across days to distributing practice within a practice session. Both of these issues are important and must be addressed before determining how the practice schedule will be organized.

The important question that must be addressed, however, before either of these scheduling decisions can be made is whether or not practice distribution schedules really make any difference in terms of learning the skill. If learning a skill is better with a particular type of practice distribution schedule than another, then it would be clear that this schedule would be the most desirable one. If, however, the practice distribution schedule doesn't really influence the quality of learning that results from practice, then the type of schedule used should not be a concern. In the discussion that follows, this practice distribution issue will be considered to provide some guidance in the scheduling decision process.

Discussion

The study of practice distribution, or the spacing of practice, has been a popular topic for research in motor learning for many years. The most popular era for this study seems to have been from the 1930s through the 1950s. Widespread attention to the topic of practice distribution appears to have been brought about by a controversy. This was based on the question of whether *massed* or *distributed* practice provided for better learning of motor skills. Some researchers argued that distributed practice was definitely better, while others maintained that it really did not make much difference which spacing strategy was followed.

An important point that must be understood about the study of massed versus distributed practice is that there are two different ways to consider the distribution of practice. These two ways were illustrated in the Application section. One way concerns the amount of practice on each day of practice. Involved in this issue is whether it is better to have fewer sessions, and therefore fewer practice days, or more sessions and therefore more practice days. The second way to consider the distribution of practice concerns the amount of rest allowed between practice trials, that is, the length of the intertrial interval. Both of these practice distribution issues will be addressed in this discussion.

Defining Massed and Distributed Practice

Although there has been considerable controversy over whether massed or distributed practice schedules lead to better skill learning, there also has been considerable controversy over the definitions of the terms *massed practice* and *distributed practice*. The most problematic is finding agreement for these terms when they relate to the interval length between trials. When these terms are used to relate to distributing practice across days, there seems to be general agreement that the terms are used in a relative way. That is, a massed practice schedule will have fewer days of practice than the distributed sessions, with each day requiring more and/or longer practice sessions. A distributed schedule, on the other hand, will distribute the same amount of practice time across more sessions, or days, so that each session is shorter than in the massed schedule and so the sessions must be over a longer period.

However, when defining these two terms is related to the length of the intertrial interval, there is not this same general agreement about an operational definition. For example, Singer (1980) defined massed practice rather narrowly as practicing "without any intermittent pauses" (p. 419). Schmidt (1987), on the other hand, defined massed practice more broadly as practice in which "the amount of practice time in a trial is greater than the amount of rest between trials" (p. 384). Distributed practice is defined by Singer as practice periods "divided by rest intervals or intervals of alternate skill learning" (p. 379). Schmidt defined distributed practice as a situation in which "the amount of rest between trials equals or exceeds the amount of time in a trial" (p. 384). For our purposes, we shall define massed practice as *practice in which the amount of rest between trials is either very short or none at all so that practice is relatively continuous*. Distributed practice, then, is *practice in which the amount of rest between trials or groups of trials is relatively large*. While "very short" and "relatively large" as used in these definitions are somewhat ambiguous, it is necessary to use these terms to permit the greatest amount of generalization from the massed vs. distributed practice research literature as applicable to motor skill learning situations. The precise meanings of these terms should be considered in relation to the skill and learning situation to which they are applied.

The Intertrial Interval and Practice Distribution

By far, the greatest amount of research concerned with the distribution of practice has been related to the length of the intertrial interval. This research has also led to the greatest amount of controversy regarding which schedule leads to better learning. It is difficult to establish a definitive answer to this question by looking at reviews of this research or at motor learning textbooks as these sources provide varying answers. For example, Ellis (1978) stated that "distributed practice facilitates the acquisition of motor skills" (p. 236). However, in another review of practice distribution research, Adams (1987) concluded that "Massed practice influences how well you perform, not how well you learn" (p. 50), indicating that although the massing of practice depresses practice performance, the amount of learning results is not affected. Thus, Adams contended that the practice distribution schedule is of little consequence for skill learning, while Ellis held that it is an important learning variable.

Two problems appear to underlie the controversy surrounding the issue of massed versus distributed practice and motor skill learning when the focus is on the length of the intertrial interval. The first problem is related to the issue of practice performance versus learning effects, an issue that was discussed at length in chapter 2. What appears to be a problem is that many of the massed vs. distributed practice experiments reported in the research literature have not included retention or transfer trials. Thus, conclusions must be based on the results during practice trial performance only. The second

problem is one that was pointed out by Schmidt (1975a) and further developed by Lee and Genovese (1988a, 1988b). This problem concerns the general failure to consider possible differences in the influence of these two practice distribution schedules on learning different types of skills. They argue that one conclusion is warranted for results investigating continuous skills while a quite different conclusion must be made when discrete skills are learned. Thus, it appears that deriving any conclusion about the effect of different practice distribution schedules on motor skill learning is dependent of looking at research involving either continuous or discrete skills.

Massed vs. distributed practice for learning continuous skills. By far the most common type of motor skill used to investigate massed vs. distributed practice effects has been continuous skills. And, the most popular continuous task has been the pursuit rotor, where the subject must keep a hand-held stylus in contact with a small disk on a rotating turntable for as long as possible. A trial is usually a specified length of time, such as 20 or 30 seconds. What makes this type of task useful for investigating the massed vs. distributed practice issue is that it is quite easy to specify massed and distributed intertrial interval lengths. Because massed practice schedules typically have few, if any, seconds of rest between trials whereas the distributed schedules are as long or longer than the trial itself, intertrial interval lengths that are readily acceptable as being distinctly massed or distributed can be readily established.

One of the consistent results from the research investigating the effect of these two practice schedules has been that at the end of the practice trials, subjects who practice under a massed practice schedule do much worse than those who practiced with a distributed schedule. Thus, when experiments include only practice trials and no retention or transfer trials, the conclusion is obvious that a distributed schedule is better than a massed schedule. However, when a retention or transfer test is added, the results become less clearcut. We will consider two experiments to illustrate this discrepancy. In both experiments, there was a transfer test in which both the massed and distributed practice groups were required to perform the task under a common distributed schedule. The use of the distributed schedule as the common transfer schedule is the most interesting transfer condition since the most interesting question here is, What will happen to the massed practice group after the massed condition has been removed? If the massing of practice is a performance rather than a learning variable, then removing this practice condition should enable those who practiced under this schedule to perform like those who practiced under a distributed schedule.

An experiment that led to the conclusion that massing practice leads to a performance but not a learning decrement was reported by Adams and Reynolds (1954). Subjects practiced the pursuit rotor task for 40 trials and began practicing the task under a massed schedule in which they had no rest between

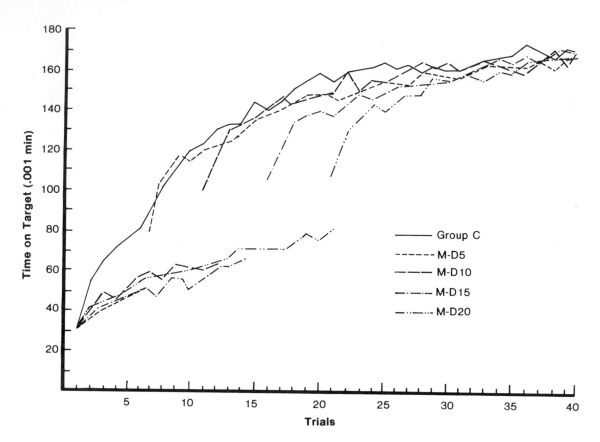

Figure 9.3-1
Results of the
experiment by
Adams and
Reynolds showing
the performance
curves for the
control group
(Group C) and the
four experimental
groups who
practiced under
massed practice
conditions for
different numbers
of trials before
shifting to a
distributed practice
condition that was
like that of the
control group.

trials. Then, one group of subjects was transferred to a distributed schedule after 5 trials. This switch in schedule occurred following a 5-minute rest. A second group of subjects transferred to the distributed schedule after 10 trials, while a third group was switched after 15 trials and a fourth group after 20 trials of massed practice. A fifth group was a control group that practiced all 40 trials in a distributed schedule. The results of this experiment are presented in Figure 9.3–1. As you can see, after being switched to a distributed schedule, all subjects showed immediate improvement and soon were performing similarly to the control group. From these results Adams and Reynolds concluded that the massing of practice only depressed practice performance and did not influence the learning of this skill.

A different conclusion was reached by Denny, Frisbey, and Weaver (1955). Subjects in their experiment practiced a pursuit rotor task for 12 trials with each trial being 30 seconds. The massed group had no rest between trials while the distributed group had a 30-second rest. Then, both groups were given a 5-minute rest and began performing 24 transfer trials with 30 seconds between trials. The results (Figure 9.3–2) showed that performance on the 12 practice trials yielded much poorer performance for the massed group than

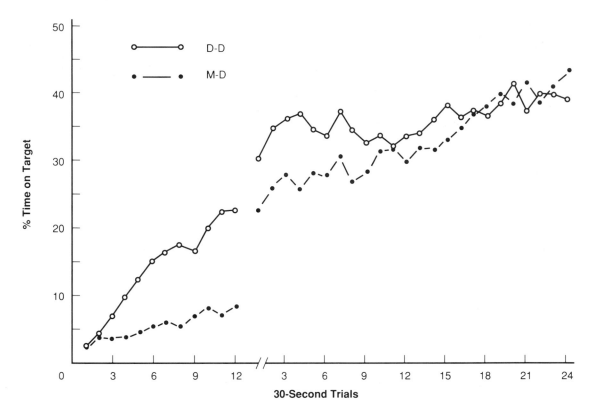

Figure 9.3-2
Results from the experiment by Denny, Frisbey, and Weaver (1955) showing the effects of massed and distributed practice on a pursuit rotor task. The first 12 trials are either massed (M) or distributed (D) practice conditions. The second set of 24 trials is distributed for both groups.

for the distributed group. And, this advantage for the distributed practice group remained for the first 11 transfer trials, at which time the two groups started to perform similarly. Thus, massing practice not only depressed practice performance, it also hindered learning.

How can the apparent discrepancy between these two experiments, which represent many others showing similar differing results, be resolved? One way is to look more closely at the Adams and Reynolds (1954) results and compare them with the results of Denny et al. (1955). The results from both experiments are actually more similar than different. In both experiments, subjects eventually performed like the group that had only experienced the distributed schedule. However, in both experiments, it took the massed practice subjects several trials to catch up. In fact, in the Adams and Reynolds experiment, the more massed practice trials that were experienced, the longer it took subjects to catch up when they were transferred to the distributed schedule. In the experiment by Denny et al., it took subjects 11 trials to catch up to the distributed group after having experienced 12 practice trials with a massed schedule. In the Adams and Reynolds experiment, a similar massed practice condition, the M-D15 group took over 15 trials to catch up to the distributed control group. Thus, it appears that the most appropriate conclusion is that

for continuous skills, the distributed schedule of practice is preferable to a massed schedule, as the massing of practice not only depresses practice performance, but also negatively affects learning.

Massed vs. distributed practice for discrete skills. A problem with using discrete skills to investigate the massed vs. distributed practice issue is directly related to the definition problem discussed earlier. For example, if a massed schedule allows no rest between trials while a distributed schedule involves a rest interval that is the same length as the practice trial, then two intertrial intervals will be essentially the same length, since a discrete response is typically very short. Consider for example a situation where subjects are practicing a rapid-aiming task that has a duration of approximately 150 msec. In this situation the distributed practice condition could, by definition, have a 150-msec intertrial interval. If the massed condition had no rest between trials, only 150 msec would separate the massed from the distributed practice schedules. Thus, the definition problem for the terms *massed* and *distributed* becomes an important concern when discrete tasks are used. Probably one reason this problem has not troubled researchers is that discrete tasks were seldom used for investigating the massed vs. distributed practice issue. In fact, in the comprehensive review by Lee and Genovese (1988b), only one study was found in the research literature in which a discrete task was used. However, the results of that one study are quite interesting and worth considering.

This single experiment was reported by Carron (1969) and involved a task that required subjects to learn to pick up a small dowel from a hole, turn it end-for-end, and reinsert it in the hole as quickly as possible. One attempt equalled one trial, which lasted on the average between 1.3 and 1.7 seconds. Carron defined massed and distributed practice conditions in a relative way. That is, the massed condition had a maximum 300-msec intertrial interval whereas the distributed group was given 5 seconds between trials. The results of this experiment showed that, as opposed to research with continuous tasks, practice performance for this discrete task was not depressed by massed practice; and, performance on a retention test two days later showed that the massed practice group actually outperformed the distributed practice group.

In an experiment that sought to further investigate Carron's (1969) results, Lee and Genovese (1988a) had subjects perform a task that required them to learn to move a hand-held stylus from one 8×8-cm metal plate to another plate 29 cm away in a goal movement time of 500 msec. The massed practice group had 0.5 seconds between trials whereas the distributed group had 25 seconds between trials. Both groups practiced this task for 50 trials, with KR given on each trial. At the end of these practice trials, each group was split into two groups, a massed and a distributed group for performance on two retention tests, one given 10 minutes after the practice trials were completed, the other given one week later.

The results of this experiment (Figure 9.3–3) confirmed to some extent what Carron had found earlier but added an important new dimension to those

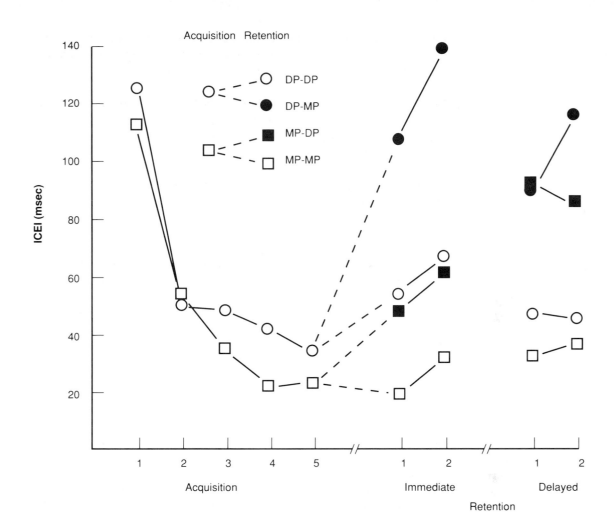

Figure 9.3-3
Results of the
experiment by Lee
and Genovese
(1988a) showing the
effects of massed
practice (MP) and
distributed practice
(DP) on the
acquisition and
retention
performance for the
discrete time-based
tapping task. Note
during retention
trials, the DP and
MP practice groups
were subdivided
into MP and DP
groups.

findings. First, notice that the massed practice group performed better than the distributed group at the end of the practice trials. But then, notice what happens to the groups that were formed for the retention tests. A strong practice-test context effect is seen. On the 10-minute retention test, the massed practice-massed retention group performs better than the other groups but the massed practice-distributed retention group performs about the same as the distributed practice-distributed retention group. The distributed practice-massed retention group performed the worst and actually made more errors than at the beginning of the practice trials. Thus, the massed practice condition led to better immediate retention performance when the retention test was also performed in a massed condition. For the one week retention test, the two groups that performed the retention test under the same conditions as they practiced performed comparably and better than both groups that were switched from their practice condition to the other condition.

Thus, it appears that massing of practice trials for discrete tasks does not hinder learning and can in fact benefit learning. However, there is a strong relationship between the practice distribution conditions during practice trials and during test trials. When the conditions are the same, the massed practice condition is advantageous for tests that follow closely in time after the end of practice, although this advantage disappears after an extended retention interval. However, the practice and test conditions are different, both practice distribution conditions suffer, with the distributed practice condition seemingly suffering more. These results, then, suggest that for learning discrete tasks, the more beneficial practice condition is to mass the distribution of practice trials.

Accounting for the intertrial practice distribution effects. The question that emerges from the discussion so far is, Why does massed practice hinder the learning of a continuous task while it benefits the learning of a discrete task? One possible reason is that fatigue effects become so severe during practice of a continuous task under a massed schedule that learning, as well as practice performance, are affected, a point to be discussed more fully in Concept 9.7. For the discrete task, where fatigue is not usually a problem, the distributed condition may lead to frustration or boredom from having to wait so long between trials. Although there may be other explanations for these differences, they await further research to be validated.

Implementing intertrial massed vs. distributed schedule results. One thing that the results of the research we have just considered make reasonably clear is that the decision about which practice schedule to use within a practice session is not an easy one. Two important points to consider are the type of skill being taught and the type of test situation. In terms of the type of skill being taught, it seems safe to recommend that if the skill is of the continuous type, that is,

if it lasts a reasonably long time and requires relatively repetitive actions, then a more distributed schedule is recommended. Thus, more gross skills like running, swimming, and bicycling, as well as repetitive, more precision-oriented skills, such as typing or piano playing, will benefit from a more distributed between-trial schedule. Of course, the key here is what constitutes the length of a trial. In most of these activities, however, a trial typically lasts several minutes. If the action required is reasonably brief, then massing practice will likely benefit. Skills such as hitting a golf ball or hitting tennis balls would not benefit from long intertrial intervals. Many industrial skills or skills being trained in an occupational therapy session fall into this category of skills and will likely benefit from practice schedules that keep intertrial intervals short.

Another way to consider the massed vs. distributed practice schedule issue is to consider how to distribute an allotted amount of practice time between days. A massed practice schedule would incorporate long practice sessions for a few days whereas a distributed schedule would spread out the same number of practice hours in shorter practice sessions across more days of practice. A potential problem that develops in considering this practice schedule concern is that many times there is little flexibility in the number of days available for practice sessions. If a teacher has only 10 days for a unit of instruction, then the practice schedule must fit that limit. Similarly, if a dancer has a performance in a set number of days, then the practice schedule must adjust accordingly. Thus, the consideration of the distribution of practice as a between-day problem may have its limitations. However, the basic question of whether it is better to have more sessions of shorter duration or fewer sessions of longer duration remains a relevant and important question, regardless of the limitations that may exist for how many days practice can occur.

The Length and
Distribution of
Practice Sessions

Unfortunately, there is not an abundance of research addressing this issue. However, one quite revealing study published by Baddely and Longman (1978) investigated the length of and distribution of practice sessions issue for learning a typing task. Subjects for this experiment were postal workers who needed to be trained to use a mail sorting machine, which required operating a typewriter-like keyboard. All trainees were provided with the 60 hours of practice time and practiced 5 days each week. However, this practice time was distributed in four different ways according to two lengths and two frequencies of training sessions. Two groups practiced for 1 hour in each session. One of these groups practiced for only 1 session each day (the 1 × 1 group), which resulted in a total training time of 12 weeks, while the second group had two sessions each day (the 2 × 1 group), thereby reducing the number of weeks in training to 6. Two other groups practiced for 2 hours in each session. One of these groups had only one session each day (the 1 × 2 group) while the other had two sessions per day (the 2 × 2 group). These latter two groups therefore had 6 weeks and 3 weeks of training, respectively. As you can see,

there are a variety of ways to distribute 60 hours of practice. The widest distribution required training to last for 12 weeks while the most massed distribution allowed training to be completed in only 3 weeks. The difference was in how long each session was and how many sessions were held each day.

Numerous performance measures were used to determine the effectiveness of the different practice schedules on learning the typing task. One of these was the amount of time it took the trainees to learn the keyboard. The 1 × 1 group took the least amount of time and learned the keyboard in 34.9 hours, while the 2 × 2 group took the most amount of time, 49.7 hours. The other two groups took approximately 43 hours each. Thus, for learning the keyboard, keeping practice sessions short and having only one session a day led to faster learning. Another interesting measure was typing speed. Here, the set goal was to learn to type 80 keystrokes a minute. Only the 1 × 1 group was able to attain this goal in less than 60 hours (actual time, 55 hours). The other groups all required additional practice time beyond the originally scheduled 60 hours. The 2 × 1 group required a total of 67 hours to attain this typing speed while the 1 × 2 group required 75 hours. The least distributed practice group, the 2 × 2 group, never did achieve this goal as they were still only doing a little better than 70 keystrokes per minute after 80 hours of practice. Retention tests were given 1, 3, and 9 months after training had finished. After 9 months, the 2 × 2 group performed the worst on the typing speed test with the other groups performing about the same. Finally, a very revealing result was obtained from the trainees' own ratings of the training schedules. Although most preferred their own schedule, the least distributed group preferred theirs the most whereas the most distributed liked theirs the least.

The results of this experiment indicate that fitting 60 hours of training into 3 weeks, where there had to be two 2-hour practice sessions each day, was a poor practice schedule. While the most distributed schedule generally attained performance goals in the least amount of time, they did not perform any better than the 1 × 2 and 2 × 1 groups on the retention tests. Given all the results, the authors concluded that the 1-hour training sessions were more desirable than the 2-hour sessions and that one session per day was only slightly more effective than two sessions per day. However, having two 2-hour sessions each day was not a good training regime.

There are distinct implications from the Baddely and Longman experiment for scheduling practice sessions for teaching motor skills. First, it is clear that practice sessions can be too long. Second, more frequent practice sessions are preferable over less frequent sessions. Third, time saved in terms of the number of days of practice can be a false savings, as massing sessions too much can lead to poorer learning. Finally, what students, trainees, or patients feel is a more desirable schedule, may not be the best schedule for learning the skill. Remember, if the postal trainees had had their way, they would have chosen the schedule that got them through with the training in the shortest amount of time, which ironically was the poorest schedule for learning the skill.

An important instruction decision is how to distribute the practice time that
has been allotted for practicing a skill. Research investigating this issue has
led to the comparison of massed and distributed schedules of practice. Two
types of practice schedule concerns are relevant to this issue. One is the length
of rest given between trials, the intertrial interval. Results of this research
have shown that for continuous tasks, distributed schedules are generally better
for learning than are massed, although the degree of difference is not a large
one. However, for discrete tasks, just the opposite has been found. For these
tasks, massed practice schedules are the preferred schedules. The second concern about the distribution of practice involves the length and frequency of
practice sessions. Although this has not been a common problem of investigation by researchers, there is evidence to suggest that practice sessions can
be too long and too frequent to lead to optimal learning.

Summary

Adams, J. A. (1987). Historical review and appraisal of research on the learning,
    retention, and transfer of human motor skills. *Psychological Bulletin, 101,*
    41–74.
Drowatzky, J. N. (1970). Effects of massed and distributed practice schedules upon
    the acquisition of pursuit rotor tracking by normal and mentally retarded
    subjects. *Research Quarterly, 41,* 32–38.
Lee, T. D., & Genovese, E. D. (1988). Distribution of practice in motor skill
    acquisition: Learning and performance effects reconsidered. *Research
    Quarterly for Exercise and Sport.*
Singer, R. N. (1965). Massed and distributed practice effects on the acquisition and
    retention of a novel basketball skill. *Research Quarterly, 36,* 68–77.

**Related
Readings**

Concept 9.4 The decision to practice a motor skill as a whole or by parts should be made on the basis of the complexity and organization of the skill

Application

An important instructional decision you must make when teaching any motor skill will be one related to how to have your students practice the skill. Should they practice the skill in its entirety or by parts? Practicing a skill as a whole would seem to help students get a better feel for the flow and timing of all of the movements. However, to practice the skill by parts would appear to place emphasis on performing each part correctly before putting the whole skill together. A major reason why this decision is an important one is related to a problem often referred to throughout this book: the efficiency of instruction. It is probably correct to state that practice method, practicing the skill as a whole or by parts, will be effective in helping the students learn the skill. However, it is equally correct to say that both methods will probably not get the student to the same level of competency in the same amount of time. One method will generally be more efficient than the other as a means of attaining competent performance. A question we will consider in the following discussion is this: Will one method always be more efficient than the other, or is the efficiency of the method related to the skill being learned?

Suppose you are teaching a beginning tennis class. You are preparing to teach the serve. Most tennis instruction books break down the serve into six or seven parts. These are generally presented as the grip, stance, backswing, ball toss, forward swing, ball contact, and follow-through. The decision you are faced with is whether to have the students practice all of these parts together as a whole or to practice each component or group of components separately.

The tennis serve situation also illustrates a further decision that you may have to make. If you decide to encourage practice of the serve by its parts, then which parts will the students practice separately? Will you attempt to set up drills and practice situations in which each part will be practiced separately? Will you combine some of the components to be practiced together, while requiring practice of other parts separately? On what basis will you combine parts for practice? There are many decisions to be made in relation to the one question "How will I have my students practice the tennis serve?"

Discussion

The issue of whole vs. part practice has been a topic of discussion in the motor learning literature since the early part of this century. Unfortunately, the research that this discussion has generated has led to more confusion than understanding. One of the primary reasons for this confusion is the nature of the

research undertaken. This research tended to be very task oriented in its approach to the problem. That is, the major question being investigated by these experiments was only whether whole or part practice was better for this task or that task. Thus we have examples of a variety of published research studies that appear almost identical. Similar experimental designs were used to test the same basic hypotheses. They differed only in the tasks that were used. Sometimes the experiments added an experimental group by modifying part practice, such as "progressive part," or combining part and whole practice as "whole-part" or "part-whole." Some examples of the published research will serve to illustrate the point being made here. Barton (1921) compared progressive part, part, and whole practice for learning a maze. Brown (1928) compared whole, part, and whole-part practice for learning a piano score. Knapp and Dixon (1952) compared whole and part-whole practice for learning to juggle. Wickstrom (1958) compared whole and a form of progressive part practice for learning gymnastic skills.

Fortunately, some attempt was finally made at trying to organize and formulate this problem so as to determine some general rule that could be followed to help in resolving the whole-part practice question. James Naylor and George Briggs (1963) concluded that the issue could be resolved if two features of the task or skill in question were considered. They called these features task organization and task complexity. *Task complexity* refers to how many parts or components are in the task and the information-processing demands of the task. A highly complex task would have many components and require much attention throughout. For example, a floor exercise routine, dance routine, or running a pass pattern and catching a pass in football could be considered as highly complex tasks. A low complexity task has relatively limited attention demands and relatively few component parts. Tasks such as shooting a rifle or arrow and a military press in weight lifting would be low in complexity. *Task organization* refers to how the components of a task are interrelated. A task in which the parts are intimately related to one another would have a high degree of organization, such as shooting a jump shot in basketball. A task in which the parts are rather independent of one another would be low in organization; this is the case in many dance routines.

Each of these features of motor skills or tasks can be regarded as being represented by a continuum of low to high. In this way, the complexity or organization of a task may be thought of as being very high or very low or somewhere in between. The precise designation along the continuum is not as important as the relative position, that is, how the task in question compares to other tasks, higher or lower.

The problem of using whole or part practice for more efficient use of practice time to learn a motor skill can be resolved, then, by a *general rule* that considers where a skill lies on each continuum. If the skill is high in complexity but low in organization, the practice of parts would be recommended. But if

First General
Rule

the skill is low in complexity and high in organization, practice of the whole skill would be the better choice. Thus, a relatively simple skill, with its component parts highly related, would be most efficiently learned by the whole practice method. Most phases of weight lifting or shooting an arrow in archery would probably fall in this category. A skill that tended to be very complex with its parts relatively independent, that is, low in organization, would be learned most efficiently by the part method.

The way to apply this general rule of motor skill complexity and organization to your own teaching situation will be to consider the skill you are teaching. Analyze it to determine its component parts and to what extent those parts are interrelated. Then decide to which end of the complexity continuum and the organization continuum the skill is more related. Your part vs. whole practice decision can then be made on the basis of how the complexity and organization features are related. For example, consider the tennis serve discussed in the application section. We determined that the serve has approximately seven component parts. Thus, the tennis serve would most appropriately lie toward the high end of the complexity continuum. Those components seem to be relatively mixed in their independence and dependence to one another. Thus, the serve would be somewhere in the middle of the organization continuum. Here, then, is a skill that is relatively high in complexity and moderate in organization. The practice method decision would seem to favor a modified part practice, where certain of the parts would be combined for practice while other parts would be practiced separately.

Second General Rule

After the decision has been made to practice the skill using a modified part method as described in the tennis serve example, you must determine how that practice will take place. What parts will be practiced separately and what parts will be combined for practice? This decision can be made on the basis of a *second general rule*. That is, parts of a skill that are highly dependent on each other should be practiced together as a unit, but parts that are relatively independent can be practiced individually. In the tennis serve, the grip, stance, backswing, and toss are relatively independent; thus these parts can be practiced individually. The forward swing, ball contact, and follow-through are strongly interdependent; these components should always be practiced as a complete unit.

The skillful instructor will be able to determine if certain parts need to be practiced individually or not. Just because the components are independent does not mean they must be practiced independently. It only means that they *can* be. Thus, when the decision is made to divide a skill into its component parts for practice, this second rule indicates that the breakdown should follow a natural division of the parts. If the learner practices certain parts of the skill separately that actually should be combined with other components as a unit, then the end result might be that he or she will require more time to learn the skill than might otherwise be necessary.

The part method seems very helpful for the practice of trouble spots. If the toss is a source of error in a student's serve, it is helpful to know that because the toss is a relatively independent part of the serve, it can be practiced alone. However, suppose the student is having difficulty with the follow-through. The practice that follows should include the forward swing, ball contact, *and* follow-through as one unit. The ball toss may or may not be included, depending on whether the instructor wants to keep this variable out of the practice. A ball suspended at the proper height from a string attached to an overhanging pole could suffice to provide a ball for contact. The benefit of this type of practice is that it allows emphasis to be placed on the phase of the skill that is causing the problem. When the follow-through is not made properly, the cause is usually with the ball contact phase of the serve. Thus, when the three-part unit is practiced, the problem can more easily be corrected.

A useful way to use the part method of teaching a complex skill and to take advantage of the "chunking" strategy that was discussed in the chapters on Memory and Attention is to employ what is traditionally known as the *progressive-part method*. In this method of teaching complex skills, the decision has been made to teach a skill by having students practice separate parts of the skill independently. However, rather than all parts being practiced separately, the parts have been organized according to the order in which each part occurs in performing the skill, and then the parts are progressively linked together. This means that after the first part has been practiced as an independent unit, the second part is practiced first as a separate part, and then together with the first part. Each independent part, then, progressively becomes a part of a larger part. As practice develops, the entire skill eventually becomes practiced as a whole skill. Thus, the parts are progressively "chunked" together as larger parts until the whole skill can be performed as one large "chunk."

The Progressive-Part Method

A simple example of the progressive-part method can be seen in a commonly used approach to teach the breaststroke in swimming. This stroke is easily subdivided into two relatively independent parts, the leg kick and the arm action. Because a difficult aspect of learning the breaststroke is the timing of the coordination of these two parts, it is helpful to reduce the attention demands of the whole skill by practicing each part independently first. This enables the student to allocate attention to just the limb action requirements, for each part can be learned without attending to how the two parts should be coordinated as a unit. After each part is practiced as independent parts, the two can then be put together to practice as a whole unit, with attention now directed toward the temporal and spatial coordination demands required for the arm and leg actions.

The tennis serve example we have been using in this discussion can also be taught with the progressive-part method. For example, the ball toss can be practiced as an independent unit, as can the backswing. However, after each

is practiced independently, they can then be combined and practiced as a separate part to help establish the coordination required of this complex action. Then, the forward swing and follow-through can be added to complete the "chunking" of the parts of the tennis serve so that it can now be practiced as a whole skill.

The distinct advantage of the progressive-part method is that it takes advantage of the benefits offered by both part and whole methods of practice. That is, the part method offers the advantage of restricting the attention demands on the individual so that specific aspects of a part of a skill can be practiced without considering how that part should be coordinated with other parts. The whole method, on the other hand, has the advantage of requiring important spatial and temporal coordination of the parts to be practiced together. In the progressive-part method, both of these qualities are combined so that attention demands of performing the skill are kept under control; the parts are progressively put together so that the important spatial and temporal coordination requirements of performing the parts as a whole can be practiced.

Summary

One of the many decisions that an instructor of motor skills must make is whether the skill being taught should be practiced as a whole or by its parts. This decision should be made according to the general rule related to the complexity and organization of the skill. This general rule recommends that whole practice is advisable when the skill tends toward the low complexity and high organization ends of the high-low skill or task complexity and organization continua. Part practice is advisable when the skill is more closely related to the opposite ends of the two continua, that is, high in complexity and low in organization. If the decision is made to follow a part practice method, then a further decision must be made. This concerns how to implement the part practice. A second general rule can be followed here. This rule recommends that the components of a skill that are significantly associated or interdependent should be practiced together as a unit. Parts of the skill that are relatively independent can be practiced separately. The progressive-part method takes advantage of the beneficial qualities of both the part and the whole methods and is an effective practice method for learning complex skills.

Related Readings

Knapp, C. G., & Dixon, W. R. (1952). Learning to juggle: A study of whole and part methods. *Research Quarterly, 23,* 389–401.

Naylor, J., & Briggs, G. (1963). Effects of task complexity and task organization on the relative efficiency of part and whole training methods. *Journal of Experimental Psychology, 65,* 217–244.

Robb, M. D. (1972). *The dynamics of motor-skill acquisition.* Englewood Cliffs, NJ: Prentice-Hall. (Read pp. 42–49.)

Singer, R. N., & Dick, W. (1979). *Teaching physical education: A systems approach* (2nd ed.). Boston: Houghton-Mifflin. (Read chapters 2 and 6.)

Modeling is an effective form of instruction for teaching motor skills

If you are teaching a new skill and want to communicate to your students how this skill should be performed, what is the most likely way that you would communicate this information? Probably you would demonstrate the skill so that the students could see for themselves how the skill should be performed. If you couldn't demonstrate the skill yourself, you might have them watch another student in the class demonstrate the skill, or, have them watch a film or video tape of someone doing the skill. In each of these situations, demonstration is the common means of communicating information about how to perform a skill. Each of these forms of demonstration is included in what is commonly referred to by learning researchers and theorists as *modeling*. This form of instruction may be the most frequently used strategy for communicating to students how a skill should be performed.

An interesting feature about the use of modeling is that it can be used in such a wide range of situations. For example, a physical education teacher may demonstrate to a large class how to putt in golf. An aerobics teacher may demonstrate to a class how to perform a particular sequence of skills. A baseball coach may show a player the correct form of bunting a ball. An occupational therapist may demonstrate to a patient how to button a shirt. In each of these situations where different types of individuals and motor skills are involved, the common goal is to communicate how to correctly perform a skill. By demonstrating a skill, the instructor indicates that he or she believes that more information is conveyed in less time than would be required if he or she verbally told the student how to perform the skill. So, whether you are teaching a large class, working with a small group, or providing individual instruction, and whether you are teaching a complex skill or a simple skill, modeling can be used as a regular instruction strategy.

Although modeling seems to be universally accepted as a form of instruction for teaching motor skills, numerous questions must be addressed to establish when modeling is effective, why modeling is effective, and what is required to most effectively use modeling as an instructional strategy for teaching motor skills. In the following discussion, these questions will be addressed so that you will have a more substantial basis for determining how to use modeling more effectively in whatever motor skill teaching situation you may find yourself.

While modeling undoubtedly has been one of the most common (if not the most common) forms of providing instructions about how to do a skill, it is ironic that there is so little research related to it. In fact, most of what we

know about modeling is related to its use in social learning. For a number of years, social behavior researchers and theorists have considered modeling to be an important means for learning values, attitudes, and other social behaviors. Much of the theoretical understanding of modeling has come from this area of study (e.g., Bandura, 1977, 1984). However, there has been a recent increase in interest in knowing more about the use of modeling for teaching motor skills, which has resulted in an increase in our understanding of how to use modeling to teach skills and why modeling works.

The Effective Model

One of the more comprehensive reviews of modeling research related to motor skill acquisition was published by Dan Gould and Glyn Roberts (1982). They identified a number of important questions that need to be answered if we are to understand conditions in which modeling is and is not effective, as well as why modeling facilitates motor skill learning. Since that time, there has been an increased interest in conducting research investigating modeling and skill acquisition, which has provided us with greater insight into the role of modeling in motor skill learning. One of the important outcomes of this research has been the finding that modeling is more effective under certain circumstances than others. This result suggests that modeling should not be used without first determining whether the instructional situation warrants its use. In the following sections, some of these circumstances will be considered to provide you with a better understanding of the use of modeling. The initial focus will be on circumstances related to the model. As you will see, the degree of effectiveness that can be achieved by the use of modeling is dependent on a number of factors related to the model, including such things as the characteristics of the model, the model's demonstration, and when the model is used.

Status of the model. One of the first things to consider when deciding about demonstrating a skill is, who should do the demonstration? It may be surprising to find that the status of who demonstrates the skill can be an influential factor in establishing the effectiveness of the demonstration. For example, consider an experiment by Landers and Landers (1973) in which they compared skilled and unskilled models that were either the teacher or student peers. In this experiment, grade-school children learned to climb the Bachman ladder, a free-standing ladder that the subject holds and then climbs as many rungs as possible before losing balance. One group of these children observed a skilled teacher while another group observed a skilled student peer. A third group observed an unskilled teacher while the last group observed an unskilled peer. All the children observed the model before beginning their 30 practice trials. Results indicated that the highest performance was achieved by those who observed the skilled teacher. However, for those who observed an unskilled model, those who observed the unskilled peer performed better than those who

observed the unskilled teacher. Thus, the status of the model was important to practice performance of this task. The teacher was more effective as the model when that person was skilled at performing the task. When the teacher could not perform the skill well, another unskilled student was the more effective model.

As you may have noticed, the Landers and Landers (1973) experiment did not include a retention or transfer test, thus limiting the potential of this study to indicate the influence of the model's status on learning. However, McCullagh (1987) reported an experiment that did include a retention test and that was designed to also look at model status. She compared the performance of college females on their performance on the Bachman ladder task after watching models portrayed as having different status. The status of the model was established by portraying the higher status model as a gymnast/dancer who had a lot of experience in balance type activities. Thus, this model was considered as being dissimilar to the subjects. The lower status model was portrayed as being similar to the subjects in that she was portrayed as a college student with no particular background related to the task. However, the model for both conditions was actually the same person and performed the skill equally well for both groups of subjects. A third group was also included as a control condition. This group did not observe a model. All subjects practiced the task for 20 trials with KR provided after every trial and then were given a 1-minute rest. Then, 10 retention trials were performed, on which no KR was given. As you can see from the results in Figure 9.5–1, the group that saw the similar status model showed higher performance during the practice trials. Also note that both model groups performed better than a control group that had not watched a model. However, this influence of the similarity of the model to the subjects did not influence learning, as all subjects performed similarly on the retention test, including the control group, which is a point that will be addressed later in this discussion.

Thus, in terms of model skill, it appears that whether the model is a peer of the students or is one who has a higher status, does not influence learning the skill. However, if the model is not skilled at performing the task, then it cannot be determined on the basis of the research that has been done what the effect on learning will be. However, based on the Landers and Landers experiment, the peer would be the better model for influencing practice performance.

Why should the model's status be expected to influence the effect of modeling on skill acquisition? Two possibilities have been suggested. First, the higher status model may influence students to pay closer attention to the demonstration and therefore positively affect the amount of information students receive from the demonstration. The second possibility is that the higher status model provides an increased motivation to perform well. The students are more motivated because of their desire to be like this person that they admire. It is also possible that both these reasons are involved in the model status influence.

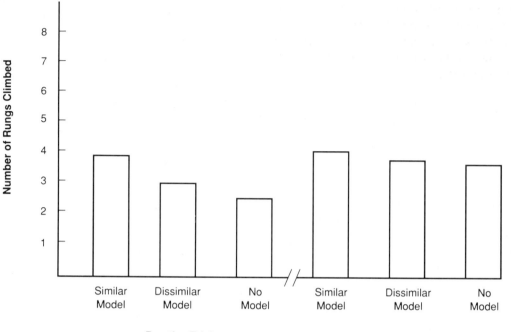

Figure 9.5-1
Results from the
experiment by
McCullagh showing
the influence of a
similar and a
dissimilar model or
no model on
performing the
Bachman ladder
task during practice
trials with KR and
on retention trials
without KR.

It is obvious that additional research is needed to address the model status question with particular attention paid to the influence of model status on learning a skill.

However, there does seem to be evidence from research outside the skill acquisition realm (see the Gould & Roberts, 1982, review of modeling research) that an important point to consider before demonstrating a skill is, How well can you perform the skill? If you can perform it well, then as a person with a respected, higher status than the student, the demonstration most likely will be more beneficial than if a student demonstrates it. However, if you cannot demonstrate the skill, you have a couple of options. One option is to use a film or tape of a well-known, skilled individual performing the skill. The second option is to use a student to demonstrate the skill. Even if the student cannot perform the skill well, he or she can be used as a visual aid that can be the basis for your verbal description of what should be done.

Correctness of the demonstration. A common conclusion about the characteristics of the model's performance of the skill being modeled is that the skill should be performed correctly. Recall that in the Landers and Landers (1973) experiment there was a comparison of skilled and unskilled models and their influence on how well the subjects acquired the ladder climbing task. The results showed that regardless of whether the model was the teacher or another

student, the skilled demonstration led to better performance than the unskilled demonstration. This result seems to be common in studies that make similar model performance comparisons. In fact, as a conclusion to their review of modeling and skill acquisition research, Gould and Roberts (1982) stated that "High-status models must accurately and skillfully portray the skill" (p. 228). Why would the more accurate demonstration lead to better learning? The most likely reason is related to what the student does after watching the demonstration. When the student is asked to try the skill after having seen a demonstration of it, the student typically tries to imitate as closely as possible what the model did.

An interesting example of research evidence supporting this point that students imitate a model after observing the model is one by Martens, Burwitz, and Zuckerman (1976, experiment 3). Subjects observed a model perform a "shoot-the-moon" task that involves moving a ball up an incline that is formed by two metal rods which are held by the subject and moved back-and-forth to make the ball move up the incline. The score obtained is based on where the ball falls through the rods to the base below. The experiment involved using different groups of subjects observing models performing the task using one of two strategies. One strategy, called the "creep strategy" involved moving the ball slowly up the incline. Although this strategy rarely led to high scores, it led to consistent scores on each trial. The other strategy, the "explosive strategy," involved moving the rods in such a way as to rapidly propel the ball up the incline. Although this strategy led to higher scores, it also was the riskier strategy since it often led to extremely low scores as well. The results of this experiment showed that the subjects typically adopted the strategy they saw used by the model they observed.

Thus, if the goal of the instructional situation is to have the student learn to perform the skill correctly, then it stands to reason that since the student will probably imitate the model, the more correctly performed skill will be learned better. However, there is an important consideration that should be taken into account before implementing this conclusion. That is, if the use of a model leads the student to imitate the model, then whether or not a model should be used may depend on how much you want the model's performance of the skill imitated. For some skills, such as a gymnastics stunt or a dance routine, there is a specified way that the skill should be performed. Thus the closer to this criterion the student can perform the skill, the better his or her performance will be evaluated. However, for most skills, there are a variety of correct ways to achieve the goal of the skill. If a student tries to imitate someone else's way of performing the skill, then his or her potential to perform the skill may be limited, since there may be a more optimal way for that student to perform. This possibility suggests, then, that for these types of skills it may be best to use the model earlier in the stages of learning. And, emphasis should be placed on those critical elements of the skill that must be performed in a certain way to achieve the task goal. For other aspects of the skill, the student should be free to modify his or her movements.

When should the model be introduced? Another important decision that must be made concerning the use of a model is when the model should be used to best facilitate learning. One possibility is that the model should be introduced before practice begins so that the students have an idea of what the skill looks like when it is performed. This approach would be in keeping with Gentile's (1972) proposal that the goal of the first stage of learning is to "get the idea of the movement." If seeing the model perform the skill before actually practicing it helps the student get the idea of the movement, then introducing the model as early in practice as possible would be more effective.

An alternative to this approach is to allow students to first try the skill on their own after being provided with information about the goal of the movement and some basic verbal instructions about how to perform the skill to accomplish this goal. This approach emphasizes initial trial-and-error practice and may help the student to develop some initial coordination capabilities, as well as to learn some movement characteristics that will not work. After some initial exploration with the skill, the model could then be introduced. The argument for the benefit of introducing the model at this time would be that the student now has a better idea of what to look for in the model's performance and will therefore benefit more by seeing the model at this time, rather than before practicing the skill.

Although this is an interesting question, there has been limited research attempting to provide an answer. And, the evidence that has been reported leads to an unsettled conclusion. Two experiments illustrate this. First, consider the experiment by Landers (1975). He had subjects practice the Bachman ladder balancing task. Observation of a model was introduced in one of three ways. One group of subjects watched the model perform 4 trials of the task before practicing 30 trials. Another group saw the model perform 4 trials before practicing 15 trials and then saw the model perform 2 more trials before practicing the second set of 15 trials. Finally, the third group practiced 15 trials and then observed the model perform 4 trials, and then did the remaining 15 trials. Results showed that the two groups that saw the model before practice began did better on the initial trials. However, after the model was introduced to the third group following 15 trials of practice, this group caught up with the other two groups. Then, on the last blocks of trials, the group that had observed the model before they began practicing and after 15 trials outperformed the other two groups. Thus, the early introduction of the model was beneficial for learning this task. However, what was even more beneficial was to have the model observed again halfway through the practice trials.

Another experiment that provides some interesting findings regarding when to introduce the model involves some developmental considerations that might be taken into account. Thomas, Pierce, and Ridsdale (1977) had 7- and 9-year-old girls practice the stabilometer task. Three groups of subjects were formed in each age group based on when the model was observed or if the model was observed at all. One group, the "beginning model" group, saw the

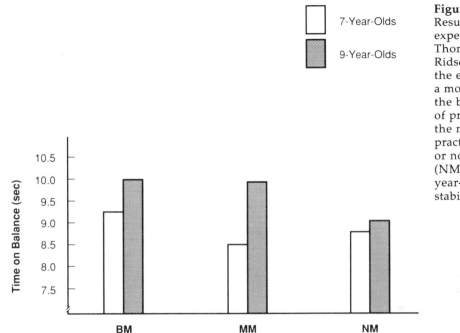

Figure 9.5-2
Results of the experiment by Thomas, Pierce, and Ridsdale showing the effect of having a model available at the beginning (BM) of practice, only at the middle of the practice trials (MM), or no model at all (NM), for 7- and 9-year-olds learning a stabilometer task.

model before beginning their 12 practice trials. Another group, the "middle model" group, saw the model after practicing 6 trials and then practiced the remaining 6 trials. The third group did not observe a model. The interesting results of this experiment (Figure 9.5–2) were that introducing a model in the middle of the practice trials led to detrimental performance by the 7-year-olds whereas it benefited the 9-year-olds. Thus, for the older children, the early opportunity to explore how to accomplish the task goal was useful practice experience.

These results suggest that introducing a model before practice begins is an appropriate use of the modeling technique. However, it is advisable to provide an opportunity for students to observe the model at other times during practice, in addition to this initial opportunity. Also, these results suggest that there are situations in which allowing students the opportunity to initially explore how the task can be done before introducing the model can be beneficial, especially if the students are old enough.

One characteristic that seems to reappear in discussions of modeling experiments is that the influence of different factors related to characteristics of the model on skill acquisition is that it depends on the skill being learned. In fact, the benefit of modeling itself seems to be characterized by this type of conclusion. Some experiments have reported that modeling leads to no better learning than no modeling, while others have concluded that modeling certain

The Effects of Modeling and the Skill Being Learned

features of a skill leads to no benefit compared with not modeling that feature of the skill. What these reports typically have in common is that the characteristics of the skill being learned may or may not lend themselves to being learned better by observing a model.

For example, the Bachman ladder task has been popular in modeling and skill acquisition research. When performance by subjects is compared when a model has been observed versus when no model was observed, results are consistent in showing a benefit for those who observed the model. The modeling benefit has also been reported for nonlaboratory tasks, such as a racquetball forehand (Southard & Higgins, 1987). However, there are other skills that have not shown this modeling benefit. For example, Doody, Bird, and Ross (1985) showed that observing a model perform a barrier knockdown timing task led to no better achievement of the criterion movement time than not observing a model. Also, Burwitz (1975) reported no modeling benefit for learning the pursuit rotor task.

What, then, can be said about what differentiates skills in how the use of a model will influence how well they are learned? One answer to this question is based on what information about the performance of the skill can be effectively conveyed by a model. For example, if the goal of a skill is to make a response in certain criterion movement time, then it is likely that a visual model will not convey useful information to the learner. However, if the model conveys the appropriate information, learning will be facilitated. Thus, rather than the skill being the key, the information about the skill conveyed by the model becomes the key.

A good example of this point is provided by the results of an experiment by Doody, Bird, and Ross (1985). They had subjects practice knocking down a specified sequence of seven 10.5 × 7-cm barriers in a criterion movement time of 2,100 msec. One group of subjects observed a videotape of a model before each practice trial. The videotape included both the video and audio aspects of the performance. Another group saw only the video portion of the tape and received no auditory modeling information. A third group received only the audio portion of the modeled performance and never saw the task performed by the model. A control group was not given any advance information other than the goal movement time. Results indicated that during 10 acquisition trials with KR and 18 no-KR retention trials, the groups that received audio modeling did better than the visual model only and the control group. In fact, the visual model only group did not do any better than the control group. Thus, although visual modeling was not effective for learning this task, auditory modeling was. The information conveyed by the auditory model was more relevant for learning this task than was the information conveyed by the visual model.

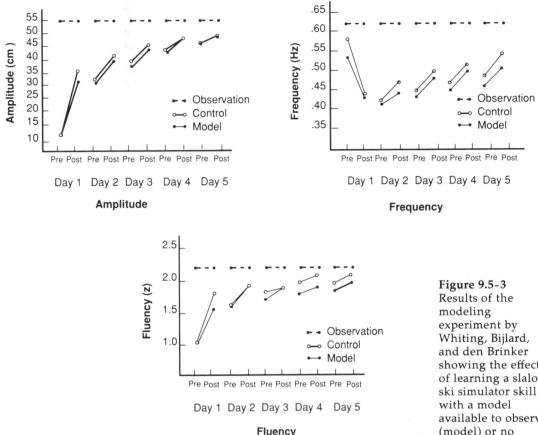

Figure 9.5-3
Results of the modeling experiment by Whiting, Bijlard, and den Brinker showing the effects of learning a slalom ski simulator skill with a model available to observe (model) or no model available (control). The model's performance (observation) is also shown in these graphs. The definitions of the measures amplitude, frequency, and fluency are in the text.

Another experiment that supports this notion that what is critical is the information conveyed by the model was reported by Whiting, Bijlard, and den Brinker (1987). Subjects practiced the slalom ski simulator task that was discussed in Concept 7.2 and shown in Figure 7.2–3. Two groups of subjects were used. One group observed a film of a skilled model demonstrating performance of the skill during their practice sessions while the other group saw no model. There were 5 days of practice with six 1.5-minute trials each day. Before and after these practice trials each day, the subjects were given a 1-minute test trial with no model available. The results of this experiment, which are presented in Figure 9.5–3, showed that the influence of the model on performance depended on what performance characteristic was measured. The observation of a model had no beneficial influence on performance "amplitude" (the average distance the subject moved the trolley on a trial). However, for both the "frequency" (how many times the subject moved the trolley side-to-side on a trial) and the "fluency" (how smooth the movement was during the trial), the group that observed the model performed better than the group that did not.

Also, it is interesting to note that for frequency, the benefit of observing a model was almost immediate, whereas for fluency this benefit was not seen until the fourth day of practice. Thus, the visual model conveyed certain task-related information that was beneficial for the frequency and fluency aspects of the performance, but not for the amplitude part of the skill.

The point of all this is that it appears possible that learning can be facilitated for any skill by modeling *if* the model conveys information that is critical for successful performance of the skill. This means that when the choice is made to demonstrate a skill, it is important to determine whether only visual information is to be provided or whether other perceptual information about performing the skill will also be provided. Also, other things that must be determined include whether the whole skill or just a part of the skill will be demonstrated and what observation angle will be provided, i.e., will the students see the skill performed from the front, side, back, above, etc.

It will help to relate this point about what information is conveyed by the model in relation to the skill being learned to a point made earlier in this text in the discussion of Kahneman's attention model (Concept 4.2). Recall that an important factor influencing a person's attention allocation policy is what Kahneman called "momentary intentions." This means that attention will be directed to those features of a skill that the student has been instructed to give attention. In addition to giving specific instructions, knowledge of results was also considered to be another example of a momentary intention device for directing attention to specific features of a skill (Concept 7.2). Now, we see another example. One of the functions served by a model is to direct the student's attention to how the skill should be performed. If no particular instructions are provided about what to observe, the student will perceive what is the most salient aspects of what is observed. Whether what is observed will facilitate learning any more than not observing that aspect of the skill will depend on how observable the important information is.

Why Does Modeling Benefit Learning?

So far in this discussion we have considered various factors that influence the benefit of modeling for skill acquisition. However, we have yet to establish *why* learning is facilitated when all the important factors have been taken into account and are a part of the use of modeling. Although there has not been extensive theoretical development of the modeling effect, two different views have emerged as explanations for why modeling facilitates skill learning. One view is based on research related to social behavior learning whereas the other view is related to how perception of visual information occurs.

The view that predominates current thinking about why the modeling effect occurs is one proposed by Bandura (1977, 1984) and is based on Bandura's work with modeling and social learning. This view of the modeling effect can be called the *cognitive mediation theory,* although it is also referred to as the mediation-contiguity theory and the stimulus-contiguity theory. This theory proposes that what happens when a person observes a model is that symbolic

coding of what is observed occurs in memory. This coding forms the basis of a representation in memory that can be accessed when the person is required to perform the skill. This representation then serves as a guide for the performance of the skill and as a standard for error detection and correction, much like Adams' perceptual trace. The key point here is that the visual information received by observing the model is transformed into a cognitive memory representation that can then be cognitively rehearsed and organized.

According to Bandura, there are four subprocesses that govern learning by observation of a model. The first is the *attention process* which determines what is observed and what information is extracted from the model act. The second subprocess is the *retention process,* which involves transforming and restructuring what is observed into symbolic codes that are stored in memory as internal models for action. Certain cognitive activities, such as rehearsal, labeling, and organization, benefit the development of this representation. The *behavior reproduction process* is the third subprocess and involves translating the memory representation of the modeled action and turning it into physical action. Successful accomplishment of this process requires the individual to possess the physical capability to perform the modeled action, otherwise, the action cannot be performed. Finally, the *motivation process* involves the incentive or motivation to perform the modeled action. This process, then, focuses on all those factors that influence a person's motivation to perform. Without this process being completed, the action will not be performed.

The second view of why modeling benefits skill acquisition is based on the direct perception view of vision proposed by Gibson (1966, 1979) and extended by Turvey (1977) to the performance of motor skills. This view has been called the *dynamic view* of modeling and has been proposed as an alternative to Bandura's theory to explain modeling effects for skill acquisition by Scully and Newell (1985). The dynamic view takes issue with the need for a symbolic coding or memory representation step between the observation of the modeled action and the physical performance of that action. This view argues that the visual system is capable of automatically processing visual information in such a way that it constrains the motor response system to act according to what is detected by vision. The visual system "picks up" salient information from the model that provides the motor response system with a basis for coordinating and controlling the various body parts required to produce the action. Thus the critical need for the observer in the early stage of learning is to be able to observe demonstrations that enable him or her to perceive the important relationships between body parts, which is termed *coordination.* Then, additional modeling will benefit the learner if information is perceived that allows for parameterizing the coordinated action, which means applying the appropriate values to such dynamic features as the force and kinematic elements required by the action.

There is no conclusive evidence available in the research literature that shows one of these two views of the modeling effect as being the more valid

one. At present, both views appear to be viable theoretical approaches to explain why modeling benefits skill acquisition. The cognitive mediation theory has been the more prominent of the two and has received the most attention in motor skills research (see Carroll & Bandura, 1985, for a discussion of some of this research). However, the dynamic view has only recently been proposed and should provide the basis for research to test its viability as an appropriate explanation of the modeling effect.

Implementing Effective Modeling

Regardless of which theoretical interpretation is adopted concerning why modeling benefits motor skill acquisition, there appear to be definite features that should characterize the effective use of modeling as a form of instruction. Perhaps the most important characteristic is that the model must convey to the observer the critical features of a skill that are important for performing that skill. Recall that certain skills have been reported that do not appear to be learned any better after observing a model than not observing a model. However, what is probably the key to this finding is that the model has not conveyed the critical performance information that is needed by the observer. This suggests that an important task of the instructor is to determine what the model should convey to the observer and how that should be accomplished. In some cases it may mean that only a certain part of the skill is modeled, or that the observer should see the skill modeled from a unique direction, or that the model should be both visual and auditory. Because modeling serves to direct attention to the skill to be performed, it is essential that steps be taken to ensure that the student's attention is directed to those aspects of the skill that will yield a benefit to performing the skill.

Another important feature of the effective use of modeling is that the skill should be demonstrated correctly. If the model is to convey essential performance information to the student, it is critical that this information be based on the correct performance of the skill. This means that if you, as the instructor, cannot perform the skill correctly, you must find someone who can. Perhaps one of the students can do the skill or ask someone to come to your class or practice the skill until you can perform it. You could also use a film or videotape of someone doing the skill correctly, since most research has shown there to be little difference, if any, between observing a live model and observing a filmed or taped model.

If only a part of the skill is to be demonstrated, it is important that you follow the guidelines presented for part practice in Concept 9.4. Recall that the important element in determining how to establish an appropriate part of a complex skill to practice was to consider if the part can be performed independently as a unit and will not be influenced by what precedes or follows it in the sequence. Although it is appropriate to demonstrate just the ball toss by itself in the tennis serve, it would not be best to just demonstrate the follow-through of the serve by itself. In the same way, if you are going to demonstrate

the pitching motion in softball, it would be best to demonstrate the backswing and the forward swing of the pitching arm action as a unit, since the transition from one to the other is such a critical part of the successful pitch.

Finally, the effective model must direct the observer's attention to what needs to be observed. Although the demonstration may convey what needs to be conveyed, which was the first point made in this section, there will be little benefit derived if the observer is not attending to that information. Make certain that everyone can see the demonstrator from the angle that you want them to observe the action. If you have people sitting in a circle around the demonstrator, then everyone is seeing the action from a different perspective. You must determine if this is appropriate for the skill being demonstrated. Also, it may be necessary to alter what would normally be done in performing the skill so that attention is not distracted by a feature of the action that is irrelevant to its performance. For example, if you are demonstrating how to shoot an arrow at a target, it is probably best not to release the arrow. If an arrow is released toward the target, it is likely that the students' attention will get directed to watching the arrow go to the target rather than on the features of drawing and releasing the arrow. This same principle can be implemented in any skill that involves an object. Try demonstrating the action without the object or without acting on the object. This approach can help direct attention to the more critical elements of the action. Finally, use verbal instructions to direct attention to what the student should observe. If you are instructing beginners, remember that they do not know what to look for to help them perform the skill. Your verbal instructions will provide them with this information.

Summary

Modeling is the demonstration of a skill to those who are learning the skill. This form of instruction is a commonly used form of conveying information to students about how a skill should be correctly performed. Several factors influence the effectiveness of using a model on skill acquisition. Such factors as the status of the model, the correctness of the demonstration, and when the model is introduced can all influence the benefit that will be derived from demonstrating a skill. Also, the information that is conveyed about the skill is critical to the effective use of modeling. Two theoretical viewpoints are prominent concerning why modeling benefits learning motor skills. One view is based on Bandura's social learning research and is called the cognitive mediation theory. The second view, called the dynamical view, holds that cognitive mediation is not needed since the visual system can automatically constrain the motor system to act in accordance with what has been modeled. The effective use of modeling requires the instructor to give close attention to several factors that were discussed related to implementing modeling as a beneficial form of instruction for skill learning.

Related Readings

Carroll, W. R., & Bandura, A. (1985). Role of timing of visual monitoring and motor rehearsal in observational learning of action patterns. *Journal of Motor Behavior, 17,* 269–282.

Gould, D. R., & Roberts, G. C. (1982). Modeling and motor skill acquisition. *Quest, 33,* 214–230.

Scully, D. M., & Newell, K. M. (1985). Observational learning and the acquisition of motor skills: Toward a visual perception perspective. *Journal of Human Movement Studies, 11,* 169–186.

Weiss, M. R., & Klint, K. A. (1987). "Show and Tell" in the gymnasium: An investigation of developmental differences in modeling and verbal rehearsal of motor skills. *Research Quarterly for Exercise and Sport, 58,* 234–241.

Practice that occurs mentally can be beneficial for learning new motor skills and for preparing to perform a skill

Situations in which mental practice can be applied abound in motor skills. These situations range from employing mental practice to help learn a new skill, to using it to assist in the performance of an activity at a world-class competitive event. Before discussing the effectiveness of mental practice and why it seems to be so effective, a few examples of how mental practice can be used in motor skill situations will help to set the stage for the discussion that follows.

A gymnast is standing beside the floor exercise mat waiting to begin his or her routine. However, before actually beginning that routine, the gymnast goes through the entire routine mentally, visualizing the performance of each stunt in the routine, from beginning to end. Following this, the gymnast then steps on the mat and begins the routine.

A young volleyball student is having difficulty learning how to spike. After several demonstrations by the instructor and several practice attempts, the student still has difficulty spiking the ball. The instructor tells the student to stop practicing and to sit down on the floor and mentally practice spiking the ball. The student is told to do this by imaging spiking the ball perfectly 15 times in a row. He or she is encouraged to go through the entire sequence of set-up, approach, and spike in his or her mind on each practice attempt. Following this procedure, the student is then instructed to go back to physically practicing the spike.

A situation that is often perplexing to a novice learner is one in which a good response is made but because of the nature of the game, it would be physically impossible to practice that response in the same way. Golf is a good example of this type of situation. If the golfer has just hit a beautiful drive right down the middle of the fairway, he or she would like to be able to hit a few more drives just to try to reproduce and reinforce the swing that produced such a beautiful result. But another type of practice can be used while walking down the fairway to the ball; the golfer can mentally practice the swing that produced the drive. As the golfer walks down the fairway, he or she can be imaging hitting that excellent drive over and over again.

Notice that in each of the examples, mental practice was applied in a slightly different way in accordance with the different goals of the mental practice. The gymnast practiced mentally to prepare for an immediate performance of a routine that had been practiced many times and was well-learned. The volleyball player was using mental practice as a means to help improve

a skill that was in the process of being learned. Finally, the golfer, although learning a new skill, was implementing the mental practice procedure to reinforce a proper response as an aid to an upcoming response.

Discussion

Mental practice is a term that has been used in a variety of types of literature for a long time. Research investigations of the relationship between mental practice and physical performance can be traced to the 1890s, while philosophic discussions can be traced back to Plato and beyond. Even the popular literature has been interested in what we call mental practice. With so much interest in this one topic for so many years, it seems paradoxical that we know relatively little about it. This is not to say, however, that we are unable to draw any conclusions from what we do know about mental practice or apply them to very practical needs. We definitely emphasize conclusions and apply them in this discussion. But it is unfortunate for all of us that we know so little about such a potentially powerful variable that is related to both learning and performance.

Defining Mental Practice

When the term *mental practice* is used in the research literature it refers to *the cognitive rehearsal of a physical skill in the absence of overt, physical movements.* Mental practice, as we are considering it here, is not to be confused with meditation, which generally connotes the involvement of the mind in deep thought in such a way as to block out the awareness of what is happening to or around the individual. Meditation can, however, be thought of as a form of mental practice; in fact, it seems to be a potentially effective means for enhancing physical performance. For example, in a *Psychology Today* article, William Morgan (1978), a sport psychologist, reported that world-class long distance runners, such as marathoners, engage in an effective form of meditation while they run. Some runners disassociate their mental concentration from their running, while others relate their mental concentration to their running by attending to finite details of the physiological status of their bodies throughout the race.

In this discussion, we are limiting the use of the term *mental practice* to cognitive or mental rehearsal. According to this use of the term, an individual is involved in mental practice when he or she is *imaging* a skill, or part of a skill, that is actually being performed. No involvement of the body's musculature is noticed by an observer. This imaging may occur while the learner is observing another person or a film; or it may occur without any visual observation.

These two different types of imaging, or mental rehearsal, have been categorized by Mahoney and Avener (1977) as internal and external imagery. *Internal imagery* involves the individual actually approximating the real-life situation in such a way that the person actually "images being inside his/her body and experiencing those sensations which might be expected in the actual

situation" (p. 137). *External imagery,* on the other hand, involves the individual viewing himself or herself from the perspective of an observer, as in watching a movie of oneself. We will not compare the efficacy of these two types of imagery conditions in this discussion. The interested reader can consult the Mahoney and Avener (1977) article or one by Hale (1982). However, be aware that these two types of imagery represent two different forms that mental rehearsal can take. Unless otherwise specified, either of these forms can be involved when mental practice is being considered.

The study of mental practice as it relates to the learning and performance of motor skills has taken two distinct research directions over the years. These approaches have followed the patterns suggested by the different situations described in the applications section. One of these directions has been the investigation of the role of mental practice in the *acquisition* of motor skills. Here the critical question is how effective mental practice is for a beginning learner who is in the initial stages of learning a motor skill. The example of the volleyball student learning to spike illustrates the orientation of this type of mental practice study.

Two Roles for Mental Practice

A second research direction has considered how mental practice can aid in the *performance* of a well-learned skill. Two approaches to this use of mental practice can be taken. The first is illustrated by the gymnast example presented earlier. Here mental practice is being used to aid in the preparation of the immediately upcoming performance. As such, mental practice can be seen as a means of response preparation, as discussed in Concept 4.1. The second use of mental practice as an aid to performance was seen in the example of the golfer mentally imaging a successful swing as he or she walks down the fairway. Here mental practice combines characteristics of both the acquisition and performance situations by providing a means of rehearsal, i.e., reinforcing a successful movement and serving to aid the retrieval from memory process necessary to produce the same swing again.

Beginning as early as the 1890s, research literature is replete with mental practice studies. Excellent reviews of this research literature have been published by Richardson (1967a; 1967b), Corbin (1972), and Feltz and Landers (1983). These reviews indicate that relatively convincing evidence is available to support the point that mental practice is an effective variable for aiding skill acquisition and performance preparation.

Most experiments investigating the effectiveness of mental practice in motor skill acquisition follow a similar design. Typically, one group is provided physical practice on a task; another group mentally practices the task for the same number of trials as the physical practice group; a third group is a control condition where subjects do not practice the task. Following these practice conditions, all groups perform the task on a retention test. In some experiments, a fourth condition is added; this involves some combination of physical and mental practice trials.

Mental Practice and Skill Acquisition

In general, comparison of the physical, mental, and no practice conditions indicate that physical practice is better than the other conditions. However, mental practice is typically better than no practice. This finding alone is interesting to support the effectiveness of mental practice in aiding acquisition. However, even more interesting is what happens when a physical-mental practice combination is compared to these three conditions.

An example of combining mental and physical practice is provided by a study reported by McBride and Rothstein (1979). An open and a closed skill were compared in terms of how mental practice related to skill acquisition. Based on the characteristics of these two types of skills, it might be expected that mental practice alone would aid the learning of closed skills but not open skills, while some combination of mental and physical practice would be necessary to show a mental practice benefit for open skills. In this experiment, all subjects were required to hit a solid whiffle golf ball at a 6-foot target that was 10 feet away. For the closed skill, the ball was placed on a batting tee 3 feet high. For the open skill, a 5-foot curved tube was placed at a 45° angle and balls were dropped down the tube at the rate of one every 10 seconds. Subjects used a forehand stroke with the nondominant arm to hit the ball with a table tennis paddle.

All subjects practiced for 40 trials. The physical practice group physically performed 40 trials. The mental practice group was given a demonstration and 3 physical practice trials. They then practiced 40 trials mentally, keeping a score for each hit. The physical and mental practice group alternated 10 physical, 10 mental, 10 physical, and 10 mental practice trials. Figure 9.6–1 shows the results of the first test trial block, which was an average of the five trials that immediately followed the 40 practice trials, and the first retention trial block, which was an average of five trials performed one day later. As you can see, for both the open and closed skills, the combination of mental and physical practice trials was superior to the mental practice and physical practice conditions for both test and retention trials.

What is interesting about these results is that the physical-mental practice group actually had only half as many physical practice trials as did the physical practice group. However, even with this much less physical practice, their retention scores were superior. This finding that a combination of mental and physical practice trials leads to better learning than physical practice alone is not uncommon in the mental practice literature. In fact, if you compare this practice situation to some points discussed throughout this text about memory and learning processes, these results would be predicted. To be more specific, consider the need to engage in effective rehearsal strategies to ensure a durable and accessible memory representation in long-term memory. Also consider the point made in Concept 9.1 that effective problem-solving activity during practice is an important element in skill acquisition. Taken together, these lead to the expectation that any practice condition that encourages an effective rehearsal strategy, which includes problem-solving activity, will lead to better

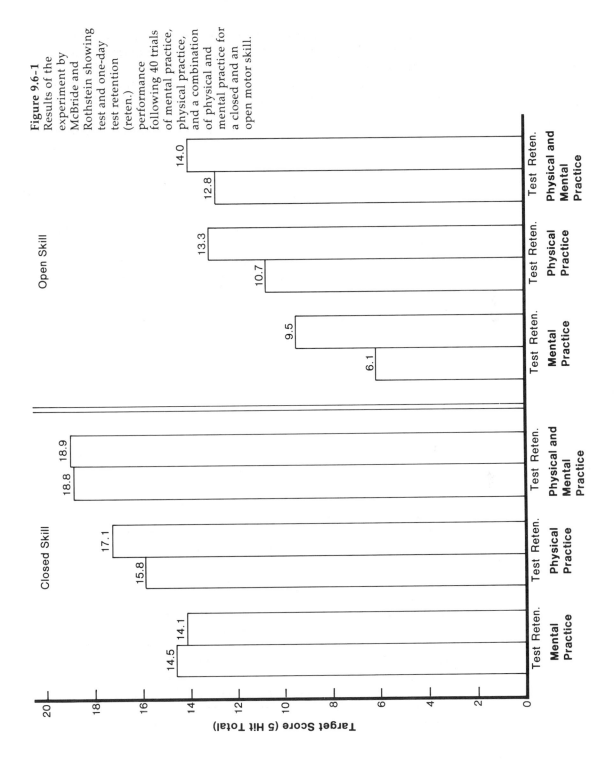

Figure 9.6-1
Results of the experiment by McBride and Rothstein showing test and one-day test retention (reten.) performance following 40 trials of mental practice, physical practice, and a combination of physical and mental practice for a closed and an open motor skill.

learning than practice conditions that do not. When mental and physical practice trials are combined, it is likely that these conditions are in effect and therefore lead to better retention performance than physical or mental practice alone.

Mental Practice as Response Preparation

In the field of sport psychology, a popular topic of interest relates to the benefit of having elite athletes image themselves performing a skill prior to actually performing it. While there is ample evidence from newspaper and sport magazines that athletes make this type of preparation, there is little research evidence to determine whether this form of preparation is better than any other form. However, some evidence does suggest that mental rehearsal is an effective form of response preparation.

In a direct test of several different methods of performance preparation, Gould, Weinberg, and Jackson (1980) examined three different preparation conditions and compared them to two control conditions. One mental preparation condition was called *attentional focus*. Here subjects were given specific instructions to concentrate on the feelings in the specific muscles involved in the task to prepare them for maximum performance. The second mental preparation condition was called *imagery,* which we have been considering in this discussion. The instructions to the subjects were to visualize themselves performing the task and setting a personal best score. The third condition was called *preparatory arousal*. In this condition, subjects were told to "psych" themselves up for maximum performance. This could be accomplished by getting mad or "pumped up" to perform as well as possible. The two control conditions involved subjects doing nothing for the 20-second preparation time or counting backwards by 7s from a four-digit number for 20 seconds.

The performance task used in this experiment was a leg-strength task in which subjects were required to exert as much power as possible with one leg on a leg-strength testing machine. Each subject was to produce a personal best score for each of four trials. A preparation interval preceded each trial during which the subjects engaged in the preparation condition assigned to their group. Results showed that the imagery and the preparatory arousal preparation conditions produced higher strength scores than the other three conditions.

The results of this study by Gould, Weinberg, and Jackson support the view that certain mental preparation strategies are better than others for producing maximum or peak performance. While imagery was not better than the arousal preparation condition, it was better than the attentional focus strategy or doing nothing at all. Since the task was an explosive strength task, it is not surprising to find that the emotional arousal strategy was effective. (Recall the discussion in Concept 4.1 concerning arousal level and performance as related to the type of task being performed.)

There have been various attempts at trying to explain why mental practice is effective as both a learning and a performance variable. The two most plausible explanations are a neuromuscular explanation and a cognitive explanation.

A neuromuscular explanation. The notion that mental practice benefits learning or response preparation for a neuromuscular reason can be traced to work by Jacobson (1931). When subjects were asked to visualize bending their right arm, he observed EMG activity in the ocular muscle but not in the biceps brachii. However, when subjects were asked to imagine bending the right arm or lifting a 10-pound weight, EMG activity was noted in the biceps brachii on more than 90% of the trials. Support from this type of electrical activity in the muscles when subjects are asked to imagine movement has been provided many times since Jacobson's early study (e.g., Hale, 1982; Lang, et al. 1980).

Evidence such as this can give us some insight into why mental practice is an effective means of aiding skill acquisition and response preparation. You saw in earlier parts of this book the importance of sensory feedback in establishing an effective memory representation for a movement. Schmidt (1975) indicated that the sensory consequences of a movement are critical in developing a strong recall schema. Adams (1971) had earlier emphasized the importance of sensory feedback for developing a strong perceptual trace. From these viewpoints, mental practice can be seen as providing sensory information that can be used to effectively learn a skill.

In the discussion of response preparation in Concept 4.1, you saw that "tuning" activity precedes a response and presets the appropriate musculature for action. Since imaging an action creates electrical activity in the musculature that is involved in the movement, imaging can be considered a form of response preparation that aids in this tuning process.

A cognitive explanation. If you will recall the discussion in Concept 2.2, the first stage of learning, according to Fitts and Posner, was termed the cognitive stage. These investigators maintained that during this stage, the learner is involved in much cognitive activity that is related to questions about "what to do" with this new task. It should not be surprising, then, that mental practice can be effective practice during this stage of learning. Mental practice can help the learner to answer some of the questions that characterize the early stage of learning, without the learner being pressured simultaneously to physically perform the skill. In the later stages of learning, mental practice would seem to be beneficial in assisting the learner to consolidate strategies as well as to correct errors.

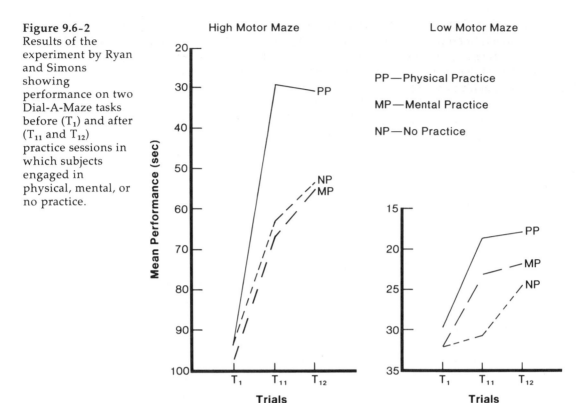

Figure 9.6-2
Results of the experiment by Ryan and Simons showing performance on two Dial-A-Maze tasks before (T_1) and after (T_{11} and T_{12}) practice sessions in which subjects engaged in physical, mental, or no practice.

An example of some support for a cognitive basis of explanation of mental practice is an experiment by Ryan and Simons (1983). They reasoned that if mental practice is essentially a cognitive phenomenon, then learning a task that is heavily cognitively oriented should benefit more from mental practice than a task that is more motor oriented. To test this, they compared acquisition on two motor tasks, one low in motor demands and the other high in motor demands. These tasks were practiced under conditions of physical practice, mental practice, and no practice. The task, called a Dial-A-Maze, resembles a child's "Etch-A-Sketch" toy. A stylus is moved through a maze pattern by rotating two handles, one controlling horizontal movement, the other controlling vertical movement. The low motor demand task consisted of moving the stylus through the maze only in horizontal and vertical directions. Motor coordination demands were minimal as the two hands did not have to work together. The high motor demand task required the two hands to work together to move the stylus in a diagonal direction. The results are seen in Figure 9.6–2. Notice that as predicted the mental practice was superior to the no practice condition for the low motor demands maze. That is, mental practice benefited the task that was heavily cognitively demanding.

Although both physiological and psychological reasons have been proposed to explain why mental practice is effective for learning and performing motor skills, another issue related to the effectiveness of mental practice is worth considering. Recall that in chapter 6 perceptual and motor abilities were identified as types of abilities related to motor skill performance. Now, when the effectiveness of mental practice is considered, we find that another type of ability is thought to come into play. This ability is the ability to image an action when requested to do so. As an individual difference characteristic, this ability differentiates people in that some have great difficulty imaging a described action while others can image with a high degree of vividness and control.

An interesting hypothesis has been proposed by Craig Hall (1980, 1985) concerning the relationship between imagery ability and the effectiveness of mental practice. He proposed that imagery ability is a critical variable in determining the success that can be expected to result from mental practice. That is, those individuals who have a high level of imagery ability will benefit from mental practice of motor skills, while those with a low level will not benefit as much from mental practice. A problem with testing this hypothesis has been the lack of appropriate tests of imagery ability relevant to motor skill performance (see Hall, Pongrac, & Buckolz, 1985, for a discussion of imagery ability tests). To overcome this problem, Hall and Pongrac (1983) developed the Movement Imagery Questionnaire (MIQ).

The MIQ consists of 18 action situations that a person is asked to physically perform. Then, the person is asked to do either one of two mental tasks, either "form as clear and vivid a mental image as possible of the movement just performed" or, "attempt to positively feel yourself making the movement just performed without actually doing it." In this test, the first mental task is called "mental imagery" while the second mental task is called "kinesthetic imagery." After one of these mental imagery tasks has been performed, the individual is asked to rate how easy or difficult it was to do the mental task. The individual is not to rate how good or bad their performance was of the mental task but how easy or difficult the mental task was to do. An example of two items from the MIQ, one from the visual and one from the kinesthetic imagery subscales, are presented in Figure 9.6–3. The two rating scales for each can also be seen in this figure. As you can see, specific action instructions are provided in each item. The ratings of all items in the test are tallied and an imagery score is obtained that indicates if the individual has a high or a low level of imagery ability or is somewhere between these two extremes.

To test the hypothesis that imagery ability relates to the effectiveness of mental practice for learning a motor skill, Goss, Hall, Buckolz, and Fishburne (1986) selected individuals for participation in a mental practice experiment on the basis of their scores on the MIQ. Three categories of imagery ability individuals were selected, high visual/high kinesthetic (HH), high visual/low kinesthetic (HL), low visual/low kinesthetic (LL). These subjects practiced four complex arm movement patterns to a criterion level of performance. Before each of the practice trials, subjects were required to kinesthetically image the

Starting Position: Stand with your feet slightly apart and your hands at your sides.

Action: Bend down low and then jump straight up in the air as high as possible with both arms extended above your head. Land with your feet apart and lower your arms to your sides.

Mental Task: Assume the starting position. Form as clear and vivid a mental image as possible of the movement just performed. Now rate the ease/difficulty with which you were able to do this mental task.

Rating

Starting Position: Stand with your feet slightly apart and your arms at your sides.

Action: Jump upwards and rotate your entire body to the left such that in the same position in which you started. That is, rotate to the left in a complete (360°) circle.

Mental Task: Assume the standing position. Attempt to feel yourself making the movement just performed without actually doing it. Now rate the ease/difficulty with which you were able to do this mental task.

Rating

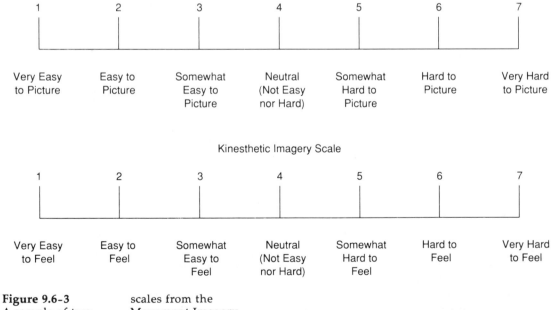

Rating Scales
Visual Imagery Scale

1	2	3	4	5	6	7
Very Easy to Picture	Easy to Picture	Somewhat Easy to Picture	Neutral (Not Easy nor Hard)	Somewhat Hard to Picture	Hard to Picture	Very Hard to Picture

Kinesthetic Imagery Scale

1	2	3	4	5	6	7
Very Easy to Feel	Easy to Feel	Somewhat Easy to Feel	Neutral (Not Easy nor Hard)	Somewhat Hard to Feel	Hard to Feel	Very Hard to Feel

Figure 9.6-3
A sample of two items and the rating scales from the Movement Imagery Questionnaire.

movement about which they were given instructions. Visual feedback, which showed the subjects their response in comparison to the criterion pattern, was provided after each trial. Two days later, all subjects returned for a retention test on the four movement patterns. During this test, no visual feedback was provided on the first 3 trials but was provided for the remainder of the trials until the subjects achieved the performance criterion that was used during the acquisition trials.

The results of this experiment showed that the HH group performed the patterns to criterion in the fewest number of trials (11.0), with the HL group next (15.4), and the LL group taking the greatest number of trials to achieve criterion (23.7). During the retention phase, the three groups again showed this same order, although the differences were not as dramatic. The HH group required 6.3 trials, while the HL and LL groups required 6.7 and 9.2 trials, respectively, to reattain the performance criterion. Another interesting analysis was based on how many subjects in each group performed at least one of the movement patterns correctly during the retention test. The results of this analysis showed that again, the HH group did the best with half of these subjects performing at least one pattern correctly while no subjects in the LL group could do this.

The results of this experiment indicate that there is a relationship between imagery ability and the effectiveness of mental practice. However, the results also show that individuals who are low in imagery ability can still benefit from mental practice for learning motor skills. These individuals may need to practice more than those with high imagery ability, but they will still be able to take advantage of the use of mental practice as an effective learning strategy. Hopefully more research will be done to help increase our understanding of imagery ability and its relationship to the effectiveness of mental practice for both learning and performing motor skills.

Mental Practice as an Instructional Strategy

A very practical benefit to be derived from using mental practice as a part of instruction is that it can help alleviate problems of what to do with students because the class is too large, or because there is not enough equipment, or because a student is injured. Students who are waiting their turn can be instructed to practice mentally a certain number of movements or exercises. It is important, however, that the teacher be very specific, instructing the students how the mental practice should be performed. The teacher should tell the students to imagine themselves doing the skill correctly. This imagining can include the entire skill or a specific part of the skill that is being worked on. The teacher should instruct them to go through this procedure a specific number of times, such as five or ten mental practices. Following these guidelines for implementing mental practice, the teacher not only keeps inactive students occupied but also provides them with an opportunity to be involved in an activity that will help them learn the skill they are practicing.

An interesting example of incorporating mental practice into a practice or performance preparation routine can be seen in some work that has come

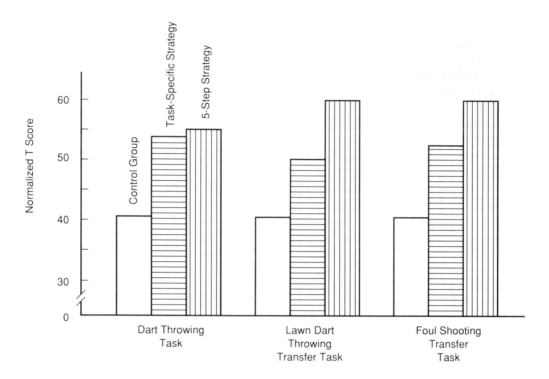

Figure 9.6-4
Results of the experiment by Singer and Suwanthada showing the influence of a generalized learning strategy (5-step strategy), a task-specific strategy, and no strategy for initial practice with a dart throwing task and transfer performance on a lawn dart throwing task and a foul shooting task.

out of Robert Singer's laboratory. Singer (1986) proposed that the learning of closed motor skills could be facilitated if persons engaged in a general learning strategy. This learning strategy involves five steps, three of which involve elements of mental practice. The first step is to get ready physically, mentally and emotionally. The second step involves mentally imaging performing the action, both visually and kinesthetically. The third step involves concentrating intensely on only one relevant cue related to the action, such as the seams of a tennis ball. The fourth step is to execute the action. Finally, the fifth step is to evaluate the performance outcome.

To test whether this general strategy could be an effective strategy for learning a specific motor skill, Singer and Suwanthada (1986) compared subjects who used this strategy with those who used more task-specific strategies and with those who were not given a strategy. The task involved underhand throwing of a dart at a rifle target that was on a wall 3 meters from the subject. Following 50 practice trials with the dart throwing task, all subjects were required to perform two related tasks, a lawn dart throwing task and a type of basketball foul shooting task. The lawn dart task involved throwing a lawn dart underhand to the rifle target that was on the ground 6 meters from the subject. The foul shooting task involved shooting a soccer ball one-handed at a target attached to a basketball backboard from a distance of 4.5 meters. As you can see in Figure 9.6–4, subjects who used the five-step general strategy

to practice the dart throwing task performed as well as those who used task-specific strategies. Also note the strategy groups performed better than the no strategy control group. However, on both transfer tasks, the subjects who had practiced the dart throwing task with the general five-step strategy performed better than the other groups. Thus, a general strategy that involved subjects in using mental practice to prepare for each practice response was an effective means to aid learning the skill for which the strategy was used, but it also was beneficial for effective transfer to related tasks.

Mental practice is by no means recommended as a panacea. It is presented, however, as a means of practice that, when used properly, can be effective in the learning and performance of motor skills. Furthermore, mental practice is not being recommended as a substitute for physical practice. But mental practice can be an effective instructional strategy, though proper implementation is critical to its effectiveness.

Summary

Mental practice is the cognitive rehearsal of a physical skill in the absence of overt, physical practice. It involves imaging the actual performance of a movement. Experimental evidence has shown that mental practice can be an effective aid in the acquisition, performance and retention of motor skills. Explanations as to why mental practice is effective relate to neuromuscular and cognitively based views. Evidence supporting both viewpoints has been discussed. The effectiveness of mental practice can be related to a person's ability to mentally image action. Mental practice can be an effective instructional strategy. However, its implementation requires effective planning by the teacher and use by the students.

Related Readings

Corbin, C. B. (1972). Mental practice. In W. P. Morgan (Ed.), *Ergogenic and muscular performance* (pp. 93–118). New York: Academic Press.

Feltz, D. L., & Landers, D. M. (1983). The effects of mental practice on motor skill learning and performance: A meta-analysis. *Journal of Sport Psychology, 5,* 25–57.

Gould, D., Weinberg, R., & Jackson, A. (1980). Mental preparation strategies, cognitions, and strength performance. *Journal of Sport Psychology, 2,* 329–335.

Hall, C. R. (1985). Individual differences in the mental practice and imagery of motor skill performance. *Canadian Journal of Applied Sport Sciences, 10,* 175–215.

Singer, R. N., & Cauraugh, J. H. (1985). The generalizability effect of learning strategies for categories of psychomotor skills. *Quest, 37,* 103–119.

Concept 9.7   Practicing while being physically fatigued appears to affect performance to a greater degree than learning, although learning can be affected

Application

A characteristic of most motor skills is that practicing them can be physically fatiguing. Activities such as dance, wrestling, gymnastics, swimming, many motor skill rehabilitation activities, and a host of others demand much from the participant in terms of physical energy. The person responsible for organizing and conducting the practice sessions for these activities is often confronted with the problem of what can be accomplished when the participants are fatigued. Can learning occur even though they are fatigued? Should something new be introduced at this time, or could the time be better spent?

For example, a dance class has been practicing very hard for an entire class period. They are obviously quite fatigued. However, as the instructor, you feel that in order to maintain a time schedule, a new movement should be introduced to the class before they are dismissed. Although your calendar indicates the need for you to present this new information at this time, does learning theory support it? If learning theory does not support this procedure, then you will, in effect, be wasting your time and that of your students by introducing this new movement while they are fatigued. However, if there is evidence to show that some benefit can be derived from practicing the new movement even while fatigued, the time will not be wasted.

Situations similar to this dance class example can be proposed for a variety of motor skills in many instructional settings. Common to all these situations is the need for the instructor to know whether a person can learn while fatigued or whether practice while fatigued is a waste of time. The concept we are considering here indicates a positive response to this question. That is, learning does appear to be possible, even though an individual is fatigued. In the following discussion we shall consider this conclusion more critically to determine what it can mean to instructors of motor skills.

Discussion

The problem that we are considering here is similar in nature to the problem discussed in previous sections of this book. That is, does fatigue affect learning or performance or both? We have already considered the fatigue problem to some degree in Concept 2.1 and have in effect set the stage for this discussion. That is, the research literature seems to indicate that fatigue has a primary impact in inhibiting performance but not learning. This means that performance scores can be expected to be depressed during the practice in which

the individual is fatigued. However, as soon as the person is given an opportunity to rest, thus reducing or eliminating the fatigue, performance during the following practice session will be similar to that of a person who had been previously practicing the skill in a nonfatigued condition.

Evidence that supports the detrimental influence of fatigue on performance is abundant. There is also ample evidence to suggest that learning is generally unaffected by fatigue. However, the research on which these conclusions are based is not without its problems, which will be discussed later. To complicate matters, an unequivocal conclusion seems impossible at this time because of some evidence which indicates that learning can also be affected by fatigue.

A good example demonstrating fatigue as a performance rather than a learning variable is the one by Godwin and Schmidt (1971) discussed in Concept 2.1. This experiment was presented in that discussion as an example of how practice performance effects can sometimes lead to incorrect inferences about learning effects. We can briefly consider it again here to consider what it has to say about fatigue and learning.

In the Godwin and Schmidt experiment, women subjects formed two groups, a fatigued group (F) and a nonfatigued group (NF). Each subject was required to perform on the sigma task, which involves rotating a handle in a clockwise direction for one revolution until hitting a stop, then reversing the direction of the handle for one more revolution, and then finally releasing the handle and knocking down a wooden barrier 11 inches away. Subjects were scored on the total amount of time it took to complete the task, that is, movement time. Subjects in the fatigue group were required to crank a hand-crank ergometer for 2 minutes before every trial of the first session of the experiment, which involved 20 trials. All subjects were asked to return to the laboratory three days later to perform 10 more trials on the sigma task but with no fatiguing condition. The results, which were presented in Figure 2.1–4, indicated that while the fatigued group performed the task more slowly than the nonfatigued group during day 1, there was no difference between groups on the no-fatigue transfer trials on day 2.

The Godwin and Schmidt experiment is a good example of several experiments which indicate that fatigue is a performance variable and not a learning variable. Since performance on the task being learned was not impaired on the second day of trials when there was no fatigue condition, the inference is that learning was not impaired during the practice trials that were performed while fatigued. Before determining how conclusive these results are, it will be necessary to consider an example of some other research that points to some different results.

Evidence Supporting Fatigue as a Performance Variable

Figure 9.7-1
Results of the
experiment by
Carron showing the
performance curves
for the fatigued
group (open circles)
and nonfatigued
group (closed
circles) for the free-
standing ladder
climbing task.

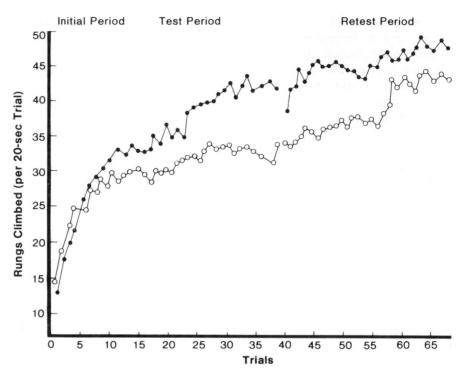

Evidence
Supporting
Fatigue as a
Performance
and Learning
Variable

A study conducted by Carron (1972) presented results which indicated that
fatigue could be considered as both a performance and a learning variable. In
that experiment, male subjects learned a balancing task, the free-standing
ladder; this task requires the subject to climb as many rungs as possible on
the ladder within a certain period of time. Each time the subject begins to fall,
he must begin again and continue until the practice trial is over. The performance measure is the total number of rungs climbed in a practice trial. Every
subject was given 68 trials of 20 seconds each. One group of subjects was
fatigued by having them ride a bicycle ergometer for 10 minutes prior to the
first 18 trials. Each practice trial was also followed by 2 minutes of this exercise. The other group, the control group, did not exercise. This procedure
was followed for two days, or 36 trials. On the final two days of 18 trials each,
neither group exercised. The results of this experiment can be seen in Figure
9.7–1. The group that was physically fatigued showed poorer performance on
all four days of the practice trials. Thus, fatigue during practice affected both
performance *and* learning.

The Issue
Reconsidered

The two experiments that have been described in this discussion indicate quite
opposite results. This leads to the obvious question of which one is correct in
its findings. Unfortunately, the answer to that question is a very difficult one.

The cause of that difficulty lies in the procedures followed in experiments investigating the fatigue and learning issue. The primary problem in the procedures is the absence of consideration of individual fitness levels of the subjects. In most experiments, the fatigue condition is based on all subjects doing an exercise for a certain amount of time or to a certain heart rate. To be truly fatiguing for all subjects, it would seem that all subjects should be given exercise bouts that would be fatiguing for each person.

A second procedural problem apparent in many of these studies is that the exercise is not specific to the muscle groups used in the task being learned. In an actual teaching situation, students generally become fatigued from using muscles involved in the task being learned. It would only seem reasonable to make the conditions of the experimental situation similar in nature to those of the instructional situation.

Finally, the issue is difficult to resolve because various fatigue levels have not been adequately considered. It appears that light to moderate fatigue affects performance but has little influence on learning, while heavy or extreme fatigue affects both performance and learning. Thus, there seems to be a *threshold of fatigue* that should be used as a guideline for instructors. If fatigue levels appear to be below that threshold, practice of a new aspect of the skill will be beneficial in the long run. However, if fatigue levels are greater than the threshold, further practice would not be advisable. Unfortunately, no evidence has been provided in the research literature to suggest any valid criteria for determining such a threshold. Until such criteria are developed, instructors must use intuition and past experience to guide them in determining the amount of fatigue that their students can show before eliminating any further instruction. The threshold of fatigue must be considered as being related to the fitness level of the individual and the task or skill involved.

While the effect of fatigue on learning motor skills has been the primary concern in this discussion, one other factor must be taken into consideration. The risk of injury to a participant must outweigh all considerations of the effect that fatigue might have on learning. If even a slight amount of fatigue would increase the chances of injury, then further practice would not be advisable until the student has recovered from the fatigued condition.

Summary

Physical fatigue is common to many motor skills. The instructor must decide whether or not further instruction will be beneficial to students who are obviously fatigued. Research evidence seems to indicate that light to moderate levels of fatigue will produce performance decrements while practicing in the fatigued state but will not impair learning. Extreme levels of fatigue, however, may impair both performance and learning.

Related Readings

Alderman, R. B. (1965). Influence of local fatigue on speed and accuracy in motor learning. *Research Quarterly, 36,* 131–140.

Carron, A. V. (1972). Motor performance and learning under physical fatigue. *Medicine and Science in Sports, 4,* 101–106.

Godwin, M. A., & Schmidt, R. A. (1971). Muscular fatigue and discrete motor learning. *Research Quarterly, 42,* 374–383.

Study Questions for Chapter 9 (Practice)

1. Why is variety of practice beneficial for learning (a) closed motor skills? (b) open motor skills? Give an example of how you would implement variety in practice for a closed and for an open skill.
2. How is contextual interference related to the variability of practice issue in motor learning?
3. How could you incorporate contextual interference into practice sessions for a skill you might teach?
4. What are two reasons that have been proposed concerning why contextual interference benefits motor skill learning?
5. Why is the issue concerning whether errors early in practice are harmful or beneficial to learning an important one for people who teach motor skills? What does the available research suggest is the more appropriate answer to this issue?
6. How is the concept of "overlearning" related to motor skill learning? Why is overlearning beneficial to learning?
7. Describe how the concept of practice distribution can be related to the intertrial interval and to the length and distribution of practice sessions. Describe a motor skill learning situation for each.
8. How do massed and distributed practice schedules influence the learning of discrete and continuous motor skills? Why do you think there is a difference in how these two schedules influence learning these skills?
9. What two general rules can be applied to answering the whole-part practice conditions question? Give a motor skill example to show how these rules can be applied to a teaching situation.
10. What is meant by the term "modeling" as it relates to motor skill instruction? What are three important issues that must be considered when determining how to provide an effective model?
11. Describe an example of a research study that has shown that modeling can benefit motor skill learning.
12. What are two proposed reasons why modeling benefits motor learning?
13. What is "mental practice"? Describe an example of how effective mental practice procedures can be implemented to aid (a) learning a new skill, and (b) preparing to perform a motor skill.
14. What are three reasons proposed to explain why mental practice aids motor learning and performance?
15. When does fatigue appear to be (a) a performance variable? (b) a learning variable? Why do you think fatigue is related to learning motor skills in these two ways?

Motivation

10

Concept 10.1
Motivation is important to the understanding of motor skills learning and performance because of its role in the initiation, maintenance, and intensity of behavior.

Concept 10.2
Arousal and anxiety affect learning and performance according to the interrelationship between individual and situational characteristics.

Concept 10.3
Establishing an appropriate goal or level of aspiration is an effective means of motivating skill learning and performance.

Concept 10.4
The application of appropriate reinforcement techniques can serve to facilitate the learning and performance of motor skills.

<table>
<tr><td>

Concept 10.1

</td><td>

Motivation is important to the understanding of motor skills learning and performance because of its role in the initiation, maintenance, and intensity of behavior

</td></tr>
</table>

Application

You are undoubtedly familiar with the old saying that "you can lead a horse to water but you can't make him drink." Trite as that saying may seem, it provides a good example of the importance of motivation in behavior. One of the reasons you can't make the horse drink is because he probably doesn't want to. That is, he is not motivated to drink. Are there any ways in which you could manipulate things in order to make the horse want to drink? Even if you get the horse to drink, will he keep drinking the water? Suppose you have worked a long time to make the water trough as appealing as possible. Then you use all your various abilities to get the horse to the trough. But in spite of all those efforts, the horse simply will not drink the water; what then?

This simple anecdote is not so far-fetched when you consider situations in which you will find yourself when it is your responsibility to teach or coach. You will spend a lot of time making lesson plans, preparing the equipment needed for the lesson, organizing the students, etc. The students will be there, in your class. But what do you do when some of them simply aren't motivated to learn what you want them to learn?

Situations like this can occur in a variety of settings. You have planned a tumbling unit for your physical education class. On the first day of the unit, a student comes up to you and says, "I've done this stuff before. I don't like it, and I'm not going to do it." The situations are not limited to the physical education class. Suppose you are coaching a basketball team. One of your key players could improve his play by developing some different one-on-one moves. You call the player aside and suggest a move for him to work on. The response is, "No, coach, I'm doing good with the way I do it. Don't mess me up with new moves." Situations like this are all too familiar to most teachers and coaches.

In the following discussion we will examine some basic elements of the term *motivation.* We will consider both its meaning and its role in the learning and performance of motor skills. As we progress through the chapter, you should be able to develop possible approaches that could be successful in achieving the desired outcomes, using the examples just presented. This discussion will also provide you with the necessary foundation to consider the issues involved in the remaining concepts of this chapter.

The Learning Environment

One of the major problems in any discussion of motivation is that it is as diverse as the disciplines that are concerned with it. Animal behaviorists equate motivation with reward or punishment. Social psychologists speak in terms of socially related reinforcers. Educational psychologists relate motivation to achievement motivation. Others consider motivation synonymous with the term *drive* or *need,* while still others see it as being similar to *arousal* or *activation.*

Webster's Unabridged Dictionary relates motivation to the word *motive.* *Motive* comes from a Latin word, *motivum,* meaning "a moving cause." Motive is defined as "some inner drive, impulse, intention, etc., that causes a person to do something or act in a certain way." Thus, any discussion of motivation is concerned with *determining the causes of a behavior;* this in turn involves investigation of what influences those causes. Although motives are defined as being internal, the influences on these inner causes can be external. A student may not want to take a particular course, but in order to graduate he or she must take it. As a result, the behavior of taking the course has been strongly influenced by the external demand of the school.

For the purposes of this book, we will define motivation as *the causes of the initiation, maintenance, and intensity of behavior.* This concept of motivation uses the term as analogous to a variable power supply, which is like a battery that can be adjusted for varying amounts of voltage. If a bell is attached to the variable power supply, the bell will begin to ring and will continue to ring until the power supply is cut off. In addition, the loudness or intensity of the ring will vary according to the amount of voltage coming from the power supply.

Do not be misled by this analogy and conclude that all aspects of motivation originate in only one source. This is not the intent of the analogy. The sources of the three aspects of behavior in which motivation is involved are many and diverse. However, the power supply analogy serves its purpose by identifying the influence of motivation on these three parts of performance.

The study of motivation, then, is concerned with the causes and influences affecting these three aspects of behavior. But why do people initiate a form of behavior? For example: Why does a particular student begin misbehaving in class? What were the reasons or influences at work in a student's decision to take a golf class? Why did a tennis player begin to take private lessons to improve his or her serve? Second, why do people continue to behave in a certain way after they have begun? Why did the student continue to play golf in his or her leisure time after the golf class ended? What are the reasons for a boy or girl remaining on an athletic team? Why does a dancer remain a part of the ballet company? Third, what causes the variations in the intensity or success of performance of an individual? For example, why did the wide receiver catch almost every pass thrown to him in one game but drop almost every pass in another game? What are the causes for a pitcher pitching so well that a no-hitter results in one game, while the same pitcher gets "hit out

of the box" in the first inning another time? Why did the dancer who performed an entire routine almost without a flaw have many problems in another performance?

An understanding of the causes or influences that account for the initiation, maintenance, and intensity of behavior is critical to our comprehension of human behavior. As you study each of the concepts in the remainder of this chapter, you will be presented with specific facets of motivation that relate to one or more of these three aspects of behavior. Anxiety is especially critical to the understanding of the causes of the intensity of behavior. Reinforcement principles are important in determining the causes of all three aspects of behavior. Goal setting plays a prominent part in influencing both the maintenance and intensity of behavior. However, before considering the impacts of anxiety, reinforcement, and goal setting on behavior, as related to motor skill learning and performance, it will be helpful to discuss the general nature of the relationship between motivation and learning in order to provide a foundation to assist you in keeping the remainder of this chapter in proper perspective.

Motivation and Learning

A teacher is often required to try to induce a student to want to learn what is being taught. In such a situation, the teacher is concerned with motivation as it is associated with the initiation of behavior when there is a need to persuade a student to continue to develop his or her skill level. Thus the teacher is involved with motivation as it relates to the maintenance of behavior. Finally, the intensity of behavior becomes a problem in a learning situation when the teacher is trying to influence a student to learn a skill to the limit of that person's abilities.

Learning and motivation as reciprocal. One of the critical questions related to the motivation and learning relationship is whether or not learning can actually occur when an individual is *not* motivated to learn. Here the "inner drive" is not directed to the situation; that is, the individual does not "want to" learn the skill. One response to this question was made by David Ausubel (1968). He indicated that the "causal relationship between motivation and learning is typically reciprocal rather than unidirectional . . . it is unnecessary to postpone learning activities until appropriate interests and motivations have been developed" (p. 365). Rather than motivation leading to learning, the opposite sometimes occurs. That is, learning leads to becoming motivated to learn more.

Here again we see the benefit of considering motivation as involved in both the initiation and maintenance of behavior. The inner desire to learn was not present at the initiation of the situation, although the individual was present because of other, external influences. Perhaps she really had no choice since her presence was compulsory. However, because she was there, the student

developed an "inner desire" or motivation to continue. Perhaps the horse in the application section can be taught to drink after he realizes how good the water is!

Examples of this type of situation are very common in physical education classes. A student has no choice but to sign up for a badminton class, perhaps because all other classes are full. But badminton was the farthest down on the list of activities the student wanted to take. Then as this student became involved in the class, he or she realized what an exciting and challenging activity it really is. The student developed a motivation to play more and continued to be involved in playing badminton even after the course was over.

Intentional vs. incidental learning. One other condition that appears to indicate that learning can occur in the absence of motivation to learn appears in situations where intentional and incidental learning can be considered. Although some discussion of this issue occurred in chapter 5, it will be beneficial to consider it again in the present context of motivation. Research has demonstrated that learning does occur even when the student is not directed to learn. Dickinson (1978), for example, instructed some subjects to learn a series of four arm-positioning movements; the first group consisted of intentional learners. A second group of subjects experienced the same movements for the same number of trials but were informed that they were only involved in a test to see how well they could visually estimate a movement of their hand. The second group represented an incidental learning group. The intentional learners were told they would be given a recall test, while the incidental learners were not so informed. Figure 10.1–1 indicates that no differences were observed when both groups were asked to recall within 60 seconds. Only after a 10-minute (600 sec) retention interval did the incidental learners produce more errors. Thus, learning of the arm-positioning movements occurred even though the subjects had never been instructed to learn them.

There is an interesting relationship between the study of intentional and incidental learning as presented here and the concepts of attention and memory considered earlier in this book. The intentional learning group in Dickinson's experiment was given specific instructions about what to attend to in the positioning task. This group was also told that there would be a retention test following the practice trials. If these two points are related to our discussions of attention and memory, it becomes apparent that what is involved here is directing selective attention during practice of a skill and emphasizing the need to remember what was practiced so that the movement can be performed in a test. Neither of these conditions existed for the incidental learning group.

One of the features of Dickinson's experiment related to memory is that the results show that more information is stored in memory than we are consciously aware of, at least for a short period of time. This can be seen in the comparison of the incidental and intentional groups' retention performance

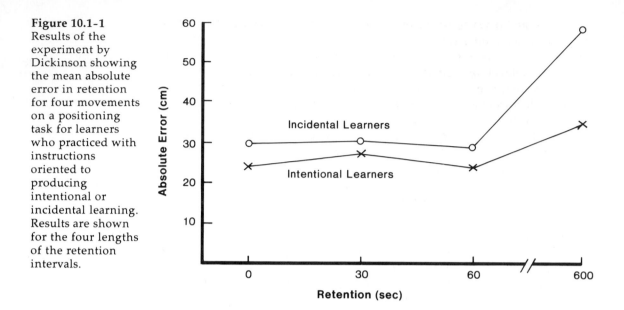

Figure 10.1-1
Results of the experiment by Dickinson showing the mean absolute error in retention for four movements on a positioning task for learners who practiced with instructions oriented to producing intentional or incidental learning. Results are shown for the four lengths of the retention intervals.

during the retention tests that were 30 and 60 seconds after practice. Notice that the final limb position of each movement was remembered as well by the group not given instructions about what to remember as it was by the intentional group. Obviously, there was information stored about the movement's end location even though the incidental group subjects had not been given any instructions about paying attention to that information. However, a comparison of the groups at the 600-second test must also be considered. While the incidental group performed as well as the intentional group for a period of time, the memory for the movement end location was not as durable as when attention was specifically directed toward that part of the movement.

An interesting way to look at the intentional vs. incidental learning issue is to relate it to the type of processing activity in which the learner engages during practice. One interesting view here is that the type of processing activity engaged in during practice may be more important for learning than the intention to learn. If this is so, then we would predict that any practice condition that engages learners in more active processing should lead to better learning under either an intentional or incidental learning situation than one that engages the learner in less processing activity. Shea and Zimny (1983) argued that this view could be related very nicely to the contextual interference effect (which was discussed in Concept 9.1) since random practice is considered to engage learners in more active processing activity than blocked practice. Thus, random vs. blocked practice under intentional and incidental learning conditions should be an effective way of testing the prediction about processing and intention to learn. As an example of an experiment supporting this view, they reported the results of Robyn Morgan's (1981) dissertation at

the University of Colorado. In Morgan's experiment, subjects were required to practice three different three-segment patterns on a barrier knock-down task like the one described for the Shea and Morgan (1979) study in Concept 9.1. These subjects were assigned to one of four experimental conditions that were a combination of either a random or blocked practice schedule of the three patterns, and an intentional or incidental learning situation. The intentional condition subjects were told that there would be a retention test; the incidental group was not told there would be a test. The results showed that regardless of whether there was an intention to learn or not, the random practice condition performed better than the blocked condition. Thus, the prediction was supported that the degree of processing activity involved in practice is more important than the intention to learn.

Summary

Motivation is related to inner drives or intentions that cause a person to behave in a certain way. While external factors may influence these inner intentions, the behavior or act is ultimately caused by some inner drive. Motivation can be defined as the causes that affect the initiation, maintenance, and intensity of behavior. The relationship between motivation and learning is best understood as being reciprocal. That is, a student may learn as a result of being motivated to learn, or he or she may become motivated to learn more as a result of becoming involved in a learning situation. It has also been demonstrated that learning may occur when individuals have not been directed to learn material that has been presented to them.

Related Readings

Ausubel, D. P. (1968). *Educational psychology: A cognitive view.* New York: Holt, Rinehart & Winston.

Dickinson, J. (1978). Retention of intentional and incidental motor learning. *Research Quarterly, 49,* 437–441.

Gagné, R. M. (1979). *The conditions of learning* (3rd ed.). New York: Holt, Rinehart & Winston. (Read chapter 10.)

Shea, J. B., & Zimny, S. T. (1983). Context information in memory and learning movement information. In R. A. Magill (Ed.), *Memory and control of action* (pp. 345–366). Amsterdam: North-Holland. (Read pp. 353–357.)

Concept 10.2

Arousal and anxiety affect learning and performance according to the interrelationship between individual and situation characteristics

Application

When you approach a situation in which you will be tested, how do you generally feel? Do you sometimes feel very nervous or worried? Do you sometimes feel very "ready" for the test and can't wait to get started on it? Do you sometimes not really care whether or not you take the test? Suppose the test we are considering is a badminton serve skill test. How do you think the results of your skill test would relate to how you felt before the test? If you were very nervous or did not care, would these result in similar scores? How would these results compare to the scores if you felt very "ready" to take the test? Intuitively, it would seem likely that different levels of feelings of anxiety or nervousness would have different effects on a person's performance in such a situation.

If you are a football player, the coaches often give you talks before a game to try to get you "ready" for the contest. How does this affect your emotional condition? Does this talk actually help you, or does it simply increase the level of anxiety you were already feeling before the pep talk? How do you think the resulting emotional state will affect your performance in the game? Should you try to get as fired up as you possibly can? Should you approach the game in a subdued manner? Or should you seek some in-between state?

Notice that in both of the situations we have considered, different levels of psychological arousal have been mentioned with reference made to anxiety. These emotional states are typically related to the performance of a physical activity. After studying the present concept, you should be able to determine the relative effects of these levels of arousal on the performance of motor skills.

There is one other point to be considered. It does not seem likely that the various levels of arousal of a performer should result in similar effects for all types of skills or tasks. For example, if a person was experiencing a high degree of arousal prior to carrying out the tasks required of a football quarterback, would you expect this player's performance levels to be as high as those of a defensive tackle who was in a similar high emotional state? Compare the types of responses required of a ballet performer and of a weight lifter? Would the same levels of arousal yield similar results for both? These examples indicate an important aspect of the relationship between arousal and physical performance. That is, the type of skill or task to be performed must be taken into account. The nature of this relationship will be considered in the following discussion.

We will examine two very important aspects of the relationship between arousal and physical performance. One is the level of arousal of the individual at the time of the performance with specific reference to anxiety and performance. The second is the type of task to be performed. It will become evident that these two conditions cannot be considered separately if the effects of arousal on the learning or performance of motor skills is to be understood.

The word *arousal* is often considered synonymous with the word *motivation*. This should be expected since *to arouse* is synonymous with such words as to *activate, awaken, alert,* or *excite.* To motivate an individual is, in effect, to arouse or activate that person in such a way as to prepare himself or herself for the task at hand. The emotional, mental, and physiological systems are activated to produce the responses necessary. The need to alert these systems was the focus of attention in Concept 4.1, which dealt with the need to prepare for a response to a "signal." In that discussion, the role of activation was considered as an important part of signal preparation.

In the first part of this discussion, there will be a general discussion of the relationship between the arousal level of the individual and level of performance that can be expected. Although this section will somewhat repeat what was discussed in Concept 4.1, it will be useful to reconsider this relationship in the present context as it will lay an important foundation for the discussion that follows on the relationship between anxiety and performance. *Anxiety,* although often used interchangably with the term *arousal,* is a more specifically defined psychological construct. In general, anxiety is a heightened level of psychological arousal that produces feelings of discomfort, both psychologically and physically. To set the stage for the discussion of anxiety and motor performance, we will first review the relationship between arousal and motor performance.

Two theories have emerged over the years as the most prominent in attempting to explain the relationship between anxiety and motor performance. *Drive theory,* developed by Hull (1943) and promoted by Spence (1958), maintains that the relationship is a linear one, that is, as state anxiety increases, performance increases proportionately. Thus, a low degree of arousal would result in a low performance level, whereas a high arousal level would yield a high performance level. One of the drawbacks of this theory is its inability to accurately predict effects in motor tasks. Rainer Martens, who must be credited as the individual primarily responsible for the development of contemporary understanding of the relationship between anxiety and motor performance, reviewed many tests of the drive theory (Martens, 1971, 1972). His review indicates a lack of support for the drive theory explanation.

Alternative to this is the *inverted-U theory.* As presented briefly in Concept 4.1, this theory postulates that the relationship between arousal and motor

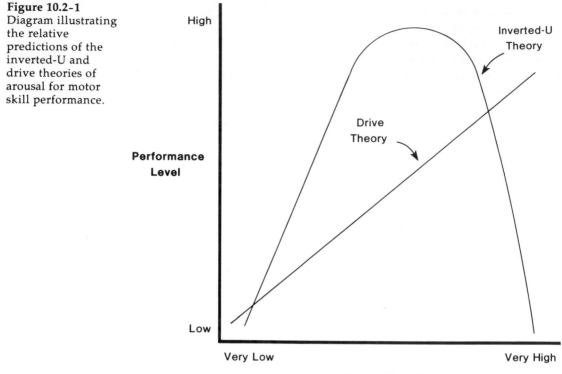

Figure 10.2-1
Diagram illustrating the relative predictions of the inverted-U and drive theories of arousal for motor skill performance.

High

Performance Level

Drive Theory

Inverted-U Theory

Low

Very Low   Very High

Arousal Level

performance is in the form of an inverted U. Thus, both too low and too high levels of arousal result in similar low performance, while a moderate level of arousal should yield high performance. (Figure 10.2–1 diagrams the differences between the drive theory and the inverted-U theory.) The inverted-U theory can be related to the Yerkes-Dodson Law concerning activation, as presented in Concept 4.1.

Trait and State Anxiety

To define *anxiety* is to reflect a theoretical bias concerning the term. Since the intent of this book is not to become involved in theoretical debates, it will be prudent to present anxiety according to the theoretical basis from which this discussion will be developed. Anxiety should be considered in terms of being a *trait* or *state* characteristic. *Trait anxiety* is similar to a personality characteristic. It is a person's general predisposition to perceive a situation as threatening or nonthreatening. A person who is characterized by a high level of trait anxiety would tend to perceive more situations as threatening than would a person who is low on the trait anxiety scale. *State anxiety,* on the other hand, involves how the individual responds to a situation. That is, it is the emotional state of an individual who experiences feelings of apprehension, tension, nervousness, worry, or fear.

The Learning Environment

Thus, state anxiety is closely allied to the concept of activation or arousal. Although arousal is a continuum of emotional conditions ranging from sleep to intense excitement, state anxiety is a form of arousal that is produced by the perception of danger. State anxiety is to be considered as a negative effect; high levels are very unpleasant for the individual. The same cannot be said for high levels of activation.

This distinction between trait anxiety and state anxiety was developed as a result of the work of Charles Spielberger (1966). He provided a useful analogy to assist in distinguishing between trait and state anxiety. State anxiety is to trait anxiety as kinetic energy is to potential energy. State anxiety is similar to kinetic energy, that is energy in motion, while trait anxiety is similar to potential energy, or energy available for action when the appropriate stimulus appears.

Trait anxiety has customarily been measured by one of two paper-pencil tests: the Taylor Manifest Anxiety Scale (MAS) and Spielberger's State-Trait Anxiety Inventory (STAI). The MAS is based on the drive theory, while the STAI follows the inverted-U hypothesis. A test that has been developed specifically to determine trait anxiety for sport situations is the Sport Competition Anxiety Test (SCAT), which was developed by Martens (1977); it follows the theoretical approach espoused by Spielberger. Each of these tests is a questionnaire that includes simple statements about how an individual generally feels in a particular situation. The person taking the test marks an appropriate space, indicating that the feeling occurs often, sometimes, or not at all. Examples of the statements from the SCAT appear in Table 10.2–1.

Measuring Anxiety

Information about an individual's trait anxiety could be useful in trying to predict the types of situations in which a high state anxiety reaction might occur. However, the indiscriminate use of the STAI or SCAT is not recommended for physical activity groups. This procedure would be of too limited practical value to justify the time spent in testing. Problems in the proper interpretation of test results also favor a more limited use of these instruments. In fact, researchers and clinicians who have been trained in the use of these tests should be the ones who use them.

State anxiety assessment can be made in a variety of ways. Since an increase in state anxiety results in increased physiological responses, monitoring the heart rate, blood pressure, or brain wave activity (EEG) can provide state anxiety information. However, these tests would not be very practical for teachers and coaches. Observation of certain characteristics of the individual can also provide state anxiety information. Thus, increased levels of state anxiety are generally associated with increased sweating of the palms of the hands, tension, and nervousness.

If a more objective measure of state anxiety is desired than observation can provide, it may be better to administer some of the available paper-pencil tests, which are simpler to administer than physiological tests. Both the STAI

Table 10.2-1.
Sample statements from the Sport Competition Anxiety Test (SCAT).

DIRECTIONS: Below are some statements about how persons feel when they compete in sports and games. Read each statement and decide if *you* HARDLY EVER, or SOMETIMES, or OFTEN feel this way when you compete in sports and games. If your choice is HARDLY EVER, blacken the square labeled A, if your choice is SOMETIMES, blacken the square labeled B, and if your choice is OFTEN, blacken the square labeled C. There are no right or wrong answers. Do not spend too much time on any one statement. Remember to choose the word that describes how you *usually* feel when competing in sports and games.

	Hardly Ever	Sometimes	Often
Competing against others is socially enjoyable.	☐A	☐B	☐C
Before I compete I feel uneasy.	☐A	☐B	☐C
Before I compete I worry about not performing well.	☐A	☐B	☐C
I am a good sportsman when I compete.	☐A	☐B	☐C
When I compete I worry about making mistakes.	☐A	☐B	☐C
Before I compete I am calm.	☐A	☐B	☐C
Before I compete I get a queasy feeling in my stomach.	☐A	☐B	☐C
I get nervous wanting to start the game.	☐A	☐B	☐C

and the SCAT include a state anxiety questionnaire that can be quickly and easily administered. Table 10.2–2 includes a sample of the statements found in the state anxiety portion of the SCAT.

Information concerning an individual's state anxiety could be very helpful in trying to determine what needs to be done for a person in a given situation. If the state anxiety level is too high, procedures can be implemented to calm down the individual. If the individual shows too low a level of anxiety, or arousal, then the individual needs to be stimulated or aroused somewhat, to prepare

Table 10.2-2.
Sample statements from the state anxiety questionnaire used with the SCAT.

DIRECTIONS: A number of statements which people have used to describe themselves are given below. Read each statement and then circle the appropriate number to the right of the statement to indicate how you *feel* right now, that is, at this moment. There are no right or wrong answers. Do not spend too much time on any one statement but give the answer which seems to describe your present feelings best.

	1	2	3	4
I feel at ease.	Not at all	Somewhat	Moderately so	Very much so
I feel nervous.	Not at all	Somewhat	Moderately so	Very much so
I am relaxed.	Not at all	Somewhat	Moderately so	Very much so
I am tense.	Not at all	Somewhat	Moderately so	Very much so
I feel over-excited and rattled.	Not at all	Somewhat	Moderately so	Very much so

him or her better for the task at hand. Again, these tests as well as the associated techniques for altering anxiety levels should only be used after adequate professional training or with proper professional supervision.

The interrelationship between trait and state anxiety must be taken into account in relating anxiety to motor performance. This is due to the nature of both trait and state anxiety. Since trait anxiety is a predisposition of an individual to find a situation threatening or not, how that person responds to any given situation must be related to state anxiety. In general, a person characterized by high trait anxiety will respond to more situations with a high degree of state anxiety than will the low trait anxiety person. This is not to say that a low trait anxiety person will never show a high level of state anxiety. What is important to understand is that the number of situations that result in a high level of state anxiety are much greater for the high trait anxiety person. Thus, when we are concerned with anxiety as it relates to a situation, the level of state anxiety is the primary focus.

Anxiety and
Motor
Performance

Levels of state anxiety and the situation. Recent investigations of the relationship between anxiety and motor performance indicate that the levels of state anxiety a person will exhibit are not only related to the trait anxiety characteristic of the individual. The trait anxiety characteristic also appears to interact with two very important situational variables, the *importance of the situation to the individual* and the *uncertainty of the outcome of the situation.* Any attempt to determine whether a person with a given level of trait anxiety will find that a particular situation will lead to a high level of state anxiety must consider these two variables.

The more importance an individual ascribes to a situation, the more likely he or she is to develop high levels of state anxiety. Of course, a high trait anxiety person would tend to consider more situations important to him or her than would a low trait anxiety person. To some individuals, a "friendly" game of racquetball becomes a very important event, while to others the same match would not appear as very important. The tension on the court of the "high importance" person can almost be felt by others on the court. An athletic event that has been given a large amount of media coverage acquires a great deal of importance to the participants as well as the fans.

The uncertainty of the outcome of an event becomes critical in sports when opponents are closely matched. In a dance performance, the uncertainty increases when the dancer is not certain how his or her performance will be received by the crowd. Students find the uncertainty of the outcome increased when they are not sure whether they have prepared adequately for the test or how difficult the test will be. You can visualize other situations in which the uncertainty of the outcome is relatively high. This uncertainty is reduced when there is any indication that the probability of the outcome is in one direction or the other. As uncertainty to the outcome increases, the expected level of state anxiety also rises. Conversely, the more likely it is that the outcome will be one way, the lower the expected level of state anxiety.

Neither the importance of the situation to the individual nor the uncertainty as to its outcome should be considered independently. Both of these variables interact with the individual's level of trait anxiety to produce a particular degree of state anxiety.

Anxiety and the task. One very important variable remains to be considered before attempting to draw conclusions as to the relationship of anxiety and motor performance. The Yerkes-Dodson Law relates activation levels to the task to be performed. A similar relationship must be considered for anxiety as well. The two characteristics of motor tasks—task difficulty and task complexity—are important here. Since task complexity concerns the number and intricacy of the components of a task, it seems quite reasonable that the complexity of a task is more related to the effects of anxiety on performance than is the difficulty of the task. For example, it could be argued that a defensive tackle's position in football is as difficult as that of the quarterback.

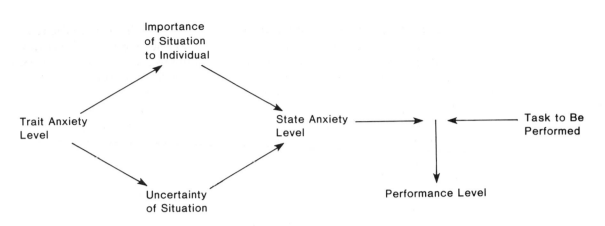

However, in terms of complexity, the quarterback's task is much more complex. With respect to anxiety levels, then, it could be predicted that a defensive tackle would exhibit better performance at much higher levels of anxiety than would a quarterback. Although, in neither case should those levels be excessively high.

With performers at the same high level of anxiety, a task that is highly complex will not be performed as well as one that is low on the complexity scale. The golfer who is at the high end of the state anxiety scale while putting will undoubtedly make a poor putt. On the other hand, it would be very advantageous for a power lifter to be located toward the high end of the state anxiety scale.

Pulling the variables together. Janet Spence (1971) noted in an article discussing the anixety-performance issue that "no simple empirical statement can be made about the relationship between anxiety and performance." After having considered the many variables involved in this relationship, you probably are in complete agreement with this statement. But rather than concluding on this pessimistic note, let us try to combine all the information about variables that influence the anxiety-performance relationship, than develop a conclusion that can be generally applied to very practical concerns.

The variables that have been considered can be divided into two groups; one group involves the individual while the other involves the situation. The *individual variables* are the levels of trait and state anxiety of the individual. These individual variables interact with the three *situation variables,* that is, the importance of the situation to the individual, the uncertainty of the situation, and the task or motor skill to be performed. Figure 10.2–2 depicts these variables as they interrelate to influence performance.

For any level of trait anxiety, as the importance and uncertainty of the situation increase, the level of state anxiety is also likely to increase. State anxiety is related in an inverse manner to the complexity of the task to be performed. Thus, higher levels of state anxiety should be associated with tasks

Figure 10.2-2
The interrelationship of individual and situation variables related to anxiety and performance.

characterized toward the lower end of the complexity scale. When these variables are considered in terms of the aforementioned interrelationships, the teacher or coach is better able to prepare the individual for optimum performance.

Implications for Learning and Performance Situations

A student in a badminton class who tends to exhibit high trait anxiety will respond to more situations in class with a high degree of state anxiety. Thus, having that person demonstrate before the class would yield performance results that would be quite different from another class member who was typically low in trait anxiety. These effects must, of course, be considered in terms of students' perception of the situation, especially the elements of importance and uncertainty. After considering all variables, the teacher or coach should have as the goal the development of an optimal level of anxiety for the task at hand to produce optimal performance.

For the instructor. Most of the concern of teachers and coaches is with anxiety levels that are too high. For optimal performance, these levels need to be reduced. Although several anxiety reduction techniques have been developed during the past few years, such as meditation, hypnosis, and relaxation, these methods are not recommended for the teacher or coach unless he or she has had professional instruction in the proper use of these techniques. Talking to the individual in calm tones can be helpful. Try to determine if the situation is being perceived as too important, thus yielding state anxiety levels that are too high. Perhaps it is the uncertainty of the situation that is related to the high anxiety. Here reassurance about the individual's own capabilities can aid in the reduction of these anxious feelings. In this connection, the teacher or coach must determine at least some of the individual's reasons for being too anxious. The perceptive educator can uncover these by means of appropriate questions and an understanding approach to the individual.

Altering the situation. Increased anxiety may also be related to the student's lack of success with the skill being practiced because of the characteristics of the task. It is possible that if the characteristics of the task were altered, the student's anxiety level would decrease so that attention could be directed where it should. For example, a young student may be having little success with hitting a pitched baseball. A closer inspection of this situation reveals that the student has a heightened level of anxiety due to fear of being hit with the ball. To reduce this anxiety, the teacher could change certain characteristics of the task. Perhaps the child should hit the ball from a batting tee or from a pitching machine where the ball would be delivered in a consistent manner. Under these conditions, the student can practice the skill at an appropriate anxiety level, achieve some success, and attend to elements of the skill necessary at this stage of his or her learning that are important for future success in hitting a pitched ball.

Focusing attention. One of the more interesting techniques that have been suggested to aid learning and performance is what is referred to as *attentional focus* (Nideffer, 1976). The idea here is to concentrate on a specific environmental cue or aspect of performance during the execution of a skill. For example, a person who is having difficulty learning to serve in tennis may be thinking about the lack of good serves he or she has had during class. This is an example of an inappropriate attention focus and can lead to increased anxiety, which in turn can lead to increasingly poorer performance rather than improvement. On a given trial this person should focus attention on one specific aspect of the performance, such as tossing the ball well, and not think about anything else. By narrowing the focus of attention to this one important performance cue, the individual has decreased the likelihood of being overly anxious and has increased the likelihood that attention will be directed to a relevant cue that will benefit performance.

There is an important connection between the benefits of attentional focus and what we discussed in chapter 4. In all three concepts of that chapter dealing with attention and performance, there is ample support for why such an approach should work. By focusing attention in the manner suggested by the attentional focus technique, the response system is sufficiently alerted to prepare a response and preparation is more likely to occur appropriately since the selection of environmental and control system information is being allowed to occur without distraction or interference. Because excessively high levels of anxiety can create a reduced attention capacity, attentional focusing helps to maintain an appropriate capacity level to deal with what demands attention in the performance of the skill.

An example of research support for the benefit of using a type of attentional focusing routine to prepare for performing a motor skill can be seen in a study with golfers by Boutcher and Crews (1987). Because the results were more clear-cut with the female than the male golfers, we will limit the discussion of that study to the results with the females. One group of university varsity golfers was given a specific attention focusing routine to use before putting while the other group was told to use their regular preparation routine. The specific routine related to concentrating on certain cues or actions in preparation for the putt, such as the number of glances at the hole or the number of practice putting strokes taken. Practice consisted of 20-minute sessions 4 days a week for 6 weeks. A pretest and a posttest of putting performance was used to determine the effects of the routine. These tests consisted of a randomized order of six putts from each of three distances (4, 12, and 20 feet) on a practice green. Results showed that the women golfers using the focusing routine increased the number of putts holed, from 5.6 on the pretest to 7.3 on the posttest, while the no-routine group actually did a little worse from pretest (5.0) to posttest (4.0). Also, the amount of error for missed putts on the posttest was 6.2 inches less for the group who had used the attention focusing routine.

Summary

Anxiety is associated with feelings of apprehension, nervousness, worry, or fear. Trait anxiety is a person's disposition to perceive a situation as threatening or nonthreatening. State anxiety reflects how the individual responds to a particular situation. Both trait and state anxiety should be understood as ranging in levels from very low to very high. Levels of state anxiety can be related to motor performance by means of the inverted-U hypothesis, which postulates that high and low levels of anxiety are related to low performance levels, while moderate levels of anxiety are related to maximum performance. The appropriate anxiety level for any task must be determined according to the complexity of the task to be performed. Highly complex tasks are performed better with levels of anxiety that are toward the lower extreme of the scale. The degree of state anxiety that can be expected in any situation must be considered in terms of the importance of the situation to the individual and the uncertainty of its outcome. These many variables must be considered together in order to determine the exact relationship between anxiety and motor performance.

Related Readings

Gould, D., Horn, T., & Spreeman, J. (1983). Competitive anxiety among elite junior wrestlers. *Journal of Sport Psychology, 5,* 58–71.

Landers, D. M., Wang, M. Q., & Courtet, P. (1985). Peripheral narrowing among experienced and inexperienced rifle shooters under low- and high-stress conditions. *Research Quarterly for Exercise and Sport, 56,* 122–130.

Martens, R. (1971). Anxiety and motor behavior. *Journal of Motor Behavior, 3,* 151–179.

Spence, J. T. (1971). What can you say about a twenty-year-old theory that won't die? *Journal of Motor Behavior, 3,* 193–203.

Spielberger, C. D. (1971). Trait-state anxiety and motor behavior. *Journal of Motor Behavior, 3,* 265–279.

Establishing an appropriate goal or level of aspiration is an effective means of motivating skill learning and performance

How do you approach a situation after you have set for yourself a specific goal to achieve in that situation? Is your approach any different than if you have no specific goal? For instance, suppose you plan to play golf on a particular afternoon. You and your opponent are fairly well matched; and you probably have in mind a goal of wanting to win the match. While winning obviously is a goal, it is a rather general goal. You could win and play very poorly or score much higher than you think you should. The goal "to win" does not include a very specific means of evaluating your performance, especially if you are in the process of trying to improve your game. You could easily choose opponents whom you know you could defeat and thereby achieve that goal. But what would happen to your game? What kind of improvement would you observe?

On the other hand, suppose you set a more specific goal. For example, you could plan to try to attain a particular score in this round. Or you set a goal of averaging a five on all holes, thus, for most golf courses, setting a goal of playing bogey golf. Another specific goal might be more directed to one aspect of your game, such as putting. Here, you could set a goal of averaging two putts per hole for the day's round. These specific objectives give you a definite means of evaluating your performance in terms of how you actually played as compared to what you think you should have done at this stage of your learning the game. From that evaluation, you would have a better understanding of how to improve the use of your practice time.

Goal setting, as it has been illustrated here, can be a very effective motivator for skill learning as well as for the maintenance and the intensity of motor skill performance. However, the proper use of goal setting is critical. To use the goal-setting technique incorrectly could lead to results quite opposite from the ones desired. In the following discussion, the approach to setting realistic goals will be considered. Also considered will be types of goal setting. Here the concern will be goal setting for a particular instance or performance, as in the golf example, or for a longer term situation, such as establishing goals for learning to play golf during the next year or six months. Goals are performance objectives that can be effective for motivating an individual to remain involved in a learning or performance situation. Goal setting can also be an effective method for obtaining an optimal level of performance from an individual. However, the proper use of this form of motivation requires an understanding of the complexities associated with its role in both learning and performance.

Discussion

The term *goal setting* is a more common or popular term than *level of aspiration,* a comparable expression that also has been used in psychology literature. We will consider these terms as interchangeable. They both mean the *level of performance on a task that a person expects to achieve in the future.* This future may be either very short-term, as in the game coming up this afternoon, or it may be very long-term, as the goal for the season or year.

Lewin and colleagues (1944) have indicated that two types of goals are important for our discussion. *Ideal goals* are ultimate goals. These are objectives the individual desires to attain as the end result of his or her practice and participation in a task. A young gymnast may have participation in the Olympic Games as an ultimate goal. A therapy patient may have as an ultimate goal the ability to walk without the aid of external support. An ultimate goal for a student learning ballet may be to perform in a community ballet company. Ideal or ultimate goals furnish a long-range end that provides the individual not only with an incentive to continue but also with a standard of performance against which points of achievement can be measured to provide information about what remains to be accomplished. *Momentary* or *action goals,* on the other hand, are the "right now" goals. These objectives are associated with performance in a situation that immediately confronts the individual. The example of the golfer, presented earlier, illustrates an action goal.

When we consider goal setting in connection with the learning and performance of motor skills, both ideal and action goals are involved. When a student enters a class in which a particular physical activity is being taught, that student may or may not have an objective in mind, that is, what he or she hopes to accomplish as a result of that class. A specific goal for the development of a certain level of skill as a result of a bowling class, for instance, can be related to the ideal goal. While the end-of-the-course goal may not be the person's lifetime ultimate goal, it is the objective that will be leading the person through the entire course, while providing him or her with a basis for the establishment of action goals. Thus, action goals are involved in the same setting as ideal goals. The bowling student can set an action goal for a particular game or class, and that goal should be in line with the ideal goal that has been set for the entire course.

Evidence That Goal Setting Is Effective

Before expanding the present discussion by suggesting how goals should be set and what to expect in return, it will be useful to consider the empirical basis for accepting the notion that goal setting is an effective means of motivating human behavior. It is essential to keep the learning-performance distinction in mind here. We will consider some examples of research evidence that support the efficacy of goal setting for learning situations and immediate performance. Learning situations should be considered as those in which an individual is attempting to acquire a new skill or to improve his or her skill level. Performance situations, on the other hand, are those more immediate situations in which an individual is performing a skill rather than practicing it. Both conditions have been shown to be influenced by goal setting.

Goal setting and performance. Since physical performance encompasses a wide range of motor activities, we will consider two experiments that have supported the role of goal setting in the performance of two different types of motor activities. First, we will examine a study by Nelson (1978), which considered the motivating effects of goal setting on muscular endurance testing. Second, in a study by Harari (1969), we will observe the effects of goal setting on the performance of distance running.

Nelson (1978) gave four groups of college men different goals to strive for in an elbow flexion strength test. These goals were an actual performance norm for the task, a fictitious norm, an obtainable performance goal, or nothing. A score for each subject was the number of repetitions the load attached to a cable tensiometer could be lifted in one attempt. The load was individualized for each subject as it was one-fourth of the predetermined maximum load that each subject could raise. The realistic norm group was told the repetition number ranges for five categories of very good to very poor. The fictitious norm group was told that the norm for people their age was 55 repetitions, while 48 and 39 repetitions were the averages for senior- and junior-high boys. Such repetitions were in fact very high. The obtainable goal group was told they should be able to do at least 40 repetitions. Results showed that the three groups which were provided with an objective standard to be used as a goal (realistic or not), performed better than the control group, which was given no norms or goals. In fact, the fictitious norm group performed better than either the realistic norm group or obtainable goal group.

The study by Harari (1969) used information about success or failure in running. Male students from a college soccer class were tested on a 750-yard run. Their time was determined at each one-third of the course as well as the entire course. One week later the class was tested again over the same course. On this occasion, one-half the class was given information about their first performance, according to their own scores (self-reference). The other half was given information in terms of the class average for the first trial (group reference). Times were announced to each runner at each one-third of the course mark to let him know how he was doing. However, these times were prearranged so that some received times indicating better performance than the trial one, while others received scores showing poorer or identical times as a trial one. Results showed that students who received times that indicated better performance and who were in the self-reference group performed better than all the other groups.

Both of these studies support the contention that goal setting is a very potent form of motivation that influences the intensity of a person's performance of physical activities. While certain questions remain from studies like these, such as which form of goal setting is the most effective, or why goal setting is effective, the point to be noted is that goal setting is effective. Not only was the setting of a goal related to better performance than when none

was set; performance was also superior when the performer knew he was exceeding the preestablished goal, even when that information was not based on actual performance.

Goal setting and learning. The benefit of successful motivation in a learning situation is evident in terms of the effectiveness and efficiency of the instruction and learning that take place. Thus, if an instructor decreases the amount of time needed to reach a given performance criterion, efficiency of instruction has been achieved since valuable instructional time has been saved. Furthermore, if the level of achievement attributable to goal setting can be shown to be higher than when no goal setting is used, we may conclude that the effective use of goal setting as an important factor of the instructional situation can be supported.

Support for the use of goal setting in a motor skill learning situation can be found in an often-cited study by Locke and Bryan (1966). By manipulating both hand and foot controls, subjects were required to match a set of light patterns on a display with another set of lights. The task was to match 13 different patterns in a sequence, as quickly and as frequently as possible. One group of subjects were told to "do their best" while a second group was given a specific goal to strive for. This latter goal was a score based on their previous test score. Results (Figure 10.3–1) showed that the specific goal group not only performed better overall but also had a faster rate of improvement.

KR and goal setting. In the discussion of Concept 7.1 you saw that one of the functions of KR is to act as a means of motivation. In this role, KR can provide information that can act as an incentive for the individual to try harder or to persist longer at a task. A common use of KR in this regard has been to relate KR as response outcome information to achievement of an established performance goal. When used in this way, KR provides the individual with information about a response that can be matched with the performance level established by the goal. On the basis of this match, the learner can then determine the needs of the next response as it relates to achieving the goal.

It is often difficult to distinguish between the functions of KR as error correction information and as information that serves as an incentive to achieve a goal. This is especially the case when KR is presented as response outcome information, i.e., a score of a response. It is likely that this information actually functions in both ways. That is, the KR provides the learner with information about the response that indicates whether response errors must be corrected and it provides information that lets the individual know how close he or she is to achieving an established goal. As such, when KR is presented to learners when a performance goal has been established, KR serves to provide more than information that can direct error correction. It can also be used to provide information that can be used as an incentive to continue pursuing the goal.

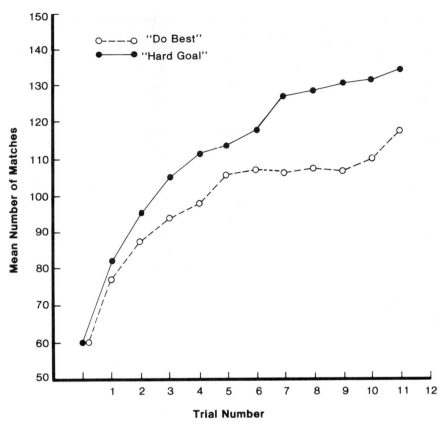

Figure 10.3-1
Results of the experiment by Locke and Bryan showing the performance curves for the two groups provided with different incentive goals for performing a complex motor task.

Summarizing goal-setting effects. As the evidence from the research presented in the preceding sections indicates, there is little doubt that goal setting is an effective motivation technique that influences both the learning of skills as well as the performance of skills in test situations. It is encouraging that the research on goal setting and its effects on performance have been consistent in supporting specific relationships between types of goals set or means of goal setting and performance. This research literature, from both laboratory-and field-based experiments, has recently been analyzed by Tubbs (1986) and can be summarized as four goal-setting characteristics that influence performance of skills in a positive way.

First, *difficult goals lead to better performance than easy goals*. There is strong support from a large number of studies indicating that goals should be difficult to achieve if they are to be effective. In keeping with this notion, the level of difficulty must be achievable by the individual. This condition adds a special concern for the person setting the goal, as it requires taking into account the capabilities of the individual and the potential to achieve a certain level of performance.

Second, *specific goals lead to better performance than do-your-best goals or no goals*. This characteristic of effective goals advances the first characteristic by establishing a requirement for the difficult goal. Not only should the goal be difficult to achieve, it should be specific in terms of what should be achieved. The experiment by Locke and Bryan (1966) is just one example of research that has supported the benefit of specific goals as an effective means of improving performance.

Third, *goal setting plus performance feedback is better than goal setting alone*. This characteristic fits well with the results of the work we just considered related to KR and goal setting. The important point here is that the effect of goal setting will be enhanced by providing the individual with information about his or her performance with specific reference to how he or she is doing in terms of reaching the set goal. Also, the effect of performance feedback appears to be stronger when it is formally given by the person who set the goal. Although there is not a lot of evidence to support this conclusion, there is sufficient evidence to suggest that this result be given consideration in performance situations. It is important to note that Tubbs indicated that the goal setting plus feedback relationship to performance is an important one that needs further research.

Fourth, *participant involvement in goal setting leads to better performance than goals assigned without participant involvement*. It is important to qualify this conclusion from the research literature. Tubbs noted that this conclusion could only be made when the goal level that was set was not held constant. This means that if the same goal is set by a participant involvement group and a group who does not participate in the goal setting, then performance of the two groups is similar. What typically happens when participants are allowed to be involved in the goal-setting process is that they will set *higher* goals than when they are not involved and someone assigns a goal to them. Thus, in the typical case, the goal-setting level is not held constant. This is an important issue in goal setting as it relates not only to the characteristic of the goal that is set, but also to who sets the goal. Participant involvement does not mean that the participants set the goal. It means that the participants are involved in the goal-setting process with the person in charge, such as the teacher, coach, or therapist.

These four goal-setting characteristics effectively summarize the current state of knowledge about the relationship between goal setting and performance of skills. Much research remains to be done to expand the knowledge of these effects, as well as to determine what other relationships may exist. However, these four characteristics establish a sufficient basis for suggesting how to effectively set goals to enhance the learning and performance of skills, which we will consider next.

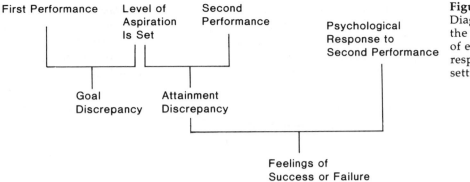

First Performance | Level of Aspiration Is Set | Second Performance

Goal Discrepancy | Attainment Discrepancy

Psychological Response to Second Performance

Feelings of Success or Failure

Figure 10.3-2
Diagram indicating the typical sequence of events and responses in a goal-setting situation.

In addition to the goal-setting characteristics we have just considered, there are some personal and situation-related factors that must be taken into account before establishing specific guidelines for setting realistic goals. An important individual characteristic is related to a personality characteristic known as "need for achievement." This characteristic will be directly related to what kind of goal a person sets, as well as the level of that goal. For example, a person with a relatively low need for achievement would tend to set a relatively low, easily attainable goal. This goal would likely be related to ensuring a high probability of avoiding failure. On the other hand, a person with a relatively high need for achievement would probably set a difficult goal that would require maximum effort to achieve. This personality characteristic becomes especially influential when the individual performer is permitted to set the performance goal without consulting the person in charge of the activity.

A situation-related factor that interacts with the need for achievement by the individual is a very powerful factor in its influence on goal setting. This factor, *past experiences,* related to prior successes or failures in achieving previously established goals, is intimately involved in influencing the type of goal the individual will set for the next attempt. The role of previous goal-setting experiences has been aptly illustrated by Alderman (1974), as adapted from Atkinson (1964), in a time-sequence diagram (Figure 10.3–2) in which each event is represented on a time line. The level of aspiration, or goal, is set following a given performance, noted as "first performance" in the diagram. The difference between these events can be interpreted as the "goal discrepancy," which is indicative of the individual's orientation toward success as well as his or her confidence. A goal level that was set rather low would indicate little confidence in being successful at achieving much beyond what has already been achieved. Then the next performance of the task occurs. The difference between the results of this performance and the goal represents the "attainment discrepancy." This reveals how accurate the individual was in the evaluation of his or her own ability, as well as his or her aspirations in the task;

Setting Realistic Goals

the person's "feelings of success or failure" follow that evaluation, which is related to the individual's "psychological response to the second performance."

Individuals with past experiences of success in achieving goals will tend to strive harder in the future. The opposite seems true for past experiences of failure. In a basketball setting, for example, if a player is always asked to defend a player who usually beats him or her, consider the influence of those experiences on future expectations. The coach who permits all players to experience a degree of success as often as possible is increasing the likelihood that his or her players will strive for goals that represent improved performance as well as require maximum effort.

Goal-setting guidelines. On the basis of what has been discussed thus far, it seems that certain guidelines can be established in using goal setting as a motivational tool. Try to apply each guideline to a motor skill learning or performance situation in which you might be involved.

1. *Set objective goals.* Goals should be in the form of a number, or some similar objective, to provide the student or performer with an objective means of evaluating his or her own performance. We have seen evidence that the statement "do your best" falls short in its effectiveness as a motivator when compared to a specific objective goal.

2. *Set goals that are meaningful.* A goal must have meaning to the person. It will be a more effective means of motivation to indicate to a student that to make 6 out of 10 shots in a basketball goal-shooting task is an above average score than to simply say, "try to make 6 out of 10." The performer not only needs an objective goal to strive for but one that is meaningful to him in order to provide an immediate point of reference for performance.

3. *Set goals that are obtainable.* While goals that are almost unattainable may lead to performance increases early in a performance experience, as in the Nelson (1978) study, failure to achieve these goals during a series of attempts will tend to lead to poorer performance than when realistic goals are used. Consideration must be given to the level of achievement that is desired by the individual. Some goals are attainable only through maximum effort, while others are attainable with little effort.

4. *Set goals according to individual differences.* Since both past experiences and the personality of the individual are intricately interrelated to the effectiveness of goal setting, the instructor must determine goals for each individual. While the coach or teacher realizes that the goal can be reached only if a maximum effort is exerted, the student or performer may not be aware of this or may not wish to exert a maximum effort for fear of not achieving the goal.

5. *Set goals on the basis of past experiences.* Goals will fit many of these guidelines if they are established in terms of past performances. The goal should be objective, it should be meaningful to the individual, and it should be individualized. Whether or not it is attainable is up to the individual and the instructor. The instructor or coach should not just "pull a number out of the air" as a performance goal. The instructor must be alert to what the individual has done in the past, not only in terms of performance levels but in terms of the amounts of improvement associated with those performance levels.

Summary

Goal setting, or level of aspiration, is a potent form of motivating individual behavior in both performance and learning situations. Research evidence has shown that when objective goals are presented to individuals, their performance in motor skills can be expected to be superior to performance when no specific goal has been provided. The commonly used phrase "do your best" does not result in as great a performance improvement as does a specific goal. The goal that an individual will establish in a situation can be related to the person's need for achievement and the individual's past experiences of success or failure in attaining goals. Specific guidelines have been presented to assist the instructor or coach in the effective use of goal setting as a means of motivating the performance and learning of motor skills.

Related Readings

Locke, E. A., Cartledge, N., & Koeppel, J. (1968). Motivational effects of knowledge of results: A goal-setting phenomenon? *Psychological Bulletin, 70,* 474–485.

Locke, E. A., Shaw, K. N., Saari, L. M., & Latham, G. P. (1981). Goal setting and task performance: 1969–1980. *Psychological Bulletin, 90,* 125–152.

Nelson, J. K. (1978). Motivating effects of the use of norms and goals with endurance testing. *Research Quarterly, 49,* 317–321.

Weinberg, R. S. (1982). Motivating athletes through goal setting. *Journal of Physical Education, Recreation, and Dance, 53* (9), 46–48.

Concept 10.4

The application of appropriate reinforcement techniques can serve to facilitate the learning and performance of motor skills

Application

Picture yourself as an elementary school physical education teacher. The young boys and girls in your class are trying to learn to dribble a soccer ball, but it is obvious to you that most of these students are having a difficult time learning this skill. You have instructed the entire class in the proper techniques of dribbling; you have also worked with many of the students in correcting wrong techniques. Besides providing technical advice or instruction about dribbling, is there anything else you can do to facilitate the learning of this skill? One thing you can do is to praise a student individually with encouraging words whenever he or she properly performs the skill or some part of the skill. From your own experience with these children, you have undoubtedly noticed that they seem to enjoy being praised by you. Your decision, then, is to apply this praise to their performance when practicing a new and difficult skill.

Let's consider a different situation and context. It is not uncommon in athletics to find a coach who believes that he or she should not praise the players too often. Such coaches have determined that it works better, for their purposes, constantly to chide the players to do better and to improve their performance. These coaches' reaction to the good execution of some aspect of the game is to say nothing. Thus, the approach is to consistently "get on" the players, but to say nothing when something is done correctly or well. It is not that praise is never used but that nothing is said which will be interpreted by the players as approval.

Another example of the use of reinforcement techniques is seen in providing an incentive for a varsity wrestling team. Suppose you are the coach. You have determined that the team needs to improve its ability in achieving takedowns. As an incentive to improve, you have devised a point system for the team; for every takedown a team member gets during a match, he will receive one point on a large chart you have placed in the wrestling room. At the end of the season, you will give a special award to the wrestler who has accumulated the most points for takedowns.

Consider one more situation. You are teaching a tennis class, but you are concerned that the class has not understood the full importance of the first serve. In fact, as you observe the class, you notice that the students seem to place very little emphasis on getting in the first serve. Instead, they seem to be satisfied with just "dinking" the ball over the net to start the rally going. You decide to have them play a game you call "one-serve tennis." In this game,

there is no second serve; any missed first serve becomes a point for the opponent. To eliminate "dinking" and to emphasize concentration on their serving skills, you further indicate that the first serves cannot be simply "patted" over; there must be a full service motion.

In each of these four situations, a different technique was used to try to improve performance or learning. The elementary school class was being verbally praised. The coach in the second situation stopped chiding a player when something was done well. The wrestling coach provided a reward as a goal to strive for. The tennis teacher devised a game that penalized incorrect performance. Each of these situations represents a technique that can be considered under the broad heading of reinforcement. In the following discussion, you will be provided with information that should help you to determine what types of results may be expected from the use of these techniques.

When the word *reinforcement* is used, what do you think of? Rats learning to push a bar in order to get a pellet of food? Pigeons learning to bowl? Programmed instruction books? Behavior modification? Each of these situations has become rather well known in most educational circles. Much media publicity for the work of B. F. Skinner has served to popularize many of the techniques in which reinforcement has been a key concept.

The role of reinforcement in human learning received its initial impetus from the studies of animal learning by Edward Thorndike in the first third of this century. Thorndike's *law of effect* set the stage for recognizing the influence of reinforcement theory in human learning. The law of effect states that learning is related to the presence of rewards or punishments following a response. A reward serves to strengthen the response, which means increased likelihood of the response occurring again. Conversely, punishment has the effect of weakening the response or lowering the probability of the response being repeated. Thus, responses apparently are made as efforts to comply with a motive, that is, to reduce a drive or need. If a reward follows a particular response then that response becomes "stronger" than any alternative response. Thus, a reward that satisfied a motive positively influences the learning of a desired response.

While other learning theorists have proposed different explanations of reinforcement in learning (such as Hull [1943] and Tolman [1932]), the individual who exerted the greatest influence on current views of reinforcement is B. F. Skinner. Skinner's view of reinforcement was not as dependent on the role of rewards; rather, he considered reinforcement to be related to an arrangement of stimulus and response conditions. Here the idea of *response contingency* is important. If a particular response is the one that should be learned, then the response must be contingent on the occurrence of a particular stimulus condition. Contingency, then, is a condition which stipulates that in order

Discussion

for a particular event to occur, it must be preceded by some other event. For example, serving an ace in tennis is contingent upon swinging the racquet. Another example would be that receiving a trophy in a golf tournament is contingent upon beating every other player's score.

Based on Skinner's view of reinforcement, the learning of a desired response will be the result of arranging the learning setting so that for the individual to receive a reinforcer, the proper response must first be made. In reinforcement theory, it is what occurs *after* a response that is important. To increase the probability of the occurrence of a desired response, a reinforcer or reinforcement should follow the desired response. The reinforcer need not be a reward. As you will see later in this discussion, a reinforcer could be *not* receiving something. To decrease the probability of a response, a punishment or penalty should follow that response.

Reinforcement and Punishment

In discussing reinforcement theory, it is important to identify and to know several terms. These relate to the events that follow a desired response or to the events that are contingent on a particular behavior. *Reinforcement is any event, action, or phenomenon that increases the probability of a response occurring again. A punishment,* on the other hand, *is any event, action, or phenomenon that decreases the probability of a response occurring again.*

Reinforcers are of two types, positive and negative. *Positive reinforcers* are events that serve as reinforcers when they are *presented* to the individual if a desired response is produced. *Negative reinforcers* serve as reinforcers when they are *withdrawn* from the individual when a desired response occurs. Remember, reinforcers always serve to strengthen a desired response. From the examples that were presented in the application section, the use of verbal praise by the teacher for the children learning to dribble a soccer ball was an example of positive reinforcement for a correct response. The wrestling coach who made a special award to the wrestler who had the most takedowns during the season was also employing positive reinforcement techniques to improve behavior. Negative reinforcement was used by the coach who withdrew or stopped chiding a player when that player produced a desired response. Thus, positive reinforcement is the presentation of a desirable stimulus, while negative reinforcement is withdrawing or terminating an adverse stimulus when a desired response is produced.

Punishment should not be confused with negative reinforcement. Punishment is always an event that follows a response in order to eliminate that response. The tennis teacher who devised a new rule for tennis provides an example of using punishment in a learning situation. The response that the teacher was trying to eliminate was the students' poor first serve. The new rule the teacher devised punished the server for making a bad first serve by giving a point to the opponent.

Reinforcers and punishment can be either *tangible* or *intangible*. A piece of candy, a trophy, or money are examples of tangible reinforcers. Tangible forms of punishment could be a paddling or an electrical shock. Intangible reinforcers would be such things as verbal praise or a smile. These are phenomena that the individual being reinforced cannot physically hold onto. An intangible punishment would be a scolding or a scowl from the teacher.

Another important characteristic of reinforcers and punishment is that they must be *important to or desired by the individual*. If a trophy is contingent on a certain performance and an individual is completely indifferent to being awarded a trophy, the effectiveness of the trophy as a reinforcement is greatly diminished. If the teacher does not permit a child to play in a game or activity following bad behavior by the child and participation is very important to the child, then the punishment will probably be effective. This characteristic of reinforcers or punishment is too often overlooked by teachers and coaches. In order for a reinforcer or punishment to be effective, the teacher must be certain that the chosen reinforcer or punishment is actually important to the individual.

Finally, the effectiveness of a reinforcer or punishment is dependent upon its *temporal association* with the response. That is, a reinforcement should closely follow, in time, the desired response. There should be no doubt on the part of the student that the reinforcer was for a particular response.

Since the primary concern in this book is the learning of motor skills, reinforcement techniques relating to instructional situations will be the focus of the discussion in this section. Unfortunately, little is known about the effectiveness of punishment in a learning situation. On the other hand, much research supports reinforcement as an effective tool in facilitating learning.

Two important questions concerning the use of reinforcement in learning will provide the basis of this discussion. One of these relates to *when* reinforcers should be used. The second question is *how often* reinforcers should be used. Although there are no unequivocal answers to these questions, positive guidelines can be furnished to assist you in using reinforcement techniques effectively.

When should reinforcers be used? From the discussion so far, it appears that a reinforcer should only be used following a proper or correct behavior or response. To adapt this statement to a learning situation would seem to lead to a rather unrealistic conclusion. If the elementary physical education teacher waited to praise a child until the child dribbled the soccer ball correctly, there would be a strong possibility that no praise would ever be given. To resolve this problem, reinforcement theorists have developed a concept they call *shaping behavior*. This means that the role of a reinforcer is to approve and

strengthen a response that is somewhat similar to the end response desired. In this way, the instructor can "shape" the behavior of the student by rewarding that student each step of the way, as he or she progresses toward the ultimate response desired. In the soccer dribbling example, the teacher should praise students who are showing responses that in some way indicate progress in learning the skill.

How often should reinforcers be used? It would not be physically or practically possible to reinforce every correct or semicorrect response of each student in a class. To solve this problem, reinforcement theorists have concluded that *partial reinforcement* can be just as effective as reinforcing every correct response. Partial reinforcement can occur in accordance with a schedule in which the reinforcement is made on the basis of some specified temporal norms. Another way to use partial reinforcement is to reinforce a student after a certain number of correct responses. The teacher should try various temporal and number-of-correct-response schedules to determine which is the most effective for his or her needs.

Summary

Reinforcement of desired behavior is an effective motivator of behavior. Reinforcement has been defined as any event, action, or phenomenon which serves to increase the probability of likelihood of a response or behavior occurring again. A reinforcer may be either positive or negative. In either case, the result is the strengthening of a desired response. A punishment is any event, action, or phenomenon which serves to decrease the probability of a behavior or response occurring again. Both reinforcers and punishment must be important to the individual and contingent on the behavior of interest, if they are to be effective. In learning situations, reinforcement should be related to responses which approximate the desired end result, in order to direct or "shape" behavior in the desired direction. Schedules of partial reinforcement, based on time or the number of correct responses, can be developed to overcome the practical problem of reinforcing each correct response.

Related Readings

Keller, F. S. (1969). *Learning: Reinforcement theory* (2nd ed.). New York: Random House.

Skinner, B. F. (1968). *The technology of teaching.* New York: Appleton-Century-Crofts. (Read chapter 7.)

Travers, R. M. W. (1979). *Essentials of learning* (4th ed.). New York: Macmillan. (Read chapter 2.)

Vallerand, R. J. (1983). The effects of differential amounts of positive verbal feedback on the intrinsic motivation of male hockey players. *Journal of Sport Psychology, 5,* 101–109.

Weinberg, R. S. (1984). The relationship between extrinsic rewards and intrinsic motivation in sport. In J. M. Silva III and R. S. Weinberg (Eds.), *Psychological foundations of sport* (pp. 177–187). Champaign, IL: Human Kinetics.

1. The study of motivation is concerned with what three aspects of behavior?
2. How are learning and motivation reciprocal?
3. How does the comparison of intentional and incidental learning conditions relate to learning and motivation and to showing that more information is stored in memory than we may realize?
4. What is the difference between trait anxiety and state anxiety?
5. What do the drive and inverted-U theories predict about the level of performance of a motor skill that can be expected for a given level of state anxiety?
6. How do individual and situation anxiety-related variables interact to influence motor skill performance levels?
7. How does attentional focus relate to influencing anxiety so that a skill can be optimally performed? Give an example of how this could occur in a skill performance situation.
8. Name four ways goal setting is related to motor skill acquisition and performance.
9. List four guidelines that should be followed to set realistic goals. Give a motor skill performance example for each.
10. How can knowledge of results (KR) be used as a source of motivation when achieving an established performance goal is involved?
11. Give an example of providing positive and negative reinforcement in a teaching situation you might be in. How does punishment differ from negative reinforcement?
12. What are three aspects of reinforcement that should be considered before applying reinforcement techniques in teaching?

References

Adams, J. A (1971). A closed-loop theory of motor learning. *Journal of Motor Behavior, 3,* 111–149.

Adams, J. A. (1987). Historical review and appraisal of research on the learning, retention, and transfer of human motor skills. *Psychological Bulletin, 101,* 41–74.

Adams, J. A., and Dijkstra, S. J. (1966). Short-term memory for motor responses. *Journal of Experimental Psychology, 71,* 314–318.

Adams, J. A., and Hufford, L. E. (1962). Contributions of a part-task trainer to the learning and relearning of a time-shared flight maneuver. *Human Factors, 4,* 159–170.

Adams, J. A., and Reynolds, B. (1954). Effects of shift of distribution of practice conditions following interpolated rest. *Journal of Experimental Psychology, 47,* 32–36.

Adams, J. A., and Xhingesse, L. V. (1960). Some determinants of two-dimensional visual tracking behavior. *Journal of Experimental Psychology, 60,* 391–403.

Alderman, R. B. (1974). *Psychological behavior in sport.* Philadelphia: W. B. Saunders.

Alderson, G. J. K., Sully, D. J., and Sully, H. G. (1974). An operational analysis of a one-handed catching task using high speed photography. *Journal of Motor Behavior, 6,* 217–226.

Allport, D. A. (1980). Attention and performance. In G. Claxton (Ed.), *Cognitive psychology: New directions* (pp. 112–153). London: Routledge & Kegan Paul.

Ammons, R. B. (1958). Le mouvement. In G. H. Steward and J. P. Steward (Eds.), *Current psychological issues* (pp. 146–183). New York: Henry Holt & Co.

Annett, J., and Sparrow, J. (1985). Transfer of training: A review of research and practical implications. *Programmed Learning and Educational Technology, 22,* 116–124.

Anson, J. G. (1982). Memory drum theory: Alternative tests and explanations for the complexity effects on simple reaction time. *Journal of Motor Behavior, 14,* 228–246.

Atkinson, J. W. (1964). An introduction to motivation. Princeton, NJ: Van Nostrand.

Atkinson, R. C., and Shiffrin, R. M. (1968). Human memory: A proposed system and its control processes. In K.W. Spence and J. T. Spence (Eds.), *The psychology of learning and motivation: Advances in research and theory* (Vol. 2, pp. 89–197). New York: Academic Press.

Ausubel, D. P. (1968). *Educational psychology: A cognitive view.* New York: Holt, Rinehart, & Winston.

Bachman, J. C. (1961). Specificity vs. generality in learning and performing two large muscle motor tasks. *Research Quarterly, 32,* 3–11.

Baddeley, A. D. (1981). The concept of working memory: A view of its current state and probable future development. *Cognition, 10,* 17–23.

Baddeley, A. D. (1986). *Working memory.* New York: Oxford University Press.

Baddeley, A. D., and Hitch, G. (1974). Working memory. In G. H. Bower (Ed.), *The psychology of learning and motivation: Advances in research and theory* (Vol. 8, pp. 47–89). New York: Academic Press.

Baddeley, A. D., and Longman, D. J. A. (1978). The influence of length and frequency of training session on the rate of learning to type. *Ergonomics, 21,* 627–635.

Bahill, A. T., and LaRitz, T. (1984). Why can't batters keep their eyes on the ball? *American Scientist, 72,* 249–252.

Ball, C. T., and Glencross, D. (1985). Developmental differences in a coincident timing task under speed and time constraints. *Human Movement Science, 4,* 1–15.

Bandura, A. (1977). Self-efficacy: Toward a unifying theory of behavioral change. *Psychological Review, 84,* 191–215.

Bandura, A. (1984). *Social foundations of thought and action.* Englewood Cliffs, NJ: Prentice-Hall.

Bartlett, F. C. (1932). *Remembering: A Study in Experimental and Social Psychology.* Cambridge: Cambridge University Press.

Barton, J. W. (1921). Smaller versus larger units in learning the maze. *Journal of Experimental Psychology, 4,* 414–424.

Basmajian, J. V. (1967). *Muscles alive* (2nd ed.). Baltimore: Williams and Wilkins.

Battig, W. F. (1979). The flexibility of human memory. In L. S. Cermak and F. I. M. Craik (Eds.), *Levels of processing in human memory* (pp. 23–44). Hillsdale, NJ: Erlbaum.

Baumgartner, T. A., and Jackson, A. S. (1982). *Measurement for evaluation in physical education* (2nd ed.). Dubuque, IA: Wm. C. Brown.

Beaubaton, D., and Hay, L. (1986). Contribution of visual information to feedfoward and feedback processes in rapid pointing movements. *Human Movement Science, 5,* 19–34.

Bell, H. M. (1950). Retention of pursuit rotor skill after one year. *Journal of Experimental Psychology, 40,* 648–649.

Benedetti, C., and McCullagh, P. (1987). Post-knowledge of results delay: Effects of interpolated activity on learning and performance. *Research Quarterly for Exercise and Sport, 58,* 375–381.

Bernstein, N. (1967). *The co-ordination and regulation of movement.* Oxford: Pergamon Press.

Bilodeau, E. A., and Bilodeau, I. M. (1958). Variable frequency of knowledge of results and the learning of a simple skill. *Journal of Experimental Psychology, 55,* 379–383.

Bilodeau, E. A., and Bilodeau, I. M. (1961). Motor skills learning. *Annual Review of Psychology, 12,* 243–280.

Bilodeau, E. A., Bilodeau, I. M., and Schumsky, D. A. (1959). Some effects of introducing and withdrawing knowledge of results early and late in practice. *Journal of Experimental Psychology, 58,* 142–144.

Bilodeau, I. M. (1969). Information feedback. In E. A. Bilodeau (Ed.), *Principles of skill acquisition* (pp. 225–285). New York: Academic Press.

Boucher, J. L. (1974). Higher processes in motor learning. *Journal of Motor Behavior, 6,* 131–137.

Boulter, L. R. (1964). Evaluations of mechanisms in delay of knowledge of results. *Canadian Journal of Psychology, 18,* 281–291.

Boutcher, S. H., and Crews, D. J. (1987). The effect of a preshot attentional routine on a well-learned skill. *International Journal of Sport Psychology, 18,* 30–39.

Brace, D. K. (1927). *Measuring motor ability.* New York: A. S. Barnes.

Brady, J. I., Jr. (1979). Surface practice, level of manual dexterity, and performance of an assembly task. *Human Factors, 21,* 25–33.

Bransford, J. D., Franks, J. J., Morris, C. D., and Stein, B. S. (1979). Some general constraints on learning and memory research. In L. S. Cermak and F. I. M. Craik (Eds.), *Levels of processing in human memory* (pp. 331–354). Hillsdale, NJ: Erlbaum.

Broadbent, D. E. (1958). *Perception and communication.* Oxford: Pergamon Press.

Brown, R. W. (1928). A comparison of the whole, part, and combination methods for learning piano music. *Journal of Experimental Psychology, 11,* 235–247.

Bryan, W. L., and Harter, N. (1987). Studies in the physiology and psychology of the telegraphic language. *Psychological Review, 4,* 27–53.

Burwitz, L. (1975). Observational learning and motor performance. *FEPSAC Conference Proceedings,* Edinburgh, Scotland.

Carlton, L. G. (1981). Processing visual feedback information for motor control. *Journal of Experimental Psychology: Human Perception and Performance, 5,* 1019–1030.

Carlton, L. G., Carlton, M. J., and Newell, K. M. (1987). Reaction time and response dynamics. *Quarterly Journal of Experimental Psychology, 39A,* 337–360.

Carroll, W. R., and Bandura, A. (1985). Role of timing of visual monitoring and motor rehearsal in observational learning of action patterns. *Journal of Motor Behavior, 17,* 269–281.

Carron, A. V. (1969). Performance and learning in a discrete motor task under massed vs. distributed practice. *Research Quarterly, 40,* 481–489.

Carron, A. V. (1972). Motor performance and learning under physical fatigue. *Medicine and Science in Sports, 4,* 101–106.

Cavanagh, P. R., and Kram, R. (1985). The efficiency of human movement—A statement of the problem. *Medicine and Science in Sports and Exercise, 17,* 304–308.

Chase, W. G., and Ericsson, K. A. (1982). Skill and working memory. In G. H. Bower (Ed.), *The psychology of learning and motivation* (Vol. 16, pp. 1–58). New York: Academic Press.

Chase, W. G., and Simon, H. A. (1973). Perception in chess. *Cognitive Psychology, 4,* 55–81.

Cherry, E. C. (1953). Some experiments on the recognition of speech with one and with two ears. *Journal of the Acoustical Society of America, 25,* 975–979.

Christina, R. W. (1973). Influence of enforced motor and sensory sets on reaction latency and movement speed. *Research Quarterly, 44,* 483–487.

Christina, R. W. (1976). Proprioception as a basis of anticipatory timing. In G. E. Stelmach (Ed.), *Motor control: Issues and trends* (pp. 187–199). New York: Academic Press.

Christina, R. W. (1977). Skilled motor performance: Anticipatory timing. In B. R. Wolman (Ed.), *International encyclopedia of psychiatry, psychology, psychoanalysis, and neurology* (Vol. 10, pp. 241–245). New York: Van Nostrand Reinhold.

Christina, R. W., and Buffan, J. L. (1976). Preview and movement as determiners of timing a discrete motor response. *Journal of Motor Behavior, 8,* 101–112.

Christina, R. W., Fischman, M. G., Lambert, A. L., and Moore, J. F. (1985). Simple reaction time as a function of response complexity: Christina et al. (1982) revisited. *Research Quarterly for Exercise and Sport, 56,* 316–322.

Christina, R. W., Fischman, M. G., Vercruyssen, M. J. P., and Anson, J. G. (1982). Simple reaction time as a function of response complexity: Memory drum theory revisited. *Journal of Motor Behavior, 14,* 301–321.

Christina, R. W., and Rose, D. J. (1985). Premotor and motor response time as a function of response complexity. *Research Quarterly for Exercise and Sport, 56,* 306–315.

Clamann, P. H. (1981). Motor units and their activity during movement. In A. L. Towe and E. S. Luschei (Eds.), *Handbook of behavioral neurobiology: Vol. 5. Motor coordination* (pp. 69–92). New York: Plenum Press.

Cook, T. W. (1933a). Studies in cross-education. I. Mirror tracing the star-shaped maze. *Journal of Experimental Psychology, 16,* 144–160.

Cook, T. W. (1933b). Studies in cross-education. II. Further experimentation in mirror tracing the star-shaped maze. *Journal of Experimental Psychology, 16,* 670–700.

Cook, T. W. (1934). Studies in cross-education. III. Kinesthetic learning of an irregular pattern. *Journal of Experimental Psychology, 17,* 749–762.

Cook, T. W. (1935). Studies in cross-education. IV. Permanence of transfer. *Journal of Experimental Psychology, 18,* 255–266.

Cook. T. W. (1936). Studies in cross-education. V. Theoretical. *Psychological Review, 43,* 149–178.

Corbin, C. (1972). Mental practice. In W. P. Morgan (Ed.), *Ergogenic aids and muscular performance* (pp. 93–118). New York: Academic Press.

Corcos, D. M. (1984). Two-handed movement control. *Research Quarterly for Exercise and Sport, 55,* 117–122.

Craik, F. I. M. (1970). The fate of primary memory items in free recall. *Journal of Verbal Learning and Verbal Behavior, 9,* 143–148.

Craik, F. I. M., and Lockhart, R. (1972). Levels of processing: A framework for memory research. *Journal of Verbal Learning and Verbal Behavior, 11,* 671–676.

Crocker, P. R. E., and Dickinson, J. (1984). Incidental psychomotor learning: The effects of number of movements, practice, and rehearsal. *Journal of Motor Behavior, 16,* 61–75.

Cronbach, L. J. (1957). The two disciplines of scientific psychology. *American Psychologist, 12,* 671–684.

Cuddy, L. J., and Jacoby, L. L. (1982). When forgetting helps memory: An analysis of repetition effects. *Journal of Verbal Learning and Verbal Behavior, 21,* 451–467.

Damos, D., and Wickens, C. D. (1980). The identification and transfer of timesharing skills. *Acta Psychologica, 46,* 15–39.

Davis, R. C. (1942). The pattern of muscular action in simple voluntary movements. *Journal of Experimental Psychology, 31,* 437–466.

Del Rey, P., Wughalter, E., and Carnes, M. (1987). Levels of expertise, interpolated activity, and contextual interference effects on memory and transfer. *Perceptual and Motor Skills, 64,* 275–284.

Del Rey, P., Wughalter, E., and Whitehurst, M. (1982). The effects of contextual interference on females with varied experience in open skills. *Research Quarterly for Exercise and Sport, 53,* 108–115.

De Lucia, P. R., and Cochran, E. L. (1985). Perceptual information for batting can be extracted throughout a ball's trajectory. *Perceptual and Motor Skills, 61,* 143–150.

den Brinker, B. P. L. M., Stabler, J. R. L. W., Whiting, H. T. A., and van Wieringen, P. C. (1986). The effect of manipulating knowledge of results in the learning of slalom-ski type ski movements. *Ergonomics, 29,* 31–40.

Denny, M. R., Frisbey, N., and Weaver, J., Jr. (1955). Rotary pursuit performance under alternate conditions of distributed and massed practice. *Journal of Experimental Psychology, 49,* 48–54.

Deutsch, J. A., and Deutsch, D. (1963). Attention: Some theoretical considerations. *Psychological Review, 70,* 80–90.

Dickinson, J. (1974). *Proprioceptive control of movement.* Princeton, NJ: Princeton Book Co.

Dickinson, J. (1978). Retention of intentional and incidental motor learning. *Research Quarterly, 49,* 437–441.

Diewart, G. L. (1975). Retention and coding in motor short-term memory: A comparison of storage codes for distance and location information. *Journal of Motor Behavior, 7,* 183–190.

Diewart, G. L., and Roy, E. A. (1978). Coding strategy for memory of movement extent information. *Journal of Experimental Psychology: Human Learning and Memory, 4,* 666–675.

Diewart, G. L., and Stelmach, G. E. (1978). Perceptual organization in motor learning. In G. E. Stelmach (Ed.), *Information processing in motor learning and control* (pp. 241–265). New York: Academic Press.

Doody, S. G., Bird, A. M., and Ross, D. (1985). The effect of auditory and visual models on acquisition of a timing task. *Human Movement Science, 4,* 271–281.

Dorfman, P. (1977). Timing and anticipation: A developmental perspective. *Journal of Motor Behavior, 9,* 67–79.

Drowatzky, J. N., and Zucatto, F. C. (1967). Interrelationships between selected measures of static and dynamic balance. *Research Quarterly, 38,* 509–510.

Duncan, J. (1977). Response selection rules in spatial choice reaction tasks. In S. Dornic (Ed.), *Attention and performance VI* (pp. 49–61). Hillsdale, NJ: Erlbaum.

Dunham, P., Jr. (1971). Learning and performance. *Research Quarterly, 42,* 334–337.

Dunham, P., Jr. (1977). Effect of practice order on the efficiency of bilateral skill acquisition. *Research Quarterly, 48,* 284–287.

Eason, R. G., Beardshall, A., and Jaffee, S. (1965). Performance and physiological indicants of activation in a vigilance situation. *Perceptual and Motor Skills, 20,* 3–13.

Eccles, J. C. (1973). *The understanding of the brain.* New York: McGraw-Hill.

Edwards, R. V., and Lee, A. M. (1985). The relationship of cognitive style and instructional strategy to learning and transfer of motor skills. *Research Quarterly for Exercise and Sport, 56,* 286–290.

Elliott, D. (1985). Manual asymmetries in the performance of sequential movements by adolescents and adults with Down Syndrome. *American Journal of Mental Deficiency, 90,* 90–97.

Elliott, D. (1986). Continuous visual information may be important after all: A failure to replicate Thomson (1983). *Journal of Experimental Psychology: Human Perception and Performance, 12,* 388–391.

Elliott, D., and Allard, F. (1985). The utilization of visual information and feedback information during rapid pointing movements. *Quarterly Journal of Experimental Psychology, 37A,* 407–425.

Ellis, H. C. (1965). *The transfer of learning.* New York: Macmillan.

Ellis, H. C. (1978). *Fundamentals of human learning, memory, and cognition* (2nd ed.). Dubuque, IA: Wm. C. Brown.

Ells, J. G. (1973). Analysis of temporal and attentional aspects of movement control. *Journal of Experimental Psychology, 99,* 10–21.

Elwell, J. L., and Grindley, G. C. (1938). The effect of knowledge of results on learning and performance. *British Journal of Psychology, 29,* 39–54.

Engle, R. W., and Buckstel, L. (1978). Memory processes among bridge players of differing experiences. *American Journal of Psychology, 91,* 673–690.

Ericsson, K. A. (1985). Memory skill. *Canadian Journal of Psychology, 39,* 188–231.

Evarts, E. V. (1980). Brain mechanisms in voluntary movements. In D. McFadden (Ed.), *Neural mechanisms in behavior* (pp. 223–259). New York: Springer-Verlag.

Fel'dman, A. G., and Latash, M. L. (1982). Interaction of afferent and efferent signals underlying joint position sense: Empirical and theoretical approaches. *Journal of Motor Behavior, 14,* 174–193.

Feltz, D., and Landers, D. M. (1983). The effects of mental practice on motor skill learning and performance: A meta-analysis. *Journal of Sport Psychology, 5,* 25–57.

Fischman, M. G. (1984). Programming time as a function of number of movement parts and changes in movement direction. *Journal of Motor Behavior, 16,* 405–423.

Fischman, M. G., and Schneider, T. (1985). Skill level, vision, and proprioception in simple one-hand catching. *Journal of Motor Behavior, 17,* 219–229.

Fitts, P. M. (1954). The information capacity of the human motor system in controlling the amplitude of movement. *Journal of Experimental Psychology, 47,* 381–391.

Fitts, P. M. (1964). Perceptual-motor skill learning. In A. W. Melton (Ed.), *Categories of human learning* (pp. 243–285). New York: Academic Press.

Fitts, P. M., Peterson, J. R., and Wolpe, G. (1963). Cognitive aspects of information processing: II. Adjustments to stimulus redundancy. *Journal of Experimental Psychology, 65,* 425–432.

Fitts, P. M., and Posner, M. I. (1967). *Human performance.* Belmont, CA: Brooks/Cole.

Fitts, P. M., and Seeger, C. M. (1953). S-R compatibility: Spatial characteristics of stimulus and response codes. *Journal of Experimental Psychology, 46,* 199–210.

Fleishman, E. A. (1972). On the relationship between abilities, learning, and human performance. *American Psychologist, 27,* 1017–1032.

Fleishman, E. A. (1978). Relating individual differences to the dimensions of human tasks. *Ergonomics, 21,* 1007–1019.

Fleishman, E. A. (1982). Systems for describing human tasks. *American Psychologist, 37,* 821–834.

Fleishman, E. A., and Hempel, W. E. (1955). The relationship between abilities and improvement with practice in a visual discrimination reaction task. *Journal of Experimental Psychology, 49,* 301–311.

Fleury, M., and Bard, C. (1985). Age, stimulus velocity, and task complexity as determinants of coincident timing behavior. *Journal of Human Movement Studies, 11,* 305–317.

Flowers, K. (1975). Handedness and controlled movement. *British Journal of Psychology, 66,* 39–52.

Franks, I. M., and Wilberg, R. B. (1982). The generation of movement patterns during the acquisition of a pursuit tracking task. *Human Movement Science, 1,* 251–272.

French, K. E., and Thomas, J. R. (1987). The relation of knowledge development to children's basketball performance. *Journal of Sport Psychology, 9,* 15–32.

Gage, N. L. (1972). *Teacher effectiveness and teacher education: The search for a scientific basis.* Palo Alto, CA: Pacific Books.

Gallagher, J. D. (1970). Motor learning characteristics of low-skilled college men. *Research Quarterly, 41,* 59–67.

Gallagher, J. D., and Thomas, J. R. (1980). Effects of varying post-KR intervals upon children's motor performance. *Journal of Motor Behavior, 12,* 41–46.

Gallahue, D. L., Werner, P. H., and Luedke, G. C. (1975). *A conceptual approach to moving and learning.* New York: John Wiley.

Gentile, A. M. (1972). A working model of skill acquisition with application to teaching. *Quest,* Monograph XVII, 3–23.

Gentile, A. M., Higgins, J. R., Miller, E. A., and Rosen, B. M. (1975). The structure of motor tasks. *Mouvement, 7,* 11–28.

Gentile, A. M., and Nemetz, K. (1978). Repetition effects: A methodological issue in motor short-term memory. *Journal of Motor Behavior, 10,* 37–44.

Gentner, D. (1987). Timing of skilled motor performance: Tests of the proportional duration model. *Psychological Review, 94,* 255–276.

Gibson, J. J. (1966). *The senses considered as perceptual systems.* Boston: Houghton Mifflin.

Gibson, J. J. (1979). *The ecological approach to visual perception.* Boston: Houghton Mifflin.

Gire, E., and Espenschade, A. (1942). The relationship between measures of motor educability and learning specific motor skills. *Research Quarterly, 13,* 43–56.

Girouard, Y., Laurencelle, L., and Proteau L. (1984). On the nature of the probe reaction-time task to uncover the attentional demands of movement. *Journal of Motor Behavior, 16,* 442–459.

Glencross, D. J. (1973). Response complexity and latency of different movement patterns. *Journal of Motor Behavior, 5,* 95–104.

Glencross, D. J. (1977). Control of skilled movements. *Psychological Bulletin, 84,* 14–29.

Glencross, D., and Tsouvallas, M. (1984). Processing of proprioceptive information in Parkinson's disease patients. *Australian Journal of Psychology, 36,* 343–354.

Godwin, M. A., and Schmidt, R. A. (1971). Muscular fatigue and discrete motor learning. *Research Quarterly, 42,* 374–383.

Goode, S. L. (1986). *The contextual interference effect in learning an open skill.* Unpublished doctoral dissertation, Louisiana State University, Baton Rouge.

Goode, S. L., and Magill, R. A. (1986). The contextual interference effect in learning three badminton serves. *Research Quarterly for Exercise and Sport, 57,* 308–314.

Goss, S., Hall, C., Buckolz, E., and Fishburne, G. (1986). Imagery ability and the acquisition and retention of motor skills. *Memory and Cognition, 14,* 469–477.

Gottsdanker, R. (1979). A psychological refractory period or an unprepared period? *Journal of Experimental Psychology: Human Perception and Performance, 5,* 208–215.

Gottsdanker, R. (1980). The ubiquitous role of preparation. In G. E. Stelmach and J. Requin (Eds.), *Tutorials in motor behavior* (pp. 355–371). Amsterdam: North-Holland.

Gould, D., and Roberts, G. C. (1982). Modeling and motor skill acquisition. *Quest, 33,* 214–230.

Gould, D., Weinberg, R., and Jackson, A. (1980). Mental preparation strategies, cognitions, and strength performance. *Journal of Sport Psychology, 2,* 329–335.

Gross, E., Griessel, D. C., and Stull, G. A. (1956). Relationship between two motor educability tests, a strength test, and wrestling ability after eight weeks of instruction. *Research Quarterly, 27,* 395–402.

Hagman, J. D. (1978). Specific-cue effects of interpolated movements on distance and location retention in short-term motor memory. *Memory and Cognition, 6,* 432–437.

Hale, B. D. (1982). The effects of internal and external imagery on muscular and ocular concomitants. *Journal of Sport Psychology, 4,* 379–387.

Hall, C. R. (1980). Imagery for movement. *Journal of Human Movement Studies, 6,* 252–264.

Hall, C. R. (1985). Individual differences in the mental practice and imagery of motor skill performance. *Canadian Journal of Applied Sport Sciences, 10,* 17S–21S.

Hall, C. R., and Buckolz, E. (1982–83). Imagery and the recall of movement patterns. *Imagination, Cognition, and Personality, 2,* 251–260.

Hall, C. R., and Pongrac, J. (1983). *Movement Imagery Questionnaire.* London, Ontario, Canada: University of Western Ontario.

Hall, C. R., Pongrac, J., and Buckolz, E. (1985). The measurement of imagery ability. *Human Movement Science, 4,* 107–118.

Hamilton, E. L. (1929). The effect of delayed incentives on the hunger drive of the white rat. *Genetic Psychology Monographs, 5,* 131–207.

Hamilton, W. (1859). *Lectures on metaphysics and logic.* Edinburgh: Blackwood.

Harari, H. (1969). Levels of aspiration and athletic performance. *Perceptual and Motor Skills, 28,* 519–524.

Hardy, C. J. (1983). The post-knowledge of results interval: Effects of interpolated activity on cognitive information processing. *Research Quarterly for Exercise and Sport, 54,* 144–148.

Hasher, L., and Zacks, R. (1979). Automatic and effortful processes in memory. *Journal of Experimental Psychology: General, 108,* 356–388.

Hay, L. (1979). Spatio-temporal analysis of movements in children: Motor programs versus feedback in the development of reaching. *Journal of Motor Behavior, 11,* 189–200.

Hebb, D. O. (1949). *The organization of behavior.* New York: John Wiley.

Henry, F. M. (1961). Reaction time-movement time correlations. *Perceptual and Motor Skills, 12,* 63–66.

Henry, F. M. (1974). Variable and constant performance errors with a group of individuals. *Journal of Motor Behavior, 6,* 149–154.

Henry, F. M., and Rogers, D. E. (1960). Increased response latency for complicated movements and the "memory drum" theory of neuromotor reaction. *Research Quarterly, 31,* 448–458.

Henry, R. A., and Hulin, C. L. (1987). Stability of skilled performance across time: Some generalizations and limitations on utilities. *Journal of Applied Psychology, 72,* 457–462.

Hick, W. E. (1952). On the rate of gain of information. *Quarterly Journal of Experimental Psychology, 4,* 11–26.

Hicks, R. E., Frank, J. M., and Kinsbourne, M. (1982). The locus of bimanual skill transfer. *Journal of General Psychology, 107,* 277–281.

Hicks, R. E., Gualtieri, T. C., and Schroeder, S. R. (1983). Cognitive and motor components of bilateral transfer. *American Journal of Psychology, 96,* 223–228.

Higgins, J. R. (1977). *Human movement: An integrated approach.* St. Louis: C. V. Mosby.

Hintzman, D. L. (1974). Theoretical implications of the spacing effect. In R. L. Solso (Ed.), *Theories in cognitive psychology: The Loyola Symposium* (pp. 77–99). Potomac, MD: Erlbaum.

Ho, L., and Shea, J. B. (1978). Levels of processing and the coding of position cues in motor short-term memory. *Journal of Motor Behavior, 10,* 113–121.

Hogan, J., and Yanowitz, B. (1978). The role of verbal estimates of movement error in ballistic skill acquisition. *Journal of Motor Behavior, 10,* 133–138.

Holding, D. H. (1965). *The principles of training.* Oxford: Pergamon Press.

Holding, D. H. (1976). An approximate transfer surface. *Journal of Motor Behavior, 8,* 1–9.

Hole, J. W., Jr. (1984). *Human anatomy and physiology* (3rd ed.). Dubuque, IA: Wm. C. Brown.

Hore, J., and Vilas, T. (1980). Arm movement performance during reversible basal ganglia lesions in the monkey. *Experimental Brain Research, 39,* 217–228.

Housner, L. D. (1981). Expert-novice knowledge structure and cognitive processing differences in badminton. (Abstract.) *Psychology of motor behavior and sport - 1981* (p. 1). Proceedings of the annual meeting of the North American Society for the Psychology of Sport and Physical Activity, Asilomar, CA.

Howe, M. J. A. (1970). *Introduction to human memory.* New York: Harper & Row.

Hubbard, A. W., and Seng, C. N. (1954). Visual movements of batters. *Research Quarterly, 25,* 42–57.

Hull, C. L. (1943). *Principles of behavior.* New York: Appleton-Century-Crofts.

Husak, W., and Reeve, T. G. (1979). Novel response production as a function of variability and amount of practice. *Research Quarterly, 50,* 215–221.

Inglis, J., Campbell, D., and Donald, M. W. (1976). Electromyographic biofeedback and neuromuscular rehabilitation. *Canadian Journal of Behavioral Science, 8,* 299–323.

Ito, M. (1970). Neurophysiological aspects of the cerebellar motor control system. *International Journal of Neurology, 7,* 162–176.

Jacobson, E. (1931). Electrical measurement of neuromuscular states during mental activities: VI. A note on mental activities concerning an amputated limb. *American Journal of Physiology, 43,* 122–125.

Jacoby, L. L. (1978). On interpreting the effects of repetitions: Solving a problem versus remembering a solution. *Journal of Verbal Learning and Verbal Behavior, 17,* 649–667.

Jahnke, J. (1963). Serial position effects in immediate serial recall. *Journal of Verbal Learning and Verbal Behavior, 2,* 284–287.

James, W. (1890). *Principles of psychology.* New York: Holt.

Johnson, B., and Nelson, J. K. (1985). *Practical measurement for evaluation in physical education* (4th ed.). Minneapolis: Burgess.

Johnson, R., and McCabe, J. (1982). Schema theory: A test of the variability of practice hypothesis. *Perceptual and Motor Skills, 55,* 231–234.

Jongsma, D. M., Elliott, D., and Lee, T. D. (1987). Experience and set in the running sprint start. *Perceptual and Motor Skills, 64,* 547–550.

Kahneman, D. (1973). *Attention and effort.* Englewood Cliffs, NJ: Prentice-Hall.

Kantowitz, B. H. (1985). Channels and stages in human information processing: A limited analysis of theory and methodology. *Journal of Mathematical Psychology, 29,* 135–174.

Kantowitz, B. H., and Knight, J. L., Jr. (1976). Testing tapping timesharing: II. Auditory secondary task. *Acta Psychologica, 40,* 343–362.

Keefe, F. J., and Surwit, R. S. (1978). Electromyographic biofeedback: Behavioral treatment of neuromuscular disorders. *Electromyography & Clinical Neurophysiology, 19,* 175–181.

Keele, S. W. (1968). Movement control in skilled motor performance. *Psychological Bulletin, 70,* 387–403.

Keele, S. W. (1982). Behavioral analysis of movement. In V. B. Brooks (Ed.), *Handbook of physiology, Sec. 1: The nervous system. Vol. II: Motor control, part 2* (pp. 1391–1414). Baltimore: American Physiological Society.

Keele, S. W., and Posner, M. I. (1968). Processing of visual feedback in rapid movements. *Journal of Experimental Psychology, 77,* 153–158.

Keller, F. S. (1958). The phantom plateau. *Journal of Experimental Analysis of Behavior, 1,* 1–13.

Kelso, J. A. S. (1977). Motor control mechanisms underlying human movement reproduction. *Journal of Experimental Psychology: Human Perception and Performance, 3,* 529–543.

Kelso, J. A. S. (1981). Contrasting perspectives on order and regulation in movement. In J. Long and A. Baddeley (Eds.), *Attention and performance IX* (pp. 437–457). Hillsdale: NJ: Erlbaum.

Kelso, J. A. S. (1984). Report of panel 3: Preparatory processes: Considerations from a theory of movement. In E. Donchin (Ed.), *Cognitive psychophysiology* (pp. 201–214). Hillsdale, NJ: Erlbaum.

Kelso, J. A. S., and Holt, K. G. (1980). Exploring a vibratory systems analysis of human movement production. *Journal of Neurophysiology, 43,* 1183–1196.

Kelso, J. A. S., Holt, K. G., and Flatt, A. E. (1980). The role of proprioception in the perception and control of human movement: Toward a theoretical reassessment. *Perception and Psychophysics, 28,* 45–52.

Kelso, J. A. S., Southard, D. L., and Goodman, D. (1979). On the coordination of two-handed movements. *Journal of Experimental Psychology: Human Perception and Performance, 5,* 229–238.

Kelso, J. A. S., and Stelmach, G. E. (1976). Central and peripheral mechanisms in motor control. In G. E. Stelmach (Ed.), *Motor control: Issues and trends* (pp. 1–40). New York: Academic Press.

Kelso, J. A. S., Stelmach, G. E., and Wanamaker, W. M. (1974). Behavioral and neurological parameters of the nerve compression block. *Journal of Motor Behavior, 6,* 179–190.

Kelso, J. A. S., Tuller, B. H., and Harris, K. S. (1983). A "dynamic pattern" perspective on the control and coordination of movement. In P. F. MacNeilage (Ed.), *The production of speech* (pp. 137–173). New York: Springer-Verlag.

Kelso, J. A. S., Tuller, B. H., Vatikiotis-Bateson, E., and Fowler, C. A. (1984). Functionally specific articulatory cooperation following jaw perturbations during speech: Evidence for coordinative structures. *Journal of Experimental Psychology: Human Perception and Performance, 10,* 812–832.

Kelso, J. A. S., and Wallace, S. A. (1978). Conscious mechanisms of control. In G. E. Stelmach (Ed.), *Information processing in motor control and learning* (pp. 79–116). New York: Academic Press.

Kelso, J. A. S., Wallace, S. A., Stelmach, G. E., and Weitz, G. A. (1975). Sensory and motor impairments in the nerve compression block. *Quarterly Journal of Experimental Psychology, 27,* 123–129.

Klapp, S. T. (1975). Feedback versus motor programming in the control of aimed movements. *Journal of Experimental Psychology, 104,* 147–153.

Knapp, C. G., and Dixon, W. R. (1952). Learning to juggle: A study of whole and part methods. *Research Quarterly, 23,* 389–401.

Kohl, R. M., and Roenker, D. L. (1980). Bilateral transfer as a function of mental imagery. *Journal of Motor Behavior, 12,* 197–206.

Kolers, P. A., and Roediger, H. L., III (1984). Procedures of mind. *Journal of Verbal Learning and Verbal Behavior, 23,* 425–449.

Kots, Ya. M. (1977). *The organization of voluntary movements.* New York: Plenum.

Laabs, G. J. (1973). Retention characteristics of different reproduction cues in motor short-term memory. *Journal of Experimental Psychology, 100,* 168–177.

Landers, D. M. (1975). Observational learning of a motor skill: Temporal spacing of demonstrations and audience presence. *Journal of Motor Behavior, 7,* 281–287.

Landers, D. M., and Landers, D. M. (1973). Teacher versus peer models: Effect of model's presence and performance level on motor behavior. *Journal of Motor Behavior, 5,* 129–139.

Landers, D. M., Boutcher, S. H., and Wang, M. Q. (1986). A psychobiological study of archery performance. *Research Quarterly for Exercise and Sport, 57,* 236–244.

Lang, P. J., Kozak, M. J., Miller, G. A., Levin, D. M., and McLean, A., Jr. (1980). Emotional imagery: Conceptual structure and pattern of somato-visceral response. *Psychophysiology, 17,* 179–192.

Larish, D. D., and Stelmach, G. E. (1982). Preprogramming, programming, and reprogramming of aimed hand movements as a function of age. *Journal of Motor Behavior, 14,* 322–340.

Lashley, K. S. (1917). The accuracy of movement in the absence of excitation from the moving organ. *American Journal of Physiology, 43,* 169–194.

Lashley, K. S. (1951). The problem of serial order in behavior. In L. A. Jeffress (Ed.), *Cerebral mechanisms in behavior* (pp. 112–136). New York: John Wiley.

Laszlo, J. L. (1966). The performance of a single motor task with kinesthetic sense loss. *Quarterly Journal of Experimental Psychology, 18,* 1–8.

Laszlo, J. L. (1967). Training of fast tapping with reduction of kinesthetic, tactile, visual, and auditory sensation. *Quarterly Journal of Experimental Psychology, 19,* 344–349.

Lavery, J. J. (1962). Retention of simple motor skills as a function of type of knowledge of results. *Canadian Journal of Psychology, 16,* 300–311.

Leavitt, J. L. (1979). Cognitive demands of skating and stickhandling in ice hockey. *Canadian Journal of Applied Sport Sciences, 4,* 46–55.

Leavitt, J. L., Lee, T. D., and Romanow, S. K. E. (1980). Proactive interference and movement attribute change in motor short-term memory. In C. H. Nadeau, W. R. Halliwell, K. M. Newell, and G. C. Roberts (Eds.), *Psychology of motor behavior and sport – 1979* (pp. 585–593). Champaign, IL: Human Kinetics.

Lee, D. N. (1974). Visual information during locomotion. In R. B. MacLeod and H. Pick (Eds.), *Perception: Essays in honor of J. J. Gibson* (pp. 250–267). Ithaca, NY: Cornell University Press.

Lee, D. N. (1976). A theory of visual control of braking based on information about time-to-collision. *Perception, 5,* 437–459.

Lee, D. N. (1980). Visuo-motor coordination in space-time. In G. E. Stelmach and J. Requin (Eds.), *Tutorials in motor behavior* (pp. 281–295). Amsterdam: North-Holland.

Lee, D. N., Lishman, J. R., and Thomson, J. A. (1984). Regulation of gait in long jumping. *Journal of Experimental Psychology: Human Perception and Performance, 8,* 448–459.

Lee, T. D., and Gallagher, J. D. (1981). A parallel between the preselection effect in psychomotor memory and the generation effect in verbal memory. *Journal of Experimental Psychology: Human Learning and Memory, 7,* 77–78.

Lee, T. D., and Genovese, E. D. (1988a). Distribution of practice in motor skill acquisition: Different effects for discrete and continuous tasks. *Research Quarterly for Exercise and Sport, 59.*

Lee, T. D., and Genovese, E. D. (1988b). Distribution of practice in motor skill acquisition: Learning and performance effects reconsidered. *Research Quarterly for Exercise and Sport, 59.*

Lee, T. D., and Hirota, T. T. (1980). Encoding specificity principle in motor short-term memory for movement extent. *Journal of Motor Behavior, 12,* 63–67.

Lee, T. D., and Magill, R. A. (1983a). Activity during the post-KR interval: Effects upon performance or learning. *Research Quarterly for Exercise and Sport, 54,* 340–345.

Lee, T. D., and Magill, R. A. (1983b). The locus of contextual interference in motor skill acquisition. *Journal of Experimental Psychology: Learning, Memory, and Cognition, 9,* 730–746.

Lee, T. D., and Magill, R. A. (1985). Can forgetting facilitate skill acquisition? In D. Goodman, R. B. Wilberg, and I. M. Franks (Eds.), *Differing perspectives in motor learning, memory and control* (pp. 3–22). Amsterdam: North-Holland.

Lee, T. D., and Magill, R. A. (1987). Effects of duration and activity during the post-KR interval on motor learning. *Psychological Research, 49,* 237–242.

Lee, T. D., Magill, R. A., and Weeks, D. J. (1985). Influence of practice schedule on testing schema theory predictions in adults. *Journal of Motor Behavior, 17,* 283–299.

Lee, T. D., and Weeks, D. J. (1987). The beneficial influence of forgetting on short-term retention of movement information. *Human Movement Science, 6,* 233–245.

Leonard, J. A. (1959). Tactual choice reactions: I. *Quarterly Journal of Experimental Psychology, 11,* 76–83.

Lewin, K., Dembo, T., Festinger, L., and Sears, P. S. (1944). Levels of aspiration. In J. M. Hunt (Ed.), *Personality and behavior disorders* (Vol. I, pp. 333–378). New York: Ronald Press.

Lindahl, L. G. (1945). Movement analysis as an industrial training method. *Journal of Applied Psychology, 29,* 420–436.

Llinas, R., and Simpson, J. (1981). Cerebellar control of movement. In A. L. Towe and E. S. Luschei (Eds.), *Handbook of behavioral neurobiology: Vol. 5. Motor coordination* (pp. 231–302). New York: Plenum.

Locke, E. A. (1968). Effects of knowledge of results feedback in relation to standards and goals on reaction-time performance. *American Journal of Psychology, 81,* 566–574.

Locke, E. A., and Bryan, J. F. (1966). Cognitive aspects of psychomotor performance: The effects of performance goals on level of performance. *Journal of Applied Psychology, 50,* 286–291.

Locke, E. A., Cartledge, N., and Koeppel, J. (1968). Motivational effects of knowledge of results: A goal-setting phenomenon. *Psychological Bulletin, 70,* 474–485.

Loftus, E. F. (1980). *Memory: Surprising new insights into how we remember and why we forget.* Reading, MA: Addison-Wesley.

Loftus, E. F., and Loftus, G. R. (1980). On the permanence of stored information in the human brain. *American Psychologist, 35,* 409–420.

Logan, G. D. (1982). On the ability to inhibit complex movements: A stop-signal study of typewriting. *Journal of Experimental Psychology: Human Perception and Performance, 8,* 778–792.

Logan, G. D. (1985). Skill and automaticity: Relations, implications, and future directions. *Canadian Journal of Psychology, 39,* 367–386.

Lorge, I., and Thorndike, E. L. (1935). The influence of the delay in the after-effect of a connection. *Journal of Experimental Psychology, 18,* 186–194.

Mackworth, N. H. (1956). Vigilance. *Nature, 178,* 1375–1377.

Magill, R. A. (1973). The post-KR interval: Time and activity effects and the relationship of motor short-term memory theory. *Journal of Motor Behavior, 5,* 49–56.

Magill, R. A. (1977). The processing of knowledge of results for a serial motor task. *Journal of Motor Behavior, 9,* 113–118.

Magill, R. A. (1983). Preface/Introduction. In R. A. Magill (Ed.), *Memory and control of action* (pp. xi–xvi). Amsterdam: North-Holland.

Magill, R. A. (1988). Activity during the post-knowledge of results interval can benefit motor skill learning. In O. G. Meijer and K. Roth (Eds.), *Complex motor behavior: The 'motor-action' controversy* (pp. 231–246). Amsterdam: Elsevier Science Publishers.

Magill, R. A., and Chamberlin, C. J. (1988). Verbal KR can be redundant information in motor skill learning (Abstract). *Psychology of motor behavior and sport–1988* (p. 64). Proceedings of the annual meeting of the North American Society for the Psychology of Sport and Physical Activity, Knoxville, TN.

Magill, R. A., and Dowell, M. N. (1977). Serial position effects in motor short-term memory. *Journal of Motor Behavior, 9,* 319–323.

Magill, R. A., and Goode, S. (1982). The representation of limb position information in memory. (Abstract). *Psychology of motor behavior and sport-1982* (p. 43). Proceedings of the annual meeting of the North American Society for the Psychology of Sport and Physical Activity, College Park, MD.

Magill, R. A., and Lee, T. D. (1987). Verbal label effects on response accuracy and organization for learning limb positioning movements. *Journal of Human Movement Studies, 13,* 285–308.

Magill, R. A., Meeuwsen, H., Lee, T. D., and Mathews, R. C. (1987). *Is the contextual interference effect in motor skill learning a spacing effect?* Unpublished manuscript, Louisiana State University, Baton Rouge.

Magill, R. A., and Parks, P. F. (1983). The psychophysics of kinesthesis for positioning responses: The physical stimulus-psychological response relationship. *Research Quarterly for Exercise and Sport, 54,* 346–351.

Magill, R. A., and Wood, C. A. (1986). Knowledge of results precision as a learning variable in motor skill acquisition. *Research Quarterly for Exercise and Sport, 57,* 170–173.

Magill, R. A., Young, D. E., Schmidt, R. A., and Shapiro, D. C. (1986). Unpublished raw data. University of California, Los Angeles.

Mahoney, M. J., and Avener, A. (1977). Psychology of the elite athlete: An exploratory study. *Cognitive Therapy and Research, 1,* 135–141.

Malina, R. M. (1984). Physical growth and maturation. In J. R. Thomas (Ed.), *Motor development during childhood and adolescence* (pp. 2–26). Minneapolis: Burgess.

Mark, L. S. (1987). Eyeheight-scaled information about affordances: A study of sitting and stair climbing. *Journal of Experimental Psychology: Human Perception and Performance, 13,* 361–370.

Marteniuk, R. G. (1986). Information processes in movement learning: Capacity and structural interference. *Journal of Motor Behavior, 5,* 249–259.

Marteniuk, R. G., and Mackenzie, C. (1980). A preliminary theory of two-handed coordinated control. In G. E. Stelmach and J. Requin (Eds.), *Tutorials in motor behavior* (pp. 185–197). Amsterdam: North-Holland.

Marteniuk, R. G., and Romanow, S. K. E. (1983). Human movement organization and learning as revealed by variability of movement, use of kinematic information and Fourier analysis. In R. A. Magill (Ed.), *Memory and control of action* (pp. 167–197). Amsterdam: North-Holland.

Martens, R. (1971). Anxiety and motor behavior: A review. *Journal of Motor Behavior, 3,* 151–179.

Martens, R. (1972). Trait and state anxiety. In W. P. Morgan (Ed.), *Ergogenic aids and muscular performance* (pp. 35–66). New York: Academic Press.

Martens, R. (1977). *Sport competition anxiety test.* Champaign, IL: Human Kinetics.

Martens, R., Burwitz, L., and Zuckerman, J. (1976). Modeling effects on motor performance. *Research Quarterly, 47,* 277–291.

Mathews, D. K. (1978). *Measurement in physical education* (4th ed.). Philadelphia: W. B. Saunders.

McBride, E., and Rothstein, A. (1979). Mental and physical practice and the learning and retention of open and closed skills. *Perceptual and Motor Skills, 49,* 359–365.

McCloy, C. H. (1934). The measurement of general motor capacity and general motor ability. *Research Quarterly, 5,* Supplement, 46–61.

McCloy, C. H. (1937). An analytic study of the stunt type tests as a measure of motor educability. *Research Quarterly, 8,* 46–55.

McCloy, C. H., and Young, N. D. (1954). *Tests and measurements in health and physical education* (3rd ed.). New York: Appleton-Century-Crofts.

McCullagh, P. (1987). Model similarity effects on motor performance. *Journal of Sports Psychology, 9,* 249–260.

McKeithern, K. B., Reitman, J. S., Reuther, H. H., and Hurtle, S. C. (1981). Knowledge organization and skill differences in computer programmers. *Cognitive Psychology, 13,* 307–325.

McLeod, P. (1978). Does probe RT measure central processing demand? *Quarterly Journal of Experimental Psychology, 30,* 83–89.

McLeod, P. (1980). What can probe RT tell us about the attention demands of movement? In G. E. Stelmach and J. Requin (Eds.), *Tutorials in motor behavior* (pp. 579–589). Amsterdam: North-Holland.

McPherson, S. L. (1987). *Development of children's expertise in tennis: Knowledge structure and sport performance.* Unpublished doctoral dissertation, Louisiana State University, Baton Rouge.

Mecuwsen, H., and Magill, R. A. (1987). *Gait control and vision in gymnastics vaulting.* Unpublished manuscript, Louisiana State University, Baton Rouge.

Melnick, M. J. (1971). Effects of overlearning on the retention of a gross motor skill. *Research Quarterly, 42,* 60–69.

Miller, G. A. (1956). The magical number seven plus or minus two: Some limits on our capacity for processing information. *Psychological Review, 63,* 81–97.

Miller, G. A., Galanter, E., and Pribram, K. H. (1960). *Plans and the structure of behavior.* New York: Holt, Rinehart, and Winston.

Moore, S. P. (1984). Systematic removal of visual feedback. *Journal of Human Movement Studies, 10,* 165–173.

Moore, S. P., and Marteniuk, R. G. (1986). Kinematic and electromyographic changes that occur as a function of learning a time-constrained aiming task. *Journal of Motor Behavior, 18,* 397–426.

Moray, N. (1959). Attention in dichotic listening: Affective cues and the influence of instructions. *Quarterly Journal of Experimental Psychology, 11,* 56–60.

Moray, N. (1967). Where is attention limited? A survey and a model. *Acta Psychologica, 27,* 84–92.

Morgan, R. L. (1981). *An examination of the memory processes underlying contextual interference in motor skills.* Unpublished doctoral dissertation, University of Colorado, Boulder.

Morgan, W. P. (1978, April). The mind of the marathoner. *Psychology Today,* 38–45.

Morris, C. D., Bransford, J. D., and Franks, J. J. (1977). Levels of processing versus transfer appropriate processing. *Journal of Verbal Learning and Verbal Behavior, 16,* 519–533.

Mosston, M. (1981). *Teaching physical education* (2nd ed.). Columbus, OH: Merrill.

Mowbray, G. H. (1960). Choice reaction times for skilled responses. *Quarterly Journal of Experimental Psychology, 12,* 193–202.

Mowbray, G. H., and Rhoades, M. U. (1959). On the reduction of choice reaction times with practice. *Quarterly Journal of Experimental Psychology, 11,* 16–23.

Mulder, T., and Hulstijn, W. (1985). Delayed sensory feedback in the learning of a novel motor skill. *Psychological Record, 47,* 203–209.

Murdock, B. B., Jr. (1957). Transfer designs and formulas. *Psychological Bulletin, 54,* 313–326.

Navon, D., and Gopher, D. (1979). On the economy of the human processing system. *Psychological Review, 86,* 214–255.

Naylor, J., and Briggs, G. (1963). Effects of task complexity and task organization on the relative efficiency of part and whole training methods. *Journal of Experimental Psychology, 65,* 217–244.

Nelson, J. K. (1978). Motivating effects of the use of norms and goals with endurance testing. *Research Quarterly, 49,* 317–321.

Neumann, E., and Ammons, R. B. (1957). Acquisition and long-term retention of a simple serial perceptual motor skill. *Journal of Experimental Psychology, 53,* 159–161.

Neumann, O. (1987). Beyond capacity: A functional view of attention. In H. Heuer and A. F. Sanders (Eds.), *Perspectives on perception and action* (pp. 361–394). Hillsdale, NJ: Erlbaum.

Newell, K. M. (1974). Knowledge of results and motor learning. *Journal of Motor Behavior, 6,* 235–244.

Newell, K. M. (1976). Knowledge of results and motor learning. In J. Keogh and R. S. Hutton (Eds.), *Exercise and sport sciences reviews* (Vol. 4, pp. 196–228). Santa Barbara, CA: Journal Publishing Affiliates.

Newell, K. M., and McGinnis, P. M. (1985). Kinematic information feedback for skilled performance. *Human Learning, 4,* 39–56.

Newell, K. M., Quinn, J. T., Jr., Sparrow, W. A., and Walter, C. B. (1983). Kinematic information feedback for learning a rapid arm movement. *Human Movement Science, 2,* 255–269.

Nideffer, R. M. (1976). *The inner athlete.* New York: Thomas Crowell.

Nissen, M. J., and Bullemer, P. (1987). Attentional requirements of learning: Evidence from performance measures. *Cognitive Psychology, 19,* 1–32.

Norman, D. A. (1968). Toward a theory of memory and attention. *Psychological Review, 75,* 522–536.

Norman, D. A. (1969). Memory while shadowing. *Quarterly Journal of Experimental Psychology, 21,* 85–93.

Norrie, M. L. (1967). Practice effects on reaction latency for simple and complex movements. *Research Quarterly, 38,* 79–85.

Osgood, C. E. (1949). The similarity paradox in human learning: A resolution. *Psychological Review, 56,* 132–143.

Paillard, J. (1980). The multichanneling of visual cues and the organization of a visually guided response. In G. E. Stelmach and J. Requin (Eds.), *Tutorials in motor behavior* (pp. 259–279). Amsterdam: North-Holland.

Penfield, W. (1954). Mechanisms of voluntary movement. *Brain, 77,* 1–17.

Peterson, L. R., and Peterson, M. J. (1959). Short term retention of individual verbal items. *Journal of Experimental Psychology, 58,* 193–198.

Pew, R. W. (1974). Levels of analysis in motor control. *Brain Research, 71,* 393–400.

Pillsbury, W. B. (1908). *Attention.* New York: Macmillan.

Polit, A., and Bizzi, E. (1978). Processes controlling arm movements in monkeys. *Science, 201,* 1235–1237.

Polit, A., and Bizzi, E. (1979). Characteristics of motor programs underlying arm movements in monkeys. *Journal of Neurophysiology, 42,* 183–194.

Popper, K., and Eccles, J. C. (1977). *The self and its brain.* New York: Springer-Verlag.

Posner, M. I. (1978). *Chronometric explorations of mind.* Hillsdale, NJ: Erlbaum.

Posner, M. I., and Boies, S. J. (1969). Components of attention. *Psychological Review, 78,* 391–408.

Posner, M. I., and Keele, S. W. (1969). Attention demands of movements. *Proceedings of the 16th Congress of Applied Psychology.* Amsterdam: Swets & Zeitlinger.

Posner, M. I., Nissen, M. J., and Klein, R. (1976). Visual dominance: An information processing account of its origins and significance. *Psychological Review, 83,* 157–171.

Poulton, E. C. (1957). On prediction in skilled movements. *Psychological Bulletin, 54,* 467–478.

Pribram, K. H. (1969). The neurophysiology of remembering. *Scientific American, 220,* 73–86.

Reeve, T. G. (1976). *Processing demands during the acquisition of motor skills requiring different feedback cues.* Unpublished doctoral dissertation, Texas A&M University.

Reeve, T. G., and Cone, S. L. (1980). Coding of learned kinesthetic location information. *Research Quarterly for Exercise and Sport, 51,* 349–358.

Reeve, T. G., and Magill, R. A. (1981). Role of components of knowledge of results information in error correction. *Research Quarterly for Exercise and Sport, 52,* 80–85.

Reeve, T. G., Mackey, L. J., and Fober, G. W. (1986). Visual dominance in the cross-modal kinesthetic to kinesthetic plus visual feedback condition. *Perceptual and Motor Skills, 62,* 243–252.

Reeve, T. G., and Mainor, R., Jr. (1983). Effects of movement context on the encoding of kinesthetic spatial information. *Research Quarterly for Exercise and Sport, 54,* 352–363.

Reeve, T. G., and Stelmach, G. E. (1982). Response feedback and movement context in retention of sequentially presented spatial information (Abstract). *Psychology of motor behavior and sport–1982* (p. 29). Proceedings of the annual meeting of the North American Society for the Psychology of Sport and Physical Activity, College Park, MD.

Reilly, R. R., Zedeck, S., and Tenopyr, M. L. (1979). Validity and fairness of physical ability tests for predicting performance in craft jobs. *Journal of Applied Psychology, 64,* 262–274.

Richardson, A. (1967a). Mental practice: A review and discussion. Part I. *Research Quarterly, 38,* 95–107.

Richardson, A. (1967b). Mental practice: A review and discussion. Part II. *Research Quarterly, 38,* 263–273.

Roberts, W. H. (1930). The effect of delayed feeding on white rats in a problem cage. *Journal of Genetic Psychology, 37,* 35–38.

Rogers, C. A. (1974). Feedback precision and post-feedback interval duration. *Journal of Experimental Psychology, 102,* 604–608.

Rosenbaum, D. A. (1980). Human movement initiation: Specification of arm, direction, and extent. *Journal of Experimental Psychology: General, 109,* 444–474.

Rosenbaum, D. A. (1983). The movement precuing technique: Assumptions, applications, and extensions. In R. A. Magill (Ed.), *Memory and control of action* (pp. 251–274). Amsterdam: North-Holland.

Rosenbaum, D. A. (1988). Successive approximations to a model of human motor programming. In G. H. Bower (Ed.), *Psychology of learning and motivation: Advances in research and theory* (Vol. 21). Orlando, FL: Academic Press.

Rothstein, A. L., and Arnold, R. K. (1976). Bridging the gap: Application of research on videotape feedback and bowling. *Motor Skills: Theory Into Practice, 1,* 36–61.

Roy, E. A. (1983). Manual performance asymmetries and motor control processes: Subject-generated changes in response parameters. *Human Movement Science, 2,* 271–277.

Roy, E. A., and Davenport, W. G. (1972). Factors in motor short-term memory: The interference effect of interpolated activity. *Journal of Experimental Psychology, 96,* 134–137.

Roy, E. A., and Elliott, D. (1986). Manual asymmetries in visually directed aiming. *Canadian Journal of Psychology, 40,* 109–121.

Rumelhart, D. E., and Norman, D. A. (1982). Simulating a skilled typist: A study of skilled cognitive-motor performance. *Cognitive Science, 6,* 1–36.

Ryan, E. D. (1965). Retention of stabilometer performance over extended periods of time. *Research Quarterly, 36,* 46–61.

Ryan, E. D., and Simons, J. (1983). What is learned in mental practice of motor skills? A test of the cognitive-motor hypothesis. *Journal of Sport Psychology, 5,* 419–426.

Salmoni, A. W., Schmidt, R. A., and Walter, C. B. (1984). Knowledge of results and motor learning: A review and reappraisal. *Psychological Bulletin, 95,* 355–386.

Salmoni, A. W., Sullivan, S. J., and Starkes, J. L. (1976). The attention demands of movements: A critique of the probe technique. *Journal of Motor Behavior, 8,* 161–169.

Schendel, J. D., and Hagman, J. D. (1982). On sustaining procedural skills over a prolonged retention interval. *Journal of Applied Psychology, 67,* 605–610.

Schmidt, R. A. (1971). Proprioception and the timing of motor responses. *Psychological Bulletin, 76,* 383–393.

Schmidt, R. A. (1975a). *Motor skills.* New York: Harper & Row.

Schmidt, R. A. (1975b). A schema theory of discrete motor skill learning. *Psychological Review, 82,* 225–260.

Schmidt, R. A. (1976). A schema as a solution to some persistent problems in motor learning theory. In G. E. Stelmach (Ed.), *Motor control: Issues and trends* (pp. 41–65). New York: Academic Press.

Schmidt, R. A. (1977). Schema theory: Implications for movement education. *Motor Skills: Theory Into Practice, 2,* 36–38.

Schmidt, R. A. (1985). The search for invariance in skilled movement behavior. *Research Quarterly for Exercise and Sport, 56,* 188–200.

Schmidt, R. A. (1987). *Motor control and learning: A behavioral emphasis* (2nd ed.). Champaign, IL: Human Kinetics.

Schmidt, R. A., and White, J. L. (1972). Evidence for an error detection mechanism in motor skills: A test of Adams' closed-loop theory. *Journal of Motor Behavior, 4,* 143–153.

Schmidt, R. A., and Young, D. E. (1987). Transfer of movement control in motor skill learning. In S. M. Cormier and J. D. Hagman (Eds.), *Transfer of learning* (pp. 47–79). Orlando, FL: Academic Press.

Schmidt, R. A., Zelaznik, H. N., Hawkins, B., Frank, J. S., and Quinn, J. T., Jr. (1979). Motor output variability: A theory for the accuracy of rapid motor acts. *Psychological Review, 86,* 415–451.

Schutz, R. W. (1977). Absolute, constant, and variable error: Problems and solutions. In D. Mood (Ed.), *Proceedings of the Colorado Measurement Symposium* (pp. 82–100). Boulder, CO: University of Colorado.

Schutz, R. W., and Roy, E. A. (1973). Absolute error: The devil in disguise. *Journal of Motor Behavior, 5,* 141–153.

Schwindt, P. C. (1981). Control of motoneurons output by pathways descending from the brain stem. In A. L. Towe and E. S. Luschei (Eds.), *Handbook of behavioral neurobiology: Vol. 5. Motor coordination* (pp. 139–230). New York: Plenum.

Scully, D. M., and Newell, K. M. (1985). Observational learning and the acquisition of motor skills: Toward a visual perception perspective. *Journal of Human Movement Studies, 11,* 169–186.

Selder, D. J., and Del Rolan, N. (1979). Knowledge of performance, skill level and performance on the balance beam. *Canadian Journal of Applied Sport Sciences, 4,* 226–229.

Shaffer, L. H. (1976). Intention and performance. *Psychological Review, 83,* 375–393.

Shaffer, L. H. (1978). Timing in the motor programming of typing. *Quarterly Journal of Experimental Psychology, 30,* 333–345.

Shaffer, L. H. (1980). Analyzing piano performance: A study of concert pianists. In G. E. Stelmach and J. Requin (Eds.), *Tutorials in motor behavior* (pp. 443–455). Amsterdam: North-Holland.

Shaffer, L. H. (1981). Performances of Chopin, Bach, and Beethoven: Studies in motor programming. *Cognitive Psychology, 13,* 326–376.

Shaffer, L. H. (1982). Rhythm and timing in skill. *Psychological Review, 89,* 109–121.

Shapiro, D. C., and Schmidt, R. A. (1982). The schema theory: Recent evidence and developmental implications. In J. A. S. Kelso and J. E. Clark (Eds.), *The development of movement control and coordination* (pp. 113–150). New York: John Wiley.

Shapiro, D. C., Zernicke, R. F., Gregor, R. J., and Diestel, J. D. (1981). Evidence for generalized motor programs using gait-pattern analysis. *Journal of Motor Behavior, 13,* 33–47.

Sharp, R. H., and Whiting, H. T. A. (1974). Exposure and occluded duration effects in a ball-catching skill. *Journal of Motor Behavior, 6,* 139–147.

Sharp, R. H., and Whiting, H. T. A. (1975). Information processing and eye movement behavior in a ball-catching skill. *Journal of Human Movement Studies, 1,* 124–131.

Shea, J. B. (1975). Interresponse interval length and the development of an error detection mechanism: A test of Adams' closed-loop theory of motor learning (Abstract). *Abstracts: Research papers 1975 AAHPERD Convention* (p. 68). Washington, DC: AAHPERD.

Shea, J. B. (1977). Effects of labelling on motor short-term memory. *Journal of Experimental Psychology: Human Learning and Memory, 3,* 92–99.

Shea, J. B., and Morgan, R. L. (1979). Contextual interference effects on the acquisition, retention, and transfer of a motor skill. *Journal of Experimental Psychology: Human Learning and Memory, 5,* 179–187.

Shea, J. B., and Upton, G. (1976). The effects of skill aquisition of an interpolated motor short-term memory task during the KR-delay interval. *Journal of Motor Behavior, 8,* 277–281.

Shea, J. B., and Zimny, S. T. (1983). Context effects in memory and learning in movement information. In R. A. Magill (Ed.), *Memory and control of action* (pp. 345–366). Amsterdam: North-Holland.

Sheridan, M. R. (1984). Response programming, response production, and fractionated reaction time. *Psychological Research, 46,* 33–47.

Sherrington, C. S. (1906). *The integrative action of the nervous system,* New York: Scribner.

Shiffrin, R. M., and Schneider, W. (1977). Controlled and automatic human information processing: II. Perceptual learning, automatic attending, and a general theory. *Psychological Review, 84,* 127–190.

Siedentop, D. (1983). *Developing teaching skills in physical education* (2nd ed.). Boston: Houghton Mifflin.

Siegel, D. (1986). Movement duration, fractionated reaction time, and response programming. *Research Quarterly for Exercise and Sport, 57,* 128–131.

Siipola, E. M. (1941). The relation of transfer to similarity in habit-structure. *Journal of Experimental Psychology, 28,* 9–14.

Simon, J. R., and Slaviero, D. P. (1975). Differential effects of a foreperiod countdown procedure on simple and choice reaction time. *Journal of Motor Behavior, 7,* 9–14.

Singer, R. N. (1966a). Comparison of inter-limb skill achievement in performing a motor skill. *Research Quarterly, 37,* 406–410.

Singer, R. N. (1966b). Transfer effects and ultimate success in archery due to degree of difficulty of the initial learning. *Research Quarterly, 37,* 532–539.

Singer, R. N. (1977). To err or not to err: A question for the instruction of psychomotor skills. *Review of Educational Research, 47,* 479–498.

Singer, R. N. (1980). *Motor learning and human performance* (3rd ed.). New York: Macmillan.

Singer, R. N. (1986). Sports performance: A five-step mental approach. *Journal of Physical Education and Recreation, 57,* 82–84.

Singer, R. N., and Dick, W. (1980). *Teaching physical education: A systems approach* (2nd ed.). Boston: Houghton Mifflin.

Singer, R. N., and Suwanthada, S. (1986). The generalizability effectiveness of a learning strategy on achievement in related closed motor skills. *Research Quarterly for Exercise and Sport, 57,* 205–214.

Skinner, B. F. (1953). *Science and human behavior.* New York: Macmillan.

Skinner, B. F. (1963). Behaviorism at fifty. *Science, 140,* 951–958.

Slater-Hammel, A. T. (1960). Reliability, accuracy, and refractoriness of a transit reaction. *Research Quarterly, 31,* 217–228.

Smith, J. L. (1969). Kinesthesis: A model for movement feedback. In R. C. Brown and B. J. Cratty (Eds.), *New perspectives of man in action* (pp. 31–50). Englewood Cliffs, NJ: Prentice-Hall.

Smith, W. M., and Bowen, K. F. (1980). The effects of delayed and displaced visual feedback on motor control. *Journal of Motor Behavior, 12,* 91–101.

Smoll, F. L. (1972). Effects of precision of information feedback upon acquisition of a motor skill. *Research Quarterly, 43,* 489–493.

Smyth, M. M., and Marriott, A. M. (1982). Vision and proprioception in simple catching. *Journal of Motor Behavior, 14,* 143–152.

Southard, D., and Higgins, T. (1987). Changing movement patterns: Effects of demonstration and practice. *Research Quarterly for Exercise and Sport, 58,* 77–80.

Sparrow, W. A. (1983). The efficiency of skilled performance. *Journal of Motor Behavior, 15,* 237–261.

Sparrow, W. A., and Irizarry-Lopez, V. M. (1987). Mechanical efficiency and metabolic cost as measures of learning a novel gross motor task. *Journal of Motor Behavior, 19,* 240–264.

Spence, J. T. (1971). What can you say about a twenty-year-old theory that won't die? *Journal of Motor Behavior, 3,* 193–203.

Spence, K. W. (1958). A theory of emotionally based drive and its relation to performance in simple learning situations. *American Psychologist, 13,* 131–141.

Spielberger, C. D. (1966). Theory and research on anxiety. In C. D. Spielberger (Ed.), *Anxiety and behavior* (pp. 3–20). New York: Academic Press.

Spray, J. A. (1986). Absolute error revisited: An accuracy measure in disguise. *Journal of Motor Behavior, 18,* 225–238.

Starkes, J. L., and Deakin, J. M. (1984). Perception in sport: A cognitive approach to skilled performance. In W. Straub and J. Williams (Eds.), *Cognitive sport psychology* (pp. 115–128). Lansing, NY: Sport Science Associates.

Starkes, J. L., Deakin, J. M., Lindley, S., and Crisp, F. (1987). Motor versus verbal recall of ballet sequences by young expert dancers. *Journal of Sport Psychology, 9,* 222–230.

Stelmach, G. E. (1969). Prior positioning responses as a factor in short-term retention of a simple motor response. *Journal of Experimental Psychology, 81,* 523–526.

Stelmach, G. E. (1970). Learning and response consistency with augmented feedback. *Ergonomics, 13,* 421–425.

Stelmach, G. E. (1974). Short-term and long-term retention of motor skills. In J. R. Wilmore (Ed.), *Exercise and sport science reviews* (Vol. 2, pp. 1–26). New York: Academic Press.

Stelmach, G. E., and Hughes, B. G. (1983). Does motor skill automation require a theory of attention? In R. A. Magill (Ed.), *Memory and control of action* (pp. 67–92). Amsterdam: North-Holland.

Stelmach, G. E., and Kelso, J. A. S. (1975). Memory trace strength and response biasing in short-term motor memory. *Memory and Cognition, 3,* 58–62.

Stelmach, G. E., and Larish, D. D. (1980). Egocentric referents in human limb orientations. In G. E. Stelmach and J. Requin (Eds.), *Tutorials in motor behavior* (pp. 167–184). Amsterdam: North-Holland.

Summers, J. J. (1975). The role of timing in motor program representation. *Journal of Motor Behavior, 7,* 229–242.

Swinnen, S. (1987). *Knowledge of results delay activities and motor learning.* Unpublished doctoral dissertation, Catholic University, Leuven, Belgium.

Taub, E., and Berman, A. J. (1963). Avoidance conditioning in the absence of relevant proprioceptive and exteroceptive feedback. *Journal of Comparative and Physiological Psychology, 56,* 1012–1016.

Taub, E., and Berman, A. J. (1968). Movement and learning in the absence of sensory feedback. In S. J. Freedman (Ed.), *The neuropsychology of spatially oriented behavior* (pp. 173–192). Homewood, IL: Dorsey Press.

Taylor, H. G., and Heilman, K. M. (1980). Left-hemisphere motor dominance in righthanders. *Cortex, 16,* 587–603.

Teichner, W. H. (1954). Recent studies of simple reaction time. *Psychological Bulletin, 51,* 128–149.

Teichner, W. H., and Krebs, M. J. (1974). Laws of visual choice reaction time. *Psychological Review, 81,* 75–98.

Thomas, J. R. (1980). Acquisition of motor skills: Information processing differences between children and adults. *Research Quarterly for Exercise and Sport, 51,* 158–173.

Thomas, J. R., French, K. E., and Humphries, C. A. (1986). Knowledge development and sport skill performance: Directions for motor behavior research. *Journal of Sport Psychology, 8,* 259–272.

Thomas, J. R., and Halliwell, W. (1976). Individual differences in motor skill acquisition. *Journal of Motor Behavior, 8,* 89–100.

Thomas, J. R., and Nelson, J. K. (1985). *Introduction to research in health, physical education, recreation, and dance.* Champaign, IL: Human Kinetics.

Thomas, J. R., Pierce, C., and Ridsdale, S. (1977). Age differences in children's ability to model motor behavior. *Research Quarterly, 48,* 592–597.

Thomas, J. R., Thomas, K. T., Lee, A. M., Testerman, E., and Ashy, M. (1983). Age differences in the use of strategy for recall of movement in a large scale environment. *Research Quarterly for Exercise and Sport, 54,* 264–272.

Thomson, J. A. (1983). Is continuous visual monitoring necessary in visually guided locomotion? *Journal of Experimental Psychology: Human Perception and Performance, 9,* 427–443.

Thorndike, E. L. (1914). *Educational psychology: Briefer course.* New York: Columbia University Press.

Titchener, E. B. (1908). *Lectures on the elementary psychology of feeling and attention.* New York: Macmillan.

Tolman, E. C. (1932). *Purposive behavior in animals and man.* New York: Appleton-Century-Crofts.

Travers, R. M. W. (1972). *Essentials of learning* (3rd ed.). New York: Macmillan.

Treisman, A. (1969). Strategies and models of selective attention. *Psychological Review, 76,* 282–289.

Treisman, A. (1971). Shifting attention between the ears. *Quarterly Journal of Experimental Psychology, 23,* 157–167.

Trussell, E. (1965). Prediction of success in a motor skill on the basis of early learning achievement. *Research Quarterly, 39,* 342–347.

Tubbs, M. E. (1986). Goal setting: A meta-analytic examination of the empirical evidence. *Journal of Applied Psychology, 71,* 474–483.

Tuller, B., Turvey, M. T., and Fitch, H. (1982). The Bernstein perspective: II. The concept of muscle linkages or coordinative structures. In J. A. S. Kelso (Ed.), *Human motor behavior: An introduction* (pp. 253–270). Hillsdale, NJ: Erlbaum.

Tulving, E. (1962). Subjective organization in free recall of "unrelated" words. *Psychological Review, 69,* 344–354.

Tulving, E. (1985). How many memory systems are there? *American Psychologist, 40,* 385–398.

Tulving, E., and Thomson, D. M. (1973). Encoding specificity and retrieval processes in episodic memory. *Psychological Review, 80,* 352–373.

Turvey, M. T. (1977). Preliminaries to a theory of action with reference to vision. In R. Shaw and J. Bransford (Eds.), *Perceiving, acting, and knowing* (pp. 211–265). Hillsdale, NJ: Erlbaum.

Von Hofsten, C. (1987). Catching. In H. Heuer and A. F. Sanders (Eds.), *Perspectives on perception and action* (pp. 33–46). Hillsdale, NJ: Erlbaum.

Vorro, J., Wilson, F. R., and Dainis, A. (1978). Multivariate analysis of biomechanical profiles for the coracobrachialis and biceps brachii (caput breve) muscles in humans. *Ergonomics, 21,* 407–418.

Wadman, W. J., Dernier van der Gon, J. J., Geuze, R. H., and Mol, C. R. (1979). Control of fast goal-directed arm movements. *Journal of Human Movement Studies, 5,* 3–17.

Wallace, S. A. (1977). The coding of location: A test of the target hypothesis. *Journal of Motor Behavior, 9,* 157–169.

Wallace, S. A., and Newell, K. M. (1983). Visual control of discrete aiming movements. *Quarterly Journal of Experimental Psychology, 35A,* 311–321.

Warren, W. H., Jr., and Whang, S. (1987). Visual guidance of walking through apertures: Body-scaled information for affordances. *Journal of Experimental Psychology: Human Perception and Performance, 13,* 371–383.

Warren, W. H., Jr., Young, D. S., and Lee, D. N. (1986). Visual control of step length during running over irregular terrain. *Journal of Experimental Psychology: Human Perception and Performance, 12,* 259–266.

Weinberg, D. R., Guy, D. E., and Tupper, R. W. (1964). Variations of post-feedback interval in simple motor learning. *Journal of Experimental Psychology, 67,* 98–99.

Welford, A. T. (1967). Single channel operations in the brain. *Acta Psychologica, 27,* 5–22.

Welford, A. T. (1968). *Fundamentals of skill.* London: Methuen.

Whiting, H. T. A. (1969). *Acquiring ball skills.* Philadelphia: Lea & Febiger.

Whiting, H. T. A. (Ed.) (1984). *Human motor actions: Bernstein reassessed.* Amsterdam: North-Holland.

Whiting, H. T. A., Bijlard, M. J., and den Brinker, B. P. L. M. (1987). The effect of the availability of a dynamic model on the acquisition of a complex cyclical action. *Quarterly Journal of Experimental Psychology, 39A,* 43–59.

Whiting, H. T. A., Gill, E. B., and Stephenson, J. M. (1970). Critical time intervals for taking in-flight information in a ball-catching task. *Ergonomics, 13,* 265–272.

Wickens, C. D. (1980). The structure of processing resources. In R. Nickerson (Ed.), *Attention and performance VII* (pp. 239–257). Hillsdale, NJ: Erlbaum.

Wickens, C. D. (1984). Processing resources in attention. In R. Parasuraman and D. R. Davies (Eds.), *Varieties of attention* (pp. 63–102). Orlando, FL: Academic Press.

Wickens, C. D., Sandry, D. L., and Vidulich, M. (1983). Compatibility and resource competition between modalities of input, control processing, and output: Testing a model of complex performance. *Human Factors, 25,* 227–248.

Wickens, D. D. (1970). Encoding categories of words: An empirical approach to meaning. *Psychological Review, 77,* 1–15.

Wickstrom, R. L. (1958). Comparative study of methodologies for teaching gymnastics and tumbling stunts. *Research Quarterly, 29,* 109–115.

Wilberg, R. B., and Girard, N. C. (1977). A further investigation into the serial position curve for short-term motor memory. *Proceedings of the IX Canadian Psychomotor Learning and Sport Psychology Symposium* (pp. 241–247). Banff, Alberta, Canada.

Wilberg, R. B., and Salmela, J. (1973). Information load and response consistency in sequential short-term motor memory. *Perceptual and Motor Skills, 37,* 23–29.

Wilkinson, R. T. (1963). Interaction of noise with knowledge of results and sleep deprivation. *Journal of Experimental Psychology, 66,* 332–337.

Williams, H. L., Beaver, W. S., Spence, M. T., and Rundell, O. R. (1969). Digital and kinesthetic memory with interpolated information processing. *Journal of Experimental Psychology, 80,* 537–541.

Winstein, C. J. (1987). *Relative frequency of information feedback in motor performance and learning.* Unpublished doctoral dissertation, University of California, Los Angeles.

Winther, K. T., and Thomas, J. R. (1981). Developmental differences in children's labeling of movement. *Journal of Motor Behavior, 13,* 77–90.

Wolf, S. L. (1983). Electromyographic biofeedback applications to stroke patients: A critical review. *Physical Therapy, 63,* 1448–1455.

Woodrow, H. (1914). The measurement of attention. *Psychological Monographs* (No. 76).

Woodworth, R. S., and Schlosberg, H. (1954). *Experimental psychology* (2nd ed.). New York: Holt, Rinehart, & Winston.

Wrisberg, C. A., Hardy, C. J., and Beitel, P. A. (1982). Stimulus velocity and movement distance as determiners of movement velocity and coincident timing accuracy. *Human Factors, 24,* 599–608.

Wrisberg, C. A., and Ragsdale, M. R. (1979). Further tests of Schmidt's schema theory: Development of a schema rule for a coincident timing task. *Journal of Motor Behavior, 11,* 159–166.

Wrisberg, C. A., and Shea, C. H. (1978). Shifts in attention demands and motor program utilization during motor learning. *Journal of Motor Behavior, 10,* 149–158.

Yerkes, R. M., and Dodson, J. D. (1908). The relation of strength of stimulus to rapidity of habit-formation. *Journal of Comparative Neurology and Psychology, 18,* 459–482.

Zelaznik, H. N. (1977). Transfer in rapid timing tasks: An examination of the role of variability of practice. In D. M. Landers and R. W. Christina (Eds.), *Psychology of motor behavior and sport* (Vol. 1, pp. 36–43). Champaign, IL: Human Kinetics.

Zelaznik, H. N., Hawkins, B., and Kisselburgh, L. (1983). Rapid visual feedback processing in single-aiming movements. *Journal of Motor Behavior, 15,* 217–236.

Zelaznik, H. N., Shapiro, D. C., and Newell, K. M. (1978). On the structure of motor recognition memory. *Journal of Motor Behavior, 10,* 313–323.

Credits

Photo Credits

Chapter Opener Photos
Chapter 1 © 1988 Ken Olson
Chapter 2 © 1988 Ken Olson
Chapter 3 © Bob Coyle
Chapter 4 © Harriet Gans/The Image Works, Inc.
Chapter 5 © 1988 Ken Olson
Chapter 6 © John Avery
Chapter 7 © Michael Siluk
Chapter 8 © John Avery
Chapter 9 © Jim Shaffer
Chapter 10 © 1988 Ken Olson

Figure 3.5–1: Courtesy Lafayette Instrument Company, Lafayette, Indiana.
Figure 7.2–3: Provided by the Department of Psychology, Faculty of Human Movement Sciences, The Free University, Amsterdam.

Figure Credits

Figure 1.2–5: Submitted by Charles Shey of Texas A & M University.
Figure 1.2–6: Marteniuk and Romanow, In Magill, ed., *Memory and Control of Action,* 1983. Reprinted by permission of the publisher.
Figure 1.2–7: Franks, I. M., Wilberg, R. B., and Fishburne, G. J., *Human Movement Science,* 1982. Reprinted by permission of the publisher.
Figure 1.2–8: Wynne Lee, *Journal of Motor Behavior,* 1980, Vol. 12. Reprinted by permission.
Figure 2.1–4: Marteniuk and Romanow, In Magill, ed., *Memory and control of action,* 1983. Reprinted by permission of the publisher.

Figure 2.1–5: Godwin, M. A., and Schmidt, R. A., *Research Quarterly,* Vol. 42. Copyright © 1971. Reprinted by permission of the publisher.
Figure 2.1–6: Adapted from figure 2 in Franks, I. M. and Wilberg, R. B. (1982). "The Generation of Movement Patterns during the Acquisition of a Pursuit Tracking Task," *Human Movement Science* 1, 251–272.
Figure 2.2–2: Schmidt, R. A. and White, J. L., "Evidence for an Error Correction Mechanism in Motor Skills: A Test of Adams' Closed-Loop Theory," *Journal of Motor Behavior* 4, pp. 143–152, 1972. Reprinted with permission of the Helen Dwight Reid Educational Foundation. Published by Heldref Publications, 4000 Albemarle St., N.W., Washington, D.C. 20016. Copyright © 1972.
Figure 2.2–3: Southard, D. and Higgins, T., "Changing Movement Patterns: Effects of Demonstration and Practice," *Research Quarterly for Exercise and Sport* 58 (1987): 77–80. Reprinted by permission of the American Alliance for Health, Physical Education, Recreation, and Dance, 1900 Association Drive, Reston, Virginia 22091.
Figure 3.1–1: Hole, John W., Jr., *Human anatomy and physiology,* © 1981 Wm. C. Brown Company Publishers, Dubuque, Iowa. Reprinted by permission.
Figure 3.1–2: Hole, John W., Jr., *Human anatomy and*

physiology, © 1981 Wm. C. Brown Company Publishers, Dubuque, Iowa. Reprinted by permission.
Figure 3.1–3: Groves, P. M. and Schlesinger, K., *Biological psychology,* © 1982 Wm. C. Brown Company Publishers, Dubuque, Iowa. Reprinted by permission.
Figure 3.1–4: Groves, P. M. and Schlesinger, K., *Biological psychology,* © 1982 Wm. C. Brown Company Publishers, Dubuque, Iowa. Reprinted by permission.
Figure 3.1–5: Butterworth, Bernard B., *Laboratory anatomy of the human body,* 2d ed., © 1979 Wm. C. Brown Company Publishers, Dubuque, Iowa. Reprinted by permission.
Figure 3.1–6: Hole, John W., Jr., *Human anatomy and physiology,* © 1981 Wm. C. Brown Company Publishers, Dubuque, Iowa. Reprinted by permission.
Figure 3.1–7: Hole, John W., Jr., *Human anatomy and physiology,* © 1981 Wm. C. Brown Company Publishers, Dubuque, Iowa. Reprinted by permission.
Figure 3.1–8: Hole, John W., Jr., *Human anatomy and physiology,* © 1981 Wm. C. Brown Company Publishers, Dubuque, Iowa. Reprinted by permission.
Figure 3.1–9: Popper and Eccles, *The self and its brain,* New York: Springer-Verlag, 1977. Reprinted by permission.
Figure 3.2–2: Schmidt, R. A., *Psychological Review,* Vol. 82;

Reprinted by permission of the publisher.

Figure 5.4–2:   Magill, R. A. and Dowell, M. N., *Journal of Motor Behavior,* Vol. 9. Copyright 1977. Reprinted by permission of the publisher.

Figure 6.1–1:   Adapted from Cronbach, L. J., "Two disciplines of scientific psychology," *American Psychologist,* Vol. 12, pp. 671–684. Copyright 1957 by the American Psychological Association. Reprinted by permission.

Table 6.2–1. From Drowatzky and Zuccato, *Research Quarterly,* Vol. 38, Copyright © 1967. Reprinted by permission of the publisher.

Figure 6.3–1:   Trussell, E., *Research Quarterly,* Vol. 36. Copyright 1965. Reprinted by permission of the publisher.

Table 6.3–1. Thomas, J. R., and Halliwell, W. "Individual Differences in Motor Skill Acquisition," *Journal of Motor Behavior* 8(1976):89–99. Reprinted with permission of the Helen Dwight Reid Educational Foundation. Published by Heldref Publications, 4000 Albemarle St., N.W., Washington, D.C. 20016. Copyright © 1976.

Figure 6.3–2:   Fleishman, E. A. and Hempel, W. E., *Journal of Experimental Psychology,* 1955, Vol. 49.

Figure 7.1–2:   Bilodeau, E. A.; Bilodeau, I., and Schumsky, D. A., *Journal of Experimental Psychology,* Vol. 58. Copyright 1959 by the American Psychological Association. Reprinted by permission.

Figure 7.1–3:   Stelmach, G. E., "Learning and response consistency with augmented feedback," *Ergonomics,* 1970, 13, 421–425. Reprinted by

permission of the publisher.

Figure 7.1–4:   Newell, K. M., *Journal of Motor Behavior,* Vol. 6. Copyright 1974. Reprinted by permission of the publisher.

Figure 7.2–1:   Smoll, F. L., *Research Quarterly,* Vol. 43. Copyright 1972. Reprinted by permission of the publisher.

Figure 7.2–2:   Magill, R. A. and Wood, C., *Research Quarterly for Exercise and Sport* 57 (1986):170–173. Reprinted by permission of the American Alliance for Health, Physical Education, Recreation, and Dance, 1900 Association Drive, Reston, Virginia 22091.

Figure 7.2–5:   Lindahl, L. G., *Journal of Applied Psychology,* 1945, Vol. 29.

Figure 7.2–6:   Newell, K. M., Quinn, J. T., Sparrow, W. A., and Walter, C. B., *Human Movement Science,* 1983, Vol. 2. Reprinted by permission of the publisher.

Figure 7.3–2:   Shea, J. and Upton, G., *Journal of Motor Behavior,* 1976, Vol. 8. Reprinted by permission of the publisher, the Helen Dwight Reid Educational Foundation.

Figure 7.3–3:   Marteniuk, R. G., *Journal of Motor Behavior* 18, pp. 55–75, 1986. Reprinted with permission of the Helen Dwight Reid Educational Foundation. Published by Heldref Publications, 4000 Albemarle St., N.W., Washington, D.C. 20016. Copyright © 1986.

Figure 7.3–4:   "Knowledge of Results Delay Activities and Motor Learning," Modified from unpublished dissertation by S. Swinnen, Catholic University, Leuven, Belgium.

Figure 7.3–5:   Hogan, J. C. and Yanowitz, B. A., *Journal of Motor Behavior,* 1977, Vol. 9. Reprinted by permission of the

publisher, the Helen Dwight Reid Educational Foundation.

Figure 7.3–7:   Lee, T. D. and Magill, R. A., *Research Quarterly for Exercise and Sport,* 1983, Vol. 54, pp. 340–345. Reprinted by permission.

Figure 8.1–1:   Holding, D., "An Approximate Transfer Surface," *Journal of Motor Behavior* 8, pp. 1–9, 1976. Reprinted with permission of the Helen Dwight Reid Educational Foundation. Published by Heldref Publications, 4000 Albemarle St., N.W., Washington, D.C. 20016. Copyright © 1976.

Figure 9.1–1:   Wrisberg, C. and Ragsdale, M. R., *Journal of Motor Behavior,* 1979, Vol. II. Reprinted by permission of the publisher, the Helen Dwight Reid Educational Foundation.

Figure 9.1–3:   Lee, T. D. and Magill, R. A., *Journal of Experimental Psychology: Learning, Memory and Cognition,* Vol. 9. Copyright 1983 by the American Psychological Association. Reprinted by permission of the author.

Figure 9.1–4:   Goode, S. L. and Magill, R. A., "Contextual Interference Effects in Learning Three Badminton Serves," *Research Quarterly for Exercise and Sport* 57 (1987):308–314. Reprinted by permission of the American Alliance for Health, Physical Education, Recreation, and Dance, 1900 Association Drive, Reston, Virginia 22091.

Figure 9.1–5:   Edwards, R. V. and Lee, A. M., "The Relationship of Cognitive Style and Instruction Strategy to Learning and Transfer of Motor Skills," *Research Quarterly for Exercise and Sport* 56 (1985):286–290. Reprinted by permission of the American

Name Index

Pillsbury, W. B., 172
Polit, A., 114, 119, 120
Pongrac, J., 465
Popper, K., 97, 105, 106, 107
Posner, M. I., 66, 67, 68, 76, 77,
    106, 123, 125, 126, 153,
    184, 195, 197, 204, 205,
    208, 213, 217, 308, 463
Poulton, E. C., 12, 158, 159
Powell, F. M., 300
Pribram, K. H., 140, 157, 230
Proteau, L., 206, 207
Prytula, R. E., 41

Quinn, J. T., Jr., 152, 344, 345,
    346, 348, 349

Ragsdale, M. R., 404, 405
Reeve, T. G., 123, 124, 125, 210,
    330, 405
Reilly, R. R., 309
Reitman, J. S., 75
Requin, J., 138, 195, 213
Reuther, H. H., 75
Reynolds, B., 429, 430, 431
Rhoades, M. U., 190
Richardson, A., 459
Ridsdale, S., 448, 449
Robb, M. D., 442
Roberts, G. C., 444, 446, 447,
    456
Roberts, W. H., 352
Roediger, H. L., 382
Roenker, D. L., 388, 389, 393
Rogers, C. A., 329, 330, 332
Rogers, D. E., 141, 143, 145,
    174, 178, 189, 208
Romanow, S. K. E., 55, 56, 70,
    71, 248, 249
Rose, D. J., 178, 189
Rosen, B. M., 13, 14
Rosenbaum, D. A., 157, 185,
    186, 187, 188, 195, 238
Ross, D., 450
Rothstein, A. L., 341, 349, 460,
    461
Roy, E. A., 25, 26, 128, 129,
    250, 260
Rubin-Rabson, G., 425
Rumelhart, D. E., 148
Rundell, O. R., 250
Ryan, E. D., 251, 252, 464

Saari, L. M., 503
Salmela, J., 235
Salmoni, A. W., 204, 318, 327,
    329, 349, 353, 360, 364
Sanders, A. F., 138, 213
Sandry, D. L., 200
Schendel, J. D., 257, 421, 422,
    424
Schlesinger, K., 107
Schlosberg, H., 118
Schmidt, K.-H., 157
Schmidt, R. A., 59, 60, 71, 72,
    78, 79, 81, 82, 83, 84, 85,
    111, 112, 113, 115, 141,
    144, 146, 149, 150, 151,
    152, 157, 166, 238, 274,
    318, 322, 323, 327, 329,
    338, 339, 349, 353, 360,
    364, 379, 383, 384, 404,
    406, 407, 415, 416, 419,
    425, 428, 429, 463, 471,
    474
Schneider, T., 133, 134
Schneider, W., 256
Schroeder, S. R., 389, 393
Schumsky, D. A., 320, 321, 323
Schutz, R. W., 25, 26, 34
Schwindt, P. C., 103
Scully, D. M., 453, 456
Sears, P. S., 496
Seeger, C. M., 184
Selder, D. J., 342, 343
Seng, C. N., 135, 136, 163, 169
Shaffer, L. H., 148, 153, 154
Shapiro, D. C., 144, 146, 150,
    151, 321, 327, 416, 419
Sharp, R. H., 135
Shaw, K. N., 503
Shea, J. B., 210, 263, 264, 336,
    354, 355, 363, 364, 408,
    409, 413, 482, 483
Sheridan, M. R., 178
Sherrington, C. S., 103, 107
Shiffrin, R. M., 231, 232, 256
Siedentop, D., 79
Siegel, D., 178
Siipola, E. M., 379, 380
Silva, J. M., 508
Simon, H. A., 75, 271
Simon, J. R., 162, 163
Simons, J., 464
Simpson, J., 97, 105

Singer, R. N., 15, 62, 297, 378,
    384, 417, 419, 428, 437,
    442, 468, 469
Skinner, B. F., 325, 352, 505,
    506, 508
Skinner, J., 41
Slater-Hammel, A. T., 147, 148,
    160
Slaviero, D. P., 162, 163
Smith, J. L., 113
Smith, W. M., 127
Smoll, F. L., 329, 330, 332
Smyth, M. M., 132, 133, 134
Southard, D. L., 73, 75, 154,
    155, 157, 450
Sparrow, J., 379, 384
Sparrow, W. A., 72, 344, 349
Spence, J. T., 491, 494
Spence, K. W., 485
Spence, M. T., 250
Spielberger, C. D., 487, 494
Spray, J. A., 26, 34
Spreeman, J., 494
Stabler, J. R. L. W., 333, 334
Stanley, J. C., 41
Starkes, J. L., 75, 77, 204, 271
Stein, B. S., 272, 372, 382
Stelmach, G. E., 16, 85, 100,
    115, 121, 122, 123, 138,
    168, 188, 195, 209, 213,
    245, 247, 248, 250, 255,
    259, 260, 270, 275, 320,
    321, 322, 340
Stephenson, J. M., 132, 133, 135
Steward, G. H., 393
Steward, J. P., 393
Straub, W. F., 77, 275
Stull, G. A., 299
Sullivan, S. J., 204
Sully, D. L., 135
Sully, H. G., 135
Summers, J. J., 380
Surwit, R. S., 347, 348
Suwanthada, S., 468
Swinnen, S., 356, 357

Taub, E., 119, 121
Taylor, H. G., 387, 388
Teichner, W. H., 174, 190
Tenopyr, M. L., 309
Testerman, E., 260

Subject Index

Motivation, 325–26, 478–83, 485, 495
Motor abilities
  cause of, 292–93
  defined and identified, 287–92
  generality vs. specificity hypotheses, 294–99
  related to motor skill performance, 290–92
  role in predicting performance, 301–10
Motor educability, 299–300
Motor pathways, 101–6
Motor programs
  characteristics of, 149–51
  defined, 140–43
  evidence for, 143–49
  function of, 151–56
  generalized motor program, 141–42, 149, 238
  invariant characteristics of, 149–51
  memory relationship, 142
  parameters of, 150–51, 390
  role in controlling movement, 151–54
Motor skill classification systems, 9–16
  basis for classifying, 10–11
  beginning and end point definition classification, 12
  movement precision classification, 11
  stability of the environment classification, 12–15
  2 × 2 classification system, 13–15
Motor unit, 103–4
Movement control systems
  closed-loop system, 80, 108–15, 126, 163
  integrating closed- and open-loop systems, 114
  open-loop system, 81, 108–11, 113–14, 145, 163
Movement education, 266–67, 396, 406

Nerve block research technique, 122
Neuromuscular control
  reflexes, 99
  voluntary movements, 99–100

Neurons
  interneurons, 93, 98
  motor (efferent), 91–93
  sensory (afferent), 91–93, 99–101
  structure and types of, 91–93
Novel response performance, 83, 274, 415–17
Novices vs. experts, 75–76, 239, 271

Open-loop control systems. *See* Movement control systems
Open motor skills, 13, 274, 404–6, 460–62

Perception, 117
Perceptual trace, 80–81, 323
Performance
  changes during learning, 47–48
  defined, 47
  distinguished from learning, 46–47, 59–64
Performance curves
  general types of, 53–55
  graphic presentation of, 50–53
  interpreting, 53–55
Performance measures
  categories of, 18–19
  ceiling and floor effects, 63
  EMG, 30–32, 74
  error measures, 22–28
  guidelines for selecting, 33–34
  kinematic measures, 29–30, 55–57
  movement time, 21
  reaction time, 18–21
  response outcome measures, 18–19
  response production measures, 18–19
  response time, 21
  root-mean-square error, 27, 29
  speed-accuracy response measurement, 32
Performance plateaus
  causes of, 62–63
  defined, 60
  examples of, 61–62
Performance variables, 63–64, 471–73

Practice
  amount of, 267, 420–24
  effects on
    attention capacity demands, 209–13
    error correction capabilities, 318–25
    movement organization, 209–10, 270–71
    response preparation, 189–90
  massed vs. distributed, 427–37
  mental practice, 457–69
  organizing practice variability, 406–12
  overlearning (overpractice), 258, 421–25
  test conditions relationship, 272–74, 372, 395, 403
  variability of, 396, 402–18
  whole vs. part, 438–42, 454
Precuing technique, 185–88
Predicting motor skill performance, 301–10
Primacy-recency effect, 277–81
Procedural knowledge, 238–39
Procedural skills, 257–58, 421–22
Progressive-part practice, 441–42
Proprioception, 116–24, 137–38
Proprioceptors
  joint receptors, 100–101
  muscle spindles, 99
Psychological refractory period (PRP), 176–77

Reaction time (RT)
  choice RT, 20–21, 182–84
  complexity of response effect on, 189
  discrimination RT, 20–21
  foreperiod, 174–76
  fractionated, 177–79
    motor time, 177–78
    pre-motor time, 177–78
  as a measure of attention, 173–74
  movement time relationship, 181–82
  as a performance measure, 18–21
  response biasing effect on, 188–89

simple RT, 20–21
stimulus predictability effect on, 185–89
Recall tests, 243
Recognition tests, 243
Regulatory and nonregulatory (relevant and irrelevant) stimuli, 68, 402–4
Reinforcement, 325, 504–8
Relationships, causal vs. noncausal, 38
Research, basic vs. applied, 40
Response biasing, 188–89
Response preparation
  attention as, 172–94
  factors influencing, 179–90
  inhibiting a prepared response, 145–49
  mental practice as, 462
  number of response choices effect on, 182–84
  practice effects on, 189–90
  response complexity effects on, 189
  sensory vs. motor set effects on, 181
  stimulus predictability effects on, 185–89
  stimulus-response compatibility effects on, 184–85
Retention tests, 57, 243

Schema theory, 81–84, 111–13, 166, 323, 338, 403–4, 407, 415–17
Scientific method, 36–41
Self-paced task, 13
Sensorimotor integration, 104
Serial motor skills, 12, 147–48
Serial position effect, 276–81
Shadowing technique, 216
Skill, 7–9, 15
Spacing of repetitions effect, 362

Speech control, 156
Speed-accuracy trade-off, 32
Stages of learning
  Adams' model, 68
  Fitts and Posner model, 66–67
  Gentile's model, 68–69
  novice vs. expert paradigm, 75–76
  performance changes during, 70–74
Superdiagonal form, 305–6
Switched-limb studies, 122–23

Task analysis, 290, 333
Theories of motor learning. *See* Adams' closed-loop theory; Schema theory
Tracking tasks performance measurement, 27–29
Transfer-appropriate processing, 382
Transfer of learning
  bilateral transfer
    causes of, 388–90
    defined, 386
    evidence for, 386–88
    practicing for, 391–92
    symmetry of, 387–88
  causes of, 380–83
  common skill components effect on, 377, 381–82
  comparing memory and transfer paradigms, 376
  complexity and organization effects on, 377–78
  conditions influencing, 376–80
  defined, 369
  importance of, 370–73
  intertask transfer, 373–75

  intratask transfer, 375–76
  measurement of, 372–76
  percentage of transfer, 374–76
  previous experience effects on, 378–79
  principles for instruction, 394–97
  processing requirements effect on, 382–83
  related to measuring learning, 373–76
  savings score, 374–75
  types of, 369–70
    negative transfer, 369, 379–80
    positive transfer, 369–70
    zero transfer, 370
Transfer surface, 381–82
Transfer tests, 58–59

Variable error, 23–27
Vigilance, 190–94
Vision
  interaction with proprioception in motor control, 137–38
  model of visual control of movement, 125–26
  role in
    aiming tasks, 126–29
    batting, 135–37
    catching, 132–35
    locomotion, 129–30
    movement control, 124–38, 453
  as sensory system, 124–25
Yerkes-Dodson Law, 180, 486, 490